Principles of

Managerial Finance

ELEVENTH EDITION

Lawrence J. GITMAN

San Diego State University

PEARSON

Addison
Wesley

Boston   San Francisco   New York
London   Toronto   Sydney   Tokyo   Singapore   Madrid
Mexico City   Munich   Paris   Cape Town   Hong Kong   Montreal

Editor-in-Chief: Denise Clinton
Senior Acquisitions Editor: Donna Battista
Senior Project Manager: Mary Clare McEwing
Development Editor: Ann Torbert
Managing Editor: Jim Rigney
Senior Production Supervisor: Nancy Fenton
Executive Marketing Manager: Stephen Frail
Media Producer: Bethany Tidd
Supplements Editor: Kirsten Dickerson
Digital Assets Manager: Jason Miranda
Permissions Editor: Dana Weightman
Project Coordination, Text Design, Art Studio,
    and Electronic Page Makeup: Thompson Steele, Inc.
Design Manager: Regina Hagen Kolenda
Cover Designer: Regina Hagen Kolenda
Cover Photographs: Masterfile
Senior Manufacturing Buyer: Hugh Crawford

For permission to use copyrighted material, grateful acknowledgment is made to the
copyright holders on p. CR-1, which are hereby made part of this copyright page.

Library of Congress Cataloging-in-Publication Data

Gitman, Lawrence J.
    Principles of managerial finance / Lawrence J. Gitman.—11th ed.
        p. cm.
    Includes bibliographical references and index.
    ISBN 0-321-26761-3 (11th ed.: alk. paper)
    1. Corporations—Finance. 2. Business enterprises—Finance.   I. Title.
HG4011.G5 2005
658.15—dc22

                                                          2004060134

For information on obtaining permission for the use of material from this
work, please submit a written request to Pearson Education, Inc., Rights and
Contracts Department, 75 Arlington Street, Suite 300, Boston, MA 02116 or
fax your request to (617) 848-7047. Printed in the United States.

ISBN 0-321-26761-3

1 2 3 4 5 6 7 8 9 10—RNT—08 07 06 05 04

Dedicated to the memory
of my mother, Dr. Edith Gitman,
who instilled in me the importance
of education and hard work

Gitman's
Proven Teaching/Learning System

Users of *Principles of Managerial Finance* have praised the effectiveness of the book's teaching/learning system, which has been hailed as one of its hallmarks. The system, driven by a set of carefully developed learning goals, has been retained and polished in the Eleventh Edition. Key elements of the teaching/learning system are illustrated and described in the "walkthrough" of features on the pages that follow. Both students and instructors are encouraged at the start of the semester to acquaint themselves with the many useful learning features the book offers.

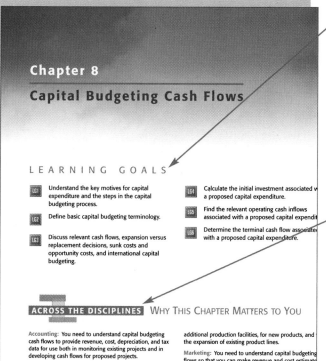

Chapter 8

Capital Budgeting Cash Flows

LEARNING GOALS

LG1 Understand the key motives for capital expenditure and the steps in the capital budgeting process.

LG2 Define basic capital budgeting terminology.

LG3 Discuss relevant cash flows, expansion versus replacement decisions, sunk costs and opportunity costs, and international capital budgeting.

LG4 Calculate the initial investment associated with a proposed capital expenditure.

LG5 Find the relevant operating cash inflows associated with a proposed capital expenditure.

LG6 Determine the terminal cash flow associated with a proposed capital expenditure.

ACROSS THE DISCIPLINES WHY THIS CHAPTER MATTERS TO YOU

Accounting: You need to understand capital budgeting cash flows to provide revenue, cost, depreciation, and tax data for use both in monitoring existing projects and in developing cash flows for proposed projects.

Information systems: You need to understand capital budgeting cash flows to maintain and facilitate the retrieval of cash flow data for both completed and existing projects.

Management: You need to understand capital budgeting

additional production facilities, for new products, and the expansion of existing product lines.

Marketing: You need to understand capital budgeting flows so that you can make revenue and cost estimate proposals for new marketing programs, for new produ and for the expansion of existing product lines.

Operations: You need to understand capital budgetin cash flows so that you can make revenue and cost esti

Six Learning Goals at the start of the chapter anchor the most important concepts and techniques to be learned in the chapter. The learning goal icons reappear next to related text sections and again in the chapter-end summary, end-of-chapter homework materials, and supplements such as the Study Guide, Test Bank, and FinanceWorks.

Every chapter opens with a feature that discusses the intersection of the finance topics covered in the chapter with the concerns of other major business disciplines. Across the Disciplines shows students majoring in accounting, information systems, management, marketing, and operations why the chapter matters to them, and it encourages them to appreciate the numerous cross-disciplinary interactions that routinely occur in business.

Each chapter opens with a short vignette that describes a recent real-company experience, event, or decision related to the aspect of managerial finance covered in the chapter. These don't take long to read, and they will raise interest in the topic by demonstrating its relevance in the business world. A critical thinking question at the end of each vignette encourages readers to give additional thought to the story.

U. S. TREASURY
A HUGE APPETITE FOR MONEY

Who is the largest debtor in the United States? Why, the federal government, of course. As of July 9, 2004, the national debt was $7,267,025,626,017. With annual deficits of $158 billion in 2002, $375 billion in 2003, and a Congressional Budget Office projection of a $477 billion deficit in 2004, the federal government has a huge need for outside financing that dwarfs any corporate bond issue.

To feed this huge demand, the **U.S. Department of Treasury** (www.ustreas.gov) can issue T-bills (debt securities that mature in less than 1 year), Treasury notes (1- to 10-year maturities), Treasury bonds (which mature in more than 10 years), and savings bonds. In addition to public auctions, Treasury securities can be purchased at banks (EE- and I-series savings bonds) and through TreasuryDirect, a Web-based system.

The Treasury Department has not offered a Treasury bond since October 2001, when it suspended issuance of the 30-year bond. With short-term rates at record low levels, it made sense to offer the short-term debt in lieu of the longer-term, higher-interest debt. The Treasury can also lower the cost of the federal debt by refinancing some of the longer-term debt. While not all 30-year Treasury bonds are *callable* (able to be repurchased at a set price at the will of the Treasury), some are, and it makes sense to swap them for lower-priced debt. For example, on May 15, 2004, the Treasury called for redemption of the 9 1/8 percent Treasury bond issued in May 1979 and scheduled to mature in May 2009. There were $4.6 billion of these bonds outstanding, and with current rates well below 9 1/8 percent, the Treasury estimated that it could save about $544 million in interest from the call and refinancing.

In fiscal year 2003, the U.S. government spent $318 billion on interest payments to holders of the national debt. If interest rates begin to rise again, the interest expense will continue to increase. Individuals can attack this interest expense directly by making payments to the U.S. Treasury for the express purpose of reducing the United States' national debt. In 2003, the Treasury received $1,277,423 from citizens wishing to reduce the federal debt. With the debt increasing at the pace of more than $1 billion per day, these contributions stopped the growth of the federal debt briefly—for just under 2 minutes.

■ *How might the issuance of large amounts of public debt affect the corporate debt market?*

277

Learning goal icons appear next to first-level text headings. The learning goal icon ties chapter content to learning goals.

376   PART THREE   Long-Term Investment Decisions

[LG1] [LG2]   8.1 | The Capital Budgeting Decision Process

Long-term investments represent sizable outlays of funds that commit a firm to some course of action. Consequently, the firm needs procedures to analyze and properly select its long-term investments. It must be able to measure cash flows and apply appropriate decision techniques. As time passes, fixed assets may become obsolete or may require an overhaul; at these points, too, financial deci-

As just stated, you want to determine the equal annual end-of-year deposits required to accumulate $30,000 at the end of 5 years, given an interest rate of 6%.

Table Use Table A–3 indicates that the future value interest factor for an ordinary annuity at 6% for 5 years ($FVIFA_{6\%,5yrs}$) is 5.637. Substituting $FVA_5 =$ $30,000 and $FVIFA_{6\%,5yrs} = 5.637$ into Equation 4.26 yields an annual required deposit, PMT, of $5,321.98. Thus, if $5,321.98 is deposited at the end of each year for 5 years at 6% interest, there will be $30,000 in the account at the end of the 5 years.

Input	Function
30000	FV
5	N
6	I
	CPT
	PMT

Solution
5,321.89

Calculator Use Using the calculator inputs shown at the left, you will find the annual deposit amount to be $5,321.89. Note that this value, except for a slight rounding difference, agrees with the value found by using Table A–3.

Spreadsheet Use The annual deposit needed to accumulate the future sum also can be calculated as shown on the following Excel spreadsheet.

	A	B
1	ANNUAL DEPOSIT NEEDED TO ACCUMULATE A FUTURE SUM	
2	Future value	$30,000
3	Number of years	5
4	Annual rate of interest	6%
5	Annual deposit	$5,321.89

Entry in Cell B5 is =-PMT(B4,B3,0,B2).
The minus sign appears before PMT because the annual deposits are cash outflows.

Examples are an important component of the book's learning system. Clearly set off from the text, they provide an immediate and concrete demonstration of how to apply financial concepts, tools, and techniques.

Examples in certain chapters, most notably in Chapter 4, demonstrate the time value of money techniques. These examples show the use of time lines, factor tables, financial calculators, and spreadsheets.

Spreadsheet solutions accompany most calculator solutions and show the inputs, solutions, and cell formulas of the spreadsheets. In this edition, spreadsheet solutions have been added in Chapters 6 and 11.

The Equation for Present Value

The present value of a future amount can be found mathematically by solving Equation 4.4 for PV. In other words, the present value, PV, of some future amount, FV^n, to be received n periods from now, assuming an opportunity cost of i, is calculated as follows:

$$PV = \frac{FV_n}{(1 + i)^n} = FV_n \times \left[\frac{1}{(1 + i)^n}\right] \qquad (4.9)$$

Note the similarity between this general equation for present value and the equation in the preceding example (Equation 4.8). Let's use this equation in an example.

Key equations are printed in blue throughout the text to help readers identify the most important mathematical relationships. The variables used in these equations are for convenience printed on the front endpapers of the book.

The Concept of Present Value

discounting cash flows
The process of finding present values; the inverse of compounding interest.

The process of finding present values is often referred to as **discounting cash flows**. It is concerned with answering the following question: If I can earn i percent on my money, what is the most I would be willing to pay now for an opportunity to receive FV_n dollars n periods from now?

This process is actually the inverse of compounding interest. Instead of finding the future value of present dollars invested at a given rate, discounting determines the present value of a future amount, assuming an opportunity to earn a certain return on the money. This annual rate of return is variously referred to as the *discount rate, required return, cost of capital,* and *opportunity cost.*⁷ These terms will be used interchangeably in this text.

For help in study and review, **key terms** and their definitions appear in the margin when they are first introduced. These terms are also boldfaced in the index and appear in the Glossary.

Electronic Spreadsheets

Hint Anyone familiar with an electronic spreadsheet, such as Excel, realizes that most of the time-value-of-money calculations can be performed expeditiously by using the special functions contained in the spreadsheet.

Like financial calculators, electronic spreadsheets have built-in routines that simplify time value calculations. We provide in the text a number of spreadsheet solutions that identify the cell entries for calculating time values. The value for each variable is entered in a cell in the spreadsheet, and the calculation is programmed using an equation that links the individual cells. If values of the variables are changed, the solution automatically changes as a result of the equation linking the cells. In the spreadsheet solutions in this book, the equation that determines the calculation is shown at the bottom of the spreadsheet.

Marginal hints add useful ideas, comments, and pieces of information to enrich the text discussion and help student learning.

Review Questions, which appear at the end of each major section of the chapter, challenge you to stop and test your understanding of key concepts, tools, techniques, and practices before you move on to the next section.

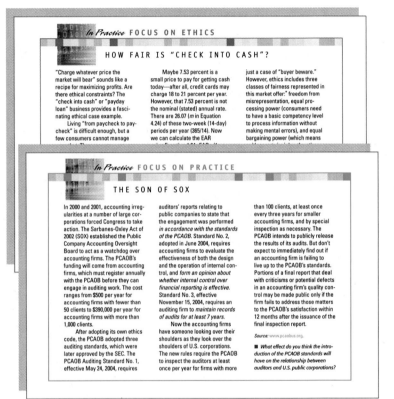

REVIEW QUESTIONS

4–8 What is the difference between an *ordinary annuity* and an *annuity due*? Which always has greater future value and present value for identical annuities and interest rates? Why?

4–9 What are the most efficient ways to calculate the present value of an ordinary annuity? What is the relationship between the *PVIF* and *PVIFA* interest factors given in Tables A–2 and A–4, respectively?

4–10 How can the future value interest factors for an ordinary annuity be modified to find the future value of an annuity due?

4–11 How can the present value interest factors for an ordinary annuity be modified to find the present value of an annuity due?

4–12 What is a *perpetuity*? How can the present value interest factor for such a stream of cash flows be determined?

In Practice boxes offer insight into important topics in finance, through the experiences of real companies, both large and small. There are two categories of boxes.

New! Focus on Ethics boxes in every chapter help you appreciate important ethical issues in finance.

Focus on Practice boxes take a corporate focus that relates a business event to a specific financial concept or technique. Boxes related to global issues are so designated.

Both types of boxes will provide you with a solid grounding in the practice of finance in the real world.

In Practice FOCUS ON ETHICS

HOW FAIR IS "CHECK INTO CASH"?

"Charge whatever price the market will bear" sounds like a recipe for maximizing profits. Are there ethical constraints? The "check into cash" or "payday loan" business provides a fascinating ethical case example.

Living "from paycheck to paycheck" is difficult enough, but a few consumers cannot manage

Maybe 7.53 percent is a small price to pay for getting cash today—after all, credit cards may charge 18 to 21 percent per year. However, that 7.53 percent is not the nominal (stated) annual rate. There are 26.07 (*m* in Equation 4.24) of these two-week (14-day) periods per year (365/14). Now we can calculate the EAR

just a case of "buyer beware." However, ethics includes three classes of fairness represented in this market offer: freedom from misrepresentation, equal processing power (consumers need to have a basic competency level to process information without making mental errors), and equal bargaining power (which means

In Practice FOCUS ON PRACTICE

THE SON OF SOX

In 2000 and 2001, accounting irregularities at a number of large corporations forced Congress to take action. The Sarbanes-Oxley Act of 2002 (SOX) established the Public Company Accounting Oversight Board to act as a watchdog over accounting firms. The PCAOB's funding will come from accounting firms, which must register annually with the PCAOB before they can engage in auditing work. The cost ranges from $500 per year for accounting firms with fewer than 50 clients to $390,000 per year for accounting firms with more than 1,000 clients.

After adopting its own ethics code, the PCAOB adopted three auditing standards, which were later approved by the SEC. The PCAOB Auditing Standard No. 1, effective May 24, 2004, requires

auditors' reports relating to public companies to state that the engagement was performed *in accordance with the standards of the PCAOB*. Standard No. 2, adopted in June 2004, requires accounting firms to evaluate the effectiveness of both the design and the operation of internal control, and *form an opinion about whether internal control over financial reporting is effective*. Standard No. 3, effective November 15, 2004, requires an auditing firm to *maintain records of audits for at least 7 years*.

Now the accounting firms have someone looking over their shoulders as they look over the shoulders of U.S. corporations. The new rules require the PCAOB to inspect the auditors at least once per year for firms with more

than 100 clients, at least once every three years for smaller accounting firms, and by special inspection as necessary. The PCAOB intends to publicly release the results of its audits. But don't expect to immediately find out if an accounting firm is failing to live up to the PCAOB's standards. Portions of a final report that deal with criticisms or potential defects in an accounting firm's quality control may be made public only if the firm fails to address those matters to the PCAOB's satisfaction within 12 months after the issuance of the final inspection report.

Source: www.pcaobus.org.

■ *What effect do you think the introduction of the PCAOB standards will have on the relationship between auditors and U.S. public corporations?*

The Summary begins with Focus on Value, which explains how the chapter's content relates to the firm's goal of maximizing owner wealth. This feature helps reinforce understanding of the link between the financial manager's actions and share value.

Summary

Focus on Value

Time value of money is an important tool that financial managers and other market participants use to assess the effects of proposed actions. Because firms have long lives and their important decisions affect their long-term cash flows, the effective application of time-value-of-money techniques is extremely important. Time value techniques enable financial managers to evaluate cash flows occurring at different times so as to combine, compare, and evaluate them and link them to the firm's **overall goal of share price maximization**. It will become clear in Chapters 6 and 7 that the application of time value techniques is a key part of the value determination process. Using them, we can measure the firm's value and evaluate the effects that various events and decisions might have on it. Clearly, an understanding of time-value-of-money techniques and an ability to apply them are needed to make intelligent value-creating decisions.

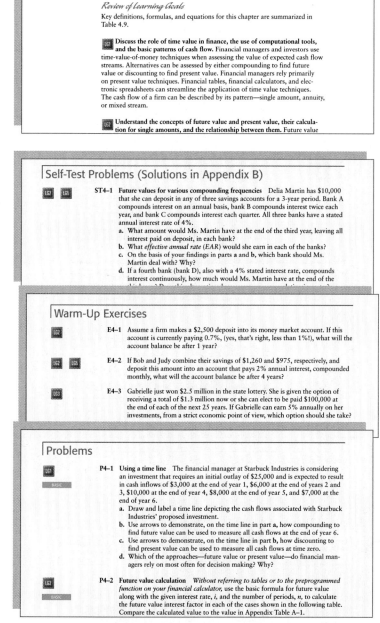

Review of Learning Goals

Key definitions, formulas, and equations for this chapter are summarized in Table 4.9.

LG1 Discuss the role of time value in finance, the use of computational tools, and the basic patterns of cash flow. Financial managers and investors use time-value-of-money techniques when assessing the value of expected cash flow streams. Alternatives can be assessed by either compounding to find future value or discounting to find present value. Financial managers rely primarily on present value techniques. Financial tables, financial calculators, and electronic spreadsheets can streamline the application of time value techniques. The cash flow of a firm can be described by its pattern—single amount, annuity, or mixed stream.

LG2 Understand the concepts of future value and present value, their calculation for single amounts, and the relationship between them. Future value

The **Review of Learning Goals** restates each learning goal and summarizes the key material that was presented to support mastery of that goal.

Self-Test Problems (Solutions in Appendix B)

LG2 **LG5** **ST4–1** **Future values for various compounding frequencies** Delia Martin has $10,000 that she can deposit in any of three savings accounts for a 3-year period. Bank A compounds interest on an annual basis, bank B compounds interest twice each year, and bank C compounds interest each quarter. All three banks have a stated annual interest rate of 4%.

a. What amount would Ms. Martin have at the end of the third year, leaving all interest paid on deposit, in each bank?
b. What *effective annual rate (EAR)* would she earn in each of the banks?
c. On the basis of your findings in parts **a** and **b**, which bank should Ms. Martin deal with? Why?
d. If a fourth bank (bank D), also with a 4% stated interest rate, compounds interest continuously, how much would Ms. Martin have at the end of the

Self-Test Problems, keyed to the learning goals, give you an opportunity to strengthen your understanding of topics by doing a sample problem. Solutions are provided in Appendix B at the back of the book.

Warm-Up Exercises

LG2 **E4–1** Assume a firm makes a $2,500 deposit into its money market account. If this account is currently paying 0.7%, (yes, that's right, less than 1%!), what will the account balance be after 1 year?

LG2 **LG5** **E4–2** If Bob and Judy combine their savings of $1,260 and $975, respectively, and deposit this amount into an account that pays 2% annual interest, compounded monthly, what will the account balance be after 4 years?

LG3 **E4–3** Gabrielle just won $2.5 million in the state lottery. She is given the option of receiving a total of $1.3 million now or she can elect to be paid $100,000 at the end of each of the next 25 years. If Gabrielle can earn 5% annually on her investments, from a strict economic point of view, which option should she take?

New! **Warm-Up Exercises** follow the Self-Test Problems. These short, numerical exercises give you practice in applying tools and techniques presented in the chapter.

Problems

LG1 **P4–1** **Using a time line** The financial manager at Starbuck Industries is considering an investment that requires an initial outlay of $25,000 and is expected to result in cash inflows of $3,000 at the end of year 1, $6,000 at the end of years 2 and 3, $10,000 at the end of year 4, $8,000 at the end of year 5, and $7,000 at the end of year 6.

BASIC
a. Draw and label a time line depicting the cash flows associated with Starbuck Industries' proposed investment.
b. Use arrows to demonstrate, on the time line in part **a**, how compounding to find future value can be used to measure all cash flows at the end of year 6.
c. Use arrows to demonstrate, on the time line in part **b**, how discounting to find present value can be used to measure all cash flows at time zero.
d. Which of the approaches—future value or present value—do financial managers rely on most often for decision making? Why?

LG2 **P4–2** **Future value calculation** *Without referring to tables or to the preprogrammed function on your financial calculator,* use the basic formula for future value along with the given interest rate, *i*, and the number of periods, *n*, to calculate the future value interest factor in each of the cases shown in the following table. Compare the calculated value to the value in Appendix Table A–1.

BASIC

A comprehensive set of **Problems**, keyed to the learning goals, contains more than one problem for each concept, tool, or technique. A short descriptor at the beginning of the problem identifies the concept or technique. Difficulty identifiers appear in the margin next to each problem. Problems labeled as "Integrative" tie together related topics. Guideline answers to selected end-of-chapter problems appear in Appendix C.

LG6 **P4–60** **ETHICS PROBLEM** A manager at a "check into cash" business (see *In Practice* box on page 191) defends his business practice as simply "charging what the market will bear." "After all," says the manager, "we don't force people to come in the door." How would you respond to this ethical defense of the payday-advance business?

INTERMEDIATE

New! The last item in the chapter problems is an **Ethics Problem**. The ethics problem gives you another opportunity to think about and apply ethics principles to financial situations.

Chapter Cases call for application of concepts and techniques to a more complex realistic situation than in the regular problems. These cases help strengthen practical application of financial tools and techniques.

Chapter 4 Case: Funding Jill Moran's Retirement Annuity

Sunrise Industries wishes to accumulate funds to provide a retirement annuity for its vice president of research, Jill Moran. Ms. Moran, by contract, will retire at the end of exactly 12 years. Upon retirement, she is entitled to receive an annual end-of-year payment of $42,000 for exactly 20 years. If she dies prior to the end of the 20-year period, the annual payments will pass to her heirs. During the 12-year "accumulation period" Sunrise wishes to fund the annuity by making equal, annual, end-of-year deposits into an account earning 9% interest. Once the 20-year "distribution period" begins, Sunrise plans to move the accumulated monies into an account earning a guaranteed 12% per year. At the end of the distribution period, the account balance will equal zero. Note that the first deposit will be made at the end of year 1 and that the first distribution payment will be received at the end of year 13.

New! Every chapter includes a Spreadsheet Exercise. This exercise gives you an opportunity to use Excel® software to create one or more spreadsheets with which to analyze a financial problem. The spreadsheet to be created often is modeled on a table in the chapter or a spreadsheet template that can be viewed at the book's Web site.

Spreadsheet Exercise

Assume that Monsanto Corporation is considering the renovation and/or replacement of some of its older and outdated carpet-manufacturing equipment. Its objective is to improve the efficiency of operations in terms of both speed and reduction in the number of defects. The company's finance department has compiled pertinent data that will allow it to conduct a marginal cost–benefit analysis for the proposed equipment replacement.

The cash outlay for new equipment would be approximately $600,000. The net book value of the old equipment and its potential net selling price is $250,000. The total benefits from the new equipment (measured in today's dollars) would be $900,000. The benefits of the old equipment over a similar period of time (measured in today's dollars) would be $300,000.

New! Every chapter offers a Group Exercise in which students work together in the context of an ongoing company. Your group will create a company and follow it through the various managerial finance topics and business activities presented in the textbook.

Group Exercise

This assignment will focus on your group's shadow corporation. As in Chapter 1, the group will be asked to utilize the latest 10-K filing.

TO DO
a. Access the latest 10-K filing. Describe the content of the letter to stockholders.
b. Calculate the basic ratios as done in the text. Sort the ratios into the five categories found in Table 2.8 (pages 72 and 73).
c. State what use each ratio has in analyzing the health of your corporation.
d. Analyze these ratios through time by calculating them over the most recent years. For any ratios that have changed, give possible explanations as to why these changes may have occurred.
e. Conclude with a financial summary of the ratios using the DuPont system.

A Web Exercise at the end of the chapter links the chapter topic to a related site on the Internet and asks you to use information there to answer questions. These exercises capture your interest while teaching about financial-related sites.

Web Exercise

Mortgage interest rates vary daily. Over a period of time, mortgage interest rates have followed definite trends based on federal interest rate policies and economic conditions. Historical interest rate information is available on the Web.

TO DO
a. For this Web exercise, direct your Internet browser to www.mbaa.org/, the home page of the Mortgage Bankers Association. View the current mortgage interest rates listed on the right side of the screen. Now direct your browser to the Mortgage and Market Data link at the top of the page, highlighting Interest rates. This page contains data for mortgage rates over the past decades. Study and comment on the levels of interest rates over the recent

An Integrative Case at the end of each Part challenges you to use what you have learned over the course of several chapters.

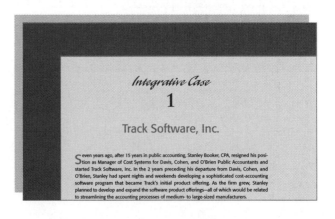

Integrative Case

1

Track Software, Inc.

Seven years ago, after 15 years in public accounting, Stanley Booker, CPA, resigned his position as Manager of Cost Systems for Davis, Cohen, and O'Brien Public Accountants and started Track Software, Inc. In the 2 years preceding his departure from Davis, Cohen, and O'Brien, Stanley had spent nights and weekends developing a sophisticated cost-accounting software program that became Track's initial product offering. As the firm grew, Stanley planned to develop and expand the software product offerings—all of which would be related to streamlining the accounting processes of medium- to large-sized manufacturers.

Brief Contents

Contents

Chapter 2

FINANCIAL STATEMENTS AND ANALYSIS

page 44

The Home Depot, Inc.—Building Strong Financials
page 45

PART TWO   IMPORTANT FINANCIAL CONCEPTS   157

Chapter 7

STOCK VALUATION
page   324

Domino's Pizza, Inc.—A Slice of the Company is Now Available to the Public
page 325

PART THREE   LONG-TERM INVESTMENT DECISIONS   373

PART FOUR   LONG-TERM FINANCIAL DECISIONS   495

Chapter 12

LEVERAGE AND CAPITAL STRUCTURE

page   536

*Krispy Kreme—Investors Eat Up
Krispy Kreme Stock
page 537*

PART FIVE   **SHORT-TERM FINANCIAL DECISIONS   625**

Chapter 15

CURRENT LIABILITIES MANAGEMENT

page 668

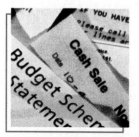

Turner Industries—Constructing a More Efficient Accounts Payable System
page 669

PART SIX   SPECIAL TOPICS IN MANAGERIAL FINANCE   705

Chapter 18

INTERNATIONAL MANAGERIAL FINANCE

page 790

General Electric Company—Growing in an Uncertain World
page 791

Preface

The desire to write *Principles of Managerial Finance* came out of my experience teaching the introductory managerial finance course early in my academic career. When I began teaching full time, I was not very far removed from my own undergraduate studies and therefore could appreciate the difficulties some of my students were having with the textbook we used. They wanted a book that spoke to them in plain English. They wanted a book that tied concepts to reality. And they wanted not just description, but demonstration of concepts, tools, and techniques. Recognizing that, I decided that I would write an introductory finance text that would effectively resolve these concerns.

Three years later, in 1976, the first edition of *Principles* was published. Its initial market success was driven by its conversational tone, wide use of examples set off in the text, and coverage of short-term finance. Building on these strengths, over ten editions, numerous translations, and more than half a million U.S. users, I've continued to listen carefully to feedback from both professors and students, from adopters, nonadopters, and practitioners. My thanks to all of those people, without whose input I could not have as effectively refined and improved the text over the years.

As before, my goal in the eleventh edition of *Principles* is to satisfy the needs of professors and students. Like the first edition, the eleventh still uses plain English, ties concepts to reality, and demonstrates concepts, tools, and techniques. It incorporates a proven learning system, which integrates pedagogy with concepts and practical applications. It concentrates on the concepts, techniques, and practices that are needed to make keen financial decisions in an increasingly competitive business environment. The strong pedagogy and generous use of examples make the text an easily accessible resource for long-distance learning and self-study programs. It has also been well received in the core M.B.A. course and in management development and executive training programs.

The text's organization, described in detail in the following pages, conceptually links the firm's actions and its value as determined in the securities market. Each major decision area is presented in terms of both risk and return factors and their potential impact on the owners' wealth. A "Focus on Value" element at the end of each chapter helps reinforce the student's understanding of the link between the financial manager's actions and share value.

Although the text is sequential, instructors can assign almost any chapter as a self-contained unit. This flexibility enables instructors to customize the text to various teaching strategies and course lengths.

We live in a world in which both international and ethical considerations cannot be divorced from the study of business in general and finance in particular. As in prior editions, discussions of international dimensions of chapter topics are integrated throughout the book. A marginal icon of a globe highlights such discussions. In each chapter in which international coverage is included, the international material is integrated into learning goals and end-of-chapter materials. In addition, for those who want to spend more time addressing the topic, a separate chapter on international finance concludes the book.

The business failures and scandals of recent years, and attempts to forestall or fix such problems by means of the Sarbanes-Oxley Act of 2002, have renewed the need for the study and application of ethics in business. Therefore, in the eleventh edition, we have included in *every* chapter an *In Practice* box that focuses on ethical issues. These boxes address some of the most significant ethical issues that financial managers face as they attempt to sail the sometimes-rough waters of the business world.

In organizing each chapter, I have adhered to a managerial decision-making perspective, relating decisions to the firm's overall goal of wealth maximization. Once a particular concept has been developed, its application is illustrated by an example. These examples demonstrate, and solidify in the student's thought, financial decision-making considerations and their consequences.

In response to suggestions of the book's users and reviewers, I have added to the already rich homework assignments several new types of assignment materials: short, numerical Warm-Up Exercises, a Spreadsheet Exercise, and a Group Exercise. These new materials expand and enrich the opportunities for instructors and students in today's classroom environment. They are explained in greater detail on pages xi–xii.

From classroom to boardroom, the eleventh edition of *Principles of Managerial Finance* can help users get to where they want to be. I hope that your review of this new edition confirms my belief that it is better than ever—more relevant, more accurate, and more effective than its prior edition. I hope you agree that *Principles of Managerial Finance*, Eleventh Edition is the most effective introductory managerial finance text available today.

Revised Content

As we made plans to publish the eleventh edition, we carefully assessed market feedback about content changes that would better meet the needs of professors teaching the course. As a result, the chapter sequence remains the same as in the tenth edition. A number of new topics have been added at appropriate places and existing discussions have been updated and/or smoothed. We now use a 365-day year for calculations throughout the text.

For those instructors who expressed a desire to assign an entire chapter on financial institutions and markets as a foundational structure in the managerial finance course, we have made available online at the book's Web site, www.aw-bc.com/gitman, a complete chapter on institutions and markets.

The following list details the chapter-by-chapter content changes in the eleventh edition.

Chapter 1 The Role and Environment of Managerial Finance

- Revised opening vignette on Starbucks.
- Expanded discussion of the role of the corporate board of directors.
- New section on corporate governance, including the influence of individual and institutional investors and discussion of the *Sarbanes-Oxley Act of 2002.*
- Revision of business taxation discussion to reflect the *Jobs and Growth Tax Relief Reconciliation Act of 2003.*
- New *In Practice* box on Warren Buffett, the "Oracle of Omaha."
- Discussion of EVA® moved out of Chapter 1 (and in to Chapter 11).

Chapter 2 Financial Statements and Analysis

- Revised opening vignette on Home Depot.
- New text discussion and *In Practice* box on the Public Company Accounting Oversight Board (PCAOB).
- New *In Practice* ethics box on how investors and the Sarbanes-Oxley Act have declared war on accounting misdeeds.

Chapter 3 Cash Flow and Financial Planning

- Revised opening vignette on Best Buy.
- New text explanation of the classification of decreases and increases in cash balances.
- New discussion and example of net operating profits after taxes (NOPAT) and its role in calculating operating cash flow (OCF) and free cash flow (FCF).
- Revised *In Practice* box on some real-world aspects of cash forecasting.
- Revised *In Practice* ethics box on ethical lapses at Critical Path.

Chapter 4 Time Value of Money

- New opening vignette on the costs of R&D at Eli Lilly and Company.
- New *In Practice* ethics box about interest rates involved in the "payday loan" business.
- Revised *In Practice* box on the effects of shorter loan periods on home mortgage payments.

Chapter 5 Risk and Return
- New opening vignette on the merger between J. P. Morgan Case and Bank One.
- Revised *In Practice* ethics box on moral risk.
- New *In Practice* box about reducing risk through international diversification.

Chapter 6 Interest Rates and Bond Valuation
- New opening vignette on the U.S. Treasury.
- New *In Practice* box on inflation-adjusted bonds (I-bonds).
- New *In Practice* ethics box about the trustworthiness of bond ratings agencies.
- Spreadsheet examples added for calculations of basic bond valuation, bond values at differing required returns, yield to maturity, and bond value with semiannual interest.

Chapter 7 Stock Valuation
- New opening vignette on the IPO of Domino's Pizza.
- New *In Practice* ethics box about whether investors require a "credibility premium."
- New text section on behavioral finance.
- Revised *In Practice* box about the efficient markets hypothesis.

Chapter 8 Capital Budgeting Cash Flows
- New opening vignette on calculating the relevant cash flows of a new FedEx terminal.
- New *In Practice* ethics box about the accuracy of cash flow estimates in practice.
- New *In Practice* box on capital investment in Russia.
- Streamlined the tax calculation necessary to find initial investment and terminal value.
- Revised the calculation of operating cash inflows for consistency with net operating profits after taxes (NOPAT) and operating cash flow (OCF) discussions introduced in Chapter 3.

Chapter 9 Capital Budgeting Techniques
- New opening vignette on value of productivity tools at Intel Corporation.
- Revised *In Practice* box on the limits of payback analysis.
- New text section on multiple IRRs.
- New *In Practice* ethics box about nonfinancial considerations in project selection.

Chapter 10   Risk and Refinements in Capital Budgeting

- New opening vignette on the use of simulation programs by Palisade Corporation to deal with project uncertainty.
- New *In Practice* box about Monte Carlo simulation programs.
- New *In Practice* ethics box about incorrect risk evaluation by the California Earthquake Authority.

Chapter 11   The Cost of Capital

- New opening vignette on how eBay has met its need for capital.
- New *In Practice* ethics box about "creative accounting" and the cost of capital at WorldCom.
- Spreadsheet example added for calculation of the before-tax cost of debt of a corporate bond.
- New discussion of economic value added (EVA®).
- Revised In Practice box about EVA®.

Chapter 12   Leverage and Capital Structure

- Revised opening vignette about Krispy Kreme Doughnuts.
- Revised *In Practice* box about operating leverage at Adobe Systems.
- New *In Practice* ethics box about overleveraging in the midst of management buyouts.
- Linked net operating profits after taxes (NOPAT), introduced in Chapter 3, to finding optimal capital structure.

Chapter 13   Dividend Policy

- New opening vignette on dividend payments by Microsoft Corporation.
- New figure to illustrate the dividend-payment time line.
- New text discussion of the tax treatment of dividends, based on the *Jobs and Growth Tax Relief Reconciliation Act of 2003*.
- New *In Practice* box on the effects of the tax law change on dividend payouts.
- Revised *In Practice* ethics box about how much cash managers should retain for growth prospects.

Chapter 14   Working Capital and Current Assets Management

- New opening vignette on AT&T's outsourcing of its prepaid phone cards operation.
- New *In Practice* box on the use of radio frequency identification (RFID) technology to monitor inventory and supply chain operations.
- Revised and expanded section on MRP systems to include MRPII and ERP systems.
- Revised section on aging of accounts receivable, including a new example of an aging schedule.
- Revised *In Practice* ethics box on remote disbursing.

Chapter 15 Current Liabilities Management

- New opening vignette on Turner Industries' use of electronic data capture to improve its accounts payable system.
- Revised *In Practice* ethics box on the ethical issues of stretching accounts payable.
- New *In Practice* box on corporations' recent use of commercial paper.

Chapter 16 Hybrid and Derivative Securities

- New opening vignette on Walt Disney Company's airplane leases to United Airlines.
- New *In Practice* box on how triple net leases work.
- New *In Practice* ethics box on the practical and political difficulties of valuing employee stock options as a form of derivative security.

Chapter 17 Mergers, LBOs, Divestitures, and Business Failure

- New opening vignette on JCPenney Company's corporate restructurings over the years.
- New text discussion of Western Europe's movement toward a U.S.-style approach to shareholder value and public capital market financing.
- New *In Practice* ethics box on some ethical considerations relating to bankruptcy.
- New *In Practice* box on the corporate makeover of WorldCom into MCI, Inc.

Chapter 18 International Managerial Finance

- New opening vignette on General Electric's plans for international growth.
- New text discussion of the Central American Free Trade Agreement (CAFTA).
- Expanded discussion of laws and regulations regarding international subsidiary and joint-venture operations.
- New *In Practice* ethics box about gift-giving and bribery in international business.
- Updated discussion of international debt.
- Revised discussion of the international stock market.
- Revised discussion of the effect of foreign currency movements on effective interest rates, including a new formula for calculating the effective interest rate for a given currency.
- Revised discussion of the use of forward contracts to hedge exchange rate risk.
- New *In Practice* box on overseas corporate assignments.

Supplements to the Eleventh Edition

The *PMF* Teaching/Learning System includes a variety of useful supplements for teachers and for students.

Teaching Tools for Instructors

The key teaching tools available to instructors are the *Instructor's Manual*, testing materials, and *PowerPoint Lecture Presentations*.

Instructor's Manual *Compiled by Frederick P. Schadler, East Carolina University.* This comprehensive resource pulls together the teaching tools so that instructors can use the textbook easily and effectively in the classroom. Each chapter provides an overview of key topics and detailed answers and solutions to all review questions, Warm-Up Exercises, end-of-chapter problems, and chapter cases, plus suggested answers to all critical thinking questions in chapter openers and boxes, Ethics Problems, Group Exercises, and Web Exercises. At the end of the manual are practice quizzes and solutions. The complete Instructor's Manual, including Spreadsheet Exercises, is available online at Supplements Central (http://suppscentral.aw.com) and on the Instructor's Resource CD-ROM.

Testing Material *Created by Daniel J. Borgia, Florida Gulf Coast University.* Thoroughly revised to accommodate changes in the text, the Test Bank consists of a mix of true/false, multiple-choice, and essay questions. Each test question includes identifiers for type of question, skill tested by learning goal, level of difficulty, and—new to this edition—key topic tested plus, where appropriate, the formula(s) or equation(s) used in deriving the answer. The Test Bank is available in both printed and electronic formats, including Windows or Macintosh *TestGen* files and Microsoft Word files. The Test Bank and TestGen are available online at Supplements Central (http://suppscentral.aw.com) and on the Instructor's Resource CD-ROM.

Instructors can download the *TestGen* version of the Test Bank into *QuizMaster*, an online testing program for Windows and Macintosh that enables users to conduct timed or untimed exams at computer workstations. After completing tests, students can see their scores and view or print a diagnostic report of those topics or objectives requiring more attention. When installed on a local area network, *QuizMaster* allows instructors to save the scores on disk, print study diagnoses, and monitor progress of students individually or by class section and by all sections of the course.

PowerPoint Lecture Presentation *Created by Daniel J. Borgia, Florida Gulf Coast University.* Available for Windows or Macintosh on the Instructor's Resource CD-ROM, this presentation combines lecture notes with art from the textbook. The PowerPoint Lecture Presentation is available online at

Supplements Central (http://suppscentral.aw.com) and on the Instructor's Resource CD-ROM.

Instructor's Resource CD-ROM Electronic files of the *Instructor's Manual, Test Bank,* and *PowerPoint Lecture Presentations* are available on one convenient CD-ROM, compatible with both Windows and Macintosh computers. The electronic versions allow instructors to customize the support materials to their individual classroom needs. All the resources on the Instructor's Resource CD-ROM are also available online at Supplements Central (http://suppscentral.aw.com).

Learning Tools for Students

Beyond the book itself, students have access to several resources for success in this course: FinanceWorks, *Study Guide,* and the *Principles of Managerial Finance,* Eleventh Edition Web site.

FinanceWorks Packaged with new copies of this text at no additional cost, the Student Access Kit for FinanceWorks opens the door to a powerful Web-based diagnostic testing and tutorial system designed specifically for the Gitman, *Principles of Managerial Finance* textbooks. With FinanceWorks, instructors can create, edit, and assign online homework, and test and track all student work in the online gradebook. FinanceWorks allows students to take practice tests correlated to the textbook and receive a customized study plan based on the test results. The problems in FinanceWorks are based on the even-numbered end-of-chapter problems. However, because the FinanceWorks problems have algorithmically generated values, no student will have the same homework as another, and there is an unlimited opportunity for practice and testing. Students get the help they need, when they need it, from the robust tutorial options, including "View an Example" and "Help Me Solve This," which breaks the problem into its steps and links to the relevant textbook page.

Students can use FinanceWorks with no instructor intervention. However, to take advantage of the full capabilities of FinanceWorks, including assigning homework and tracking student progress in the automated gradebook, instructors will want to set up their class. Please contact your local sales representative to request an Instructor Quick Start Guide for FinanceWorks. You can find your representative using the rep locator at www.aw-bc.com/replocator.

Study Guide *Prepared by Stanley G. Eakins, East Carolina University.* The *Study Guide* is an integral component of the *PMF* Learning System. It offers many tools for studying finance. Each chapter contains the following features: chapter summary enumerated by learning goals; topical chapter outline, also broken down by learning goals for quick review; sample problem solutions; study tips; a full sample exam with the answers at the end of the chapter; and a financial dictionary of key terms.

Principles of Managerial Finance, Eleventh Edition Web Site The Web site to accompany this textbook, located at www.aw-bc.com/gitman, contains many additional resources. For each chapter on the Web site you will find

- eThemes of the Times: a collection of *New York Times* articles keyed to the chapter, along with review questions
- Web Cases, which ask students to use the Web to find information and solve finance problems
- Web Exercises from the textbook
- Self-Assessment Quizzes
- Case Studies in Finance, updated by Michael Seiler of Hawaii Pacific University

In addition to the chapter resources, you will find

- A new Web chapter, "Financial Markets and Institutions," from the text *Introduction to Finance* by Lawrence J. Gitman and Jeff Madura
- An online glossary, both as review flashcards and as a quick-reference document
- Spreadsheet examples from the textbook
- A Financial Calculator Guide
- Our Online Career Center

In addition to the Companion Web site, the course content is available in Course-Compass™, Blackboard, and WebCT. The CourseCompass™ version also includes FianaceWorks (see page xxxviii). CourseCompass™ is a nationally hosted, dynamic, interactive online course management system powered by Blackboard, leaders in the development of Internet-based learning tools. This easy-to-use and customizable program enables professors to tailor content and functionality to meet individual course needs. To see a demo, visit www .coursecompass.com. Please contact your local sales representative for more information on obtaining course content in these various formats.

Acknowledgments

To My Colleagues, Friends, and Family

No textbook can consistently meet market needs without continual feedback from colleagues, students, practitioners, and members of the publishing team. Once again, I invite colleagues to relate their classroom experiences using this book and its package to me in care of the Acquisitions Editor in Finance, Addison-Wesley Publishing Company, 75 Arlington Street, Suite 300, Boston, Massachusetts 02116. Your constructive criticism will help me to continue to improve the textbook and its Teaching/Learning System still further.

Addison-Wesley and former publisher HarperCollins sought the advice of a great many excellent reviewers, all of whom strongly influenced various aspects of this book. The following individuals provided extremely thoughtful and useful comments for the preparation of the eleventh edition:

Omar Benkato, *Ball State University*
Irv DeGraw, *Washington College*
Sharon Garrison, *University of Arizona*
Deborah Giarusso, *University of Northern Iowa*
Arthur Guarino, *Stevens Institute of Technology*
Mary Hartman, *Bentley College*
Vivian F. Nazar, *Ferris State University*
Susanne Polley, *SUNY Cortland*
Fran Quinn, *Merrimack College*
Michael Schinski, *SUNY Geneseo*
Donald H. Stuhlman, *Wilmington College*

My special thanks go to the following individuals who analyzed the manuscript in previous editions:

Saul W. Adelman	Douglas S. Bible	Patrick A. Casabona
M. Fall Ainina	Charles W. Blackwell	Robert Chatfield
Gary A. Anderson	Russell L. Block	K. C. Chen
Ronald F. Anderson	Calvin M. Boardman	Roger G. Clarke
James M. Andre	Paul Bolster	Terrence M. Clauretie
Gene L. Andrusco	Robert J. Bondi	Mark Cockalingam
Antonio Apap	Jeffrey A. Born	Thomas Cook
David A. Arbeit	Jerry D. Boswell	Maurice P. Corrigan
Allen Arkins	Denis O. Boudreaux	Mike Cudd
Saul H. Auslander	Kenneth J. Boudreaux	Donnie L. Daniel
Peter W. Bacon	Wayne Boyet	Prabir Datta
Richard E. Ball	Ron Braswell	Joel J. Dauten
Thomas Bankston	Christopher Brown	Lee E. Davis
Alexander Barges	William Brunsen	Richard F. DeMong
Charles Barngrover	Samuel B. Bulmash	Peter A. DeVito
Michael Becker	Francis E. Canda	James P. D'Mello
Scott Besley	Omer Carey	R. Gordon Dippel

Carleton Donchess
Thomas W. Donohue
Shannon Donovan
Vincent R. Driscoll
Betty A. Driver
Lorna Dotts
David R. Durst
Dwayne O. Eberhardt
Ronald L. Ehresman
Ted Ellis
F. Barney English
Greg Filbeck
Ross A. Flaherty
Rich Fortin
Timothy J. Gallagher
George W. Gallinger
Gerald D. Gay
R. H. Gilmer
Anthony J. Giovino
Philip W. Glasgo
Jeffrey W. Glazer
Joel Gold
Ron B. Goldfarb
Dennis W. Goodwin
David A. Gordon
J. Charles Granicz
C. Ramon Griffin
Reynolds Griffith
Lewell F. Gunter
Melvin W. Harju
Phil Harrington
George F. Harris
George T. Harris
John D. Harris
R. Stevenson Hawkey
Roger G. Hehman
Harvey Heinowitz
Glenn Henderson
Russell H. Hereth
Kathleen T. Hevert
J. Lawrence Hexter
Douglas A. Hibbert
Roger P. Hill
Linda C. Hittle
James Hoban
Hugh A. Hobson
Keith Howe
Kenneth M. Huggins
Jerry G. Hunt
Mahmood Islam
James F. Jackson

Stanley Jacobs
Dale W. Janowsky
Jeannette R. Jesinger
Nalina Jeypalan
Timothy E. Johnson
Roger Juchau
Ashok K. Kapoor
Daniel J. Kaufman, Jr.
Joseph K. Kiely
Terrance E. Kingston
Thomas M. Krueger
Lawrence Kryzanowski
Harry R. Kuniansky
Richard E. La Near
William R. Lane
James Larsen
Rick LeCompte
B. E. Lee
Scott Lee
Michael A. Lenarcic
A. Joseph Lerro
Thomas J. Liesz
Alan Lines
Christopher K. Ma
James C. Ma
Dilip B. Madan
Judy Maese
James Mallet
Timothy A. Manuel
Brian Maris
Daniel S. Marrone
William H. Marsh
John F. Marshall
Linda J. Martin
Stanley A. Martin
Charles E. Maxwell
Timothy Hoyt
McCaughey
Jay Meiselman
Vincent A. Mercurio
Joseph Messina
John B. Mitchell
Daniel F. Mohan
Charles Mohundro
Gene P. Morris
Edward A. Moses
Tarun K. Mukherjee
William T. Murphy
Randy Myers
Lance Nail
Donald A. Nast

G. Newbould
Charles Ngassam
Gary Noreiko
Dennis T. Officer
Kathleen J. Oldfather
Kathleen F.
Oppenheimer
Richard M. Osborne
Jerome S. Osteryoung
Prasad Padmanabahn
Roger R. Palmer
Don B. Panton
John Park
Ronda S. Paul
Bruce C. Payne
Gerald W. Perritt
Gladys E. Perry
Stanley Piascik
Gregory Pierce
Mary L. Piotrowski
D. Anthony Plath
Jerry B. Poe
Gerald A. Pogue
Ronald S. Pretekin
Fran Quinn
Rich Ravichandran
David Rayone
Walter J. Reinhart
Jack H. Reubens
Benedicte Reyes
William B. Riley, Jr.
Ron Rizzuto
Gayle A. Russell
Patricia A. Ryan
Murray Sabrin
Kanwal S. Sachedeva
R. Daniel Sadlier
Hadi Salavitabar
Gary Sanger
William L. Sartoris
Carl J. Schwendiman
Carl Schweser
Jim Scott
John W. Settle
Richard A. Shick
A. M. Sibley
Surendra S. Singhvi
Stacy Sirmans
Barry D. Smith
Gerald Smolen
Ira Smolowitz

Jean Snavely	Emery A. Trahan	Richard E. Williams
Joseph V. Stanford	Pieter A. Vandenberg	Glenn A. Wilt, Jr.
John A. Stocker	Nikhil P. Varaiya	Bernard J. Winger
Lester B. Strickler	Oscar Varela	Tony R. Wingler
Elizabeth Strock	Kenneth J. Venuto	I. R. Woods
Sankar Sundarrajan	James A. Verbrugge	John C. Woods
Philip R. Swensen	Ronald P. Volpe	Robert J. Wright
S. Tabriztchi	John M. Wachowicz, Jr.	Richard H. Yanow
John C. Talbott	William H. Weber III	Seung J. Yoon
Gary Tallman	Herbert Weinraub	Charles W. Young
Harry Tamule	Jonathan B. Welch	Philip J. Young
Richard W. Taylor	Grant J. Wells	Joe W. Zeman
Rolf K. Tedefalk	Larry R. White	J. Kenton Zumwalt
Richard Teweles	Peter Wichert	John T. Zeitlow
Kenneth J. Thygerson	C. Don Wiggins	Tom Zwirlein
Robert D. Tollen	Howard A. Williams	

My special thanks go to all members of my book team whose vision, creativity, and ongoing support helped me to engineer all elements of the Teaching/Learning System: to Michael J. Woodworth of Purdue University for the chapter opening vignettes and the *In Practice*: Focus on Practice boxes; to John Zietlow of Lee University and Edward Zajicek of Winston-Salem State University for the *In Practice:* Focus on Ethics boxes; to Mehdi Salehizadeh of San Diego State University for help in revising the chapter on International Finance; to William Mosher of Clark University for the Warm-Up Exercises, Group Exercises, and Web Exercises; to Steven Lifland of High Point University for the new in-chapter spreadsheet examples and the end-of-chapter Spreadsheet Exercises; to Bernard W. Weinrich of St. Louis Community College, Forest Park Campus, for preparing the marginal annotations; to Daniel J. Borgia of Florida Gulf Coast University for revising the Test Banks and the PowerPoint Lecture Presentations; to Fred Schadler of East Carolina University for updating the *Instructor's Manual;* and to Stan Eakins of East Carolina University for revising the *Study Guide* and to Michael Seiler of Hawaii Pacific University for updating the Case Studies in Finance on the book's Web site.

I'm pleased by and proud of all their efforts.

A hearty round of applause also goes to the publishing team assembled by Addison-Wesley—including Donna Battista, Mary Clare McEwing, Gina Kolenda, Nancy Fenton, Bethany Tidd, Dana Weightman, Jason Miranda, Kirstin Dickerson, Deborah Meredith, Stephen Frail, and others who worked on the book—for the inspiration and the perspiration that define teamwork. Nancy Freihofer and all the people at Thompson Steele, Inc. deserve an equally resounding ovation. A standing ovation is due Ann Torbert, whose development expertise and hard work have contributed to the book's standard of excellence. Also, special thanks to the formidable Addison-Wesley sales force in finance, whose ongoing efforts keep the business fun!

Finally, and most important, many thanks to my wife, Robin, and to our children, Zachary and Jessica, for patiently providing support, understanding, and good humor throughout the revision process. To them, I will be forever grateful.

Lawrence J. Gitman
La Jolla, California

To the Student

Because you have a good many options for getting your assigned reading materials, I appreciate your choosing this textbook as the best means for learning. You should not be disappointed. When I wrote the first edition of this book, I was not far removed from my undergraduate studies and therefore set out to write a book that would meet the needs of students. Through its various editions over the years, I have been careful to maintain that student focus.

In this eleventh edition of the textbook, my product team and I have put together an effective learning system. It integrates a variety of learning tools with the concepts, tools, techniques, and practical applications you'll need to learn about managerial finance. We have carefully listened to the compliments and complaints of students and of professors who have used earlier editions of this textbook in their coursework, and we have worked hard to present the most important concepts and practices of managerial finance in a clear and interesting way.

This book is loaded with features designed to motivate your study of finance and to help you learn the course material. For an overview and explanation of those features, go to pages vii–xii ("Gitman's Proven Teaching/Learning System"). The page views and descriptions there will walk you through the features included in the book.

Some words of advice about a few specific features: First, pay attention to the learning goals, which will help you focus attention on what material you need to learn, where you can find it in the chapter, and whether you've mastered it by the end of the chapter.

Second, at the end of each major text section are Review Questions. It may be tempting to rush past those questions, but try to resist doing so. Pausing briefly to test your understanding of the key concepts, tools, techniques, and practices in the section you've just read will help you cement your understanding of that material. Give yourself an honest assessment of whether you've understood what you've read. If you haven't, go back (even briefly) and review anything that seemed unclear.

Third, look for (or make) opportunities to talk with classmates or friends about what you're reading and learning in the course. Being able to talk about the concepts and techniques of finance demonstrates how much you've learned, uncovers things you haven't yet understood fully, and gives you valuable practice for class and (eventually) the business world. While you're talking, don't neglect to discuss the issues raised in the *Focus on Ethics* boxes in the book, which look at some of the types of opportunities to do right (or not) that people in business sometimes face.

Packaged with new copies of the text at no additional cost, the Student Access Kit for FinanceWorks opens the door to a powerful Web-based diagnostic testing and tutorial system designed specifically for this text. FinanceWorks allows you to take practice tests correlated to the textbook and receive a customized study plan based on their results. The problems in FinanceWorks are based on the even-numbered end-of-chapter problems. However, because the FinanceWorks problems have algorithmically generated values, no student will have the same homework as another. Thus there is an unlimited opportunity for practice and testing. You will get the help you need, when you need it, from the robust tutorial options, including "View an Example" and "Help Me Solve This," which breaks the problem into steps and links to the relevant textbook page.

Given today's rapidly changing technology, who knows what might be available next? We are striving to keep pace with your needs and interests, and want to hear your ideas for improving the teaching and learning of finance. Please feel free to share your ideas with us by e-mailing finance@aw-bc.com.

I wish you all the best in this course, and in your academic and professional careers.

Lawrence J. Gitman
San Diego State University

PART ONE

Introduction to Managerial Finance

1

Chapter 1

The Role and Environment of Managerial Finance

LEARNING GOALS

LG1 Define *finance,* its major areas and opportunities, and the legal forms of business organization.

LG2 Describe the managerial finance function and its relationship to economics and accounting.

LG3 Identify the primary activities of the financial manager.

LG4 Explain the goal of the firm, corporate governance, the role of ethics, and the agency issue.

LG5 Understand financial institutions and markets, and the role they play in managerial finance.

LG6 Discuss business taxes and their importance in financial decisions.

ACROSS THE DISCIPLINES WHY THIS CHAPTER MATTERS TO YOU

Accounting: You need to understand the relationships between the firm's accounting and finance functions; how the financial statements you prepare will be used for making investment and financing decisions; ethical behavior by those responsible for a firm's funds; what agency costs are and why the firm must bear them; and how to calculate the tax effects of proposed transactions.

Information systems: You need to understand the organization of the firm; why finance personnel require both historical and projected data to support investment and financing decisions; and what data are necessary for determining the firm's tax liability.

Management: You need to understand the legal forms of business organization; the tasks that will be performed by finance personnel; the goal of the firm; the issue of man-

agement compensation; the role of ethics in the firm; the agency problem; and the firm's relationship to various financial institutions and markets.

Marketing: You need to understand how the activities you pursue will be affected by the finance function, such as the firm's cash and credit management policies; the role of ethics in promoting a sound corporate image; and the role the financial markets play in the firm's ability to raise capital for new projects.

Operations: You need to understand the organization of the firm and of the finance function in particular; why maximizing profit is not the main goal of the firm; the role of financial institutions and markets in financing the firm's production capacity; and the role of ethics and the agency problem.

STARBUCKS

CREATING NEW FLAVORS FOR GROWTH

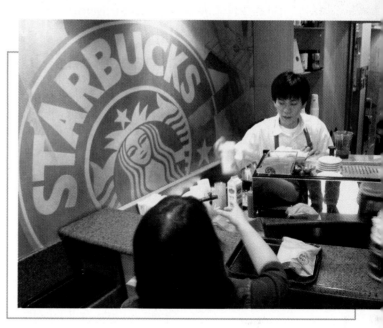

Sometimes it seems that there's a **Starbucks** (www.starbucks.com) on every corner—and now in supermarkets and hospitals as well. The company that revolutionized the way we think about coffee now has more than 7,500 retail locations worldwide and millions of customers each week lining up for lattes and other concoctions.

Founded in 1985, the chain's success is tied to its somewhat unusual business strategies. Its mission statement emphasizes, first, creating a better work environment for employees and, second, satisfying customers and promoting good corporate citizenship within its communities. For example, Starbucks was one of the first companies to offer health benefits and equity (ownership) to its part-time employees. The company's goal is to create an experience, including happy employees, that builds trust with the customer. Profits are among the last of its guiding principles.

Starbucks' bond with employees and customers has translated into sales and earnings that are as strong as its coffee. Sales growth for the 10-year period from 1994 to 2003 averaged more than 35 percent compounded per year, and growth in earnings averaged more than 41 percent per year. A share of Starbucks' stock purchased in January 1994 increased in value by 27.8 percent per year over the 10 years ended in January 2004, easily beating the S&P 500 return of 9.1 percent per year over the same 10-year period.

Although some fear that Starbucks has saturated the domestic market, same-store sales keep rising as the company introduces new beverage products and adds new customer services, including a retail digital music service, gift cards, and Internet "hot spots" in many of its stores. Expansion into the international market is a key element in the company's long-term goal of reaching 25,000 retail outlets. By early 2004, Starbucks had retail outlets in 37 countries, including three stores in Paris and nearly 200 in Tokyo.

Accomplishing its business objectives while building shareholder value requires that Starbucks practices sound financial management—raising funds to open new stores and build more roasting plants, deciding when and where to put them, managing cash collections, reducing purchasing costs, and dealing with the fluctuations in the value of foreign currency and other risks as it buys coffee beans and expands overseas.

Like Starbucks, every company must deal with many different issues to keep its financial condition solid. Chapter 1 introduces managerial finance and its key role in helping an organization meet its financial and business objectives.

■ *What additional concerns might a chief financial officer (CFO) face when a company expands into international markets?*

[LG1] 1.1 | Finance and Business

The field of finance is broad and dynamic. It directly affects the life of every person and of every organization. There are many areas and career opportunities in the field of finance. Basic principles of finance, such as those you will learn in this textbook, can be universally applied in business organizations of different types.

What Is Finance?

finance
The art and science of managing money.

Finance can be defined as the art and science of managing money. Virtually all individuals and organizations earn or raise money and spend or invest money. Finance is concerned with the process, institutions, markets, and instruments involved in the transfer of money among individuals, businesses, and governments. Most adults will benefit from an understanding of finance, which will enable them to make better personal financial decisions. Those who work in financial jobs will benefit by being able to interact effectively with the firm's financial personnel, processes, and procedures.

Major Areas and Opportunities in Finance

The major areas of finance can be summarized by reviewing the career opportunities in finance. These opportunities can, for convenience, be divided into two broad areas: financial services and managerial finance.

Financial Services

financial services
The area of finance concerned with the design and delivery of advice and financial products to individuals, business, and government.

Financial services is the area of finance concerned with the design and delivery of advice and financial products to individuals, business, and government. It involves a variety of interesting career opportunities within the areas of banking and related institutions, personal financial planning, investments, real estate, and insurance. Career opportunities available in each of these areas are described at this textbook's Web site www.aw-bc.com/gitman.

Managerial Finance

managerial finance
Concerns the duties of the *financial manager* in the business firm.

financial manager
Actively manages the financial affairs of any type of business, whether financial or nonfinancial, private or public, large or small, profit-seeking or not-for-profit.

Managerial finance is concerned with the duties of the financial manager in the business firm. **Financial managers** actively manage the financial affairs of any type of businesses—financial and nonfinancial, private and public, large and small, profit-seeking and not-for-profit. They perform such varied financial tasks as planning, extending credit to customers, evaluating proposed large expenditures, and raising money to fund the firm's operations. In recent years, changing economic, competitive, and regulatory environments have increased the importance and complexity of the financial manager's duties. Today's financial manager is more actively involved in developing and implementing corporate strategies aimed at "growing the firm" and improving its competitive position. As a result, many top executives have come from the finance area.

Another ongoing trend has been the globalization of business activity. U.S. corporations have dramatically increased their sales, purchases, investments, and fund raising in other countries, and foreign corporations have likewise increased their corresponding activities in the United States. These changes have increased the need for financial managers who can manage cash flows in different currencies and protect against the risks that naturally arise from international transactions. Although these changes make the managerial finance function more complex, they can lead to a more rewarding and fulfilling career.

Legal Forms of Business Organization

The three most common legal forms of business organization are the *sole proprietorship*, the *partnership*, and the *corporation*. Other specialized forms of business organization also exist. Sole proprietorships are the most numerous. However, corporations are overwhelmingly dominant with respect to business receipts and net profits. Corporations are given primary emphasis in this textbook.

Sole Proprietorships

sole proprietorship
A business owned by one person and operated for his or her own profit.

A **sole proprietorship** is a business owned by one person who operates it for his or her own profit. About 75 percent of all business firms are sole proprietorships. The typical sole proprietorship is a small business, such as a bike shop, personal trainer, or plumber. The majority of sole proprietorships are found in the wholesale, retail, service, and construction industries.

unlimited liability
The condition of a sole proprietorship (or general partnership) allowing the owner's total wealth to be taken to satisfy creditors.

Typically, the proprietor, along with a few employees, operates the proprietorship. He or she normally raises capital from personal resources or by borrowing and is responsible for all business decisions. The sole proprietor has **unlimited liability;** his or her total wealth—not merely the amount originally invested—can be taken to satisfy creditors. The key strengths and weaknesses of sole proprietorships are summarized in Table 1.1 (see page 6).

Partnerships

partnership
A business owned by two or more people and operated for profit.

A **partnership** consists of two or more owners doing business together for profit. Partnerships account for about 10 percent of all businesses, and they are typically larger than sole proprietorships. Finance, insurance, and real estate firms are the most common types of partnership. Public accounting and stock brokerage partnerships often have large numbers of partners.

articles of partnership
The written contract used to formally establish a business partnership.

Most partnerships are established by a written contract known as **articles of partnership.** In a *general* (or *regular*) *partnership*, all partners have unlimited liability, and each partner is legally liable for *all* of the debts of the partnership. Strengths and weaknesses of partnerships are summarized in Table 1.1.

Corporations

corporation
An artificial being created by law (often called a "legal entity").

A **corporation** is an artificial being created by law. Often called a "legal entity," a corporation has the powers of an individual in that it can sue and be sued, make and be party to contracts, and acquire property in its own name. Although only about 15 percent of all businesses are incorporated, the corporation is the dominant form of business organization in terms of receipts and profits. It accounts for nearly 90 percent of business receipts and 80 percent of net profits. Although corporations are involved in all types of businesses, manufacturing corporations account for the largest portion of corporate business receipts and net profits. The key strengths and weaknesses of large corporations are summarized in Table 1.1.

Hint Many small corporations, as well as small proprietorships and partnerships, have no access to financial markets. In addition, whenever the owners take out a loan, they usually must personally cosign the loan.

TABLE 1.1

Strengths and Weaknesses of the Common Legal Forms of Business Organization

	Sole proprietorship	Partnership	Corporation
Strengths	• Owner receives all profits (and sustains all losses) • Low organizational costs • Income included and taxed on proprietor's personal tax return • Independence • Secrecy • Ease of dissolution	• Can raise more funds than sole proprietorships • Borrowing power enhanced by more owners • More available brain power and managerial skill • Income included and taxed on partner's personal tax return	• Owners have *limited liability,* which guarantees that they cannot lose more than they invested • Can achieve large size via sale of ownership (stock) • Ownership (stock) is readily transferable • Long life of firm • Can hire professional managers • Has better access to financing • Can offer attractive retirement plans
Weaknesses	• Owner has *unlimited liability*—total wealth can be taken to satisfy debts • Limited fund-raising power tends to inhibit growth • Proprietor must be jack-of-all-trades • Difficult to give employees long-run career opportunities • Lacks continuity when proprietor dies	• Owners have *unlimited liability* and may have to cover debts of other partners • Partnership is dissolved when a partner dies • Difficult to liquidate or transfer partnership	• Taxes generally higher, because corporate income is taxed, and dividends paid to owners are also taxed at a maximum 15% rate • More expensive to organize than other business forms • Subject to greater government regulation • Lacks secrecy, because stockholders must receive financial reports

stockholders
The owners of a corporation, whose ownership, or *equity,* is evidenced by either common stock or preferred stock.

common stock
The purest and most basic form of corporate ownership.

dividends
Periodic distributions of earnings to the stockholders of a firm.

board of directors
Group elected by the firm's stockholders and typically responsible for developing strategic goals and plans, setting general policy, guiding corporate affairs, approving major expenditures, and hiring/firing, compensating, and monitoring key officers and executives.

The owners of a corporation are its **stockholders,** whose ownership, or *equity,* is evidenced by either common stock or preferred stock.[1] These forms of ownership are defined and discussed in Chapter 7; at this point it is enough to say that **common stock** is the purest and most basic form of corporate ownership. Stockholders expect to earn a return by receiving **dividends**—periodic distributions of earnings—or by realizing gains through increases in share price.

As noted in the upper portion of Figure 1.1, control of the corporation is structured as a democracy. The stockholders (owners) vote periodically to elect members of the board of directors and to decide other issues such as amending the corporate charter. The **board of directors** is typically responsible for developing strategic goals and plans, setting general policy, guiding corporate affairs, approving major expenditures, and hiring/firing, compensating, and monitoring key officers and executives. The directors typically include both "inside directors," such as key corporate executives, and "outside directors," such as executives from other companies, major shareholders, and national or community leaders. Outside directors for major corporations are generally paid an annual fee of $15,000 to $25,000 or more. Also, they are frequently granted options to buy a specified number of shares of the firm's stock at a stated—and often attractive—price.

1. Some corporations do not have stockholders but rather have "members" who often have rights similar to those of stockholders—that is, they are entitled to vote and receive dividends. Examples include mutual savings banks, credit unions, mutual insurance companies, and a whole host of charitable organizations.

FIGURE 1.1

Corporate Organization
The general organization
of a corporation and the
finance function (which is
shown in yellow)

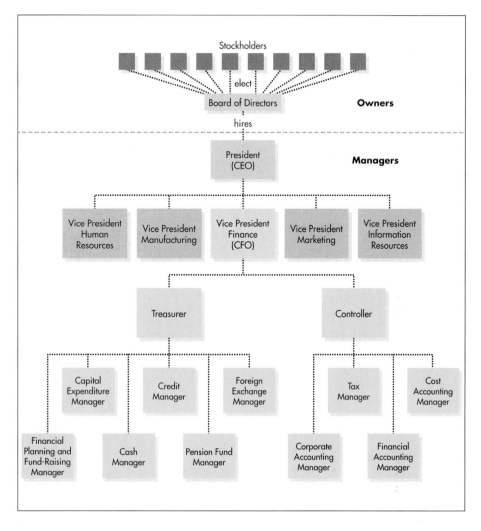

The **president or chief executive officer (CEO)** is responsible for managing day-to-day operations and carrying out the policies established by the board of directors. The CEO is required to report periodically to the firm's directors.

It is important to note the division between owners and managers in a large corporation, as shown by the dashed horizontal line in Figure 1.1. This separation and some of the issues surrounding it will be addressed in the discussion of *the agency issue* later in this chapter.

president or chief executive officer (CEO)
Corporate official responsible for managing the firm's day-to-day operations and carrying out the policies established by the *board of directors.*

Other Limited Liability Organizations

A number of other organizational forms provide owners with limited liability. The most popular are **limited partnerships (LPs)**, **S corporations (S corps)**, **limited liability corporations (LLCs)**, and **limited liability partnerships (LLPs)**. Each represents a specialized form or blending of the characteristics of the organizational forms described previously. What they have in common is that their owners enjoy limited liability, and they typically have fewer than 100 owners. Each of these limited liability organizations is briefly described in Table 1.2 (see page 8).

limited partnership (LP)
S corporation (S corp)
limited liability corporation (LLC)
limited liability partnership (LLP)
See Table 1.2.

Other Limited Liability Organizations

Organization	Description
Limited partnership (LP)	A partnership in which one or more partners have limited liability as long as at least *one* partner (the general partner) has unlimited liability. The *limited partners* cannot take an active role in the firm's management; they are passive investors.
S corporation (S corp)	A tax-reporting entity that (under Subchapter S of the Internal Revenue Code) allows certain corporations with 100 or fewer stockholders to choose to be taxed as partnerships. Its stockholders receive the organizational benefits of a corporation and the tax advantages of a partnership. But S corps lose certain tax advantages related to pension plans.
Limited liability corporation (LLC)	Permitted in most states, the LLC gives its owners, like those of S corps, limited liability and taxation as a partnership. But unlike an S corp, the LLC can own more than 80% of another corporation, and corporations, partnerships, or non-U.S. residents can own LLC shares. LLCs work well for corporate joint ventures or projects developed through a subsidiary.
Limited liability partnership (LLP)	A partnership permitted in many states; governing statutes vary by state. All LLP partners have limited liability. They are liable for their own acts of malpractice, but not for those of other partners. The LLP is taxed as a partnership. LLPs are frequently used by legal and accounting professionals.

Why Study Managerial Finance?

An understanding of the concepts, techniques, and practices presented throughout this text will fully acquaint you with the financial manager's activities and decisions. Because most business decisions are measured in financial terms, the financial manager plays a key role in the operation of the firm. People in all areas of responsibility—accounting, information systems, management, marketing, operations, and so forth—need a basic understanding of the managerial finance function.

Okay, so you're not planning to major in finance! You still will need to understand the activities of the financial manager to improve your chance of success in your chosen business career. All managers in the firm, regardless of their job descriptions, work with financial personnel to justify labor requirements, negotiate operating budgets, deal with financial performance appraisals, and sell proposals at least partly on the basis of their financial merits. Clearly, those managers who understand the financial decision-making process will be better able to address financial concerns and will therefore more often get the resources they need to attain their own goals. The "Across the Disciplines" element that appears on each chapter-opening page should help you understand some of the many interactions between managerial finance and other business careers. These features should help you understand the importance of finance to all business careers.

As you study this text, you will learn about the career opportunities in managerial finance, which are briefly described in Table 1.3. Although this text focuses on publicly held profit-seeking firms, the principles presented here are equally applicable to private and not-for-profit organizations. The decision-making prin-

TABLE 1.3

Career Opportunities in Managerial Finance

Position	Description
Financial analyst	Primarily prepares the firm's financial plans and budgets. Other duties include financial forecasting, performing financial comparisons, and working closely with accounting.
Capital expenditures manager	Evaluates and recommends proposed asset investments. May be involved in the financial aspects of implementing approved investments.
Project finance manager	In large firms, arranges financing for approved asset investments. Coordinates consultants, investment bankers, and legal counsel.
Cash manager	Maintains and controls the firm's daily cash balances. Frequently manages the firm's cash collection and disbursement activities and short-term investments; coordinates short-term borrowing and banking relationships.
Credit analyst/manager	Administers the firm's credit policy by evaluating credit applications, extending credit, and monitoring and collecting accounts receivable.
Pension fund manager	In large companies, oversees or manages the assets and liabilities of the employees' pension fund.
Foreign exchange manager	Manages specific foreign operations and the firm's exposure to fluctuations in exchange rates.

ciples developed in this text can also be applied to personal financial decisions. I hope that this first exposure to the exciting field of finance will provide the foundation and initiative for further study and possibly even a future career.

REVIEW QUESTIONS

1–1 What is *finance?* Explain how this field affects the life of everyone and of every organization.

1–2 What is the *financial services* area of finance? Describe the field of *managerial finance.*

1–3 Which legal form of business organization is most common? Which form is dominant in terms of business receipts and net profits?

1–4 Describe the roles and the basic relationship among the major parties in a corporation—stockholders, board of directors, and president. How are corporate owners compensated?

1–5 Briefly name and describe some organizational forms other than corporations that provide owners with limited liability.

1–6 Why is the study of managerial finance important regardless of the specific area of responsibility one has within the business firm?

LG2   LG3   1.2 | The Managerial Finance Function

People in all areas of responsibility within the firm must interact with finance personnel and procedures to get their jobs done. For financial personnel to make useful forecasts and decisions, they must be willing and able to talk to individuals in other areas of the firm. For example, when considering a new product, the financial manager needs to obtain sales forecasts, pricing guidelines, and advertising and promotion budget estimates from marketing personnel. The managerial finance function can be broadly described by considering its role within the organization, its relationship to economics and accounting, and the primary activities of the financial manager.

Organization of the Finance Function

treasurer
The firm's chief financial manager, who is responsible for the firm's financial activities, such as financial planning and fund raising, making capital expenditure decisions, and managing cash, credit, the pension fund, and foreign exchange.

controller
The firm's chief accountant, who is responsible for the firm's accounting activities, such as corporate accounting, tax management, financial accounting, and cost accounting.

Hint A *controller* is sometimes referred to as a *comptroller*. Not-for-profit and governmental organizations frequently use the title of comptroller.

The size and importance of the managerial finance function depend on the size of the firm. In small firms, the finance function is generally performed by the accounting department. As a firm grows, the finance function typically evolves into a separate department linked directly to the company president or CEO through the chief financial officer (CFO). The lower portion of the organizational chart in Figure 1.1 (on page 7) shows the structure of the finance function in a typical medium-to-large-size firm.

Reporting to the CFO are the treasurer and the controller. The **treasurer** (the chief financial manager) is commonly responsible for handling financial activities, such as financial planning and fund raising, making capital expenditure decisions, managing cash, managing credit activities, managing the pension fund, and managing foreign exchange. The **controller** (the chief accountant) typically handles the accounting activities, such as corporate accounting, tax management, financial accounting, and cost accounting. The treasurer's focus tends to be more external, the controller's focus more internal. *The activities of the treasurer, or financial manager, are the primary concern of this text.*

If international sales or purchases are important to a firm, it may well employ one or more finance professionals whose job is to monitor and manage the firm's exposure to loss from currency fluctuations. A trained financial manager can "hedge," or protect against such a loss, at reasonable cost by using a variety of financial instruments. These **foreign exchange managers** typically report to the firm's treasurer.

Relationship to Economics

foreign exchange manager
The manager responsible for monitoring and managing the firm's exposure to loss from currency fluctuations.

marginal cost–benefit analysis
Economic principle that states that financial decisions should be made and actions taken only when the added benefits exceed the added costs.

The field of finance is closely related to economics. Financial managers must understand the economic framework and be alert to the consequences of varying levels of economic activity and changes in economic policy. They must also be able to use economic theories as guidelines for efficient business operation. Examples include supply-and-demand analysis, profit-maximizing strategies, and price theory. The primary economic principle used in managerial finance is **marginal cost–benefit analysis,** the principle that financial decisions should be made and actions taken only when the added benefits exceed the added costs. Nearly all financial decisions ultimately come down to an assessment of their marginal benefits and marginal costs.

EXAMPLE   Jamie Teng is a financial manager for Nord Department Stores, a large chain of upscale department stores operating primarily in the western United States. She is currently trying to decide whether to replace one of the firm's online computers

FIG

Finan
Prima
financ

with a new, more sophisticated one that would both speed processing and handle a larger volume of transactions. The new computer would require a cash outlay of $80,000, and the old computer could be sold to net $28,000. The total benefits from the new computer (measured in today's dollars) would be $100,000. The benefits over a similar time period from the old computer (measured in today's dollars) would be $35,000. Applying marginal cost–benefit analysis, Jamie organizes the data as follows:

Benefits with new computer	$100,000	
Less: Benefits with old computer	35,000	
(1) Marginal (added) benefits		$65,000
Cost of new computer	$ 80,000	
Less: Proceeds from sale of old computer	28,000	
(2) Marginal (added) costs		52,000
Net benefit [(1) − (2)]		$13,000

Because the marginal (added) benefits of $65,000 exceed the marginal (added) costs of $52,000, Jamie recommends that the firm purchase the new computer to replace the old one. The firm will experience a net benefit of $13,000 as a result of this action. ■

Relationship to Accounting

The firm's finance (treasurer) and accounting (controller) activities are closely related and generally overlap. Indeed, managerial finance and accounting are often not easily distinguishable. In small firms the controller often carries out the finance function, and in large firms many accountants are closely involved in various finance activities. However, there are two basic differences between finance and accounting; one is related to the emphasis on cash flows and the other to decision making.

Emphasis on Cash Flows

The accountant's primary function is to develop and report data for measuring the performance of the firm, assess its financial position, comply with and file reports required by securities regulators, and file and pay taxes. Using certain standardized and generally accepted principles, the accountant prepares financial statements that recognize revenue at the time of sale (whether payment has been received or not) and recognize expenses when they are incurred. This approach is referred to as the **accrual basis.**

The financial manager, on the other hand, places primary emphasis on *cash flows,* the intake and outgo of cash. He or she maintains the firm's solvency by planning the cash flows necessary to satisfy its obligations and to acquire assets needed to achieve the firm's goals. The financial manager uses this **cash basis** to recognize the revenues and expenses only with respect to actual inflows and outflows of cash. Regardless of its profit or loss, *a firm must have a sufficient flow of cash to meet its obligations as they come due.*

accrual basis
In preparation of financial statements, recognizes revenue at the time of sale and recognizes expenses when they are incurred.

cash basis
Recognizes revenues and expenses only with respect to actual inflows and outflows of cash.

earnings
The amou
the perioc
outstandi
stock, calc
the perioc
available f
common s
the numbe
common s

EXAMPLE   Nick Dukakis, the financial manager of Neptune Manufacturing, a producer of marine engine components, is choosing between two investments, Rotor and Valve. The following table shows the EPS that each investment is expected to have over its 3-year life.

| Investment | Earnings per share (EPS) | | | |
	Year 1	Year 2	Year 3	Total for years 1, 2, and 3
Rotor	$1.40	$1.00	$0.40	$2.80
Valve	0.60	1.00	1.40	3.00

In terms of the profit maximization goal, Valve would be preferred over Rotor, because it results in higher total earnings per share over the 3-year period ($3.00 EPS compared with $2.80 EPS). ■

But is profit maximization a reasonable goal? No. It fails for a number of reasons: It ignores (1) the timing of returns, (2) cash flows available to stockholders, and (3) risk.[2]

Timing

Because the firm can earn a return on funds it receives, *the receipt of funds sooner rather than later is preferred.* In our example, in spite of the fact that the total earnings from Rotor are smaller than those from Valve, Rotor provides much greater earnings per share in the first year. The larger returns in year 1 could be reinvested to provide greater future earnings.

Cash Flows

Profits do *not* necessarily result in cash flows available to the stockholders. Owners receive cash flow in the form of either cash dividends paid them or the proceeds from selling their shares for a higher price than initially paid. Greater EPS do not necessarily mean that a firm's board of directors will vote to increase dividend payments.

Furthermore, higher EPS do not necessarily translate into a higher stock price. Firms sometimes experience earnings increases without any correspondingly favorable change in stock price. Only when earnings increases are accompanied by increased future cash flows would a higher stock price be expected. For example, a firm with a high-quality product sold in a very competitive market could increase its earnings by significantly reducing its equipment maintenance expenditures. As a result the firm's expenses would be reduced, thereby increasing its profits. But because the reduced maintenance will result in lower product quality, the firm would impair its competitive position and its stock price would drop as many well-informed investors sell the stock in recognition of lower future cash flows. In this case, the earnings increase was accompanied by lower future cash flows and therefore a lower stock price.

_____

2. Another criticism of profit maximization is the potential for profit manipulation through the creative use of elective accounting practices. This issue has received close scrutiny from securities regulators during recent years.

Risk

risk
The chance that actual outcomes may differ from those expected.

Profit maximization also disregards **risk**—the chance that actual outcomes may differ from those expected. A basic premise in managerial finance is that a tradeoff exists between return (cash flow) and risk. *Return and risk are, in fact, the key determinants of share price, which represents the wealth of the owners in the firm.*

Hint The relationship between risk and return is one of the most important concepts in the book. Investors who seek to avoid risk will *always* require a bigger return for taking bigger risks.

Cash flow and risk affect share price differently: Higher cash flow is generally associated with a higher share price. Higher risk tends to result in a lower share price because the stockholder must be compensated for the greater risk. For example, if a firm's highly successful CEO dies suddenly and a suitable successor is not available, its share price typically will drop immediately. This occurs not because of any near-term cash flow reduction but in response to the firm's increased risk—there's a chance that the firm's lack of near-term leadership could result in reduced future cash flows. Simply put, the increased risk reduces the firm's share price. In general, stockholders are **risk-averse**—that is, they want to avoid risk. When risk is involved, stockholders expect to earn higher rates of return on investments of higher risk and lower rates on lower-risk investments. The key point, which will be fully developed in Chapter 5, is that differences in risk can significantly affect the value of an investment.

risk-averse
Seeking to avoid risk.

Because profit maximization does not achieve the objectives of the firm's owners, it should *not* be the primary goal of the financial manager.

Maximize Shareholder Wealth

The goal of the firm, and therefore of all managers and employees, is *to maximize the wealth of the owners for whom it is being operated.* The wealth of corporate owners is measured by the share price of the stock, which in turn is based on the timing of returns (cash flows), their magnitude, and their risk.

When considering each financial decision alternative or possible action in terms of its effect on the share price of the firm's stock, *financial managers should accept only those actions that are expected to increase share price.* Figure 1.3 depicts this process. Because share price represents the owners' wealth in the firm, maximizing share price will maximize owner wealth. Note that *return (cash flows) and risk are the key decision variables in maximizing owner wealth.* It is important

FIGURE 1.3

Share Price Maximization
Financial decisions and share price

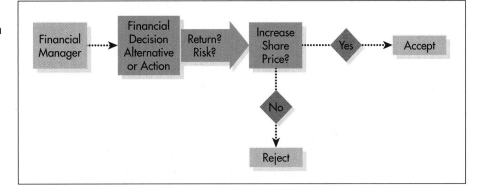

to recognize that earnings per share, because they are viewed as an indicator of the firm's future returns (cash flows), often appear to affect share price.

What About Stakeholders?

Although maximization of shareholder wealth is the primary goal, many firms broaden their focus to include the interests of *stakeholders* as well as shareholders. **Stakeholders** are groups such as employees, customers, suppliers, creditors, owners, and others who have a direct economic link to the firm. A firm with a *stakeholder focus* consciously avoids actions that would prove detrimental to stakeholders. The goal is not to maximize stakeholder well-being but to preserve it.

stakeholders
Groups such as employees, customers, suppliers, creditors, owners, and others who have a direct economic link to the firm.

The stakeholder view does not alter the goal of maximizing shareholder wealth. Such a view is often considered part of the firm's "social responsibility." It is expected to provide long-run benefit to shareholders by maintaining positive stakeholder relationships. Such relationships should minimize stakeholder turnover, conflicts, and litigation. Clearly, the firm can better achieve its goal of shareholder wealth maximization by fostering cooperation with its other stakeholders, rather than conflict with them.

Corporate Governance

The system used to direct and control a corporation is referred to as **corporate governance.** It defines the rights and responsibilities of the key corporate participants such as the shareholders, board of directors, officers and managers, and other stakeholders, and the rules and procedures for making corporate decisions. It also typically specifies the structure through which the company sets objectives, develops plans for achieving them, and establishes procedures for monitoring performance.

corporate governance
The system used to direct and control a corporation. Defines the rights and responsibilities of key corporate participants, decision-making procedures, and the way in which the firm will set, achieve, and monitor its objectives.

Figure 1.1 on page 7 depicts the typical corporate governance structure, in which the stockholders (owners) elect a board of directors (their representatives), who in turn hire officers and managers (professional managers) to operate the firm in a manner consistent with the goals, plans, and policies established and monitored by the board on behalf of the shareholders. Typically, the board's policies specify ethical practices and provide for the protection of stakeholder interests.

Individual Versus Institutional Investors

Clearly, the corporate board's first responsibility is to the shareholders. To better understand this responsibility it is helpful to differentiate between the two broad classes of owners—individuals and institutions. **Individual investors** are investors who buy relatively small quantities of shares so as to earn a return on idle funds, build a source of retirement income, or provide financial security. **Institutional investors** are investment professionals that are paid to manage other people's money. They hold and trade large quantities of securities for individuals, businesses, and governments. Institutional investors include banks, insurance companies, mutual funds, and pension funds, which invest large sums of money to earn competitive returns for their clients/plan participants.

individual investors
Investors who buy relatively small quantities of shares so as to meet personal investment goals.

institutional investors
Investment professionals, such as insurance companies, mutual funds, and pension funds, that are paid to manage other people's money and that trade large quantities of securities.

Because they hold and trade large blocks of stock, institutional investors tend to have a much greater influence on corporate governance than do individual investors. Simply stated, because they own large amounts of common stock and have the resources to buy and sell large blocks of shares, institutional investors are able to maintain management's attention. If a large institutional investor sells or buys a sizable block of shares, the share price will likely be driven down or up, respectively. Clearly, these large investors speak in a much louder voice than does the individual investor.

The Sarbanes-Oxley Act of 2002

Beginning in 2000, numerous corporate misdeeds were uncovered and disclosed by various regulatory bodies. The misdeeds derived from two main types of issues: (1) false disclosures in financial reporting and other information releases, and (2) undisclosed conflicts of interest between corporations and their analysts, auditors, and attorneys and between corporate directors, officers, and shareholders. In response to these fraudulent disclosures and conflicts of interest, in July 2002 Congress passed the **Sarbanes-Oxley Act of 2002** (commonly called **SOX**).

Sarbanes-Oxley focused on eliminating the many disclosure and conflict of interest problems that had surfaced. It did the following: established an oversight board to monitor the accounting industry; tightened audit regulations and controls; toughened penalties against executives who commit corporate fraud; strengthened accounting disclosure requirements and ethical guidelines for corporate officers; established corporate board structure and membership guidelines; established guidelines with regard to analyst conflicts of interest; mandated instant disclosure of stock sales by corporate executives; and increased securities regulation authority and budgets for auditors and investigators. Although it is too soon to know the full effect of SOX, most commentators believe it will be effective in eliminating fraudulent disclosures and conflicts of interest by corporations.

Sarbanes-Oxley Act of 2002 (SOX)
An act aimed at eliminating corporate disclosure and conflict of interest problems. Contains provisions about corporate financial disclosures and the relationships among corporations, analysts, auditors, attorneys, directors, officers, and shareholders.

The Role of Ethics

In recent years, the ethics of actions taken by certain businesses have received major media attention. Examples include aircraft manufacturer Boeing Co.'s receiving billions of dollars of contracts with the Pentagon as a result of its questionable dealings with an Air Force acquisitions official, who later became a Boeing vice president and in 2004 was sentenced to nine months in prison for her actions; auditing firm KPMG's 2004 agreement to pay $115 million, one of the largest settlements ever paid by an auditing firm, to settle a shareholder lawsuit claiming they had failed in their audit work for Lernout & Hauspie Speech Products NV, a now-defunct Belgian maker of speech-recognition software; the late 2002 agreement by ten of Wall Street's largest firms to pay $1.4 billion to settle allegations by state and federal regulators that they provided misleading stock advice to investors for the benefit of their coprorate invesment banking clients; an agreement by financial services company American Express Co. in early 2002 to pay $31 million to settle a sex- and age-discrimination lawsuit filed on behalf of more than 4,000 women who said they were denied equal pay and promotions; and energy company Enron Corp.'s key executives indicating to employee-shareholders in mid-2001 that the firm's then-depressed stock price would soon recover while, at the same time, selling their own shares and, not long after, taking the firm into bankruptcy.

ethics
Standards of conduct or moral judgment.

Clearly, these and similar actions have raised the question of **ethics**—standards of conduct or moral judgment. Today, the business community in general and the financial community in particular are developing and enforcing ethical standards. The goal of these ethical standards is to motivate business and market participants to adhere to both the letter and the spirit of laws and regulations concerned with business and professional practice. Most business leaders believe businesses actually strengthen their competitive positions by maintaining high ethical standards.

Considering Ethics

Robert A. Cooke, a noted ethicist, suggests that the following questions be used to assess the ethical viability of a proposed action.[3]

1. Is the action arbitrary or capricious? Does it unfairly single out an individual or group?
2. Does the action violate the moral or legal rights of any individual or group?
3. Does the action conform to accepted moral standards?
4. Are there alternative courses of action that are less likely to cause actual or potential harm?

Clearly, considering such questions before taking an action can help to ensure its ethical viability. Specifically, Cooke suggests that the effects of a proposed decision should be evaluated from a number of perspectives before it is finalized:

1. Are the rights of any stakeholder being violated?
2. Does the firm have any overriding duties to any stakeholder?
3. Will the decision benefit any stakeholder to the detriment of another stakeholder?
4. If there is detriment to any stakeholder, how should it be remedied, if at all?
5. What is the relationship between stockholders and other stakeholders?

Today, an increasing number of firms are directly addressing the issue of ethics by establishing corporate ethics policies and requiring employee compliance with them. The *In Practice* box on the facing page, for example, describes ethics concerns at Hewlett-Packard. A major impetus toward the development of corporate ethics policies has been the *Sarbanes-Oxley Act of 2002* described earlier. Frequently, employees are required to sign a formal pledge to uphold the firm's ethics policies. Such policies typically apply to employee actions in dealing with all corporate stakeholders, including the public. Many companies also require employees to participate in ethics seminars and training programs. To provide further insight into the ethical dilemmas and issues sometimes facing the financial manager, one of the two *In Practice* boxes in each chapter focuses on ethics.

Ethics and Share Price

An effective ethics program is believed to enhance corporate value. An ethics program can produce a number of positive benefits. It can reduce potential litigation and judgment costs; maintain a positive corporate image; build shareholder confidence; and gain the loyalty, commitment, and respect of the firm's stakeholders. Such actions, by maintaining and enhancing cash flow and reducing perceived risk, can positively affect the firm's share price. *Ethical behavior is therefore viewed as necessary for achieving the firm's goal of owner wealth maximization.*[4]

---

3. Robert A. Cooke, "Business Ethics: A Perspective," in *Arthur Andersen Cases on Business Ethics* (Chicago: Arthur Andersen, September 1991), pp. 2 and 5.

4. For an excellent discussion of this and related issues by a number of finance academics and practitioners who have given a lot of thought to financial ethics, see James S. Ang, "On Financial Ethics," *Financial Management* (Autumn 1993), pp. 32–59.

In Practice FOCUS ON ETHICS

ETHICS AT HEWLETT-PACKARD

In 1939, long before anyone coined the expression "corporate social responsibility," Bill Hewlett and Dave Packard started a company, **Hewlett-Packard,** based on principles of fair dealing and respect. HP credits its ongoing commitment to "doing well by doing good" as a major reason why employees, suppliers, customers, and shareholders seek it out. HP is clear on its obligation to increase the market value of its common stock, yet it strives to maintain the integrity of each employee in every country in which it does business. HP's "Standards of Business Conduct" includes the following warning to employees, especially finance staffers (p. 1):

> HP employees at every level must comply with these Standards, and associated policies and guidelines. Failure to do so is considered misconduct and may lead to termination of employment. In particular, all executive officers and senior financial officers, their staffs, and all managers and other employees contributing to HP's financial record-keeping must comply strictly with HP finance and accounting standards, policies, and guidelines.

CEO Carly Fiorina, in her "CEO's Message" at the beginning of the "Standards of Business Conduct," states (p. iii): "Unethical or illegal business conduct on the part of HP is simply unacceptable and will not be tolerated."

Such a stance puts the company under the microscope. When HP began its publicity blitz to gain stockholder acceptance of its eventual merger with **Compaq,** Walter Hewlett, a member of both the board and the Hewlett family, filed suit alleging misstatement of financial facts and improper pressure of shareholder Deutsche Bank on the part of the HP management team. Although a Delaware judge dismissed the lawsuit, its mere existence underscored the fact that a company's ethics constantly face the scrutiny of the public and investors. HP's reputation was reaffirmed in 2003 when it was one of three companies awarded the Society of Financial Service Professionals' American Business Ethics Awards.

Maximizing shareholder wealth is what some call a "moral imperative," in that stockholders are owners who have property rights, and managers are stewards who are obliged to look out for owners' interests. Many times, doing what is right is consistent with maximizing the stock price. But what if integrity concerns cause a company to lose a contract or result in analysts reducing their rating of the stock from "buy" to "sell"? Despite the risk of such setbacks, the objective (maximizing shareholder wealth) holds, and company officers must pursue the objective within the ethical constraints. Those constraints occasionally limit the menu of actions from which managers may choose. Some critics have mistakenly assumed that the objective was the cause of unethical

behavior, ignoring the fact that *any* business goal might be cited as a factor pressuring individuals to be unethical.

American business professionals have tended to operate from within a strong moral foundation, based on early childhood moral development that takes place in families and religious institutions. This ethos does not prevent all ethical lapses, of course: After news of a major bond price manipulation episode broke, a Treasury Department official was quoted in the *Wall Street Journal* as saying the traders "broke lessons you learned in Sunday school in second grade." It's not surprising that chief financial officers declare that the number 1 personal attribute finance grads need is ethics—more than interpersonal skills, communication skills, decision-making ability, or computer skills. HP is aware of this, and has institutionalized it in its culture and policies.

■ *Can you come up with three or four basic ethics "lessons" (perhaps learned from your family and/or a religious institution) that might be said to form the basis of your ethical foundation? (It might be interesting to search out an acquaintance or two in your finance class later and compare notes.)*

The Agency Issue

We have seen that the goal of the financial manager should be to maximize the wealth of the firm's owners. Thus managers can be viewed as *agents* of the owners who have hired them and given them decision-making authority to manage the firm. Technically, any manager who owns less than 100 percent of the firm is to some degree an agent of the other owners. This separation of owners and managers is shown by the dashed horizontal line in Figure 1.1 on page 7.

In theory, most financial managers would agree with the goal of owner wealth maximization. In practice, however, managers are also concerned with their personal wealth, job security, and fringe benefits. Such concerns may make managers reluctant or unwilling to take more than moderate risk if they perceive that taking too much risk might jeopardize their jobs or reduce their personal wealth. The result is a less-than-maximum return and a potential loss of wealth for the owners.

Hint A stockbroker confronts the same issue. If she gets you to buy and sell more stock, it's good for *her,* but it may *not* be good for you.

The Agency Problem

agency problem
The likelihood that managers may place personal goals ahead of corporate goals.

From this conflict of owner and personal goals arises what has been called the **agency problem,** the likelihood that managers may place personal goals ahead of corporate goals.[5] Two factors—market forces and *agency costs*—serve to prevent or minimize agency problems.

Market Forces   One market force is major shareholders, particularly large *institutional investors* such as life insurance companies, mutual funds, and pension funds. These holders of large blocks of a firm's stock exert pressure on management to perform, by communicating their concerns to the firm's board. They often threaten to exercise their voting rights or liquidate their holdings if the board does not respond positively to their concerns.

Another market force is the *threat of takeover* by another firm that believes it can enhance the target firm's value by restructuring its management, operations, and financing.[6] The constant threat of a takeover tends to motivate management to act in the best interests of the firm's owners.

agency costs
The costs borne by stockholders to maintain a *governance structure* that minimizes agency problems and contributes to the maximization of owner wealth.

Agency Costs   To minimize agency problems and contribute to the maximization of owners' wealth, stockholders incur **agency costs.** These are the costs of maintaining a *corporate governance* structure that monitors management behavior, ensures against dishonest acts of management, and gives managers the financial incentive to maximize share price.

The most popular, powerful, and expensive approach is to *structure management compensation* to correspond with share price maximization. The objective is to give managers incentives to act in the best interests of the owners. In addition, the resulting compensation packages allow firms to compete for and hire the

5. The agency problem and related issues were first addressed by Michael C. Jensen and William H. Meckling, "Theory of the Firm: Managerial Behavior, Agency Costs and Ownership Structure," *Journal of Financial Economics* 3 (October 1976), pp. 305–306. For an excellent discussion of Jensen and Meckling and subsequent research on the agency problem, see William L. Megginson, *Corporate Finance Theory* (Boston, MA: Addison Wesley, 1997), Chapter 2.

6. Detailed discussion of the important aspects of corporate takeovers is included in Chapter 17, "Mergers, LBOs, Divestitures, and Business Failure."

best managers available. The two key types of compensation plans are incentive plans and performance plans.

Incentive plans tend to tie management compensation to share price. The most popular incentive plan is the granting of **stock options** to management. These options allow managers to purchase stock at the market price set at the time of the grant. If the market price rises, managers will be rewarded by being able to resell the shares at the higher market price.

Many firms also offer **performance plans,** which tie management compensation to measures such as earnings per share (EPS), growth in EPS, and other ratios of return. **Performance shares,** shares of stock given to management as a result of meeting the stated performance goals, are often used in these plans. Another form of performance-based compensation is **cash bonuses,** cash payments tied to the achievement of certain performance goals.

The Current View of Management Compensation

The execution of many compensation plans has been closely scrutinized in recent years. Both individuals and institutional stockholders, as well as the Securities and Exchange Commission (SEC), continue to publicly question the appropriateness of the multimillion-dollar compensation packages that many corporate executives receive. For example, the three highest-paid CEOs in 2003 were (1) Reuben Mark of Colgate-Palmolive, who earned $141.1 million; (2) Steven P. Jobs of Apple Computer, who earned $74.8 million; and (3) George David of United Technologies, who earned $70.5 million. Tenth on the same list was Richard M. Kovacevich of Wells Fargo, who earned $35.9 million. During 2003, the compensation of the average CEO of a major U.S. corporation increased by about 9 percent from 2002. CEOs of 365 of the largest U.S. companies surveyed by *Business Week,* using data from Standard & Poor's EXECUCOMP, earned an average of $8.1 million in total compensation; the average for the 20 highest paid CEOs was $46.5 million.

Recent studies have failed to find a strong relationship between CEO compensation and share price. During the past few years, publicity surrounding these large compensation packages (without corresponding share price performance) has driven down executive compensation. Contributing to this publicity is the SEC requirement that publicly traded companies disclose to shareholders and others both the amount of compensation to their highest-paid executives and the method used to determine it. At the same time, new compensation plans that better link managers' performance with regard to shareholder wealth to their compensation are being developed and implemented.

Unconstrained, managers may have other goals in addition to share price maximization, but much of the evidence suggests that share price maximization—the focus of this book—is the primary goal of most firms.

REVIEW QUESTIONS

1–11 For what three basic reasons is profit maximization inconsistent with wealth maximization?

1–12 What is *risk?* Why must risk as well as return be considered by the financial manager who is evaluating a decision alternative or action?

---

incentive plans
Management compensation plans that tend to tie management compensation to share price; the most popular incentive plan involves the grant of *stock options.*

stock options
An incentive allowing managers to purchase stock at the market price set at the time of the grant.

performance plans
Plans that tie management compensation to measures such as EPS, growth in EPS, and other ratios of return. *Performance shares* and/or *cash bonuses* are used as compensation under these plans.

performance shares
Shares of stock given to management for meeting stated performance goals.

cash bonuses
Cash paid to management for achieving certain performance goals.

1–13   What is the goal of the firm and, therefore, of all managers and employees? Discuss how one measures achievement of this goal.

1–14   What is *corporate governance?* How has the Sarbanes-Oxley Act of 2002 affected it? Explain.

1–15   Describe the role of corporate ethics policies and guidelines, and discuss the relationship that is believed to exist between ethics and share price.

1–16   How do market forces—both shareholder activism and the threat of takeover—act to prevent or minimize the *agency problem?* What role do *institutional investors* play in shareholder activism?

1–17   Define *agency costs*, and explain their relationship to a firm's *corporate governance* structure. How can the firm *structure management compensation* to minimize agency problems? What is the current view with regard to the execution of many compensation plans?

LG5   # 1.4 | Financial Institutions and Markets

Most successful firms have ongoing needs for funds. They can obtain funds from external sources in three ways. The first source is through a *financial institution* that accepts savings and transfers them to those that need funds. A second source is through *financial markets,* organized forums in which the suppliers and demanders of various types of funds can make transactions. A third source is through *private placement.* Because of the unstructured nature of private placements, here we focus primarily on the role of financial institutions and financial markets in facilitating business financing.

Financial Institutions

financial institution
An intermediary that channels the savings of individuals, businesses, and governments into loans or investments.

Hint Think about how inefficient it would be if each individual saver had to negotiate with each potential user of savings. Institutions make the process very efficient by becoming intermediaries between savers and users.

Financial institutions serve as intermediaries by channeling the savings of individuals, businesses, and governments into loans or investments. Many financial institutions directly or indirectly pay savers interest on deposited funds; others provide services for a fee (for example, checking accounts for which customers pay service charges). Some financial institutions accept customers' savings deposits and lend this money to other customers or to firms; others invest customers' savings in earning assets such as real estate or stocks and bonds; and some do both. Financial institutions are required by the government to operate within established regulatory guidelines.

Key Customers of Financial Institutions

The key suppliers of funds to financial institutions and the key demanders of funds from financial institutions are individuals, businesses, and governments. The savings that individual consumers place in financial institutions provide these institutions with a large portion of their funds. Individuals not only supply funds to financial institutions but also demand funds from them in the form of loans. However, individuals as a group are the *net suppliers* for financial institutions: They save more money than they borrow.

Business firms also deposit some of their funds in financial institutions, primarily in checking accounts with various commercial banks. Like individuals, firms borrow funds from these institutions, but firms are *net demanders* of funds: They borrow more money than they save.

Governments maintain deposits of temporarily idle funds, certain tax payments, and Social Security payments in commercial banks. They do not borrow funds *directly* from financial institutions, although by selling their debt securities to various institutions, governments indirectly borrow from them. The government, like business firms, is typically a *net demander* of funds: It typically borrows more than it saves. We've all heard about the federal budget deficit.

Major Financial Institutions

The major financial institutions in the U.S. economy are commercial banks, savings and loans, credit unions, savings banks, insurance companies, mutual funds, and pension funds. These institutions attract funds from individuals, businesses, and governments, combine them, and make loans available to individuals and businesses. Descriptions of the major financial institutions are found at the textbook's Web site at www.aw-bc.com/gitman.

Financial Markets

financial markets
Forums in which suppliers of funds and demanders of funds can transact business directly.

private placement
The sale of a new security issue, typically bonds or preferred stock, directly to an investor or group of investors.

public offering
The nonexclusive sale of either bonds or stocks to the general public.

primary market
Financial market in which securities are initially issued; the only market in which the issuer is directly involved in the transaction.

secondary market
Financial market in which preowned securities (those that are not new issues) are traded.

Financial markets are forums in which suppliers of funds and demanders of funds can transact business directly. Whereas the loans and investments of institutions are made without the direct knowledge of the suppliers of funds (savers), suppliers in the financial markets know where their funds are being lent or invested. The two key financial markets are the money market and the capital market. Transactions in short-term debt instruments, or marketable securities, take place in the *money market*. Long-term securities—bonds and stocks—are traded in the *capital market*.

To raise money, firms can use either private placements or public offerings. **Private placement** involves the sale of a new security issue, typically bonds or preferred stock, directly to an investor or group of investors, such as an insurance company or pension fund. Most firms, however, raise money through a **public offering** of securities, which is the nonexclusive sale of either bonds or stocks to the general public.

All securities are initially issued in the **primary market**. This is the only market in which the corporate or government issuer is directly involved in the transaction and receives direct benefit from the issue. That is, the company actually receives the proceeds from the sale of securities. Once the securities begin to trade between savers and investors, they become part of the **secondary market**. The primary market is the one in which "new" securities are sold. The secondary market can be viewed as a "preowned" securities market.

The Relationship Between Institutions and Markets

Financial institutions actively participate in the financial markets as both suppliers and demanders of funds. Figure 1.4 (see page 24) depicts the general flow of funds through and between financial institutions and financial markets; private placement transactions are also shown. The individuals, businesses, and governments that supply and demand funds may be domestic or foreign. We next

FIGURE 1.4

Flow of Funds
Flow of funds for financial institutions and markets

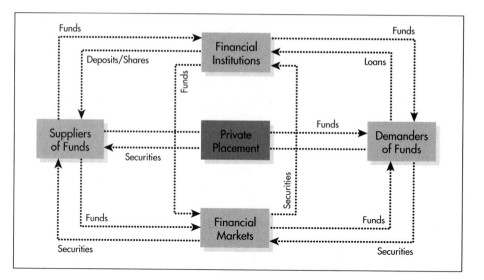

briefly discuss the money market, including its international equivalent—the *Eurocurrency market*. We then end this section with a discussion of the capital market, which is of key importance to the firm.

The Money Market

money market
A financial relationship created between suppliers and demanders of *short-term funds.*

The **money market** is created by a financial relationship between suppliers and demanders of *short-term funds* (funds with maturities of one year or less). The money market exists because some individuals, businesses, governments, and financial institutions have temporarily idle funds that they wish to put to some interest-earning use. At the same time, other individuals, businesses, governments, and financial institutions find themselves in need of seasonal or temporary financing. The money market brings together these suppliers and demanders of short-term funds.

marketable securities
Short-term debt instruments, such as U.S. Treasury bills, commercial paper, and negotiable certificates of deposit issued by government, business, and financial institutions, respectively.

Most money market transactions are made in **marketable securities**—short-term debt instruments, such as U.S. Treasury bills, commercial paper, and negotiable certificates of deposit issued by government, business, and financial institutions, respectively. (Marketable securities are described in Chapter 14.)

The Operation of the Money Market

The money market is not an actual organization housed in some central location. How, then, are suppliers and demanders of short-term funds brought together? Typically, they are matched through the facilities of large New York banks and through government securities dealers. A number of stock brokerage firms purchase money market instruments for resale to customers. Also, financial institutions purchase money market instruments for their portfolios so as to provide attractive returns on their customers' deposits and share purchases. Additionally, the Federal Reserve banks become involved in loans from one commercial bank to another; these loans are referred to as transactions in **federal funds**.

federal funds
Loan transactions between commercial banks in which the Federal Reserve banks become involved.

In the money market, businesses and governments demand short-term funds (borrow) by *issuing* a money market instrument. Parties that supply short-term

Hint Remember that the *money market* is for short-term fund raising and is represented by current liabilities on the balance sheet. The *capital market* is for long-term fund raising and is reflected by long-term debt and equity on the balance sheet.

Eurocurrency market
International equivalent of the domestic money market.

funds (invest) *purchase* the money market instruments. To issue or purchase a money market instrument, one party must go directly to another party or use an intermediary, such as a bank or brokerage firm, to make the transaction. The secondary (resale) market for marketable securities is no different from the primary (initial issue) market with respect to the basic transactions that are made. Individuals also participate in the money market as purchasers and sellers of money market instruments. Although individuals do not issue marketable securities, they may sell them in the money market to liquidate them prior to maturity.

The Eurocurrency Market

The international equivalent of the domestic money market is called the **Eurocurrency market.** This is a market for short-term bank deposits denominated in U.S. dollars or other easily convertible currencies. Historically, the Eurocurrency market has been centered in London, but it has evolved into a truly global market.

Eurocurrency deposits arise when a corporation or individual makes a bank deposit in a currency other than the local currency of the country where the bank is located. If, for example, a multinational corporation were to deposit U.S. dollars in a London bank, this would create a Eurodollar deposit (a dollar deposit at a bank in Europe). Nearly all Eurodollar deposits are *time deposits.* This means that the bank would promise to repay the deposit, with interest, at a fixed date in the future—say, in 6 months. During the interim, the bank is free to lend this dollar deposit to creditworthy corporate or government borrowers. If the bank cannot find a borrower on its own, it may lend the deposit to another international bank. The rate charged on these "interbank loans" is called the **London Interbank Offered Rate (LIBOR),** and it is the base rate that is used to price all Eurocurrency loans.

London Interbank Offered Rate (LIBOR)
The base rate that is used to price all Eurocurrency loans.

The Eurocurrency market has grown rapidly, primarily because it is an unregulated, wholesale, and global market that fills the needs of both borrowers and lenders. Investors with excess cash to lend are able to make large, short-term, and safe deposits at attractive interest rates. Likewise, borrowers are able to arrange large loans, quickly and confidentially, also at attractive interest rates.

The Capital Market

capital market
A market that enables suppliers and demanders of *long-term funds* to make transactions.

The **capital market** is a market that enables suppliers and demanders of *long-term funds* to make transactions. Included are securities issues of business and government. The backbone of the capital market is formed by the various *securities exchanges* that provide a forum for bond and stock transactions.

Key Securities Traded: Bonds and Stocks

The key capital market securities are *bonds* (long-term debt) and both *common stock* and *preferred stock* (equity, or ownership).

bond
Long-term debt instrument used by business and government to raise large sums of money, generally from a diverse group of lenders.

Bonds are long-term debt instruments used by business and government to raise large sums of money, generally from a diverse group of lenders. *Corporate bonds* typically pay interest *semiannually* (every 6 months) at a stated *coupon interest rate.* They have an initial *maturity* of from 10 to 30 years, and a *par,* or *face, value* of $1,000 that must be repaid at maturity. Bonds are described in detail in Chapter 6.

EXAMPLE   Lakeview Industries, a major microprocessor manufacturer, has issued a 9 percent coupon interest rate, 20-year bond with a $1,000 par value that pays interest semiannually. Investors who buy this bond receive the contractual right to $90 annual interest (9% coupon interest rate × $1,000 par value) distributed as $45 at the end of each 6 months (1/2 × $90) for 20 years, plus the $1,000 par value at the end of year 20. ■

As noted earlier, shares of *common stock* are units of ownership, or equity, in a corporation. Common stockholders earn a return by receiving dividends—periodic distributions of earnings—or by realizing increases in share price. **Preferred stock** is a special form of ownership that has features of both a bond and common stock. Preferred stockholders are promised a fixed periodic dividend that must be paid prior to payment of any dividends to common stockholders. In other words, preferred stock has "preference" over common stock. Preferred and common stock are described in detail in Chapter 7.

preferred stock
A special form of ownership having a fixed periodic dividend that must be paid prior to payment of any dividends to common stockholders.

Major Securities Exchanges

Securities exchanges provide the marketplace in which firms can raise funds through the sale of new securities and purchasers of securities can easily resell them when necessary. Many people call securities exchanges "stock markets," but this label is misleading because bonds, common stock, preferred stock, and a variety of other investment vehicles are all traded on these exchanges. The two key types of securities exchanges are the organized exchange and the over-the-counter exchange. In addition, important markets exist outside the United States.

securities exchanges
Organizations that provide the marketplace in which firms can raise funds through the sale of new securities and purchasers can resell securities.

Organized Securities Exchanges   **Organized securities exchanges** are tangible organizations that act as *secondary markets* where outstanding securities are resold. Organized exchanges account for about 62 percent of the *total dollar volume* (about 46 percent of the *total share volume*) of domestic shares traded. The best-known organized exchanges are the New York Stock Exchange (NYSE) and the American Stock Exchange (AMEX), both headquartered in New York City. There are also regional exchanges, such as the Chicago Stock Exchange and the Pacific Exchange.

organized securities exchanges
Tangible organizations that act as *secondary markets* where outstanding securities are resold.

Most exchanges are modeled after the New York Stock Exchange, which is the dominant *organized* U.S. exchange. For a firm's securities to be listed for trading on an organized exchange, a firm must file an application for listing and meet a number of requirements. For example, to be eligible for listing on the NYSE, a firm must have at least 2,200 stockholders owning 100 or more shares; a minimum of 1.1 million shares of publicly held stock outstanding; pretax earnings of at least $6.5 million over the previous 3 years, with no loss in the previous 2 years; and a minimum market value of public shares of $100 million. Clearly, only large, widely held firms are candidates for NYSE listing.

To make transactions on the "floor" of the New York Stock Exchange, an individual or firm must own a "seat" on the exchange. There are a total of 1,366 seats on the NYSE, most of which are owned by brokerage firms. Trading is carried out on the floor of the exchange through an *auction process*. The goal of trading is to fill *buy orders* at the lowest price and to fill *sell orders* at the highest price, thereby giving both purchasers and sellers the best possible deal.

Once placed, an order to buy or sell can be executed in minutes, thanks to sophisticated telecommunication devices. New Internet-based brokerage systems enable investors to place their buy and sell orders electronically. Information on publicly traded securities is reported in various media, both print, such as the *Wall Street Journal,* and electronic, such as MSN Money (www.moneycentral .msn.com).

over-the-counter (OTC) exchange
An intangible market for the purchase and sale of securities not listed by the organized exchanges.

The Over-the-Counter Exchange   The **over-the-counter (OTC) exchange** is an intangible market for the purchase and sale of securities not listed by the organized exchanges. OTC traders, known as *dealers,* are linked with the purchasers and sellers of securities through the *National Association of Securities Dealers Automated Quotation (Nasdaq) system.*

This sophisticated telecommunications network provides current bid and ask prices on thousands of actively traded OTC securities. The *bid price* is the highest price offered by a dealer to purchase a given security, and the *ask price* is the lowest price at which the dealer is willing to sell the security. The dealer in effect adds securities to his or her inventory by purchasing them at the bid price and sells securities from the inventory at the ask price. The dealer expects to profit from the *spread* between the bid and ask prices. Unlike the auction process on the organized securities exchanges, the prices at which securities are traded in the OTC market result from both competitive bids and negotiation.

Unlike the organized exchanges, the OTC handles *both* outstanding securities and new public issues, making it both a *secondary* and a *primary market.* The OTC accounts for about 38 percent of the *total dollar volume* (about 54 percent of the *total share volume*) of domestic shares traded.

Eurobond market
The market in which corporations and governments typically issue bonds denominated in dollars and sell them to investors located outside the United States.

International Capital Markets   Although U.S. capital markets are by far the world's largest, there are important debt and equity markets outside the United States. In the **Eurobond market,** corporations and governments typically issue bonds denominated in dollars and sell them to investors located outside the United States. A U.S. corporation might, for example, issue dollar-denominated bonds that would be purchased by investors in Belgium, Germany, or Switzerland. Through the Eurobond market, issuing firms and governments can tap a much larger pool of investors than would be generally available in the local market.

foreign bond
Bond that is issued by a foreign corporation or government and is denominated in the investor's home currency and sold in the investor's home market.

The foreign bond market is another international market for long-term debt securities. A **foreign bond** is a bond issued by a foreign corporation or government that is denominated in the investor's home currency and sold in the investor's home market. A bond issued by a U.S. company that is denominated in Swiss francs and sold in Switzerland is an example of a foreign bond. Although the foreign bond market is much smaller than the Eurobond market, many issuers have found it to be an attractive way of tapping debt markets in Germany, Japan, Switzerland, and the United States.

international equity market
A market that allows corporations to sell blocks of shares to investors in a number of different countries simultaneously.

Finally, the **international equity market** allows corporations to sell blocks of shares to investors in a number of different countries simultaneously. This market enables corporations to raise far larger amounts of capital than they could raise in any single national market. International equity sales have also proven to be indispensable to governments that have sold state-owned companies to private investors during recent years.

The Role of Securities Exchanges

efficient market
A market that allocates funds
to their most productive uses
as a result of competition
among wealth-maximizing
investors that determines
and publicizes prices that are
believed to be close to their
true value.

Securities exchanges create continuous liquid markets in which firms can obtain needed financing. They also create **efficient markets** that allocate funds to their most productive uses. This is especially true for securities that are actively traded on major exchanges, where the competition among wealth-maximizing investors determines and publicizes prices that are believed to be close to their true value. See *In Practice* box below for the story of one legendary stock price, and the equally legendary man who brought it about.

The price of an individual security is determined by the demand for and supply of the security. Figure 1.5 depicts the interaction of the forces of demand (represented by line D_0) and supply (represented by line S) for a given security currently selling at an equilibrium price P_0. At that price, Q_0 shares of the stock are traded.

In Practice FOCUS ON PRACTICE

WARREN BUFFETT: THE ORACLE OF OMAHA

In early 1980, investors could buy one share of Berkshire Hathaway Class A (BRKA) common stock for $285. That may have seemed expensive at the time, but by mid-2004 the price of just one share had climbed to more than $86,500. The wizard behind this phenomenal growth in shareholder value is the Chairman of **Berkshire Hathaway,** Warren Buffett, nicknamed the "Oracle of Omaha."

Born in 1930, Buffett practiced his entrepreneurial skills as a teenager by delivering newspapers in Omaha, Nebraska, and he made his first stock purchase at the age of 11. Buffett studied economics at Columbia University, under two professors, Benjamin Graham and David Dodd, who were proponents of value investing. Graham was particularly noted for advocating the principle of intrinsic business value, the measure of a company's true worth independent of the stock price. After finishing his formal education, Buffett began his invest-

ment career in earnest. While running several investment partnerships, he purchased a struggling New Bedford, Massachusetts, textile mill called Berkshire Hathaway. By deploying the company's capital in other ventures, Berkshire Hathaway soon became an investment vehicle rather than a textile mill. Indeed, the original textile mill assets were disposed of in 1985.

In the years since then, Buffett has pursued a strategy of buying up entire companies or taking a large stock position if he feels a company's stock is underpriced relative to the true value of its assets. For example, consider some of Berkshire Hathaway's holdings in mid-2004: 8.2 percent of **Coca-Cola** (since 1994), 11.8 percent of **American Express Company** (1998), 9.5 percent of **Gillette** (1989), and 18.1 percent of **The Washington Post** (1973). Ignoring hot investment trends, Buffett looks for undervalued companies with low overhead, high growth

potential, strong market share, and a low ratio of the stock price to the company's earnings (called the *P/E ratio;* see Chapter 2).

Berkshire Hathaway's annual report is a "must-read" for many investors, due to the popularity of Buffet's annual letter to shareholders with his homespun take on such topics as investing, corporate governance, and corporate leadership. Berkshire Hathaway's annual shareholder meetings in Omaha have turned into a cult-like gathering each year, with thousands traveling to listen to Buffett answer questions from shareholders. One question that has been firmly answered is the question of Buffett's ability to create shareholder value.

■ *The share price of BRKA has never been split to make the shares more affordable to average investors. Why might the company refuse to split its shares?*

FIGURE 1.5

Supply and Demand
Supply and demand for
a security

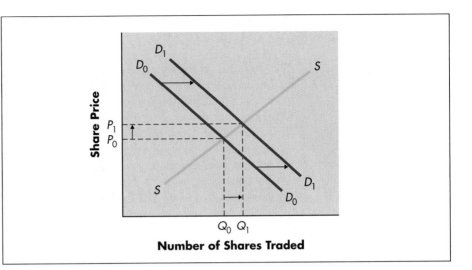

Changing evaluations of a firm's prospects cause changes in the demand for and supply of its securities and ultimately result in a new price for the securities. Suppose, for example, that the firm shown in Figure 1.5 announces a favorable discovery. Investors expect rewarding results from the discovery, so they increase their valuations of the firm's shares. The changing evaluation results in a shift in demand from D_0 to D_1. At that new level of demand, Q_1 shares will be traded, and a new, higher equilibrium price of P_1 will result. The competitive market created by the major securities exchanges provides a forum in which share prices are continuously adjusted to changing demand and supply.

For an in-depth, chapter-length discussion of financial institutions and financial markets, see the online chapter at the book's Web site (www.aw-bc.com/gitman).

REVIEW QUESTIONS

1–18   Who are the key participants in the transactions of financial institutions? Who are *net suppliers* and who are *net demanders*?

1–19   What role do *financial markets* play in our economy? What are *primary* and *secondary* markets? What relationship exists between financial institutions and financial markets?

1–20   What is the *money market*? How does it work?

1–21   What is the *Eurocurrency market*? What is the *London Interbank Offered Rate (LIBOR)* and how is it used in this market?

1–22   What is the *capital market*? What are the primary securities traded in it?

1–23   What role do securities exchanges play in the capital market? How does the *over-the-counter exchange* operate? How does it differ from the *organized securities exchanges*?

1–24   Briefly describe the international capital markets, particularly the *Eurobond market* and the *international equity market.*

1–25   What are *efficient markets*? What determines the price of an individual security in such a market?

1.5 | Business Taxes

Taxes are a fact of life, and businesses, like individuals, must pay taxes on income. The income of sole proprietorships and partnerships is taxed as the income of the individual owners; corporate income is subject to corporate taxes. Regardless of their legal form, all businesses can earn two types of income: ordinary and capital gains. Under current law, these two types of income are treated differently in the taxation of individuals; they are not treated differently for entities subject to corporate taxes. Frequent amendments are made to the tax code. As this book goes to press (Nov. 2004), a bill, which is likely to pass, is before Congress that proposes cuts to the top corporate tax rate from the current 35% to 34% in 2005 and 2006 and a further reduction to 32% starting in 2007.

Ordinary Income

ordinary income
Income earned through the sale of a firm's goods or services.

The **ordinary income** of a corporation is income earned through the sale of goods or services. Ordinary income is currently taxed subject to the rates depicted in the corporate tax rate schedule in Table 1.4.

EXAMPLE Webster Manufacturing, Inc., a small manufacturer of kitchen knives, has before-tax earnings of $250,000. The tax on these earnings can be found by using the tax rate schedule in Table 1.4:

$$\text{Total taxes due} = \$22,250 + [0.39 \times (\$250,000 - \$100,000)]$$
$$= \$22,250 + (0.39 \times \$150,000)$$
$$= \$22,250 + \$58,500 = \underline{\$80,750}$$

From a financial point of view, it is important to understand the difference between average and marginal tax rates, the treatment of interest and dividend income, and the effects of tax deductibility.

TABLE 1.4

Corporate Tax Rate Schedule

Range of taxable income		Tax calculation
	Base tax +	(Marginal rate × amount over base bracket)
$ 0 to $ 50,000	$ 0 +	(15% × amount over $ 0)
50,000 to 75,000	7,500 +	(25 × amount over 50,000)
75,000 to 100,000	13,750 +	(34 × amount over 75,000)
100,000 to 335,000	22,250 +	(39 × amount over 100,000)
335,000 to 10,000,000	113,900 +	(34 × amount over 335,000)
10,000,000 to 15,000,000	3,400,000 +	(35 × amount over 10,000,000)
15,000,000 to 18,333,333	5,150,000 +	(38 × amount over 15,000,000)
Over 18,333,333	6,416,667 +	(35 × amount over 18,333,333)

Average Versus Marginal Tax Rates

average tax rate
A firm's taxes divided by its taxable income.

The **average tax rate** paid on the firm's ordinary income can be calculated by dividing its taxes by its taxable income. For firms with taxable income of $10,000,000 or less, the average tax rate ranges from 15 to 34 percent, reaching 34 percent when taxable income equals or exceeds $335,000. For firms with taxable income in excess of $10,000,000, the average tax rate ranges between 34 and 35 percent. The average tax rate paid by Webster Manufacturing, Inc., in the preceding example was 32.3 percent ($80,750 ÷ $250,000). As a corporation's taxable income increases, its average tax rate approaches and finally reaches 34 percent. It remains at that level up to $10,000,000 of taxable income, beyond which it rises toward and reaches 35 percent at $18,333,333.

marginal tax rate
The rate at which *additional income* is taxed.

The **marginal tax rate** represents the rate at which *additional income* is taxed. In the current corporate tax structure, the marginal tax rate on income up to $50,000 is 15 percent; from $50,000 to $75,000 it is 25 percent; and so on, as shown in Table 1.4. Webster Manufacturing's marginal tax rate is currently 39 percent because its next dollar of taxable income (bringing its before-tax earnings to $250,001) would be taxed at that rate. To simplify calculations in the text, *a fixed 40 percent tax rate is assumed to be applicable to ordinary corporate income.* Given our focus on financial decision making, this rate is assumed to represent the firm's *marginal tax rate.*

Interest and Dividend Income

double taxation
Occurs when the already once-taxed earnings of a corporation are distributed as cash dividends to stockholders, who must pay taxes of up to a maximum rate of 15 percent on them.

In the process of determining taxable income, any *interest received* by the corporation is included as ordinary income. Dividends, on the other hand, are treated differently. This different treatment moderates the effect of **double taxation,** which occurs when the already once-taxed earnings of a corporation are distributed as cash dividends to stockholders, who must pay taxes of up to a maximum rate of 15 percent on them. Therefore, dividends that the firm receives on common and preferred stock held in other corporations, and representing less than 20 percent ownership in them, are subject to a 70 percent exclusion for tax purposes.[7]

intercorporate dividends
Dividends received by one corporation on common and preferred stock held in other corporations.

Because of the dividend exclusion, only 30 percent of these **intercorporate dividends** are included as ordinary income. The tax law provides this exclusion to avoid *triple taxation.* Triple taxation would occur if the first and second corporations were taxed on income before the second corporation paid dividends to its shareholders, who must then pay taxes up to a maximum rate of 15 percent on them. The dividend exclusion in effect eliminates most of the potential tax liability from the dividends received by the second and any subsequent corporations.

EXAMPLE   Charnes Industries, a large foundry that makes custom castings for the automobile industry, during the year just ended received $100,000 in interest on bonds it held and $100,000 in dividends on common stock it owned in other corporations. The firm is subject to a 40% marginal tax rate and is eligible for a 70%

7. The exclusion is 80% if the corporation owns between 20% and 80% of the stock in the corporation paying it dividends; 100% of the dividends received are excluded if it owns more than 80% of the corporation paying it dividends. For convenience, we are assuming here that the ownership interest in the dividend-paying corporation is less than 20%.

exclusion on its intercorporate dividend receipts. The after-tax income realized by Charnes from each of these sources of investment income is found as follows:

	Interest income	Dividend income
(1) Before-tax amount	$100,000	$100,000
Less: Applicable exclusion	0	$(0.70 \times \$100,000) =$ 70,000
Taxable amount	$100,000	$ 30,000
(2) Tax (40%)	40,000	12,000
After-tax amount [(1) − (2)]	$ 60,000	$ 88,000

As a result of the 70% dividend exclusion, the after-tax amount is greater for the dividend income than for the interest income. Clearly, the dividend exclusion enhances the attractiveness of stock investments relative to bond investments made by one corporation in another. ■

Tax-Deductible Expenses

In calculating their taxes, corporations are allowed to deduct operating expenses, as well as interest expense. The tax deductibility of these expenses reduces their after-tax cost. The following example illustrates the benefit of tax deductibility.

EXAMPLE

Two companies, Debt Co. and No Debt Co., both expect in the coming year to have earnings before interest and taxes of $200,000. Debt Co. during the year will have to pay $30,000 in interest. No Debt Co. has no debt and therefore will have no interest expense. Calculation of the earnings after taxes for these two firms is as follows:

	Debt Co.	No Debt Co.
Earnings before interest and taxes	$200,000	$200,000
Less: Interest expense	30,000	0
Earnings before taxes	$170,000	$200,000
Less: Taxes (40%)	68,000	80,000
Earnings after taxes	$102,000	$120,000
Difference in earnings after taxes		$18,000

Whereas Debt Co. had $30,000 more interest expense than No Debt Co., Debt Co.'s earnings after taxes are only $18,000 less than those of No Debt Co. ($102,000 for Debt Co. versus $120,000 for No Debt Co.). This difference is attributable to the fact that Debt Co.'s $30,000 interest expense deduction provided a tax savings of $12,000 ($68,000 for Debt Co. versus $80,000 for No Debt Co.). This amount can be calculated directly by multiplying the tax rate by the amount of interest expense $(0.40 \times \$30,000 = \$12,000)$. Similarly, the $18,000 *after-tax cost* of the interest expense can be calculated directly by multiplying one minus the tax rate by the amount of interest expense $[(1 − 0.40) \times \$30,000 = \$18,000]$. ■

The tax deductibility of certain expenses reduces their actual (after-tax) cost to the profitable firm. Note that both for accounting and tax purposes *interest is a tax-deductible expense, whereas dividends are not.* Because dividends are not tax deductible, their after-tax cost is equal to the amount of the dividend. Thus a $30,000 cash dividend has an after-tax cost of $30,000.

Capital Gains

capital gain
The amount by which the sale price of an asset exceeds the asset's initial purchase price.

If a firm sells a capital asset (such as stock held as an investment) for more than its initial purchase price, the difference between the sale price and the purchase price is called a **capital gain.** For corporations, capital gains are added to ordinary corporate income and taxed at the regular corporate rates, with a maximum marginal tax rate of 39 percent. To simplify the computations presented in the text, as for ordinary income, *a fixed 40 percent tax rate is assumed to be applicable to corporate capital gains.*

EXAMPLE   Ross Company, a manufacturer of pharmaceuticals, has pretax operating earnings of $500,000 and has just sold for $150,000 an asset that was purchased 2 years ago for $125,000. Because the asset was sold for more than its initial purchase price, there is a capital gain of $25,000 ($150,000 sale price − $125,000 initial purchase price). The corporation's taxable income will total $525,000 ($500,000 ordinary income plus $25,000 capital gain). Because this total exceeds $335,000, the capital gain will be taxed at the 34% rate (see Table 1.4), resulting in a tax of $8,500 (0.34 × $25,000).   ■

REVIEW QUESTIONS

1–26   Describe the tax treatment of *ordinary income* and that of *capital gains.* What is the difference between the *average tax rate* and the *marginal tax rate?*

1–27   Why might the *intercorporate dividend* exclusion make corporate stock investments by one corporation in another more attractive than bond investments?

1–28   What benefit results from the tax deductibility of certain corporate expenses?

1.6 | Using This Text

The organization of this textbook links the firm's activities to its value, as determined in the securities markets. The activities of the financial manager are described in the six parts of the book. Each major decision area is presented in terms of both return and risk factors and their potential effects on owners' wealth. Coverage of international events and topics is integrated into the chapter discussions, and a separate chapter on international managerial finance is included.

The text has been developed around a group of learning goals—six per chapter. Mastery of these goals results in a broad understanding of managerial finance. These goals have been carefully integrated into a learning system. Each chapter begins with a numbered list of learning goals. Next to each major text heading is a "toolbox," which notes by number the specific learning goal(s) addressed in that section. At the end of each section of the chapter (positioned before the next major heading) are review questions that test your understanding of the material in that section. At the end of each chapter, the chapter summaries, self-test problems, warm-up exercises, and problems are also keyed by number to each chapter's learning goals. By linking all elements to the learning goals, the integrated learning system facilitates your mastery of the goals.

Each chapter ends with a case that integrates the chapter materials, and each part ends with an integrative case that ties together the key topical material covered in the chapters within that part. Both the chapter-end and the part-end cases can be used to synthesize and apply related concepts and techniques. Following the chapter case, you will find a spreadsheet exercise, a group exercise, and a Web exercise. These exercises will help you apply the chapter material and polish needed business skills by using Excel Software, working in teams, and mining the Web for financial information.

Summary

Focus on Value

Chapter 1 established the primary goal of the firm—**to maximize the wealth of the owners for whom the firm is being operated.** For public companies, which are the focus of this text, value at any time is reflected in the stock price. Therefore, management should act only on those alternatives or opportunities that are expected to create value for owners by increasing the stock price. Doing this requires management to consider the returns (magnitude and timing of cash flows) and the risk of each proposed action and their combined effect on value.

Review of Learning Goals

LG1 Define *finance*, its major areas and opportunities, and the legal forms of business organization. Finance is the art and science of managing money. It affects the life of every person and of every organization. Major opportunities in financial services exist within banking and related institutions, personal financial planning, investments, real estate, and insurance. Managerial finance is concerned with the duties of the financial manager in the business firm. It offers numerous career opportunities. The recent trend toward globalization of business activity has created new demands and opportunities in managerial finance.

The legal forms of business organization are the sole proprietorship, the partnership, and the corporation. The corporation is dominant in terms of business receipts and profits, and its owners are its common and preferred stockholders. Stockholders expect to earn a return by receiving dividends or by realizing gains through increases in share price.

LG2 Describe the managerial finance function and its relationship to economics and accounting. All areas of responsibility within a firm interact with finance personnel and procedures. The financial manager must understand the economic environment and relies heavily on the economic principle of marginal cost–benefit analysis to make financial decisions. Financial managers use accounting but concentrate on cash flows and decision making.

LG3 **Identify the primary activities of the financial manager.** The primary activities of the financial manager, in addition to ongoing involvement in financial analysis and planning, are making investment decisions and making financing decisions.

LG4 **Explain the goal of the firm, corporate governance, the role of ethics, and the agency issue.** The goal of the financial manager is to maximize the owners' wealth, as evidenced by stock price. Profit maximization ignores the timing of returns, does not directly consider cash flows, and ignores risk, so it is an inappropriate goal. Both return and risk must be assessed by the financial manager who is evaluating decision alternatives. The wealth-maximizing actions of financial managers should also reflect the interests of stakeholders, groups who have a direct economic link to the firm.

The corporate governance structure is used to direct and control the corporation by defining the rights and responsibilities of the key corporate participants. Both individual and institutional investors hold the stock of most companies, but the institutional investors tend to have much greater influence on corporate governance. The Sarbanes-Oxley Act of 2002 (commonly called SOX) was passed to eliminate fraudulent financial disclosure and conflict of interest problems. Positive ethical practices help a firm and its managers to achieve the firm's goal of owner wealth maximization. SOX has provided impetus toward such practices.

An agency problem results when managers, as agents for owners, place personal goals ahead of corporate goals. Market forces, in the form of shareholder activism and the threat of takeover, tend to prevent or minimize agency problems. Institutional investors often exert pressure on management to perform. Firms incur agency costs to maintain a corporate governance structure that monitors managers' actions and provides incentives for them to act in the best interests of owners. Stock options and performance plans are examples of such agency costs.

LG5 **Understand financial institutions and markets, and the role they play in managerial finance.** Financial institutions serve as intermediaries by channeling into loans or investments the savings of individuals, businesses, and governments. The financial markets are forums in which suppliers and demanders of funds can transact business directly. Financial institutions actively participate in the financial markets as both suppliers and demanders of funds.

In the money market, marketable securities (short-term debt instruments) are traded, typically through large New York banks and government securities dealers. The Eurocurrency market is the international equivalent of the domestic money market.

In the capital market, transactions in long-term debt (bonds) and equity (common and preferred stock) are made. The organized securities exchanges provide secondary markets for securities. The over-the-counter (OTC) exchange offers a secondary market for securities and is a primary market in which new public issues are sold. Important international debt and equity markets are the Eurobond market and the international equity market. The securities exchanges create continuous liquid markets for needed financing and allocate funds to their most productive uses.

LG6 **Discuss business taxes and their importance in financial decisions.**
Corporate income is subject to corporate taxes. Corporate tax rates are applicable to both ordinary income (after deduction of allowable expenses) and capital gains. The average tax rate paid by a corporation ranges from 15 to 35 percent. Corporate taxpayers can reduce their taxes through certain provisions in the tax code: intercorporate dividend exclusions and tax-deductible expenses. A capital gain occurs when an asset is sold for more than its initial purchase price; they are added to ordinary corporate income and taxed at regular corporate tax rates. (For convenience, we assume a 40 percent marginal tax rate in this book.)

Self-Test Problem (Solution in Appendix B)

LG6   **ST1–1** **Corporate taxes**   Montgomery Enterprises, Inc., had operating earnings of $280,000 for the year just ended. During the year the firm sold stock that it held in another company for $180,000, which was $30,000 above its original purchase price of $150,000, paid 1 year earlier.
a. What is the amount, if any, of capital gains realized during the year?
b. How much total taxable income did the firm earn during the year?
c. Use the corporate tax rate schedule given in Table 1.4 to calculate the firm's total taxes due.
d. Calculate both the *average tax rate* and the *marginal tax rate* on the basis of your findings.

Warm-Up Exercises

LG1   **E1–1** Ann and Jack have been partners for several years. Their firm, A & J Tax Preparation, has been very successful, as the pair agree on most business-related questions. One disagreement, however, concerns the legal form of their business. Ann has tried for the past 2 years to get Jack to agree to incorporate. She believes that there is no downside to incorporating and sees only benefits. Jack strongly disagrees; he thinks that the business should remain a partnership forever.
First, take Ann's side and explain the positive side to incorporating the business. Next, take Jack's side and state the advantages to remaining a partnership. Lastly, what information would you want if you were asked to make the decision for Ann and Jack?

LG2   **E1–2** You have been made treasurer for a day at AIMCO, Inc. AIMCO develops technology for video conferencing. A manager of the satellite division has asked you to authorize a capital expenditure in the amount of $10,000. The manager states that this expenditure is necessary to continue a long-running project designed to use satellites to allow video conferencing anywhere on the planet. The manager admits that the satellite concept has been surpassed by recent technological advances in telephony, but he feels that AIMCO should continue the project. His reasoning is based on the fact that $2.5 million has already been spent over the past 15 years on this project. Although the project has little chance to be viable, the manager believes it would be a shame to waste the money and time already spent.

Use marginal cost–benefit analysis to make your decision regarding whether you should authorize the $10,000 expenditure to continue the project.

LG3

E1–3 The end-of-the-year parties at Yearling, Inc., are known for their extravagance. Management provides the best food and entertainment to thank the employees for their hard work. During the planning for this year's bash, a disagreement broke out between the treasurer's staff and the controller's staff. The treasurer's staff contended that the firm was running low on cash and might have trouble paying its bills over the coming months; they requested that cuts be made to the budget for the party. The controller's staff felt that any cuts were unwarranted as the firm continued to be very profitable.

Can both sides be right? Explain your answer.

LG4

E1–4 Recently, some branches of Donut Shop, Inc., have dropped the practice of allowing employees to accept tips. Customers who once said, "Keep the change," now have to get used to waiting for their nickels. Management even instituted a policy of requiring that the change be thrown out if a customer drives off without it. As a frequent customer who gets coffee and doughnuts for the office, you notice that the lines are longer and that more mistakes are being made in your order.

Explain why tips could be viewed as similar to stock options and why the delays and incorrect orders could represent a case of agency cost. If tips are gone forever, how could Donut Shop reduce these agency costs?

LG6

E1–5 Reston, Inc., has asked your corporation, Pruro, Inc., for financial assistance. As a long-time customer of Reston, your firm has decided to give that assistance. The question you are debating is whether Pruro should take Reston stock with a 5% dividend yield or a promissory note paying 5%.

Assuming payment is guaranteed and the dollar amounts for annual interest and dividend income are identical, which option will result in greater after-tax income for the first year?

Problems

LG1

BASIC

P1–1 **Liability comparisons**   Merideth Harper has invested $25,000 in Southwest Development Company. The firm has recently declared bankruptcy and has $60,000 in unpaid debts. Explain the nature of payments, if any, by Ms. Harper in each of the following situations.
   a. Southwest Development Company is a sole proprietorship owned by Ms. Harper.
   b. Southwest Development Company is a 50–50 partnership of Ms. Harper and Christopher Black.
   c. Southwest Development Company is a corporation.

P1–2   Marginal cost–benefit analysis and the goal of the firm   Ken Allen, capital budgeting analyst for Bally Gears, Inc., has been asked to evaluate a proposal. The manager of the automotive division believes that replacing the robotics used on the heavy truck gear line will produce total benefits of $560,000 (in today's dollars) over the next 5 years. The existing robotics would produce benefits of $400,000 (also in today's dollars) over that same time period. An initial cash investment of $220,000 would be required to install the new equipment. The manager estimates that the existing robotics can be sold for $70,000. Show how Ken will apply marginal cost–benefit analysis techniques to determine the following:

a. The marginal (added) benefits of the proposed new robotics.
b. The marginal (added) cost of the proposed new robotics.
c. The net benefit of the proposed new robotics.
d. What should Ken Allen recommend that the company do? Why?
e. What factors besides the costs and benefits should be considered before the final decision is made?

P1–3   Accrual income versus cash flow for a period   Thomas Book Sales, Inc., supplies textbooks to college and university bookstores. The books are shipped with a proviso that they must be paid for within 30 days but can be returned for a full refund credit within 90 days. In 2006, Thomas shipped and billed book titles totaling $760,000. Collections, net of return credits, during the year totaled $690,000. The company spent $300,000 acquiring the books that it shipped.

a. Using accrual accounting and the preceding values, show the firm's net profit for the past year.
b. Using cash accounting and the preceding values, show the firm's net cash flow for the past year.
c. Which of these statements is more useful to the financial manager? Why?

P1–4   Identifying agency problems, costs, and resolutions   Explain why each of the following situations is an agency problem and what costs to the firm might result from it. Suggest how the problem might be dealt with short of firing the individual(s) involved.

a. The front desk receptionist routinely takes an extra 20 minutes of lunch to run personal errands.
b. Division managers are padding cost estimates so as to show short-term efficiency gains when the costs come in lower than the estimates.
c. The firm's chief executive officer has secret talks with a competitor about the possibility of a merger in which (s)he would become the CEO of the combined firms.
d. A branch manager lays off experienced full-time employees and staffs customer service positions with part-time or temporary workers to lower employment costs and raise this year's branch profit. The manager's bonus is based on profitability.

P1–5   Corporate taxes   Tantor Supply, Inc., is a small corporation acting as the exclusive distributor of a major line of sporting goods. During 2006 the firm earned $92,500 before taxes.

a. Calculate the firm's tax liability using the corporate tax rate schedule given in Table 1.4. (p. 30)
b. How much are Tantor Supply's 2006 after-tax earnings?

c. What was the firm's *average tax rate*, based on your findings in part **a**?

d. What is the firm's *marginal tax rate*, based on your findings in part **a**?

P1–6   Average corporate tax rates   Using the corporate tax rate schedule given in Table 1.4, perform the following:

a. Calculate the tax liability, after-tax earnings, and average tax rates for the following levels of corporate earnings before taxes: $10,000; $80,000; $300,000; $500,000; $1.5 million; $10 million; and $20 million.

b. Plot the average tax rates (measured on the *y* axis) against the pretax income levels (measured on the *x* axis). What generalization can be made concerning the relationship between these variables?

P1–7   Marginal corporate tax rates   Using the corporate tax rate schedule given in Table 1.4, perform the following:

a. Find the marginal tax rate for the following levels of corporate earnings before taxes: $15,000; $60,000; $90,000; $200,000; $400,000; $1 million; and $20 million.

b. Plot the marginal tax rates (measured on the *y* axis) against the pretax income levels (measured on the *x* axis). Explain the relationship between these variables.

P1–8   Interest versus dividend income   During the year just ended, Shering Distributors, Inc., had pretax earnings from operations of $490,000. In addition, during the year it received $20,000 in income from interest on bonds it held in Zig Manufacturing and received $20,000 in income from dividends on its 5% common stock holding in Tank Industries, Inc. Shering is in the 40% tax bracket and is eligible for a 70% dividend exclusion on its Tank Industries stock.

a. Calculate the firm's tax on its operating earnings only.

b. Find the tax and the after-tax amount attributable to the interest income from Zig Manufacturing bonds.

c. Find the tax and the after-tax amount attributable to the dividend income from the Tank Industries, Inc., common stock.

d. Compare, contrast, and discuss the after-tax amounts resulting from the interest income and dividend income calculated in parts **b** and **c**.

e. What is the firm's total tax liability for the year?

P1–9   Interest versus dividend expense   Michaels Corporation expects earnings before interest and taxes to be $40,000 for this period. Assuming an ordinary tax rate of 40%, compute the firm's earnings after taxes and earnings available for common stockholders (earnings after taxes and preferred stock dividends, if any) under the following conditions:

a. The firm pays $10,000 in interest.

b. The firm pays $10,000 in preferred stock dividends.

P1–10   Capital gains taxes   Perkins Manufacturing is considering the sale of two non-depreciable assets, X and Y. Asset X was purchased for $2,000 and will be sold today for $2,250. Asset Y was purchased for $30,000 and will be sold today for $35,000. The firm is subject to a 40% tax rate on capital gains.

a. Calculate the amount of capital gain, if any, realized on each of the assets.

b. Calculate the tax on the sale of each asset.

P1–11   Capital gains taxes   The following table contains purchase and sale prices for the nondepreciable capital assets of a major corporation. The firm paid taxes of 40% on capital gains.

Asset	Purchase price	Sale price
A	$ 3,000	$ 3,400
B	12,000	12,000
C	62,000	80,000
D	41,000	45,000
E	16,500	18,000

a. Determine the amount of capital gain realized on each of the five assets.
b. Calculate the amount of tax paid on each of the assets.

P1–12   ETHICS PROBLEM   What does it mean to say that managers should maximize shareholder wealth "subject to ethical constraints"? What ethical considerations might enter into decisions that result in cash flow and stock price effects that are less than they might otherwise have been?

Chapter 1 Case: Assessing the Goal of Sports Products, Inc.

Loren Seguara and Dale Johnson both work for Sports Products, Inc., a major producer of boating equipment and accessories. Loren works as a clerical assistant in the Accounting Department, and Dale works as a packager in the Shipping Department. During their lunch break one day, they began talking about the company. Dale complained that he had always worked hard trying not to waste packing materials and efficiently and cost-effectively performing his job. In spite of his efforts and those of his co-workers in the department, the firm's stock price had declined nearly $2 per share over the past 9 months. Loren indicated that she shared Dale's frustration, particularly because the firm's profits had been rising. Neither could understand why the firm's stock price was falling as profits rose.

Loren indicated that she had seen documents describing the firm's profit-sharing plan under which all managers were partially compensated on the basis of the firm's profits. She suggested that maybe it was profit that was important to management, because it directly affected their pay. Dale said, "That doesn't make sense, because the stockholders own the firm. Shouldn't management do what's best for stockholders? Something's wrong!" Loren responded, "Well, maybe that explains why the company hasn't concerned itself with the stock price. Look, the only profits that stockholders receive are in the form of cash dividends, and this firm has never paid dividends during its 20-year history. We as stockholders therefore don't directly benefit from profits. The only way we benefit is for the stock price to rise." Dale chimed in, "That probably explains why the firm is being sued by state and federal environmental officials for dumping pollutants in the adjacent stream. Why spend money for pollution control? It increases costs, lowers profits, and therefore lowers management's earnings!"

Loren and Dale realized that the lunch break had ended and they must quickly return to work. Before leaving, they decided to meet the next day to continue their discussion.

TO DO

a. What should the management of Sports Products, Inc., pursue as its overriding goal? Why?
b. Does the firm appear to have an *agency problem?* Explain.
c. Evaluate the firm's approach to pollution control. Does it seem to be *ethical?* Why might incurring the expense to control pollution be in the best interests of the firm's owners despite its negative effect on profits?
d. Does the firm appear to have an effective *corporate governance* structure? Explain any shortcomings.
e. On the basis of the information provided, what specific recommendations would you offer the firm?

Spreadsheet Exercise

Assume that Monsanto Corporation is considering the renovation and/or replacement of some of its older and outdated carpet-manufacturing equipment. Its objective is to improve the efficiency of operations in terms of both speed and reduction in the number of defects. The company's finance department has compiled pertinent data that will allow it to conduct a marginal cost–benefit analysis for the proposed equipment replacement.

The cash outlay for new equipment would be approximately $600,000. The net book value of the old equipment and its potential net selling price is $250,000. The total benefits from the new equipment (measured in today's dollars) would be $900,000. The benefits of the old equipment over a similar period of time (measured in today's dollars) would be $300,000.

TO DO

Create a spreadsheet to conduct a marginal cost–benefit analysis for Monsanto Corporation and determine the following:

a. The marginal (added) benefits of the proposed new equipment.
b. The marginal (added) cost of the proposed new equipment.
c. The net benefit of the proposed new equipment.
d. What would you recommend that the firm do? Why?

Group Exercise

You may not recall it, but in kindergarten one yardstick of your development was summarized as "plays well with others." As you moved through your school years, this explicit characteristic was deleted, and you were graded based on your attainment of more concrete learning goals such as addition, spelling, and, eventually, logical thinking. Of course, playing well—getting along with others—is not a skill that disappears along with our baby teeth. Humans are social animals, and as such we spend much of our day in close proximity to other people. This is particularly true in the workplace. Most jobs include at least some component of teamwork. Working well within groups is necessary for success in most firms.

With this fact in mind, in each chapter you will be asked to complete a group assignment linked to the learning goals of each chapter. The size of the groups is flexible, although groups of 3 to 5 students are probably most appropriate. These assignments will be continuous in the sense that the groups will be establishing a firm and, in each chapter, will attempt to simulate decisions made by corporations in their normal course of financial management. The group assignments begin with this chapter, and each subsequent chapter will build on your previous work.

Your group must first form a fictitious partnership. Assume that this partnership has existed for several years and is in the process of going public. This "firm-group" will continue throughout the semester. You will also follow a real, publicly traded firm throughout the semester, which should be related in some way to your fictitious business.

TO DO

LG1 a. Name your firm, describe the business it is in, and state what advantages you (as management) see in going public.

LG3 b. Discuss the necessary managerial roles of your fictitious firm, and explain the responsibilities for each within the firm. (Although individual roles could be assigned here, the *group* is responsible for all parts of all assignments.)

LG3 LG4 LG5 LG6 c. Choose a publicly traded corporation to act as a "shadow firm."
   (1) Go to the SEC's Web site (www.sec.gov/) and look up the most recent annual report for your shadow firm.
   (2) Find the exchange on which your firm's stock trades.
   (3) Check for profitability by looking solely at recent movements in earnings per share (EPS).
   (4) Note any taxation issues that are apparent in the annual report.

Web Exercise

The World Wide Web (a part of the larger Internet) has become such a powerful force in every aspect of our society that to ignore its potential would lessen your learning experience. As a source of timely information, the Web is unrivaled. Anyone in the world now has the ability to do in-depth research into almost any topic with just a few mouse clicks. The Web exercise in each chapter of this book will continue the work done within the chapter, applying real-world and real-time data to the subjects taught therein. A relatively brief "deliverable" is attached with the assigned searches. These documents are meant to serve as verification of your time spent online. Often the exercises will build on past exercises and match closely the work done in the group exercises; this correspondence is created purposefully. The chapter, its examples and problems, and the group and Web exercises should all be seen as continuous tools whereby overlap reinforces the key elements of the material.

TO DO

Go to the SEC's Web site at www.sec.gov/. There, click on the link under Filings and Forms for Descriptions of SEC Forms (commonly called "Edgar"). Scroll down to Table 3 Securities and Exchange Act. Summarize several of the more pertinent reports listed in this table. More importantly, after returning to the SEC's home page, locate examples of these forms as filed by a corporation of your choosing. Catalogue what you notice regarding these filings.

Remember to check the book's Web site at

www.aw-bc.com/gitman

for additional resources, including additional Web exercises.

Chapter 2

Financial Statements and Analysis

LEARNING GOALS

LG1 Review the contents of the stockholders' report and the procedures for consolidating international financial statements.

LG2 Understand who uses financial ratios, and how.

LG3 Use ratios to analyze a firm's liquidity and activity.

LG4 Discuss the relationship between debt and financial leverage and the ratios used to analyze a firm's debt.

LG5 Use ratios to analyze a firm's profitability and its market value.

LG6 Use a summary of financial ratios and the DuPont system of analysis to perform a complete ratio analysis.

ACROSS THE DISCIPLINES   WHY THIS CHAPTER MATTERS TO YOU

Accounting: You need to understand the stockholders' report and preparation of the four key financial statements; how firms consolidate international financial statements; and how to calculate and interpret financial ratios for decision making.

Information systems: You need to understand what data are included in the firm's financial statements to design systems that will supply such data to those who prepare the statements and to those in the firm who use the data for ratio calculations.

Management: You need to understand what parties are interested in the stockholders' report and why; how the financial statements will be analyzed by those both inside and outside the firm to assess various aspects of perform-

ance; the caution that should be exercised in using financial ratio analysis; and how the financial statements affect the value of the firm.

Marketing: You need to understand the effects your decisions will have on the financial statements, particularly the income statement and the statement of cash flows, and how analysis of ratios, especially those involving sales figures, will affect the firm's decisions about levels of inventory, credit policies, and pricing decisions.

Operations: You need to understand how the costs of operations are reflected in the firm's financial statements and how analysis of ratios, particularly those involving assets, cost of goods sold, or inventory, may affect requests for new equipment or facilities.

THE HOME DEPOT, INC.
BUILDING STRONG FINANCIALS

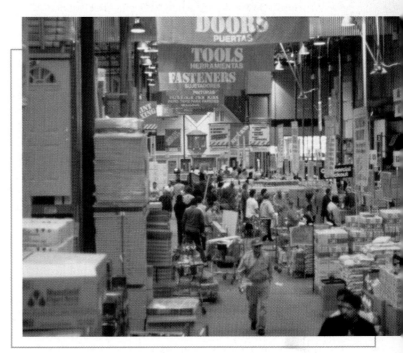

The primary responsibility of the chief financial officer (CFO) is no longer just financial reporting. Today's CFO—a key member of the executive team—is also involved in strategic planning and, at many companies, information management. Managing a company's financial operations takes many different skills.

Home Depot (www.homedepot.com) is the world's largest home-improvement retailer and the second largest retailer in the United States. Its CFO and Executive Vice President, Carol Tome, reports directly to Chief Executive Officer Robert L. Nardinelli. She works closely with him to guide the giant firm's future growth. One of Tome's objectives is to improve the company's *return on investment* (*ROI*), a measure of management's effectiveness in generating profits with its available assets. In early 2004, Home Depot's ROI was 20.49 percent, compared to 20.34 percent for the home-improvement retail industry as a whole and 13.07 percent for the services sector in general.

Activity ratios that measure how quickly accounts are converted into cash are another focus of CFOs. Particularly important to a retail chain are inventory turnover, receivables collection period, and accounts payable periods. "We're looking for processing efficiencies," Tome says. Improved new-store productivity and lower preopening costs per store, together with attention to cost control, help boost margins. In the first quarter of 2004, Home Depot reported a year-over-year same-store sales increase of 7.7 percent, the highest in 5 years.

The company's measures of debt also indicate that it enjoys a strong financial position. In mid-2004, only 7 percent of Home Depot's total long-term financing was debt, a very low degree of indebtedness. This strength gives Home Depot more flexibility to pursue new projects and more opportunities to raise funds from banks.

With knowledge of the financial fitness of the company, a CFO can make recommendations on the deployment of capital. Home Depot plans capital spending of $3.7 billion in 2004, including $1 billion to support its modernization program. In addition, the company spent $3.6 billion to repurchase shares during 2002 and 2003. In this chapter, you will learn how to use financial ratios to analyze a firm's financial fitness as shown in its financial statements.

■ *Increased same-store sales are often a bellwether of improving financial strength. What are two methods of raising same-store sales? Does either, or both, actually help the company?*

2.1 | The Stockholders' Report

generally accepted accounting principles (GAAP)
The practice and procedure guidelines used to prepare and maintain financial records and reports; authorized by the *Financial Accounting Standards Board (FASB)*.

Financial Accounting Standards Board (FASB)
The accounting profession's rule-setting body, which authorizes *generally accepted accounting principles (GAAP)*.

Public Company Accounting Oversight Board (PCAOB)
A not-for-profit corporation established by the *Sarbanes-Oxley Act of 2002* to protect the interests of investors and further the public interest in the preparation of informative, fair, and independent audit reports.

Securities and Exchange Commission (SEC)
The federal regulatory body that governs the sale and listing of securities.

stockholders' report
Annual report that publicly owned corporations must provide to stockholders; it summarizes and documents the firm's financial activities during the past year.

letter to stockholders
Typically, the first element of the annual stockholders' report and the primary communication from management.

Every corporation has many and varied uses for the standardized records and reports of its financial activities. Periodically, reports must be prepared for regulators, creditors (lenders), owners, and management. The guidelines used to prepare and maintain financial records and reports are known as **generally accepted accounting principles (GAAP)**. These accounting practices and procedures are authorized by the accounting profession's rule-setting body, the **Financial Accounting Standards Board (FASB)**. The *Sarbanes-Oxley Act of 2002*, enacted in an effort to eliminate the many disclosure and conflict of interest problems of corporations, established the **Public Company Accounting Oversight Board (PCAOB)**, which is a not-for-profit corporation that oversees auditors of public corporations. The PCAOB is charged with protecting the interests of investors and furthering the public interest in the preparation of informative, fair, and independent audit reports. The expectation is that it will instill confidence in investors with regard to the accuracy of the audited financial statements of public companies. For more about the PCAOB, see the *In Practice* box on the facing page.

Publicly owned corporations with more than $5 million in assets and 500 or more stockholders[1] are required by the **Securities and Exchange Commission (SEC)**—the federal regulatory body that governs the sale and listing of securities—to provide their stockholders with an annual **stockholders' report**. The stockholders' report summarizes and documents the firm's financial activities during the past year. It begins with a letter to the stockholders from the firm's president and/or chairman of the board.

The Letter to Stockholders

The **letter to stockholders** is the primary communication from management. It describes the events that are considered to have had the greatest effect on the firm during the year. It also generally discusses management philosophy, strategies, and actions, as well as plans for the coming year. Links at this book's Web site (www.aw-bc.com/gitman) will take you to some representative letters to stockholders.

The Four Key Financial Statements

The four key financial statements required by the SEC for reporting to shareholders are (1) the income statement, (2) the balance sheet, (3) the statement of stockholders' equity, and (4) the statement of cash flows.[2] The financial statements from the 2006 stockholders' report of Bartlett Company, a manufacturer of metal fasteners, are presented and briefly discussed. Note that an abbreviated form of the statement of stockholders' equity—the statement of retained earnings—is described in the following discussions.

---

1. Although the Securities and Exchange Commission (SEC) does not have an official definition of *publicly owned,* these financial measures mark the cutoff point it uses to require informational reporting, regardless of whether the firm publicly sells its securities. Firms that do not meet these requirements are commonly called "closely owned" firms.

2. Whereas these statement titles are consistently used throughout this text, it is important to recognize that in practice, companies frequently use different titles. For example, General Electric uses "Statement of Earnings" rather than "Income Statement" and "Statement of Financial Position" rather than "Balance Sheet." Both Nextel and Qualcomm use "Statement of Operations" rather than "Income Statement."

In Practice FOCUS ON PRACTICE

THE SON OF SOX

In 2000 and 2001, accounting irregularities at a number of large corporations forced Congress to take action. The Sarbanes-Oxley Act of 2002 (SOX) established the Public Company Accounting Oversight Board to act as a watchdog over accounting firms. The PCAOB's funding will come from accounting firms, which must register annually with the PCAOB before they can engage in auditing work. The cost ranges from $500 per year for accounting firms with fewer than 50 clients to $390,000 per year for accounting firms with more than 1,000 clients.

After adopting its own ethics code, the PCAOB adopted three auditing standards, which were later approved by the SEC. The PCAOB Auditing Standard No. 1, effective May 24, 2004, requires

auditors' reports relating to public companies to state that the engagement was performed *in accordance with the standards of the PCAOB*. Standard No. 2, adopted in June 2004, requires accounting firms to evaluate the effectiveness of both the design and the operation of internal control, and *form an opinion about whether internal control over financial reporting is effective*. Standard No. 3, effective November 15, 2004, requires an auditing firm to *maintain records of audits for at least 7 years*.

Now the accounting firms have someone looking over their shoulders as they look over the shoulders of U.S. corporations. The new rules require the PCAOB to inspect the auditors at least once per year for firms with more

than 100 clients, at least once every three years for smaller accounting firms, and by special inspection as necessary. The PCAOB intends to publicly release the results of its audits. But don't expect to immediately find out if an accounting firm is failing to live up to the PCAOB's standards. Portions of a final report that deal with criticisms or potential defects in an accounting firm's quality control may be made public only if the firm fails to address those matters to the PCAOB's satisfaction within 12 months after the issuance of the final inspection report.

Source: www.pcaobus.org.

■ *What effect do you think the introduction of the PCAOB standards will have on the relationship between auditors and U.S. public corporations?*

Income Statement

income statement
Provides a financial summary of the firm's operating results during a specified period.

The **income statement** provides a financial summary of the firm's operating results during a specified period. Most common are income statements covering a 1-year period ending at a specified date, ordinarily December 31 of the calendar year. Many large firms, however, operate on a 12-month financial cycle, or *fiscal year,* that ends at a time other than December 31. In addition, monthly income statements are typically prepared for use by management, and quarterly statements must be made available to the stockholders of publicly owned corporations.

Hint Some firms, such as retailers and agricultural firms, end their fiscal year at the end of their operating cycle rather than at the end of the calendar year—for example, retailers at the end of January and agricultural firms at the end of September.

Table 2.1 (see page 48) presents Bartlett Company's income statements for the years ended December 31, 2006 and 2005. The 2006 statement begins with *sales revenue*—the total dollar amount of sales during the period—from which the *cost of goods sold* is deducted. The resulting *gross profits* of $986,000 represent the amount remaining to satisfy operating, financial, and tax costs. Next, *operating expenses,* which include selling expense, general and administrative expense, lease expense, and depreciation expense, are deducted from gross profits.[3] The resulting *operating profits* of $418,000 represent the profits earned from producing and selling products; this amount does not consider financial and

---

3. Depreciation expense can be, and frequently is, included in manufacturing costs—cost of goods sold—to calculate gross profits. Depreciation is shown as an expense in this text to isolate its effect on cash flows.

TABLE 2.1

Bartlett Company Income Statements ($000)

	For the years ended December 31	
	2006	2005
Sales revenue	$3,074	$2,567
Less: Cost of goods sold	2,088	1,711
Gross profits	$ 986	$ 856
Less: Operating expenses		
Selling expense	$ 100	$ 108
General and administrative expenses	194	187
Lease expense[a]	35	35
Depreciation expense	239	223
Total operating expense	$ 568	$ 553
Operating profits	$ 418	$ 303
Less: Interest expense	93	91
Net profits before taxes	$ 325	$ 212
Less: Taxes (rate = 29%)[b]	94	64
Net profits after taxes	$ 231	$ 148
Less: Preferred stock dividends	10	10
Earnings available for common stockholders	$ 221	$ 138
Earnings per share (EPS)[c]	$ 2.90	$ 1.81
Dividend per share (DPS)[d]	$ 1.29	$ 0.75

[a]Lease expense is shown here as a separate item rather than being included as part of interest expense, as specified by the FASB for financial reporting purposes. The approach used here is consistent with tax reporting rather than financial reporting procedures.

[b]The 29% tax rate for 2006 results because the firm has certain special tax write-offs that do not show up directly on its income statement.

[c]Calculated by dividing the earnings available for common stockholders by the number of shares of common stock outstanding—76,262 in 2006 and 76,244 in 2005. Earnings per share in 2006: $221,000 ÷ 76,262 = $2.90; in 2005: $138,000 ÷ 76,244 = $1.81.

[d]Calculated by dividing the dollar amount of dividends paid to common stockholders by the number of shares of common stock outstanding. Dividends per share in 2006: $98,000 ÷ 76,262 = $1.29; in 2005: $57,183 ÷ 76,244 = $0.75.

tax costs. (Operating profit is often called *earnings before interest and taxes,* or *EBIT.*) Next, the financial cost—*interest expense*—is subtracted from operating profits to find *net profits* (or *earnings*) *before taxes*. After subtracting $93,000 in 2006 interest, Bartlett Company had $325,000 of net profits before taxes.

Next, taxes are calculated at the appropriate tax rates and deducted to determine *net profits* (or *earnings*) *after taxes*. Bartlett Company's net profits after taxes for 2006 were $231,000. Any preferred stock dividends must be subtracted from net profits after taxes to arrive at *earnings available for common stockholders*. This is the amount earned by the firm on behalf of the common stockholders during the period.

Dividing earnings available for common stockholders by the number of shares of common stock outstanding results in *earnings per share (EPS)*. EPS represent the number of dollars earned during the period on behalf of each outstanding share of common stock. In 2006, Bartlett Company earned $221,000 for its common stockholders, which represents $2.90 for each outstanding share. The actual cash **dividend per share (DPS),** which is the dollar amount of cash distributed during the period on behalf of each outstanding share of common stock, paid in 2006 was $1.29.

Balance Sheet

The **balance sheet** presents a summary statement of the firm's financial position at a given point in time. The statement balances the firm's *assets* (what it owns) against its financing, which can be either *debt* (what it owes) or *equity* (what was provided by owners). Bartlett Company's balance sheets as of December 31 of 2006 and 2005 are presented in Table 2.2 (see page 50). They show a variety of asset, liability (debt), and equity accounts.

An important distinction is made between short-term and long-term assets and liabilities. The **current assets** and **current liabilities** are *short-term* assets and liabilities. This means that they are expected to be converted into cash (current assets) or paid (current liabilities) within 1 year or less. All other assets and liabilities, along with stockholders' equity, which is assumed to have an infinite life, are considered *long-term,* or *fixed,* because they are expected to remain on the firm's books for more than 1 year.

As is customary, the assets are listed from the most liquid—*cash*—down to the least liquid. *Marketable securities* are very liquid short-term investments, such as U.S. Treasury bills or certificates of deposit, held by the firm. Because they are highly liquid, marketable securities are viewed as a form of cash ("near cash"). *Accounts receivable* represent the total monies owed the firm by its customers on credit sales made to them. *Inventories* include raw materials, work in process (partially finished goods), and finished goods held by the firm. The entry for *gross fixed assets* is the original cost of all fixed (long-term) assets owned by the firm.[4] *Net fixed assets* represent the difference between gross fixed assets and *accumulated depreciation*—the total expense recorded for the depreciation of fixed assets. (The net value of fixed assets is called their *book value.*)

Like assets, the liabilities and equity accounts are listed from short-term to long-term. Current liabilities include *accounts payable,* amounts owed for credit purchases by the firm; *notes payable,* outstanding short-term loans, typically from commercial banks; and *accruals,* amounts owed for services for which a bill may not or will not be received. (Examples of accruals include taxes due the government and wages due employees.) **Long-term debt** represents debt for which payment is not due in the current year. *Stockholders' equity* represents the owners' claims on the firm. The *preferred stock* entry shows the historical proceeds from the sale of preferred stock ($200,000 for Bartlett Company).

Next, the amount paid by the original purchasers of common stock is shown by two entries: common stock and paid-in capital in excess of par on common stock. The *common stock* entry is the *par value* of common stock. **Paid-in capital in excess of par** represents the amount of proceeds in excess of the par value received from the original sale of common stock. The sum of the common stock

dividend per share (DPS) The dollar amount of cash distributed during the period on behalf of each outstanding share of common stock.

balance sheet Summary statement of the firm's financial position at a given point in time.

current assets Short-term assets, expected to be converted into cash within 1 year or less.

current liabilities Short-term liabilities, expected to be paid within 1 year or less.

Hint Another interpretation of the balance sheet is that on one side are the assets that have been purchased to be used to increase the profit of the firm. The other side indicates how these assets were acquired, either by borrowing or by investing the owners' money.

long-term debt Debts for which payment is not due in the current year.

paid-in capital in excess of par The amount of proceeds in excess of the par value received from the original sale of common stock.

---

4. For convenience the term *fixed assets* is used throughout this text to refer to what, in a strict accounting sense, is captioned "property, plant, and equipment." This simplification of terminology permits certain financial concepts to be more easily developed.

TABLE 2.2

Bartlett Company Balance Sheets ($000)

	December 31	
Assets	2006	2005
Current assets		
Cash	$ 363	$ 288
Marketable securities	68	51
Accounts receivable	503	365
Inventories	289	300
Total current assets	$1,223	$1,004
Gross fixed assets (at cost)[a]		
Land and buildings	$2,072	$1,903
Machinery and equipment	1,866	1,693
Furniture and fixtures	358	316
Vehicles	275	314
Other (includes financial leases)	98	96
Total gross fixed assets (at cost)	$4,669	$4,322
Less: Accumulated depreciation	2,295	2,056
Net fixed assets	$2,374	$2,266
Total assets	$3,597	$3,270

Liabilities and Stockholders' Equity		
Current liabilities		
Accounts payable	$ 382	$ 270
Notes payable	79	99
Accruals	159	114
Total current liabilities	$ 620	$ 483
Long-term debt (includes financial leases)[b]	$1,023	$ 967
Total liabilities	$1,643	$1,450
Stockholders' equity		
Preferred stock—cumulative 5%, $100 par, 2,000 shares authorized and issued[c]	$ 200	$ 200
Common stock—$2.50 par, 100,000 shares authorized, shares issued and outstanding in 2006: 76,262; in 2005: 76,244	191	190
Paid-in capital in excess of par on common stock	428	418
Retained earnings	1,135	1,012
Total stockholders' equity	$1,954	$1,820
Total liabilities and stockholders' equity	$3,597	$3,270

[a]In 2006, the firm has a 6-year financial lease requiring annual beginning-of-year payments of $35,000. Four years of the lease have yet to run.

[b]Annual principal repayments on a portion of the firm's total outstanding debt amount to $71,000.

[c]The annual preferred stock dividend would be $5 per share (5% × $100 par), or a total of $10,000 annually ($5 per share × 2,000 shares).

and paid-in capital accounts divided by the number of shares outstanding represents the original price per share received by the firm on a single issue of common stock. Bartlett Company therefore received about $8.12 per share [($191,000 par + $428,000 paid-in capital in excess of par) ÷ 76,262 shares] from the sale of its common stock.

Finally, **retained earnings** represent the cumulative total of all earnings, net of dividends, that have been retained and reinvested in the firm since its inception. It is important to recognize that retained earnings *are not cash* but rather have been utilized to finance the firm's assets.

Bartlett Company's balance sheets in Table 2.2 show that the firm's total assets increased from $3,270,000 in 2005 to $3,597,000 in 2006. The $327,000 increase was due primarily to the $219,000 increase in current assets. The asset increase, in turn, appears to have been financed primarily by an increase of $193,000 in total liabilities. Better insight into these changes can be derived from the statement of cash flows, which we will discuss shortly.

Statement of Retained Earnings

The *statement of retained earnings* is an abbreviated form of the statement of stockholders' equity. Unlike the **statement of stockholders' equity,** which shows all equity account transactions that occurred during a given year, the **statement of retained earnings** reconciles the net income earned during a given year, and any cash dividends paid, with the change in retained earnings between the start and the end of that year. Table 2.3 presents this statement for Bartlett Company for the year ended December 31, 2006. The statement shows that the company began the year with $1,012,000 in retained earnings and had net profits after taxes of $231,000, from which it paid a total of $108,000 in dividends, resulting in year-end retained earnings of $1,135,000. Thus the net increase for Bartlett Company was $123,000 ($231,000 net profits after taxes minus $108,000 in dividends) during 2006.

Statement of Cash Flows

The **statement of cash flows** is a summary of the cash flows over the period of concern. The statement provides insight into the firm's operating, investment, and financing cash flows and reconciles them with changes in its cash and marketable securities during the period. Bartlett Company's statement of cash flows for the year ended December 31, 2006, is presented in Table 2.4 (see page 52). Further insight into this statement is included in the discussion of cash flow in Chapter 3.

retained earnings
The cumulative total of all earnings, net of dividends, that have been retained and reinvested in the firm since its inception.

statement of stockholders' equity
Shows all equity account transactions that occurred during a given year.

statement of retained earnings
Reconciles the net income earned during a given year, and any cash dividends paid, with the change in retained earnings between the start and the end of that year. An abbreviated form of the *statement of stockholders' equity.*

statement of cash flows
Provides a summary of the firm's operating, investment, and financing cash flows and reconciles them with changes in its cash and marketable securities during the period.

TABLE 2.3

Bartlett Company Statement of Retained Earnings ($000) for the Year Ended December 31, 2006

Retained earnings balance (January 1, 2006)		$1,012
Plus: Net profits after taxes (for 2006)		231
Less: Cash dividends (paid during 2006)		
Preferred stock	$10	
Common stock	98	
Total dividends paid		108
Retained earnings balance (December 31, 2006)		$1,135

TABLE 2.4		

Bartlett Company Statement of Cash Flows ($000) for the Year Ended December 31, 2006

Cash Flow from Operating Activities		
Net profits after taxes	$231	
Depreciation	239	
Increase in accounts receivable	(138)[a]	
Decrease in inventories	11	
Increase in accounts payable	112	
Increase in accruals	45	
Cash provided by operating activities		$500
Cash Flow from Investment Activities		
Increase in gross fixed assets	($347)	
Change in business interests	0	
Cash provided by investment activities		(347)
Cash Flow from Financing Activities		
Decrease in notes payable	($ 20)	
Increase in long-term debts	56	
Changes in stockholders' equity[b]	11	
Dividends paid	(108)	
Cash provided by financing activities		(61)
Net increase in cash and marketable securities		$ 92

[a]As is customary, parentheses are used to denote a negative number, which in this case is a cash outflow.

[b]Retained earnings are excluded here, because their change is actually reflected in the combination of the "net profits after taxes" and "dividends paid" entries.

Notes to the Financial Statements

Included with published financial statements are explanatory notes keyed to the relevant accounts in the statements. These **notes to the financial statements** provide detailed information on the accounting policies, procedures, calculations, and transactions underlying entries in the financial statements. Common issues addressed by these notes include revenue recognition, income taxes, breakdowns of fixed asset accounts, debt and lease terms, and contingencies. Professional securities analysts use the data in the statements and notes to develop estimates of the value of securities that the firm issues, and these estimates influence the actions of investors and therefore the firm's share value. The *In Practice* box on the facing page discusses some common corporate accounting misdeeds, their potential impact on investors, and how SOX has helped to eliminate them.

Consolidating International Financial Statements

So far, we've discussed financial statements involving only one currency, the U.S. dollar. The issue of how to consolidate a company's foreign and domestic financial statements has bedeviled the accounting profession for many years. The current policy is described in **Financial Accounting Standards Board (FASB) Standard No. 52,** which mandates that U.S.-based companies translate their foreign-currency-

In Practice FOCUS ON ETHICS

INVESTORS AND SOX DECLARE WAR ON ACCOUNTING MISDEEDS

If you are a student at Rutgers University, you may have taken the new course "Cooking the Books," which is entirely focused on financial fraud. If you study business at Seton Hall University (ex-Tyco CFO Dennis Kozlowski's alma mater), you may enroll in a class showing how accounting numbers can be altered by manipulation. New courses such as these may help deter future accounting fiascos: According to Professors Richard McKenzie (University of California at Irvine) and Tibor Machan (Chapman University), knowing which accounting and finance practices are proper is key to keeping companies honest, as is the personal integrity of accountants and financial managers.

Financial statements are often misstated—and not just by the Tycos, Enrons, and WorldComs of the business world. The SEC has implemented a special effort to prevent fraudulent earnings-management practices. Marianne Jennings, an expert in this area, asserts that common techniques used by corporate accountants to increase or reduce a year's revenues or expenses include the following: writing down inventory, writing up inventory valuation to meet profit target, recording sup-

plies or expenses early, delaying invoices, selling excess assets, and deferring expenditures. Arthur Levitt, chairman of the SEC, also sees evidence of "cookie jar reserves"—a practice in which unrealistic assumptions are used to overstate or understate expenses for the period, so as to reduce earnings in some years and to increase earnings in "down years." The result is a more stable yearly pattern of earnings.

What about the auditors of the financial statements in these cases, you ask? One study of 33 companies that experienced accounting problems indicated that 31 of those companies were handed a clean bill of health by their auditors. When an independent research firm called RateFinancials studied the annual stockholders' reports and other financial documents of 120 major companies, it estimated that as many as one-third do not accurately depict their true financial condition in one or more of their financial reports.

Is shareholder wealth being maximized by these practices? Jennings cites evidence that when earnings manipulation is discovered, the companies' stock prices drop by 9 percent, on average. For

the 33 companies cited previously, shareholder wealth dropped from *$1.8 trillion* to $527 billion following the revelation of the accounting misdeeds.

Investors were cheered by the passage in 2002 of the Sarbanes-Oxley Act (SOX), whose subtitle is "The Public Company Accounting Reform and Investor Protection Act" (see Chapter 1). Included in SOX are provisions for criminal penalties for altering documents, requirement for a code of ethics for the senior financial officers, requirement for the CEO and CFO to sign off on annual reports, new requirements for auditor independence, and certification of a company's internal controls. More accurate and truthful information will reduce the uncertainty of the information flow that investors appraise in valuing stock.

Sources: Marianne M. Jennings, "Earnings Management: The Ethical Issues Remain," *Corporate Finance Review* 3(5), pp. 39–41 (March/April 1999); Jennifer Oladip, "Business Ethics 101," *The Columbus Dispatch,* July 28, 2002, pp. F1–F2; Bruce Meyerson, "Efforts at Transparency Too Obscure for Words," *Seattle Times,* June 23, 2004. Accessed online at: seattletimes .nwsource.com.

■ *What difference might the requirement of auditor independence be expected to make in improving the accuracy of financial reporting?*

current rate (translation) method
Technique used by U.S.-based companies to translate their foreign-currency-denominated assets and liabilities into dollars, for consolidation with the parent company's financial statements, using the year-end (current) exchange rate.

denominated assets and liabilities into dollars, for consolidation with the parent company's financial statements. This is done by using a technique called the **current rate (translation) method,** under which all of a U.S. parent company's foreign-currency-denominated assets and liabilities are converted into dollar values using the exchange rate prevailing at the fiscal year ending date (the current rate). Income statement items are treated similarly. Equity accounts, on the other hand, are translated into dollars by using the exchange rate that prevailed when the parent's equity investment was made (the historical rate). Retained earnings are adjusted to reflect each year's operating profits or losses.

REVIEW QUESTIONS

2–1 What roles do GAAP, the FASB, and the PCAOB play in the financial reporting activities of public companies?

2–2 Describe the purpose of each of the four major financial statements.

2–3 Why are the notes to the financial statements important to professional securities analysts?

2–4 How is the *current rate (translation) method* used to consolidate a firm's foreign and domestic financial statements?

LG2 ## 2.2 | Using Financial Ratios

ratio analysis
Involves methods of calculating and interpreting financial ratios to analyze and monitor the firm's performance.

The information contained in the four basic financial statements is of major significance to a variety of interested parties who regularly need to have relative measures of the company's operating efficiency. *Relative* is the key word here, because the analysis of financial statements is based on the use of *ratios* or *relative values*. **Ratio analysis** involves methods of calculating and interpreting financial ratios to analyze and monitor the firm's performance. The basic inputs to ratio analysis are the firm's income statement and balance sheet.

Interested Parties

Hint Management should be the most interested party of this group. Managers not only have to worry about the financial situation of the firm, but they are also critically interested in what the other parties think about the firm.

Ratio analysis of a firm's financial statements is of interest to shareholders, creditors, and the firm's own management. Both current and prospective shareholders are interested in the firm's current and future level of risk and return, which directly affect share price. The firm's creditors are interested primarily in the short-term liquidity of the company and its ability to make interest and principal payments. A secondary concern of creditors is the firm's profitability; they want assurance that the business is healthy. Management, like stockholders, is concerned with all aspects of the firm's financial situation, and it attempts to produce financial ratios that will be considered favorable by both owners and creditors. In addition, management uses ratios to monitor the firm's performance from period to period.

Types of Ratio Comparisons

cross-sectional analysis
Comparison of different firms' financial ratios at the same point in time; involves comparing the firm's ratios to those of other firms in its industry or to industry averages.

Ratio analysis is not merely the calculation of a given ratio. More important is the *interpretation* of the ratio value. A meaningful basis for comparison is needed to answer such questions as "Is it too high or too low?" and "Is it good or bad?" Two types of ratio comparisons can be made: cross-sectional and time-series.

Cross-Sectional Analysis

benchmarking
A type of *cross-sectional analysis* in which the firm's ratio values are compared to those of a key competitor or group of competitors that it wishes to emulate.

Cross-sectional analysis involves the comparison of different firms' financial ratios at the same point in time. Analysts are often interested in how well a firm has performed in relation to other firms in its industry. Frequently, a firm will compare its ratio values to those of a key competitor or group of competitors that it wishes to emulate. This type of cross-sectional analysis, called **benchmarking**, has become very popular.

Comparison to industry averages is also popular. These figures can be found in the *Almanac of Business and Industrial Financial Ratios, Dun & Bradstreet's Industry Norms and Key Business Ratios, Business Month, FTC Quarterly Reports, RMA Annual Statement Studies, Value Line,* and industry sources.[5] A sample from one available source of industry averages is given in Table 2.5 (see page 56).

Many people mistakenly believe that as long as the firm being analyzed has a value "better than" the industry average, it can be viewed favorably. However, this "better than average" viewpoint can be misleading. Quite often a ratio value that is far better than the norm can indicate problems that, on more careful analysis, may be more severe than had the ratio been worse than the industry average. It is therefore important to investigate significant deviations *to either side* of the industry standard.

Hint Industry averages are not particularly useful for analyzing firms with multiproduct lines. In the case of multiproduct firms, it is difficult to select the appropriate benchmark industry.

EXAMPLE

In early 2007, Mary Boyle, the chief financial analyst at Caldwell Manufacturing, a producer of heat exchangers, gathered data on the firm's financial performance during 2006, the year just ended. She calculated a variety of ratios and obtained industry averages. She was especially interested in inventory turnover, which reflects the speed with which the firm moves its inventory from raw materials through production into finished goods and to the customer as a completed sale. Generally, higher values of this ratio are preferred, because they indicate a quicker turnover of inventory. Caldwell Manufacturing's calculated inventory turnover for 2006 and the industry average inventory turnover were as follows:

	Inventory turnover, 2006
Caldwell Manufacturing	14.8
Industry average	9.7

Mary's initial reaction to these data was that the firm had managed its inventory significantly *better than* the average firm in the industry. The turnover was nearly 53% faster than the industry average. Upon reflection, however, she realized that a very high inventory turnover could also mean very low levels of inventory. The consequence of low inventory could be excessive stockouts (insufficient inventory). Discussions with people in the manufacturing and marketing departments did, in fact, uncover such a problem: Inventories during the year were extremely low, the result of numerous production delays that hindered the firm's ability to meet demand and resulted in lost sales. A ratio that initially appeared to reflect extremely efficient inventory management was actually the symptom of a major problem. ■

Time-Series Analysis

time-series analysis
Evaluation of the firm's financial performance over time using financial ratio analysis.

Time-series analysis evaluates performance over time. Comparison of current to past performance, using ratios, enables analysts to assess the firm's progress. Developing trends can be seen by using multiyear comparisons. Any significant year-to-year changes may be symptomatic of a major problem.

---

5. Cross-sectional comparisons of firms operating in several lines of business are difficult to perform. Weighted-average industry average ratios based on the firm's product-line mix can be used or, if data are available, analysis of the firm on a product-line basis can be performed to evaluate a multiproduct firm.

TABLE 2.5

Industry Average Ratios (2003) for Selected Lines of Business[a]

Line of business (number of concerns reporting)[b]	Current ratio (X)	Quick ratio (X)	Sales to inventory (X)	Collection period (days)	Total assets to sales (%)	Total liabilities to net worth (%)	Return on sales (%)	Return on total assets (%)	Return on net worth (%)
Department	4.9	1.4	6.6	1.8	32.0	25.1	2.8	6.8	16.2
stores	2.6	0.6	4.6	6.1	43.8	76.6	1.0	2.3	4.5
(143)	1.6	0.2	3.5	21.2	64.9	176.9	0.1	0.1	0.2
Electronic	2.3	1.5	31.6	27.4	24.6	54.3	3.4	7.3	20.6
computers	1.6	0.9	11.3	40.9	58.9	114.3	0.5	1.3	4.6
(76)	1.2	0.7	6.8	68.5	104.1	238.3	(9.7)	(10.4)	(20.6)
Grocery	2.6	1.0	29.6	1.1	15.3	48.5	2.2	9.4	24.8
stores	1.6	0.5	19.6	2.9	21.3	105.2	1.0	4.4	10.0
(455)	1.1	0.2	13.9	6.9	31.2	277.3	0.3	1.4	3.5
Motor	2.9	1.1	11.4	16.1	27.8	56.4	4.2	10.3	26.9
vehicles	1.7	0.7	8.3	24.1	37.4	150.8	1.5	4.1	9.6
(42)	1.2	0.5	5.5	40.5	47.3	357.2	0.2	0.8	1.2

[a]These values are given for each ratio for each line of business. The center value is the median, and the values immediately above and below it are the upper and lower quartiles, respectively.

[b]Standard Industrial Classification (SIC) codes for the lines of business shown are, respectively: SIC #5311, SIC #3571, SIC #5411, SIC #3711.

Source: "Industry Norms and Key Business Ratios," Copyright © 2003 Dun & Bradstreet, Inc. Reprinted with permission.

Combined Analysis

The most informative approach to ratio analysis combines cross-sectional and time-series analyses. A combined view makes it possible to assess the trend in the behavior of the ratio in relation to the trend for the industry. Figure 2.1 depicts this type of approach using the average collection period ratio of Bartlett Company, over the years 2003–2006. This ratio reflects the average amount of time (in days) it takes the firm to collect bills, and lower values of this ratio generally are preferred. The figure quickly discloses that (1) Bartlett's effectiveness in collecting its receivables is poor in comparison to the industry, and (2) Bartlett's trend is toward longer collection periods. Clearly, Bartlett needs to shorten its collection period.

Cautions About Using Ratio Analysis

Before discussing specific ratios, we should consider the following cautions about their use:

1. Ratios that reveal large deviations from the norm merely indicate *symptoms* of a problem. Additional analysis is typically needed to isolate the *causes* of the problem. The fundamental point is this: Ratio analysis directs attention to potential areas of concern; it does not provide conclusive evidence as to the existence of a problem.

2. A single ratio does not generally provide sufficient information from which to judge the *overall* performance of the firm. Only when a group of ratios is

FIGURE 2.1

Combined Analysis
Combined cross-sectional and time-series view of Bartlett Company's average collection period, 2003–2006

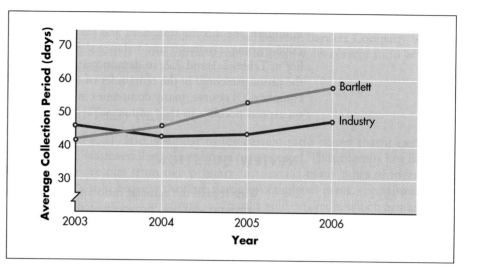

used can reasonable judgments be made. However, if an analysis is concerned only with certain *specific* aspects of a firm's financial position, one or two ratios may suffice.

3. The ratios being compared should be calculated using financial statements dated at the same point in time during the year. If they are not, the effects of *seasonality* may produce erroneous conclusions and decisions. For example, comparison of the inventory turnover of a toy manufacturer at the end of June with its end-of-December value can be misleading. Clearly, the seasonal impact of the December holiday selling season would skew any comparison of the firm's inventory management.

4. It is preferable to use *audited financial statements* for ratio analysis. If the statements have not been audited, the data contained in them may not reflect the firm's true financial condition.

5. The financial data being compared should have been developed in the same way. The use of differing accounting treatments—especially relative to inventory and depreciation—can distort the results of ratio comparisons, regardless of whether cross-sectional or time-series analysis is used.

6. Results can be distorted by *inflation*, which can cause the book values of inventory and depreciable assets to differ greatly from their true (replacement) values. Additionally, inventory costs and depreciation write-offs can differ from their true values, thereby distorting profits. Without adjustment, inflation tends to cause older firms (older assets) to appear more efficient and profitable than newer firms (newer assets). Clearly, in using ratios, care must be taken when comparing older to newer firms or a firm to itself over a long period of time.

Categories of Financial Ratios

Financial ratios can be divided for convenience into five basic categories: liquidity, activity, debt, profitability, and market ratios. Liquidity, activity, and debt ratios primarily measure risk. Profitability ratios measure return. Market ratios capture both risk and return.

industry norms) may result in unnecessarily low risk and return. In general, the lower the firm's coverage ratios, the less certain it is to be able to pay fixed obligations. If a firm is unable to pay these obligations, its creditors may seek immediate repayment, which in most instances would force a firm into bankruptcy. Two popular coverage ratios are the times interest earned ratio and the fixed-payment coverage ratio.[13]

Debt Ratio

debt ratio
Measures the proportion of total assets financed by the firm's creditors.

The **debt ratio** measures the proportion of total assets financed by the firm's creditors. The higher this ratio, the greater the amount of other people's money being used to generate profits. The ratio is calculated as follows:

$$\text{Debt ratio} = \frac{\text{Total liabilities}}{\text{Total assets}}$$

The debt ratio for Bartlett Company in 2006 is

$$\frac{\$1,643,000}{\$3,597,000} = 0.457 = 45.7\%$$

This value indicates that the company has financed close to half of its assets with debt. The higher this ratio, the greater the firm's degree of indebtedness and the more financial leverage it has.

Times Interest Earned Ratio

times interest earned ratio
Measures the firm's ability to make contractual interest payments; sometimes called the *interest coverage ratio.*

The **times interest earned ratio,** sometimes called the *interest coverage ratio,* measures the firm's ability to make contractual interest payments. The higher its value, the better able the firm is to fulfill its interest obligations. The times interest earned ratio is calculated as follows:

$$\text{Times interest earned ratio} = \frac{\text{Earnings before interest and taxes}}{\text{Interest}}$$

The figure for *earnings before interest and taxes* is the same as that for *operating profits* shown in the income statement. Applying this ratio to Bartlett Company yields the following 2006 value:

$$\text{Times interest earned ratio} = \frac{\$418,000}{\$93,000} = 4.5$$

The times interest earned ratio for Bartlett Company seems acceptable. A value of at least 3.0—and preferably closer to 5.0—is often suggested. The firm's earnings before interest and taxes could shrink by as much as 78 percent $[(4.5 - 1.0) \div 4.5]$, and the firm would still be able to pay the $93,000 in interest it owes. Thus it has a good margin of safety.

---

13. Coverage ratios use data that are derived on an *accrual basis* (discussed in Chapter 1) to measure what in a strict sense should be measured on a *cash basis.* This occurs because debts are serviced by using cash flows, not the accounting values shown on the firm's financial statements. But because it is difficult to determine cash flows available for debt service from the firm's financial statements, the calculation of coverage ratios as presented here is quite common thanks to the ready availability of financial statement data.

Fixed-Payment Coverage Ratio

fixed-payment coverage ratio
Measures the firm's ability to meet all fixed-payment obligations.

The **fixed-payment coverage ratio** measures the firm's ability to meet all fixed-payment obligations, such as loan interest and principal, lease payments, and preferred stock dividends.[14] As is true of the times interest earned ratio, the higher this value, the better. The formula for the fixed-payment coverage ratio is

$$\begin{array}{l} \text{Fixed-} \\ \text{payment} \\ \text{coverage} \\ \text{ratio} \end{array} = \dfrac{\text{Earnings before interest and taxes} + \text{Lease payments}}{\begin{array}{c} \text{Interest} + \text{Lease payments} \\ + \{(\text{Principal payments} + \text{Preferred stock dividends}) \times [1/(1 - T)]\} \end{array}}$$

where T is the corporate tax rate applicable to the firm's income. The term $1/(1 - T)$ is included to adjust the after-tax principal and preferred stock dividend payments back to a before-tax equivalent that is consistent with the before-tax values of all other terms. Applying the formula to Bartlett Company's 2006 data yields

$$\begin{array}{l} \text{Fixed-payment} \\ \text{coverage ratio} \end{array} = \dfrac{\$418,000 + \$35,000}{\$93,000 + \$35,000 + \{(\$71,000 + \$10,000) \times [1/(1 - 0.29)]\}}$$

$$= \dfrac{\$453,000}{\$242,000} = 1.9$$

Because the earnings available are nearly twice as large as its fixed-payment obligations, the firm appears safely able to meet the latter.

Like the times interest earned ratio, the fixed-payment coverage ratio measures risk. The lower the ratio, the greater the risk to both lenders and owners; the greater the ratio, the lower the risk. This ratio allows interested parties to assess the firm's ability to meet additional fixed-payment obligations without being driven into bankruptcy.

REVIEW QUESTIONS

2–11   What is *financial leverage?*

2–12   What ratio measures the firm's *degree of indebtedness?* What ratios assess the firm's *ability to service debts?*

LG5   2.6 | Profitability Ratios

There are many measures of profitability. As a group, these measures enable the analyst to evaluate the firm's profits with respect to a given level of sales, a certain level of assets, or the owners' investment. Without profits, a firm could not attract outside capital. Owners, creditors, and management pay close attention to boosting profits because of the great importance placed on earnings in the marketplace.

---

14. Although preferred stock dividends, which are stated at the time of issue, can be "passed" (not paid) at the option of the firm's directors, it is generally believed that the payment of such dividends is necessary. *This text therefore treats the preferred stock dividend as a contractual obligation, to be paid as a fixed amount, as scheduled.*

Common-Size Income Statements

common-size income statement
An income statement in which each item is expressed as a percentage of sales.

A popular tool for evaluating profitability in relation to sales is the **common-size income statement**.[15] Each item on this statement is expressed as a percentage of sales. Common-size income statements are especially useful in comparing performance across years. Three frequently cited ratios of profitability that can be read directly from the common-size income statement are (1) the gross profit margin, (2) the operating profit margin, and (3) the net profit margin.

Common-size income statements for 2006 and 2005 for Bartlett Company are presented and evaluated in Table 2.7. These statements reveal that the firm's cost of goods sold increased from 66.7 percent of sales in 2005 to 67.9 percent in 2006, resulting in a worsening gross profit margin. However, thanks to a decrease in total operating expenses, the firm's net profit margin rose from 5.4 percent of sales in 2005 to 7.2 percent in 2006. The decrease in expenses more than com-

TABLE 2.7

Bartlett Company Common-Size Income Statements

	For the years ended December 31		Evaluation[a]
	2006	2005	2005–2006
Sales revenue	100.0%	100.0%	same
Less: Cost of goods sold	67.9	66.7	worse
(1) Gross profit margin	32.1%	33.3%	worse
Less: Operating expenses			
Selling expense	3.3%	4.2%	better
General and administrative expenses	6.8	6.7	better
Lease expense	1.1	1.3	better
Depreciation expense	7.3	9.3	better
Total operating expense	18.5%	21.5%	better
(2) Operating profit margin	13.6%	11.8%	better
Less: Interest expense	3.0	3.5	better
Net profits before taxes	10.6%	8.3%	better
Less: Taxes	3.1	2.5	worse[b]
Net profits after taxes	7.5%	5.8%	better
Less: Preferred stock dividends	0.3	0.4	better
(3) Net profit margin	7.2%	5.4%	better

[a]Subjective assessments based on data provided.

[b]Taxes as a percentage of sales increased noticeably between 2005 and 2006 because of differing costs and expenses, whereas the average tax rates (taxes ÷ net profits before taxes) for 2005 and 2006 remained about the same—30% and 29%, respectively.

---

15. This statement is sometimes called a *percent income statement*. The same treatment is often applied to the firm's balance sheet to make it easier to evaluate changes in the asset and financial structures of the firm. In addition to measuring profitability, these statements in effect can be used as an alternative or supplement to liquidity, activity, and debt-ratio analysis.

pensated for the increase in the cost of goods sold. A decrease in the firm's 2006 interest expense (3.0 percent of sales versus 3.5 percent in 2005) added to the increase in 2006 profits.

Gross Profit Margin

gross profit margin
Measures the percentage of each sales dollar remaining after the firm has paid for its goods.

The **gross profit margin** measures the percentage of each sales dollar remaining after the firm has paid for its goods. The higher the gross profit margin, the better (that is, the lower the relative cost of merchandise sold). The gross profit margin is calculated as follows:

$$\text{Gross profit margin} = \frac{\text{Sales} - \text{Cost of goods sold}}{\text{Sales}} = \frac{\text{Gross profits}}{\text{Sales}}$$

Bartlett Company's gross profit margin for 2006 is

$$\frac{\$3,074,000 - \$2,088,000}{\$3,074,000} = \frac{\$986,000}{\$3,074,000} = 32.1\%$$

This value is labeled (1) on the common-size income statement in Table 2.7.

Hint This is a very significant ratio for small retailers, especially during times of inflationary prices. If the owner of the firm does not raise prices when the cost of sales is rising, the gross profit margin will erode.

Operating Profit Margin

operating profit margin
Measures the percentage of each sales dollar remaining after all costs and expenses *other than* interest, taxes, and preferred stock dividends are deducted; the "pure profits" earned on each sales dollar.

The **operating profit margin** measures the percentage of each sales dollar remaining after all costs and expenses *other than* interest, taxes, and preferred stock dividends are deducted. It represents the "pure profits" earned on each sales dollar. Operating profits are "pure" because they measure only the profits earned on operations and ignore interest, taxes, and preferred stock dividends. A high operating profit margin is preferred. The operating profit margin is calculated as follows:

$$\text{Operating profit margin} = \frac{\text{Operating profits}}{\text{Sales}}$$

Bartlett Company's operating profit margin for 2006 is

$$\frac{\$418,000}{\$3,074,000} = 13.6\%$$

This value is labeled (2) on the common-size income statement in Table 2.7.

Net Profit Margin

net profit margin
Measures the percentage of each sales dollar remaining after all costs and expenses, *including* interest, taxes, and preferred stock dividends, have been deducted.

The **net profit margin** measures the percentage of each sales dollar remaining after all costs and expenses, *including* interest, taxes, and preferred stock dividends, have been deducted. The higher the firm's net profit margin, the better. The net profit margin is calculated as follows:

$$\text{Net profit margin} = \frac{\text{Earnings available for common stockholders}}{\text{Sales}}$$

Bartlett Company's net profit margin for 2006 is

$$\frac{\$221,000}{\$3,074,000} = 7.2\%$$

Hint The net profit margin is sometimes defined as net profits after taxes divided by sales. The formula used here places greater emphasis on the common stockholders.

This value is labeled (3) on the common-size income statement in Table 2.7.

The net profit margin is a commonly cited measure of the firm's success with respect to earnings on sales. "Good" net profit margins differ considerably across industries. A net profit margin of 1 percent or less would not be unusual for a grocery store, whereas a net profit margin of 10 percent would be low for a retail jewelry store.

Earnings per Share (EPS)

Hint EPS represents the dollar amount earned *on behalf of* each outstanding share of common stock—not the amount of earnings *actually distributed* to shareholders.

The firm's *earnings per share (EPS)* is generally of interest to present or prospective stockholders and management. As we noted earlier, EPS represents the number of dollars earned during the period on behalf of each outstanding share of common stock. Earnings per share is calculated as follows:

$$\text{Earnings per share} = \frac{\text{Earnings available for common stockholders}}{\text{Number of shares of common stock outstanding}}$$

Bartlett Company's earnings per share in 2006 is

$$\frac{\$221,000}{76,262} = \$2.90$$

This figure represents the dollar amount earned *on behalf of* each outstanding share of common stock. The dollar amount of cash *actually distributed* to each shareholder is the *dividend per share (DPS)*, which, as noted in Bartlett Company's income statement (Table 2.1), rose to $1.29 in 2006 from $0.75 in 2005. EPS is closely watched by the investing public and is considered an important indicator of corporate success.

Return on Total Assets (ROA)

return on total assets (ROA)
Measures the overall effectiveness of management in generating profits with its available assets; also called the *return on investment (ROI)*.

The **return on total assets (ROA)**, often called the *return on investment (ROI)*, measures the overall effectiveness of management in generating profits with its available assets. The higher the firm's return on total assets, the better. The return on total assets is calculated as follows:

$$\text{Return on total assets} = \frac{\text{Earnings available for common stockholders}}{\text{Total assets}}$$

Hint Some firms use this measure as a simple decision technique for evaluating proposed fixed-asset investments.

Bartlett Company's return on total assets in 2006 is

$$\frac{\$221,000}{\$3,597,000} = 6.1\%$$

This value indicates that the company earned 6.1 cents on each dollar of asset investment.

Return on Common Equity (ROE)

return on common equity (ROE)
Measures the return earned on the common stockholders' investment in the firm.

The **return on common equity (ROE)** measures the return earned on the common stockholders' investment in the firm. Generally, the higher this return, the better off are the owners. Return on common equity is calculated as follows:

$$\text{Return on common equity} = \frac{\text{Earnings available for common stockholders}}{\text{Common stock equity}}$$

This ratio for Bartlett Company in 2006 is

$$\frac{\$221,000}{\$1,754,000} = 12.6\%$$

Note that the value for common stock equity ($1,754,000) was found by subtracting the $200,000 of preferred stock equity from the total stockholders' equity of $1,954,000 (see Bartlett Company's 2006 balance sheet in Table 2.2). The calculated ROE of 12.6 percent indicates that during 2006 Bartlett earned 12.6 cents on each dollar of common stock equity.

REVIEW QUESTIONS

2–13 What three ratios of profitability are found on a *common-size income statement?*

2–14 What would explain a firm's having a high gross profit margin and a low net profit margin?

2–15 Which measure of profitability is probably of greatest interest to the investing public? Why?

LG5 2.7 Market Ratios

market ratios
Relate a firm's market value, as measured by its current share price, to certain accounting values.

Market ratios relate the firm's market value, as measured by its current share price, to certain accounting values. These ratios give insight into how well investors in the marketplace feel the firm is doing in terms of risk and return. They tend to reflect, on a relative basis, the common stockholders' assessment of all aspects of the firm's past and expected future performance. Here we consider two popular market ratios, one that focuses on earnings and another that considers book value.

Price/Earnings (P/E) Ratio

price/earnings (P/E) ratio
Measures the amount that investors are willing to pay for each dollar of a firm's earnings; the higher the P/E ratio, the greater the investor confidence.

The **price/earnings (P/E) ratio** is commonly used to assess the owners' appraisal of share value.[16] The P/E ratio measures the amount that investors are willing to pay for each dollar of a firm's earnings. The level of this ratio indicates the degree of

---

16. Use of the price/earnings ratio to estimate the value of the firm is part of the discussion of "Other approaches to common stock valuation" in Chapter 7.

confidence that investors have in the firm's future performance. The higher the P/E ratio, the greater the investor confidence. The P/E ratio is calculated as follows:

$$\text{Price/earnings (P/E) ratio} = \frac{\text{Market price per share of common stock}}{\text{Earnings per share}}$$

If Bartlett Company's common stock at the end of 2006 was selling at $32.25, using the EPS of $2.90, the P/E ratio at year-end 2006 is

$$\frac{\$32.25}{\$2.90} = 11.1$$

This figure indicates that investors were paying $11.10 for each $1.00 of earnings. The P/E ratio is most informative when applied in cross-sectional analysis using an industry average P/E ratio or the P/E ratio of a benchmark firm.

Market/Book (M/B) Ratio

market/book (M/B) ratio
Provides an assessment of how investors view the firm's performance. Firms expected to earn high returns relative to their risk typically sell at higher M/B multiples.

The **market/book (M/B) ratio** provides an assessment of how investors view the firm's performance. It relates the market value of the firm's shares to their book—strict accounting—value. To calculate the firm's M/B ratio, we first need to find the *book value per share of common stock*:

$$\frac{\text{Book value per share}}{\text{of common stock}} = \frac{\text{Common stock equity}}{\text{Number of shares of common stock outstanding}}$$

Substituting the appropriate values for Bartlett Company from its 2006 balance sheet, we get

$$\frac{\text{Book value per share}}{\text{of common stock}} = \frac{\$1,754,000}{76,262} = \$23.00$$

The formula for the market/book ratio is

$$\text{Market/book (M/B) ratio} = \frac{\text{Market price per share of common stock}}{\text{Book value per share of common stock}}$$

Substituting Bartlett Company's end of 2006 common stock price of $32.25 and its $23.00 book value per share of common stock (calculated above) into the M/B ratio formula, we get

$$\text{Market/book (M/B) ratio} = \frac{\$32.25}{\$23.00} = 1.40$$

This M/B ratio means that investors are currently paying $1.40 for each $1.00 of book value of Bartlett Company's stock.

The stocks of firms that are expected to perform well—improve profits, increase their market share, or launch successful products—typically sell at higher M/B ratios than the stocks of firms with less attractive outlooks. Simply stated, firms expected to earn high returns relative to their risk typically sell at higher M/B multiples. Clearly, Bartlett's future prospects are being viewed favorably by investors, who are willing to pay more than its book value for the firm's shares. Like P/E ratios, M/B ratios are typically assessed cross-sectionally, to get a feel for the firm's risk and return compared to peer firms.

REVIEW QUESTION

2–16   How do the *price/earnings (P/E) ratio* and the *market/book (M/B) ratio* provide a feel for the firm's risk and return?

LG6 2.8 | A Complete Ratio Analysis

Analysts frequently wish to take an overall look at the firm's financial performance and status. Here we consider two popular approaches to a complete ratio analysis: (1) summarizing all ratios and (2) the DuPont system of analysis. The summary analysis approach tends to view *all aspects* of the firm's financial activities to isolate key areas of responsibility. The DuPont system acts as a search technique aimed at finding the *key areas* responsible for the firm's financial condition.

Summarizing All Ratios

We can use Bartlett Company's ratios to perform a complete ratio analysis using both cross-sectional and time-series analysis approaches. The 2006 ratio values calculated earlier and the ratio values calculated for 2004 and 2005 for Bartlett Company, along with the industry average ratios for 2006, are summarized in Table 2.8 (see pages 72 and 73), which also shows the formula used to calculate each ratio. Using these data, we can discuss the five key aspects of Bartlett's performance—liquidity, activity, debt, profitability, and market.

Liquidity

The overall liquidity of the firm seems to exhibit a reasonably stable trend, having been maintained at a level that is relatively consistent with the industry average in 2006. The firm's liquidity seems to be good.

Activity

Bartlett Company's inventory appears to be in good shape. Its inventory management seems to have improved, and in 2006 it performed at a level above that of the industry. The firm may be experiencing some problems with accounts receivable. The average collection period seems to have crept up above that of the industry. Bartlett also appears to be slow in paying its bills; it pays nearly 30 days slower than the industry average. This could adversely affect the firm's credit standing. Although overall liquidity appears to be good, the management of receivables and payables should be examined. Bartlett's total asset turnover reflects a decline in the efficiency of total asset utilization between 2004 and 2005. Although in 2006 it rose to a level considerably above the industry average, it appears that the pre-2005 level of efficiency has not yet been achieved.

TABLE 2.8   Summary of Bartlett Company Ratios (2004–2006, Including 2006 Industry Averages)

Ratio	Formula	Year 2004[a]	Year 2005[b]	Year 2006[b]	Industry average 2006[c]	Evaluation[d] Cross-sectional 2006	Evaluation[d] Time-series 2004–2006	Overall
Liquidity								
Current ratio	$\dfrac{\text{Current assets}}{\text{Current liabilities}}$	2.04	2.08	1.97	2.05	OK	OK	OK
Quick (acid-test) ratio	$\dfrac{\text{Current assets} - \text{Inventory}}{\text{Current liabilities}}$	1.32	1.46	1.51	1.43	OK	good	good
Activity								
Inventory turnover	$\dfrac{\text{Cost of goods sold}}{\text{Inventory}}$	5.1	5.7	7.2	6.6	good	good	good
Average collection period	$\dfrac{\text{Accounts receivable}}{\text{Average sales per day}}$	43.9 days	51.2 days	59.7 days	44.3 days	poor	poor	poor
Average payment period	$\dfrac{\text{Accounts payable}}{\text{Average purchases per day}}$	75.8 days	81.2 days	95.4 days	66.5 days	poor	poor	poor
Total asset turnover	$\dfrac{\text{Sales}}{\text{Total assets}}$	0.94	0.79	0.85	0.75	OK	OK	OK
Debt								
Debt ratio	$\dfrac{\text{Total liabilities}}{\text{Total assets}}$	36.8%	44.3%	45.7%	40.0%	OK	OK	OK
Times interest earned ratio	$\dfrac{\text{Earnings before interest and taxes}}{\text{Interest}}$	5.6	3.3	4.5	4.3	good	OK	OK
Fixed-payment coverage ratio	$\dfrac{\text{Earnings before interest and taxes} + \text{Lease payments}}{\text{Int.} + \text{Lease pay.} + \{(\text{Prin.} + \text{Pref. div.}) \times [1/(1 - T)]\}}$	2.4	1.4	1.9	1.5	good	OK	good

Ratio	Formula	Year 2004[a]	2005[b]	2006[b]	Industry average 2006[c]	Evaluation[d] Cross-sectional 2006	Time-series 2004–2006	Overall
Profitability								
Gross profit margin	$\dfrac{\text{Gross profits}}{\text{Sales}}$	31.4%	33.3%	32.1%	30.0%	OK	OK	OK
Operating profit margin	$\dfrac{\text{Operating profits}}{\text{Sales}}$	14.6%	11.8%	13.6%	11.0%	good	OK	good
Net profit margin	$\dfrac{\text{Earnings available for common stockholders}}{\text{Sales}}$	8.2%	5.4%	7.2%	6.2%	good	OK	good
Earnings per share (EPS)	$\dfrac{\text{Earnings available for common stockholders}}{\text{Number of shares of common stock outstanding}}$	$3.26	$1.81	$2.90	$2.26	good	OK	good
Return on total assets (ROA)	$\dfrac{\text{Earnings available for common stockholders}}{\text{Total assets}}$	7.8%	4.2%	6.1%	4.6%	good	OK	good
Return on common equity (ROE)	$\dfrac{\text{Earnings available for common stockholders}}{\text{Common stock equity}}$	13.7%	8.5%	12.6%	8.5%	good	OK	good
Market								
Price/earnings (P/E) ratio	$\dfrac{\text{Market price per share of common stock}}{\text{Earnings per share}}$	10.5	10.0[e]	11.1	12.5	OK	OK	OK
Market/book (M/B) ratio	$\dfrac{\text{Market price per share of common stock}}{\text{Book value per share of common stock}}$	1.25	0.85[e]	1.40	1.30	OK	OK	OK

[a]Calculated from data not included in the chapter.
[b]Calculated by using the financial statements presented in Tables 2.1 and 2.2
[c]Obtained from sources not included in this chapter.
[d]Subjective assessments based on data provided.
[e]The market price per share at the end of 2005 was $18.06.

Debt

Bartlett Company's indebtedness increased over the 2004–2006 period and is currently above the industry average. Although this increase in the debt ratio could be cause for alarm, the firm's ability to meet interest and fixed-payment obligations improved, from 2005 to 2006, to a level that outperforms the industry. The firm's increased indebtedness in 2005 apparently caused a deterioration in its ability to pay debt adequately. However, Bartlett has evidently improved its income in 2006 so that it is able to meet its interest and fixed-payment obligations at a level consistent with the average in the industry. In summary, it appears that although 2005 was an off year, the company's improved ability to pay debts in 2006 compensates for its increased degree of indebtedness.

Profitability

Bartlett's profitability relative to sales in 2006 was better than the average company in the industry, although it did not match the firm's 2004 performance. Although the *gross* profit margin was better in 2005 and 2006 than in 2004, higher levels of operating and interest expenses in 2005 and 2006 appear to have caused the 2006 *net* profit margin to fall below that of 2004. However, Bartlett Company's 2006 net profit margin is quite favorable when compared to the industry average.

The firm's earnings per share, return on total assets, and return on common equity behaved much as its net profit margin did over the 2004–2006 period. Bartlett appears to have experienced either a sizable drop in sales between 2004 and 2005 or a rapid expansion in assets during that period. The exceptionally high 2006 level of return on common equity suggests that the firm is performing quite well. The firm's above-average returns—net profit margin, EPS, ROA, and ROE—may be attributable to the fact that it is more risky than average. A look at market ratios is helpful in assessing risk.

Market

Investors have greater confidence in the firm in 2006 than in the prior two years, as reflected in the price/earnings (P/E) ratio of 11.1. However, this ratio is below the industry average. The P/E ratio suggests that the firm's risk has declined but remains above that of the average firm in its industry. The firm's market/book (M/B) ratio has increased over the 2004–2006 period, and in 2006 it exceeds the industry average. This implies that investors are optimistic about the firm's future performance. The P/E and M/B ratios reflect the firm's increased profitability over the 2004–2006 period: Investors expect to earn high future returns as compensation for the firm's above-average risk.

In summary, the firm appears to be growing and has recently undergone an expansion in assets, financed primarily through the use of debt. The 2005–2006 period seems to reflect a phase of adjustment and recovery from the rapid growth in assets. Bartlett's sales, profits, and other performance factors seem to be growing with the increase in the size of the operation. In addition, the market response to these accomplishments appears to have been positive. In short, the firm seems to have done well in 2006.

DuPont System of Analysis

DuPont system of analysis
System used to dissect the firm's financial statements and to assess its financial condition.

The **DuPont system of analysis** is used to dissect the firm's financial statements and to assess its financial condition. It merges the income statement and balance sheet into two summary measures of profitability: return on total assets (ROA) and return on common equity (ROE). Figure 2.2 (see page 76) depicts the basic DuPont system with Bartlett Company's 2006 monetary and ratio values. The upper portion of the chart summarizes the income statement activities; the lower portion summarizes the balance sheet activities.

Dupont Formula

DuPont formula
Multiplies the firm's *net profit margin* by its *total asset turnover* to calculate the firm's *return on total assets (ROA)*.

The DuPont system first brings together the *net profit margin*, which measures the firm's profitability on sales, with its *total asset turnover*, which indicates how efficiently the firm has used its assets to generate sales. In the **DuPont formula**, the product of these two ratios results in the *return on total assets (ROA)*:

$$ROA = \text{Net profit margin} \times \text{Total asset turnover}$$

Substituting the appropriate formulas into the equation and simplifying results in the formula given earlier,

$$ROA = \frac{\text{Earnings available for common stockholders}}{\text{Sales}} \times \frac{\text{Sales}}{\text{Total assets}} = \frac{\text{Earnings available for common stockholders}}{\text{Total assets}}$$

When the 2006 values of the net profit margin and total asset turnover for Bartlett Company, calculated earlier, are substituted into the DuPont formula, the result is

$$ROA = 7.2\% \times 0.85 = 6.1\%$$

This value is the same as that calculated directly in an earlier section (page 68). The DuPont formula enables the firm to break down its return into profit-on-sales and efficiency-of-asset-use components. Typically, a firm with a low net profit margin has a high total asset turnover, which results in a reasonably good return on total assets. Often, the opposite situation exists.

Modified Dupont Formula

modified DuPont formula
Relates the firm's *return on total assets (ROA)* to its *return on common equity (ROE)* using the *financial leverage multiplier (FLM)*.

financial leverage multiplier (FLM)
The ratio of the firm's total assets to its common stock equity.

The second step in the DuPont system employs the **modified DuPont formula.** This formula relates the firm's *return on total assets (ROA)* to its *return on common equity (ROE)*. The latter is calculated by multiplying the return on total assets (ROA) by the **financial leverage multiplier (FLM)**, which is the ratio of total assets to common stock equity:

$$ROE = ROA \times FLM$$

Substituting the appropriate formulas into the equation and simplifying results in the formula given earlier,

$$ROE = \frac{\text{Earnings available for common stockholders}}{\text{Total assets}} \times \frac{\text{Total assets}}{\text{Common stock equity}} = \frac{\text{Earnings available for common stockholders}}{\text{Common stock equity}}$$

FIGURE 2.2   **Dupont System of Analysis**

The DuPont system of analysis with application to Bartlett Company (2006)

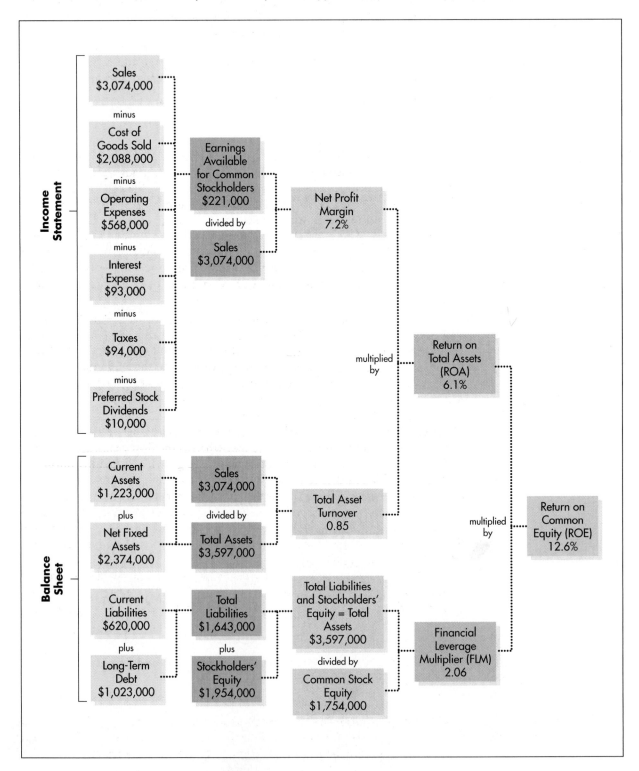

Use of the financial leverage multiplier (FLM) to convert the ROA into the ROE reflects the impact of financial leverage on owners' return. Substituting the values for Bartlett Company's ROA of 6.1 percent, calculated earlier, and Bartlett's FLM of 2.06 ($3,597,000 total assets ÷ $1,754,000 common stock equity) into the modified DuPont formula yields

$$\text{ROE} = 6.1\% \times 2.06 = 12.6\%$$

The 12.6 percent ROE calculated by using the modified DuPont formula is the same as that calculated directly (page 69).

Applying the Dupont System

The advantage of the DuPont system is that it allows the firm to break its return on equity into a profit-on-sales component (net profit margin), an efficiency-of-asset-use component (total asset turnover), and a use-of-financial-leverage component (financial leverage multiplier). The total return to owners therefore can be analyzed in these important dimensions.

The use of the DuPont system of analysis as a diagnostic tool is best explained using Figure 2.2. Beginning with the rightmost value—the ROE—the financial analyst moves to the left, dissecting and analyzing the inputs to the formula to isolate the probable cause of the resulting above-average (or below-average) value.

EXAMPLE   For the sake of demonstration, let's ignore all industry average data in Table 2.8 and assume that Bartlett's ROE of 12.6 % is actually below the industry average. Moving to the left in Figure 2.2, we would examine the inputs to the ROE—the ROA and the FLM—relative to the industry averages. Let's assume that the FLM is in line with the industry average, but the ROA is below the industry average. Moving farther to the left, we examine the two inputs to the ROA—the net profit margin and total asset turnover. Assume that the net profit margin is in line with the industry average, but the total asset turnover is below the industry average. Moving still farther to the left, we find that whereas the firm's sales are consistent with the industry value, Bartlett's total assets have grown significantly during the past year. Looking farther to the left, we would review the firm's activity ratios for current assets. Let's say that whereas the firm's inventory turnover is in line with the industry average, its average collection period is well above the industry average.

We can readily trace the possible problem back to its cause: Bartlett's low ROE is primarily the consequence of slow collections of accounts receivable, which resulted in high levels of receivables and therefore high levels of total assets. The high total assets slowed Bartlett's total asset turnover, driving down its ROA, which then drove down its ROE. By using the DuPont system of analysis to dissect Bartlett's overall returns as measured by its ROE, we found that slow collections of receivables caused the below-industry-average ROE. Clearly, the firm needs to better manage its credit operations. ■

REVIEW QUESTIONS

2–17   Financial ratio analysis is often divided into five areas: *liquidity, activity, debt, profitability,* and *market* ratios. Differentiate each of these areas of analysis from the others. Which is of the greatest concern to creditors?

2–18 Describe how you would use a large number of ratios to perform a complete ratio analysis of the firm.

2–19 What three areas of analysis are combined in the *modified DuPont formula?* Explain how the *DuPont system of analysis* is used to dissect the firm's results and isolate their causes.

Summary

Focus on Value

Financial managers review and analyze the firm's financial statements periodically, both to uncover developing problems and to assess the firm's progress toward achieving its goals. These actions are aimed at **preserving and creating value for the firm's owners.** Financial ratios enable financial managers to monitor the pulse of the firm and its progress toward its strategic goals. Although financial statements and financial ratios rely on accrual concepts, they can provide useful insights into important aspects of risk and return (cash flow) that affect share price, which management is attempting to maximize.

Review of Learning Goals

LG1 Review the contents of the stockholders' report and the procedures for consolidating international financial statements. The annual stockholders' report, which publicly owned corporations must provide to stockholders, documents the firm's financial activities of the past year. It includes the letter to stockholders and various subjective and factual information, as well as four key financial statements: the income statement, the balance sheet, the statement of stockholders' equity (or its abbreviated form, the statement of retained earnings), and the statement of cash flows. Notes describing the technical aspects of the financial statements follow. Financial statements of companies that have operations whose cash flows are denominated in one or more foreign currencies must be translated into dollars in accordance with *FASB Standard No. 52.*

LG2 Understand who uses financial ratios, and how. Ratio analysis enables stockholders and lenders and the firm's managers to evaluate the firm's financial performance. It can be performed on a cross-sectional or a time-series basis. Benchmarking is a popular type of cross-sectional analysis. Key cautions for applying financial ratios are as follow: (1) Ratios with large deviations from the norm merely indicate symptoms of a problem. (2) A single ratio does not generally provide sufficient information. (3) The ratios being compared should be calculated using financial statements dated at the same point in time during the year. (4) Audited financial statements should be used. (5) Data should be checked for consistency of accounting treatment. (6) Inflation and different asset ages can distort ratio comparisons.

LG3 Use ratios to analyze a firm's liquidity and activity. Liquidity, or the ability of the firm to pay its bills as they come due, can be measured by the current ratio and the quick (acid-test) ratio. Activity ratios measure the speed with which accounts are converted into sales or cash—inflows or outflows. The activity of inventory can be measured by its turnover; that of accounts receivable by the average collection period; and that of accounts payable by the average payment period. Total asset turnover measures the efficiency with which the firm uses its assets to generate sales.

LG4 **Discuss the relationship between debt and financial leverage and the ratios used to analyze a firm's debt.** The more debt a firm uses, the greater its financial leverage, which magnifies both risk and return. Financial debt ratios measure both the degree of indebtedness and the ability to service debts. A common measure of indebtedness is the debt ratio. The ability to pay fixed charges can be measured by times interest earned and fixed-payment coverage ratios.

LG5 **Use ratios to analyze a firm's profitability and its market value.** The common-size income statement, which shows all items as a percentage of sales, can be used to determine gross profit margin, operating profit margin, and net profit margin. Other measures of profitability include earnings per share, return on total assets, and return on common equity. Market ratios include the price/earnings ratio and the market/book ratio.

LG6 **Use a summary of financial ratios and the DuPont system of analysis to perform a complete ratio analysis.** A summary of all ratios—liquidity, activity, debt, profitability, and market—can be used to perform a complete ratio analysis using cross-sectional and time-series analysis. The DuPont system of analysis is a diagnostic tool used to find the key areas responsible for the firm's financial performance. It enables the firm to break the return on common equity into three components: profit on sales, efficiency of asset use, and use of financial leverage.

Self-Test Problems (Solutions in Appendix B)

LG3 **LG4** **LG5** ST2–1 **Ratio formulas and interpretations** Without referring to the text, indicate for each of the following ratios the formula for calculating it and the kinds of problems, if any, the firm is likely to have if that ratio is too high relative to the industry average. What if the ratio is too low relative to the industry average? Create a table similar to the one that follows and fill in the empty blocks.

Ratio	Too high	Too low
Current ratio =		
Inventory turnover =		
Times interest earned =	✕	
Gross profit margin =		
Return on total assets =	✕	
Price/earnings(P/E)ratio =		

LG3 LG4 LG5 **ST2–2 Balance sheet completion using ratios** Complete the 2006 balance sheet for O'Keefe Industries using the information that follows it.

<table>
<tr><td colspan="4" align="center">O'Keefe Industries
Balance Sheet
December 31, 2006</td></tr>
<tr><td colspan="2">**Assets**</td><td colspan="2">**Liabilities and Stockholders' Equity**</td></tr>
<tr><td>Cash</td><td>$32,720</td><td>Accounts payable</td><td>$120,000</td></tr>
<tr><td>Marketable securities</td><td>25,000</td><td>Notes payable</td><td>_____</td></tr>
<tr><td>Accounts receivable</td><td>_____</td><td>Accruals</td><td>20,000</td></tr>
<tr><td>Inventories</td><td>_____</td><td>Total current liabilities</td><td>_____</td></tr>
<tr><td>Total current assets</td><td>_____</td><td>Long-term debt</td><td>_____</td></tr>
<tr><td>Net fixed assets</td><td>_____</td><td>Stockholders' equity</td><td>$600,000</td></tr>
<tr><td>Total assets</td><td>$_____</td><td>Total liabilities and
stockholders' equity</td><td>$_____</td></tr>
</table>

The following financial data for 2006 are also available:
(1) Sales totaled $1,800,000.
(2) The gross profit margin was 25%.
(3) Inventory turnover was 6.0.
(4) There are 365 days in the year.
(5) The average collection period was 40 days.
(6) The current ratio was 1.60.
(7) The total asset turnover ratio was 1.20.
(8) The debt ratio was 60%.

Warm-Up Exercises

LG1 **E2–1** You are a summer intern at the office of a local tax-preparer. To test your basic knowledge of financial statements, your manager, who graduated from your alma mater 2 years ago, gives you the following list of accounts and asks you to prepare a simple income statement using those accounts.

	Accounts ($000,000)
Depreciation	25
General and administrative expenses	22
Sales	345
Sales expenses	18
Cost of goods sold	255
Lease expense	4
Interest expense	3

a. Arrange the accounts into a well-labeled income statement. Make sure you label and solve for gross profit, operating profit, and net profit before taxes.
b. Using a 35% tax rate, calculate taxes paid and net profit after taxes.

c. Assuming a dividend of $1.10 per share with 4.25 million shares outstanding, calculate EPS and additions to retained earnings.

LG1

E2–2   Explain why the income statement can also be called a "profit and loss statement." What exactly does the word "balance" mean in the title of the balance sheet? Why do we balance the two halves?

LG1

E2–3   Cooper Industries, Inc., began 2006 with retained earnings of $25.32 million. During the year it paid four quarterly dividends of $0.35 per share to 2.75 million common stockholders. Preferred stockholders, holding 500,000 shares, were paid two semiannual dividends of $0.75 per share. The firm had a net profit after taxes of $5.15 million. Prepare the statement of retained earnings for the year ended December 31, 2006.

LG3

E2–4   Bluestone Metals, Inc., is a metal fabrication firm which manufactures prefabricated metal parts for customers in a variety of industries. The firm's motto is "If you need it, we can make it." The CEO of Bluestone recently held a board meeting during which he extolled the virtues of the corporation. The company, he stated confidently, had the capability to build any product and could do so using a lean manufacturing model. The firm would soon be profitable, claimed the CEO, because the company used state of the art technology to build a variety of products while keeping inventory levels low. As a business press reporter, you have calculated some ratios to analyze the financial health of the firm. Bluestone's current ratios and quick ratios for the past six years are shown in the table below:

	2001	2002	2003	2004	2005	2006
Current ratio	1.2	1.4	1.3	1.6	1.8	2.2
Quick ratio	1.1	1.3	1.2	0.8	0.6	0.4

What do you think of the CEO's claim that the firm is lean and soon to be profitable? (*Hint:* Is there a possible warning sign in the relationship between the two ratios?)

LG5

E2–5   If we know that a firm has a net profit margin of 4.5%, total asset turnover of 0.72, and an equity multiplier of 1.43, what is its ROE? What is the advantage to using the DuPont system to calculate ROE over the direct calculation of earnings available for common stockholders ÷ common stock equity?

Problems

LG1

BASIC

P2–1   **Reviewing basic financial statements**   The income statement for the year ended December 31, 2006, the balance sheets for December 31, 2006 and 2005, and the statement of retained earnings for the year ended December 31, 2006, for Technica, Inc., are given on pages 82 and 83. Briefly discuss the form and informational content of each of these statements.

Technica, Inc.
Income Statement
for the Year Ended December 31, 2006

Sales revenue		$600,000
Less: Cost of goods sold		460,000
Gross profits		$140,000
Less: Operating expenses		
General and administrative expenses	$30,000	
Depreciation expense	30,000	
Total operating expense		60,000
Operating profits		$ 80,000
Less: Interest expense		10,000
Net profits before taxes		$ 70,000
Less: Taxes		27,100
Earnings available for common stockholders		$ 42,900
Earnings per share (EPS)		$2.15

Technica, Inc.
Balance Sheets

	December 31	
Assets	**2006**	**2005**
Cash	$ 15,000	$ 16,000
Marketable securities	7,200	8,000
Accounts receivable	34,100	42,200
Inventories	82,000	50,000
Total current assets	$138,300	$116,200
Land and buildings	$150,000	$150,000
Machinery and equipment	200,000	190,000
Furniture and fixtures	54,000	50,000
Other	11,000	10,000
Total gross fixed assets	$415,000	$400,000
Less: Accumulated depreciation	145,000	115,000
Net fixed assets	$270,000	$285,000
Total assets	$408,300	$401,200
Liabilities and Stockholders' Equity		
Accounts payable	$ 57,000	$ 49,000
Notes payable	13,000	16,000
Accruals	5,000	6,000
Total current liabilities	$ 75,000	$ 71,000
Long-term debt	$150,000	$160,000
Stockholders' equity		
Common stock equity (shares outstanding: 19,500 in 2006 and 20,000 in 2005)	$110,200	$120,000
Retained earnings	73,100	50,200
Total stockholders' equity	$183,300	$170,200
Total liabilities and stockholders' equity	$408,300	$401,200

Technica, Inc.
Statement of Retained Earnings
for the Year Ended December 31, 2006

Retained earnings balance (January 1, 2006)	$50,200
Plus: Net profits after taxes (for 2006)	42,900
Less: Cash dividends (paid during 2006)	20,000
Retained earnings balance (December 31, 2006)	$73,100

LG1

BASIC

P2–2 **Financial statement account identification** Mark each of the accounts listed in the following table as follows:

a. In column (1), indicate in which statement—income statement (IS) or balance sheet (BS)—the account belongs.

b. In column (2), indicate whether the account is a current asset (CA), current liability (CL), expense (E), fixed asset (FA), long-term debt (LTD), revenue (R), or stockholders' equity (SE).

Account name	(1) Statement	(2) Type of account
Accounts payable	BS	CL
Accounts receivable	BS	CA
Accruals	BS	CL
Accumulated depreciation	BS	E
Administrative expense		
Buildings		
Cash		
Common stock (at par)		
Cost of goods sold		
Depreciation		
Equipment		
General expense		
Interest expense		
Inventories		
Land		
Long-term debts		
Machinery		
Marketable securities		
Notes payable		
Operating expense		
Paid-in capital in excess of par		
Preferred stock		
Preferred stock dividends		
Retained earnings		
Sales revenue		
Selling expense		
Taxes	IS	E
Vehicles		

P2–3   Income statement preparation   On December 31, 2006, Cathy Chen, a self-employed certified public accountant (CPA), completed her first full year in business. During the year, she billed $360,000 for her accounting services. She had two employees: a bookkeeper and a clerical assistant. In addition to her *monthly* salary of $8,000, Ms. Chen paid *annual* salaries of $48,000 and $36,000 to the bookkeeper and the clerical assistant, respectively. Employment taxes and benefit costs for Ms. Chen and her employees totaled $34,600 for the year. Expenses for office supplies, including postage, totaled $10,400 for the year. In addition, Ms. Chen spent $17,000 during the year on tax-deductible travel and entertainment associated with client visits and new business development. Lease payments for the office space rented (a tax-deductible expense) were $2,700 *per month*. Depreciation expense on the office furniture and fixtures was $15,600 for the year. During the year, Ms. Chen paid interest of $15,000 on the $120,000 borrowed to start the business. She paid an average tax rate of 30 percent during 2006.

a. Prepare an income statement for Cathy Chen, CPA, for the year ended December 31, 2006.

b. Evaluate her 2006 financial performance.

P2–4   Calculation of EPS and retained earnings   Philagem, Inc., ended 2006 with a net profit *before* taxes of $218,000. The company is subject to a 40% tax rate and must pay $32,000 in preferred stock dividends before distributing any earnings on the 85,000 shares of common stock currently outstanding.

a. Calculate Philagem's 2006 earnings per share (EPS).

b. If the firm paid common stock dividends of $0.80 per share, how many dollars would go to retained earnings?

P2–5   Balance sheet preparation   Use the *appropriate items* from the following list to prepare in good form Owen Davis Company's balance sheet at December 31, 2006.

Item	Value ($000) at December 31, 2006	Item	Value ($000) at December 31, 2006
Accounts payable	$ 220	Inventories	$ 375
Accounts receivable	450	Land	100
Accruals	55	Long-term debts	420
Accumulated depreciation	265	Machinery	420
Buildings	225	Marketable securities	75
Cash	215	Notes payable	475
Common stock (at par)	90	Paid-in capital in excess	
Cost of goods sold	2,500	of par	360
Depreciation expense	45	Preferred stock	100
Equipment	140	Retained earnings	210
Furniture and fixtures	170	Sales revenue	3,600
General expense	320	Vehicles	25

P2–6   Impact of net income on a firm's balance sheet   Conrad Air, Inc., reported net income of $1,365,000 for the year ended December 31, 2006. Show the effect of these funds on the firm's balance sheet for the previous year (below) in each of the scenarios following the balance sheet.

Conrad Air, Inc.
Balance Sheet
as of December 31, 2006

Assets		Liabilities and Stockholders' Equity	
Cash	$ 120,000	Accounts payable	$ 70,000
Marketable securities	35,000	Short-term notes	55,000
Accounts receivable	45,000	Current liabilities	$ 125,000
Inventories	130,000	Long-term debt	$2,700,000
Current assets	$ 330,000	Total liabilities	$2,825,000
Equipment	$2,970,000	Common stock	$ 500,000
Buildings	1,600,000	Retained earnings	1,575,000
Fixed assets	$4,570,000	Stockholders' equity	$2,075,000
Total assets	$4,900,000	Total liabilities and equity	$4,900,000

a. Conrad paid no dividends during the year and invested the funds in marketable securities.
b. Conrad paid dividends totaling $500,000 and used the balance of the net income to retire (pay off) long-term debt.
c. Conrad paid dividends totaling $500,000 and invested the balance of the net income in building a new hangar.
d. Conrad paid out all $1,365,000 as dividends to its stockholders.

P2–7   Initial sale price of common stock   Beck Corporation has one issue of preferred stock and one issue of common stock outstanding. Given Beck's stockholders' equity account that follows, determine the original price per share at which the firm sold its single issue of common stock.

Stockholders' Equity ($000)	
Preferred stock	$ 125
Common stock ($0.75 par, 300,000 shares outstanding)	225
Paid-in capital in excess of par on common stock	2,625
Retained earnings	900
Total stockholders' equity	$3,875

P2–8   Statement of retained earnings   Hayes Enterprises began 2006 with a retained earnings balance of $928,000. During 2006, the firm earned $377,000 after taxes. From this amount, preferred stockholders were paid $47,000 in dividends. At year-end 2006, the firm's retained earnings totaled $1,048,000. The firm had 140,000 shares of common stock outstanding during 2006.

a. Prepare a statement of retained earnings for the year ended December 31, 2006, for Hayes Enterprises. (*Note:* Be sure to calculate and include the amount of cash dividends paid in 2006.)
b. Calculate the firm's 2006 earnings per share (EPS).
c. How large a per-share cash dividend did the firm pay on common stock during 2006?

P2–9 Changes in stockholders' equity Listed are the equity sections of balance sheets for years 2005 and 2006 as reported by Mountain Air Ski Resorts, Inc. The overall value of stockholders' equity has risen from $2,000,000 to $7,500,000. Use the statements to discover how and why this happened.

Mountain Air Ski Resorts, Inc. Balance Sheets (partial)		
Stockholders' Equity	**2005**	**2006**
Common stock ($1.00 par)		
Authorized—5,000,000 shares		
Outstanding—1,500,000 shares 2006		$1,500,000
— 500,000 shares 2005	$ 500,000	
Paid-in capital in excess of par	500,000	4,500,000
Retained earnings	1,000,000	1,500,000
Total stockholders' equity	$2,000,000	$7,500,000

The company paid total dividends of $200,000 during fiscal 2006.
a. What was Mountain Air's net income for fiscal 2006?
b. How many new shares did the corporation issue and sell during the year?
c. At what average price per share did the new stock sold during 2006 sell?
d. At what price per share did Mountain Air's original 500,000 shares sell?

P2–10 Ratio comparisons Robert Arias recently inherited a stock portfolio from his uncle. Wishing to learn more about the companies in which he is now invested, Robert performs a ratio analysis on each one and decides to compare them to each other. Some of his ratios are listed below.

Ratio	Island Electric Utility	Burger Heaven	Fink Software	Roland Motors
Current ratio	1.10	1.3	6.8	4.5
Quick ratio	0.90	0.82	5.2	3.7
Debt ratio	0.68	0.46	0	0.35
Net profit margin	6.2%	14.3%	28.5%	8.4%

Assuming that his uncle was a wise investor who assembled the portfolio with care, Robert finds the wide differences in these ratios confusing. Help him out.

a. What problems might Robert encounter in comparing these companies to one another on the basis of their ratios?
b. Why might the current and quick ratios for the electric utility and the fast-food stock be so much lower than the same ratios for the other companies?
c. Why might it be all right for the electric utility to carry a large amount of debt, but not the software company?
d. Why wouldn't investors invest all of their money in software companies instead of in less profitable companies? (Focus on risk and return.)

LG3

BASIC

P2–11 Liquidity management   Bauman Company's total current assets, total current liabilities, and inventory for each of the past 4 years follow:

Item	2003	2004	2005	2006
Total current assets	$16,950	$21,900	$22,500	$27,000
Total current liabilities	9,000	12,600	12,600	17,400
Inventory	6,000	6,900	6,900	7,200

a. Calculate the firm's current and quick ratios for each year. Compare the resulting time series for these measures of liquidity.
b. Comment on the firm's liquidity over the 2003–2006 period.
c. If you were told that Bauman Company's inventory turnover for each year in the 2003–2006 period and the industry averages were as follows, would this information support or conflict with your evaluation in part **b**? Why?

Inventory turnover	2003	2004	2005	2006
Bauman Company	6.3	6.8	7.0	6.4
Industry average	10.6	11.2	10.8	11.0

LG3

BASIC

P2–12 Inventory management   Wilkins Manufacturing has annual sales of $4 million and a gross profit margin of 40%. Its *end-of-quarter inventories* are

Quarter	Inventory
1	$ 400,000
2	800,000
3	1,200,000
4	200,000

a. Find the average quarterly inventory and use it to calculate the firm's inventory turnover and the average age of inventory.
b. Assuming that the company is in an industry with an average inventory turnover of 2.0, how would you evaluate the activity of Wilkins' inventory?

LG3

BASIC

P2–13 **Accounts receivable management** An evaluation of the books of Blair Supply, which follows, gives the end-of-year accounts receivable balance, which is believed to consist of amounts originating in the months indicated. The company had annual sales of $2.4 million. The firm extends 30-day credit terms.

Month of origin	Amounts receivable
July	$ 3,875
August	2,000
September	34,025
October	15,100
November	52,000
December	193,000
Year-end accounts receivable	$300,000

a. Use the year-end total to evaluate the firm's collection system.
b. If 70% of the firm's sales occur between July and December, would this affect the validity of your conclusion in part **a**? Explain.

LG3

INTERMEDIATE

P2–14 **Interpreting liquidity and activity ratios** The new owners of Bluegrass Natural Foods, Inc., have hired you to help them diagnose and cure problems that the company has had in maintaining adequate liquidity. As a first step, you perform a liquidity analysis. You then do an analysis of the company's short-term activity ratios. Your calculations and appropriate industry norms are listed.

Ratio	Bluegrass	Industry norm
Current ratio	4.5	4.0
Quick ratio	2.0	3.1
Inventory turnover	6.0	10.4
Average collection period	73 days	52 days
Average payment period	31 days	40 days

a. What recommendations relative to the amount and the handling of inventory could you make to the new owners?
b. What recommendations relative to the amount and the handling of accounts receivable could you make to the new owners?
c. What recommendations relative to the amount and the handling of accounts payable could you make to the new owners?
d. What results, overall, would you hope your recommendations would achieve? Why might your recommendations not be effective?

LG4

BASIC

P2–15 **Debt analysis** Springfield Bank is evaluating Creek Enterprises, which has requested a $4,000,000 loan, to assess the firm's financial leverage and financial risk. On the basis of the debt ratios for Creek, along with the industry averages and Creek's recent financial statements (see the facing page), evaluate and recommend appropriate action on the loan request.

Creek Enterprises
Income Statement
for the Year Ended December 31, 2006

Sales revenue		$30,000,000
Less: Cost of goods sold		21,000,000
Gross profits		$ 9,000,000
Less: Operating expenses		
Selling expense	$3,000,000	
General and administrative expenses	1,800,000	
Lease expense	200,000	
Depreciation expense	1,000,000	
Total operating expense		6,000,000
Operating profits		$ 3,000,000
Less: Interest expense		1,000,000
Net profits before taxes		$ 2,000,000
Less: Taxes (rate = 40%)		800,000
Net profits after taxes		$ 1,200,000
Less: Preferred stock dividends		100,000
Earnings available for common stockholders		$ 1,100,000

Creek Enterprises
Balance Sheet
December 31, 2006

Assets		Liabilities and Stockholders' Equity	
Current assets		Current liabilities	
Cash	$ 1,000,000	Accounts payable	$ 8,000,000
Marketable securities	3,000,000	Notes payable	8,000,000
Accounts receivable	12,000,000	Accruals	500,000
Inventories	7,500,000	Total current liabilities	$16,500,000
Total current assets	$23,500,000	Long-term debt (includes financial leases)[b]	$20,000,000
Gross fixed assets (at cost)[a]		Stockholders' equity	
Land and buildings	$11,000,000	Preferred stock (25,000 shares,	
Machinery and equipment	20,500,000	$4 dividend)	$ 2,500,000
Furniture and fixtures	8,000,000	Common stock (1 million shares at $5 par)	5,000,000
Gross fixed assets	$39,500,000	Paid-in capital in excess of par value	4,000,000
Less: Accumulated depreciation	13,000,000	Retained earnings	2,000,000
Net fixed assets	$26,500,000	Total stockholders' equity	$13,500,000
Total assets	$50,000,000	Total liabilities and stockholders' equity	$50,000,000

[a]The firm has a 4-year financial lease requiring annual beginning-of-year payments of $200,000. Three years of the lease have yet to run.
[b]Required annual principal payments are $800,000.

Note: Industry averages appear at the top of page 90.

Industry averages	
Debt ratio	0.51
Times interest earned ratio	7.30
Fixed-payment coverage ratio	1.85

P2–16 Common-size statement analysis A common-size income statement for Creek Enterprises' 2005 operations follows. Using the firm's 2006 income statement presented in Problem 2–15, develop the 2006 common-size income statement and compare it to the 2005 statement. Which areas require further analysis and investigation?

Creek Enterprises
Common-Size Income Statement
for the Year Ended December 31, 2005

Sales revenue ($35,000,000)		100.0%
Less: Cost of goods sold		65.9
Gross profits		34.1%
Less: Operating expenses		
Selling expense	12.7%	
General and administrative expenses	6.3	
Lease expense	0.6	
Depreciation expense	3.6	
Total operating expense		23.2
Operating profits		10.9%
Less: Interest expense		1.5
Net profits before taxes		9.4%
Less: Taxes (rate = 40%)		3.8
Net profits after taxes		5.6%
Less: Preferred stock dividends		0.1
Earnings available for common stockholders		5.5%

P2–17 The relationship between financial leverage and profitability Pelican Paper, Inc., and Timberland Forest, Inc., are rivals in the manufacture of craft papers. Some financial statement values for each company follow. Use them in a ratio analysis that compares the firms' financial leverage and profitability.

Item	Pelican Paper, Inc.	Timberland Forest, Inc.
Total assets	$10,000,000	$10,000,000
Total equity (all common)	9,000,000	5,000,000
Total debt	1,000,000	5,000,000
Annual interest	100,000	500,000
Total sales	$25,000,000	$25,000,000
EBIT	6,250,000	6,250,000
Net income	3,690,000	3,450,00

a. Calculate the following debt and coverage ratios for the two companies. Discuss their financial risk and ability to cover the costs in relation to each other.
   (1) Debt ratio
   (2) Times interest earned ratio
b. Calculate the following profitability ratios for the two companies. Discuss their profitability relative to each other.
   (1) Operating profit margin
   (2) Net profit margin
   (3) Return on total assets
   (4) Return on common equity
c. In what way has the larger debt of Timberland Forest made it more profitable than Pelican Paper? What are the risks that Timberland's investors undertake when they choose to purchase its stock instead of Pelican's?

LG6

BASIC

P2–18 **Ratio proficiency**   McDougal Printing, Inc., had sales totaling $40,000,000 in fiscal year 2006. Some ratios for the company are listed below. Use this information to determine the dollar values of various income statement and balance sheet accounts as requested.

McDougal Printing, Inc. Year Ended December 31, 2006	
Sales	$40,000,000
Gross profit margin	80%
Operating profit margin	35%
Net profit margin	8%
Return on total assets	16%
Return on common equity	20%
Total asset turnover	2
Average collection period	62.2 days

Calculate values for the following:
a. Gross profits
b. Cost of goods sold
c. Operating profits
d. Operating expenses
e. Earnings available for common stockholders
f. Total assets
g. Total common stock equity
h. Accounts receivable

LG6

INTERMEDIATE

P2–19 **Cross-sectional ratio analysis**   Use the financial statements on page 92 for Fox Manufacturing Company for the year ended December 31, 2006, along with the industry average ratios also given in what follows, to:
a. Prepare and interpret a complete ratio analysis of the firm's 2006 operations.
b. Summarize your findings and make recommendations.

Fox Manufacturing Company
Income Statement
for the Year Ended December 31, 2006

Sales revenue		$600,000
Less: Cost of goods sold		460,000
Gross profits		$140,000
Less: Operating expenses		
General and administrative expenses	$30,000	
Depreciation expense	30,000	
Total operating expense		60,000
Operating profits		$ 80,000
Less: Interest expense		10,000
Net profits before taxes		$ 70,000
Less: Taxes		27,100
Net profits after taxes (earnings available for common stockholders)		$ 42,900
Earnings per share (EPS)		$2.15

Fox Manufacturing Company
Balance Sheet
December 31, 2006

Assets

Cash	$ 15,000
Marketable securities	7,200
Accounts receivable	34,100
Inventories	82,000
Total current assets	$138,300
Net fixed assets	270,000
Total assets	$408,300

Liabilities and Stockholders' Equity

Accounts payable	$ 57,000
Notes payable	13,000
Accruals	5,000
Total current liabilities	$ 75,000
Long-term debt	$150,000
Stockholders' equity	
Common stock equity (20,000 shares outstanding)	$110,200
Retained earnings	73,100
Total stockholders' equity	$183,300
Total liabilities and stockholders' equity	$408,300

Note: Industry averages appear at the top of the facing page.

Ratio	Industry average, 2006
Current ratio	2.35
Quick ratio	0.87
Inventory turnover[a]	4.55
Average collection period[a]	35.8 days
Total asset turnover	1.09
Debt ratio	0.300
Times interest earned ratio	12.3
Gross profit margin	0.202
Operating profit margin	0.135
Net profit margin	0.091
Return on total assets (ROA)	0.099
Return on common equity (ROE)	0.167
Earnings per share (EPS)	$3.10

[a]Based on a 365-day year and on end-of-year figures.

P2–20 Financial statement analysis The financial statements of Zach Industries for the year ended December 31, 2006, follow.

INTERMEDIATE

Zach Industries
Income Statement
for the Year Ended December 31, 2006

Sales revenue	$160,000
Less: Cost of goods sold	106,000
Gross profits	$ 54,000
Less: Operating expenses	
Selling expense	$ 16,000
General and administrative expenses	10,000
Lease expense	1,000
Depreciation expense	10,000
Total operating expense	$ 37,000
Operating profits	$ 17,000
Less: Interest expense	6,100
Net profits before taxes	$ 10,900
Less: Taxes	4,360
Net profits after taxes	$ 6,540

Zach Industries
Balance Sheet
December 31, 2006

Assets

Cash	$ 500
Marketable securities	1,000
Accounts receivable	25,000
Inventories	45,500
Total current assets	$ 72,000
Land	$ 26,000
Buildings and equipment	90,000
Less: Accumulated depreciation	38,000
Net fixed assets	$ 78,000
Total assets	$150,000

Liabilities and Stockholders' Equity

Accounts payable	$ 22,000
Notes payable	47,000
Total current liabilities	$ 69,000
Long-term debt	$ 22,950
Common stock[a]	$ 31,500
Retained earnings	$ 26,550
Total liabilities and stockholders' equity	$150,000

[a]The firm's 3,000 outstanding shares of common stock closed 2006 at a price of $25 per share.

a. Use the preceding financial statements to complete the following table. Assume that the industry averages given in the table are applicable for both 2005 and 2006.

Ratio	Industry average	Actual 2005	Actual 2006
Current ratio	1.80	1.84	_____
Quick ratio	0.70	0.78	_____
Inventory turnover[a]	2.50	2.59	_____
Average collection period[a]	37.5 days	36.5 days	_____
Debt ratio	65%	67%	_____
Times interest earned ratio	3.8	4.0	_____
Gross profit margin	38%	40%	_____
Net profit margin	3.5%	3.6%	_____
Return on total assets	4.0%	4.0%	_____
Return on common equity	9.5%	8.0%	_____
Market/book ratio	1.1	1.2	_____

[a]Based on a 365-day year and on end-of-year figures.

b. Analyze Zach Industries' financial condition as it is related to (1) liquidity, (2) activity, (3) debt, (4) profitability, and (5) market. Summarize the company's overall financial condition.

P2–21 **Integrative—Complete ratio analysis** Given the following financial statements (below and on the facing page), historical ratios, and industry averages, calculate Sterling Company's financial ratios for the most recent year. (Assume a 365-day year.) Analyze its overall financial situation from both a cross-sectional and a time-series viewpoint. Break your analysis into evaluations of the firm's liquidity, activity, debt, profitability, and market.

Sterling Company
Income Statement
for the Year Ended December 31, 2006

Sales revenue		$10,000,000
Less: Cost of goods sold		7,500,000
Gross profits		$ 2,500,000
Less: Operating expenses		
Selling expense	$300,000	
General and administrative expenses	650,000	
Lease expense	50,000	
Depreciation expense	200,000	
Total operating expense		1,200,000
Operating profits		$ 1,300,000
Less: Interest expense		200,000
Net profits before taxes		$ 1,100,000
Less: Taxes (rate = 40%)		440,000
Net profits after taxes		$ 660,000
Less: Preferred stock dividends		50,000
Earnings available for common stockholders		$ 610,000
Earnings per share (EPS)		$3.05

Sterling Company
Balance Sheet
December 31, 2006

Assets		Liabilities and Stockholders' Equity	
Current assets		Current liabilities	
Cash	$ 200,000	Accounts payable[b]	$ 900,000
Marketable securities	50,000	Notes payable	200,000
Accounts receivable	800,000	Accruals	100,000
Inventories	950,000	Total current liabilities	$ 1,200,000
Total current assets	$ 2,000,000	Long-term debt (includes financial leases)[c]	$ 3,000,000
Gross fixed assets (at cost)[a] $12,000,000		Stockholders' equity	
Less: Accumulated depreciation 3,000,000		Preferred stock (25,000 shares, $2 dividend)	$ 1,000,000
Net fixed assets	$ 9,000,000	Common stock (200,000 shares at $3 par)[d]	600,000
Other assets	$ 1,000,000	Paid-in capital in excess of par value	5,200,000
Total assets	$12,000,000	Retained earnings	1,000,000
		Total stockholders' equity	$ 7,800,000
		Total liabilities and stockholders' equity	$12,000,000

[a]The firm has an 8-year financial lease requiring annual beginning-of-year payments of $50,000. Five years of the lease have yet to run.
[b]Annual credit purchases of $6,200,000 were made during the year.
[c]The annual principal payment on the long-term debt is $100,000.
[d]On December 31, 2006, the firm's common stock closed at $39.50 per share.

Historical and Industry Average Ratios for Sterling Company

Ratio	Actual 2004	Actual 2005	Industry average, 2006
Current ratio	1.40	1.55	1.85
Quick ratio	1.00	0.92	1.05
Inventory turnover	9.52	9.21	8.60
Average collection period	45.6 days	36.9 days	35.5 days
Average payment period	59.3 days	61.6 days	46.4 days
Total asset turnover	0.74	0.80	0.74
Debt ratio	0.20	0.20	0.30
Times interest earned ratio	8.2	7.3	8.0
Fixed-payment coverage ratio	4.5	4.2	4.2
Gross profit margin	0.30	0.27	0.25
Operating profit margin	0.12	0.12	0.10
Net profit margin	0.062	0.062	0.053
Return on total assets (ROA)	0.045	0.050	0.040
Return on common equity (ROE)	0.061	0.067	0.066
Earnings per share (EPS)	$1.75	$2.20	$1.50
Price/earnings (P/E) ratio	12.0	10.5	11.2
Market/book (M/B) ratio	1.20	1.05	1.10

P2–22 DuPont system of analysis Use the following ratio information for Johnson International and the industry averages for Johnson's line of business to:
  a. Construct the DuPont system of analysis for both Johnson and the industry.
  b. Evaluate Johnson (and the industry) over the 3-year period.
  c. Indicate in which areas Johnson requires further analysis. Why?

	2004	2005	2006
Johnson			
Financial leverage multiplier	1.75	1.75	1.85
Net profit margin	0.059	0.058	0.049
Total asset turnover	2.11	2.18	2.34
Industry Averages			
Financial leverage multiplier	1.67	1.69	1.64
Net profit margin	0.054	0.047	0.041
Total asset turnover	2.05	2.13	2.15

P2–23 Complete ratio analysis, recognizing significant differences Home Health, Inc., has come to Jane Ross for a yearly financial checkup. As a first step, Jane has prepared a complete set of ratios for fiscal years 2005 and 2006. She will use them to look for significant changes in the company's situation from one year to the next.

Home Health, Inc. Financial Ratios		
Ratio	2005	2006
Current ratio	3.25	3.00
Quick ratio	2.50	2.20
Inventory turnover	12.80	10.30
Average collection period	42.6 days	31.4 days
Total asset turnover	1.40	2.00
Debt ratio	0.45	0.62
Times interest earned ratio	4.00	3.85
Gross profit margin	68%	65%
Operating profit margin	14%	16%
Net profit margin	8.3%	8.1%
Return on total assets	11.6%	16.2%
Return on common equity	21.1%	42.6%
Price/earnings ratio	10.7	9.8
Market/book ratio	1.40	1.25

  a. To focus on the degree of change, calculate the year-to-year proportional change by subtracting the year 2005 ratio from the year 2006 ratio, then dividing the difference by the year 2005 ratio. Multiply the result by 100.

Preserve the positive or negative sign. The result is the percentage change in the ratio from 2005 to 2006. Calculate the proportional change for the ratios shown here.

b. For any ratio that shows a year-to-year difference of 10% or more, state whether the difference is in the company's favor or not.

c. For the most significant changes (25% or more), look at the other ratios and cite at least one other change that may have contributed to the change in the ratio that you are discussing.

P2–24 **ETHICS PROBLEM**   Do some reading in periodicals and/or on the Internet to find out more about the Sarbanes-Oxley Act's provisions for companies. Select one of those provisions, and indicate why you think financial statements will be more trustworthy if company financial executives implement this provision of SOX.

Chapter 2 Case: Assessing Martin Manufacturing's Current Financial Position

Terri Spiro, an experienced budget analyst at Martin Manufacturing Company, has been charged with assessing the firm's financial performance during 2006 and its financial position at year-end 2006. To complete this assignment, she gathered the firm's 2006 financial statements (below and on page 98). In addition, Terri obtained the firm's ratio values for 2004 and 2005, along with the 2006 industry average ratios (also applicable to 2004 and 2005). These are presented in the table on page 99.

Martin Manufacturing Company
Income Statement
for the Year Ended December 31, 2006

Sales revenue		$5,075,000
Less: Cost of goods sold		3,704,000
Gross profits		$1,371,000
Less: Operating expenses		
Selling expense	$650,000	
General and administrative expenses	416,000	
Depreciation expense	152,000	
Total operating expense		1,218,000
Operating profits		$ 153,000
Less: Interest expense		93,000
Net profits before taxes		$ 60,000
Less: Taxes (rate = 40%)		24,000
Net profits after taxes		$ 36,000
Less: Preferred stock dividends		3,000
Earnings available for common stockholders		$ 33,000
Earnings per share (EPS)		$0.33

Annual Income Statement (Values in millions)		
	For the year ended	
	December 31, 2006	December 31, 2005
Sales	$178,909.00	$187,510.00
Cost of goods sold	?	111,631.00
Selling, general, and administrative expenses	12,356.00	12,900.00
Other tax expense	33,572.00	33,377.00
Depreciation and amortization	12,103.00	7,944.00
Other income (add to EBIT to arrive at EBT)	3,147.00	3,323.00
Interest expense	398	293
Income tax rate (average)	35.324%	37.945%
Dividends paid per share	$1.47	$0.91
Basic EPS from total operations	$1.71	$2.25

You also have the following balance sheet information as of December 31, 2006 and 2005, respectively.

Annual Balance Sheet (Values in millions)		
	December 31, 2006	December, 31, 2005
Cash and equivalents	$ 7,229.00	$ 6,547.00
Receivables	21,163.00	19,549.00
Inventories	8,068.00	7,904.00
Other current assets	1,831.00	1,681.00
Property, plant, and equipment, gross	204,960.00	187,519.00
Accumulated depreciation and depletion	110,020.00	97,917.00
Other noncurrent assets	19,413.00	17,891.00
Accounts payable	$13,792.00	$22,862.00
Short-term debt payable	4,093.00	3,703.00
Other current liabilities	15,290.00	3,549.00
Long-term debt payable	6,655.00	7,099.00
Deferred income taxes	16,484.00	16,359.00
Other noncurrent liabilities	21,733.00	16,441.00
Retained earnings	$74,597.00	$73,161.00
Total common shares outstanding	6.7 billion	6.8 billion

TO DO

a. Create a spreadsheet similar to the spreadsheet in Table 2.1 (which can be viewed at www.aw-bc.com/gitman) to model the following:
  (1) A multiple-step comparative income statement for Dayton, Inc., for the periods ending December 31, 2006 and 2005. You must calculate the cost of goods sold for the year 2006.
  (2) A common-size income statement for Dayton, Inc., covering the years 2006 and 2005.

b. Create a spreadsheet similar to the spreadsheet in Table 2.2 (which can be viewed at www.aw-bc.com/gitman) to model the following:
   (1) A detailed, comparative balance sheet for Dayton, Inc., for the years ended December 31, 2006 and 2005.
   (2) A common-size balance sheet for Dayton, Inc., covering the years 2006 and 2005.

c. Create a spreadsheet similar to the spreadsheet in Table 2.8 (which can be viewed at www.aw-bc.com/gitman) to perform the following analysis:
   (1) Create a table that reflects both 2006 and 2005 operating ratios for Dayton, Inc., segmented into (a) liquidity, (b) activity, (c) debt, (d) profitability, and (e) market. Assume that the current market price for the stock is $90.
   (2) Compare the 2006 ratios to the 2005 ratios. Indicate whether the results "outperformed the prior year" or "underperformed relative to the prior year."

Group Exercise

This assignment will focus on your group's shadow corporation. As in Chapter 1, the group will be asked to utilize the latest 10-K filing.

TO DO

a. Access the latest 10-K filing. Describe the content of the letter to stockholders.
b. Calculate the basic ratios as done in the text. Sort the ratios into the five categories found in Table 2.8 (pages 72 and 73).
c. State what use each ratio has in analyzing the health of your corporation.
d. Analyze these ratios through time by calculating them over the most recent years. For any ratios that have changed, give possible explanations as to why these changes may have occurred.
e. Conclude with a financial summary of the ratios using the DuPont system.

Web Exercise

For this assignment, you will need a Web-based search engine such as Google.

TO DO

a. Enter the term "stock market" as a search keyword. Scan the results for the New York Stock Exchange and Nasdaq home sites. Compare and contrast the two stock markets' home pages.
b. Return to your search engine and search for "financial markets." Report on your findings, including a synopsis of a free site that you feel had very usable financial market news and analysis. This site should be used as a source of information in future assignments, so spend some time looking for a good site.

Remember to check the book's Web site at

www.aw-bc.com/gitman

for additional resources, including additional Web exercises.

Chapter 3

Cash Flow and Financial Planning

LEARNING GOALS

LG1 Understand tax depreciation procedures and the effect of depreciation on the firm's cash flows.

LG2 Discuss the firm's statement of cash flows, operating cash flow, and free cash flow.

LG3 Understand the financial planning process, including long-term (strategic) financial plans and short-term (operating) financial plans.

LG4 Discuss the cash-planning process and the preparation, evaluation, and use of the cash budget.

LG5 Explain the simplified procedures used to prepare and evaluate the pro forma income statement and the pro forma balance sheet.

LG6 Evaluate the simplified approaches to pro forma financial statement preparation and the common uses of pro forma statements.

ACROSS THE DISCIPLINES WHY THIS CHAPTER MATTERS TO YOU

Accounting: You need to understand how depreciation is used for both tax and financial reporting purposes; how to develop the statement of cash flows; the primary focus on cash flows, rather than accruals, in financial decision making; and how pro forma financial statements are used within the firm.

Information systems: You need to understand the data that must be kept to record depreciation for tax and financial reporting; the information needs for strategic and operating plans; and what data are needed as inputs for preparing cash plans and profit plans.

Management: You need to understand the difference between strategic and operating plans, and the role of

each; the importance of focusing on the firm's cash flows; and how use of pro forma statements can head off trouble for the firm.

Marketing: You need to understand the central role that marketing plays in formulating the firm's long-term, strategic plans, and the importance of the sales forecast as the key input for both cash planning and profit planning.

Operations: You need to understand how depreciation affects the value of the firm's plant assets; how the results of operations are captured in the statement of cash flows; that operations provide key inputs into the firm's short-term financial plans; and the distinction between fixed and variable operating costs.

BEST BUY
A TALE OF TWO STRATEGIES

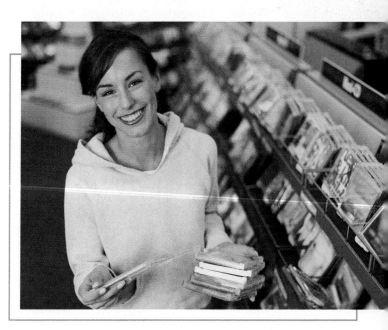

What should a company's management do with a $1 billion "war chest"? In the case of **Best Buy** (www.bestbuy.com), a specialty retailer of consumer electronics, personal computers, entertainment software, and appliances, the strategy from late 2000 through 2001 was to "grow the company" by purchasing other retail chains. In late 2000, the company purchased **Magnolia Hi-Fi,** a Seattle-based retail chain. Several months later, in the face of a falling stock market, Best Buy completed the acquisition of the 1,300-store **Musicland Group, Inc.,** for $685 million in cash. In August 2001, Best Buy continued its expansion strategy by purchasing **Future Shop,** an 88-store Canadian retailer of consumer electronics, for $377 million.

Within two years, both the corporate management and the corporate strategy for Best Buy had changed. In 2003, noting that "as a result of a strategic study that commenced a few months ago, it was determined that Musicland would not be capable of meeting our original expectations," CEO Brad Anderson announced that Musicland was for sale. With the sale of Musicland, Best Buy began to focus its efforts in a new direction—efficiency. Its new initiative, which it calls *customer centricity,* was launched in 32 "lab" stores to test whether the program should be expanded throughout the chain. In 2004, Best Buy planned to extend the initiative to 110 additional stores.

Customer centricity identifies five customer segments: the affluent professional, the younger male customer who wants the latest technology, the "family man" who uses technology to improve his life, the busy "suburban mom" who wants to enrich her children's lives, and the small business customer. The idea is that each store will focus its products on one or more of the five target markets according to the demographics of the surrounding area.

In addition to customer centricity, Best Buy introduced a long-term incentive program in 2003, offering employees stock options and restricted shares linked to total shareholder return. By mid-2004, the company had accumulated $2.1 billion in cash and marketable securities. Instead of going on an acquisitions binge, as it had in the past, Best Buy announced that it would increase its cash dividend and undertake a $500 million share repurchase program.

Like Best Buy, companies must make strategic plans and implement those plans. As you will see in this chapter, part of that decision-making process involves planning a company's cash flows.

■ *What other options might a company have for using its cash and marketable securities?*

LG1 LG2 3.1 | Analyzing the Firm's Cash Flow

Cash flow, the lifeblood of the firm, is the primary focus of the financial manager both in managing day-to-day finances and in planning and making strategic decisions focused on creating shareholder value. We therefore place major emphasis on estimating and analyzing the cash flows associated with the major financial decisions discussed and demonstrated throughout this book.

An important factor affecting a firm's cash flow is depreciation (and any other noncash charges). From an accounting perspective, a firm's cash flows can be summarized in the statement of cash flows, which was described in Chapter 2. From a strict financial perspective, firms often focus on both *operating cash flow,* which is used in managerial decision making, and *free cash flow,* which is closely watched by participants in the capital market. We begin our analysis of cash flow by considering the key aspects of depreciation, which is closely related to the firm's cash flow.

Depreciation

depreciation
The systematic charging of a portion of the costs of fixed assets against annual revenues over time.

Business firms are permitted for tax and financial reporting purposes to charge a portion of the costs of fixed assets systematically against annual revenues. This allocation of historical cost over time is called **depreciation.** For tax purposes, the depreciation of business assets is regulated by the Internal Revenue Code. Because the objectives of financial reporting sometimes differ from those of tax legislation, firms often use different depreciation methods for financial reporting than those required for tax purposes. Tax laws are used to accomplish economic goals such as providing incentives for business investment in certain types of assets, whereas the objectives of financial reporting are, of course, quite different. Keeping two different sets of records for these two different purposes is legal.

modified accelerated cost recovery system (MACRS)
System used to determine the depreciation of assets for tax purposes.

Depreciation for tax purposes is determined by using the **modified accelerated cost recovery system (MACRS);** a variety of depreciation methods are available for financial reporting purposes. Before we discuss the methods of depreciating an asset, you must understand the depreciable value of an asset and the depreciable life of an asset.

Depreciable Value of an Asset

Under the basic MACRS procedures, the depreciable value of an asset (the amount to be depreciated) is its *full* cost, including outlays for installation.[1] No adjustment is required for expected salvage value.

EXAMPLE Baker Corporation acquired a new machine at a cost of $38,000, with installation costs of $2,000. Regardless of its expected salvage value, the depreciable value of the machine is $40,000: $38,000 cost + $2,000 installation cost. ■

Depreciable Life of an Asset

depreciable life
Time period over which an asset is depreciated.

The time period over which an asset is depreciated—its **depreciable life**—can significantly affect the pattern of cash flows. The shorter the depreciable life, the

---

1. Land values are *not* depreciable. Therefore, to determine the depreciable value of real estate, the value of the land is subtracted from the cost of real estate. In other words, only buildings and other improvements are depreciable.

TABLE 3.1

First Four Property Classes Under MACRS

Property class (recovery period)	Definition
3 years	Research equipment and certain special tools
5 years	Computers, typewriters, copiers, duplicating equipment, cars, light-duty trucks, qualified technological equipment, and similar assets
7 years	Office furniture, fixtures, most manufacturing equipment, railroad track, and single-purpose agricultural and horticultural structures
10 years	Equipment used in petroleum refining or in the manufacture of tobacco products and certain food products

more quickly the cash flow created by the depreciation write-off will be received. Given the financial manager's preference for faster receipt of cash flows, a shorter depreciable life is preferred to a longer one. However, the firm must abide by certain Internal Revenue Service (IRS) requirements for determining depreciable life. These MACRS standards, which apply to both new and used assets, require the taxpayer to use as an asset's depreciable life the appropriate MACRS **recovery period.**[2] There are six MACRS recovery periods—3, 5, 7, 10, 15, and 20 years—excluding real estate. It is customary to refer to the property classes, in accordance with their recovery periods, as 3-, 5-, 7-, 10-, 15-, and 20-year property. The first four property classes—those routinely used by business—are defined in Table 3.1.

recovery period
The appropriate depreciable life of a particular asset as determined by MACRS.

Depreciation Methods

For *financial reporting purposes,* a variety of depreciation methods (straight-line, double-declining balance, and sum-of-the-years'-digits[3]) can be used. For *tax purposes,* using MACRS recovery periods, assets in the first four property classes are depreciated by the double-declining balance (200 percent) method, using the half-year convention and switching to straight-line when advantageous. Although tables of depreciation percentages are not provided by law, the *approximate percentages* (rounded to the nearest whole percent) written off each year for the first four property classes are shown in Table 3.2 (see page 106). Rather than using the percentages in the table, the firm can either use straight-line depreciation over the asset's recovery period with the half-year convention or use the alternative depreciation system. For purposes of this text, we will use the MACRS depreciation percentages, because they generally provide for the fastest write-off and therefore the best cash flow effects for the profitable firm.

Because MACRS requires use of the half-year convention, assets are assumed to be acquired in the middle of the year, and therefore only one-half of the first year's depreciation is recovered in the first year. As a result, the final half-year of depreciation is recovered in the year immediately following the asset's stated recovery period. In Table 3.2, the depreciation percentages for an *n*-year class

---

2. An exception occurs in the case of assets depreciated under the *alternative depreciation system.* For convenience, in this text we ignore the depreciation of assets under this system.

3. For a review of these depreciation methods as well as other aspects of financial reporting, see any recently published financial accounting text.

| TABLE 3.2 | Rounded Depreciation Percentages by Recovery Year Using MACRS for First Four Property Classes |

	Percentage by recovery year[a]			
Recovery year	3 years	5 years	7 years	10 years
1	33%	20%	14%	10%
2	45	32	25	18
3	15	19	18	14
4	7	12	12	12
5		12	9	9
6		5	9	8
7			9	7
8			4	6
9				6
10				6
11				4
Totals	100%	100%	100%	100%

[a]These percentages have been rounded to the nearest whole percent to simplify calculations while retaining realism. To calculate the *actual* depreciation for tax purposes, be sure to apply the actual unrounded percentages or directly apply double-declining balance (200%) depreciation using the half-year convention.

asset are given for $n + 1$ years. For example, a 5-year asset is depreciated over 6 recovery years. The application of the tax depreciation percentages given in Table 3.2 can be demonstrated by a simple example.

EXAMPLE

Baker Corporation acquired, for an installed cost of $40,000, a machine having a recovery period of 5 years. Using the applicable percentages from Table 3.2, Baker calculates the depreciation in each year as follows:

Year	Cost (1)	Percentages (from Table 3.2) (2)	Depreciation [(1) × (2)] (3)
1	$40,000	20%	$ 8,000
2	40,000	32	12,800
3	40,000	19	7,600
4	40,000	12	4,800
5	40,000	12	4,800
6	40,000	5	2,000
Totals		100%	$40,000

Column 3 shows that the full cost of the asset is written off over 6 recovery years. ■

Because financial managers focus primarily on cash flows, *only tax depreciation methods will be utilized throughout this textbook.*

Developing the Statement of Cash Flows

The *statement of cash flows,* introduced in Chapter 2, summarizes the firm's cash flow over a given period of time. Before discussing the statement and its interpretation, we will review the cash flow through the firm and the classification of inflows and outflows of cash.

Hint In finance, cash is king. Income statement profits are good, but they don't pay the bills, nor do asset owners accept them in place of cash.

The Firm's Cash Flows

Figure 3.1 illustrates the firm's cash flows. Note that marketable securities are considered the same as cash because of their highly liquid nature. Both cash and

FIGURE 3.1   **Cash Flows**

The firm's cash flows

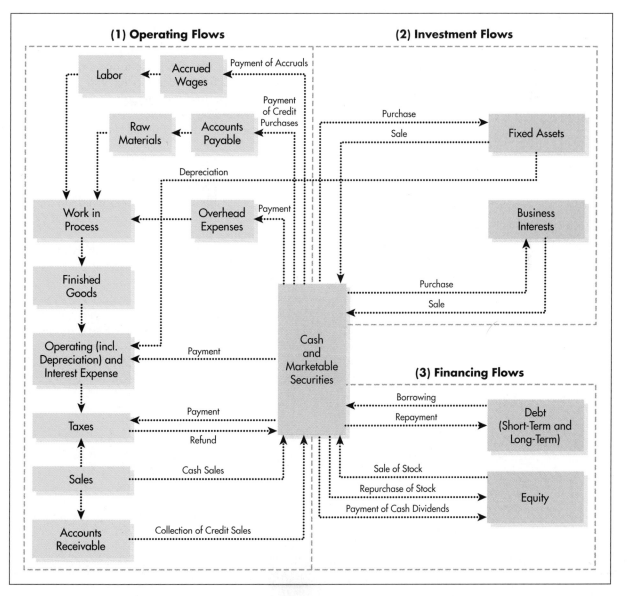

operating flows
Cash flows directly related to sale and production of the firm's products and services.

investment flows
Cash flows associated with purchase and sale of both fixed assets and business interests.

financing flows
Cash flows that result from debt and equity financing transactions; include incurrence and repayment of debt, cash inflow from the sale of stock, and cash outflows to pay cash dividends or repurchase stock.

marketable securities represent a reservoir of liquidity that is *increased by cash inflows* and *decreased by cash outflows*. Also note that the firm's cash flows can be divided into (1) operating flows, (2) investment flows, and (3) financing flows. The **operating flows** are cash inflows and outflows directly related to the sale and production of the firm's products and services. **Investment flows** are cash flows associated with the purchase and sale of both fixed assets and business interests. Clearly, purchase transactions would result in cash outflows, whereas sales transactions would generate cash inflows. The **financing flows** result from debt and equity financing transactions. Incurring (or repaying) either short-term or long-term debt would result in a corresponding cash inflow (or outflow). Similarly, the sale of stock would result in a cash inflow; the payment of cash dividends or repurchase of stock would result in a financing outflow. In combination, the firm's operating, investment, and financing cash flows during a given period affect the firm's cash and marketable securities balances.

Classifying Inflows and Outflows of Cash

The statement of cash flows, in effect, summarizes the inflows and outflows of cash during a given period. Table 3.3 classifies the basic inflows (sources) and outflows (uses) of cash. For example, if a firm's accounts payable increased by $1,000 during the year, the change would be an *inflow of cash*. If the firm's inventory increased by $2,500, the change would be an *outflow of cash*.

A few additional points can be made with respect to the classification scheme in Table 3.3:

1. A *decrease* in an asset, such as the firm's cash balance, is an *inflow of cash,* because cash that has been tied up in the asset is released and can be used for some other purpose, such as repaying a loan. On the other hand, an *increase* in the firm's cash balance is an *outflow of cash,* because additional cash is being tied up in the firm's cash balance.

   The classification of decreases and increases in a firm's cash balance is difficult for many to grasp. To clarify, imagine that you store all your cash in a bucket. Your cash balance is represented by the amount of cash in the bucket. When you need cash, you withdraw it from the bucket, which *decreases your cash balance and provides an inflow* of cash to you. Conversely, when you have excess cash, you deposit it in the bucket, which *increases your cash balance and represents an outflow* of cash from you. Focus on the movement of funds *in and out of your pocket*: Clearly, a decrease in cash (from the bucket) is an inflow (to your pocket); an increase in cash (in the bucket) is an outflow (from your pocket).

TABLE 3.3

The Inflows and Outflows of Cash

Inflows (sources)	Outflows (uses)
Decrease in any asset	Increase in any asset
Increase in any liability	Decrease in any liability
Net profits after taxes	Net loss
Depreciation and other noncash charges	Dividends paid
Sale of stock	Repurchase or retirement of stock

noncash charge
An expense that is deducted on the income statement but does not involve the actual outlay of cash during the period; includes depreciation, amortization, and depletion.

2. Depreciation (like amortization and depletion) is a **noncash charge**—an expense that is deducted on the income statement but does not involve the actual outlay of cash during the period. Because it shields the firm from taxes by lowering taxable income, the noncash charge is considered a cash inflow. From a strict accounting perspective, adding depreciation back to the firm's net profits after taxes provides an estimate of cash flow from operations[4]:

$$\text{Cash flow from operations} = \\ \text{Net profits after taxes} + \text{Depreciation and other noncash charges} \quad (3.1)$$

   Note that a firm can have a *net loss* (negative net profits after taxes) and still have positive cash flow from operations when depreciation (and other non-cash charges) during the period is greater than the net loss. In the statement of cash flows, net profits after taxes (or net losses) and depreciation (and other noncash charges) are therefore treated as separate entries.
3. We will refine Equation 3.1 in the next section and apply the revised equation (Equation 3.4) in Chapter 8 to estimate the relevant operating cash inflows associated with a firm's present and proposed fixed-asset investments.
4. Because depreciation is treated as a separate cash inflow, only *gross* rather than *net* changes in fixed assets appear on the statement of cash flows. This treatment avoids the potential double counting of depreciation.
5. Direct entries of changes in retained earnings are not included on the statement of cash flows. Instead, entries for items that affect retained earnings appear as net profits or losses after taxes and dividends paid.

Preparing the Statement of Cash Flows

The statement of cash flows for a given period is developed using the income statement for the period, along with the beginning- and end-of-period balance sheets. The income statement for the year ended December 31, 2006, and the December 31 balance sheets for 2005 and 2006 for Baker Corporation are given in Tables 3.4 (see page 110) and 3.5 (see page 111), respectively. The statement of cash flows for the year ended December 31, 2006, for Baker Corporation is presented in Table 3.6 (see page 112). Note that all cash inflows as well as net profits after taxes and depreciation are treated as positive values. All cash outflows, any losses, and dividends paid are treated as negative values. The items in each category—operating, investment, and financing—are totaled, and the three totals are added to get the "Net increase (decrease) in cash and marketable securities" for the period. As a check, this value should reconcile with the actual change in cash and marketable securities for the year, which is obtained from the beginning- and end-of-period balance sheets.

Interpreting the Statement

The statement of cash flows allows the financial manager and other interested parties to analyze the firm's cash flow. The manager should pay special attention both to the major categories of cash flow and to the individual items of cash inflow and outflow, to assess whether any developments have occurred that are contrary to the company's financial policies. In addition, the statement can be

---

4. This equation is merely an estimate because it is based on the assumption that the firm's accounts receivable, inventory, accounts payable, and accruals remain unchanged during the period. Generally, these account balances will change over the period.

TABLE 3.4	Baker Corporation Income Statement ($000) for the Year Ended December 31, 2006	
Sales revenue		$1,700
Less: Cost of goods sold		1,000
Gross profits		$ 700
Less: Operating expenses		
Selling expense	$ 70	
General and administrative expenses	120	
Lease expense[a]	40	
Depreciation expense	100	
Total operating expense		$ 330
Earnings before interest and taxes (EBIT)		$ 370
Less: Interest expense		70
Net profits before taxes		$ 300
Less: Taxes (rate = 40%)		120
Net profits after taxes		$ 180
Less: Preferred stock dividends		10
Earnings available for common stockholders		$ 170
Earnings per share (EPS)[b]		$1.70

[a]Lease expense is shown here as a separate item rather than included as interest expense as specified by the FASB for financial reporting purposes. The approach used here is consistent with tax reporting rather than financial reporting procedures.

[b]Calculated by dividing the earnings available for common stockholders by the number of shares of common stock outstanding ($170,000 ÷ 100,000 shares = $1.70 per share).

used to evaluate progress toward projected goals or to isolate inefficiencies. For example, increases in accounts receivable or inventories resulting in major cash outflows may signal credit or inventory problems, respectively. The financial manager also can prepare a statement of cash flows developed from projected financial statements. This approach can be used to determine whether planned actions are desirable in view of the resulting cash flows.

Because *an understanding of the basic financial principles presented throughout this text is absolutely essential to the effective interpretation of the statement of cash flows*, detailed interpretation of the statement is not included here.

Operating Cash Flow

operating cash flow (OCF)
The cash flow a firm generates from its normal operations; calculated as *net operating profits after taxes (NOPAT)*.

A firm's **operating cash flow (OCF)** is the cash flow it generates from its normal operations—producing and selling its output of goods or services. A variety of definitions of OCF can be found in the financial literature. Equation 3.1 introduced the simple accounting definition of cash flow from operations. Here we refine this definition to estimate cash flows more accurately. Unlike the earlier definition, this one excludes interest and taxes to enable us to focus on the true cash flow resulting from operations without regard to interest expense and taxes.

TABLE 3.5

Baker Corporation Balance Sheets ($000)

	December 31	
Assets	2006	2005
Current assets		
Cash	$ 400	$ 300
Marketable securities	600	200
Accounts receivable	400	500
Inventories	600	900
Total current assets	$2,000	$1,900
Gross fixed assets (at cost)		
Land and buildings	$1,200	$1,050
Machinery and equipment	850	800
Furniture and fixtures	300	220
Vehicles	100	80
Other (includes certain leases)	50	50
Total gross fixed assets (at cost)	$2,500	$2,200
Less: Accumulated depreciation	1,300	1,200
Net fixed assets	$1,200	$1,000
Total assets	$3,200	$2,900
Liabilities and Stockholders' Equity		
Current liabilities		
Accounts payable	$ 700	$ 500
Notes payable	600	700
Accruals	100	200
Total current liabilities	$1,400	$1,400
Long-term debt	$ 600	$ 400
Total liabilities	$2,000	$1,800
Stockholders' equity		
Preferred stock	$ 100	$ 100
Common stock—$1.20 par, 100,000 shares outstanding in 2006 and 2005	120	120
Paid-in capital in excess of par on common stock	380	380
Retained earnings	600	500
Total stockholders' equity	$1,200	$1,100
Total liabilities and stockholders' equity	$3,200	$2,900

net operating profits after taxes (NOPAT)
A firm's earnings before interest and after taxes, EBIT $\times (1 - T)$.

The first step is to calculate **net operating profits after taxes (NOPAT)**, which represent the firm's earnings before interest and after taxes. Letting T equal the applicable corporate tax rate, NOPAT is calculated as follows:

$$\text{NOPAT} = \text{EBIT} \times (1 - T) \qquad (3.2)$$

To convert NOPAT to operating cash flow (OCF), we merely add back depreciation:

$$\text{OCF} = \text{NOPAT} + \text{Depreciation} \qquad (3.3)$$

TABLE 3.6

Baker Corporation Statement of Cash Flows ($000) for the Year Ended December 31, 2006

Cash Flow from Operating Activities		
Net profits after taxes	$180	
Depreciation	100	
Decrease in accounts receivable	100	
Decrease in inventories	300	
Increase in accounts payable	200	
Decrease in accruals	(100)[a]	
Cash provided by operating activities		$780
Cash Flow from Investment Activities		
Increase in gross fixed assets	($300)	
Changes in business interests	0	
Cash provided by investment activities		(300)
Cash Flow from Financing Activities		
Decrease in notes payable	($100)	
Increase in long-term debts	200	
Changes in stockholders' equity[b]	0	
Dividends paid	(80)	
Cash provided by financing activities		20
Net increase in cash and marketable securities		$500

[a]As is customary, parentheses are used to denote a negative number, which in this case is a cash outflow.

[b]Retained earnings are excluded here, because their change is actually reflected in the combination of the "Net profits after taxes" and "Dividends paid" entries.

We can substitute the expression for NOPAT from Equation 3.2 into Equation 3.3 to get a single equation for OCF:

$$OCF = [EBIT \times (1 - T)] + \text{Depreciation} \qquad (3.4)$$

EXAMPLE

Substituting the values for Baker Corporation from its income statement (Table 3.4) into Equation 3.4, we get

$$OCF = [\$370 \times (1.00 - 0.40)] + \$100 = \$222 + \$100 = \$322$$

During 2006, Baker Corporation generated $322,000 of cash flow from producing and selling its output. Therefore, we can conclude that Baker's operations are generating positive cash flows. ■

Comparing Equations 3.1 and 3.4 reveals the key difference between the accounting and finance definitions of operating cash flow: The finance definition excludes interest—a financing cost—as an operating cash flow, whereas the accounting definition includes it as an operating flow. In the unlikely case that a firm has no interest expense, the accounting definition (Equation 3.1) and the finance definition (Equation 3.4) of operating cash flow would be the same.

Free Cash Flow

free cash flow (FCF)
The amount of cash flow available to investors (creditors and owners) after the firm has met all operating needs and paid for investments in net fixed assets and net current assets.

The firm's **free cash flow** (FCF) represents the amount of cash flow available to investors—the providers of debt (creditors) and equity (owners)—after the firm has met all operating needs and paid for investments in net fixed assets and net current assets. It represents the summation of the net amount of cash flow available to creditors and owners during the period. Free cash flow can be defined as follows:

$$\text{FCF} = \text{OCF} - \text{Net fixed asset investment (NFAI)}$$
$$- \text{Net current asset investment (NCAI)} \qquad (3.5)$$

The *net fixed asset investment (NFAI)* can be calculated as shown here:

$$\text{NFAI} = \text{Change in net fixed assets} + \text{Depreciation} \qquad (3.6)$$

EXAMPLE

Using the Baker Corporation's balance sheets in Table 3.5, we see that its change in net fixed assets between 2005 and 2006 was +$200 ($1,200 in 2006 − $1,000 in 2005). Substituting this value and the $100 of depreciation for 2006 into Equation 3.6, we get Baker's net fixed asset investment (NFAI) for 2006:

$$\text{NFAI} = \$200 + \$100 = \$300$$

Baker Corporation therefore invested a net $300,000 in fixed assets during 2006. This amount would, of course, represent a net cash outflow to acquire fixed assets during 2006. ∎

Looking at Equation 3.6, we can see that if the depreciation during a year is less than the *decrease* during that year in net fixed assets, the NFAI would be negative. A negative NFAI represents a net cash *inflow* attributable to the fact that the firm sold more assets than it acquired during the year.

The *net current asset investment (NCAI)* represents the net investment made by the firm in its current (operating) assets. "Net" refers to the difference between current assets and the sum of accounts payable and accruals. Notes payable are not included in the NCAI calculation because they represent a negotiated creditor claim on the firm's free cash flow. Equation 3.7 shows the NCAI calculation.

$$\text{NCAI} = \text{Change in current assets} -$$
$$\text{Change in (accounts payable} + \text{accruals)} \qquad (3.7)$$

EXAMPLE

Looking at the Baker Corporation's balance sheets for 2005 and 2006 in Table 3.5, we see that the change in current assets between 2005 and 2006 is +$100 ($2,000 in 2006 − $1,900 in 2005). The difference between Baker's accounts payable plus accruals of $800 in 2006 ($700 in accounts payable + $100 in accruals) and of $700 in 2005 ($500 in accounts payable + $200 in accruals) is +$100 ($800 in 2006 − $700 in 2005). Substituting into Equation 3.7 the change in current assets and the change in the sum of accounts payable plus accruals for Baker Corporation, we get its 2006 NCAI:

$$\text{NCAI} = \$100 - \$100 = \$0$$

This means that during 2006 Baker Corporation made no investment ($0) in its current assets net of accounts payable and accruals.

Now we can substitute Baker Corporation's 2006 operating cash flow (OCF) of $322, its net fixed asset investment (NFAI) of $300, and its net current asset investment (NCAI) of $0 into Equation 3.5 to find its free cash flow (FCF):

$$FCF = \$322 - \$300 - \$0 = \$22$$

We can see that during 2006 Baker generated $22,000 of free cash flow, which it can use to pay its investors—creditors (payment of interest) and owners (payment of dividends). Thus, the firm generated adequate cash flow to cover all of its operating costs and investments and had free cash flow available to pay investors. ■

Further analysis of free cash flow is beyond the scope of this initial introduction to cash flow. Clearly, cash flow is the lifeblood of the firm. We next consider various aspects of financial planning for cash flow and profit.

REVIEW QUESTIONS

3–1   Briefly describe the first four *modified accelerated cost recovery system (MACRS)* property classes and recovery periods. Explain how the depreciation percentages are determined by using the MACRS recovery periods.

3–2   Describe the overall cash flow through the firm in terms of operating flows, investments flows, and financing flows.

3–3   Explain why a decrease in cash is classified as a *cash inflow (source)* and why an increase in cash is classified as a *cash outflow (use)* in preparing the statement of cash flows.

3–4   Why is depreciation (as well as amortization and depletion) considered a *noncash charge?* How do accountants estimate *cash flow from operations?*

3–5   Describe the general format of the statement of cash flows. How are cash inflows differentiated from cash outflows on this statement?

3–6   What is the difference between the accounting and finance definitions of *operating cash flow?* Under what circumstances are they the same?

3–7   From a strict financial perspective, define and differentiate between a firm's *operating cash flow (OCF)* and its *free cash flow (FCF).*

LG3   ## 3.2 | The Financial Planning Process

Financial planning is an important aspect of the firm's operations because it provides road maps for guiding, coordinating, and controlling the firm's actions to achieve its objectives. Two key aspects of the financial planning process are *cash planning* and *profit planning*. Cash planning involves preparation of the firm's cash budget. Profit planning involves preparation of pro forma statements. Both the cash budget and the pro forma statements are useful for internal financial planning; they also are routinely required by existing and prospective lenders.

financial planning process
Planning that begins with long-term, or *strategic*, financial plans that in turn guide the formulation of short-term, or *operating*, plans and budgets.

The **financial planning process** begins with long-term, or *strategic*, financial plans. These, in turn, guide the formulation of short-term, or *operating*, plans and budgets. Generally, the short-term plans and budgets implement the firm's long-term strategic objectives. Although the remainder of this chapter places primary emphasis on short-term financial plans and budgets, a few preliminary comments on long-term financial plans are in order.

Long-Term (Strategic) Financial Plans

long-term (strategic) financial plans
Lay out a company's planned financial actions and the anticipated impact of those actions over periods ranging from 2 to 10 years.

Long-term (strategic) financial plans lay out a company's planned financial actions and the anticipated impact of those actions over periods ranging from 2 to 10 years. Five-year strategic plans, which are revised as significant new information becomes available, are common. Generally, firms that are subject to high degrees of operating uncertainty, relatively short production cycles, or both, tend to use shorter planning horizons.

Hint Preparation of the annual budget is an important part of the firm's planning process that involves all managers. It represents a tedious but important management activity.

Long-term financial plans are part of an integrated strategy that, along with production and marketing plans, guides the firm toward strategic goals. Those long-term plans consider proposed outlays for fixed assets, research and development activities, marketing and product development actions, capital structure, and major sources of financing. Also included would be termination of existing projects, product lines, or lines of business; repayment or retirement of outstanding debts; and any planned acquisitions. Such plans tend to be supported by a series of annual budgets and profit plans.

Short-Term (Operating) Financial Plans

short-term (operating) financial plans
Specify short-term financial actions and the anticipated impact of those actions.

Short-term (operating) financial plans specify short-term financial actions and the anticipated impact of those actions. These plans most often cover a 1- to 2-year period. Key inputs include the sales forecast and various forms of operating and financial data. Key outputs include a number of operating budgets, the cash budget, and pro forma financial statements. The entire short-term financial planning process is outlined in Figure 3.2. Here we ignore operating budgets, which focus on the accounting aspects of short-term business plans, and instead focus solely on cash and profit planning from the financial manager's perspective.

FIGURE 3.2
Short-Term Financial Planning
The short-term (operating) financial planning process

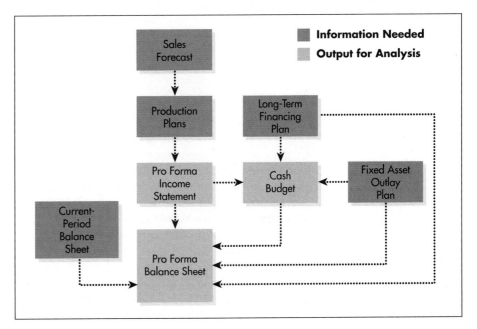

Hint Excel spreadsheets are widely used to streamline the process of preparing and evaluating these short-term financial planning statements.

Short-term financial planning begins with the sales forecast. From it, production plans are developed that take into account lead (preparation) times and include estimates of the required raw materials. Using the production plans, the firm can estimate direct labor requirements, factory overhead outlays, and operating expenses. Once these estimates have been made, the firm's pro forma income statement and cash budget can be prepared. With the basic inputs (pro forma income statement, cash budget, fixed asset outlay plan, long-term financing plan, and current-period balance sheet), the pro forma balance sheet can finally be developed.

Throughout the remainder of this chapter, we will concentrate on the key outputs of the short-term financial planning process: the cash budget, the pro forma income statement, and the pro forma balance sheet.

REVIEW QUESTIONS

3–8   What is the *financial planning process?* Contrast *long-term (strategic) financial plans* and *short-term (operating) financial plans*.

3–9   Which three statements result as part of the short-term (operating) financial planning process?

LG4 3.3 | Cash Planning: Cash Budgets

cash budget (cash forecast) A statement of the firm's planned inflows and outflows of cash that is used to estimate its short-term cash requirements.

The **cash budget,** or **cash forecast,** is a statement of the firm's planned inflows and outflows of cash. It is used by the firm to estimate its short-term cash requirements, with particular attention being paid to planning for surplus cash and for cash shortages.

Typically, the cash budget is designed to cover a 1-year period, divided into smaller time intervals. The number and type of intervals depend on the nature of the business. The more seasonal and uncertain a firm's cash flows, the greater the number of intervals. Because many firms are confronted with a seasonal cash flow pattern, the cash budget is quite often presented on a monthly basis. Firms with stable patterns of cash flow may use quarterly or annual time intervals.

The Sales Forecast

sales forecast The prediction of the firm's sales over a given period, based on external and/or internal data; used as the key input to the short-term financial planning process.

The key input to the short-term financial planning process is the firm's **sales forecast.** This prediction of the firm's sales over a given period is ordinarily prepared by the marketing department. On the basis of the sales forecast, the financial manager estimates the monthly cash flows that will result from projected sales receipts and from outlays related to production, inventory, and sales. The manager also determines the level of fixed assets required and the amount of financing, if any, needed to support the forecast level of sales and production. In practice, obtaining good data is the most difficult aspect of forecasting.[5] The sales

---

5. Calculation of the various forecasting techniques, such as regression, moving averages, and exponential smoothing, is not included in this text. For a description of the technical side of forecasting, refer to a basic statistics, econometrics, or management science text.

forecast may be based on an analysis of external data, internal data, or a combination of the two.

An **external forecast** is based on the relationships observed between the firm's sales and certain key external economic indicators such as the gross domestic product (GDP), new housing starts, consumer confidence, and disposable personal income. Forecasts containing these indicators are readily available. Because the firm's sales are often closely related to some aspect of overall national economic activity, a forecast of economic activity should provide insight into future sales.

external forecast
A sales forecast based on the relationships observed between the firm's sales and certain key external economic indicators.

internal forecast
A sales forecast based on a buildup, or consensus, of sales forecasts through the firm's own sales channels.

Internal forecasts are based on a buildup, or consensus, of sales forecasts through the firm's own sales channels. Typically, the firm's salespeople in the field are asked to estimate how many units of each type of product they expect to sell in the coming year. These forecasts are collected and totaled by the sales manager, who may adjust the figures using knowledge of specific markets or of the salesperson's forecasting ability. Finally, adjustments may be made for additional internal factors, such as production capabilities.

Hint The firm needs to spend a great deal of time and effort to make the sales forecast as precise as possible. An "after-the-fact" analysis of the prior year's forecast can help the firm determine which approach or combination of approaches will give it the most accurate forecasts.

Firms generally use a combination of external and internal forecast data to make the final sales forecast. The internal data provide insight into sales expectations, and the external data provide a means of adjusting these expectations to take into account general economic factors. The nature of the firm's product also often affects the mix and types of forecasting methods used.

Preparing the Cash Budget

The general format of the cash budget is presented in Table 3.7. We will discuss each of its components individually. In addition, the *In Practice* box on page 118 discusses some real-world aspects of cash forecasting.

Cash Receipts

cash receipts
All of a firm's inflows of cash during a given financial period.

Cash receipts include all of a firm's inflows of cash during a given financial period. The most common components of cash receipts are cash sales, collections of accounts receivable, and other cash receipts.

TABLE 3.7

The General Format of the Cash Budget

	Jan.	Feb.	...	Nov.	Dec.
Cash receipts	$XXX	$XXG		$XXM	$XXT
Less: Cash disbursements	XXA	XXH	...	XXN	XXU
Net cash flow	$XXB	$XXI		$XXO	$XXV
Add: Beginning cash	XXC	XXD	XXJ	XXP	XXQ
Ending cash	$XXD	$XXJ		$XXQ	$XXW
Less: Minimum cash balance	XXE	XXK	...	XXR	XXY
Required total financing		$XXL		$XXS	
Excess cash balance	$XXF				$XXZ

In Practice FOCUS ON PRACTICE

CASH FORECASTS: EASIER SAID THAN DONE

Given the importance of cash to sound financial management, it is surprising how many companies ignore the cash forecasting process. Three reasons for this omission come up most often: Cash forecasts are always wrong; they are hard to do; and managers don't see the benefits of these forecasts unless the company is already in the midst of a cash crunch. In addition, each company has its own methodology for cash forecasting. If the firm's cash inflows and outflows don't form a pattern that managers can graph, it's tough to develop successful forecasts.

Yet the reasons to forecast cash are equally compelling: Cash forecasts allow the firm to plan for adequate liquidity, enable a company to minimize its borrowing costs or maximize its investment income, and help financial executives manage currency exposures more effectively. In times of tight credit, lenders expect borrowers to monitor cash carefully and will favor a company that prepares good cash forecasts. When cash needs and forecasted cash positions don't match, financial managers can plan to borrow funds to close the gap.

According to a 2003 survey conducted by Visa USA, fewer than 10 percent of corporate treasurers, CFOs, and controllers believe that their current cash flow and cash management processes are very efficient. In a separate survey conducted by GTNews and sponsored by REL Consultancy Group, 75 percent of multinational corporations admitted to having little or no confidence in the accuracy of their own cash flow forecasts. Poor internal communication was blamed for cash flow forecasting errors by more than half of the respondents. Poor sales projections and collection policies were noted by almost half of the treasurers responding to the survey, who cited problems in pricing, billing, and logistics that led to poor cash collections from customers.

Many companies are using technology to demystify cash forecasts and increase forecast accuracy. Software can apply statistical techniques, graph historical data, or build models based on each customer's payment patterns. It can also tap corporate databases for the firm's purchases, payment information, and shipments to customers. Even so, installing new and powerful budgeting and planning software is not the final answer to predicting cash flows. The next—and often difficult—step is getting the workforce to abandon their old methods, spreadsheets, or even pencil-and-paper forecasts and to utilize the new technology.

Sources: Adapted from Richard H. Gamble, "Cash Forecast: Cloudy But Clearing," *Business Finance* (May 2001), downloaded from www.businessfinancemag.com; and from Laurie Brannen, "Cash Forecasting Gets Short Shrift" and "The Trouble with Cash Management," downloaded from www.businessfinancemag.com on July 1, 2004.

■ *How might cash flow forecasts vary among the marketing, sales, and finance departments within a large corporation?*

EXAMPLE   Coulson Industries, a defense contractor, is developing a cash budget for October, November, and December. Coulson's sales in August and September were $100,000 and $200,000, respectively. Sales of $400,000, $300,000, and $200,000 have been forecast for October, November, and December, respectively. Historically, 20% of the firm's sales have been for cash, 50% have generated accounts receivable collected after 1 month, and the remaining 30% have generated accounts receivable collected after 2 months. Bad-debt expenses (uncollectible accounts) have been negligible.[6] In December, the firm will receive a $30,000 dividend from stock in a subsidiary. The schedule of expected cash receipts for the company is presented in Table 3.8. It contains the following items:

---

6. Normally, it would be expected that the collection percentages would total slightly less than 100%, because some of the accounts receivable would be uncollectible. In this example, the sum of the collection percentages is 100% (20% + 50% + 30%), which reflects the fact that all sales are assumed to be collected.

TABLE 3.8   A Schedule of Projected Cash Receipts for Coulson Industries ($000)

	Aug. $100	Sept. $200	Oct. $400	Nov. $300	Dec. $200
Forecast sales					
Cash sales (0.20)	$20	$40	$ 80	$ 60	$ 40
Collections of A/R:					
Lagged 1 month (0.50)		50	100	200	150
Lagged 2 months (0.30)			30	60	120
Other cash receipts					30
Total cash receipts			$210	$320	$340

Forecast sales   This initial entry is *merely informational*. It is provided as an aid in calculating other sales-related items.

Cash sales   The cash sales shown for each month represent 20% of the total sales forecast for that month.

Collections of A/R   These entries represent the collection of accounts receivable (A/R) resulting from sales in earlier months.

Lagged 1 month   These figures represent sales made in the preceding month that generated accounts receivable collected in the current month. Because 50% of the current month's sales are collected 1 month later, the collections of A/R with a 1-month lag shown for September represent 50% of the sales in August, collections for October represent 50% of September sales, and so on.

Lagged 2 months   These figures represent sales made 2 months earlier that generated accounts receivable collected in the current month. Because 30% of sales are collected 2 months later, the collections with a 2-month lag shown for October represent 30% of the sales in August, and so on.

Other cash receipts   These are cash receipts expected from sources other than sales. Interest received, dividends received, proceeds from the sale of equipment, stock and bond sale proceeds, and lease receipts may show up here. For Coulson Industries, the only other cash receipt is the $30,000 dividend due in December.

Total cash receipts   This figure represents the total of all the cash receipts listed for each month. For Coulson Industries, we are concerned only with October, November, and December, as shown in Table 3.8.   ■

Cash Disbursements

cash disbursements
All outlays of cash by the firm during a given financial period.

Cash disbursements include all outlays of cash by the firm during a given financial period. The most common cash disbursements are

Cash purchases	Fixed-asset outlays
Payments of accounts payable	Interest payments
Rent (and lease) payments	Cash dividend payments
Wages and salaries	Principal payments (loans)
Tax payments	Repurchases or retirements of stock

It is important to recognize that *depreciation and other noncash charges are NOT included in the cash budget,* because they merely represent a scheduled write-off of an earlier cash outflow. The impact of depreciation, as we noted earlier, is reflected in the reduced cash outflow for tax payments.

EXAMPLE Coulson Industries has gathered the following data needed for the preparation of a cash disbursements schedule for October, November, and December.

Purchases The firm's purchases represent 70% of sales. Of this amount, 10% is paid in cash, 70% is paid in the month immediately following the month of purchase, and the remaining 20% is paid 2 months following the month of purchase.[7]

Rent payments Rent of $5,000 will be paid each month.

Wages and salaries Fixed salary cost for the year is $96,000, or $8,000 per month. In addition, wages are estimated as 10% of monthly sales.

Tax payments Taxes of $25,000 must be paid in December.

Fixed-asset outlays New machinery costing $130,000 will be purchased and paid for in November.

Interest payments An interest payment of $10,000 is due in December.

Cash dividend payments Cash dividends of $20,000 will be paid in October.

Principal payments (loans) A $20,000 principal payment is due in December.

Repurchases or retirements of stock No repurchase or retirement of stock is expected between October and December.

The firm's cash disbursements schedule, using the preceding data, is shown in Table 3.9. Some items in the table are explained in greater detail below.

Purchases This entry is *merely informational.* The figures represent 70% of the forecast sales for each month. They have been included to facilitate calculation of the cash purchases and related payments.

Cash purchases The cash purchases for each month represent 10% of the month's purchases.

Payments of A/P These entries represent the payment of accounts payable (A/P) resulting from purchases in earlier months.

Lagged 1 month These figures represent purchases made in the preceding month that are paid for in the current month. Because 70% of the firm's purchases are paid for 1 month later, the payments with a 1-month lag shown for September represent 70% of the August purchases, payments for October represent 70% of September purchases, and so on.

Lagged 2 months These figures represent purchases made 2 months earlier that are paid for in the current month. Because 20% of the firm's purchases are paid for 2 months later, the payments with a 2-month lag for October represent 20% of the August purchases, and so on.

---

7. Unlike the collection percentages for sales, the total of the payment percentages should equal 100%, because it is expected that the firm will pay off all of its accounts payable.

TABLE 3.9

A Schedule of Projected Cash Disbursements for Coulson Industries ($000)

	Aug.	Sept.	Oct.	Nov.	Dec.
Purchases (0.70 × sales)	$70	$140	$280	$210	$140
Cash purchases (0.10)	$7	$14	$ 28	$ 21	$ 14
Payments of A/P:					
Lagged 1 month (0.70)		49	98	196	147
Lagged 2 months (0.20)			14	28	56
Rent payments			5	5	5
Wages and salaries			48	38	28
Tax payments					25
Fixed-asset outlays				130	
Interest payments					10
Cash dividend payments			20		
Principal payments					20
Total cash disbursements			$213	$418	$305

net cash flow
The mathematical difference between the firm's cash receipts and its cash disbursements in each period.

ending cash
The sum of the firm's beginning cash and its net cash flow for the period.

required total financing
Amount of funds needed by the firm if the ending cash for the period is less than the desired minimum cash balance; typically represented by notes payable.

excess cash balance
The (excess) amount available for investment by the firm if the period's ending cash is greater than the desired minimum cash balance; assumed to be invested in marketable securities.

Wages and salaries   These amounts were obtained by adding $8,000 to 10% of the *sales* in each month. The $8,000 represents the salary component; the rest represents wages.

The remaining items on the cash disbursements schedule are self-explanatory. ■

Net Cash Flow, Ending Cash, Financing, and Excess Cash

Look back at the general-format cash budget in Table 3.7. We have inputs for the first two entries, and we now continue calculating the firm's cash needs. The firm's **net cash flow** is found by subtracting the cash disbursements from cash receipts in each period. Then we add beginning cash to the firm's net cash flow to determine the **ending cash** for each period. Finally, we subtract the desired minimum cash balance from ending cash to find the **required total financing** or the **excess cash balance**. If the ending cash is less than the minimum cash balance, *financing* is required. Such financing is typically viewed as short-term and is therefore represented by notes payable. If the ending cash is greater than the minimum cash balance, *excess cash* exists. Any excess cash is assumed to be invested in a liquid, short-term, interest-paying vehicle—that is, in marketable securities.

EXAMPLE

Table 3.10 (see page 122) presents Coulson Industries' cash budget, based on the data already developed. At the end of September, Coulson's cash balance was $50,000, and its notes payable and marketable securities equaled $0.[8] The company wishes to maintain, as a reserve for unexpected needs, a minimum cash balance of $25,000.

8. If Coulson either had outstanding notes payable or held marketable securities at the end of September, its "beginning cash" value would be misleading. It could be either overstated or understated, depending on whether the firm had notes payable or marketable securities on its books at that time. For simplicity, the cash budget discussions and problems presented in this chapter assume that the firm's notes payable and marketable securities equal $0 at the beginning of the period of concern.

TABLE 3.10

A Cash Budget for Coulson Industries ($000)

	Oct.	Nov.	Dec.
Total cash receipts[a]	$210	$320	$340
Less: Total cash disbursements[b]	213	418	305
Net cash flow	($ 3)	($ 98)	$ 35
Add: Beginning cash	50	47	(51)
Ending cash	$ 47	($ 51)	($ 16)
Less: Minimum cash balance	25	25	25
Required total financing (notes payable)[c]	—	$ 76	$ 41
Excess cash balance (marketable securities)[d]	$ 22	—	—

[a]From Table 3.8.
[b]From Table 3.9.
[c]Values are placed in this line when the ending cash is less than the desired minimum cash balance. These amounts are typically financed short-term and therefore are represented by notes payable.
[d]Values are placed in this line when the ending cash is greater than the desired minimum cash balance. These amounts are typically assumed to be invested short-term and therefore are represented by marketable securities.

For Coulson Industries to maintain its required $25,000 ending cash balance, it will need total borrowing of $76,000 in November and $41,000 in December. In October the firm will have an excess cash balance of $22,000, which can be held in an interest-earning marketable security. The required total financing figures in the cash budget refer to *how much will be owed at the end of the month*; they do *not* represent the monthly changes in borrowing.

The monthly changes in borrowing and in excess cash can be found by further analyzing the cash budget. In October the $50,000 beginning cash, which becomes $47,000 after the $3,000 net cash outflow, results in a $22,000 excess cash balance once the $25,000 minimum cash is deducted. In November the $76,000 of required total financing resulted from the $98,000 net cash outflow less the $22,000 of excess cash from October. The $41,000 of required total financing in December resulted from reducing November's $76,000 of required total financing by the $35,000 of net cash inflow during December. Summarizing, the *financial activities for each month* would be as follows:

October: **Invest the $22,000** excess cash balance in marketable securities.

November: Liquidate the $22,000 of marketable securities and **borrow $76,000** (notes payable).

December: **Repay $35,000** of notes payable to leave $41,000 of outstanding required total financing.

Evaluating the Cash Budget

Hint Not only is the cash budget a great tool to let management know when it has cash shortages or excesses, but it may be a document required by potential creditors. It communicates to them what the money will be used for, and how and when their loans will be repaid.

The cash budget indicates whether a cash shortage or surplus is expected in each of the months covered by the forecast. Each month's figure is based on the internally imposed requirement of a minimum cash balance and *represents the total balance at the end of the month*.

At the end of each of the 3 months, Coulson expects the following balances in cash, marketable securities, and notes payable:

Account	End-of-month balance ($000)		
	Oct.	Nov.	Dec.
Cash	$25	$25	$25
Marketable securities	22	0	0
Notes payable	0	76	41

Hint Because of the uncertainty of the ending cash values, the financial manager will usually seek to borrow more than the maximum financing indicated in the cash budget.

Note that the firm is assumed first to liquidate its marketable securities to meet deficits and then to borrow with notes payable if additional financing is needed. As a result, it will not have marketable securities and notes payable on its books at the same time.

Because it may be necessary to borrow up to $76,000 for the 3-month period, the financial manager should be certain that some arrangement is made to ensure the availability of these funds.

Coping with Uncertainty in the Cash Budget

Aside from careful estimation of cash budget inputs, there are two ways of coping with the uncertainty of the cash budget.[9] One is to prepare several cash budgets—based on pessimistic, most likely, and optimistic forecasts. From this range of cash flows, the financial manager can determine the amount of financing necessary to cover the most adverse situation. The use of several cash budgets, based on differing assumptions, also should give the financial manager a sense of the riskiness of the various alternatives. This *sensitivity analysis,* or "what if" approach, is often used to analyze cash flows under a variety of circumstances. Clearly the use of electronic spreadsheets simplifies the process of performing sensitivity analysis.

EXAMPLE   Table 3.11 (see page 124) presents the summary of Coulson Industries' cash budget prepared for each month of concern using pessimistic, most likely, and optimistic estimates of total cash receipts and disbursements. The most likely estimate is based on the expected outcomes presented earlier.

During October, Coulson will, at worst, need a maximum of $15,000 of financing and, at best, will have a $62,000 excess cash balance. During November, its financing requirement will be between $0 and $185,000, or it could experience an excess cash balance of $5,000. The December projections show maximum borrowing of $190,000 with a possible excess cash balance of $107,000. By considering the extreme values in the pessimistic and optimistic outcomes, Coulson Industries should be better able to plan its cash requirements. For the 3-month period, the peak borrowing requirement under the worst circumstances would be $190,000, which happens to be considerably greater than the most likely estimate of $76,000 for this period.

---

9. The term *uncertainty* is used here to refer to the variability of the cash flow outcomes that may actually occur.

TABLE 3.11

A Sensitivity Analysis of Coulson Industries' Cash Budget ($000)

	October			November			December		
	Pessi- mistic	Most likely	Opti- mistic	Pessi- mistic	Most likely	Opti- mistic	Pessi- mistic	Most likely	Opti- mistic
Total cash receipts	$160	$210	$285	$210	$320	$410	$275	$340	$422
Less: Total cash disbursements	200	213	248	380	418	467	280	305	320
Net cash flow	($ 40)	($ 3)	$ 37	($170)	($ 98)	($ 57)	($ 5)	$ 35	$102
Add: Beginning cash	50	50	50	10	47	87	(160)	(51)	30
Ending cash	$ 10	$ 47	$ 87	($160)	($ 51)	$ 30	($165)	($ 16)	$132
Less: Minimum cash balance	25	25	25	25	25	25	25	25	25
Required total financing	$ 15	—	—	$185	$ 76	—	$190	$ 41	—
Excess cash balance	—	$ 22	$ 62	—	—	$ 5	—	—	$107

A second and much more sophisticated way of coping with uncertainty in the cash budget is *simulation* (discussed in Chapter 10). By simulating the occurrence of sales and other uncertain events, the firm can develop a probability distribution of its ending cash flows for each month. The financial decision maker can then use the probability distribution to determine the amount of financing needed to protect the firm adequately against a cash shortage.

Cash Flow Within the Month

Because the cash budget shows cash flows only on a total monthly basis, the information provided by the cash budget is not necessarily adequate for ensuring solvency. A firm must look more closely at its pattern of daily cash receipts and cash disbursements to ensure that adequate cash is available for paying bills as they come due. For an example related to this topic, see the book's Web site at www.aw-bc.com/gitman.

The synchronization of cash flows in the cash budget at month-end does not ensure that the firm will be able to meet its daily cash requirements. Because a firm's cash flows are generally quite variable when viewed on a daily basis, effective cash planning requires a look *beyond* the cash budget. The financial manager must therefore plan and monitor cash flow more frequently than on a monthly basis. The greater the variability of cash flows from day to day, the greater the amount of attention required.

REVIEW QUESTIONS

3–10   What is the purpose of the *cash budget?* What role does the sales forecast play in its preparation?

3–11   Briefly describe the basic format of the cash budget.

3–12   How can the two "bottom lines" of the cash budget be used to determine the firm's short-term borrowing and investment requirements?

3–13   What is the cause of uncertainty in the cash budget, and what two techniques can be used to cope with this uncertainty?

 3.4 | Profit Planning: Pro Forma Statements

pro forma statements
Projected, or forecast, income statements and balance sheets.

Whereas cash planning focuses on forecasting cash flows, *profit planning* relies on accrual concepts to project the firm's profit and overall financial position. Shareholders, creditors, and the firm's management pay close attention to the **pro forma statements,** which are projected, or forecast, income statements and balance sheets. The basic steps in the short-term financial planning process were shown in the flow diagram of Figure 3.2. The approaches for estimating the pro forma statements are all based on the belief that the financial relationships reflected in the firm's past financial statements will not change in the coming period. The commonly used simplified approaches are presented in subsequent discussions.

Hint A key point in understanding pro forma statements is that they reflect the goals and objectives of the firm for the planning period. For these goals and objectives to be achieved, operational plans will have to be developed. Financial plans can be realized only if the correct actions are implemented.

Two inputs are required for preparing pro forma statements: (1) financial statements for the preceding year and (2) the sales forecast for the coming year. A variety of assumptions must also be made. The company that we will use to illustrate the simplified approaches to pro forma preparation is Vectra Manufacturing, which manufactures and sells one product. It has two basic product models—X and Y—which are produced by the same process but require different amounts of raw material and labor.

Preceding Year's Financial Statements

The income statement for the firm's 2006 operations is given in Table 3.12 (see page 126). It indicates that Vectra had sales of $100,000, total cost of goods sold of $80,000, net profits before taxes of $9,000, and net profits after taxes of $7,650. The firm paid $4,000 in cash dividends, leaving $3,650 to be transferred to retained earnings. The firm's balance sheet for 2006 is given in Table 3.13 (see page 126).

Sales Forecast

Just as for the cash budget, the key input for pro forma statements is the sales forecast. Vectra Manufacturing's sales forecast for the coming year (2007), based on both external and internal data, is presented in Table 3.14 (see page 126). The unit sale prices of the products reflect an increase from $20 to $25 for model X and from $40 to $50 for model Y. These increases are necessary to cover anticipated increases in costs.

REVIEW QUESTION

3–14   What is the purpose of *pro forma statements?* What inputs are required for preparing them using the simplified approaches?

TABLE 3.12

Vectra Manufacturing's Income Statement for the Year Ended December 31, 2006

Sales revenue		
Model X (1,000 units at $20/unit)	$20,000	
Model Y (2,000 units at $40/unit)	80,000	
Total sales		$100,000
Less: Cost of goods sold		
Labor	$28,500	
Material A	8,000	
Material B	5,500	
Overhead	38,000	
Total cost of goods sold		80,000
Gross profits		$ 20,000
Less: Operating expenses		10,000
Operating profits		$ 10,000
Less: Interest expense		1,000
Net profits before taxes		$ 9,000
Less: Taxes (0.15 × $9,000)		1,350
Net profits after taxes		$ 7,650
Less: Common stock dividends		4,000
To retained earnings		$ 3,650

TABLE 3.13

Vectra Manufacturing's Balance Sheet, December 31, 2006

Assets		Liabilities and Stockholders' Equity	
Cash	$ 6,000	Accounts payable	$ 7,000
Marketable securities	4,000	Taxes payable	300
Accounts receivable	13,000	Notes payable	8,300
Inventories	16,000	Other current liabilities	3,400
Total current assets	$39,000	Total current liabilities	$19,000
Net fixed assets	$51,000	Long-term debt	$18,000
Total assets	$90,000	Stockholders' equity	
		Common stock	$30,000
		Retained earnings	$23,000
		Total liabilities and stockholders' equity	$90,000

TABLE 3.14

2007 Sales Forecast for Vectra Manufacturing

Unit sales	
Model X	1,500
Model Y	1,950
Dollar sales	
Model X ($25/unit)	$ 37,500
Model Y ($50/unit)	97,500
Total	$135,000

3.5 | # Preparing the Pro Forma Income Statement

percent-of-sales method
A simple method for developing the pro forma income statement; it forecasts sales and then expresses the various income statement items as percentages of projected sales.

A simple method for developing a pro forma income statement is the **percent-of-sales method.** It forecasts sales and then expresses the various income statement items as percentages of projected sales. The percentages used are likely to be the percentages of sales for those items in the previous year. By using dollar values taken from Vectra's 2006 income statement (Table 3.12), we find that these percentages are

$$\frac{\text{Cost of goods sold}}{\text{Sales}} = \frac{\$80,000}{\$100,000} = 80.0\%$$

$$\frac{\text{Operating expenses}}{\text{Sales}} = \frac{\$10,000}{\$100,000} = 10.0\%$$

$$\frac{\text{Interest expense}}{\text{Sales}} = \frac{\$1,000}{\$100,000} = 1.0\%$$

Applying these percentages to the firm's forecast sales of $135,000 (developed in Table 3.14), we get the 2007 pro forma income statement shown in Table 3.15 (see page 128). We have assumed that Vectra will pay $4,000 in common stock dividends, so the expected contribution to retained earnings is $6,327. This represents a considerable increase over $3,650 in the preceding year (see Table 3.12).

Considering Types of Costs and Expenses

The technique that is used to prepare the pro forma income statement in Table 3.15 assumes that all the firm's costs and expenses are *variable.* That is, we assumed that for a given percentage increase in sales, the same percentage increase in cost of goods sold, operating expenses, and interest expense would result. For example, as Vectra's sales increased by 35 percent (from $100,000 in 2006 to $135,000 projected for 2007), we assumed that its costs of goods sold also increased by 35 percent (from $80,000 in 2006 to $108,000 in 2007). On the basis of this assumption, the firm's net profits before taxes also increased by 35 percent (from $9,000 in 2006 to $12,150 projected for 2007).

This approach implies that the firm will not receive the benefits that result from fixed costs when sales are increasing.[10] Clearly, though, if the firm has fixed costs, these costs do not change when sales increase; the result is increased profits. But by remaining unchanged when sales decline, these costs tend to lower profits. Therefore, the use of past cost and expense ratios generally *tends to understate profits when sales are increasing.* (Likewise, it *tends to overstate profits when sales are decreasing.*) The best way to adjust for the presence of fixed costs when preparing a pro forma income statement is to break the firm's historical costs and expenses into *fixed* and *variable* components.[11]

---

10. The potential returns as well as risks resulting from use of fixed (operating and financial) costs to create "leverage" are discussed in Chapter 12. The key point to recognize here is that when the firm's revenue is *increasing,* fixed costs can magnify returns.

11. The application of *regression analysis*—a statistically based technique for measuring the relationship between variables—to past cost data as they relate to past sales could be used to develop equations that recognize the fixed and variable nature of each cost. Such equations could be employed when preparing the pro forma income statement from the sales forecast. The use of the regression approach in pro forma income statement preparation is widespread, and many computer software packages for use in pro forma preparation rely on this technique. Expanded discussions of the application of this technique can be found in most second-level managerial finance texts.

TABLE 3.15	A Pro Forma Income Statement, Using the Percent-of-Sales Method, for Vectra Manufacturing for the Year Ended December 31, 2007	
Sales revenue		$135,000
Less: Cost of goods sold (0.80)		108,000
Gross profits		$ 27,000
Less: Operating expenses (0.10)		13,500
Operating profits		$ 13,500
Less: Interest expense (0.01)		1,350
Net profits before taxes		$ 12,150
Less: Taxes (0.15 × $12,150)		1,823
Net profits after taxes		$ 10,327
Less: Common stock dividends		4,000
To retained earnings		$ 6,327

EXAMPLE   Vectra Manufacturing's 2006 actual and 2007 pro forma income statements, broken into fixed and variable cost and expense components, follow:

Vectra Manufacturing Income Statements	2006 Actual	2007 Pro forma
Sales revenue	$100,000	$135,000
Less: Cost of good sold		
Fixed cost	40,000	40,000
Variable cost (0.40 × sales)	40,000	54,000
Gross profits	$ 20,000	$ 41,000
Less: Operating expenses		
Fixed expense	5,000	5,000
Variable expense (0.05 × sales)	5,000	6,750
Operating profits	$ 10,000	$ 29,250
Less: Interest expense (all fixed)	1,000	1,000
Net profits before taxes	$ 9,000	$ 28,250
Less: Taxes (0.15 × net profits before taxes)	1,350	4,238
Net profits after taxes	$ 7,650	$ 24,012

Breaking Vectra's costs and expenses into fixed and variable components provides a more accurate projection of its pro forma profit. By assuming that *all* costs are variable (as shown in Table 3.15), we find that projected net profits before taxes would continue to equal 9 percent of sales (in 2006, $9,000 net profits before taxes ÷ $100,000 sales). Therefore, the 2007 net profits before taxes would have been $12,150 (0.09 × $135,000 projected sales) instead of the $28,250 obtained by using the firm's fixed-cost–variable-cost breakdown. ■

CRITICAL ETHICAL LAPSE AT CRITICAL PATH

Critical Path provides a fascinating study in how managers can seem to maximize shareholder wealth by making financial projections that primarily benefit the managers. This Silicon Valley dot-com publicized wildly optimistic sales projections for its leading-edge corporate e-mail services, even as its CEO was privately trying to sell the company. As the fiscal year-end neared, and no buyer took the bait, sales personnel and accountants were pressured by management into doing whatever was necessary to try to approach the projected numbers. *Business Week* quoted a former sales manager: "The line between right and wrong wasn't just blurred—it was wiped out."

Stockholders at Critical Path saw the stock price plummet from $114 in March 2000 to about $2 after the financial statements were corrected. So much for maximizing shareholder wealth! David Thatcher, the company's former president, pleaded guilty to conspiracy to commit securities fraud by inflating the firm's revenues in an attempt to meet the predicted financial results for the third and fourth quarters of 2000. He got off easy—receiving only a year in jail and a fine of $7,500—but the publicity surrounding this and similar cases sent a message to financial officers. So, too, did a shareholder class action lawsuit against the company that resulted in a payment of $17.5 million in cash—covered by the company's liability insurance—and issuance of stock options controlling 850,000 shares of stock for the shareholders who were most adversely affected by the deception.

The Private Securities Litigation Reform Act of 1995 offers some protection against unrealistic financial forecasts by requiring that companies disclose risks and uncertainties that may cause public "forward-looking statements" not to materialize. Accordingly, **Fifth Third Bancorp** was careful to note six reasons why the anticipated benefits from its acquisition of **Old Kent Financial** might not come to pass. Furthermore, to keep companies from selectively disclosing key developments to Wall Street securities analysts but not to the general public, the SEC in 2000 adopted Regulation FD ("fair disclosure"). Unfortunately, companies do not have to release revisions of forecasts, leaving room for the ethical lapses similar to those seen with Critical Path.

One thing is for sure: The best way for financial managers to avoid misleading investors when publicizing rosy forecasts is to ask themselves if they would want to invest their own money based on such overoptimistic projections.

■ *What other strategies could regulators and/or investors use to curb the misuse of funds and limit the manipulation of information by managers?*

Clearly, when using a simplified approach to prepare a pro forma income statement, we should break down costs and expenses into fixed and variable components.

The *In Practice* box above demonstrates the importance of making accurate and honest financial projections.

REVIEW QUESTIONS

3–15   How is the *percent-of-sales method* used to prepare pro forma income statements?

3–16   Why does the presence of fixed costs cause the percent-of-sales method of pro forma income statement preparation to fail? What is a better method?

3.6 | # Preparing the Pro Forma Balance Sheet

judgmental approach
A simplified approach for preparing the pro forma balance sheet under which the values of certain balance sheet accounts are estimated, some as a percentage of sales and others by management assumption, and the firm's external financing is used as a balancing, or "plug," figure.

A number of simplified approaches are available for preparing the pro forma balance sheet. One involves estimating all balance sheet accounts as a strict percentage of sales. A better and more popular approach is the **judgmental approach**,[12] under which the values of certain balance sheet accounts are estimated, some as a percentage of sales and others by management assumption, and the firm's external financing is used as a balancing, or "plug," figure. To apply the judgmental approach to prepare Vectra Manufacturing's 2007 pro forma balance sheet, a number of assumptions must be made about levels of various balance sheet accounts:

1. A minimum cash balance of $6,000 is desired.
2. Marketable securities are assumed to remain unchanged from their current level of $4,000.
3. Accounts receivable on average represent about 45 days of sales. Because Vectra's annual sales are projected to be $135,000, accounts receivable should average $16,875 (1/8 × $135,000). (Forty-five days expressed fractionally is about one-eighth of a year: 45/365 ≈ 1/8.)
4. The ending inventory should remain at a level of about $16,000, of which 25 percent (approximately $4,000) should be raw materials and the remaining 75 percent (approximately $12,000) should consist of finished goods.
5. A new machine costing $20,000 will be purchased. Total depreciation for the year is $8,000. Adding the $20,000 acquisition to the existing net fixed assets of $51,000 and subtracting the depreciation of $8,000 yields net fixed assets of $63,000.
6. Purchases are expected to represent approximately 30% of annual sales, which in this case is approximately $40,500 (0.30 × $135,000). The firm estimates that it can take 73 days on average to satisfy its accounts payable. Thus accounts payable should equal one-fifth (73 days ÷ 365 days) of the firm's purchases, or $8,100 (1/5 × $40,500).
7. Taxes payable are expected to equal one-fourth of the current year's tax liability, which equals $455 (one-fourth of the tax liability of $1,823 shown in the pro forma income statement in Table 3.15).
8. Notes payable are assumed to remain unchanged from their current level of $8,300.
9. No change in other current liabilities is expected. They remain at the level of the previous year: $3,400.
10. The firm's long-term debt and its common stock are expected to remain unchanged at $18,000 and $30,000, respectively; no issues, retirements, or repurchases of bonds or stocks are planned.
11. Retained earnings will increase from the beginning level of $23,000 (from the balance sheet dated December 31, 2006, in Table 3.13) to $29,327. The increase of $6,327 represents the amount of retained earnings calculated in the year-end 2007 pro forma income statement in Table 3.15.

---

12. The judgmental approach represents an improved version of the *percent-of-sales approach* to pro forma balance sheet preparation. Because the judgmental approach requires only slightly more information and should yield better estimates than the somewhat naive percent-of-sales approach, it is presented here.

TABLE 3.16

A Pro Forma Balance Sheet, Using the Judgmental Approach, for Vectra Manufacturing (December 31, 2007)

Assets			Liabilities and Stockholders' Equity	
Cash		$ 6,000	Accounts payable	$ 8,100
Marketable securities		4,000	Taxes payable	455
Accounts receivable		16,875	Notes payable	8,300
Inventories			Other current liabilities	3,400
Raw materials	$ 4,000		Total current liabilities	$ 20,255
Finished goods	12,000		Long-term debt	$ 18,000
Total inventory		16,000	Stockholders' equity	
Total current assets		$ 42,875	Common stock	$ 30,000
Net fixed assets		$ 63,000	Retained earnings	$ 29,327
Total assets		$105,875	Total	$ 97,582
			External financing required[a]	$ 8,293
			Total liabilities and	
			stockholders' equity	$105,875

[a]The amount of external financing needed to force the firm's balance sheet to balance. Because of the nature of the judgmental approach, the balance sheet is not expected to balance without some type of adjustment.

external financing required ("plug" figure) Under the judgmental approach for developing a pro forma balance sheet, the amount of external financing needed to bring the statement into balance. It can be either a positive or a negative value.

A 2007 pro forma balance sheet for Vectra Manufacturing based on these assumptions is presented in Table 3.16. A **"plug" figure**—called the **external financing required**—of $8,293 is needed to bring the statement into balance. This means that the firm will have to obtain about $8,293 of additional external financing to support the increased sales level of $135,000 for 2007.

A *positive* value for "external financing required," like that shown in Table 3.16, means that, based on its plans, the firm will not generate enough internal financing to support its forecast growth in assets. To support the forecast level of operation, the firm must raise funds externally by using debt and/or equity financing or by reducing dividends. Once the form of financing is determined, the pro forma balance sheet is modified to replace "external financing required" with the planned increases in the debt and/or equity accounts.

A *negative* value for "external financing required" indicates that, based on its plans, the firm will generate more financing internally than it needs to support its forecast growth in assets. In this case, funds are available for use in repaying debt, repurchasing stock, or increasing dividends. Once the specific actions are determined, "external financing required" is replaced in the pro forma balance sheet with the planned reductions in the debt and/or equity accounts. Obviously, besides being used to prepare the pro forma balance sheet, the judgmental approach is frequently used specifically to estimate the firm's financing requirements.

REVIEW QUESTIONS

3–17   Describe the *judgmental approach* for simplified preparation of the pro forma balance sheet.

(2) The firm receives other income of $2,000 per month.

(3) The firm's actual or expected purchases, all made for cash, are $50,000, $70,000, and $80,000 for the months of May through July, respectively.

(4) Rent is $3,000 per month.

(5) Wages and salaries are 10% of the previous month's sales.

(6) Cash dividends of $3,000 will be paid in June.

(7) Payment of principal and interest of $4,000 is due in June.

(8) A cash purchase of equipment costing $6,000 is scheduled in July.

(9) Taxes of $6,000 are due in June.

[LG4]

[CHALLENGE]

P3–10 Cash budget—Advanced   The actual sales and purchases for Xenocore, Inc., for September and October 2006, along with its forecast sales and purchases for the period November 2006 through April 2007, follow.

Year	Month	Sales	Purchases
2006	September	$210,000	$120,000
2006	October	250,000	150,000
2006	November	170,000	140,000
2006	December	160,000	100,000
2007	January	140,000	80,000
2007	February	180,000	110,000
2007	March	200,000	100,000
2007	April	250,000	90,000

The firm makes 20% of all sales for cash and collects on 40% of its sales in each of the 2 months following the sale. Other cash inflows are expected to be $12,000 in September and April, $15,000 in January and March, and $27,000 in February. The firm pays cash for 10% of its purchases. It pays for 50% of its purchases in the following month and for 40% of its purchases 2 months later.

Wages and salaries amount to 20% of the preceding month's sales. Rent of $20,000 per month must be paid. Interest payments of $10,000 are due in January and April. A principal payment of $30,000 is also due in April. The firm expects to pay cash dividends of $20,000 in January and April. Taxes of $80,000 are due in April. The firm also intends to make a $25,000 cash purchase of fixed assets in December.

a. Assuming that the firm has a cash balance of $22,000 at the beginning of November, determine the end-of-month cash balances for each month, November through April.

b. Assuming that the firm wishes to maintain a $15,000 minimum cash balance, determine the required total financing or excess cash balance for each month, November through April.

c. If the firm were requesting a line of credit to cover needed financing for the period November to April, how large would this line have to be? Explain your answer.

P3–11 Cash flow concepts   The following represent financial transactions that Johnsfield & Co. will be undertaking in the next planning period. For each transaction, check the statement or statements that will be affected immediately.

	Statement		
Transaction	Cash budget	Pro forma income statement	Pro forma balance sheet
Cash sale			
Credit sale			
Accounts receivable are collected			
Asset with 5-year life is purchased			
Depreciation is taken			
Amortization of goodwill is taken			
Sale of common stock			
Retirement of outstanding bonds			
Fire insurance premium is paid for the next 3 years			

P3–12 Cash budget—Sensitivity analysis   Trotter Enterprises, Inc., has gathered the following data to plan for its cash requirements and short-term investment opportunities for October, November, and December. All amounts are shown in thousands of dollars.

	October			November			December		
	Pessi-mistic	Most likely	Opti-mistic	Pessi-mistic	Most likely	Opti-mistic	Pessi-mistic	Most likely	Opti-mistic
Total cash receipts	$260	$342	$462	$200	$287	$366	$191	$294	$353
Total cash disbursements	285	326	421	203	261	313	287	332	315

a. Prepare a sensitivity analysis of Trotter's cash budget using −$20,000 as the beginning cash balance for October and a minimum required cash balance of $18,000.

b. Use the analysis prepared in part **a** to predict Trotter's financing needs and investment opportunities over the months of October, November, and December. Discuss how knowledge of the timing and amounts involved can aid the planning process.

per unit of finished product. Terri Spiro, an experienced budget analyst, has been charged with preparing a forecast of the firm's 2007 financial position, assuming replacement and modernization of manufacturing equipment. She plans to use the 2006 financial statements presented on pages 97 and 98, along with the key projected financial data summarized in the following table.

Martin Manufacturing Company Key Projected Financial Data (2007)	
Data item	Value
Sales revenue	$6,500,000
Minimum cash balance	$25,000
Inventory turnover (times)	7.0
Average collection period	50 days
Fixed-asset purchases	$400,000
Total dividend payments (preferred and common)	$20,000
Depreciation expense	$185,000
Interest expense	$97,000
Accounts payable increase	20%
Accruals and long-term debt	Unchanged
Notes payable, preferred and common stock	Unchanged

TO DO

a. Use the historical and projected financial data provided to prepare a pro forma income statement for the year ended December 31, 2007. (*Hint:* Use the *percent-of-sales method* to estimate all values *except* depreciation expense and interest expense, which have been estimated by management and included in the table.)

b. Use the projected financial data along with relevant data from the pro forma income statement prepared in part **a** to prepare the pro forma balance sheet at December 31, 2007. (*Hint:* Use the *judgmental approach.*)

c. Will Martin Manufacturing Company need to obtain *external financing* to fund the proposed equipment modernization program? Explain.

Spreadsheet Exercise

You have been assigned the task of putting together a statement for the ACME Company that shows its expected inflows and outflows of cash over the months of July 2007 through December 2007.

You have been given the following data for ACME Company:

1. Expected gross sales for May through December are $300,000, $400,000, $450,000, $400,000, $425,000, $400,000, $435,000, and $400,000, respectively.

2. 12% of the sales in any given month are collected during that month. The firm offers its customers a cash discount for early payment of their accounts and as a result factors a 3% discount into the current month's sales collection.

3. 75% of the sales in any given month are collected during the following month after the sale.

4. 13% of the sales in any given month are collected during the second month following the sale.

5. The expected purchases of raw materials in any given month are based on 80% of the expected sales during the following month.

6. The firm pays 100% of its current month's raw materials purchases in the following month.

7. Wages and salaries are paid on a monthly basis and are based on 6% of the current month's expected sales.

8. Monthly lease payments are 2% of the current month's expected sales.

9. The monthly advertising expense amounts to 3% of sales.

10. R&D expenditures are expected to be allocated to August, September, and October at the rate of 12% of sales in those months.

11. During December a prepayment of insurance for the following year will be made in the amount of $24,000.

12. During the months of July through December, the firm expects to have miscellaneous expenditures of $15,000, $20,000, $25,000, $30,000, $35,000, and $40,000, respectively.

13. Taxes will be paid in September in the amount of $40,000 and in December in the amount of $45,000.

14. Property, plant, and equipment expenditures of $180,000 are expected in September.

15. The beginning cash balance in July is $15,000.

16. The target cash balance is $15,000.

17. The firm can invest its surplus cash and earn a 6% annual return.

TO DO

a. Prepare a cash budget for July 2007 through December 2007 by creating a combined spreadsheet that incorporates spreadsheets similar to those in Tables 3.8, 3.9, and 3.10. Divide your spreadsheet into three sections:
   (1) Collections from sales and payments to purchase inventory
   (2) Operating expenditures over the time period
   (3) Cash budget covering the period of July through December

   The cash budget should reflect the following:
   (1) Beginning and ending monthly cash balances
   (2) The month(s) in which there will be a cash shortage
   (3) The month(s) which there will be a cash surplus
   (4) The cumulative cash shortage and/or cash surplus

b. Based on your analysis, briefly describe the outlook for this company over the next six months. Discuss its specific obligations and the funds available to meet them. What could the firm do in the case of a cash shortage? (Where could it get the money?) What should the firm do if it has a cash surplus?

Integrative Case

1

Track Software, Inc.

Seven years ago, after 15 years in public accounting, Stanley Booker, CPA, resigned his position as Manager of Cost Systems for Davis, Cohen, and O'Brien Public Accountants and started Track Software, Inc. In the 2 years preceding his departure from Davis, Cohen, and O'Brien, Stanley had spent nights and weekends developing a sophisticated cost-accounting software program that became Track's initial product offering. As the firm grew, Stanley planned to develop and expand the software product offerings—all of which would be related to streamlining the accounting processes of medium- to large-sized manufacturers.

Although Track experienced losses during its first 2 years of operation—2000 and 2001—its profit has increased steadily from 2002 to the present (2006). The firm's profit history, including dividend payments and contributions to retained earnings, is summarized in Table 1.

Stanley started the firm with a $100,000 investment—his savings of $50,000 as equity and a $50,000 long-term loan from the bank. He had hoped to maintain his initial 100 percent ownership in the corporation, but after experiencing a $50,000 loss during the first year of operation (2000), he sold 60 percent of the stock to a group of investors to obtain needed funds. Since then, no other stock transactions have taken place. Although he owns only

Table 1

Track Software, Inc.
Profit, Dividends, and Retained Earnings, 2000–2006

Year	Net profits after taxes (1)	Dividends paid (2)	Contribution to retained earnings [(1) − (2)] (3)
2000	($50,000)	$ 0	($50,000)
2001	(20,000)	0	(20,000)
2002	15,000	0	15,000
2003	35,000	0	35,000
2004	40,000	1,000	39,000
2005	43,000	3,000	40,000
2006	48,000	5,000	43,000

40 percent of the firm, Stanley actively manages all aspects of its activities; the other stockholders are not active in management of the firm. The firm's stock was valued at $4.50 per share in 2005 and at $5.28 per share in 2006.

Stanley has just prepared the firm's 2006 income statement, balance sheet, and statement of retained earnings, shown in Tables 2 (below), 3, and 4 (on page 154), along with the 2005 balance sheet. In addition, he has compiled the 2005 ratio values and industry average ratio values for 2006, which are applicable to both 2005 and 2006 and are summarized in Table 5 (on page 155). He is quite pleased to have achieved record earnings of $48,000 in 2006, but he is concerned about the firm's cash flows. Specifically, he is finding it more and more difficult to pay the firm's bills in a timely manner and generate cash flows to investors—both creditors and owners. To gain insight into these cash flow problems, Stanley is planning to determine the firm's 2006 operating cash flow (OCF) and free cash flow (FCF).

Stanley is further frustrated by the firm's inability to afford to hire a software developer to complete development of a cost estimation package that is believed to have "blockbuster" sales potential. Stanley began development of this package 2 years ago, but the firm's growing complexity has forced him to devote more of his time to administrative duties, thereby halting the development of this product. Stanley's reluctance to fill this position stems from his concern that the added $80,000 per year in salary and benefits for the position would certainly lower the firm's earnings per share (EPS) over the next couple of years. Although the project's success is in no way guaranteed, Stanley believes that if the money were spent to hire the software developer, the firm's sales and earnings would significantly rise once the 2- to 3-year development, production, and marketing process was completed.

Table 2

Track Software, Inc.
Income Statement ($000)
for the Year Ended December 31, 2006

Sales revenue		$1,550
Less: Cost of goods sold		1,030
Gross profits		$ 520
Less: Operating expenses		
Selling expense	$150	
General and administrative expenses	270	
Depreciation expense	11	
Total operating expense		431
Operating profits (EBIT)		$ 89
Less: Interest expense		29
Net profits before taxes		$ 60
Less: Taxes (20%)		12
Net profits after taxes		$ 48

Table 3

Track Software, Inc.
Balance Sheet ($000)

Assets	December 31 2006	December 31 2005
Current assets		
Cash	$ 12	$ 31
Marketable securities	66	82
Accounts receivable	152	104
Inventories	191	145
Total current assets	$421	$362
Gross fixed assets	$195	$180
Less: Accumulated depreciation	63	52
Net fixed assets	$132	$128
Total assets	$553	$490
Liabilities and Stockholders' Equity		
Current liabilities		
Accounts payable	$136	$126
Notes payable	200	190
Accruals	27	25
Total current liabilities	$363	$341
Long-term debt	$ 38	$ 40
Total liabilities	$401	$381
Stockholders' equity		
Common stock (50,000 shares outstanding at $0.40 par value)	$ 20	$ 20
Paid-in capital in excess of par	30	30
Retained earnings	102	59
Total stockholders' equity	$152	$109
Total liabilities and stockholders' equity	$553	$490

Table 4

Track Software, Inc.
Statement of Retained Earnings ($000)
for the Year Ended December 31, 2006

Retained earnings balance (January 1, 2006)	$ 59
Plus: Net profits after taxes (for 2006)	48
Less: Cash dividends on common stock (paid during 2006)	5
Retained earnings balance (December 31, 2006)	$102

Table 5

Ratio	Actual 2005	Industry average 2006
Current ratio	1.06	1.82
Quick ratio	0.63	1.10
Inventory turnover	10.40	12.45
Average collection period	29.6 days	20.2 days
Total asset turnover	2.66	3.92
Debt ratio	0.78	0.55
Times interest earned ratio	3.0	5.6
Gross profit margin	32.1%	42.3%
Operating profit margin	5.5%	12.4%
Net profit margin	3.0%	4.0%
Return on total assets (ROA)	8.0%	15.6%
Return on common equity (ROE)	36.4%	34.7%
Price/earnings (P/E) ratio	5.2	7.1
Market/book (M/B) ratio	2.1	2.2

With all of these concerns in mind, Stanley set out to review the various data to develop strategies that would help to ensure a bright future for Track Software. Stanley believed that as part of this process, a thorough ratio analysis of the firm's 2006 results would provide important additional insights.

TO DO

a. (1) Upon what financial goal does Stanley seem to be focusing? Is it the correct goal? Why or why not?

(2) Could a potential agency problem exist in this firm? Explain.

b. Calculate the firm's earnings per share (EPS) for each year, recognizing that the number of shares of common stock outstanding has remained *unchanged* since the firm's inception. Comment on the EPS performance in view of your response in part **a.**

c. Use the financial data presented to determine Track's *operating cash flow (OCF)* and *free cash flow (FCF)* in 2006. Evaluate your findings in light of Track's current cash flow difficulties.

d. Analyze the firm's financial condition in 2006 as it relates to (1) liquidity, (2) activity, (3) debt, (4) profitability, and (5) market, using the financial statements provided in Tables 2 and 3 and the ratio data included in Table 5. Be sure to *evaluate* the firm on both a cross-sectional and a time-series basis.

e. What recommendation would you make to Stanley regarding hiring a new software developer? Relate your recommendation here to your responses in part **a.**

PART TWO

Important Financial Concepts

Chapter 4

Time Value of Money

LEARNING GOALS

LG1 Discuss the role of time value in finance, the use of computational tools, and the basic patterns of cash flow.

LG2 Understand the concepts of future value and present value, their calculation for single amounts, and the relationship between them.

LG3 Find the future value and the present value of both an ordinary annuity and an annuity due, and find the present value of a perpetuity.

LG4 Calculate both the future value and the present value of a mixed stream of cash flows.

LG5 Understand the effect that compounding interest more frequently than annually has on future value and on the effective annual rate of interest.

LG6 Describe the procedures involved in (1) determining deposits needed to accumulate a future sum, (2) loan amortization, (3) finding interest or growth rates, and (4) finding an unknown number of periods.

ACROSS THE DISCIPLINES WHY THIS CHAPTER MATTERS TO YOU

Accounting: You need to understand time-value-of-money calculations to account for certain transactions such as loan amortization, lease payments, and bond interest rates.

Information systems: You need to understand time-value-of-money calculations to design systems that accurately measure and value the firm's cash flows.

Management: You need to understand time-value-of-money calculations so that you can manage cash receipts and disbursements in a way that will enable the firm to receive the greatest value from its cash flows.

Marketing: You need to understand time value of money because funding for new programs and products must be justified financially using time-value-of-money techniques.

Operations: You need to understand time value of money because the value of investments in new equipment, in new processes, and in inventory will be affected by the time value of money.

ELI LILLY AND COMPANY

RIDING THE PIPELINE

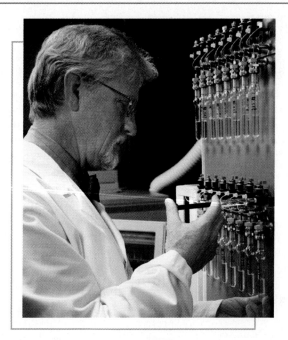

Before a company will approve a project or venture, it must be sure that the capital expenditures will be repaid by future cash flows. Specifically, the expected cash inflows from a project must exceed the project's cash outflows. For pharmaceutical companies, this calculation is complicated by the lengthy process of research and development, which they hope ends with the approval of the Food and Drug Administration (FDA).

For **Eli Lilly and Company** (www.lilly.com), maker of Prozac, Cialis, and Humulin, the average length of time from the discovery of a new drug until delivery to a patient is 15 years. After the research process produces a promising lead, researchers must determine what dosage will be required for the medicine to be effective and at what level it might be toxic to patients. They also must explore practical issues, such as whether Eli Lilly will be able to manufacture the compound on a large scale and whether the compound will be stable enough to remain effective and safe in patients' hands. The clinical trials themselves can take years.

To help recoup its investment, a drug manufacturer can get a 20-year patent, which grants the company exclusive rights to make and sell the new drug. Given that the research and approval process often lasts from 10 to 15 years, the useful patent life after approval may dwindle to less than 10 years. Once patent protection expires, generic drug manufacturers can flood the market with low-priced alternatives to the name-brand drug. Generic drug manufacturers' share of the prescription market has grown from 19 percent of the volume in 1984 to 47 percent in 2000 and is expected to rise to around 50 percent by 2006.

For Eli Lilly, the cost of bringing a new drug to market averages $800 million. To keep its drug pipeline full, the company plows some 19 percent of its sales back into the R&D programs on which its future depends. With large cash expenditures occurring years before any cash return, the time value of money is an important factor in assessing the economic viability of a new drug. In this chapter you will learn how to determine the present value of future cash flows and how to perform other time-value-of-money calculations.

■ *In December 2003, national legislation was enacted to provide a prescription drug benefit under the Medicare program beginning in 2006. What effect might this benefit have on prescription drug prices and on drug company return on investment?*

4.1 | The Role of Time Value in Finance

Financial managers and investors are always confronted with opportunities to earn positive rates of return on their funds, whether through investment in attractive projects or in interest-bearing securities or deposits. Therefore, the timing of cash outflows and inflows has important economic consequences, which financial managers explicitly recognize as the *time value of money*. Time value is based on the belief that a dollar today is worth more than a dollar that will be received at some future date. We begin our study of time value in finance by considering the two views of time value—future value and present value, the computational tools used to streamline time value calculations, and the basic patterns of cash flow.

> **Hint** The time value of money is one of the most important concepts in finance. Money that the firm has in its possession today is more valuable than money in the future because the money it now has can be invested and earn positive returns.

Future Value Versus Present Value

Financial values and decisions can be assessed by using either future value or present value techniques. Although these techniques will result in the same decisions, they view the decision differently. Future value techniques typically measure cash flows at the *end* of a project's life. Present value techniques measure cash flows at the *start* of a project's life (time zero). *Future value* is cash you will receive at a given future date, and *present value* is just like cash in hand today.

A **time line** can be used to depict the cash flows associated with a given investment. It is a horizontal line on which time zero appears at the leftmost end and future periods are marked from left to right. A time line covering five periods (in this case, years) is given in Figure 4.1. The cash flows occurring at time zero and at the end of each year are shown above the line; the negative values represent *cash outflows* ($10,000 at time zero) and the positive values represent *cash inflows* ($3,000 inflow at the end of year 1, $5,000 inflow at the end of year 2, and so on).

> **time line**
> A horizontal line on which time zero appears at the leftmost end and future periods are marked from left to right; can be used to depict investment cash flows.

Because money has a time value, all of the cash flows associated with an investment, such as those in Figure 4.1, must be measured at the same point in time. Typically, that point is either the end or the beginning of the investment's life. The future value technique uses *compounding* to find the *future value* of each cash flow at the end of the investment's life and then sums these values to find the investment's future value. This approach is depicted above the time line in Figure 4.2. The figure shows that the future value of each cash flow is measured at the end of the investment's 5-year life. Alternatively, the present value technique uses *discounting* to find the *present value* of each cash flow at time zero and then sums these values to find the investment's value today. Application of this approach is depicted below the time line in Figure 4.2.

FIGURE 4.1

Time Line
Time line depicting an investment's cash flows

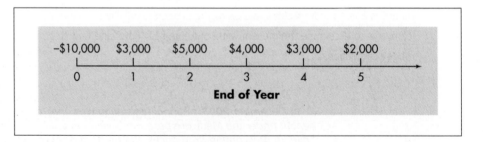

FIGURE 4.2

Compounding and Discounting

Time line showing compounding to find future value and discounting to find present value

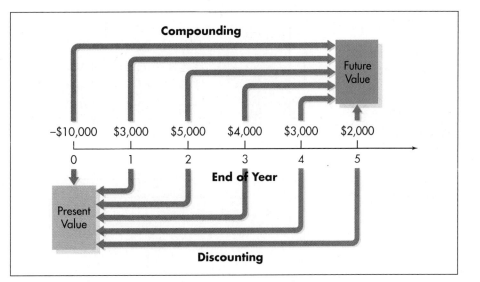

The meaning and mechanics of compounding to find future value and of discounting to find present value are covered in this chapter. Although future value and present value result in the same decisions, *financial managers—because they make decisions at time zero—tend to rely primarily on present value techniques.*

Computational Tools

Time-consuming calculations are often involved in finding future and present values. Although you should understand the concepts and mathematics underlying these calculations, the application of time value techniques can be streamlined. We focus on the use of financial tables, hand-held financial calculators, and electronic spreadsheets as aids in computation.

Financial Tables

Financial tables include various future and present value interest factors that simplify time value calculations. The values shown in these tables are easily developed from formulas, with various degrees of rounding. The tables are typically indexed by the interest rate (in columns) and the number of periods (in rows). Figure 4.3 (see page 162) shows this general layout. The interest factor at a 20 percent interest rate for 10 years would be found at the intersection of the 20% column and the 10-period row, as shown by the dark blue box. A full set of the four basic financial tables is included in Appendix A at the end of the book. These tables are described more fully later in the chapter.

Financial Calculators

Financial calculators also can be used for time value computations. Generally, *financial calculators* include numerous preprogrammed financial routines. This chapter and those that follow show the keystrokes for calculating interest factors and making other financial computations. For convenience, we use the important financial keys, labeled in a fashion consistent with most major financial calculators.

FIGURE 4.3
Financial Tables
Layout and use of
a financial table

	Interest Rate ↓							
Period	1%	2%	...	10%	...	**20%**	...	50%
1			...		...	⋮	...	
2			...		...	⋮	...	
3			...		...	⋮	...	
⋮	⋮	⋮	...	⋮	...	⋮	...	⋮
→ **10**	...	...	...	...	...	**X.XXX**	...	...
⋮	⋮	⋮	...	⋮	...	⋮	...	⋮
20			...		...		...	
⋮	⋮	⋮	...	⋮	...	⋮	...	⋮
50			...		...		...	

We focus primarily on the keys pictured and defined in Figure 4.4. We typically use four of the first five keys shown in the left column, along with the compute (**CPT**) key. One of the four keys represents the unknown value being calculated. (Occasionally, all five of the keys are used, with one representing the unknown value.) The keystrokes on some of the more sophisticated calculators are menu-driven: After you select the appropriate routine, the calculator prompts you to input each value; on these calculators, a compute key is not needed to obtain a solution. Regardless, any calculator with the basic future and present value functions can be used in lieu of financial tables. See Appendix A for keystrokes for some of the more popular calculators. The keystrokes for other financial calculators are explained in the reference guides that accompany them.

Once you understand the basic underlying concepts, you probably will want to use a calculator to streamline routine financial calculations. With a little practice, you can increase both the speed and the accuracy of your financial computations. Note that because of a calculator's greater precision, slight differences are likely to exist between values calculated by using financial tables and those found with a financial calculator. Remember that *conceptual understanding of the material is the objective*. An ability to solve problems with the aid of a calculator does not necessarily reflect such an understanding, so don't just settle for answers. Work with the material until you are sure you also understand the concepts.

FIGURE 4.4
Calculator Keys
Important financial keys
on the typical calculator

Key		Description
N	—	Number of periods
I	—	Interest rate per period
PV	—	Present value
PMT	—	Amount of payment (used only for annuities)
FV	—	Future value
CPT	—	Compute key used to initiate financial calculation once all values are input

Electronic Spreadsheets

Like financial calculators, electronic spreadsheets have built-in routines that simplify time value calculations. We provide in the text a number of spreadsheet solutions that identify the cell entries for calculating time values. The value for each variable is entered in a cell in the spreadsheet, and the calculation is programmed using an equation that links the individual cells. If values of the variables are changed, the solution automatically changes as a result of the equation linking the cells. In the spreadsheet solutions in this book, the equation that determines the calculation is shown at the bottom of the spreadsheet.

It is important that you become familiar with the use of electronic spreadsheets for several reasons.

- Spreadsheets go far beyond the computational abilities of calculators. They offer a host of routines for important financial and statistical relationships. They **perform complex analyses,** for example, that evaluate the probabilities of success and the risks of failure for management decisions.

- Spreadsheets have the ability to program logical decisions. They make it possible to **automate the choice of the best option** from among two or more alternatives. We give several examples of this ability to identify the optimal selection among alternative investments and to decide what level of credit to extend to customers.

- Spreadsheets display not only the calculated values of solutions but also the input conditions on which solutions are based. The linkage between a spreadsheet's cells **makes it possible to do sensitivity analysis**—that is, to evaluate the effects of changes in conditions on the values of the solutions. Managers, after all, are seldom interested simply in determining a single value for a given set of conditions. Conditions change, and managers who are not prepared to react quickly to take advantage of changes must suffer their consequences.

- Spreadsheets **encourage teamwork.** They assemble details from different corporate divisions and consolidate them into a firm's financial statements and cash budgets. They integrate information from marketing, manufacturing, and other functional organizations to evaluate capital investments. Laptop computers provide the portability to transport these abilities and use spreadsheets wherever one might be—attending an important meeting at a firm's headquarters or visiting a distant customer or supplier.

- Spreadsheets **enhance learning.** Creating spreadsheets promotes one's understanding of a subject. Because spreadsheets are interactive, one gets an immediate response to one's entries. The interplay between computer and user becomes a game that many find both enjoyable and instructive.

- Spreadsheets **communicate as well as calculate.** Their output includes tables and charts that can be incorporated into reports. They interplay with immense databases that corporations use for directing and controlling global operations. They are the nearest thing we have to a universal business language.

The ability to use electronic spreadsheets has become a prime skill for today's managers. As the saying goes, "Get aboard the bandwagon, or get run over." The spreadsheet solutions we present in this book will help you climb up onto that bandwagon!

Basic Patterns of Cash Flow

The cash flow—both inflows and outflows—of a firm can be described by its general pattern. It can be defined as a single amount, an annuity, or a mixed stream.

Single amount: A lump-sum amount either currently held or expected at some future date. Examples include $1,000 today and $650 to be received at the end of 10 years.

Annuity: A level periodic stream of cash flow. For our purposes, we'll work primarily with *annual* cash flows. Examples include either paying out or receiving $800 at the end of each of the next 7 years.

Mixed stream: A stream of cash flow that is *not* an annuity; a stream of unequal periodic cash flows that reflect no particular pattern. Examples include the following two cash flow streams A and B.

| | Mixed cash flow stream | |
End of year	A	B
1	$ 100	−$ 50
2	800	100
3	1,200	80
4	1,200	− 60
5	1,400	
6	300	

Note that neither cash flow stream has equal, periodic cash flows and that A is a 6-year mixed stream and B is a 4-year mixed stream.

In the next three sections of this chapter, we develop the concepts and techniques for finding future and present values of single amounts, annuities, and mixed streams, respectively. Detailed demonstrations of these cash flow patterns are included.

REVIEW QUESTIONS

4–1   What is the difference between *future value* and *present value*? Which approach is generally preferred by financial managers? Why?

4–2   Define and differentiate among the three basic patterns of cash flow: (1) a single amount, (2) an annuity, and (3) a mixed stream.

LG2   4.2 | Single Amounts

Imagine that at age 25 you began making annual purchases of $2,000 of an investment that earns a guaranteed 5 percent annually. At the end of 40 years, at age 65, you would have invested a total of $80,000 (40 years × $2,000 per year). Assuming that all funds remain invested, how much would you have accumulated at the end of the fortieth year? $100,000? $150,000? $200,000? No, your $80,000 would have grown to $242,000! Why? Because the time value of money allowed your investments to generate returns that built on each other over the 40 years.

Future Value of a Single Amount

The most basic future value and present value concepts and computations concern single amounts, either present or future amounts. We begin by considering the future value of present amounts. Then we will use the underlying concepts to determine the present value of future amounts. You will see that although future value is more intuitively appealing, present value is more useful in financial decision making.

future value
The value at a given future date of a present amount placed on deposit today and earning interest at a specified rate. Found by applying *compound interest* over a specified period of time.

We often need to find the value at some future date of a given amount of money placed on deposit today. For example, if you deposit $500 today into an account that pays 5 percent annual interest, how much would you have in the account at the end of exactly 10 years? **Future value** is the value at a given future date of a present amount placed on deposit today and earning interest at a specified rate. It depends on the rate of interest earned and the length of time a given amount is left on deposit. Here we explore the future value of a single amount.

The Concept of Future Value

compound interest
Interest that is earned on a given deposit and has become part of the *principal* at the end of a specified period.

principal
The amount of money on which interest is paid.

We speak of **compound interest** to indicate that the amount of interest earned on a given deposit has become part of the principal at the end of a specified period. The term **principal** refers to the amount of money on which the interest is paid. Annual compounding is the most common type.

The *future value* of a present amount is found by applying *compound interest* over a specified period of time. Savings institutions advertise compound interest returns at a rate of x percent, or x percent interest, compounded annually, semiannually, quarterly, monthly, weekly, daily, or even continuously. The concept of future value with annual compounding can be illustrated by a simple example.

EXAMPLE If Fred Moreno places $100 in a savings account paying 8% interest compounded annually, at the end of 1 year he will have $108 in the account—the initial principal of $100 plus 8% ($8) in interest. The future value at the end of the first year is calculated by using Equation 4.1:

$$\text{Future value at end of year 1} = \$100 \times (1 + 0.08) = \$108 \tag{4.1}$$

If Fred were to leave this money in the account for another year, he would be paid interest at the rate of 8% on the new principal of $108. At the end of this second year there would be $116.64 in the account. This amount would represent the principal at the beginning of year 2 ($108) plus 8% of the $108 ($8.64) in interest. The future value at the end of the second year is calculated by using Equation 4.2:

$$\text{Future value at end of year 2} = \$108 \times (1 + 0.08) \tag{4.2}$$
$$= \$116.64$$

Substituting the expression between the equals signs in Equation 4.1 for the $108 figure in Equation 4.2 gives us Equation 4.3:

$$\text{Future value at end of year 2} = \$100 \times (1 + 0.08) \times (1 + 0.08) \qquad (4.3)$$
$$= \$100 \times (1 + 0.08)^2$$
$$= \$116.64 \qquad \blacksquare$$

The equations in the preceding example lead to a more general formula for calculating future value.

The Equation for Future Value

The basic relationship in Equation 4.3 can be generalized to find the future value after any number of periods. We use the following notation for the various inputs:

FV_n = future value at the end of period n

PV = initial principal, or present value

i = annual rate of interest paid. (*Note:* On financial calculators, **I** is typically used to represent this rate.)

n = number of periods (typically years) that the money is left on deposit

The general equation for the future value at the end of period n is

$$FV_n = PV \times (1 + i)^n \qquad (4.4)$$

A simple example will illustrate how to apply Equation 4.4.

EXAMPLE Jane Farber places $800 in a savings account paying 6% interest compounded annually. She wants to know how much money will be in the account at the end of 5 years. Substituting $PV = \$800$, $i = 0.06$, and $n = 5$ into Equation 4.4 gives the amount at the end of year 5.

$$FV_5 = \$800 \times (1 + 0.06)^5 = \$800 \times (1.338) = \$1,070.40$$

This analysis can be depicted on a time line as follows:

Time line for future value of a single amount ($800 initial principal, earning 6%, at the end of 5 years)

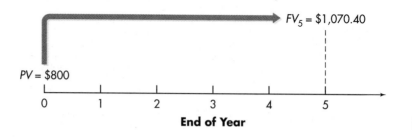

Using Computational Tools to Find Future Value

Solving the equation in the preceding example involves raising 1.06 to the fifth power. Using a future value interest table, a financial calculator, or an electronic spreadsheet greatly simplifies the calculation. A table that provides values for $(1 + i)^n$ in Equation 4.4 is included near the back of the book in Appendix Table A–1. The value in each cell of the table is called the **future value interest factor**. This factor is the multiplier used to calculate, at a specified interest rate, the future value of a present amount as of a given time. The future value interest

future value interest factor
The multiplier used to calculate, at a specified interest rate, the future value of a present amount as of a given time.

factor for an initial principal of $1 compounded at i percent for n periods is referred to as $FVIF_{i,n}$.

$$\text{Future value interest factor} = FVIF_{i,n} = (1 + i)^n \qquad (4.5)$$

By finding the intersection of the annual interest rate, i, and the appropriate periods, n, you will find the future value interest factor that is relevant to a particular problem.[1] Using $FVIF_{i,n}$ as the appropriate factor, we can rewrite the general equation for future value (Equation 4.4) as follows:

$$FV_n = PV \times (FVIF_{i,n}) \qquad (4.6)$$

This expression indicates that to find the future value at the end of period n of an initial deposit, we have merely to multiply the initial deposit, PV, by the appropriate future value interest factor.[2]

EXAMPLE   In the preceding example, Jane Farber placed $800 in her savings account at 6% interest compounded annually and wishes to find out how much will be in the account at the end of 5 years.

Table Use   The future value interest factor for an initial principal of $1 on deposit for 5 years at 6% interest compounded annually, $FVIF_{6\%,\ 5yrs}$, found in Table A–1, is 1.338. Using Equation 4.6, $800 \times 1.338 = 1,070.40$. Therefore, the future value of Jane's deposit at the end of year 5 will be $1,070.40.

Calculator Use[3]   The financial calculator can be used to calculate the future value directly.[4] First punch in $800 and depress **PV**; next punch in 5 and depress **N**; then punch in 6 and depress **I** (which is equivalent to "i" in our notation)[5]; finally, to calculate the future value, depress **CPT** and then **FV**. The future value of $1,070.58 should appear on the calculator display as shown at the left. On many calculators, this value will be preceded by a minus sign ($-1,070.58$). *If a minus sign appears on your calculator, ignore it here as well as in all other "Calculator Use" illustrations in this text.*[6]

Because the calculator is more accurate than the future value factors, which have been rounded to the nearest 0.001, a slight difference—in this case, $0.18—

Input   Function
800   PV
5   N
6   I
    CPT
    FV

Solution
1,070.58

---

1. Although we commonly deal with years rather than periods, financial tables are frequently presented in terms of periods to provide maximum flexibility.

2. Occasionally, you may want to estimate roughly how long a given sum must earn at a given annual rate to double the amount. The *Rule of 72* is used to make this estimate; dividing the annual rate of interest into 72 results in the approximate number of periods it will take to double one's money at the given rate. For example, to double one's money at a 10% annual rate of interest will take about 7.2 years ($72 \div 10 = 7.2$). Looking at Table A–1, we can see that the future value interest factor for 10% and 7 years is slightly less than 2 (1.949); this approximation therefore appears to be reasonably accurate.

3. Many calculators allow the user to set the number of payments per year. Most of these calculators are preset for monthly payments—12 payments per year. Because we work primarily with annual payments—one payment per year—it is important to *be sure that your calculator is set for one payment per year*. And although most calculators are preset to recognize that all payments occur at the end of the period, it is important to *make sure that your calculator is correctly set on the END mode*. Consult the reference guide that accompanies your calculator for instructions for setting these values.

4. To avoid including previous data in current calculations, *always clear all registers of your calculator before inputting values and making each computation.*

5. The known values *can be punched into the calculator in any order;* the order specified in this as well as other demonstrations of calculator use included in this text merely reflects convenience and personal preference.

6. The calculator differentiates inflows from outflows by preceding the outflows with a negative sign. For example, in the problem just demonstrated, the $800 present value (PV), because it was keyed as a positive number (800), is considered an inflow or deposit. Therefore, the calculated future value (FV) of $-1,070.58$ is preceded by a minus sign to show that it is the resulting outflow or withdrawal. Had the $800 present value been keyed in as a negative number (-800), the future value of $1,070.58 would have been displayed as a positive number (1,070.58). Simply stated, *the cash flows—present value (PV) and future value (FV)—will have opposite signs.*

will frequently exist between the values found by these alternative methods. Clearly, the improved accuracy and ease of calculation tend to favor the use of the calculator. (*Note:* In future examples of calculator use, we will use only a display similar to that shown on the preceding page. If you need a reminder of the procedures involved, go back and review the preceding paragraph.)

Spreadsheet Use The future value of the single amount also can be calculated as shown on the following Excel spreadsheet.

	A	B
1	**FUTURE VALUE OF A SINGLE AMOUNT**	
2	Present value	$800
3	Interest rate, pct per year compounded annually	6%
4	Number of years	5
5	Future value	$1,070.58

Entry in Cell B5 is =FV(B3,B4,0,−B2,0).
The minus sign appears before B2 because the present value is an outflow (i.e., a deposit made by Jane Farber).

A Graphical View of Future Value

Remember that we measure future value at the *end* of the given period. Figure 4.5 illustrates the relationship among various interest rates, the number of periods interest is earned, and the future value of one dollar. The figure shows that (1) the higher the interest rate, the higher the future value, and (2) the longer the period of time, the higher the future value. Note that for an interest rate of 0 percent, the future value always equals the present value ($1.00). But for any interest rate greater than zero, the future value is greater than the present value of $1.00.

Present Value of a Single Amount

It is often useful to determine the value today of a future amount of money. For example, how much would I have to deposit today into an account paying 7 percent annual interest to accumulate $3,000 at the end of 5 years? **Present value** is

present value
The current dollar value of a future amount—the amount of money that would have to be invested today at a given interest rate over a specified period to equal the future amount.

FIGURE 4.5

Future Value Relationship
Interest rates, time periods, and future value of one dollar

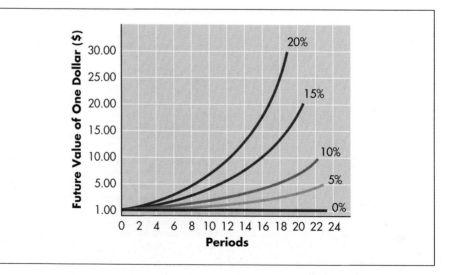

the current dollar value of a future amount—the amount of money that would have to be invested today at a given interest rate over a specified period to equal the future amount. Present value depends largely on the investment opportunities and the point in time at which the amount is to be received. This section explores the present value of a single amount.

The Concept of Present Value

discounting cash flows
The process of finding present values; the inverse of compounding interest.

The process of finding present values is often referred to as **discounting cash flows.** It is concerned with answering the following question: If I can earn i percent on my money, what is the most I would be willing to pay now for an opportunity to receive FV_n dollars n periods from today?

This process is actually the inverse of compounding interest. Instead of finding the future value of present dollars invested at a given rate, discounting determines the present value of a future amount, assuming an opportunity to earn a certain return on the money. This annual rate of return is variously referred to as the *discount rate, required return, cost of capital,* and *opportunity cost.*[7] These terms will be used interchangeably in this text.

EXAMPLE   Paul Shorter has an opportunity to receive $300 one year from now. If he can earn 6% on his investments in the normal course of events, what is the most he should pay now for this opportunity? To answer this question, Paul must determine how many dollars he would have to invest at 6% today to have $300 one year from now. Letting PV equal this unknown amount and using the same notation as in the future value discussion, we have

$$PV \times (1 + 0.06) = \$300 \tag{4.7}$$

Solving Equation 4.7 for PV gives us Equation 4.8:

$$PV = \frac{\$300}{(1 + 0.06)} \tag{4.8}$$

$$= \$283.02$$

The value today ("present value") of $300 received one year from today, given an opportunity cost of 6%, is $283.02. That is, investing $283.02 today at the 6% opportunity cost would result in $300 at the end of one year.   ■

The Equation for Present Value

The present value of a future amount can be found mathematically by solving Equation 4.4 for PV. In other words, the present value, PV, of some future amount, FV^n, to be received n periods from now, assuming an opportunity cost of i, is calculated as follows:

$$PV = \frac{FV_n}{(1 + i)^n} = FV_n \times \left[\frac{1}{(1 + i)^n} \right] \tag{4.9}$$

Note the similarity between this general equation for present value and the equation in the preceding example (Equation 4.8). Let's use this equation in an example.

---

7. The theoretical underpinning of this "required return" is introduced in Chapter 5 and further refined in subsequent chapters.

EXAMPLE

Pam Valenti wishes to find the present value of $1,700 that will be received 8 years from now. Pam's opportunity cost is 8%. Substituting $FV_8 = \$1,700$, $n = 8$, and $i = 0.08$ into Equation 4.9 yields Equation 4.10:

$$PV = \frac{\$1,700}{(1 + 0.08)^8} = \frac{\$1,700}{1.851} = \$918.42 \qquad (4.10)$$

The following time line shows this analysis.

Time line for present value of a single amount ($1,700 future amount, discounted at 8%, from the end of 8 years)

End of Year

```
0     1     2     3     4     5     6     7     8
|     |     |     |     |     |     |     |     |
                                          FV_8 = $1,700

PV = $918.42  ◄──────────────────────────────┘
```

Using Computational Tools to Find Present Value

present value interest factor

The multiplier used to calculate, at a specified discount rate, the present value of an amount to be received in a future period.

The present value calculation can be simplified by using a **present value interest factor**. This factor is the multiplier used to calculate, at a specified discount rate, the present value of an amount to be received in a future period. The present value interest factor for the present value of $1 discounted at i percent for n periods is referred to as $PVIF_{i,n}$.

$$\text{Present value interest factor} = PVIF_{i,n} = \frac{1}{(1 + i)^n} \qquad (4.11)$$

Appendix Table A–2 presents present value interest factors for $1. By letting $PVIF_{i,n}$ represent the appropriate factor, we can rewrite the general equation for present value (Equation 4.9) as follows:

$$PV = FV_n \times (PVIF_{i,n}) \qquad (4.12)$$

This expression indicates that to find the present value of an amount to be received in a future period, n, we have merely to multiply the future amount, FV_n, by the appropriate present value interest factor.

EXAMPLE

Input	Function
1700	FV
8	N
8	I
	CPT
	PV

Solution
918.46

As noted, Pam Valenti wishes to find the present value of $1,700 to be received 8 years from now, assuming an 8% opportunity cost.

Table Use   The present value interest factor for 8% and 8 years, $PVIF_{8\%,8\text{ yrs}}$, found in Table A–2, is 0.540. Using Equation 4.12, $\$1,700 \times 0.540 = \$918$. The present value of the $1,700 Pam expects to receive in 8 years is $918.

Calculator Use   Using the calculator's financial functions and the inputs shown at the left, you should find the present value to be $918.46. The value obtained with the calculator is more accurate than the values found using the equation or the table, although for the purposes of this text, these differences are insignificant.

Spreadsheet Use   The present value of the single future amount also can be calculated as shown on the following Excel spreadsheet.

	A	B
1	**PRESENT VALUE OF A SINGLE AMOUNT**	
2	Future value	$1,700
3	Interest rate, pct per year compounded annually	8%
4	Number of years	8
5	Present value	$918.46

Entry in Cell B5 is =−PV(B3,B4,0,B2).
The minus sign appears before PV to change
the present value to a positive amount.

A Graphical View of Present Value

Remember that present value calculations assume that the future values are measured at the *end* of the given period. The relationships among the factors in a present value calculation are illustrated in Figure 4.6. The figure clearly shows that, everything else being equal, (1) the higher the discount rate, the lower the present value, and (2) the longer the period of time, the lower the present value. Also note that given a discount rate of 0 percent, the present value always equals the future value ($1.00). But for any discount rate greater than zero, the present value is less than the future value of $1.00.

Comparing Present Value and Future Value

We will close this section with some important observations about present values. One is that the expression for the present value interest factor for i percent and n periods, $1/(1 + i)^n$, is the *inverse* of the future value interest factor for i percent and n periods, $(1 + i)^n$. You can confirm this very simply: Divide a present value interest factor for i percent and n periods, $PVIF_{i,n}$, given in Table A–2, into 1.0, and compare the resulting value to the future value interest factor given in Table A–1 for i percent and n periods, $FVIF_{i,n}$. The two values should be equivalent.

FIGURE 4.6

Present Value Relationship
Discount rates, time periods, and present value of one dollar

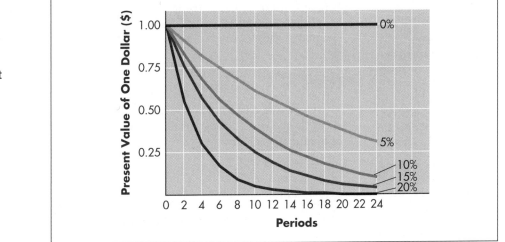

Second, because of the relationship between present value interest factors and future value interest factors, we can find the present value interest factors given a table of future value interest factors, and vice versa. For example, the future value interest factor (from Table A–1) for 10 percent and 5 periods is 1.611. Dividing this value into 1.0 yields 0.621, which is the present value interest factor (given in Table A–2) for 10 percent and 5 periods.

REVIEW QUESTIONS

4–3   How is the *compounding process* related to the payment of interest on savings? What is the general equation for future value?

4–4   What effect would a *decrease* in the interest rate have on the future value of a deposit? What effect would an *increase* in the holding period have on future value?

4–5   What is meant by "the present value of a future amount"? What is the general equation for present value?

4–6   What effect does *increasing* the required return have on the present value of a future amount? Why?

4–7   How are present value and future value calculations related?

LG3 4.3 | Annuities

annuity
A stream of equal periodic cash flows, over a specified time period. These cash flows can be *inflows* of returns earned on investments or *outflows* of funds invested to earn future returns.

ordinary annuity
An annuity for which the cash flow occurs at the *end* of each period.

annuity due
An annuity for which the cash flow occurs at the *beginning* of each period.

How much will you have at the end of 5 years if your employer withholds and invests $1,000 of your year-end bonus at the end of *each* of the next 5 years, guaranteeing you a 9 percent annual rate of return? How much would you pay today, given that you can earn 7 percent on low-risk investments, to receive a guaranteed $3,000 at the end of *each* of the next 20 years? To answer these questions, you need to understand the application of the time value of money to *annuities*.

An **annuity** is a stream of equal periodic cash flows, over a specified time period. These cash flows are usually annual but can occur at other intervals, such as monthly (rent, car payments). The cash flows in an annuity can be *inflows* (the $3,000 received at the end of each of the next 20 years) or *outflows* (the $1,000 invested at the end of each of the next 5 years).

Types of Annuities

There are two basic types of annuities. For an **ordinary annuity,** the cash flow occurs at the *end* of each period. For an **annuity due,,** the cash flow occurs at the *beginning* of each period.

EXAMPLE   Fran Abrams is choosing which of two annuities to receive. Both are 5-year, $1,000 annuities; annuity A is an ordinary annuity, and annuity B is an annuity due. To better understand the difference between these annuities, she has listed their cash flows in Table 4.1. Note that the amount of each annuity totals $5,000. The two annuities differ in the timing of their cash flows: The cash flows are received sooner with the annuity due than with the ordinary annuity. ■

	TABLE 4.1	Comparison of Ordinary Annuity and Annuity Due Cash Flows ($1,000, 5 Years)	

	Annual cash flows	
End of year[a]	Annuity A (*ordinary*)	Annuity B (*annuity due*)
0	$ 0	$1,000
1	1,000	1,000
2	1,000	1,000
3	1,000	1,000
4	1,000	1,000
5	1,000	0
Totals	$5,000	$5,000

[a]The ends of years 0, 1, 2, 3, and 4 are equivalent to the beginnings of years 1, 2, 3, 4, and 5, respectively.

Although the cash flows of both annuities in Table 4.1 total $5,000, the annuity due would have a higher future value than the ordinary annuity, because each of its five annual cash flows can earn interest for one year more than each of the ordinary annuity's cash flows. In general, as will be demonstrated later in this chapter, *both the future value and the present value of an annuity due are always greater than the future value and the present value, respectively, of an otherwise identical ordinary annuity.*

Because ordinary annuities are more frequently used in finance, *unless otherwise specified, the term* annuity *is intended throughout this book to refer to ordinary annuities.*

Finding the Future Value of an Ordinary Annuity

The calculations required to find the future value of an ordinary annuity are illustrated in the following example.

EXAMPLE   Fran Abrams wishes to determine how much money she will have at the end of 5 years if she chooses annuity A, the ordinary annuity. It represents deposits of $1,000 annually, at the *end of each* of the next 5 years, into a savings account paying 7% annual interest. This situation is depicted on the following time line:

Time line for future value of an ordinary annuity ($1,000 end-of-year deposit, earning 7%, at the end of 5 years)

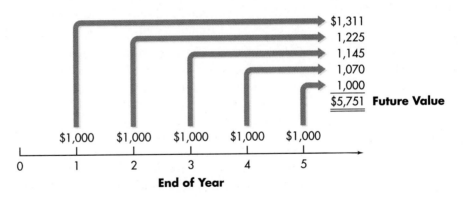

As the figure shows, at the end of year 5, Fran will have $5,751 in her account. Note that because the deposits are made at the end of the year, the first deposit will earn interest for 4 years, the second for 3 years, and so on. ■

Using Computational Tools to Find the Future Value of an Ordinary Annuity

Annuity calculations can be simplified by using an interest table, a financial calculator, or an electronic spreadsheet. A table for the future value of a $1 *ordinary annuity* is given in Appendix Table A–3. The factors in the table are derived by summing the future value interest factors for the appropriate number of years. For example, the factor for the annuity in the preceding example is the sum of the factors for the five years (years 4 through 0): $1.311 + 1.225 + 1.145 + 1.070 + 1.000 = 5.751$. Because the deposits occur at the end of each year, they will earn interest from the end of the year in which each occurs to the end of year 5. Therefore, the first deposit earns interest for 4 years (end of year 1 through end of year 5), and the last deposit earns interest for zero years. The future value interest factor for zero years at any interest rate, $FVIF_{i,0}$, is 1.000, as we have noted. The formula for the **future value interest factor for an ordinary annuity** when interest is compounded annually at i percent for n periods, $FVIFA_{i,n}$, is[8]

future value interest factor for an ordinary annuity The multiplier used to calculate the future value of an *ordinary annuity* at a specified interest rate over a given period of time.

$$FVIFA_{i,n} = \sum_{t=1}^{n} (1 + i)^{t-1} \qquad (4.13)$$

This factor is the multiplier used to calculate the future value of an *ordinary annuity* at a specified interest rate over a given period of time.

Using FVA_n for the future value of an n-year annuity, PMT for the amount to be deposited annually at the *end* of each year, and $FVIFA_{i,n}$ for the appropriate *future value interest factor for a one-dollar ordinary annuity compounded at i percent for* n *years,* we can express the relationship among these variables alternatively as

$$FVA_n = PMT \times (FVIFA_{i,n}) \qquad (4.14)$$

The following example illustrates this calculation using a table, a calculator, and a spreadsheet.

EXAMPLE

Input	Function
1000	PMT
5	N
7	I
	CPT
	FV
Solution	
5,750.74	

As noted earlier, Fran Abrams wishes to find the future value (FVA_n) at the end of 5 years (n) of an annual *end-of-year deposit* of $1,000 ($PMT$) into an account paying 7% annual interest (i) during the next 5 years.

Table Use   The future value interest factor for an ordinary 5-year annuity at 7% ($FVIFA_{7\%,5yrs}$), found in Table A–3, is 5.751. Using Equation 4.14, the $1,000 deposit $\times 5.751$ results in a future value for the annuity of $5,751.

Calculator Use   Using the calculator inputs shown at the left, you will find the future value of the ordinary annuity to be $5,750.74, a slightly more precise answer than that found using the table.

---

8. A mathematical expression that can be applied to calculate the future value interest factor for an ordinary annuity more efficiently is

$$FVIFA_{i,n} = \frac{1}{i} \times [(1 + i)^n - 1] \qquad (4.13a)$$

The use of this expression is especially attractive in the absence of the appropriate financial tables and of any financial calculator or electronic spreadsheet.

Spreadsheet Use   The future value of the ordinary annuity also can be calculated as shown on the following Excel spreadsheet.

	A	B
1	**FUTURE VALUE OF AN ORDINARY ANNUITY**	
2	Annual payment	$1,000
3	Annual rate of interest, compounded annually	7%
4	Number of years	5
5	Future value of an ordinary annuity	$5,750.74

Entry in Cell B5 is =FV(B3,B4,–B2)
The minus sign appears before B2 because
the annual payment is a cash outflow.

Finding the Present Value of an Ordinary Annuity

Quite often in finance, there is a need to find the present value of a *stream* of cash flows to be received in future periods. An annuity is, of course, a stream of equal periodic cash flows. (We'll explore the case of mixed streams of cash flows in a later section.) The method for finding the present value of an ordinary annuity is similar to the method just discussed. There are long and short methods for making this calculation.

EXAMPLE   Braden Company, a small producer of plastic toys, wants to determine the most it should pay to purchase a particular ordinary annuity. The annuity consists of cash flows of $700 at the end of each year for 5 years. The firm requires the annuity to provide a minimum return of 8%. This situation is depicted on the following time line:

Time line for present value of an ordinary annuity ($700 end-of-year cash flows, discounted at 8%, over 5 years)

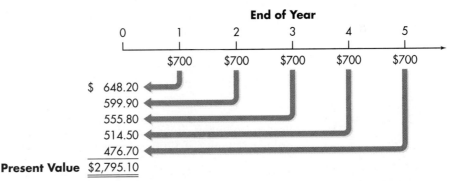

Table 4.2 (see page 176) shows the long method for finding the present value of the annuity. This method involves finding the present value of each payment and summing them. This procedure yields a present value of $2,795.10.

Using Computational Tools to Find the Present Value of an Ordinary Annuity

Annuity calculations can be simplified by using an interest table for the present value of an annuity, a financial calculator, or an electronic spreadsheet. The values for the present value of a $1 ordinary annuity are given in Appendix Table A–4. The factors in the table are derived by summing the present value interest factors

TABLE 4.2

The Long Method for Finding the Present Value of an Ordinary Annuity

Year (n)	Cash flow (1)	$PVIF_{8\%,n}{}^{a}$ (2)	Present value [(1) × (2)] (3)
1	$700	0.926	$ 648.20
2	700	0.857	599.90
3	700	0.794	555.80
4	700	0.735	514.50
5	700	0.681	476.70
		Present value of annuity	$2,795.10

^{a}Present value interest factors at 8% are from Table A–2.

present value interest factor for an ordinary annuity
The multiplier used to calculate the present value of an *ordinary annuity* at a specified discount rate over a given period of time.

(in Table A–2) for the appropriate number of years at the given discount rate. The formula for the **present value interest factor for an ordinary annuity** with cash flows that are discounted at i percent for n periods, $PVIFA_{i,n}$, is[9]

$$PVIFA_{i,n} = \sum_{t=1}^{n} \frac{1}{(1 + i)^t} \qquad (4.15)$$

This factor is the multiplier used to calculate the present value of an *ordinary annuity* at a specified discount rate over a given period of time.

By letting PVA_n equal the present value of an n-year *ordinary annuity*, letting PMT equal the amount to be received annually at the *end* of each year, and letting $PVIFA_{i,n}$ represent the appropriate *present value interest factor for a one-dollar ordinary annuity discounted at* i *percent for* n *years*, we can express the relationship among these variables as

$$PVA_n = PMT \times (PVIFA_{i,n}) \qquad (4.16)$$

The following example illustrates this calculation using a table, a calculator, and a spreadsheet.

EXAMPLE

Braden Company, as we have noted, wants to find the present value of a 5-year ordinary annuity of $700, assuming an 8% opportunity cost.

Table Use   The present value interest factor for an ordinary annuity at 8% for 5 years ($PVIFA_{8\%,5yrs}$), found in Table A–4, is 3.993. If we use Equation 4.16, $700 annuity $\times$ 3.993 results in a present value of $2,795.10.

Calculator Use   Using the calculator's inputs shown at the left, you will find the present value of the ordinary annuity to be $2,794.90. The value obtained with the calculator is more accurate than those found using the equation or the table.

9. A mathematical expression that can be applied to calculate the present value interest factor for an ordinary annuity more efficiently is

$$PVIFA_{i,n} = \frac{1}{i} \times \left[1 - \frac{1}{(1 + i)^n} \right] \qquad (4.15a)$$

The use of this expression is especially attractive in the absence of the appropriate financial tables and of any financial calculator or an electronic spreadsheet.

Spreadsheet Use The present value of the ordinary annuity also can be calculated as shown on the following Excel spreadsheet.

	A	B
1	**PRESENT VALUE OF AN ORDINARY ANNUITY**	
2	Annual payment	$700
3	Annual rate of interest, compounded annually	8%
4	Number of years	5
5	Present value of an ordinary annuity	$2,794.90
	Entry in Cell B5 is =PV(B3,B4,–B2). The minus sign appears before B2 because the annual payment is a cash outflow.	

Finding the Future Value of an Annuity Due

We now turn our attention to annuities due. Remember that the cash flows of an annuity due occur at the *start of the period*. A simple conversion is applied to use the future value interest factors for an ordinary annuity (in Table A–3) with annuities due. Equation 4.17 presents this conversion:

$$FVIFA_{i,n}(\text{annuity due}) = FVIFA_{i,n} \times (1 + i) \qquad (4.17)$$

This equation says that the future value interest factor for an annuity due can be found merely by multiplying the future value interest factor for an ordinary annuity at the same percent and number of periods by $(1 + i)$. Why is this adjustment necessary? Because each cash flow of an annuity due earns interest for one year more than an ordinary annuity (from the start to the end of the year). Multiplying $FVIFA_{i,n}$ by $(1 + i)$ simply adds an additional year's interest to *each* annuity cash flow. The following example demonstrates how to find the future value of an annuity due.

EXAMPLE Recall from an earlier example that Fran Abrams wanted to choose between an ordinary annuity and an annuity due, both offering similar terms except for the timing of cash flows. We calculated the future value of the ordinary annuity in the example on pages 173 and 174. We now will calculate the future value of the annuity due, using the cash flows represented by annuity B in Table 4.1 (page 173).

Table Use Substituting $i = 7\%$ and $n = 5$ years into Equation 4.17, with the aid of the appropriate interest factor from Table A–3, we get

$$FVIFA_{7\%,5\text{yrs}}(\text{annuity due}) = FVIFA_{7\%,5\text{yrs}} \times (1 + 0.07)$$
$$= 5.751 \times 1.07 = 6.154$$

Then, substituting $PMT = \$1,000$ and $FVIFA_{7\%,5\text{ yrs}}$ (annuity due) $= 6.154$ into Equation 4.14, we get a future value for the annuity due:

$$FVA_5 = \$1,000 \times 6.154 = \$6,154$$

Calculator Use Before using your calculator to find the future value of an annuity due, depending on the specific calculator, you must either switch it to BEGIN mode or use the DUE key. Then, using the inputs shown at the left, you will find the future value of the annuity due to be $6,153.29. (*Note:* Because we nearly always assume end-of-period cash flows, *be sure to switch your calculator back to END mode when you have completed your annuity-due calculations.*)

Note: Switch calculator to BEGIN mode.

Input	Function
1000	PMT
5	N
7	I
	CPT
	FV

Solution
6,153.29

Spreadsheet Use The future value of the annuity due also can be calculated as shown on the following Excel spreadsheet.

	A	B
1	**FUTURE VALUE OF AN ANNUITY DUE**	
2	Annual payment	$1,000
3	Annual rate of interest, compounded annually	7%
4	Number of years	5
5	Future value of an annuity due	$6,153.29
	Entry in Cell B5 is =FV(B3,B4,–B2,0,1). The minus sign appears before B2 because the annual payment is a cash outflow.	

Comparison of an Annuity Due with an Ordinary Annuity Future Value

The future value of an annuity due is *always greater* than the future value of an otherwise identical ordinary annuity. We can see this by comparing the future values at the end of year 5 of Fran Abrams's two annuities:

Ordinary annuity = $5,750.74   Annuity due = $6,153.29

Because the cash flow of the annuity due occurs at the beginning of the period rather than at the end, its future value is greater. In the example, Fran would earn about $400 more with the annuity due.

Finding the Present Value of an Annuity Due

We can also find the present value of an annuity due. This calculation can be easily performed by adjusting the ordinary annuity calculation. Because the cash flows of an annuity due occur at the beginning rather than the end of the period, to find their present value, each annuity due cash flow is discounted back one less year than for an ordinary annuity. A simple conversion can be applied to use the present value interest factors for an ordinary annuity (in Table A–4) with annuities due.

$$PVIFA_{i,n}(\text{annuity due}) = PVIFA_{i,n} \times (1 + i) \tag{4.18}$$

The equation indicates that the present value interest factor for an annuity due can be obtained by multiplying the present value interest factor for an ordinary annuity at the same percent and number of periods by $(1 + i)$. This conversion adjusts for the fact that each cash flow of an annuity due is discounted back one less year than a comparable ordinary annuity. Multiplying $PVIFA_{i,n}$ by $(1 + i)$ effectively adds back one year of interest to *each* annuity cash flow. Adding back one year of interest to each cash flow in effect reduces by 1 the number of years *each* annuity cash flow is discounted.

EXAMPLE In the earlier example of Braden Company on page 175, we found the present value of Braden's $700, 5-year ordinary annuity discounted at 8% to be about $2,795. If we now assume that Braden's $700 annual cash flow occurs at the *start* of each year and is thereby an annuity due, we can calculate its present value using a table, a calculator, or a spreadsheet.

Table Use   Substituting $i = 8\%$ and $n = 5$ years into Equation 4.18, with the aid of the appropriate interest factor from Table A–4, we get

$$PVIFA_{8\%,5\text{yrs}}(\text{annuity due}) = PVIFA_{8\%,5\text{yrs}} \times (1 + 0.08)$$
$$= 3.993 \times 1.08 = 4.312$$

Then, substituting $PMT = \$700$ and $PVIFA_{8\%,5\text{yrs}}(\text{annuity due}) = 4.312$ into Equation 4.16, we get a present value for the annuity due:

$$PVA_5 = \$700 \times 4.312 = \$3,018.40$$

Note: Switch calculator to BEGIN mode.

Input	Function
700	PMT
5	N
8	I
	CPT
	PV

Solution
3,018.49

Calculator Use   Before using your calculator to find the present value of an annuity due, depending on the specifics of your calculator, you must either switch it to BEGIN mode or use the DUE key. Then, using the inputs shown at the left, you will find the present value of the annuity due to be $3,018.49 (*Note:* Because we nearly always assume end-of-period cash flows, *be sure to switch your calculator back to END mode when you have completed your annuity-due calculations.*)

Spreadsheet Use   The present value of the annuity due also can be calculated as shown on the following Excel spreadsheet.

	A	B
1	**PRESENT VALUE OF AN ANNUITY DUE**	
2	Annual payment	$700
3	Annual rate of interest, compounded annually	8%
4	Number of years	5
5	Present value of an annuity due	$3,018.49
	Entry in Cell B5 is =PV(B3,B4,−B2,0,1). The minus sign appears before B2 because the annual payment is a cash outflow.	

Comparison of an Annuity Due with an Ordinary Annuity Present Value

The present value of an annuity due is always greater than the present value of an otherwise identical ordinary annuity. We can see this by comparing the present values of the Braden Company's two annuities:

$$\text{Ordinary annuity} = \$2,794.90 \qquad \text{Annuity due} = \$3,018.49$$

Because the cash flow of the annuity due occurs at the beginning of the period rather than at the end, its present value is greater. In the example, Braden Company would realize about $200 more in present value with the annuity due.

Finding the Present Value of a Perpetuity

perpetuity
An annuity with an infinite life, providing continual annual cash flow.

A **perpetuity** is an annuity with an infinite life—in other words, an annuity that never stops providing its holder with a cash flow at the end of each year (for example, the right to receive $500 at the end of each year forever).

It is sometimes necessary to find the present value of a perpetuity. The present value interest factor for a perpetuity discounted at the rate i is

$$PVIFA_{i,\infty} = \frac{1}{i} \qquad (4.19)$$

As the equation shows, the appropriate factor, $PVIFA_{i,\infty}$, is found simply by dividing the discount rate, i (stated as a decimal), into 1. The validity of this method can be seen by looking at the factors in Table A–4 for 8, 10, 20, and 40 percent: As the number of periods (typically years) approaches 50, these factors approach the values calculated using Equation 4.19: $1 \div 0.08 = 12.50$; $1 \div 0.10 = 10.00$; $1 \div 0.20 = 5.00$; and $1 \div 0.40 = 2.50$.

EXAMPLE   Ross Clark wishes to endow a chair in finance at his alma mater. The university indicated that it requires $200,000 per year to support the chair, and the endowment would earn 10% per year. To determine the amount Ross must give the university to fund the chair, we must determine the present value of a $200,000 perpetuity discounted at 10%. The appropriate present value interest factor can be found by dividing 1 by 0.10, as noted in Equation 4.19. Substituting the resulting factor, $PVIFA_{10\%,\infty} = 10$, and the amount of the perpetuity, $PMT = \$200,000$, into Equation 4.16 results in a present value of $2,000,000 for the perpetuity. In other words, to generate $200,000 every year for an indefinite period requires $2,000,000 today if Ross Clark's alma mater can earn 10% on its investments. If the university earns 10% interest annually on the $2,000,000, it can withdraw $200,000 per year indefinitely without touching the initial $2,000,000, which would never be drawn upon.   ∎

REVIEW QUESTIONS

4–8   What is the difference between an *ordinary annuity* and an *annuity due?* Which always has greater future value and present value for identical annuities and interest rates? Why?

4–9   What are the most efficient ways to calculate the present value of an ordinary annuity? What is the relationship between the *PVIF* and *PVIFA* interest factors given in Tables A–2 and A–4, respectively?

4–10   How can the future value interest factors for an ordinary annuity be modified to find the future value of an annuity due?

4–11   How can the present value interest factors for an ordinary annuity be modified to find the present value of an annuity due?

4–12   What is a *perpetuity?* How can the present value interest factor for such a stream of cash flows be determined?

4.4 | Mixed Streams

mixed stream
A stream of unequal periodic cash flows that reflect no particular pattern.

Two basic types of cash flow streams are possible: the annuity and the mixed stream. Whereas an *annuity* is a pattern of equal periodic cash flows, a **mixed stream** is a stream of unequal periodic cash flows that reflect no particular pattern. Financial managers frequently need to evaluate opportunities that are expected to provide mixed streams of cash flows. Here we consider both the future value and the present value of mixed streams.

Future Value of a Mixed Stream

Determining the future value of a mixed stream of cash flows is straightforward. We determine the future value of each cash flow at the specified future date and then add all the individual future values to find the total future value.

EXAMPLE   Shrell Industries, a cabinet manufacturer, expects to receive the following mixed stream of cash flows over the next 5 years from one of its small customers.

End of year	Cash flow
1	$11,500
2	14,000
3	12,900
4	16,000
5	18,000

If Shrell expects to earn 8% on its investments, how much will it accumulate by the end of year 5 if it immediately invests these cash flows when they are received? This situation is depicted on the following time line:

Time line for future value of a mixed stream (end-of-year cash flows, compounded at 8% to the end of year 5)

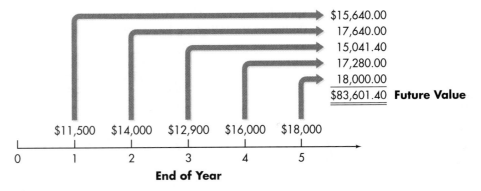

Table Use   To solve this problem, we determine the future value of each cash flow compounded at 8% for the appropriate number of years. Note that the first cash flow of $11,500, received at the end of year 1, will earn interest for 4 years (end of year 1 through end of year 5); the second cash flow of $14,000, received at the end of year 2, will earn interest for 3 years (end of year 2 through end of year 5); and so on. The sum of the individual end-of-year-5 future values is the future value of the mixed cash flow stream. The future value interest factors required are those shown in Table A–1. Table 4.3 (see page 182) presents the calculations needed to find the future value of the cash flow stream, which turns out to be $83,601.40.

Calculator Use   You can use your calculator to find the future value of each individual cash flow, as demonstrated earlier (pages 167 and 168), and then sum the future values, to get the future value of the stream. Unfortunately, unless you can program your calculator, most calculators lack a function that would allow you to input *all of the cash flows*, specify the interest rate, and directly calculate the future value of the entire cash flow stream. Had you used your calculator to find

Calculator Use You can use a calculator to find the present value of each individual cash flow, as demonstrated earlier (page 170), and then sum the present values, to get the present value of the stream. However, most financial calculators have a function that allows you to punch in *all cash flows*, specify the discount rate, and then directly calculate the present value of the entire cash flow stream. Because calculators provide solutions more precise than those based on rounded table factors, the present value of Frey Company's cash flow stream found using a calculator is $1,904.76, which is close to the $1,904.60 value calculated before.

Spreadsheet Use The present value of the mixed stream of future cash flows also can be calculated as shown on the following Excel spreadsheet.

	A	B
1	PRESENT VALUE OF A MIXED STREAM OF CASH FLOWS	
2	Interest Rate, pct/year	9%
3	Year	Year-End Cash Flow
4	1	$400
5	2	$800
6	3	$500
7	4	$400
8	5	$300
9	Present value	$1,904.76
	Entry in Cell B9 is =NPV(B2,B4:B8).	

Paying about $1,905 would provide exactly a 9% return. Frey should pay no more than that amount for the opportunity to receive these cash flows. ∎

REVIEW QUESTION

4–13 How is the future value of a mixed stream of cash flows calculated? How is the present value of a mixed stream of cash flows calculated?

LG5 4.5 | # Compounding Interest More Frequently Than Annually

Interest is often compounded more frequently than once a year. Savings institutions compound interest semiannually, quarterly, monthly, weekly, daily, or even continuously. This section discusses various issues and techniques related to these more frequent compounding intervals.

Semiannual Compounding

semiannual compounding
Compounding of interest over two periods within the year.

Semiannual compounding of interest involves two compounding periods within the year. Instead of the stated interest rate being paid once a year, one-half of the stated interest rate is paid twice a year.

TABLE 4.5

The Future Value from Investing $100 at 8% Interest Compounded Semiannually Over 24 Months (2 Years)

Period	Beginning principal (1)	Future value interest factor (2)	Future value at end of period [(1) × (2)] (3)
6 months	$100.00	1.04	$104.00
12 months	104.00	1.04	108.16
18 months	108.16	1.04	112.49
24 months	112.49	1.04	116.99

EXAMPLE Fred Moreno has decided to invest $100 in a savings account paying 8% interest *compounded semiannually.* If he leaves his money in the account for 24 months (2 years), he will be paid 4% interest compounded over four periods, each of which is 6 months long. Table 4.5 uses interest factors to show that at the end of 12 months (1 year) with 8% semiannual compounding, Fred will have $108.16; at the end of 24 months (2 years), he will have $116.99. ∎

Quarterly Compounding

quarterly compounding
Compounding of interest over four periods within the year.

Quarterly compounding of interest involves four compounding periods within the year. One-fourth of the stated interest rate is paid four times a year.

EXAMPLE Fred Moreno has found an institution that will pay him 8% interest *compounded quarterly.* If he leaves his money in this account for 24 months (2 years), he will be paid 2% interest compounded over eight periods, each of which is 3 months long. Table 4.6 uses interest factors to show the amount Fred will have at the end of each period. At the end of 12 months (1 year), with 8% quarterly compounding, Fred will have $108.24; at the end of 24 months (2 years), he will have $117.17. ∎

TABLE 4.6

The Future Value from Investing $100 at 8% Interest Compounded Quarterly Over 24 Months (2 Years)

Period	Beginning principal (1)	Future value interest factor (2)	Future value at end of period [(1) × (2)] (3)
3 months	$100.00	1.02	$102.00
6 months	102.00	1.02	104.04
9 months	104.04	1.02	106.12
12 months	106.12	1.02	108.24
15 months	108.24	1.02	110.41
18 months	110.40	1.02	112.62
21 months	112.61	1.02	114.87
24 months	114.86	1.02	117.17

TABLE 4.7

The Future Value at the End of Years 1 and 2 from Investing $100 at 8% Interest, Given Various Compounding Periods

End of year	Compounding period		
	Annual	Semiannual	Quarterly
1	$108.00	$108.16	$108.24
2	116.64	116.99	117.17

Table 4.7 compares values for Fred Moreno's $100 at the end of years 1 and 2 given annual, semiannual, and quarterly compounding periods at the 8 percent rate. As shown, *the more frequently interest is compounded, the greater the amount of money accumulated.* This is true for *any interest rate* for *any period of time.*

A General Equation for Compounding More Frequently Than Annually

The interest-factor formula for annual compounding (Equation 4.5) can be rewritten for use when compounding takes place more frequently. If *m* equals the number of times per year interest is compounded, the interest-factor formula for annual compounding can be rewritten as

$$FVIF_{i,n} = \left(1 + \frac{i}{m}\right)^{m \times n} \tag{4.20}$$

The basic equation for future value (Equation 4.4) can now be rewritten as

$$FV_n = PV \times \left(1 + \frac{i}{m}\right)^{m \times n} \tag{4.21}$$

If *m* = 1, Equation 4.21 reduces to Equation 4.4. Thus, if interest is compounded annually (once a year), Equation 4.21 will provide the same result as Equation 4.4. The general use of Equation 4.21 can be illustrated with a simple example.

EXAMPLE   The preceding examples calculated the amount that Fred Moreno would have at the end of 2 years if he deposited $100 at 8% interest compounded semiannually and compounded quarterly. For semiannual compounding, *m* would equal 2 in Equation 4.21; for quarterly compounding, *m* would equal 4. Substituting the appropriate values for semiannual and quarterly compounding into Equation 4.21, we find that

1. *For semiannual compounding:*

$$FV_2 = \$100 \times \left(1 + \frac{0.08}{2}\right)^{2 \times 2} = \$100 \times (1 + 0.04)^4 = \$116.99$$

2. *For quarterly compounding:*

$$FV_2 = \$100 \times \left(1 + \frac{0.08}{4}\right)^{4 \times 2} = \$100 \times (1 + 0.02)^8 = \$117.17$$

These results agree with the values for FV_2 in Tables 4.5 and 4.6. ◼

If the interest were compounded monthly, weekly, or daily, m would equal 12, 52, or 365, respectively.

Using Computational Tools for Compounding More Frequently Than Annually

We can use the future value interest factors for one dollar, given in Table A–1, when interest is compounded m times each year. Instead of indexing the table for i percent and n years, as we do when interest is compounded annually, we index it for $(i \div m)$ percent and $(m \times n)$ periods. However, the table is less useful, because it includes only selected rates for a limited number of periods. Instead, a financial calculator or an electronic spreadsheet is typically required.

EXAMPLE   Fred Moreno wished to find the future value of $100 invested at 8% interest compounded both semiannually and quarterly for 2 years. The number of compounding periods m, the interest rate $(i \div m)$, and the number of periods $(m \times n)$ used in each case, along with the future value interest factor, are as follows:

Compounding period	m	Interest rate $(i \div m)$	Periods $(m \times n)$	Future value interest factor from Table A–1
Semiannual	2	8% ÷ 2 = 4%	2 × 2 = 4	1.170
Quarterly	4	8% ÷ 4 = 2%	4 × 2 = 8	1.172

Table Use   Multiplying each of the future value interest factors by the initial $100 deposit results in a value of $117.00 (1.170 × $100) for semiannual compounding and a value of $117.20 (1.172 × $100) for quarterly compounding.

Calculator Use   If the calculator were used for the semiannual compounding calculation, the number of periods would be 4 and the interest rate would be 4%. The future value of $116.99 will appear on the calculator display as shown at the top left.

For the quarterly compounding case, the number of periods would be 8 and the interest rate would be 2%. The future value of $117.17 will appear on the calculator display as shown in the second display at the left.

Spreadsheet Use   The future value of the single amount with semiannual and quarterly compounding also can be calculated as shown on the following Excel spreadsheet.

	A	B
1	**FUTURE VALUE OF A SINGLE AMOUNT WITH SEMIANNUAL AND QUARTERLY COMPOUNDING**	
2	Present value	$100
3	Interest rate, pct per year compounded semiannually	8%
4	Number of years	2
5	Future value with semiannual compounding	$116.99
6	Present value	$100
7	Interest rate, pct per year compounded quarterly	8%
8	Number of years	2
9	Future value with quarterly compounding	$117.17

Entry in Cell B5 is =FV(B3/2,B4*2,0,–B2,0).
Entry in Cell B9 is =FV(B7/4,B8*4,0,–B2,0).
The minus sign appears before B2 because the present value
is a cash outflow (i.e., a deposit made by Fred Moreno).

Comparing the calculator, table, and spreadsheet values, we can see that the calculator and spreadsheet values agree with the values in Table 4.7 but are more precise because the table factors have been rounded. ■

Continuous Compounding

continuous compounding
Compounding of interest an infinite number of times per year at intervals of microseconds.

In the extreme case, interest can be compounded continuously. **Continuous compounding** involves compounding over every microsecond—the smallest time period imaginable. In this case, m in Equation 4.20 would approach infinity. Through the use of calculus, we know that as m approaches infinity, the interest-factor equation becomes

$$FVIF_{i,n} \text{ (continuous compounding)} = e^{i \times n} \qquad (4.22)$$

where e is the exponential function,[10] which has a value of 2.7183. The future value for continuous compounding is therefore

$$FV_n \text{ (continuous compounding)} = PV \times (e^{i \times n}) \qquad (4.23)$$

EXAMPLE   To find the value at the end of 2 years ($n = 2$) of Fred Moreno's $100 deposit ($PV = \$100$) in an account paying 8% annual interest ($i = 0.08$) compounded continuously, we can substitute into Equation 4.23:

$$FV_2 \text{ (continuous compounding)} = \$100 \times e^{0.08 \times 2}$$
$$= \$100 \times 2.7183^{0.16}$$
$$= \$100 \times 1.1735 = \$117.35$$

Calculator Use   To find this value using the calculator, you need first to find the value of $e^{0.16}$ by punching in 0.16 and then pressing **2nd** and then e^x to get 1.1735. Next multiply this value by $100 to get the future value of $117.35 as shown at the left. (*Note:* On some calculators, you may not have to press **2nd** before pressing e^x.)

---

10. Most calculators have the exponential function, typically noted by e^x, built into them. The use of this key is especially helpful in calculating future value when interest is compounded continuously.

Spreadsheet Use   The future value of the single amount with continuous compounding of Fred's deposit also can be calculated as shown on the following Excel spreadsheet.

	A	B
1	**FUTURE VALUE OF A SINGLE AMOUNT WITH CONTINUOUS COMPOUNDING**	
2	Present value	$100
3	Annual rate of interest, compounded continuously	8%
4	Number of years	2
5	Future value with continuous compounding	$117.35
	Entry in Cell B5 is =B2*EXP(B3*B4).	

The future value with continuous compounding therefore equals $117.35. As expected, the continuously compounded value is larger than the future value of interest compounded semiannually ($116.99) or quarterly ($117.17). Continuous compounding results in the largest future value that would result from compounding interest more frequently than annually at a given rate over a stated period of time.

Nominal and Effective Annual Rates of Interest

Both businesses and investors need to make objective comparisons of loan costs or investment returns over different compounding periods. To put interest rates on a common basis, so as to allow comparison, we distinguish between nominal and effective annual rates. The **nominal, or stated, annual rate** is the contractual annual rate of interest charged by a lender or promised by a borrower. The **effective, or true, annual rate (EAR)** is the annual rate of interest actually paid or earned. The effective annual rate reflects the effects of compounding frequency, whereas the nominal annual rate does not.

Using the notation introduced earlier, we can calculate the effective annual rate, EAR, by substituting values for the nominal annual rate, i, and the compounding frequency, m, into Equation 4.24:

$$EAR = \left(1 + \frac{i}{m}\right)^m - 1 \tag{4.24}$$

We can apply this equation using data from preceding examples.

nominal (stated) annual rate
Contractual annual rate of interest charged by a lender or promised by a borrower.

effective (true) annual rate (EAR)
The annual rate of interest actually paid or earned.

EXAMPLE   Fred Moreno wishes to find the effective annual rate associated with an 8% nominal annual rate ($i = 0.08$) when interest is compounded (1) annually ($m = 1$); (2) semiannually ($m = 2$); and (3) quarterly ($m = 4$). Substituting these values into Equation 4.24, we get

1. *For annual compounding:*

$$EAR = \left(1 + \frac{0.08}{1}\right)^1 - 1 = (1 + 0.08)^1 - 1 = 1 + 0.08 - 1 = 0.08 = 8\%$$

Spreadsheet Use   The annual payment to repay the loan also can be calculated as shown on the first Excel spreadsheet. The amortization schedule allocating each loan payment to interest and principal can be calculated precisely as shown on the second spreadsheet.

	A	B
1	**ANNUAL PAYMENT TO REPAY A LOAN**	
2	Loan principal (present value)	$6,000
3	Annual rate of interest	10%
4	Number of years	4
5	Annual payment	$1,892.82

Entry in Cell B5 is =–PMT(B3,B4,B2).
The minus sign appears before PMT because
the annual payments are cash outflows.

	A	B	C	D	E
1	**LOAN AMORTIZATION SCHEDULE**				
2		Data: Loan principal		$6,000	
3		Annual rate of interest		10%	
4		Number of years		4	
5		Annual Payments			
6	Year	Total	To Interest	To Principal	Year-End Principal
7	0				$ 6,000.00
8	1	$1,892.82	$600.00	$1,292.82	4,707.18
9	2	$1,892.82	$470.72	$1,422.11	3,285.07
10	3	$1,892.82	$328.51	$1,564.32	1,720.75
11	4	$1,892.82	$172.07	$1,720.75	0.00

Key Cell Entries
Cell B8: =–PMT(D3,D4,D2), copy to B9:B11
Cell C8: =–CUMIPMT(D3,D4,D2,A8,A8,0), copy to C9:C11
Cell D8: =–CUMPRINC(D3,D4,D2,A8,A8,0), copy to D9:D11
Cell E8: =E7–D8, copy to E9:E11
The minus signs appear before the entries in Cells B8, C8, and D8
because these are cash outflows.

TABLE 4.8

Loan Amortization Schedule
($6,000 Principal, 10% Interest, 4-Year Repayment Period)

End of year	Beginning-of-year principal (1)	Loan payment (2)	Payments		End-of-year principal [(1) − (4)] (5)
			Interest [0.10 × (1)] (3)	Principal [(2) − (3)] (4)	
1	$6,000.00	$1,892.74	$600.00	$1,292.74	$4,707.26
2	4,707.26	1,892.74	470.73	1,422.01	3,285.25
3	3,285.25	1,892.74	328.53	1,564.21	1,721.04
4	1,721.04	1,892.74	172.10	1,720.64	—[a]

[a]Because of rounding, a slight difference ($0.40) exists between the beginning-of-year-4 principal (in column 1) and the year-4 principal payment (in column 4).

In Practice FOCUS ON PRACTICE

REFINANCE WHEN IT IS IN YOUR BEST INTEREST

Beginning in 2001, falling interest rates encouraged millions of homeowners to refinance their mortgages. For many years, the 30-year, fixed-rate mortgage was the traditional choice when buying a home. In recent years, however, more homeowners have chosen fixed-rate mortgages with a 15-year term when purchasing a new home or refinancing their current residence. They were often pleasantly surprised to discover that they could pay off the loan in half the time with a monthly payment that is only about 38 percent higher. Not only will they own the home free and clear sooner with this scheme, but they also pay considerably less interest over the life of the loan.

Assume you need a $200,000 mortgage and can borrow at fixed rates. The shorter loan would carry a lower rate (because it presents less risk for the lender). The accompanying table shows how the two mortgages compare: The extra $451 per month, or total of $81,180 during the life of the 15-year loan, saves $212,954 in interest and principal payments over the remaining 15 years of the 30-year loan, for net savings of $131,774!

Why doesn't everyone take out a shorter mortgage? Many homeowners either can't afford the higher monthly payment or would rather have the extra spending money now. Others hope to do even better by investing the difference themselves. Suppose you invested $451 each month in a mutual fund that offers an average annual return of 7 percent. At the end of 15 years, your cumulative $81,180 investment would have grown to $142,950, or $61,770 more than you had contributed! Of course, many people lack the self-discipline needed to save rather than spend that money. For them, the 15-year mortgage represents a way to discipline themselves to save.

■ *Why does a dollar-for-dollar comparison of mortgage interest savings fail to give a complete picture when comparing mortgages? (Hint: Consider the time value of money and taxes.)*

Term	Rate	Monthly principal and interest	Total interest paid over the term of the loan
15 years	5.500%	$1,634.17	$ 94,150
30 years	5.875%	$1,183.08	$225,907

For discussion of the effect of shorter loan periods on home mortgage payments, see the *In Practice* box above.

Finding Interest or Growth Rates

It is often necessary to calculate the compound annual interest or *growth rate* (that is, the annual rate of change in values) of a series of cash flows. Examples include finding the interest rate on a loan, the rate of growth in sales, and the rate of growth in earnings. In doing this, we can use either future value or present value interest factors. The use of present value interest factors is described in this section. The simplest situation is one in which a person wishes to find the rate of interest or growth in a *series of cash flows.*[12]

---

12. Because the calculations required for finding interest rates and growth rates, given the series of cash flows, are the same, this section refers to the calculations as those required to find interest *or* growth rates.

EXAMPLE

Ray Noble wishes to find the rate of interest or growth reflected in the stream of cash flows he received from a real estate investment over the period 2002 through 2006. The following table lists those cash flows:

Year	Cash flow
2006	$1,520
2005	1,440
2004	1,370
2003	1,300
2002	1,250

By using the first year (2002) as a base year, we see that interest has been earned (or growth experienced) for 4 years.

Table Use   The first step in finding the interest or growth rate is to divide the amount received in the earliest year (PV) by the amount received in the latest year (FV_n). Looking back at Equation 4.12, we see that this results in the present value interest factor for a *single amount* for 4 years, $PVIF_{i,4yrs}$, which is 0.822 ($1,250 ÷ $1,520). The interest rate in Table A–2 associated with the factor closest to 0.822 for 4 years is the interest or growth rate of Ray's cash flows. In the row for year 4 in Table A–2, the factor for 5 percent is 0.823—almost exactly the 0.822 value. Therefore, the interest or growth rate of the given cash flows is approximately (to the nearest whole percent) 5%.[13]

Input	Function
1250	PV
−1520	FV
4	N
	CPT
	I

Solution
5.01

Calculator Use   Using the calculator, we treat the earliest value as a present value, PV, and the latest value as a future value, FV_n. (*Note:* Most calculators require *either* the PV or the FV value to be input as a negative number to calculate an unknown interest or growth rate. That approach is used here.) Using the inputs shown at the left, you will find the interest or growth rate to be 5.01%, which is consistent with, but more precise than, the value found using Table A–2.

Spreadsheet Use   The interest or growth rate for the series of cash flows also can be calculated as shown on the following Excel spreadsheet.

	A	B
1	INTEREST OR GROWTH RATE – SERIES OF CASH FLOWS	
2	Year	Cash Flow
3	2006	$1,520
4	2005	$1,440
5	2004	$1,370
6	2003	$1,300
7	2002	$1,250
8	Annual growth rate	5.01%

Entry in Cell B8 is =RATE((A3–A7),0,B7,B3,0). The expression A3–A7 in the entry calculates the number of years of growth. The minus sign appears before B3 because the investment in 2006 is treated as a cash outflow.

13. To obtain more precise estimates of interest or growth rates, *interpolation*—a mathematical technique for estimating unknown intermediate values—can be applied. For information on how to interpolate a more precise answer in this example, see the book's home page at www.aw-bc.com/gitman.

Another type of interest-rate problem involves finding the interest rate associated with an *annuity*, or equal-payment loan.

EXAMPLE

Jan Jacobs can borrow $2,000 to be repaid in equal annual end-of-year amounts of $514.14 for the next 5 years. She wants to find the interest rate on this loan.

Table Use   Substituting $PVA_5 = \$2,000$ and $PMT = \$514.14$ into Equation 4.27 and rearranging the equation to solve for $PVIFA_{i,5yrs}$, we get

$$PVIFA_{i,5\text{yrs}} = \frac{PVA_5}{PMT} = \frac{\$2,000}{\$514.14} = 3.890 \qquad (4.29)$$

The interest rate for 5 years associated with the annuity factor closest to 3.890 in Table A–4 is 9%. Therefore, the interest rate on the loan is approximately (to the nearest whole percent) 9%.

Calculator Use   (*Note:* Most calculators require *either* the *PMT* or the *PV* value to be input as a negative number to calculate an unknown interest rate on an equal-payment loan. That approach is used here.) Using the inputs shown at the left, you will find the interest rate to be 9.00%, which is consistent with the value found using Table A–4.

Spreadsheet Use   The interest or growth rate for the annuity also can be calculated as shown on the following Excel spreadsheet.

	A	B
1	INTEREST OR GROWTH RATE – ANNUITY	
2	Present value (loan principal)	$2,000
3	Number of years	5
4	Annual payment	$514.14
5	Annual interest rate	9.00%
	Entry in Cell B5 is =RATE(B3,B4,–B2). The minus sign appears before B2 because the loan principal is treated as a cash outflow.	

Finding an Unknown Number of Periods

Sometimes it is necessary to calculate the number of time periods needed to generate a given amount of cash flow from an initial amount. Here we briefly consider this calculation for both single amounts and annuities. This simplest case is when a person wishes to determine the number of periods, n, it will take for an initial deposit, PV, to grow to a specified future amount, FV_n, given a stated interest rate, i.

EXAMPLE

Ann Bates wishes to determine the number of years it will take for her initial $1,000 deposit, earning 8% annual interest, to grow to equal $2,500. Simply stated, at an 8% annual rate of interest, how many years, n, will it take for Ann's $1,000, PV, to grow to $2,500, FV_n?

Table Use In a manner similar to our approach for finding an unknown interest or growth rate in a series of cash flows, we begin by dividing the amount deposited in the earliest year by the amount received in the latest year. This results in the present value interest factor for 8% and n years, $PVIF_{8\%,n}$, which is 0.400 ($\$1,000 \div \$2,500$). The number of years (periods) in Table A–2 associated with the factor closest to 0.400 for an 8% interest rate is the number of years required for $\$1,000$ to grow to $\$2,500$ at 8%. In the 8% column of Table A–2, the factor for 12 years is 0.397—almost exactly the 0.400 value. Therefore, the number of years necessary for the $\$1,000$ to grow to a future value of $\$2,500$ at 8% is approximately (to the nearest year) 12.

Input	Function
1000	PV
−2500	FV
8	I
	CPT
	N

Solution
11.91

Calculator Use Using the calculator, we treat the initial value as the present value, PV, and the latest value as the future value, FV_n. (*Note:* Most calculators require *either* the PV or the FV value to be input as a negative number to calculate an unknown number of periods. That approach is used here.) Using the inputs shown at the left, we find the number of periods to be 11.91 years, which is consistent with, but more precise than, the value found using Table A–2.

Spreadsheet Use The number of years for the present value to grow to a specified future value also can be calculated as shown on the following Excel spreadsheet.

	A	B
1	YEARS FOR A PRESENT VALUE TO GROW TO A SPECIFIED FUTURE VALUE	
2	Present value (deposit)	$1,000
3	Annual rate of interest, compounded annually	8%
4	Future value	$2,500
5	Number of years	11.91
	Entry in Cell B5 is =NPER(B3,0,B2,−B4). The minus sign appears before B4 because the future value is treated as a cash outflow.	

Another type of number-of-periods problem involves finding the number of periods associated with an *annuity*. Occasionally we wish to find the unknown life, n, of an annuity, PMT, that is intended to achieve a specific objective, such as repaying a loan of a given amount, PVA_n, with a stated interest rate, i.

EXAMPLE Bill Smart can borrow $25,000 at an 11% annual interest rate; equal, annual, end-of-year payments of $4,800 are required. He wishes to determine how long it will take to fully repay the loan. In other words, he wishes to determine how many years, n, it will take to repay the $25,000, 11% loan, PVA_n, if the payments of $4,800, PMT, are made at the end of each year.

Table Use Substituting $PVA_n = \$25,000$ and $PMT = \$4,800$ into Equation 4.27 and rearranging the equation to solve $PVIFA_{11\%,n}$, we get

$$PVIFA_{11\%,n} = \frac{PVA_n}{PMT} = \frac{\$25,000}{\$4,800} = 5.208 \tag{4.30}$$

The number of periods for an 11% interest rate associated with the annuity factor closest to 5.208 in Table A–4 is 8 years. Therefore, the number of periods necessary to repay the loan fully is approximately (to the nearest year) 8 years.

Calculator Use (*Note:* Most calculators require *either* the *PV* or the *PMT* value to be input as a negative number to calculate an unknown number of periods. That approach is used here.) Using the inputs shown at the left, you will find the number of periods to be 8.15 years, which is consistent with the value found using Table A–4.

Spreadsheet Use The number of years to pay off the loan also can be calculated as shown on the following Excel spreadsheet.

	A	B
1	**YEARS TO PAY OFF A LOAN**	
2	Annual payment	$4,800
3	Annual rate of interest, compounded annually	11%
4	Present value (loan principal)	$25,000
5	Number of years to pay off the loan	8.15

Entry in Cell B5 is =NPER(B3,–B2,B4).
The minus sign appears before B2 because
the payments are treated as cash outflows.

REVIEW QUESTIONS

4–17   How can you determine the size of the equal, annual, end-of-period deposits necessary to accumulate a certain future sum at the end of a specified future period at a given annual interest rate?

4–18   Describe the procedure used to amortize a loan into a series of equal periodic payments.

4–19   Which present value interest factors would be used to find (**a**) the growth rate associated with a series of cash flows and (**b**) the interest rate associated with an equal-payment loan?

4–20   How can you determine the unknown number of periods when you know the present and future values—single amount or annuity—and the applicable rate of interest?

Summary

Focus on Value

Time value of money is an important tool that financial managers and other market participants use to assess the effects of proposed actions. Because firms have long lives and their important decisions affect their long-term cash flows, the effective application of time-value-of-money techniques is extremely important. Time value techniques enable financial managers to evaluate cash flows occurring at different times so as to combine, compare, and evaluate them and link them to the firm's **overall goal of share price maximization.** It will become clear in Chapters 6 and 7 that the application of time value techniques is a key part of the value determination process. Using them, we can measure the firm's value and evaluate the effects that various events and decisions might have on it. Clearly, an understanding of time-value-of-money techniques and an ability to apply them are needed to make intelligent value-creating decisions.

Review of Learning Goals

Key definitions, formulas, and equations for this chapter are summarized in Table 4.9.

LG1 **Discuss the role of time value in finance, the use of computational tools, and the basic patterns of cash flow.** Financial managers and investors use time-value-of-money techniques when assessing the value of expected cash flow streams. Alternatives can be assessed by either compounding to find future value or discounting to find present value. Financial managers rely primarily on present value techniques. Financial tables, financial calculators, and electronic spreadsheets can streamline the application of time value techniques. The cash flow of a firm can be described by its pattern—single amount, annuity, or mixed stream.

LG2 **Understand the concepts of future value and present value, their calculation for single amounts, and the relationship between them.** Future value (FV) relies on compound interest to measure future amounts: The initial principal or deposit in one period, along with the interest earned on it, becomes the beginning principal of the following period.

The present value (PV) of a future amount is the amount of money today that is equivalent to the given future amount, considering the return that can be earned. Present value is the inverse of future value.

LG3 **Find the future value and the present value of both an ordinary annuity and an annuity due, and find the present value of a perpetuity.** An annuity is a pattern of equal periodic cash flows. For an ordinary annuity, the cash flows occur at the end of the period. For an annuity due, cash flows occur at the beginning of the period.

The future value of an ordinary annuity can be found by using the future value interest factor for an annuity. The present value of an ordinary annuity can be found by using the present value interest factor for an annuity. A simple conversion can be applied to use the FV and PV interest factors for an ordinary annuity to find, respectively, the future value and the present value of an annuity due. The present value of a perpetuity—an infinite-lived annuity—is found using 1 divided by the discount rate to represent the present value interest factor.

LG4 **Calculate both the future value and the present value of a mixed stream of cash flows.** A mixed stream of cash flows is a stream of unequal periodic cash flows that reflect no particular pattern. The future value of a mixed stream of cash flows is the sum of the future values of each individual cash flow. Similarly, the present value of a mixed stream of cash flows is the sum of the present values of the individual cash flows.

LG5 **Understand the effect that compounding interest more frequently than annually has on future value and on the effective annual rate of interest.** Interest can be compounded at intervals ranging from annually to daily, and even continuously. The more often interest is compounded, the larger the future amount that will be accumulated, and the higher the effective, or true, annual rate (EAR).

TABLE 4.9

Summary of Key Definitions, Formulas, and Equations for Time Value of Money

Definitions of variables

e = exponential function = 2.7183
EAR = effective annual rate
FV_n = future value or amount at the end of period n
FVA_n = future value of an n-year annuity
i = annual rate of interest
m = number of times per year interest is compounded
n = number of periods—typically years—over which money earns a return
PMT = amount deposited or received annually at the end of each year
PV = initial principal or present value
PVA_n = present value of an n-year annuity
t = period number index

Interest factor formulas

Future value of a single amount with annual compounding:

$$FVIF_{i,n} = (1 + i)^n$$ [Equation 4.5; factors in Table A–1]

Present value of a single amount:

$$PVIF_{i,n} = \frac{1}{(1 + i)^n}$$ [Equation 4.11; factors in Table A–2]

Future value of an ordinary annuity:

$$FVIFA_{i,n} = \sum_{t=1}^{n} (1 + i)^{t-1}$$ [Equation 4.13; factors in Table A–3]

Present value of an ordinary annuity:

$$PVIFA_{i,n} = \sum_{t=1}^{n} \frac{1}{(1 + i)^t}$$ [Equation 4.15; factors in Table A–4]

Future value of an annuity due:

$$FVIFA_{i,n} \text{ (annuity due)} = FVIFA_{i,n} \times (1 + i)$$ [Equation 4.17]

Present value of an annuity due:

$$PVIFA_{i,n} \text{ (annuity due)} = PVIFA_{i,n} \times (1 + i)$$ [Equation 4.18]

Present value of a perpetuity:

$$PVIFA_{i,\infty} = \frac{1}{i}$$ [Equation 4.19]

Future value with compounding more frequently than annually:

$$FVIF_{i,n} = \left(1 + \frac{i}{m}\right)^{m \times n}$$ [Equation 4.20]

For continuous compounding, $m = \infty$:

$$FVIF_{i,n} \text{ (continuous compounding)} = e^{i \times n}$$ [Equation 4.22]

To find the effective annual rate:

$$EAR = \left(1 + \frac{i}{m}\right)^m - 1$$ [Equation 4.24]

Basic equations

Future value (single amount):	$FV_n = PV \times (FVIF_{i,n})$	[Equation 4.6]
Present value (single amount):	$PV = FV_n \times (PVIF_{i,n})$	[Equation 4.12]
Future value (annuity):	$FVA_n = PMT \times (FVIFA_{i,n})$	[Equation 4.14]
Present value (annuity):	$PVA_n = PMT \times (PVIFA_{i,n})$	[Equation 4.16]

The annual percentage rate (APR)—a nominal annual rate—is quoted on credit cards and loans. The annual percentage yield (APY)—an effective annual rate—is quoted on savings products.

LG6 Describe the procedures involved in (1) determining deposits needed to accumulate a future sum, (2) loan amortization, (3) finding interest or growth rates, and (4) finding an unknown number of periods. (1) The periodic deposit to accumulate a given future sum can be found by solving the equation for the future value of an annuity for the annual payment. (2) A loan can be amortized into equal periodic payments by solving the equation for the present value of an annuity for the periodic payment. (3) Interest or growth rates can be estimated by finding the unknown interest rate in the equation for the present value of a single amount or an annuity. (4) An unknown number of periods can be estimated by finding the unknown number of periods in the equation for the present value of a single amount or an annuity.

Self-Test Problems (Solutions in Appendix B)

LG2 LG5   **ST4–1 Future values for various compounding frequencies**   Delia Martin has $10,000 that she can deposit in any of three savings accounts for a 3-year period. Bank A compounds interest on an annual basis, bank B compounds interest twice each year, and bank C compounds interest each quarter. All three banks have a stated annual interest rate of 4%.
a. What amount would Ms. Martin have at the end of the third year, leaving all interest paid on deposit, in each bank?
b. What *effective annual rate* (*EAR*) would she earn in each of the banks?
c. On the basis of your findings in parts **a** and **b**, which bank should Ms. Martin deal with? Why?
d. If a fourth bank (bank D), also with a 4% stated interest rate, compounds interest continuously, how much would Ms. Martin have at the end of the third year? Does this alternative change your recommendation in part **c**? Explain why or why not.

LG3   **ST4–2 Future values of annuities**   Ramesh Abdul wishes to choose the better of two equally costly cash flow streams: annuity X and annuity Y. X is an *annuity due* with a cash inflow of $9,000 for each of 6 years. Y is an *ordinary annuity* with a cash inflow of $10,000 for each of 6 years. Assume that Ramesh can earn 15% on his investments.
a. On a purely subjective basis, which annuity do you think is more attractive? Why?
b. Find the future value at the end of year 6, FVA_6, for both annuity X and annuity Y.
c. Use your finding in part **b** to indicate which annuity is more attractive. Why? Compare your finding to your subjective response in part **a**.

LG2 LG3 LG4   **ST4–3 Present values of single amounts and streams**   You have a choice of accepting either of two 5-year cash flow streams or single amounts. One cash flow stream is an ordinary annuity, and the other is a mixed stream. You may accept alternative A or B—either as a cash flow stream or as a single amount. Given the cash flow stream and single amounts associated with each (see the following table), and assuming a 9% opportunity cost, which alternative (A or B) and in which form (cash flow stream or single amount) would you prefer?

	Cash flow stream	
End of year	Alternative A	Alternative B
1	$700	$1,100
2	700	900
3	700	700
4	700	500
5	700	300
	Single amount	
At time zero	$2,825	$2,800

LG6

ST4–4   Deposits needed to accumulate a future sum   Judi Janson wishes to accumulate $8,000 by the end of 5 years by making equal, annual, end-of-year deposits over the next 5 years. If Judi can earn 7% on her investments, how much must she deposit at the *end of each year* to meet this goal?

Warm-Up Exercises

LG2

E4–1   Assume a firm makes a $2,500 deposit into its money market account. If this account is currently paying 0.7%, (yes, that's right, less than 1%!), what will the account balance be after 1 year?

LG2 **LG5**

E4–2   If Bob and Judy combine their savings of $1,260 and $975, respectively, and deposit this amount into an account that pays 2% annual interest, compounded monthly, what will the account balance be after 4 years?

LG3

E4–3   Gabrielle just won $2.5 million in the state lottery. She is given the option of receiving a total of $1.3 million now or she can elect to be paid $100,000 at the end of each of the next 25 years. If Gabrielle can earn 5% annually on her investments, from a strict economic point of view which option should she take?

LG4

E4–4   Your firm has the option of making an investment in new software that will cost $130,000 today and is estimated to provide the savings shown in the following table over its 5-year life:

Year	Savings estimate
1	$35,000
2	50,000
3	45,000
4	25,000
5	15,000

Should the firm make this investment if it requires a minimum annual return of 9% on all investments?

LG5   E4–5   Joseph is a friend of yours. He has plenty of money but little financial sense. He received a gift of $12,000 for his recent graduation and is looking for a bank in which to deposit the funds. Partners' Savings Bank offers an account with an annual interest rate of 3% compounded semiannually, while Selwyn's offers an account with a 2.75% annual interest rate compounded continuously. Calculate the value of the two accounts at the end of one year and recommend to Joseph which account he should choose.

LG6   E4–6   Jack and Jill have just had their first child. If college is expected to cost $150,000 per year in 18 years, how much should the couple begin depositing annually at the end of each year to accumulate enough funds to pay the first year's tuition at the beginning of the 19th year? Assume that they can earn a 6% annual rate of return on their investment.

Problems

LG1

BASIC

P4–1   **Using a time line**   The financial manager at Starbuck Industries is considering an investment that requires an initial outlay of $25,000 and is expected to result in cash inflows of $3,000 at the end of year 1, $6,000 at the end of years 2 and 3, $10,000 at the end of year 4, $8,000 at the end of year 5, and $7,000 at the end of year 6.

a. Draw and label a time line depicting the cash flows associated with Starbuck Industries' proposed investment.

b. Use arrows to demonstrate, on the time line in part **a**, how compounding to find future value can be used to measure all cash flows at the end of year 6.

c. Use arrows to demonstrate, on the time line in part **b**, how discounting to find present value can be used to measure all cash flows at time zero.

d. Which of the approaches—future value or present value—do financial managers rely on most often for decision making? Why?

LG2

BASIC

P4–2   **Future value calculation**   *Without referring to tables or to the preprogrammed function on your financial calculator,* use the basic formula for future value along with the given interest rate, i, and the number of periods, n, to calculate the future value interest factor in each of the cases shown in the following table. Compare the calculated value to the value in Appendix Table A–1.

Case	Interest rate, i	Number of periods, n
A	12%	2
B	6	3
C	9	2
D	3	4

LG2

BASIC

P4–3   **Future value tables**   Use the future value interest factors in Appendix Table A–1 in each of the cases shown in the table on the facing page to estimate, to the nearest year, how long it would take an initial deposit, assuming no withdrawals,

a. To double.
b. To quadruple.

Case	Interest rate
A	7%
B	40
C	20
D	10

P4–4 **Future values**   For each of the cases shown in the following table, calculate the future value of the single cash flow deposited today that will be available at the end of the deposit period if the interest is compounded annually at the rate specified over the given period.

Case	Single cash flow	Interest rate	Deposit period (years)
A	$ 200	5%	20
B	4,500	8	7
C	10,000	9	10
D	25,000	10	12
E	37,000	11	5
F	40,000	12	9

P4–5 **Time value**   You have $1,500 to invest today at 7% interest compounded annually.
a. Find how much you will have accumulated in the account at the end of (1) 3 years, (2) 6 years, and (3) 9 years.
b. Use your findings in part **a** to calculate the amount of interest earned in (1) the first 3 years (years 1 to 3), (2) the second 3 years (years 4 to 6), and (3) the third 3 years (years 7 to 9).
c. Compare and contrast your findings in part **b**. Explain why the amount of interest earned increases in each succeeding 3-year period.

P4–6 **Time value**   As part of your financial planning, you wish to purchase a new car exactly 5 years from today. The car you wish to purchase costs $14,000 today, and your research indicates that its price will increase by 2% to 4% per year over the next 5 years.
a. Estimate the price of the car at the end of 5 years if inflation is (1) 2% per year and (2) 4% per year.
b. How much more expensive will the car be if the rate of inflation is 4% rather than 2%?

P4–7 **Time value**   You can deposit $10,000 into an account paying 9% annual interest either today or exactly 10 years from today. How much better off will you be at the end of 40 years if you decide to make the initial deposit today rather than 10 years from today?

P4–8   Time value   Misty needs to have $15,000 at the end of 5 years to fulfill her goal of purchasing a small sailboat. She is willing to invest the funds as a single amount today but wonders what sort of investment return she will need to earn. Use your calculator or the time value tables to figure out the approximate annually compounded rate of return needed in each of these cases:

a. Misty can invest $10,200 today.
b. Misty can invest $8,150 today.
c. Misty can invest $7,150 today.

P4–9   Single-payment loan repayment   A person borrows $200 to be repaid in 8 years with 14% annually compounded interest. The loan may be repaid at the end of any earlier year with no prepayment penalty.

a. What amount will be due if the loan is repaid at the end of year 1?
b. What is the repayment at the end of year 4?
c. What amount is due at the end of the eighth year?

P4–10   Present value calculation   *Without referring to tables or to the preprogrammed function on your financial calculator,* use the basic formula for present value, along with the given opportunity cost, *i*, and the number of periods, *n*, to calculate the present value interest factor in each of the cases shown in the accompanying table. Compare the calculated value to the table value.

Case	Opportunity cost, i	Number of periods, n
A	2%	4
B	10	2
C	5	3
D	13	2

P4–11   Present values   For each of the cases shown in the following table, calculate the present value of the cash flow, discounting at the rate given and assuming that the cash flow is received at the end of the period noted.

Case	Single cash flow	Discount rate	End of period (years)
A	$ 7,000	12%	4
B	28,000	8	20
C	10,000	14	12
D	150,000	11	6
E	45,000	20	8

P4–12   Present value concept   Answer each of the following questions.

a. What single investment made today, earning 12% annual interest, will be worth $6,000 at the end of 6 years?
b. What is the present value of $6,000 to be received at the end of 6 years if the discount rate is 12%?

    c. What is the most you would pay today for a promise to repay you $6,000 at the end of 6 years if your opportunity cost is 12%?

    d. Compare, contrast, and discuss your findings in parts **a** through **c.**

P4–13 **Time value** Jim Nance has been offered a future payment of $500 three years from today. If his opportunity cost is 7% compounded annually, what value should he place on this opportunity today? What is the most he should pay to purchase this payment today?

P4–14 **Time value** An Iowa state savings bond can be converted to $100 at maturity 6 years from purchase. If the state bonds are to be competitive with U.S. savings bonds, which pay 8% annual interest (compounded annually), at what price must the state sell its bonds? Assume no cash payments on savings bonds prior to redemption.

P4–15 **Time value and discount rates** You just won a lottery that promises to pay you $1,000,000 exactly 10 years from today. Because the $1,000,000 payment is guaranteed by the state in which you live, opportunities exist to sell the claim today for an immediate single cash payment.

    a. What is the least you will sell your claim for if you can earn the following rates of return on similar-risk investments during the 10-year period?

        (1) 6%

        (2) 9%

        (3) 12%

    b. Rework part **a** under the assumption that the $1,000,000 payment will be received in 15 rather than 10 years.

    c. On the basis of your findings in parts **a** and **b,** discuss the effect of both the size of the rate of return and the time until receipt of payment on the present value of a future sum.

P4–16 **Time value comparisons of single amounts** In exchange for a $20,000 payment today, a well-known company will allow you to choose *one* of the alternatives shown in the following table. Your opportunity cost is 11%.

Alternative	Single amount
A	$28,500 at end of 3 years
B	$54,000 at end of 9 years
C	$160,000 at end of 20 years

    a. Find the value today of each alternative.

    b. Are all the alternatives acceptable—that is, worth $20,000 today?

    c. Which alternative, if any, will you take?

P4–17 **Cash flow investment decision** Tom Alexander has an opportunity to purchase any of the investments shown in the following table. The purchase price, the amount of the single cash inflow, and its year of receipt are given for each investment. Which purchase recommendations would you make, assuming that Tom can earn 10% on his investments?

Investment	Price	Single cash inflow	Year of receipt
A	$18,000	$30,000	5
B	600	3,000	20
C	3,500	10,000	10
D	1,000	15,000	40

LG3

INTERMEDIATE

P4–18 Future value of an annuity   For each case in the accompanying table, answer the questions that follow.

Case	Amount of annuity	Interest rate	Deposit period (years)
A	$ 2,500	8%	10
B	500	12	6
C	30,000	20	5
D	11,500	9	8
E	6,000	14	30

a. Calculate the future value of the annuity assuming that it is
   (1) An ordinary annuity.
   (2) An annuity due.
b. Compare your findings in parts a(1) and a(2). All else being identical, which type of annuity—ordinary or annuity due—is preferable? Explain why.

LG3

INTERMEDIATE

P4–19 Present value of an annuity   Consider the following cases.

Case	Amount of annuity	Interest rate	Period (years)
A	$ 12,000	7%	3
B	55,000	12	15
C	700	20	9
D	140,000	5	7
E	22,500	10	5

a. Calculate the present value of the annuity assuming that it is
   (1) An ordinary due.
   (2) An annuity due.
b. Compare your findings in parts a(1) and a(2). All else being identical, which type of annuity—ordinary or annuity due—is preferable? Explain why.

LG3

CHALLENGE

P4–20 Time value—Annuities   Marian Kirk wishes to select the better of two 10-year annuities, C and D. Annuity C is an *ordinary annuity* of $2,500 per year for 10 years. Annuity D is an *annuity due* of $2,200 per year for 10 years.
a. Find the *future value* of both annuities at the end of year 10, assuming that Marian can earn (1) 10% annual interest and (2) 20% annual interest.

b. Use your findings in part **a** to indicate which annuity has the greater future value at the end of year 10 for both the (1) 10% and (2) 20% interest rates.

c. Find the *present value* of both annuities, assuming that Marian can earn (1) 10% annual interest and (2) 20% annual interest.

d. Use your findings in part **c** to indicate which annuity has the greater present value for both (1) 10% and (2) 20% interest rates.

e. Briefly compare, contrast, and explain any differences between your findings using the 10% and 20% interest rates in parts **b** and **d**.

P4–21 Retirement planning   Hal Thomas, a 25-year-old college graduate, wishes to retire at age 65. To supplement other sources of retirement income, he can deposit $2,000 each year into a tax-deferred individual retirement arrangement (IRA). The IRA will be invested to earn an annual return of 10%, which is assumed to be attainable over the next 40 years.

a. If Hal makes annual end-of-year $2,000 deposits into the IRA, how much will he have accumulated by the end of his sixty-fifth year?

b. If Hal decides to wait until age 35 to begin making annual end-of-year $2,000 deposits into the IRA, how much will he have accumulated by the end of his sixty-fifth year?

c. Using your findings in parts **a** and **b,** discuss the impact of delaying making deposits into the IRA for 10 years (age 25 to age 35) on the amount accumulated by the end of Hal's sixty-fifth year.

d. Rework parts **a, b,** and **c,** assuming that Hal makes all deposits at the beginning, rather than the end, of each year. Discuss the effect of beginning-of-year deposits on the future value accumulated by the end of Hal's sixty-fifth year.

P4–22 Value of a retirement annuity   An insurance agent is trying to sell you an immediate-retirement annuity, which for a single amount paid today will provide you with $12,000 at the end of each year for the next 25 years. You currently earn 9% on low-risk investments comparable to the retirement annuity. Ignoring taxes, what is the most you would pay for this annuity?

P4–23 Funding your retirement   You plan to retire in exactly 20 years. Your goal is to create a fund that will allow you to receive $20,000 at the end of each year for the 30 years between retirement and death (a psychic told you would die exactly 30 years after you retire). You know that you will be able to earn 11% per year during the 30-year retirement period.

a. How large a fund will you need *when you retire* in 20 years to provide the 30-year, $20,000 retirement annuity?

b. How much will you need *today* as a single amount to provide the fund calculated in part **a** if you earn only 9% per year during the 20 years preceding retirement?

c. What effect would an increase in the rate you can earn both during and prior to retirement have on the values found in parts **a** and **b**? Explain.

P4–24 Value of an annuity versus a single amount   Assume that you just won the state lottery. Your prize can be taken either in the form of $40,000 at the end of each of the next 25 years (i.e., $1,000,000 over 25 years) or as a single amount of $500,000 paid immediately.

a. If you expect to be able to earn 5% annually on your investments over the next 25 years, ignoring taxes and other considerations, which alternative should you take? Why?

b. Would your decision in part **a** change if you could earn 7% rather than 5% on your investments over the next 25 years? Why?

c. On a strictly economic basis, at approximately what earnings rate would you be indifferent between the two plans?

P4–25 **Perpetuities** Consider the data in the following table.

Perpetuity	Annual amount	Discount rate
A	$ 20,000	8%
B	100,000	10
C	3,000	6
D	60,000	5

Determine, for each of the perpetuities:
a. The appropriate present value interest factor.
b. The present value.

P4–26 **Creating an endowment** Upon completion of her introductory finance course, Marla Lee was so pleased with the amount of useful and interesting knowledge she gained that she convinced her parents, who were wealthy alumni of the university she was attending, to create an endowment. The endowment is to allow three needy students to take the introductory finance course each year in perpetuity. The guaranteed annual cost of tuition and books for the course is $600 per student. The endowment will be created by making a single payment to the university. The university expects to earn exactly 6% per year on these funds.

a. How large an initial single payment must Marla's parents make to the university to fund the endowment?

b. What amount would be needed to fund the endowment if the university could earn 9% rather than 6% per year on the funds?

P4–27 **Value of a mixed stream** For each of the mixed streams of cash flows shown in the following table, determine the future value at the end of the final year if deposits are made into an account paying annual interest of 12%, assuming that no withdrawals are made during the period and that the deposits are made:

a. At the *end* of each year.
b. At the *beginning* of each year.

	Cash flow stream		
Year	A	B	C
1	$ 900	$30,000	$1,200
2	1,000	25,000	1,200
3	1,200	20,000	1,000
4		10,000	1,900
5		5,000	

P4–28 **Value of a single amount versus a mixed stream** Gina Vitale has just contracted to sell a small parcel of land that she inherited a few years ago. The buyer is willing to pay $24,000 at the closing of the transaction or will pay the amounts shown in the following table at the *beginning* of each of the next 5 years. Because Gina doesn't really need the money today, she plans to let it accumulate in an account that earns 7% annual interest. Given her desire to buy a house at the end of 5 years after closing on the sale of the lot, she decides to choose the payment alternative—$24,000 single amount or the mixed stream of payments in the following table—that provides the higher future value at the end of 5 years. Which alternative will she choose?

Mixed stream	
Beginning of year	Cash flow
1	$ 2,000
2	4,000
3	6,000
4	8,000
5	10,000

P4–29 **Value of mixed streams** Find the present value of the streams of cash flows shown in the following table. Assume that the firm's opportunity cost is 12%.

A		B		C	
Year	Cash flow	Year	Cash flow	Year	Cash flow
1	−$2,000	1	$10,000	1–5	$10,000/yr
2	3,000	2–5	5,000/yr	6–10	8,000/yr
3	4,000	6	7,000		
4	6,000				
5	8,000				

P4–30 **Present value—Mixed streams** Consider the mixed streams of cash flows shown in the following table.

	Cash flow stream	
Year	A	B
1	$ 50,000	$ 10,000
2	40,000	20,000
3	30,000	30,000
4	20,000	40,000
5	10,000	50,000
Totals	$150,000	$150,000

a. Find the present value of each stream using a 15% discount rate.
b. Compare the calculated present values and discuss them in light of the fact that the undiscounted cash flows total $150,000 in each case.

P4–31   **Value of a mixed stream**   Harte Systems, Inc., a maker of electronic surveillance equipment, is considering selling to a well-known hardware chain the rights to market its home security system. The proposed deal calls for the hardware chain to pay Harte $30,000 and $25,000 at the end of years 1 and 2 and to make annual year-end payments of $15,000 in years 3 through 9. A final payment to Harte of $10,000 would be due at the end of year 10.

    a. Lay out the cash flows involved in the offer on a time line.

    b. If Harte applies a required rate of return of 12% to them, what is the present value of this series of payments?

    c. A second company has offered Harte an immediate one-time payment of $100,000 for the rights to market the home security system. Which offer should Harte accept?

P4–32   **Funding budget shortfalls**   As part of your personal budgeting process, you have determined that in each of the next 5 years you will have budget shortfalls. In other words, you will need the amounts shown in the following table at the end of the given year to balance your budget—that is, to make inflows equal outflows. You expect to be able to earn 8% on your investments during the next 5 years and wish to fund the budget shortfalls over the next 5 years with a single amount.

End of year	Budget shortfall
1	$ 5,000
2	4,000
3	6,000
4	10,000
5	3,000

    a. How large must the single deposit today into an account paying 8% annual interest be to provide for full coverage of the anticipated budget shortfalls?

    b. What effect would an increase in your earnings rate have on the amount calculated in part **a**? Explain.

P4–33   **Relationship between future value and present value—Mixed stream**   Using *only* the information in the accompanying table, answer the questions that follow.

Year (t)	Cash flow	Future value interest factor at 5% ($FVIF_{5\%,n}$)
1	$ 800	1.050
2	900	1.102
3	1,000	1.158
4	1,500	1.216
5	2,000	1.276

    a. Determine the *present value* of the mixed stream of cash flows using a 5% discount rate.

    b. How much would you be willing to pay for an opportunity to buy this stream, assuming that you can at best earn 5% on your investments?

c. What effect, if any, would a 7% rather than a 5% opportunity cost have on your analysis? (Explain verbally.)

P4–34 Changing compounding frequency   Using annual, semiannual, and quarterly compounding periods, for each of the following, (1) calculate the future value if $5,000 is deposited initially, and (2) determine the *effective annual rate (EAR)*.
   a. At 12% annual interest for 5 years.
   b. At 16% annual interest for 6 years.
   c. At 20% annual interest for 10 years.

P4–35 Compounding frequency, time value, and effective annual rates   For each of the cases in the following table:
   a. Calculate the future value at the end of the specified deposit period.
   b. Determine the *effective annual rate, EAR*.
   c. Compare the nominal annual rate, *i*, to the effective annual rate, EAR. What relationship exists between compounding frequency and the nominal and effective annual rates?

Case	Amount of initial deposit	Nominal annual rate, *i*	Compounding frequency, *m* (times/year)	Deposit period (years)
A	$ 2,500	6%	2	5
B	50,000	12	6	3
C	1,000	5	1	10
D	20,000	16	4	6

P4–36 Continuous compounding   For each of the cases in the following table, find the future value at the end of the deposit period, assuming that interest is compounded continuously at the given nominal annual rate.

Case	Amount of initial deposit	Nominal annual rate, *i*	Deposit period (years), *n*
A	$1,000	9%	2
B	600	10	10
C	4,000	8	7
D	2,500	12	4

P4–37 Compounding frequency and time value   You plan to invest $2,000 in an individual retirement arrangement (IRA) today at a *nominal annual rate* of 8%, which is expected to apply to all future years.
   a. How much will you have in the account at the end of 10 years if interest is compounded (1) annually? (2) Semiannually? (3) Daily (assume a 365-day year)? (4) Continuously?
   b. What is the *effective annual rate, EAR*, for each compounding period in part **a**?
   c. How much greater will your IRA balance be at the end of 10 years if interest is compounded continuously rather than annually?

c. How large must Sunrise's equal, annual, end-of-year deposits into the account be over the 12-year accumulation period to fund fully Ms. Moran's retirement annuity?

d. How much would Sunrise have to deposit annually during the accumulation period if it could earn 10% rather than 9% during the accumulation period?

e. How much would Sunrise have to deposit annually during the accumulation period if Ms. Moran's retirement annuity were a perpetuity and all other terms were the same as initially described?

Spreadsheet Exercise

At the end of 2005, Uma Corporation was considering undertaking a major long-term project in an effort to remain competitive in its industry. The production and sales departments determined the potential annual cash flow savings that could accrue to the firm if it acts soon. Specifically, they estimate that a mixed stream of future cash flow savings will occur at the end of the years 2006 through 2011. The years 2012 through 2016 will see consecutive and equal cash flow savings at the end of each year. The firm estimates that its discount rate over the first 6 years will be 7%. The expected discount rate over the years 2012 through 2016 will be 11%.

The project managers will find the project acceptable if it results in present cash flow savings of at least $860,000. The following cash flow savings data are supplied to the finance department for analysis:

End of Year	Cash Flow Savings
2006	$110,000
2007	120,000
2008	130,000
2009	150,000
2010	160,000
2011	150,000
2012	90,000
2013	90,000
2014	90,000
2015	90,000
2016	90,000

TO DO

Create a spreadsheet similar to Tables 4.2 and 4.4 (or to one that can be viewed at www.aw-bc.com/gitman), and then answer the following questions:

a. Determine the value (at the beginning of 2006) of the future cash flow savings expected to be generated by this project.

b. Based solely on the one criterion set by management, should the firm undertake this specific project? Explain.

c. What is the "interest rate risk," and how might it influence the recommendation made in part b? Explain.

Group Exercise

"Cash is king." This statement was uttered by Donald Trump at the end of the 1980s, referring to the climate for real estate investment. Most people would agree that in life, cash is, indeed, king. The management and proper valuation of cash flows is the most important factor in the survival of a business. Almost all businesses receive cash payments in spurts but must make cash payments at regular intervals. Many businesses have failed not for a lack of sales success, but rather for a lack of *timely* cash. Therefore, the timing of cash flows and implied time value are of utmost importance.

TO DO

In this assignment, you will evaluate scenarios involving your group's fictitious firm.

a. Your firm has a single copy machine for the tenth floor, and it has broken down yet again. Your firm must decide how to proceed in replacing the copier. So far, you have received two competing offers for comparable machines. Both offers are 3-year leases.

> *Option A* requires an up-front payment of $1,700 with additional annual payments of $1,200 at the beginning of years two and three. The firm is also charged one-half of 1 cent, ($0.005), for each sheet printed, payable at the end of each year.

> *Option B* has no up-front cost. Its lease payment is $1,300, payable at the beginning of the year, and the per-sheet charge is 1 cent ($0.01), payable at the end of each year.

You estimate that monthly use of the copy machine will amount to 1,500 copies. Determine an appropriate discount rate and discount the cash flows for each lease. Choose the best lease based on which lease costs less in present value terms. Be prepared to defend your choice.

b. A second option is to purchase the machine outright. In fact, after the lease expires, you are considering buying your firm's next copier.

(1) You need to obtain a minimum of two offers before buying a copy machine. Your needs include a multifunction machine capable of copying, faxing, and printing, with networking capability because all workers on the tenth floor will be sharing it. The purchase price should approximate the present value calculations from part **a.** In your search, you must consider not only the purchase price of the machine, but also the cost of any warranty/service agreement. In addition, you must adjust the current price for expected inflation. Take the price for the machine today and find out what the price will be in 3 years given a 3% compound annual inflation rate. Alternatively, you could calculate what the price would be given a 5% annual rate of decrease, as that is the observed trend over recent years.

(2) Because you want to save for this expenditure (rather than take out a loan for it), you need information about savings rates at a local bank. (Here "bank" refers to any depository institution, including those that are strictly online operations.) After getting a rate for a savings account,

calculate what amount you would have to deposit today to have the dollar value of the machine you wish to buy at the end of 3 years. If, instead, you wanted to make annual deposits at the end of each of the next 3 years, how much should you deposit? What if those three equal deposits were made at the beginning of each year?

[LG6]   c.   Your firm plans to upgrade its computer systems. The computers will be financed with a 5-year bank loan totaling $25,000. Your firm can obtain a loan at the prime rate and you are asked to provide this information to your firm's management. Obtain this information from a local bank and use that interest rate to prepare an amortization schedule for the loan.

[LG4]   d.   A recent court ruling concluded that a competitor had violated one of your patents without properly paying for its use. The court-ordered settlement provides the following annual payments to your firm:

Year	Payment
1	$150,000
2	125,000
3	100,000
4	75,000
5	50,000

Find the present value of these cash flows using a 6% discount rate.

Web Exercise

Mortgage interest rates vary daily. Over a period of time, mortgage interest rates have followed definite trends based on federal interest rate policies and economic conditions. Historical interest rate information is available on the Web.

TO DO

a.   For this Web exercise, direct your Internet browser to www.mbaa.org/, the home page of the Mortgage Bankers Association. View the current mortgage interest rates listed on the right side of the screen. Now direct your browser to the Mortgage and Market Data link at the top of the page, highlighting Interest rates. This page contains data for mortgage rates over the past decades. Study and comment on the levels of interest rates over the recent past. The Freddie Mac Average Rate for 30-Year Fixed Rate Mortgages, 1971— present (Monthly) link is a good place to start. How do interest rates recently—in the past year, for example—compare with those that prevailed during the 1970s, 1980s, and 1990s? Do you see any trends in the level of interest rates?

One way to perform this analysis would be to graph the monthly data. While this can be accomplished by hand, the use of a graphing tool such as that found in Excel would facilitate the process. Here graphing the entire series in one graph is feasible, but dividing the data into three or more graphs along decade lines should make the analysis clearer.

b. A second set of data can be found at the Federal Reserve System's Web site. Point your browser to www.federalreserve.gov/. Go to the Economic and Research Data link on the left side of the page. Next, go to the Statistics: Releases and Historical Data link at the top of the page. At this page, look at G.13 Selected Interest Rates, choosing Historical Data. Now scan about one-third of the way down the page, under U.S. Government Securities, Treasury constant maturities, 10-year, and highlight monthly frequency. (The Web address to access these data directly is www.federalreserve.gov/releases/ h15/data/m/tcm10y.txt.) This data set goes back to April 1953. (The data shown are actually yields, not interest rates. This topic will be covered in Chapter 6, but for now you can treat the yield as an interest rate.) Compare the trend in the U.S. government 10-year rates and your earlier analysis of mortgage rates. Because mortgage data went back only to 1971, begin your comparison there. Nevertheless, you should look closely at today's rates and the rates that prevailed in the late 1950s and early 1960s. Graphs are required for a complete comparison of the two series.

Remember to check the book's Web site at

www.aw-bc.com/gitman

for additional resources, including additional Web exercises.

LG1 5.1 | Risk and Return Fundamentals

To maximize share price, the financial manager must learn to assess two key determinants: risk and return.[1] Each financial decision presents certain risk and return characteristics, and the unique combination of these characteristics has an impact on share price. Risk can be viewed as it is related either to a single asset or to a **portfolio**—a collection, or group, of assets. We will look at both, beginning with the risk of a single asset. First, though, it is important to introduce some fundamental ideas about risk, return, and risk preferences.

portfolio
A collection, or group, of assets.

Risk Defined

risk
The chance of financial loss or, more formally, the *variability of returns associated with a given asset.*

In the most basic sense, **risk** is the chance of financial loss. Assets having greater chances of loss are viewed as more risky than those with lesser chances of loss. More formally, the term *risk* is used interchangeably with *uncertainty* to refer to the *variability of returns associated with a given asset.* A $1,000 government bond that guarantees its holder $5 interest after 30 days has no risk, because there is no variability associated with the return. A $1,000 investment in a firm's common stock, which over the same 30 days may earn anywhere from $0 to $10, is very risky because of the high variability of its return. The more nearly certain the return from an asset, the less variability and therefore the less risk.

Some risks directly affect both financial managers and shareholders. Table 5.1 briefly describes the common sources of risk that affect both firms and their shareholders. As you can see, business risk and financial risk are more firm-specific and therefore are of greatest interest to financial managers. Interest rate, liquidity, and market risks are more shareholder-specific and therefore are of greatest interest to stockholders. Event, exchange rate, purchasing-power, and tax risk directly affect both firms and shareholders. The *In Practice* box on page 228 focuses on another risk that affects both firms and shareholders—moral risk. A number of these risks are discussed in more detail later in this text. Clearly, both financial managers and shareholders must assess these and other risks as they make investment decisions.

Return Defined

return
The total gain or loss experienced on an investment over a given period of time; calculated by dividing the asset's cash distributions during the period, plus change in value, by its beginning-of-period investment value.

Obviously, if we are going to assess risk on the basis of variability of return, we need to be certain we know what *return* is and how to measure it. The **return** is the total gain or loss experienced on an investment over a given period of time. It is commonly measured as cash distributions during the period plus the change in value, expressed as a percentage of the beginning-of-period investment value. The expression for calculating the rate of return earned on any asset over period t, k_t, is commonly defined as

$$k_t = \frac{C_t + P_t - P_{t-1}}{P_{t-1}} \tag{5.1}$$

---

1. Two important points should be recognized here: (1) Although for convenience the publicly traded corporation is being discussed, the risk and return concepts presented apply to all firms; and (2) concern centers only on the wealth of common stockholders, because they are the "residual owners" whose returns are in no way specified in advance.

TABLE 5.1

Popular Sources of Risk Affecting Financial Managers and Shareholders

Source of risk	Description
Firm-Specific Risks	
Business risk	The chance that the firm will be unable to cover its operating costs. Level is driven by the firm's revenue stability and the structure of its operating costs (fixed versus variable).
Financial risk	The chance that the firm will be unable to cover its financial obligations. Level is driven by the predictability of the firm's operating cash flows and its fixed-cost financial obligations.
Shareholder-Specific Risks	
Interest rate risk	The chance that changes in interest rates will adversely affect the value of an investment. Most investments lose value when the interest rate rises and increase in value when it falls.
Liquidity risk	The chance that an investment cannot be easily liquidated at a reasonable price. Liquidity is significantly affected by the size and depth of the market in which an investment is customarily traded.
Market risk	The chance that the value of an investment will decline because of market factors that are independent of the investment (such as economic, political, and social events). In general, the more a given investment's value responds to the market, the greater its risk; the less it responds, the smaller its risk.
Firm and Shareholder Risks	
Event risk	The chance that a totally unexpected event will have a significant effect on the value of the firm or a specific investment. These infrequent events, such as government-mandated withdrawal of a popular prescription drug, typically affect only a small group of firms or investments.
Exchange rate risk	The exposure of future expected cash flows to fluctuations in the currency exchange rate. The greater the chance of undesirable exchange rate fluctuations, the greater the risk of the cash flows and therefore the lower the value of the firm or investment.
Purchasing-power risk	The chance that changing price levels caused by inflation or deflation in the economy will adversely affect the firm's or investment's cash flows and value. Typically, firms or investments with cash flows that move with general price levels have a low purchasing-power risk, and those with cash flows that do not move with general price levels have a high purchasing-power risk.
Tax risk	The chance that unfavorable changes in tax laws will occur. Firms and investments with values that are sensitive to tax law changes are more risky.

where

k_t = actual, expected, or required rate of return[2] during period t

C_t = cash (flow) received from the asset investment in the time period $t - 1$ to t

P_t = price (value) of asset at time t

P_{t-1} = price (value) of asset at time $t - 1$

---

2. The terms *expected return* and *required return* are used interchangeably throughout this text, because in an efficient market (discussed later) they would be expected to be equal. The actual return is an *ex post* value, whereas expected and required returns are *ex ante* values. Therefore, the actual return may be greater than, equal to, or less than the expected/required return.

WHAT ABOUT MORAL RISK?

The poster boy for "moral risk," exemplifying the devastating effects of unethical behavior for a company's investors, has to be Nick Leeson. This 28-year-old trader violated his bank's investing rules while secretly placing huge bets on the direction of the Japanese stock market. When those bets proved to be wrong, the $1.24 billion losses resulted in the demise of the centuries-old Barings Bank. More than any other single episode in world financial history, Leeson's misdeeds proved the importance of character in the financial industry.

Forty-one percent of surveyed chief financial officers admit ethical problems in their organizations, and 48 percent of surveyed employees admit to engaging in unethical practices such as cheating on expense accounts or forging signatures. (The real numbers may actually be higher, as self-reported percentages are often low.) One of the main reasons cited for accounting fraud uncovered in recent years was the pressure to "hit the numbers" expected by some security analysts on Wall Street. In a 2004 survey, 47 percent of CFOs said that they felt pressure from CEOs to use aggressive accounting to "make the numbers work,"

according to *CFO Magazine*. The good news was that the same *CFO* survey found the CFOs standing up to CEO pressure and improving ethical standards in their departments, thanks to the 2002 Sarbanes-Oxley Act.

What can be done to minimize moral risk? A first step is to build awareness through a code of ethics. Almost all *Fortune* 500 companies and about half of all companies have an ethics code spelling out general principles of right and wrong conduct. Companies such as **Texas Instruments** have gone into specifics, because ethical codes are often faulted for being vague and abstract.

Organizations also reveal their ethical commitment in other ways: Some companies are administering honesty tests prior to hiring new workers. Others talk about ethical values periodically and attempt to weed out employees who do not share those values before they can harm the company's reputation or culture. Still others include ethics in mid-level managers' required training (as at **Proctor & Gamble**) or model ethics throughout top management and the board (termed "tone at the top," especially notable at **Johnson & Johnson**). Building on the whistle-blowing protection that

is now mandated by the Sarbanes-Oxley legislation, some companies promote openness for employees who have ethics-related concerns. Another approach is to have a person designated as *ethics director*, as is now done at **Boeing** (as required by a key customer, the U.S. Air Force, following ethical problems at Boeing). **Merck & Co.** evaluates leaders' ethics in performance reviews.

The Leeson saga underscores the difficulty of dealing with the "moral hazard" problem, when the consequences of an individual's actions are largely borne by others. John Boatright argues in his book *Ethics in Finance* that the best antidote is to attract loyal, hardworking employees (although loyalty can be used as an excuse for doing wrong). Ethicists Scott Rae and Kenman L. Wong tell us that debating ethical issues is fruitless if we continue to ignore the character traits that empower people for moral behavior.

Source: Don Durfee, "It's Better (and Worse) Than You Think," *CFO* (May 2004) p. 29.

■ *Is "hitting the numbers" an appropriate goal, given the Chapter 1 contrast of profit and shareholder wealth maximization? If not, why do executives emphasize it?*

The return, k_t, reflects the combined effect of cash flow, C_t, and changes in value, $P_t - P_{t-1}$, over period t.[3]

Equation 5.1 is used to determine the rate of return over a time period as short as 1 day or as long as 10 years or more. However, in most cases, t is 1 year, and k therefore represents an annual rate of return.

---

3. The beginning-of-period value, P_{t-1}, and the end-of-period value, P_t, are not necessarily *realized values*. They are often *unrealized*, which means that although the asset was *not* actually purchased at time $t-1$ and sold at time t, values P_{t-1} and P_t *could* have been realized had those transactions been made.

EXAMPLE   Robin's Gameroom, a high-traffic video arcade, wishes to determine the return on two of its video machines, Conqueror and Demolition. Conqueror was purchased 1 year ago for $20,000 and currently has a market value of $21,500. During the year, it generated $800 of after-tax cash receipts. Demolition was purchased 4 years ago; its value in the year just completed declined from $12,000 to $11,800. During the year, it generated $1,700 of after-tax cash receipts. Substituting into Equation 5.1, we can calculate the annual rate of return, k, for each video machine.

Conqueror (C):

$$k_C = \frac{\$800 + \$21,500 - \$20,000}{\$20,000} = \frac{\$2,300}{\$20,000} = \underline{\underline{11.5\%}}$$

Demolition (D):

$$k_D = \frac{\$1,700 + \$11,800 - \$12,000}{\$12,000} = \frac{\$1,500}{\$12,000} = \underline{\underline{12.5\%}}$$

Although the market value of Demolition declined during the year, its cash flow caused it to earn a higher rate of return than Conqueror earned during the same period. Clearly, the combined impact of cash flow and changes in value, as measured by the rate of return, is important.   ■

Historical Returns

Investment returns vary both over time and between different types of investments. By averaging historical returns over a long period of time, it becomes possible to eliminate the impact of market and other types of risk. This enables the financial decision maker to focus on the differences in return that are attributable primarily to the types of investment. Table 5.2 shows the average annual rates of return for a number of popular security investments (and inflation) over the 78-year period January 1, 1926, through December 31, 2003. Each rate represents the average annual rate of return an investor would have realized had he or she purchased the investment on January 1, 1926, and sold it on December 31, 2003. You can see that significant differences exist between the average annual

TABLE 5.2

Historical Returns for Selected Security Investments (1926–2003)

Investment	Average annual return
Large-company stocks	12.4%
Small-company stocks	17.5
Long-term corporate bonds	6.2
Long-term government bonds	5.8
U.S. Treasury bills	3.8
Inflation	3.1%

Source: Stocks, Bonds, Bills, and Inflation, 2004 Yearbook (Chicago: Ibbotson Associates, Inc., 2004).

rates of return realized on the various types of stocks, bonds, and bills shown. Later in this chapter, we will see how these differences in return can be linked to differences in the risk of each of these investments.

Risk Preferences

Feelings about risk differ among managers (and firms).[4] Thus it is important to specify a generally acceptable level of risk. The three basic risk preference behaviors—risk-averse, risk-indifferent, and risk-seeking—are depicted graphically in Figure 5.1.

risk-indifferent
The attitude toward risk in which no change in return would be required for an increase in risk.

risk-averse
The attitude toward risk in which an increased return would be required for an increase in risk.

risk-seeking
The attitude toward risk in which a decreased return would be accepted for an increase in risk.

- For the **risk-indifferent** manager, the required return does not change as risk goes from x_1 to x_2. In essence, no change in return would be required for the increase in risk. Clearly, this attitude is nonsensical in almost any business context.

- For the **risk-averse** manager, the required return increases for an increase in risk. Because they shy away from risk, these managers require higher expected returns to compensate them for taking greater risk.

- For the **risk-seeking** manager, the required return decreases for an increase in risk. Theoretically, because they enjoy risk, these managers are willing to give up some return to take more risk. However, such behavior would not be likely to benefit the firm.

Hint Remember that most *shareholders* are risk-averse. Like risk-averse managers, for a given increase in risk, they require an increase in return on their investment in that firm.

Most managers are risk-averse; for a given increase in risk, they require an increase in return. They generally tend to be conservative rather than aggressive when accepting risk for their firm. Accordingly, a *risk-averse financial manager requiring higher returns for greater risk is assumed throughout this text.*

FIGURE 5.1

Risk Preferences
Risk preference behaviors

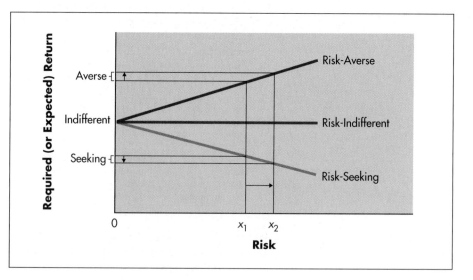

---

4. The risk preferences of the managers should, in theory, be consistent with the risk preferences of the firm. Although the *agency problem* suggests that, in practice, managers may not behave in a manner consistent with the firm's risk preferences, it is assumed here that they do. Therefore, the managers' risk preferences and those of the firm are assumed to be identical.

FIGURE 5.3

Continuous Probability Distributions

Continuous probability distributions for asset A's and asset B's returns

continuous probability distribution
A and B have the same most likely
for asset B has much greater *disper*
asset B is more risky than asset A.

Risk Measurement

In addition to considering its *range*
tatively by using statistics. Here w
tion and the coefficient of variation
of asset returns.

Standard Deviation

standard deviation (σ_k)
The most common statistical indicator of an asset's risk; it measures the dispersion around the *expected value*.

expected value of a return ($\bar{k}$)
The most likely return on a given asset.

The most common statistical indica
σ_k, which measures the dispersion
value of a return, $\bar{k}$, is the most l
follows:[9]

$$\bar{k} =$$

where

k_j = return for the jth outcome
Pr_j = probability of occurrence
n = number of outcomes cons

7. The continuous distribution's probabilities chan
ered. The area under each of the curves is equal to
outcomes, are considered.

8. Although risk is typically viewed as determined
people believe that risk exists only when outcome
expected value are considered bad. Nevertheless, th
ability on either side of the expected value, because
outcomes associated with an investment.

9. The formula for finding the expected value of ret
probabilities are assumed to be equal, is a simple ar

where n is the number of observations. Equation 5.2
abilities are often available.

5–1   What is *risk* in the context of financial decision making?
5–2   Define *return*, and describe how to find the rate of return on an investment.
5–3   Compare the following risk preferences: (**a**) risk-averse, (**b**) risk-indifferent, and (**c**) risk-seeking. Which is most common among financial managers?

LG2   5.2 | Risk of a Single Asset

The concept of risk can be developed by first considering a single asset held in isolation. We can look at expected-return behaviors to assess risk, and statistics can be used to measure it.

Risk Assessment

Sensitivity analysis and probability distributions can be used to assess the general level of risk embodied in a given asset.

sensitivity analysis
An approach for assessing risk that uses several possible-return estimates to obtain a sense of the variability among outcomes.

range
A measure of an asset's risk, which is found by subtracting the pessimistic (worst) outcome from the optimistic (best) outcome.

Sensitivity Analysis

Sensitivity analysis uses several possible-return estimates to obtain a sense of the variability among outcomes.[5] One common method involves making pessimistic (worst), most likely (expected), and optimistic (best) estimates of the returns associated with a given asset. In this case, the asset's risk can be measured by the range of returns. The **range** is found by subtracting the pessimistic outcome from the optimistic outcome. The greater the range, the more variability, or risk, the asset is said to have.

EXAMPLE   Norman Company, a custom golf equipment manufacturer, wants to choose the better of two investments, A and B. Each requires an initial outlay of $10,000, and each has a *most likely* annual rate of return of 15%. Management has made *pessimistic* and *optimistic* estimates of the returns associated with each. The three estimates for each asset, along with its range, are given in Table 5.3 (see page 232). Asset A appears to be less risky than asset B; its range of 4% (17% − 13%) is less than the range of 16% (23% − 7%) for asset B. The risk-averse decision maker would prefer asset A over asset B, because A offers the same most likely return as B (15%) with lower risk (smaller range). ■

Although the use of sensitivity analysis and the range is rather crude, it does give the decision maker a feel for the behavior of returns, which can be used to estimate the risk involved.

5. The term *sensitivity analysis* is intentionally used in a general rather than a technically correct fashion here to simplify this discussion. A more technical and precise definition and discussion of this technique and of "scenario analysis" are presented in Chapter 10.

TABLE 5.3

Asset...

Initial investment	
Annual rate of return	
Pessimistic	
Most likely	
Optimistic	
Range	

probability
The *chance* that a given outcome will occur.

probability distribution
A model that relates probabilities to the associated outcomes.

Probability Distributions

Probability distributions provide...
The **probability** of a given outcome...
80 percent probability of occurre...
An outcome with a probability o...
a probability of zero will never o...

EXAMPLE

Norman Company's past estim...
simistic, most likely, and optimis...
tively. Note that the sum of the...
must be based on all the alternat...

A **probability distribution** is...
ated outcomes. The simplest ty...
which shows only a limited numl...
charts for Norman Company's a...
both assets have the same most l...
or more dispersed, for asset B th...

If we knew all the possible o...
develop a **continuous probabilit**...
thought of as a bar chart for a ver...

bar chart
The simplest type of probability distribution; shows only a limited number of outcomes and associated probabilities for a given event.

continuous probability distribution
A probability distribution showing all the possible outcomes and associated probabilities for a given event.

FIGURE 5.2

Bar Charts
Bar charts for asset A's and asset B's returns

6. To develop a continuous probability distribu...
for a given event. Then, by developing a free...
occurred over the given time horizon, one can...
butions for risky events can also be developed...

TABLE 5.4

Expected Values of Returns for Assets A and B

Possible outcomes	Probability (1)	Returns (2)	Weighted value [(1) × (2)] (3)
Asset A			
Pessimistic	.25	13%	3.25%
Most likely	.50	15	7.50
Optimistic	.25	17	4.25
Total	1.00	Expected return	15.00%
Asset B			
Pessimistic	.25	7%	1.75%
Most likely	.50	15	7.50
Optimistic	.25	23	5.75
Total	1.00	Expected return	15.00%

EXAMPLE

The expected values of returns for Norman Company's assets A and B are presented in Table 5.4. Column 1 gives the Pr_j's and column 2 gives the k_j's. In each case n equals 3. The expected value for each asset's return is 15%.

The expression for the *standard deviation of returns*, σ_k, is[10]

$$\sigma_k = \sqrt{\sum_{j=1}^{n} (k_j - \overline{k})^2 \times Pr_j} \quad (5.3)$$

In general, the higher the standard deviation, the greater the risk.

EXAMPLE

Table 5.5 presents the standard deviations for Norman Company's assets A and B, based on the earlier data. The standard deviation for asset A is 1.41%, and the standard deviation for asset B is 5.66%. The higher risk of asset B is clearly reflected in its higher standard deviation.

Historical Returns and Risk We can now use the standard deviation as a measure of risk to assess the historical (1926–2003) investment return data in Table 5.2. Table 5.6 repeats the historical returns in column 1 and shows the standard deviations associated with each of them in column 2. A close relationship can be seen between the investment returns and the standard deviations: Investments with higher returns have higher standard deviations. Because higher standard deviations are associated with greater risk, the historical data confirm the existence of a positive relationship between risk and return. That relationship

10. The formula that is commonly used to find the standard deviation of returns, σ_k, in a situation in which *all* outcomes are known *and* their related probabilities are assumed equal, is

$$\sigma_k = \sqrt{\frac{\sum_{j=1}^{n} (k_j - \overline{k})^2}{n - 1}} \quad (5.3a)$$

where n is the number of observations. Equation 5.3 is emphasized in this chapter because returns and related probabilities are often available.

TABLE 5.5

The Calculation of the Standard Deviation of the Returns for Assets A and B[a]

j	k_j	$\bar{k}$	$k_j - \bar{k}$	$(k_j - \bar{k})^2$	Pr_j	$(k_j - \bar{k})^2 \times Pr_j$
			Asset A			
1	13%	15%	−2%	4%	.25	1%
2	15	15	0	0	.50	0
3	17	15	2	4	.25	<u>1</u>

$$\sum_{j=1}^{3}(k_j - \bar{k})^2 \times Pr_j = 2\%$$

$$\sigma_{k_A} = \sqrt{\sum_{j=1}^{n}(k_j - \bar{k})^2 \times Pr_j} = \sqrt{2\%} = \underline{\underline{1.41\%}}$$

j	k_j	$\bar{k}$	$k_j - \bar{k}$	$(k_j - \bar{k})^2$	Pr_j	$(k_j - \bar{k})^2 \times Pr_j$
			Asset B			
1	7%	15%	−8%	64%	.25	16%
2	15	15	0	0	.50	0
3	23	15	8	64	.25	<u>16</u>

$$\sum_{j=1}^{k}(k_j - \bar{k})^2 \times Pr_j = 32\%$$

$$\sigma_{k_B} = \sqrt{\sum_{j=1}^{3}(k_j - \bar{k})^2 \times Pr_j} = \sqrt{32\%} = \underline{\underline{5.66\%}}$$

[a]Calculations in this table are made in percentage form rather than decimal form—e.g., 13% rather than 0.13. As a result, some of the intermediate computations may appear to be inconsistent with those that would result from using decimal form. Regardless, the resulting standard deviations are correct and identical to those that would result from using decimal rather than percentage form.

TABLE 5.6

Historical Returns, Standard Deviations, and Coefficients of Variation for Selected Security Investments (1926–2003)

Investment	Average annual return (1)	Standard deviation (2)	Coefficient of variation[a] (3)
Large-company stocks	12.4%	20.4%	1.65
Small-company stocks	17.5	33.3	1.90
Long-term corporate bonds	6.2	8.6	1.39
Long-term government bonds	5.8	9.4	1.62
U.S. Treasury bills	3.8	3.1	0.82
Inflation	3.1%	4.3%	1.39

[a]Calculated by dividing the standard deviation in column 2 by the average annual return in column 1.
Source: Stocks, Bonds, Bills, and Inflation, 2004 Yearbook (Chicago: Ibbotson Associates, Inc., 2004).

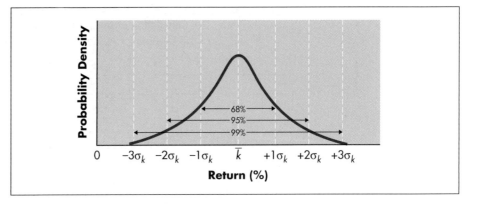

reflects *risk aversion* by market participants, who require higher returns as compensation for greater risk. The historical data in columns 1 and 2 of Table 5.6 clearly show that during the 1926–2003 period, investors were rewarded with higher returns on higher-risk investments.

normal probability distribution
A symmetrical probability distribution whose shape resembles a "bell-shaped" curve.

Normal Distribution   A **normal probability distribution,** depicted in Figure 5.4, always resembles a "bell-shaped" curve. It is symmetrical: From the peak of the graph, the curve's extensions are mirror images (reflections) of each other. The symmetry of the curve means that half the probability is associated with the values to the left of the peak and half with the values to the right. As noted on the figure, for normal probability distributions, 68 percent of the possible outcomes will lie between ±1 standard deviation from the expected value, 95 percent of all outcomes will lie between ±2 standard deviations from the expected value, and 99 percent of all outcomes will lie between ±3 standard deviations from the expected value.[11]

EXAMPLE   If we assume that the probability distribution of returns for the Norman Company is normal, 68% of the possible outcomes would have a return ranging between 13.59% and 16.41% for asset A and between 9.34% and 20.66% for asset B; 95% of the possible return outcomes would range between 12.18% and 17.82% for asset A and between 3.68% and 26.32% for asset B; and 99% of the possible return outcomes would range between 10.77% and 19.23% for asset A and between −1.98% and 31.98% for asset B. The greater risk of asset B is clearly reflected in its much wider range of possible returns for each level of confidence (68%, 95%, and so on).

Coefficient of Variation

coefficient of variation (CV)
A measure of relative dispersion that is useful in comparing the risks of assets with differing expected returns.

The **coefficient of variation, CV,** is a measure of relative dispersion that is useful in comparing the risks of assets with differing expected returns. Equation 5.4 gives the expression for the coefficient of variation:

$$CV = \frac{\sigma_k}{\bar{k}} \quad \text{—must li} \, \text{kon}$$

(5.4)

11. Tables of values indicating the probabilities associated with various deviations from the expected value of a normal distribution can be found in any basic statistics text. These values can be used to establish confidence limits and make inferences about possible outcomes. Such applications can be found in most basic statistics and upper-level managerial finance textbooks.

The higher the coefficient of variation, the greater the risk and therefore the higher the expected return. This relationship can be seen by comparing the coefficients of variation in column 3 of Table 5.6, which shows historical 1926–2003 investment data, with the average annual returns in column 1. As with the standard deviations in column 2, higher returns are associated with higher coefficients of variation.

EXAMPLE   When the standard deviations (from Table 5.5) and the expected returns (from Table 5.4) for assets A and B are substituted into Equation 5.4, the coefficients of variation for A and B are 0.094 (1.41% ÷ 15%) and 0.377 (5.66% ÷ 15%), respectively. Asset B has the higher coefficient of variation and is therefore more risky than asset A—which we already know from the standard deviation. (Because both assets have the same expected return, the coefficient of variation has not provided any new information.) ■

The real utility of the coefficient of variation comes in comparing the risks of assets that have *different* expected returns.

EXAMPLE   A firm wants to select the less risky of two alternative assets—C and D. The expected return, standard deviation, and coefficient of variation for each of these assets' returns are

Statistics	Asset C	Asset D
(1) Expected return	12%	20%
(2) Standard deviation	9%[a]	10%
(3) Coefficient of variation [(2) ÷ (1)]	0.75	0.50[a]

[a]Preferred asset using the given risk measure.

Judging solely on the basis of their standard deviations, the firm would prefer asset C, which has a lower standard deviation than asset D (9% versus 10%). However, management would be making a serious error in choosing asset C over asset D, because the dispersion—the risk—of the asset, as reflected in the coefficient of variation, is lower for D (0.50) than for C (0.75). Clearly, using the coefficient of variation to compare asset risk is effective because it also considers the relative size, or expected return, of the assets. ■

REVIEW QUESTIONS

5–4   Explain how the *range* is used in sensitivity analysis.

5–5   What does a plot of the *probability distribution* of outcomes show a decision maker about an asset's risk?

5–6   What relationship exists between the size of the *standard deviation* and the degree of asset risk?

5–7   When is the *coefficient of variation* preferred over the standard deviation for comparing asset risk?

LG3   LG4   5.3 | Risk of a Portfolio

efficient portfolio
A portfolio that maximizes return for a given level of risk or minimizes risk for a given level of return.

In real-world situations, the risk of any single investment would not be viewed independently of other assets. (We did so for teaching purposes.) New investments must be considered in light of their impact on the risk and return of the *portfolio* of assets.[12] The financial manager's goal is to create an **efficient portfolio,** one that maximizes return for a given level of risk or minimizes risk for a given level of return. We therefore need a way to measure the return and the standard deviation of a portfolio of assets. Once we can do that, we will look at the statistical concept of *correlation,* which underlies the process of diversification that is used to develop an efficient portfolio.

Portfolio Return and Standard Deviation

The *return on a portfolio* is a weighted average of the returns on the individual assets from which it is formed. We can use Equation 5.5 to find the portfolio return, k_p:

$$k_p = (w_1 \times k_1) + (w_2 \times k_2) + \cdots + (w_n \times k_n) = \sum_{j=1}^{n} w_j \times k_j \qquad (5.5)$$

where

w_j = proportion of the portfolio's total dollar value represented by asset j

k_j = return on asset j

Of course, $\sum_{j=1}^{n} w_j = 1$, which means that 100 percent of the portfolio's assets must be included in this computation.

The *standard deviation of a portfolio's returns* is found by applying the formula for the standard deviation of a single asset. Specifically, Equation 5.3 is used when the probabilities of the returns are known, and Equation 5.3a (from footnote 10) is applied when the outcomes are known and their related probabilities of occurrence are assumed to be equal.

EXAMPLE   Assume that we wish to determine the expected value and standard deviation of returns for portfolio XY, created by combining equal portions (50%) of assets X and Y. The forecasted returns of assets X and Y for each of the next 5 years (2007–2011) are given in columns 1 and 2, respectively, in part A of Table 5.7. In column 3, the weights of 50% for both assets X and Y along with their respective returns from columns 1 and 2 are substituted into Equation 5.5. Column 4 shows the results of the calculation—an expected portfolio return of 12% for each year, 2007 to 2011.

Furthermore, as shown in part B of Table 5.7, the expected value of these portfolio returns over the 5-year period is also 12% (calculated by using Equation 5.2a, in footnote 9). In part C of Table 5.7, portfolio XY's standard

---

12. The portfolio of a firm, which would consist of its total assets, is not differentiated from the portfolio of an owner, which would probably contain a variety of different investment vehicles (i.e., assets). The differing characteristics of these two types of portfolios should become clear upon completion of Chapter 10.

AN INTERNATIONAL FLAVO

What do the Dodge Caravan, Kit Kat chocolate bars, aspirin, and Fox TV have in common? While they may be products with which you are familiar, all are products of non-U.S. corporations. The Dodge Caravan is a product of **DaimlerChrysler,** a German company. Kit Kat bars are a product of Swiss company **Nestlé.** Aspirin is produced by **Bayer AG,** a German company, and Fox TV is part of **News Corp,** an Australian company. Just as Americans use many products and services created by companies headquartered in foreign countries, so many U.S. corporations seek to expand internationally. The result is a more globally integrated economy.

One method of reducing investment risk is diversification. Allocating a portion of one's portfolio to non-U.S. equities has historically provided better risk-adjusted returns than a portfolio

consisting solely of U.S. assets. As you have learned in this chapter, the benefit of diversification between two assets is enhanced the two asset classes are not highly correlated, and it is larges when two asset classes are perfectly negatively correlated.

From the mid-1990s through 2000, when the technology bubble burst, international and U.S. markets moved more closely together than usual. The increased correlation between the U.S. asset and international asset classes cause some to question the wisdom of international diversification. Compounding the issue was the effect that the poor performance of international markets had in a diversified portfolio during the heady days of the bull market in the late 1990s. Although investors are often willing to accept less risk in the form of less volatility of their portfolios, it is not as easy to rec-

banks rather than individuals, foreign in country experiences political or economic

For more discussion of reducing risk see the *In Practice* box above.

REVIEW QUESTIONS

5–8 What is an *efficient portfolio?* How of a portfolio be determined?

5–9 Why is the *correlation* between ass sification allow risky assets to be c folio is less than the risk of the indi

5–10 How does international diversifica might international diversification *political risks,* and how do they aff

TABLE 5.7 Expected Return, Expected Value, and Standard Deviation of Returns for Portfolio XY

A. Expected portfolio returns

Year	Asset X (1)	Asset Y (2)	Portfolio return calculation[a] (3)	Expected portfolio return, k_p (4)
2007	8%	16%	$(.50 \times 8\%) + (.50 \times 16\%) =$	12%
2008	10	14	$(.50 \times 10\%) + (.50 \times 14\%) =$	12
2009	12	12	$(.50 \times 12\%) + (.50 \times 12\%) =$	12
2010	14	10	$(.50 \times 14\%) + (.50 \times 10\%) =$	12
2011	16	8	$(.50 \times 16\%) + (.50 \times 8\%) =$	12

B. Expected value of portfolio returns, 2007–2011[b]

$$\bar{k}_p = \frac{12\% + 12\% + 12\% + 12\% + 12\%}{5} = \frac{60\%}{5} = 12\%$$

C. Standard deviation of expected portfolio returns[c]

$$\sigma_{k_p} = \sqrt{\frac{(12\% - 12\%)^2 + (12\% - 12\%)^2 + (12\% - 12\%)^2 + (12\% - 12\%)^2 + (12\% - 12\%)^2}{5 - 1}}$$

$$= \sqrt{\frac{0\% + 0\% + 0\% + 0\% + 0\%}{4}}$$

$$= \sqrt{\frac{0\%}{4}} = 0\%$$

[a]Using Equation 5.5.
[b]Using Equation 5.2a found in footnote 9.
[c]Using Equation 5.3a found in footnote 10.

correlation
A statistical measure of the relationship between any two series of numbers representing data of any kind.

positively correlated
Describes two series that move in the same direction.

negatively correlated
Describes two series that move in opposite directions.

deviation is calculated to be 0% (using Equation 5.3a, in footnote 10). This value should not be surprising because the expected return each year is the same—12%. No variability is exhibited in the expected returns from year to year. ■

Correlation

Correlation is a statistical measure of the relationship between any two series of numbers. The numbers may represent data of any kind, from returns to test scores. If two series move in the same direction, they are **positively correlated.** If the series move in opposite directions, they are **negatively correlated.**[13]

13. The general *long-term trends* of two series could be the same (both increasing or both decreasing) or different (one increasing, the other decreasing), and the correlation of their *short-term (point-to-point) movements* in both situations could be either positive or negative. In other words, the pattern of movement around the trends could be correlated independent of the actual relationship between the trends. Further clarification of this seemingly inconsistent behavior can be found in most basic statistics texts.

International Diversificati

The ultimate example of portfolio d
in a portfolio. The inclusion of asset
not highly correlated with the U.S.
siveness to market movements and t

Returns from International Diver:

Over long periods, returns from int
superior to those of purely domes
economy is performing relatively p
against most foreign currencies. At s
on a portfolio of foreign assets can
short or intermediate period, inte
returns, particularly during periods
tive to other currencies. When the U.
a foreign-currency-denominated port
yields a satisfactory return in local c
reduced when translated into dollar
coupled with an appreciating dollar,
investors.

Overall, though, the logic of int
that these fluctuations in currency v
out over long periods. Compared to s
nationally diversified portfolio will t
level of risk.

Risks of International Diversificatic

political risk
Risk that arises from the
possibility that a host
government will take actions
harmful to foreign investors
or that political turmoil in
a country will endanger
investments there.

U.S. investors should also be aware
investing. In addition to the risk indu
financial risks are unique to internati
risk, which arises from the possibilit
harmful to foreign investors or that p
investments there. Political risks are
where unstable or ideologically moti
return of profits by foreign investors c
host country. An example of politica
2003–2004 that Operation Enduring
facilities in Iraq and cause a worldwi
concern was indeed validated by the
2004 and continued throughout the ye

Even where governments do not
international investors may suffer if a s
of dividends or interest to foreigners.
scarce foreign exchange, they rarely g
investors. Instead, hard-currency reser
imports such as food, medicine, and inc
government's debt. Because most of th

LG5 LG6 5.4

Risk and Return: The Capital Asset Pricing Model (CAPM)

capital asset pricing model (CAPM)
The basic theory that links risk and return for all assets.

The most important aspect of risk is the *overall risk* of the firm as viewed by investors in the marketplace. Overall risk significantly affects investment opportunities and—even more important—the owners' wealth. The basic theory that links risk and return for all assets is the **capital asset pricing model (CAPM).**[16] We will use CAPM to understand the basic risk–return tradeoffs involved in all types of financial decisions.

Types of Risk

To understand the basic types of risk, consider what happens to the risk of a portfolio consisting of a single security (asset), to which we add securities randomly selected from, say, the population of all actively traded securities. Using the standard deviation of return, σ_{k_p}, to measure the total portfolio risk, Figure 5.8 depicts the behavior of the total portfolio risk (y axis) as more securities are added (x axis). With the addition of securities, the total portfolio risk declines, as a result of the effects of diversification, and tends to approach a lower limit. Research has shown that, on average, most of the risk-reduction benefits of diversification can be gained by forming portfolios containing 15 to 20 randomly selected securities.[17]

FIGURE 5.8

Risk Reduction
Portfolio risk and diversification

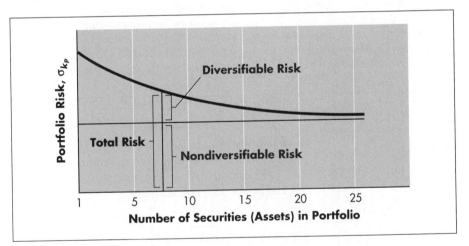

---

16. The initial development of this theory is generally attributed to William F. Sharpe, "Capital Asset Prices: A Theory of Market Equilibrium Under Conditions of Risk," *Journal of Finance* 19 (September 1964), pp. 425–442, and John Lintner, "The Valuation of Risk Assets and the Selection of Risky Investments in Stock Portfolios and Capital Budgets," *Review of Economics and Statistics* 47 (February 1965), pp. 13–37. A number of authors subsequently advanced, refined, and tested this now widely accepted theory.

17. See, for example, W. H. Wagner and S. C. Lau, "The Effect of Diversification on Risk," *Financial Analysts Journal* 26 (November–December 1971), pp. 48–53, and Jack Evans and Stephen H. Archer, "Diversification and the Reduction of Dispersion: An Empirical Analysis," *Journal of Finance* 23 (December 1968), pp. 761–767. A more recent study, Gerald D. Newbould and Percy S. Poon, "The Minimum Number of Stocks Needed for Diversification," *Financial Practice and Education* (Fall 1993), pp. 85–87, shows that because an investor holds but one of a large number of possible x-security portfolios, it is unlikely that he or she will experience the average outcome. As a consequence, the study suggests that a minimum of 40 stocks is needed to diversify a portfolio fully. This study tends to support the widespread popularity of mutual fund investments.

total risk
The combination of a security's *nondiversifiable risk* and *diversifiable risk*.

diversifiable risk
The portion of an asset's risk that is attributable to firm-specific, random causes; can be eliminated through diversification. Also called *unsystematic risk.*

nondiversifiable risk
The relevant portion of an asset's risk attributable to market factors that affect all firms; cannot be eliminated through diversification. Also called *systematic risk.*

The **total risk** of a security can be viewed as consisting of two parts:

$$\text{Total security risk} = \text{Nondiversifiable risk} + \text{Diversifiable risk} \qquad (5.6)$$

Diversifiable risk (sometimes called *unsystematic risk*) represents the portion of an asset's risk that is associated with random causes that can be eliminated through diversification. It is attributable to firm-specific events, such as strikes, lawsuits, regulatory actions, and loss of a key account. **Nondiversifiable risk** (also called *systematic risk*) is attributable to market factors that affect all firms; it cannot be eliminated through diversification. (It is the shareholder-specific *market risk* described in Table 5.1.) Factors such as war, inflation, international incidents, and political events account for nondiversifiable risk.

Because any investor can create a portfolio of assets that will eliminate virtually all diversifiable risk, *the only relevant risk is nondiversifiable risk.* Any investor or firm therefore must be concerned solely with nondiversifiable risk. The measurement of nondiversifiable risk is thus of primary importance in selecting assets with the most desired risk–return characteristics.

The Model: CAPM

The capital asset pricing model (CAPM) links nondiversifiable risk and return for all assets. We will discuss the model in five sections. The first deals with the beta coefficient, which is a measure of nondiversifiable risk. The second section presents an equation of the model itself, and the third graphically describes the relationship between risk and return. The fourth section discusses the effects of changes in inflationary expectations and risk aversion on the relationship between risk and return. The final section offers some comments on the CAPM.

Beta Coefficient

beta coefficient (*b*)
A relative measure of non-diversifiable risk. An *index* of the degree of movement of an asset's return in response to a change in the *market return.*

market return
The return on the market portfolio of all traded securities.

The **beta coefficient,** *b,* is a relative measure of nondiversifiable risk. It is an *index* of the degree of movement of an asset's return in response to a change in the *market return.* An asset's historical returns are used in finding the asset's beta coefficient. The **market return** is the return on the market portfolio of all traded securities. The *Standard & Poor's 500 Stock Composite Index* or some similar stock index is commonly used as the market return. Betas for actively traded stocks can be obtained from a variety of sources, but you should understand how they are derived and interpreted and how they are applied to portfolios.

Deriving Beta from Return Data   An asset's historical returns are used in finding the asset's beta coefficient. Figure 5.9 (see page 248) plots the relationship between the returns of two assets—R and S—and the market return. Note that the horizontal (*x*) axis measures the historical market returns and that the vertical (*y*) axis measures the individual asset's historical returns. The first step in deriving beta involves plotting the coordinates for the market return and asset returns from various points in time. Such annual "market return–asset return" coordinates are shown *for asset S only* for the years 1999 through 2006. For example, in 2006, asset S's return was 20 percent when the market return was 10 percent. By use of statistical techniques, the "characteristic line" that best explains the relationship between the asset return and the market return coordinates is fit to

FIGURE 5.9

Beta Derivation^a
Graphical derivation of beta
for assets R and S

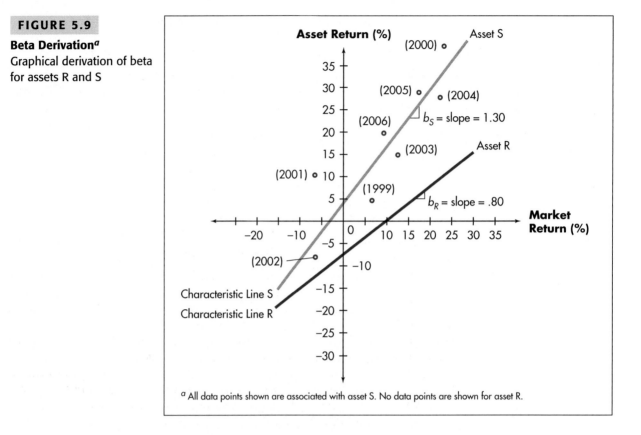

^{a} All data points shown are associated with asset S. No data points are shown for asset R.

the data points.[18] The slope of this line is *beta*. The beta for asset R is about .80 and that for asset S is about 1.30. Asset S's higher beta (steeper characteristic line slope) indicates that its return is more responsive to changing market returns. *Therefore asset S is more risky than asset R.*[19]

---

18. The empirical measurement of beta is approached by using *least-squares regression analysis* to find the regression coefficient (b_j) in the equation for the "characteristic line":

$$k_j = a_j + b_j k_m + e_j$$

where

k_j = return on asset j

a_j = intercept

b_j = beta coefficient, which equals $\dfrac{Cov\ (k_j,\ k_m)}{\sigma_m^2}$

where

$Cov\ (k_j,\ k_m)$ = covariance of the return on asset j, k_j, and the return on the market portfolio, k_m

σ_m^2 = variance of the return on the market portfolio

k_m = required rate of return on the market portfolio of securities

e_j = random error term, which reflects the diversifiable, or unsystematic, risk of asset j

The calculations involved in finding betas are somewhat rigorous. If you want to know more about these calculations, consult an advanced managerial finance or investments text.

19. The values of beta also depend on the time interval used for return calculations and on the number of returns used in the regression analysis. In other words, betas calculated using monthly returns would not necessarily be comparable to those calculated using a similar number of daily returns.

The Equation

Using the beta coefficient to measure nondiversifiable risk, the *capital asset pricing model (CAPM)* is given in Equation 5.8:

$$k_j = R_F + [b_j \times (k_m - R_F)] \tag{5.8}$$

market risk premium

where

k_j = required return on asset *j*

R_F = risk-free rate of return, commonly measured by the return on a U.S. Treasury bill

b_j = beta coefficient or index of nondiversifiable risk for asset *j*

k_m = market return; return on the market portfolio of assets

risk-free rate of return, (R_F)
The required return on a *risk-free asset,* typically a 3-month U.S. Treasury bill.

U.S. Treasury bills (T-bills)
Short-term IOUs issued by the U.S. Treasury; considered the *risk-free asset.*

The CAPM can be divided into two parts: (1) the **risk-free rate of return, R_F,** which is the required return on a *risk-free asset,* typically a 3-month **U.S. Treasury bill (T-bill),** a short-term IOU issued by the U.S. Treasury, and (2) the *risk premium.* These are, respectively, the two elements on either side of the plus sign in Equation 5.8. The $(k_m - R_F)$ portion of the risk premium is called the *market risk premium,* because it represents the premium the investor must receive for taking the average amount of risk associated with holding the market portfolio of assets.[20]

Historical Risk Premiums   Using the historical return data for selected security investments for the 1926–2003 period shown in Table 5.2, we can calculate the risk premiums for each investment category. The calculation (consistent with Equation 5.8) involves merely subtracting the historical U.S. Treasury bill's average return from the historical average return for a given investment:

Investment	Risk premium[a]		
Large-company stocks	12.4%	− 3.8% =	8.6%
Small company stocks	17.5	− 3.8	= 13.7
Long-term corporate bonds	6.2	− 3.8	= 2.4
Long-term government bonds	5.8	− 3.8	= 2.0
U.S. Treasury bills	3.8	− 3.8	= 0.0

[a]Return values obtained from Table 5.2.

Reviewing the risk premiums calculated above, we can see that the risk premium is highest for small-company stocks, followed by large-company stocks, long-term corporate bonds, and long-term government bonds. This outcome makes sense intuitively because small-company stocks are riskier than large-company stocks, which are riskier than long-term corporate bonds (equity is riskier than debt investment). Long-term corporate bonds are riskier than long-term

---

20. Although CAPM has been widely accepted, a broader theory, *arbitrage pricing theory (APT),* first described by Stephen A. Ross, "The Arbitrage Theory of Capital Asset Pricing," *Journal of Economic Theory* (December 1976), pp. 341–360, has received a great deal of attention in the financial literature. The theory suggests that the risk premium on securities may be better explained by a number of factors underlying and in place of the market return used in CAPM. The CAPM in effect can be viewed as being derived from APT. Although testing of APT confirms the importance of the market return, it has thus far failed to identify other risk factors clearly. As a result of this failure, as well as APT's lack of practical acceptance and usage, we concentrate our attention here on CAPM.

government bonds (because the government is less likely to renege on debt). And of course, U.S. Treasury bills, because of their lack of default risk and their very short maturity, are virtually risk-free, as indicated by their lack of any risk premium.

EXAMPLE Benjamin Corporation, a growing computer software developer, wishes to determine the required return on an asset Z, which has a beta of 1.5. The risk-free rate of return is 7%; the return on the market portfolio of assets is 11%. Substituting $b_Z = 1.5$, $R_F = 7\%$, and $k_m = 11\%$ into the capital asset pricing model given in Equation 5.8 yields a required return of

$$k_Z = 7\% + [1.5 \times (11\% - 7\%)] = 7\% + 6\% = \underline{\underline{13\%}}$$

The market risk premium of 4% (11% − 7%), when adjusted for the asset's index of risk (beta) of 1.5, results in a risk premium of 6% (1.5 × 4%). That risk premium, when added to the 7% risk-free rate, results in a 13% required return. ■

Other things being equal, *the higher the beta, the higher the required return, and the lower the beta, the lower the required return.*

The Graph: The Security Market Line (SML)

security market line (SML)
The depiction of the *capital asset pricing model (CAPM)* as a graph that reflects the required return in the marketplace for each level of nondiversifiable risk (beta).

When the capital asset pricing model (Equation 5.8) is depicted graphically, it is called the **security market line (SML)**. The SML will, in fact, be a straight line. It reflects the required return in the marketplace for each level of nondiversifiable risk (beta). In the graph, risk as measured by beta, b, is plotted on the x axis, and required returns, k, are plotted on the y axis. The risk–return tradeoff is clearly represented by the SML.

EXAMPLE In the preceding example for Benjamin Corporation, the risk-free rate, R_F, was 7%, and the market return, k_m, was 11%. The SML can be plotted by using the two sets of coordinates for the betas associated with R_F and k_m, b_{R_F} and b_m (that is, $b_{R_F} = 0$,[21] $R_F = 7\%$; and $b_m = 1.0$, $k_m = 11\%$). Figure 5.10 presents the resulting security market line. As traditionally shown, the security market line in Figure 5.10 presents the required return associated with all positive betas. The market risk premium of 4% (k_m of 11% − R_F of 7%) has been highlighted. For a beta for asset Z, b_Z, of 1.5, its corresponding required return, k_Z, is 13%. Also shown in the figure is asset Z's risk premium of 6% (k_Z of 13% − R_F of 7%). It should be clear that for assets with betas greater than 1, the risk premium is greater than that for the market; for assets with betas less than 1, the risk premium is less than that for the market. ■

Shifts in the Security Market Line

The security market line is not stable over time, and shifts in the security market line can result in a change in required return. The position and slope of the SML are affected by two major forces—inflationary expectations and risk aversion—which are analyzed next.[22]

---

21. Because R_F is the rate of return on a risk-free asset, the beta associated with the risk-free asset, b_{R_F}, would equal 0. The zero beta on the risk-free asset reflects not only its absence of risk but also that the asset's return is unaffected by movements in the market return.

22. A firm's beta can change over time as a result of changes in the firm's asset mix, in its financing mix, or in external factors not within management's control, such as earthquakes, toxic spills, and so on. The impacts of changes in beta on value are discussed in Chapter 7.

FIGURE 5.10

Security Market Line
Security market line (SML)
with Benjamin Corporation's
asset Z data shown

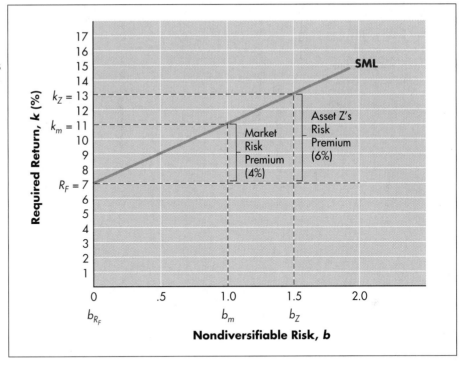

Changes in Inflationary Expectations   Changes in inflationary expectations affect the risk-free rate of return, R_F. The equation for the risk-free rate of return is

$$R_F = k^* + IP \qquad (5.9)$$

This equation shows that, assuming a constant real rate of interest, k^*, changes in inflationary expectations, reflected in an inflation premium, IP, will result in corresponding changes in the risk-free rate. Therefore, a change in inflationary expectations that results from events such as international trade embargoes or major changes in Federal Reserve policy will result in a shift in the SML. Because the risk-free rate is a basic component of all rates of return, any change in R_F will be reflected in *all* required rates of return.

Changes in inflationary expectations result in parallel shifts in the SML in direct response to the magnitude and direction of the change. This effect can best be illustrated by an example.

EXAMPLE   In the preceding example, using CAPM, the required return for asset Z, k_Z, was found to be 13%. Assuming that the risk-free rate of 7% includes a 2% real rate of interest, k^*, and a 5% inflation premium, IP, then Equation 5.9 confirms that

$$R_F = 2\% + 5\% = 7\%$$

Now assume that recent economic events have resulted in an *increase of 3% in inflationary expectations, raising the inflation premium* to 8% (IP_1). As a result, all returns likewise rise by 3%. In this case, the new returns (noted by subscript 1) are

$$R_{F_1} = 10\% \text{ (rises from 7\% to 10\%)}$$
$$k_{m_1} = 14\% \text{ (rises from 11\% to 14\%)}$$

FIGURE 5.11

Inflation Shifts SML
Impact of increased
inflationary expectations
on the SML

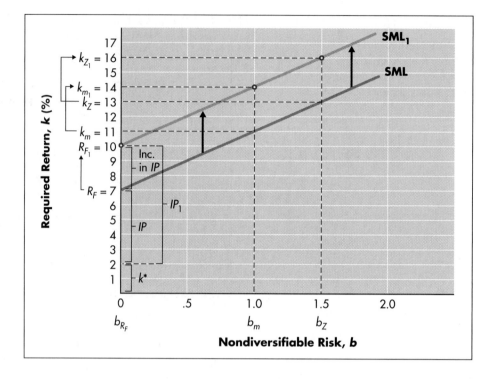

Substituting these values, along with asset Z's beta (b_Z) of 1.5, into the CAPM (Equation 5.8), we find that asset Z's new required return (k_{Z_1}) can be calculated:

$$k_{Z_1} = 10\% + [1.5 \times (14\% - 10\%)] = 10\% + 6\% = \underline{\underline{16\%}}$$

Comparing k_{Z_1} of 16% to k_Z of 13%, we see that the change of 3% in asset Z's required return exactly equals the change in the inflation premium. The same 3% increase results for all assets.

Figure 5.11 depicts the situation just described. It shows that the 3% increase in inflationary expectations results in a parallel shift upward of 3% in the SML. Clearly, the required returns on all assets rise by 3%. Note that the rise in the inflation premium from 5% to 8% (*IP* to IP_1) causes the risk-free rate to rise from 7% to 10% (R_F to R_{F_1}) and the market return to increase from 11% to 14% (k_m to k_{m_1}). The security market line therefore shifts upward by 3% (SML to SML$_1$), causing the required return on all risky assets, such as asset Z, to rise by 3%. It should now be clear that *a given change in inflationary expectations will be fully reflected in a corresponding change in the returns of all assets, as reflected graphically in a parallel shift of the SML.* ◼

Changes in Risk Aversion The slope of the security market line reflects the general risk preferences of investors in the marketplace. As discussed earlier and shown in Figure 5.1, most investors are *risk-averse*—they require increased returns for increased risk. This positive relationship between risk and return is graphically represented by the SML, which depicts the relationship between non-diversifiable risk as measured by beta (*x* axis) and the required return (*y* axis). The slope of the SML reflects the degree of risk aversion: *the steeper its slope, the greater the degree of risk aversion,* because a higher level of return will be required for each level of risk as measured by beta. In other words, *risk premiums increase with increasing risk avoidance.*

Changes in risk aversion, and therefore shifts in the SML, result from changing preferences of investors, which generally result from economic, political, and social events. Examples of events that *increase* risk aversion include a stock market crash, assassination of a key political leader, and the outbreak of war. In general, widely accepted expectations of hard times ahead tend to cause investors to become more risk-averse, requiring higher returns as compensation for accepting a given level of risk. The impact of increased risk aversion on the SML can best be demonstrated by an example.

EXAMPLE   In the preceding examples, the SML in Figure 5.10 reflected a risk-free rate (R_F) of 7%, a market return (k_m) of 11%, a market risk premium $(k_m - R_F)$ of 4%, and a required return on asset Z (k_Z) of 13% with a beta (b_Z) of 1.5. Assume that recent economic events have made investors more risk-averse, causing a new higher market return (k_{m_1}) of 14%. Graphically, this change would cause the SML to shift upward as shown in Figure 5.12, causing a new market risk premium $(k_{m_1} - R_F)$ of 7%. As a result, the required return on all risky assets will increase. For asset Z, with a beta of 1.5, the new required return (k_{Z_1}) can be calculated by using CAPM (Equation 5.8):

$$k_{Z_1} = 7\% + [1.5 \times (14\% - 7\%)] = 7\% + 10.5\% = \underline{\underline{17.5\%}}$$

This value can be seen on the new security market line (SML₁) in Figure 5.12. Note that although asset Z's risk, as measured by beta, did not change, its required return has increased because of the increased risk aversion reflected in

FIGURE 5.12

Risk Aversion Shifts SML
Impact of increased risk aversion on the SML

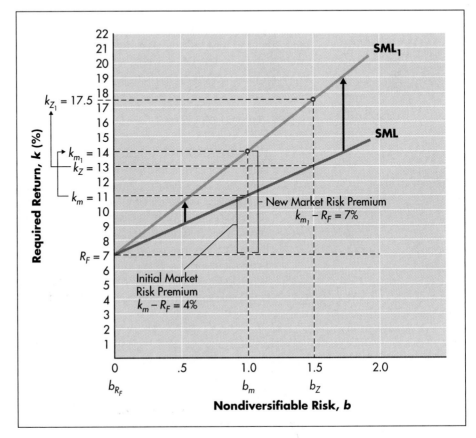

the market risk premium. It should now be clear that *greater risk aversion results in higher required returns for each level of risk. Similarly, a reduction in risk aversion causes the required return for each level of risk to decline.* ■

Some Comments on CAPM

The capital asset pricing model generally relies on historical data. The betas may or may not actually reflect the *future* variability of returns. Therefore, the required returns specified by the model can be viewed only as rough approximations. Users of betas commonly make subjective adjustments to the historically determined betas to reflect their expectations of the future.

The CAPM was developed to explain the behavior of security prices and provide a mechanism whereby investors could assess the impact of a proposed security investment on their portfolio's overall risk and return. It is based on an assumed **efficient market** with the following characteristics: many small investors, all having the same information and expectations with respect to securities; no restrictions on investment, no taxes, and no transaction costs; and rational investors, who view securities similarly and are risk-averse, preferring higher returns and lower risk.

Although the perfect world of the efficient market appears to be unrealistic, studies have provided support for the existence of the expectational relationship described by CAPM in active markets such as the New York Stock Exchange.[23] In the case of real corporate assets, such as plant and equipment, research thus far has failed to prove the general applicability of CAPM because of indivisibility, relatively large size, limited number of transactions, and absence of an efficient market for such assets.

Despite the limitations of CAPM, it provides a useful conceptual framework for evaluating and linking risk and return. An awareness of this tradeoff and an attempt to consider risk as well as return in financial decision making should help financial managers achieve their goals.

efficient market
A market with the following characteristics: many small investors, all having the same information and expectations with respect to securities; no restrictions on investment, no taxes, and no transaction costs; and rational investors, who view securities similarly and are risk-averse, preferring higher returns and lower risk.

REVIEW QUESTIONS

5–11 How are total risk, nondiversifiable risk, and diversifiable risk related? Why is nondiversifiable risk the *only relevant risk?*

5–12 What risk does *beta* measure? How can you find the beta of a portfolio?

5–13 Explain the meaning of each variable in the *capital asset pricing model (CAPM)* equation. What is the *security market line (SML)?*

5–14 What impact would the following changes have on the security market line and therefore on the required return for a given level of risk? (a) An *increase* in inflationary expectations. (b) Investors become *less* risk-averse.

5–15 Why do financial managers have some difficulty applying CAPM in financial decision making? Generally, what benefit does CAPM provide them?

23. A study by Eugene F. Fama and Kenneth R. French, "The Cross-Section of Expected Stock Returns," *Journal of Finance* 47 (June 1992), pp. 427–465, raised serious questions about the validity of CAPM. The study failed to find a significant relationship between the *historical* betas and *historical* returns on over 2,000 stocks during 1963–1990. In other words, it found that the magnitude of a stock's *historical* beta had no relationship to the level of its *historical* return. Although Fama and French's study continues to receive attention, CAPM has not been abandoned because its rejection as a *historical* model fails to discredit its validity as an *expectational* model. Therefore, in spite of this challenge, CAPM continues to be viewed as a logical and useful framework—both conceptually and operationally—for linking *expected* nondiversifiable risk and return.

Summary

Focus on Value

A firm's risk and expected return directly affect its share price. As we shall see in Chapter 7, risk and return are the two key determinants of the firm's value. It is therefore the financial manager's responsibility to assess carefully the risk and return of all major decisions so as to ensure that the expected returns justify the level of risk being introduced.

The way the financial manager can expect to achieve **the firm's goal of increasing its share price** (and thereby benefiting its owners) is to take only those actions that earn returns at least commensurate with their risk. Clearly, financial managers need to recognize, measure, and evaluate risk–return tradeoffs to ensure that their decisions contribute to the creation of value for owners.

Review of Learning Goals

Key definitions and formulas for this chapter are summarized in Table 5.13 (see page 258).

LG1 **Understand the meaning and fundamentals of risk, return, and risk preferences.** Risk is the chance of loss or, more formally, the variability of returns. A number of sources of firm-specific and shareholder-specific risks exist. Return is any cash distributions plus the change in value expressed as a percentage of the initial value. Investment returns vary both over time and between different types of investments. Managers may be risk-averse, risk-indifferent, or risk-seeking. Most financial decision makers are risk-averse. They generally prefer less risky alternatives, and they require higher expected returns in exchange for taking on greater risk.

LG2 **Describe procedures for assessing and measuring the risk of a single asset.** The risk of a single asset is measured in much the same way as the risk of a portfolio of assets. Sensitivity analysis and probability distributions can be used to assess risk. The range, the standard deviation, and the coefficient of variation can be used to measure risk quantitatively.

LG3 **Discuss the measurement of return and standard deviation for a portfolio and the concept of correlation.** The return of a portfolio is calculated as the weighted average of returns on the individual assets from which it is formed. The portfolio standard deviation is found by using the formula for the standard deviation of a single asset.

Correlation—the statistical relationship between any two series of numbers—can be positive, negative, or uncorrelated. At the extremes, the series can be perfectly positively correlated or perfectly negatively correlated.

LG4 **Understand the risk and return characteristics of a portfolio in terms of correlation and diversification, and the impact of international assets on a portfolio.** Diversification involves combining assets with low correlation to reduce the risk of the portfolio. The range of risk in a two-asset portfolio depends on the correlation between the two assets. If they are perfectly positively correlated, the portfolio's risk will be between the individual assets' risks. If they are uncorrelated, the portfolio's risk will be between the risk of the more

TABLE 5.13

Summary of Key Definitions and Formulas for Risk and Return

Definitions of variables

b_j = beta coefficient or index of nondiversifiable risk for asset j

b_p = portfolio beta

C_t = cash received from the asset investment in the time period $t-1$ to t

CV = coefficient of variation

$\bar{k}$ = expected value of a return

k_j = return for the jth outcome; return on asset j; required return on asset j

k_m = market return; the return on the market portfolio of assets

k_p = portfolio return

k_t = actual, expected, or required rate of return during period t

n = number of outcomes considered

P_t = price (value) of asset at time t

P_{t-1} = price (value) of asset at time $t-1$

Pr_j = probability of occurrence of the jth outcome

R_F = risk-free rate of return

σ_k = standard deviation of returns

w_j = proportion of total portfolio dollar value represented by asset j

---

Risk and return formulas

Rate of return during period t:

$$k_t = \frac{C_t + P_t - P_{t-1}}{P_{t-1}}$$ [Equation 5.1]

Expected value of a return:
  For probabilistic data:

$$\bar{k} = \sum_{j=1}^{n} k_j \times Pr_j$$ [Equation 5.2]

  General formula:

$$\bar{k} = \frac{\sum_{j=1}^{n} k_j}{n}$$ [Equation 5.2a]

Standard deviation of return:
  For probabilistic data:

$$\sigma_k = \sqrt{\sum_{j=1}^{n} (k_j - \bar{k})^2 \times Pr_j}$$ [Equation 5.3]

  General formula:

$$\sigma_k = \sqrt{\frac{\sum_{j=1}^{n} (k_j - \bar{k})^2}{n - 1}}$$ [Equation 5.3a]

Coefficient of variation:

$$CV = \frac{\sigma_k}{\bar{k}}$$ [Equation 5.4]

Portfolio return:

$$k_p = \sum_{j=1}^{n} w_j \times k_j$$ [Equation 5.5]

Total security risk = Nondiversifiable risk + Diversifiable risk [Equation 5.6]

Portfolio beta:

$$b_p = \sum_{j=1}^{n} w_j \times b_j$$ [Equation 5.7]

Capital asset pricing model (CAPM):

$$k_j = R_F + [b_j \times (k_m - R_F)]$$ [Equation 5.8]

risky asset and an amount less than the risk of the less risky asset but greater than zero. If they are perfectly negatively correlated, the portfolio's risk will be between the risk of the more risky asset and zero.

International diversification can be used to reduce a portfolio's risk further. Foreign assets have the risk of currency fluctuation and political risks.

LG5 **Review the two types of risk and the derivation and role of beta in measuring the relevant risk of both a security and a portfolio.** The total risk of a security consists of nondiversifiable and diversifiable risk. Diversifiable risk can be eliminated through diversification. Nondiversifiable risk is the only relevant risk.

Nondiversifiable risk is measured by the beta coefficient, which is a relative measure of the relationship between an asset's return and the market return. Beta is derived by finding the slope of the "characteristic line" that best explains the historical relationship between the asset's return and the market return. The beta of a portfolio is a weighted average of the betas of the individual assets that it includes.

LG6 **Explain the capital asset pricing model (CAPM), its relationship to the security market line (SML), and the major forces causing shifts in the SML.** The capital asset pricing model (CAPM) uses beta to relate an asset's risk relative to the market to the asset's required return. The graphical depiction of CAPM is the security market line (SML), which shifts over time in response to changing inflationary expectations and/or changes in investor risk aversion. Changes in inflationary expectations result in parallel shifts in the SML. Increasing risk aversion results in a steepening in the slope of the SML. Decreasing risk aversion reduces the slope of the SML. Although it has some shortcomings, CAPM provides a useful conceptual framework for evaluating and linking risk and return.

Self-Test Problems (Solutions in Appendix B)

ST5–1   Portfolio analysis   You have been asked for your advice in selecting a portfolio of assets and have been given the following data:

	Expected return		
Year	Asset A	Asset B	Asset C
2007	12%	16%	12%
2008	14	14	14
2009	16	12	16

No probabilities have been supplied. You have been told that you can create two portfolios—one consisting of assets A and B and the other consisting of assets A and C—by investing equal proportions (50%) in each of the two component assets.

a. What is the expected return for each asset over the 3-year period?

b. What is the standard deviation for each asset's return?

    c. What is the expected return for each of the two portfolios?

    d. How would you characterize the correlations of returns of the two assets making up each of the two portfolios identified in part **c**?

    e. What is the standard deviation for each portfolio?

    f. Which portfolio do you recommend? Why?

 ST5–2 **Beta and CAPM**   Currently under consideration is a project with a beta, b, of 1.50. At this time, the risk-free rate of return, R_F, is 7%, and the return on the market portfolio of assets, k_m, is 10%. The project is actually *expected* to earn an annual rate of return of 11%.

    a. If the return on the market portfolio were to increase by 10%, what would you expect to happen to the project's *required return?* What if the market return were to decline by 10%?

    b. Use the capital asset pricing model (CAPM) to find the *required return* on this investment.

    c. On the basis of your calculation in part **b**, would you recommend this investment? Why or why not?

    d. Assume that as a result of investors becoming less risk-averse, the market return drops by 1% to 9%. What impact would this change have on your responses in parts **b** and **c**?

Warm-Up Exercises

E5–1 An analyst predicted last year that the stock of Logistics, Inc., would offer a total return of at least 10% in the coming year. At the beginning of the year, the firm had a stock market value of $10 million. At the end of the year, it had a market value of $12 million even though it experienced a loss, or negative net income, of $2.5 million. Did the analyst's prediction prove correct? Explain using the values for total annual return.

E5–2 Four analysts cover the stock of Fluorine Chemical. One forecasts a 5% return for the coming year. A second expects the return to be negative 5%. A third predicts a 10% return. A fourth expects a 3% return in the coming year. You are relatively confident that the return will be positive but not large, so you arbitrarily assign probabilities of being correct of 35%, 5%, 20%, and 40%, respectively, to the analysts' forecasts. Given these probabilities, what is Fluorine Chemical's *expected return* for the coming year?

E5–3 The expected annual returns are 15% for investment 1 and 12% for investment 2. The standard deviation of the first investment's return is 10%; the second investment's return has a standard deviation of 5%. Which investment is less risky based solely on *standard deviation?* Which investment is less risky based on *coefficient of variation?* Which is a better measure given that the expected returns of the two investments are not the same?

E5–4 Your portfolio has three asset classes. U.S. government T-bills account for 45% of the portfolio, large-company stocks constitute another 40%, and small-company stocks make up the remaining 15%. If the expected returns are 3.8% for the T-bills, 12.4% for the large-company stocks, and 17.5% for the small-company stocks, what is the expected return of the portfolio?

LG5

E5–5 You wish to calculate the risk level of your portfolio based on its beta. The five stocks in the portfolio with their respective weights and betas are as follows:

Stock	Portfolio weight	Beta
Alpha	20%	1.15
Centauri	10	.85
Zen	15	1.6
Wren	20	1.35
Yukos	35	1.85

Calculate the beta of your portfolio.

E5–6 **a.** Calculate the required rate of return for an asset that has a beta of 1.8, given a risk-free rate of 5% and a market return of 10%.
 b. If investors have become more risk-averse due to recent geopolitical events, and the market return rises to 13%, what is the required rate of return for the same asset?
 c. Use your findings in part **a.** to graph the initial *security market line (SML),* and then use your findings in part **b.** to graph (on the same set of axes) the shift in the SML.

Problems

BASIC

P5–1 **Rate of return** Douglas Keel, a financial analyst for Orange Industries, wishes to estimate the rate of return for two similar-risk investments, X and Y. Douglas's research indicates that the immediate past returns will serve as reasonable estimates of future returns. A year earlier, investment X had a market value of $20,000; investment Y had a market value of $55,000. During the year, investment X generated cash flow of $1,500 and investment Y generated cash flow of $6,800. The current market values of investments X and Y are $21,000 and $55,000, respectively.
 a. Calculate the expected rate of return on investments X and Y using the most recent year's data.
 b. Assuming that the two investments are equally risky, which one should Douglas recommend? Why?

LG1

BASIC

P5–2 **Return calculations** For each of the investments shown in the following table, calculate the rate of return earned over the unspecified time period.

Investment	Cash flow during period	Beginning-of-period value	End-of-period value
A	− $ 100	$ 800	$ 1,100
B	15,000	120,000	118,000
C	7,000	45,000	48,000
D	80	600	500
E	1,500	12,500	12,400

LG1

INTERMEDIATE

P5–3   Risk preferences   Sharon Smith, the financial manager for Barnett Corporation, wishes to evaluate three prospective investments: X, Y, and Z. Currently, the firm earns 12% on its investments, which have a risk index of 6%. The expected return and expected risk of the investments are as follows:

Investment	Expected return	Expected risk index
X	14%	7%
Y	12	8
Z	10	9

a. If Sharon were *risk-indifferent,* which investments would she select? Explain why.
b. If she were *risk-averse,* which investments would she select? Why?
c. If she were *risk-seeking,* which investments would she select? Why?
d. Given the traditional risk preference behavior exhibited by financial managers, which investment would be preferred? Why?

LG2

INTERMEDIATE

P5–4   Risk analysis   Solar Designs is considering an investment in an expanded product line. Two possible types of expansion are being considered. After investigating the possible outcomes, the company made the estimates shown in the following table:

	Expansion A	Expansion B
Initial investment	$12,000	$12,000
Annual rate of return		
Pessimistic	16%	10%
Most likely	20%	20%
Optimistic	24%	30%

a. Determine the *range* of the rates of return for each of the two projects.
b. Which project is less risky? Why?
c. If you were making the investment decision, which one would you choose? Why? What does this imply about your feelings toward risk?
d. Assume that expansion B's most likely outcome is 21% per year and that all other facts remain the same. Does this change your answer to part c? Why?

LG2

INTERMEDIATE

P5–5   Risk and probability   Micro-Pub, Inc., is considering the purchase of one of two microfilm cameras, R and S. Both should provide benefits over a 10-year period, and each requires an initial investment of $4,000. Management has constructed the table (at the top of the facing page) of estimates of rates of return and probabilities for pessimistic, most likely, and optimistic results.

a. Determine the *range* for the rate of return for each of the two cameras.
b. Determine the *expected value* of return for each camera.
c. Purchase of which camera is riskier? Why?

	Camera R		Camera S	
	Amount	Probability	Amount	Probability
Initial investment	$4,000	1.00	$4,000	1.00
Annual rate of return				
Pessimistic	20%	.25	15%	.20
Most likely	25%	.50	25%	.55
Optimistic	30%	.25	35%	.25

INTERMEDIATE

P5–6   Bar charts and risk   Swan's Sportswear is considering bringing out a line of designer jeans. Currently, it is negotiating with two different well-known designers. Because of the highly competitive nature of the industry, the two lines of jeans have been given code names. After market research, the firm has established the expectations shown in the following table about the annual rates of return:

		Annual rate of return	
Market acceptance	Probability	Line J	Line K
Very poor	.05	.0075	.010
Poor	.15	.0125	.025
Average	.60	.0850	.080
Good	.15	.1475	.135
Excellent	.05	.1625	.150

Use the table to:
a. Construct a bar chart for each line's annual rate of return.
b. Calculate the *expected value* of return for each line.
c. Evaluate the relative riskiness for each jean line's rate of return using the bar charts.

BASIC

P5–7   Coefficient of variation   Metal Manufacturing has isolated four alternatives for meeting its need for increased production capacity. The data gathered relative to each of these alternatives are summarized in the following table:

Alternative	Expected return	Standard deviation of return
A	20%	7.0%
B	22	9.5
C	19	6.0
D	16	5.5

a. Calculate the *coefficient of variation* for each alternative.
b. If the firm wishes to minimize risk, which alternative do you recommend? Why?

P5–8   Standard deviation versus coefficient of variation as measures of risk
Greengage, Inc., a successful nursery, is considering several expansion projects. All of the alternatives promise to produce an acceptable return. The owners are extremely risk-averse; therefore, they will choose the least risky of the alternatives. Data on four possible projects follow.

Project	Expected return	Range	Standard deviation
A	12.0%	.040	.029
B	12.5	.050	.032
C	13.0	.060	.035
D	12.8	.045	.030

a. Which project is least risky, judging on the basis of range?
b. Which project has the lowest standard deviation? Explain why standard deviation is not an appropriate measure of risk for purposes of this comparison.
c. Calculate the coefficient of variation for each project. Which project will Greengage's owners choose? Explain why this may be the best measure of risk for comparing this set of opportunities.

P5–9   Assessing return and risk   Swift Manufacturing must choose between two asset purchases. The annual rate of return and the related probabilities given in the following table summarize the firm's analysis to this point.

Project 257		Project 432	
Rate of return	Probability	Rate of return	Probability
− 10%	.01	10%	.05
10	.04	15	.10
20	.05	20	.10
30	.10	25	.15
40	.15	30	.20
45	.30	35	.15
50	.15	40	.10
60	.10	45	.10
70	.05	50	.05
80	.04		
100	.01		

a. For each project, compute:
   (1) The range of possible rates of return.
   (2) The expected value of return.
   (3) The standard deviation of the returns.
   (4) The coefficient of variation of the returns.
b. Construct a bar chart of each distribution of rates of return.
c. Which project would you consider less risky? Why?

P5–10   Integrative—Expected return, standard deviation, and coefficient of variation
Three assets—F, G, and H—are currently being considered by Perth Industries. The probability distributions of expected returns for these assets are shown in the table at the top of the facing page:

	Asset F		Asset G		Asset H	
j	Pr_j	Return, k_j	Pr_j	Return, k_j	Pr_j	Return, k_j
1	.10	40%	.40	35%	.10	40%
2	.20	10	.30	10	.20	20
3	.40	0	.30	−20	.40	10
4	.20	− 5			.20	0
5	.10	−10			.10	−20

a. Calculate the expected value of return, $\overline{k}$, for each of the three assets. Which provides the largest expected return?
b. Calculate the standard deviation, σ_k, for each of the three assets' returns. Which appears to have the greatest risk?
c. Calculate the coefficient of variation, CV, for each of the three assets' returns. Which appears to have the greatest *relative* risk?

P5–11 **Normal probability distribution**   Assuming that the rates of return associated with a given asset investment are normally distributed and that the expected return, $\overline{k}$, is 18.9% and the coefficient of variation, CV, is .75, answer the following questions:

a. Find the standard deviation of returns, σ_k.
b. Calculate the range of expected return outcomes associated with the following probabilities of occurrence: (1) 68%, (2) 95%, (3) 99%.
c. Draw the probability distribution associated with your findings in parts **a** and **b**.

P5–12 **Portfolio return and standard deviation**   Jamie Wong is considering building a portfolio containing two assets, L and M. Asset L will represent 40% of the dollar value of the portfolio, and asset M will account for the other 60%. The expected returns over the next 6 years, 2007–2012, for each of these assets, are shown in the following table:

	Expected return	
Year	Asset L	Asset M
2007	14%	20%
2008	14	18
2009	16	16
2010	17	14
2011	17	12
2012	19	10

a. Calculate the expected portfolio return, k_p, for *each* of the 6 years.
b. Calculate the expected value of portfolio returns, $\overline{k}_p$, over the 6-year period.
c. Calculate the standard deviation of expected portfolio returns, σ_{k_p}, over the 6-year period.
d. How would you characterize the correlation of returns of the two assets L and M?
e. Discuss any benefits of diversification achieved through creation of the portfolio.

P5–13   **Portfolio analysis**   You have been given the return data shown in the first table on three assets—F, G, and H—over the period 2007–2010.

	Expected return		
Year	Asset F	Asset G	Asset H
2007	16%	17%	14%
2008	17	16	15
2009	18	15	16
2010	19	14	17

Using these assets, you have isolated the three investment alternatives shown in the following table:

Alternative	Investment
1	100% of asset F
2	50% of asset F and 50% of asset G
3	50% of asset F and 50% of asset H

a. Calculate the expected return over the 4-year period for each of the three alternatives.
b. Calculate the standard deviation of returns over the 4-year period for each of the three alternatives.
c. Use your findings in parts a and b to calculate the coefficient of variation for each of the three alternatives.
d. On the basis of your findings, which of the three investment alternatives do you recommend? Why?

P5–14   **Correlation, risk, and return**   Matt Peters wishes to evaluate the risk and return behaviors associated with various combinations of assets V and W under three assumed degrees of correlation: perfect positive, uncorrelated, and perfect negative. The expected return and risk values calculated for each of the assets are shown in the following table.

Asset	Expected return, $\bar{k}$	Risk (standard deviation), σ_k
V	8%	5%
W	13	10

a. If the returns of assets V and W are *perfectly positively correlated* (correlation coefficient = +1), describe the *range* of (1) expected return and (2) risk associated with all possible portfolio combinations.
b. If the returns of assets V and W are *uncorrelated* (correlation coefficient = 0), describe the *approximate range* of (1) expected return and (2) risk associated with all possible portfolio combinations.
c. If the returns of assets V and W are *perfectly negatively correlated* (correlation coefficient = −1), describe the *range* of (1) expected return and (2) risk associated with all possible portfolio combinations.

INTERMEDIATE

P5–15 **International investment returns**   Joe Martinez, a U.S. citizen living in Brownsville, Texas, invested in the common stock of Telmex, a Mexican corporation. He purchased 1,000 shares at 20.50 pesos per share. Twelve months later, he sold them at 24.75 pesos per share. He received no dividends during that time.

    a. What was Joe's investment return (in percentage terms) for the year, on the basis of the peso value of the shares?

    b. The exchange rate for pesos was 9.21 pesos per US$1.00 at the time of the purchase. At the time of the sale, the exchange rate was 9.85 pesos per US$1.00. Translate the purchase and sale prices into US$.

    c. Calculate Joe's investment return on the basis of the US$ value of the shares.

    d. Explain why the two returns are different. Which one is more important to Joe? Why?

LG5

INTERMEDIATE

P5–16 **Total, nondiversifiable, and diversifiable risk**   David Talbot randomly selected securities from all those listed on the New York Stock Exchange for his portfolio. He began with a single security and added securities one by one until a total of 20 securities were held in the portfolio. After each security was added, David calculated the portfolio standard deviation, σ_{k_p}. The calculated values are shown in the following table.

Number of securities	Portfolio risk, σ_{k_p}	Number of securities	Portfolio risk, σ_{k_p}
1	14.50%	11	7.00%
2	13.30	12	6.80
3	12.20	13	6.70
4	11.20	14	6.65
5	10.30	15	6.60
6	9.50	16	6.56
7	8.80	17	6.52
8	8.20	18	6.50
9	7.70	19	6.48
10	7.30	20	6.47

    a. On a set of "number of securities in portfolio (x axis)–portfolio risk (y axis)" axes, plot the portfolio risk data given in the preceding table.

    b. Divide the total portfolio risk in the graph into its *nondiversifiable* and *diversifiable* risk components and label each of these on the graph.

    c. Describe which of the two risk components is the *relevant risk,* and explain why it is relevant. How much of this risk exists in David Talbot's portfolio?

LG5

INTERMEDIATE

P5–17 **Graphical derivation of beta**   A firm wishes to estimate graphically the betas for two assets, A and B. It has gathered the return data shown in the table at the top of page 268 for the market portfolio and for both assets over the last 10 years, 1997–2006.

    a. On a set of "market return (x axis)–asset return (y axis)" axes, use the data given to draw the characteristic line for asset A and for asset B.

    b. Use the characteristic lines from part **a** to estimate the betas for assets A and B.

c. Use the betas found in part **b** to comment on the relative risks of assets A and B.

	Actual return		
Year	Market portfolio	Asset A	Asset B
1997	6%	11%	16%
1998	2	8	11
1999	−13	− 4	−10
2000	− 4	3	3
2001	− 8	0	− 3
2002	16	19	30
2003	10	14	22
2004	15	18	29
2005	8	12	19
2006	13	17	26

P5–18 Interpreting beta A firm wishes to assess the impact of changes in the market return on an asset that has a beta of 1.20.

a. If the market return increased by 15%, what impact would this change be expected to have on the asset's return?

b. If the market return decreased by 8%, what impact would this change be expected to have on the asset's return?

c. If the market return did not change, what impact, if any, would be expected on the asset's return?

d. Would this asset be considered more or less risky than the market? Explain.

P5–19 Betas Answer the following questions for assets A to D shown in the following table.

Asset	Beta
A	.50
B	1.60
C	− .20
D	.90

a. What impact would a *10% increase* in the market return be expected to have on each asset's return?

b. What impact would a *10% decrease* in the market return be expected to have on each asset's return?

c. If you were certain that the market return would *increase* in the near future, which asset would you prefer? Why?

d. If you were certain that the market return would *decrease* in the near future, which asset would you prefer? Why?

P5–20 Betas and risk rankings Stock A has a beta of .80, stock B has a beta of 1.40, and stock C has a beta of − .30.

a. Rank these stocks from the most risky to the least risky.

b. If the return on the market portfolio increased by 12%, what change would you expect in the return for each of the stocks?

c. If the return on the market portfolio decreased by 5%, what change would you expect in the return for each of the stocks?

d. If you felt that the stock market was getting ready to experience a significant decline, which stock would you probably add to your portfolio? Why?

e. If you anticipated a major stock market rally, which stock would you add to your portfolio? Why?

P5–21 **Portfolio betas**   Rose Berry is attempting to evaluate two possible portfolios, which consist of the same five assets held in different proportions. She is particularly interested in using beta to compare the risks of the portfolios, so she has gathered the data shown in the following table.

		Portfolio weights	
Asset	Asset beta	Portfolio A	Portfolio B
1	1.30	10%	30%
2	.70	30	10
3	1.25	10	20
4	1.10	10	20
5	.90	40	20
Totals		100%	100%

a. Calculate the betas for portfolios A and B.

b. Compare the risks of these portfolios to the market as well as to each other. Which portfolio is more risky?

P5–22 **Capital asset pricing model (CAPM)**   For each of the cases shown in the following table, use the capital asset pricing model to find the required return.

Case	Risk-free rate, R_F	Market return, k_m	Beta, b
A	5%	8%	1.30
B	8	13	.90
C	9	12	− .20
D	10	15	1.00
E	6	10	.60

P5–23 **Beta coefficients and the capital asset pricing model**   Katherine Wilson is wondering how much risk she must undertake to generate an acceptable return on her portfolio. The risk-free return currently is 5%. The return on the average stock (market return) is 16%. Use the CAPM to calculate the beta coefficient associated with each of the following portfolio returns.

a. 10%

b. 15%

c. 18%

d. 20%

e. Katherine is risk-averse. What is the highest return she can expect if she is unwilling to take more than an average risk?

P5–24 Manipulating CAPM   Use the basic equation for the capital asset pricing model (CAPM) to work each of the following problems.

a. Find the *required return* for an asset with a beta of .90 when the risk-free rate and market return are 8% and 12%, respectively.

b. Find the *risk-free rate* for a firm with a required return of 15% and a beta of 1.25 when the market return is 14%.

c. Find the *market return* for an asset with a required return of 16% and a beta of 1.10 when the risk-free rate is 9%.

d. Find the *beta* for an asset with a required return of 15% when the risk-free rate and market return are 10% and 12.5%, respectively.

P5–25 Portfolio return and beta   Jamie Peters invested $100,000 to set up the following portfolio one year ago:

Asset	Cost	Beta at purchase	Yearly income	Value today
A	$20,000	.80	$1,600	$20,000
B	35,000	.95	1,400	36,000
C	30,000	1.50	—	34,500
D	15,000	1.25	375	16,500

a. Calculate the portfolio beta on the basis of the original cost figures.

b. Calculate the percentage return of each asset in the portfolio for the year.

c. Calculate the percentage return of the portfolio on the basis of original cost, using income and gains during the year.

d. At the time Jamie made his investments, investors were estimating that the market return for the coming year would be 10%. The estimate of the risk-free rate of return averaged 4% for the coming year. Calculate an expected rate of return for each stock on the basis of its beta and the expectations of market and risk-free returns.

e. On the basis of the actual results, explain how each stock in the portfolio performed relative to those CAPM-generated expectations of performance. What factors could explain these differences?

P5–26 Security market line (SML)   Assume that the risk-free rate, R_F, is currently 9% and that the market return, k_m, is currently 13%.

a. Draw the security market line (SML) on a set of "nondiversifiable risk (x axis)–required return (y axis)" axes.

b. Calculate and label the *market risk premium* on the axes in part **a.**

c. Given the previous data, calculate the required return on asset A having a beta of .80 and asset B having a beta of 1.30.

d. Draw in the betas and required returns from part **c** for assets A and B on the axes in part **a.** Label the *risk premium* associated with each of these assets, and discuss them.

P5–27 Shifts in the security market line   Assume that the risk-free rate, R_F, is currently 8%, the market return, k_m, is 12%, and asset A has a beta, b_A, of 1.10.

a. Draw the security market line (SML) on a set of "nondiversifiable risk (x axis)–required return (y axis)" axes.

b. Use CAPM to calculate the required return, k_A, on asset A, and depict asset A's beta and required return on the SML drawn in part **a.**

c. Assume that as a result of recent economic events, inflationary expectations have declined by 2%, lowering R_F and k_m to 6% and 10%, respectively. Draw the new SML on the axes in part **a,** and calculate and show the new required return for asset A.

d. Assume that as a result of recent events, investors have become more risk-averse, causing the market return to rise by 1%, to 13%. Ignoring the shift in part **c,** draw the new SML on the same set of axes that you used before, and calculate and show the new required return for asset A.

e. From the previous changes, what conclusions can be drawn about the impact of (1) decreased inflationary expectations and (2) increased risk aversion on the required returns of risky assets?

P5–28 Integrative—Risk, return, and CAPM Wolff Enterprises must consider several investment projects, A through E, using the capital asset pricing model (CAPM) and its graphical representation, the security market line (SML). Relevant information is presented in the following table.

Item	Rate of return	Beta, b
Risk-free asset	9%	0
Market portfolio	14	1.00
Project A	—	1.50
Project B	—	.75
Project C	—	2.00
Project D	—	0
Project E	—	− .5

a. Calculate (1) the required rate of return and (2) the risk premium for each project, given its level of nondiversifiable risk.

b. Use your findings in part **a** to draw the security market line (required return relative to nondiversifiable risk).

c. Discuss the relative nondiversifiable risk of projects A through E.

d. Assume that recent economic events have caused investors to become less risk-averse, causing the market return to decline by 2%, to 12%. Calculate the new required returns for assets A through E, and draw the new security market line on the same set of axes that you used in part **b.**

e. Compare your findings in parts **a** and **b** with those in part **d.** What conclusion can you draw about the impact of a decline in investor risk aversion on the required returns of risky assets?

P5–29 ETHICS PROBLEM Integrity, especially honesty, is trait number one for being hired as a CFO in corporate America today. How might you assess a job candidate's honesty if you were interviewing a potential CFO candidate?

Chapter 5 Case: Analyzing Risk and Return on Chargers Products' Investments

Junior Sayou, a financial analyst for Chargers Products, a manufacturer of stadium benches, must evaluate the risk and return of two assets, X and Y. The firm is considering adding these assets to its diversified asset portfolio. To assess the return and risk of each asset, Junior gathered data on the annual cash flow and beginning- and end-of-year values of each asset over the immediately preceding 10 years, 1997–2006. These data are summarized in the table below. Junior's investigation suggests that both assets, on average, will tend to perform in the future just as they have during the past 10 years. He therefore believes that the expected annual return can be estimated by finding the average annual return for each asset over the past 10 years.

		Return Data for Assets X and Y, 1997–2006					
		Asset X			Asset Y		
		Value				Value	
Year	Cash flow	Beginning	Ending	Cash flow	Beginning	Ending
1997	$1,000	$20,000	$22,000	$1,500	$20,000	$20,000
1998	1,500	22,000	21,000	1,600	20,000	20,000
1999	1,400	21,000	24,000	1,700	20,000	21,000
2000	1,700	24,000	22,000	1,800	21,000	21,000
2001	1,900	22,000	23,000	1,900	21,000	22,000
2002	1,600	23,000	26,000	2,000	22,000	23,000
2003	1,700	26,000	25,000	2,100	23,000	23,000
2004	2,000	25,000	24,000	2,200	23,000	24,000
2005	2,100	24,000	27,000	2,300	24,000	25,000
2006	2,200	27,000	30,000	2,400	25,000	25,000

Junior believes that each asset's risk can be assessed in two ways: in isolation and as part of the firm's diversified portfolio of assets. The risk of the assets in isolation can be found by using the standard deviation and coefficient of variation of returns over the past 10 years. The capital asset pricing model (CAPM) can be used to assess the asset's risk as part of the firm's portfolio of assets. Applying some sophisticated quantitative techniques, Junior estimated betas for assets X and Y of 1.60 and 1.10, respectively. In addition, he found that the risk-free rate is currently 7% and that the market return is 10%.

TO DO

a. Calculate the annual rate of return for each asset in *each* of the 10 preceding years, and use those values to find the average annual return for each asset over the 10-year period.

b. Use the returns calculated in part a to find (1) the standard deviation and (2) the coefficient of variation of the returns for each asset over the 10-year period 1997–2006.

c. Use your findings in parts a and b to evaluate and discuss the return and risk associated with each asset. Which asset appears to be preferable? Explain.

    d. Use the CAPM to find the required return for each asset. Compare this value with the average annual returns calculated in part **a.**

    e. Compare and contrast your findings in parts **c** and **d.** What recommendations would you give Junior with regard to investing in either of the two assets? Explain to Junior why he is better off using beta rather than the standard deviation and coefficient of variation to assess the risk of each asset.

    f. Rework parts **d** and **e** under each of the following circumstances:

        (1) A rise of 1% in inflationary expectations causes the risk-free rate to rise to 8% and the market return to rise to 11%.

        (2) As a result of favorable political events, investors suddenly become less risk-averse, causing the market return to drop by 1%, to 9%.

Spreadsheet Exercise

Jane is considering investing in three different stocks or creating three distinct two-stock portfolios. Jane considers herself to be a rather conservative investor. She is able to obtain forecasted returns for the three securities for the years 2007 through 2013. The data are as follows:

Year	Stock A	Stock B	Stock C
2007	10%	10%	12%
2008	13	11	14
2009	15	8	10
2010	14	12	11
2011	16	10	9
2012	14	15	9
2013	12	15	10

In any of the possible two-stock portfolios, the weight of each stock in the portfolio will be 50%. The three possible portfolio combinations are AB, AC, and BC.

TO DO

Create a spreadsheet similar to Tables 5.7 and 5.8 (or the spreadsheets that can be viewed at www.aw-bc.com/gitman) to answer the following:

a. Calculate the expected return for each individual stock.

b. Calculate the standard deviation for each individual stock.

c. Calculate the expected returns for portfolio AB, AC, and BC.

d. Calculate the standard deviations for portfolios AB, AC, and BC.

e. Would you recommend that Jane invest in the single stock A or the portfolio consisting of stocks A and B? Explain your answer from a risk–return viewpoint.

f. Would you recommend that Jane invest in the single stock B or the portfolio consisting of stocks B and C? Explain your answer from a risk–return viewpoint.

Group Exercise

This chapter begins the book's exploration of the important topics of risk and return. This assignment will bring the group back to an analysis of your real-world firm. Many Web sites provide the necessary type of market information, such as historical price data, returns, and betas. You should always be careful, as with any research, about the source of information; it is safest to stick to the more well-known or government-sponsored sites. One small part of this exercise will be to compare different sources of information and the information contained therein.

TO DO

a. Obtain financial information for both broad market indices and your shadow firm. Begin by checking several Web sites, which will serve as a good way to compare these sites. At each site, look up your shadow firm and investigate what information each Web site has available. It should include current, historical, and market index information. As there are many quality sites with publicly available, free information, the following is merely a short list of suggestions. You will use some of these data in the other parts of this assignment.

Point your browser to the Nasdaq home page, www.nasdaq.com/. Begin by asking for financial data on your shadow firm. To do so, use the stock symbol for your firm. Ask for a "summary quote," which will give you basic financial information along with options for other data and charts. Next, look up information on broader indices. Now, direct your browser to the home page of the NYSE, www.nyse.com/. Repeat the steps from the Nasdaq site. A very useful site is Yahoo's finance site http://finance.yahoo.com/. Next, go to Bloomberg's Web page, www.bloomberg.com/index.html, and repeat the steps. MSN's site, at www.moneycentral.msn.com/home.asp, is also useful. You may also use www.bigcharts.com to find historical stock prices and graphs. Lastly, you could visit Reuters' Web site at www.reuters.com/.

b. Using the site of your choice, find the price of your shadow corporation's stock one year earlier. Calculate its 1-year return based solely on the change in the price of a share of stock. Compare this return to the return for a market benchmark—for example, the Dow Jones Industrial Average, the S&P 500, or a Nasdaq-based metric such as the Nasdaq 100. Next, calculate the return for your stock over the past 5 years. How does the return over 5 years compare to the recent 1-year return? Now compare the 5-year return on your benchmark to your corporation's stock.

c. Using the same data as part **b**, calculate the annual return for each of the past 5 years for your stock. Use these data to compute the expected return and the standard deviation of the returns.

d. You can graphically check for correlation by eyeballing a 5-year chart that contains the past history of your stock and the benchmark you have chosen. Discuss the degree of correlation and any changes you notice over the period.

e. Use recent data to calculate the required return on your corporation. You will need to get the rate on 3-month T-bills to be used as the risk-free rate. You can use the beta reported by a site of your choice and use the historical return for your benchmark as the market return.

f. Using your answers from part **c**, graph the SML.

Web Exercise

One risk mentioned in the text is inflation risk. We have looked previously at interest rates on mortgages and yields on 10-year U.S. Treasury bonds. Here we will look at inflation rates in the United States over the past decades.

TO DO

Point your browser to the Bureau of Labor Statistics' home page at www.bls.gov/. Inflation and Consumer Spending is the first heading; under it you will find the link for the consumer price index (CPI). Here you can find information and data covering this most-familiar consumer inflation measure.

a. After acclimating yourself with this page and the general information on the CPI, go to Get Detailed CPI Statistics and highlight All Urban Consumers (Current Series). Select the first box, US All Items. At the bottom of the page, click "Retrieve Data." The table that is retrieved produces the index numbers with the time period of 1982–1984 = 100. You will need to convert this index into a percentage change at an annual rate. Choose More Formatting Options at the top of the page. On the next page, you will highlight the box for 12 months percent change. You also will change the data range to 1953 to the present. Now retrieve data again.

   At this point, you should have two tables, with the new one appearing at the bottom. Find the annual column that calculates the inflation rate for each year over the past 5 decades. Note the pattern of annual inflation rates. Compare it to the pattern exhibited in the 10-year Treasury bonds and the mortgage rate data from Chapter 4. While this is an annual series and you are comparing it to monthly data, you should still be able to discern a pattern between rising and falling rates of interest over time, as exhibited both in the 10-year series and the 30-year mortgage rate series, and rates of inflation, as measured by the CPI series.

b. Return to the CPI series, and look for any trends in the monthly rates that foretold the rising or falling rates shown in the annual column. For example, look at the 1972–1974 period. Rates of inflation at the annual level appear to have risen almost without warning from 3.2% to 6.2% to 11% over the 3 years. However, if you look at the monthly rates for the 3 years, you will see the increasing trend more clearly. Interest rates and yields would not be set only once a year with solely annual data. Instead, changes are incorporated minute by minute. A monthly frequency is better than an annual review and does capture much of any changing trend(s).

Remember to check the book's Web site at

www.aw-bc.com/gitman

for additional resources, including additional Web exercises.

Chapter 6

Interest Rates and Bond Valuation

LEARNING GOALS

LG1 Describe interest rate fundamentals, the term structure of interest rates, and risk premiums.

LG2 Review the legal aspects of bond financing and bond cost.

LG3 Discuss the general features, quotations, ratings, popular types, and international issues of corporate bonds.

LG4 Understand the key inputs and basic model used in the valuation process.

LG5 Apply the basic valuation model to bonds and describe the impact of required return and time to maturity on bond values.

LG6 Explain yield to maturity (YTM), its calculation, and the procedure used to value bonds that pay interest semiannually.

ACROSS THE DISCIPLINES WHY THIS CHAPTER MATTERS TO YOU

Accounting: You need to understand interest rates and the various types of bonds to be able to account properly for amortization of bond premiums and discounts and for bond purchases and retirements.

Information systems: You need to understand the data that you will need to track in bond amortization schedules and bond valuation.

Management: You need to understand the behavior of interest rates and how they will affect the types of funds the

firm can raise and the timing and cost of bond issues and retirements.

Marketing: You need to understand how the interest rate level and the firm's ability to issue bonds may affect the availability of financing for marketing research projects and new-product development.

Operations: You need to understand how the interest rate level may affect the firm's ability to raise funds to maintain and grow the firm's production capacity.

U. S. TREASURY
A HUGE APPETITE FOR MONEY

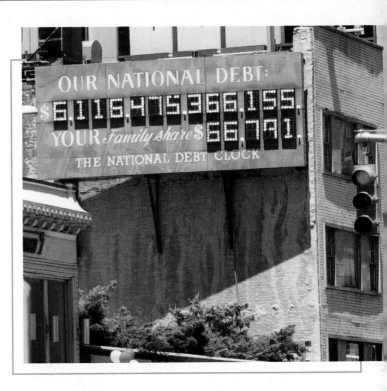

Who is the largest debtor in the United States? Why, the federal government, of course. As of July 9, 2004, the national debt was $7,267,025,626,017. With annual deficits of $158 billion in 2002, $375 billion in 2003, and a Congressional Budget Office projection of a $477 billion deficit in 2004, the federal government has a huge need for outside financing that dwarfs any corporate bond issue.

To feed this huge demand, the **U.S. Department of Treasury** (www.ustreas.gov) can issue T-bills (debt securities that mature in less than 1 year), Treasury notes (1- to 10-year maturities), Treasury bonds (which mature in more than 10 years), and savings bonds. In addition to public auctions, Treasury securities can be purchased at banks (EE- and I-series savings bonds) and through TreasuryDirect, a Web-based system.

The Treasury Department has not offered a Treasury bond since October 2001, when it suspended issuance of the 30-year bond. With short-term rates at record low levels, it made sense to offer the short-term debt in lieu of the longer-term, higher-interest debt. The Treasury can also lower the cost of the federal debt by refinancing some of the longer-term debt. While not all 30-year Treasury bonds are *callable* (able to be repurchased at a set price at the will of the Treasury), some are, and it makes sense to swap them for lower-priced debt. For example, on May 15, 2004, the Treasury called for redemption of the 9 1/8 percent Treasury bond issued in May 1979 and scheduled to mature in May 2009. There were $4.6 billion of these bonds outstanding, and with current rates well below 9 1/8 percent, the Treasury estimated that it could save about $544 million in interest from the call and refinancing.

In fiscal year 2003, the U.S. government spent $318 billion on interest payments to holders of the national debt. If interest rates begin to rise again, the interest expense will continue to increase. Individuals can attack this interest expense directly by making payments to the U.S. Treasury for the express purpose of reducing the United States' national debt. In 2003, the Treasury received $1,277,423 from citizens wishing to reduce the federal debt. With the debt increasing at the pace of more than $1 billion per day, these contributions stopped the growth of the federal debt briefly—for just under 2 minutes.

■ *How might the issuance of large amounts of public debt affect the corporate debt market?*

6.1 | Interest Rates and Required Returns

As noted in Chapter 1, financial institutions and markets create the mechanism through which funds flow between savers (funds suppliers) and investors (funds demanders). The level of funds flow between suppliers and demanders can significantly affect economic growth. Growth results from the interaction of a variety of economic factors (such as the money supply, trade balances, and economic policies) that affect the cost of money—the interest rate or required return.

The interest rate level acts as a regulating device that controls the flow of funds between suppliers and demanders. The *Board of Governors of the Federal Reserve System* regularly assesses economic conditions and, when necessary, initiates actions to raise or lower interest rates to control inflation and economic growth. Generally, the lower the interest rate, the greater the funds flow and therefore the greater the economic growth; the higher the interest rate, the lower the funds flow and economic growth.

Interest Rate Fundamentals

interest rate
The compensation paid by the borrower of funds to the lender; from the borrower's point of view, the cost of borrowing funds.

required return
The cost of funds obtained by selling an ownership interest; it reflects the funds supplier's level of expected return.

liquidity preferences
General preferences of investors for shorter-term securities.

real rate of interest
The rate that creates an equilibrium between the supply of savings and the demand for investment funds in a perfect world, without inflation, where funds suppliers and demanders are indifferent to the term of loans or investments and have no *liquidity preference,* and where all outcomes are certain.

The **interest rate** or required return represents the cost of money. It is the compensation that a demander of funds must pay a supplier. When funds are lent, the cost of borrowing the funds is the interest rate. When funds are obtained by selling an ownership interest—as in the sale of stock—the cost to the issuer (demander) is commonly called the **required return,** which reflects the funds supplier's level of expected return. In both cases the supplier is compensated for providing funds. Ignoring risk factors, the cost of funds results from the *real rate of interest* adjusted for inflationary expectations and **liquidity preferences**—general preferences of investors for shorter-term securities.

The Real Rate of Interest

Assume a *perfect world* in which there is no inflation and in which funds suppliers and demanders are indifferent to the term of loans or investments because they have no *liquidity preference* and all outcomes are certain.[1] At any given point in time in that perfect world, there would be one cost of money—the **real rate of interest.** The real rate of interest creates an equilibrium between the supply of savings and the demand for investment funds. It represents the most basic cost of money. The real rate of interest in the United States is assumed to be stable and equal to around 1 percent.[2] This supply–demand relationship is shown in Figure 6.1 by the supply function (labeled S_0) and the demand function (labeled D). An equilibrium between the supply of funds and the demand for funds ($S_0 = D$) occurs at a rate of interest k_0^*, the real rate of interest.

Clearly, the real rate of interest changes with changing economic conditions, tastes, and preferences. A trade surplus could result in an increased supply of

---

1. These assumptions are made to describe the most basic interest rate, the *real rate of interest.* Subsequent discussions relax these assumptions to develop the broader concept of the interest rate and required return.

2. Data in *Stocks, Bonds, Bills and Inflation, 2004 Yearbook* (Chicago: Ibbotson Associates, Inc., 2004), show that over the period 1926–2003, U.S. Treasury bills provided an average annual real rate of return of about 0.70 percent. Because of certain major economic events that occurred during the 1926–2003 period, many economists believe that the real rate of interest during recent years has been about 1 percent.

FIGURE 6.1

Supply–Demand Relationship
Supply of savings and demand for investment funds

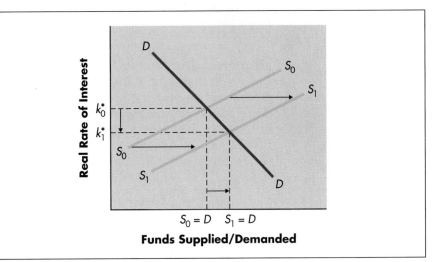

funds, causing the supply function in Figure 6.1 to shift to, say, S_1. This could result in a lower real rate of interest, k_1^*, at equilibrium ($S_1 = D$). Likewise, a change in tax laws or other factors could affect the demand for funds, causing the real rate of interest to rise or fall to a new equilibrium level.

Nominal or Actual Rate of Interest (Return)

nominal rate of interest
The actual rate of interest charged by the supplier of funds and paid by the demander.

The **nominal rate of interest** is the actual rate of interest charged by the supplier of funds and paid by the demander. *Throughout this book, interest rates and required rates of return are nominal rates unless otherwise noted.* The nominal rate of interest differs from the real rate of interest, k^*, as a result of two factors: (1) inflationary expectations reflected in an inflation premium (IP), and (2) issuer and issue characteristics, such as default risk and contractual provisions, reflected in a risk premium (RP). When this notation is adopted, the nominal rate of interest for security 1, k_1, is given in Equation 6.1:

$$k_1 = \underbrace{k^* + IP}_{\substack{\text{risk-free} \\ \text{rate, } R_F}} + \underbrace{RP_1}_{\substack{\text{risk} \\ \text{premium}}} \tag{6.1}$$

As the horizontal braces below the equation indicate, the nominal rate, k_1, can be viewed as having two basic components: a risk-free rate of return, R_F, and a risk premium, RP_1:

$$k_1 = R_F + RP_1 \tag{6.2}$$

To simplify the discussion, we will assume that the risk premium, RP_1, is equal to zero. By drawing from Equation 6.1,[3] the risk-free rate can (as earlier noted in Equation 5.9) be represented as

$$R_F = k^* + IP \tag{6.3}$$

---

3. This equation is commonly called the *Fisher equation,* named for the renowned economist Irving Fisher, who first presented this approximate relationship between nominal interest and the rate of inflation. See Irving Fisher, *The Theory of Interest* (New York: Macmillan, 1930).

Thus we concern ourselves only with the *risk-free rate of return, R_F,* which was defined in Chapter 5 as the required return on a risk-free asset.[4] The risk-free rate (as shown in Equation 6.3) embodies the real rate of interest plus the inflationary expectation. Three-month *U.S. Treasury bills (T-bills)*, which are (as noted in Chapter 5) short-term IOUs issued by the U.S. Treasury, are commonly considered the risk-free asset. *The real rate of interest can be estimated by subtracting the inflation premium from the nominal rate of interest.* For the risk-free asset in Equation 6.3, the real rate of interest, k^*, would equal $R_F - IP$. A simple example can demonstrate the practical distinction between nominal and real rates of interest.

EXAMPLE

Marilyn Carbo has $10 that she can spend on candy costing $0.25 per piece. She could therefore buy 40 pieces of candy ($10.00/$0.25) today. The nominal rate of interest on a 1-year deposit is currently 7%, and the expected rate of inflation over the coming year is 4%. Instead of buying the 40 pieces of candy today, Marilyn could invest the $10 in a 1-year deposit account now. At the end of 1 year she would have $10.70 because she would have earned 7% interest—an additional $0.70 ($0.07 \times 10.00)—on her $10 deposit. The 4% inflation rate would over the 1-year period increase the cost of the candy by 4%—an additional $0.01 ($0.04 \times 0.25)—to $0.26 per piece. As a result, at the end of the 1-year period Marilyn would be able to buy about 41.2 pieces of candy ($10.70/$0.26), or roughly 3% more (41.2/40.0 = 1.03). The increase in the amount of money available to Marilyn at the end of 1 year is merely her nominal rate of return (7%), which must be reduced by the rate of inflation (4%) during the period to determine her real rate of return of 3%. Marilyn's increased buying power therefore equals her 3% real rate of return. ■

The premium for *inflationary expectations* in Equation 6.3 represents the average rate of *inflation* expected over the life of a loan or investment. It is *not* the rate of inflation experienced over the immediate past; rather, it reflects the forecasted rate. Take, for example, the risk-free asset. During the week ended May 17, 2004, 3-month T-bills earned a 1.06 percent rate of return. Assuming an approximate 0.70 percent real rate of interest, funds suppliers were forecasting a 0.36 percent (annual) rate of inflation (1.06% − 0.70%) over the next 3 months. This expectation was in striking contrast to the expected rate of inflation 23 years earlier in the week ending May 22, 1981. At that time the 3-month T-bill rate was 16.60 percent, which meant an expected (annual) inflation rate of 15.90 percent (16.60% − 0.70%). The inflationary expectation premium changes over time in response to many factors, including recent rates, government policies, and international events. For discussion of a U.S. debt security whose interest rate is adjusted for inflation, see the *In Practice* box on the facing page.

Figure 6.2 (see page 282) illustrates the annual movement of the rate of inflation and the risk-free rate of return during the period 1978–2004. During this period the two rates tended to move in a similar fashion. Between 1978 and the early 1980s, inflation and interest rates were quite high, peaking at over 13 percent in 1980–1981. Since 1981 these rates have declined to levels generally below those in 1978. Note that during 2003 and 2004 the annual rate of inflation actu-

---

4. The risk premium and its effect on the nominal rate of interest are discussed and illustrated in a later part of this section.

In Practice FOCUS ON PRACTICE

BEAUTY IS IN THE EYE OF THE I-BOND HOLDER

One of the negative features of debt instruments when compared with equity assets is that once issued, fixed-rate debt instruments cannot be adjusted to take inflation into account. In fact, rising inflation generally raises the risk-free rate of return, and new bond issues command a higher coupon rate than previously issued bonds. From your study of the time value of money in Chapter 4, you may have discovered that when interest rates rise, the market (that is, present) value of previously issued bonds falls.

The **U.S. Department of Treasury** now offers the I Bond, which is an inflation-adjusted savings bond. A Series-I Bond earns interest through the application of a *composite rate*. The composite rate consists of a *fixed* rate that remains the same for the life of the bond and an *inflation* rate that is subject to change twice a year. Interest accrues monthly and compounds semiannually. Interest

earnings are payable only upon redemption. As with all federal debt instruments, interest earnings are exempt from state and local income taxes. Unlike Series-EE Bonds, which are issued at one-half of face value, I Bonds are issued at face value in denominations ranging from $50 to $10,000.

To adjust the inflation portion of the I Bond's interest rate, the Treasury uses the *Consumer Price Index for All Urban Consumers* (CPI-U) as the inflation rate. The CPI-U rate is announced semi-annually in May and November. The May and November figures are applicable for a 6-month period for any bonds issued before the next composite rate announcement. The I Bond's composite rate will be *higher* than its fixed rate if the semiannual inflation rate reflects any *inflation*. Conversely, an I Bond's composite rate will be *lower* than its fixed rate if the semiannual inflation rate reflects any *deflation*. However, even if

deflation becomes so great that it would reduce the composite rate below zero, the Treasury will not allow the value of the bond to decrease from its most recent redemption value.

The I Bond is not without its drawbacks. First, any redemption within the first 5 years results in a 3-month interest penalty. Also, you should redeem an I Bond only at the first of the month because none of the interest earned during a month is included in the redemption value until the first day of the following month. Nevertheless, if inflation ever comes back as aggressively as it did in the late 1970s, I Bond holders will enjoy the benefit of its inflation-protection feature.

Source: Information on the I Bond can be found at www.publicdebt.treas.gov.

■ *What effect do you think the inflation-adjusted interest rate has on the cost of an I Bond in comparison with similar bonds that make no allowance for inflation?*

ally exceeded the average 3-month Treasury bill rate. The data in Figure 6.2 clearly illustrate the significant impact of inflation on the nominal rate of interest for the risk-free asset.

Term Structure of Interest Rates

term structure of interest rates
The relationship between the interest rate or rate of return and the time to maturity.

For any class of similar-risk securities, the **term structure of interest rates** relates the interest rate or rate of return to the time to maturity. For convenience we will use Treasury securities as an example, but other classes could include securities that have similar overall quality or risk. The riskless nature of Treasury securities also provides a laboratory in which to develop the term structure.

Yield Curves

yield to maturity
Annual rate of return earned on a debt security purchased on a given day and held to maturity.

A debt security's **yield to maturity** (discussed later in this chapter) represents the annual rate of return earned on a debt security purchased on a given day and held to maturity. At any point in time, the relationship between the debt's remaining

FIGURE 6.2

Impact of Inflation
Relationship between annual rate of inflation and 3-month U.S. Treasury bill average annual returns, 1978–2004

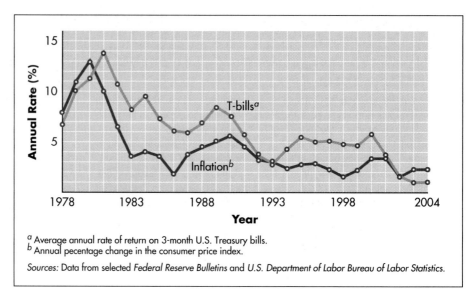

ᵃ Average annual rate of return on 3-month U.S. Treasury bills.
ᵇ Annual pecentage change in the consumer price index.

Sources: Data from selected *Federal Reserve Bulletins* and *U.S. Department of Labor Bureau of Labor Statistics.*

yield curve
A graph of the relationship between the debt's remaining time to maturity (*x* axis) and its yield to maturity (*y* axis); it shows the yield to maturity for debts of equal quality and different maturities. Graphically depicts the *term structure of interest rates.*

inverted yield curve
A *downward-sloping* yield curve that indicates generally cheaper long-term borrowing costs than short-term borrowing costs.

normal yield curve
An *upward-sloping* yield curve that indicates generally cheaper short-term borrowing costs than long-term borrowing costs.

flat yield curve
A yield curve that reflects relatively similar borrowing costs for both short- and longer-term loans.

expectations theory
The theory that the yield curve reflects investor expectations about future interest rates and inflation; an increasing inflation expectation results in an upward-sloping yield curve, and a decreasing inflation expectation results in a downward-sloping yield curve.

time to maturity and its yield to maturity is represented by the **yield curve.** The yield curve shows the yield to maturity for debts of equal quality and different maturities; it is a graphical depiction of the *term structure of interest rates.* Figure 6.3 shows three yield curves for all U.S. Treasury securities: one at May 22, 1981, a second at September 29, 1989, and a third at May 17, 2004.

Note that both the position and the shape of the yield curves change over time. The yield curve of May 22, 1981, indicates that short-term interest rates at that time were above longer-term rates. This curve is described as *downward-sloping,* reflecting long-term borrowing costs generally cheaper than short-term borrowing costs. Historically, the downward-sloping yield curve, which is often called an **inverted yield curve,** has been the exception. More frequently, yield curves similar to that of May 17, 2004, have existed. These *upward-sloping* or **normal yield curves** indicate that short-term borrowing costs are below long-term borrowing costs. Sometimes, a **flat yield curve,** similar to that of September 29, 1989, exists. It reflects relatively similar borrowing costs for both short- and longer-term loans.

The shape of the yield curve may affect the firm's financing decisions. A financial manager who faces a downward-sloping yield curve is likely to rely more heavily on cheaper, long-term financing; when the yield curve is upward-sloping, the manager is more likely to use cheaper, short-term financing. Although a variety of other factors influence the choice of loan maturity, the shape of the yield curve provides useful insights into future interest rate expectations.

Theories of Term Structure

Three theories are frequently cited to explain the general shape of the yield curve: the expectations theory, the liquidity preference theory, and the market segmentation theory.

Expectations Theory   One theory of the term structure of interest rates, the **expectations theory,** suggests that the yield curve reflects investor expectations about future interest rates and inflation. Higher future rates of expected inflation

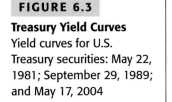

FIGURE 6.3

Treasury Yield Curves
Yield curves for U.S.
Treasury securities: May 22,
1981; September 29, 1989;
and May 17, 2004

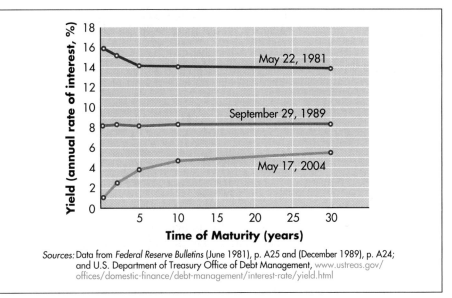

Sources: Data from *Federal Reserve Bulletins* (June 1981), p. A25 and (December 1989), p. A24; and U.S. Department of Treasury Office of Debt Management, www.ustreas.gov/offices/domestic-finance/debt-management/interest-rate/yield.html

will result in higher long-term interest rates; the opposite occurs with lower future rates. This widely accepted explanation of the term structure can be applied to the securities of any issuer.

For example, take the case of U.S. Treasury securities. Thus far, we have concerned ourselves solely with the 3-month Treasury bill. In fact, all Treasury securities are *riskless* in terms of (1) the chance that the Treasury will default on the issue and (2) the ease with which they can be liquidated for cash without losing value. Because it is believed to be easier to forecast inflation over shorter periods of time, the shorter-term 3-month U.S. Treasury bill is considered the risk-free asset. Of course, differing inflation expectations associated with different maturities will cause nominal interest rates to vary. With the addition of a maturity subscript, *t*, Equation 6.3 can be rewritten as

$$R_{F_t} = k^* + IP_t \tag{6.4}$$

In other words, for U.S. Treasury securities the nominal, or risk-free, rate for a given maturity varies with the inflation expectation over the term of the security.[5]

EXAMPLE   The nominal interest rate, R_F, for four maturities of U.S. Treasury securities on May 17, 2004, is given in column 1 of the table on page 284. Assuming that the real rate of interest is 0.70%, as noted in column 2, the inflation expectation for each maturity in column 3 is found by solving Equation 6.4 for IP_t. Although a 0.36% rate of inflation was expected over the 3-month period beginning May 17, 2004, a 1.81% average rate of inflation was expected over the 2-year period, and so on. An analysis of the inflation expectations in column 3 for May 17, 2004, suggests that at that time a general expectation of increasing inflation existed. Simply stated, the May 17, 2004, yield curve for U.S. Treasury securities shown

5. Although U.S. Treasury securities have no risk of default or illiquidity, they do suffer from "maturity, or interest rate, risk"—the risk that interest rates will change in the future and thereby affect longer maturities more than shorter maturities. Therefore, the longer the maturity of a Treasury (or any other) security, the greater its interest rate risk. The impact of interest rate changes on bond values is discussed later in this chapter; here we ignore this effect.

in Figure 6.3 was upward-sloping as a result of the expectation that the rate of inflation would increase in the future.[6]

Maturity, t	Nominal interest rate, R_{F_t} (1)	Real interest rate, k^* (2)	Inflation expectation, IP_t [(1) − (2)] (3)
3 months	1.06%	0.70%	0.36%
2 years	2.51	0.70	1.81
5 years	3.83	0.70	3.13
30 years	5.49	0.70	4.79

Generally, under the expectations theory, an increasing inflation expectation results in an upward-sloping yield curve; a decreasing inflation expectation results in a downward-sloping yield curve; and a stable inflation expectation results in a flat yield curve. Although, as we'll see, other theories exist, the observed strong relationship between inflation and interest rates (see Figure 6.2) supports this widely accepted theory.

Liquidity Preference Theory   The tendency for yield curves to be upward-sloping can be further explained by the **liquidity preference theory**. This theory holds that for a given issuer, such as the U.S. Treasury, long-term rates tend to be higher than short-term rates. This belief is based on two behavioral facts:

liquidity preference theory
Theory suggesting that for any given issuer, long-term interest rates tend to be higher than short-term rates because (1) lower liquidity and higher responsiveness to general interest rate movements of longer-term securities exists and (2) borrower willingness to pay a higher rate for long-term financing cause the yield curve to be upward-sloping.

1. Investors perceive less risk in short-term securities than in longer-term securities and are therefore willing to accept lower yields on them. The reason is that shorter-term securities are more liquid and less responsive to general interest rate movements.[7]
2. Borrowers are generally willing to pay a higher rate for long-term than for short-term financing. By locking in funds for a longer period of time, they can eliminate the potential adverse consequences of having to roll over short-term debt at unknown costs to obtain long-term financing.

Investors (lenders) tend to require a premium for tying up funds for longer periods, whereas borrowers are generally willing to pay a premium to obtain longer-term financing. These preferences of lenders and borrowers cause the yield curve to tend to be upward-sloping. Simply stated, longer maturities tend to have higher interest rates than shorter maturities.

market segmentation theory
Theory suggesting that the market for loans is segmented on the basis of maturity and that the supply of and demand for loans within each segment determine its prevailing interest rate; the slope of the yield curve is determined by the general relationship between the prevailing rates in each market segment.

Market Segmentation Theory   The **market segmentation theory** suggests that the market for loans is segmented on the basis of maturity and that the supply of and demand for loans within each segment determine its prevailing interest rate. In other words, the equilibrium between suppliers and demanders of short-term funds, such as seasonal business loans, would determine prevailing short-

6. It is interesting to note (in Figure 6.3) that the expectations reflected by the September 29, 1989, yield curve were not fully borne out by actual events. By May 2004, interest rates had fallen for all maturities, and the yield curve at that time had shifted downward and become upward-sloping, reflecting an expectation of increasing future interest rates and inflation rates.

7. Later in this chapter we demonstrate that debt instruments with longer maturities are more sensitive to changing market interest rates. For a given change in market rates, the price or value of longer-term debts will be more significantly changed (up or down) than the price or value of debts with shorter maturities.

term interest rates, and the equilibrium between suppliers and demanders of long-term funds, such as real estate loans, would determine prevailing long-term interest rates. The slope of the yield curve would be determined by the general relationship between the prevailing rates in each market segment. Simply stated, low rates in the short-term segment and high rates in the long-term segment cause the yield curve to be upward-sloping. The opposite occurs for high short-term rates and low long-term rates.

All three theories of term structure have merit. From them we can conclude that at any time, the slope of the yield curve is affected by (1) inflationary expectations, (2) liquidity preferences, and (3) the comparative equilibrium of supply and demand in the short- and long-term market segments. Upward-sloping yield curves result from higher future inflation expectations, lender preferences for shorter-maturity loans, and greater supply of short-term loans than of long-term loans relative to demand. The opposite behaviors would result in a downward-sloping yield curve. At any time, the interaction of these three forces determines the prevailing slope of the yield curve.

Risk Premiums: Issuer and Issue Characteristics

So far we have considered only risk-free U.S. Treasury securities. We now reintroduce the risk premium and assess it in view of risky non-Treasury issues. Recall Equation 6.1:

$$k_1 = \underbrace{k^* + IP}_{\substack{\text{risk-free} \\ \text{rate, } R_F}} + \underbrace{RP_1}_{\substack{\text{risk} \\ \text{premium}}}$$

In words, the nominal rate of interest for security 1 (k_1) is equal to the risk-free rate, consisting of the real rate of interest (k^*) plus the inflation expectation premium (IP), plus the risk premium (RP_1). The *risk premium* varies with specific issuer and issue characteristics; it causes similar-maturity securities[8] to have differing nominal rates of interest.

EXAMPLE   The nominal interest rates on a number of classes of long-term securities on May 17, 2004, were as follows:[9]

Security	Nominal interest rate
U.S. Treasury bonds (average)	5.44%
Corporate bonds (by ratings):	
High quality (Aaa–Aa)	6.04
Medium quality (A–Baa)	6.82
Speculative (Ba–C)	11.32
Utility bonds (average rating)	6.61

8. To provide for the same risk-free rate of interest, $k^* + IP$, it is necessary to assume equal maturities. When we do so, the inflationary expectations premium, IP, and therefore R_F, will be held constant, and the issuer and issue characteristics premium, RP, becomes the key factor differentiating the nominal rates of interest on various securities.

9. These yields were obtained from yields and spreads from Reuters as posted on the Bondsonline Web site, www.bondsonline.com, on May 17, 2004. Note that bond ratings are explained later in this chapter, beginning on page 291.

Because the U.S. Treasury bond would represent the risk-free, long-term security, we can calculate the risk premium of the other securities by subtracting the risk-free rate, 5.44%, from each nominal rate (yield):

Security	Risk premium
Corporate bonds (by ratings):	
High quality (Aaa–Aa)	$6.04\% - 5.44\% = 0.60\%$
Medium quality (A–Baa)	$6.82 \quad - 5.44 \quad = 1.38$
Speculative (Ba–C)	$11.32 \quad - 5.44 \quad = 5.88$
Utility bonds (average rating)	$6.61 \quad - 5.44 \quad = 1.17$

These risk premiums reflect differing issuer and issue risks. The lower-rated corporate issues (speculative) have a far higher risk premium than that of the higher-rated corporates (high quality and medium quality), and the utility issue has a risk premium near that of the medium-quality corporates. ■

The risk premium consists of a number of issuer- and issue-related components, including business risk, financial risk, interest rate risk, liquidity risk, and tax risk, which were defined in Table 5.1 on page 227, and the purely debt-specific risks—default risk, maturity risk, and contractual provision risk, briefly defined in Table 6.1. In general, the highest risk premiums and therefore the highest returns result from securities issued by firms with a high risk of default and from long-term maturities that have unfavorable contractual provisions.

TABLE 6.1

Debt-Specific Issuer- and Issue-Related Risk Premium Components

Component	Description
Default risk	The possibility that the issuer of debt will not pay the contractual interest or principal as scheduled. The greater the uncertainty as to the borrower's ability to meet these payments, the greater the risk premium. High bond ratings reflect low default risk, and low bond ratings reflect high default risk.
Maturity risk	The fact that the longer the maturity, the more the value of a security will change in response to a given change in interest rates. If interest rates on otherwise similar-risk securities suddenly rise as a result of a change in the money supply, the prices of long-term bonds will decline by more than the prices of short-term bonds, and vice versa.[a]
Contractual provision risk	Conditions that are often included in a debt agreement or a stock issue. Some of these reduce risk, whereas others may increase risk. For example, a provision allowing a bond issuer to retire its bonds prior to their maturity under favorable terms increases the bond's risk.

[a]A detailed discussion of the effects of interest rates on the price or value of bonds and other fixed-income securities is presented later in this chapter.

REVIEW QUESTIONS

6–1   What is the *real rate of interest?* Differentiate it from the *nominal rate of interest* for the risk-free asset, a 3-month U.S. Treasury bill.

6–2   What is the *term structure of interest rates,* and how is it related to the *yield curve?*

6–3   For a given class of similar-risk securities, what does each of the following yield curves reflect about interest rates: (**a**) downward-sloping; (**b**) upward-sloping; and (**c**) flat? Which form has been historically dominant?

6–4   Briefly describe the following theories of the general shape of the yield curve: (**a**) expectations theory; (**b**) liquidity preference theory; and (**c**) market segmentation theory.

6–5   List and briefly describe the potential issuer- and issue-related risk components that are embodied in the risk premium. Which are the purely debt-specific risks?

LG2   LG3   6.2 | Corporate Bonds

corporate bond
A long-term debt instrument indicating that a corporation has borrowed a certain amount of money and promises to repay it in the future under clearly defined terms.

A **corporate bond** is a long-term debt instrument indicating that a corporation has borrowed a certain amount of money and promises to repay it in the future under clearly defined terms. Most bonds are issued with maturities of 10 to 30 years and with a par value, or face value, of $1,000. The **coupon interest rate** on a bond represents the percentage of the bond's par value that will be paid annually, typically in two equal semiannual payments, as interest. The bondholders, who are the lenders, are promised the semiannual interest payments and, at maturity, repayment of the principal amount.

coupon interest rate
The percentage of a bond's par value that will be paid annually, typically in two equal semiannual payments, as interest.

Legal Aspects of Corporate Bonds

Certain legal arrangements are required to protect purchasers of bonds. Bondholders are protected primarily through the indenture and the trustee.

Bond Indenture

bond indenture
A legal document that specifies both the rights of the bondholders and the duties of the issuing corporation.

A **bond indenture** is a legal document that specifies both the rights of the bondholders and the duties of the issuing corporation. Included in the indenture are descriptions of the amount and timing of all interest and principal payments, various standard and restrictive provisions, and, frequently, sinking-fund requirements and security interest provisions.

standard debt provisions
Provisions in a *bond indenture* specifying certain record-keeping and general business practices that the bond issuer must follow; normally, they do not place a burden on a financially sound business.

Standard Provisions   The **standard debt provisions** in the bond indenture specify certain record-keeping and general business practices that the bond issuer must follow. Standard debt provisions do not normally place a burden on a financially sound business.

The borrower commonly must (1) *maintain satisfactory accounting records* in accordance with generally accepted accounting principles (GAAP); (2) periodically *supply audited financial statements;* (3) *pay taxes and other liabilities when due;* and (4) *maintain all facilities in good working order.*

restrictive covenants
Provisions in a *bond indenture* that place operating and financial constraints on the borrower.

Restrictive Provisions Bond indentures also normally include certain **restrictive covenants,** which place operating and financial constraints on the borrower. These provisions help protect the bondholder against increases in borrower risk. Without them, the borrower could increase the firm's risk but not have to pay increased interest to compensate for the increased risk.

The most common restrictive covenants do the following:

1. Require a *minimum level of liquidity,* to ensure against loan default.
2. *Prohibit the sale of accounts receivable* to generate cash. Selling receivables could cause a long-run cash shortage if proceeds were used to meet current obligations.
3. Impose *fixed-asset restrictions.* The borrower must maintain a specified level of fixed assets to guarantee its ability to repay the bonds.
4. *Constrain subsequent borrowing.* Additional long-term debt may be prohibited, or additional borrowing may be *subordinated* to the original loan. **Subordination** means that subsequent creditors agree to wait until all claims of the *senior debt* are satisfied.
5. *Limit the firm's annual cash dividend payments* to a specified percentage or amount.

subordination
In a bond indenture, the stipulation that subsequent creditors agree to wait until all claims of the *senior debt* are satisfied.

Other restrictive covenants are sometimes included in bond indentures.

The violation of any standard or restrictive provision by the borrower gives the bondholders the right to demand immediate repayment of the debt. Generally, bondholders evaluate any violation to determine whether it jeopardizes the loan. They may then decide to demand immediate repayment, continue the loan, or alter the terms of the bond indenture.

sinking-fund requirement
A restrictive provision often included in a bond indenture, providing for the systematic retirement of bonds prior to their maturity.

Sinking-Fund Requirements Another common restrictive provision is a **sinking-fund requirement.** Its objective is to provide for the systematic retirement of bonds prior to their maturity. To carry out this requirement, the corporation makes semiannual or annual payments that are used to retire bonds by purchasing them in the marketplace.

Security Interest The bond indenture identifies any collateral pledged against the bond and specifies how it is to be maintained. The protection of bond collateral is crucial to guarantee the safety of a bond issue.

Trustee

trustee
A paid individual, corporation, or commercial bank trust department that acts as the third party to a *bond indenture* and can take specified actions on behalf of the bondholders if the terms of the indenture are violated.

A **trustee** is a third party to a *bond indenture.* The trustee can be an individual, a corporation, or (most often) a commercial bank trust department. The trustee is paid to act as a "watchdog" on behalf of the bondholders and can take specified actions on behalf of the bondholders if the terms of the indenture are violated.

Cost of Bonds to the Issuer

The cost of bond financing is generally greater than the issuer would have to pay for short-term borrowing. The major factors that affect the cost, which is the rate of interest paid by the bond issuer, are the bond's maturity, the size of the offering, the issuer's risk, and the basic cost of money.

Impact of Bond Maturity on Bond Cost

Generally, as we noted earlier, long-term debt pays higher interest rates than short-term debt. In a practical sense, the longer the maturity of a bond, the less accuracy there is in predicting future interest rates, and therefore the greater the bondholders' risk of giving up an opportunity to lend money at a higher rate. In addition, the longer the term, the greater the chance that the issuer might default.

Impact of Offering Size on Bond Cost

The size of the bond offering also affects the interest cost of borrowing, but in an inverse manner: Bond flotation and administration costs per dollar borrowed are likely to decrease with increasing offering size. On the other hand, the risk to the bondholders may increase, because larger offerings result in greater risk of default.

Impact of Issuer's Risk

The greater the issuer's *default risk,* the higher the interest rate. Some of this risk can be reduced through inclusion of appropriate restrictive provisions in the bond indenture. Clearly, bondholders must be compensated with higher returns for taking greater risk. Frequently, bond buyers rely on bond ratings (discussed later) to determine the issuer's overall risk.

Impact of the Cost of Money

The cost of money in the capital market is the basis for determining a bond's coupon interest rate. Generally, the rate on U.S. Treasury securities of equal maturity is used as the lowest-risk cost of money. To that basic rate is added a *risk premium* (as described earlier in this chapter) that reflects the factors mentioned above (maturity, offering size, and issuer's risk).

General Features of a Bond Issue

conversion feature
A feature of *convertible bonds* that allows bondholders to change each bond into a stated number of shares of common stock.

call feature
A feature included in nearly all corporate bond issues that gives the issuer the opportunity to repurchase bonds at a stated *call price* prior to maturity.

call price
The stated price at which a bond may be repurchased, by use of a *call feature,* prior to maturity.

Three features sometimes included in a corporate bond issue are a conversion feature, a call feature, and stock purchase warrants. These features provide the issuer or the purchaser with certain opportunities for replacing or retiring the bond or supplementing it with some type of equity issue.

Convertible bonds offer a **conversion feature** that allows bondholders to change each bond into a stated number of shares of common stock. Bondholders convert their bonds into stock only when the market price of the stock is such that conversion will provide a profit for the bondholder. Inclusion of the conversion feature by the issuer lowers the interest cost and provides for automatic conversion of the bonds to stock if future stock prices appreciate noticeably.

The **call feature** is included in nearly all corporate bond issues. It gives the issuer the opportunity to repurchase bonds prior to maturity. The **call price** is the stated price at which bonds may be repurchased prior to maturity. Sometimes the call feature can be exercised only during a certain period. As a rule, the call price exceeds the par value of a bond by an amount equal to 1 year's interest. For example, a $1,000 bond with a 10 percent coupon interest rate would be callable for around $1,100 [$1,000 + (10% × $1,000)]. The amount by which the call

call premium
The amount by which a bond's *call price* exceeds its par value.

stock purchase warrants
Instruments that give their holders the right to purchase a certain number of shares of the issuer's common stock at a specified price over a certain period of time. Occasionally attached to bonds as "sweeteners."

quotations
Information on bonds, stocks, and other securities, including current price data and statistics on recent price behavior.

price exceeds the bond's par value is commonly referred to as the **call premium.** This premium compensates bondholders for having the bond called away from them; to the issuer, it is the cost of calling the bonds.

The call feature enables an issuer to call an outstanding bond when interest rates fall and issue a new bond at a lower interest rate. When interest rates rise, the call privilege will not be exercised, except possibly to meet *sinking-fund requirements.* Of course, to sell a callable bond in the first place, the issuer must pay a higher interest rate than on noncallable bonds of equal risk, to compensate bondholders for the risk of having the bonds called away from them.

Bonds occasionally have stock purchase warrants attached as "sweeteners" to make them more attractive to prospective buyers. **Stock purchase warrants** are instruments that give their holders the right to purchase a certain number of shares of the issuer's common stock at a specified price over a certain period of time. Their inclusion typically enables the issuer to pay a slightly lower coupon interest rate than would otherwise be required.

Interpreting Bond Quotations

The financial manager needs to stay abreast of the market values of the firm's outstanding securities, whether they are traded on an organized exchange, over the counter, or in international markets. Similarly, existing and prospective investors in the firm's securities need to monitor the prices of the securities they own because these prices represent the current value of their investment. Information on bonds, stocks, and other securities is contained in **quotations,** which include current price data along with statistics on recent price behavior. Security price quotations are readily available for actively traded bonds and stocks. The most up-to-date "quotes" can be obtained electronically, via a personal computer. Price information is available from stockbrokers and is widely published in news media. Popular sources of daily security price quotations include financial newspapers, such as the *Wall Street Journal* and *Investor's Business Daily,* and the business sections of daily general newspapers. Here we focus on bond quotations; stock quotations are reviewed in Chapter 7.

Figure 6.4 includes an excerpt from the "Forty most active fixed-coupon corporate bonds" quotations reported in the *Wall Street Journal* for transactions through the close of trading on Tuesday, May 18, 2004. We will look at the corporate bonds quotation for General Motors (GM), which is highlighted in Figure 6.4. The first column following the company name gives the bond's coupon interest rate (7.200%), and the next column gives the bond's maturity date (January 15, 2011). This information allows investors to differentiate between the various bonds issued by a corporation. Note that on the day of this quote, GM had two bonds listed (the other one is the first one listed in the quote).

The next column, labeled "Last Price," gives the last price at which the bond traded on May 18, 2004. Although most corporate bonds are issued with a *par,* or *face, value* of $1,000, *all bonds are quoted as a percentage of par.* A $1,000-par-value bond quoted at 92.543 is priced at $925.43 (92.543% × $1,000). Corporate bonds are quoted in dollars and cents. Thus GM's last price of 103.143 for the day was $1,031.43—that is, 103.143% × $1,000.

The next column, labeled "Last Yield," represents the bond's *yield,* or *compound annual rate of return.* For the GM bond, this yield is 6.606%. The last yield

FIGURE 6.4 **Bond Quotations**

Selected bond quotations for May 18, 2004

Corporate Bonds

Tuesday, May 18, 2004

Forty most active fixed-coupon corporate bonds

COMPANY (TICKER)	COUPON	MATURITY	LAST PRICE	LAST YIELD	*EST SPREAD	UST†	EST $ VOL (000's)
General Motors (GM)	8.375	Jul 15, 2033	102.655	8.134	268	30	334,869
Ford Motor Credit (F)	7.000	Oct 01, 2013	100.002	6.998	227	10	229,101
Altria Group (MO)	7.000	Nov 04, 2013	100.049	6.992	226	10	166,186
General Motors Acceptance (GMAC)	6.875	Sep 15, 2011	101.623	6.590	185	10	164,077
Liberty Media (L)	3.500	Sep 25, 2006	99.865	3.559	104	2	124,704
General Motors Acceptance (GMAC)	7.750	Jan 19, 2010	108.318	5.993	214	5	120,744
Wyeth (WYE)	5.500	Feb 01, 2014	96.782	5.939	121	10	116,133
Ford Motor Credit (F)	7.375	Oct 28, 2009	105.747	6.115	227	5	111,809
General Motors Acceptance (GMAC)	6.875	Aug 28, 2012	100.781	6.748	201	10	107,817
Credit Suisse First Boston (USA) (CRDSUI)	6.500	Jan 15, 2012	107.043	5.364	64	10	106,127
Medtronic (MDT)-c	1.250	Sep 15, 2021	102.797	0.220	n.a.	n.a.	100,167
Sprint Capital (FON)	6.125	Nov 15, 2008	105.336	4.788	95	5	98,221
Citigroup (C)	6.000	Oct 31, 2033	94.007	6.454	101	30	80,490
General Motors (GM)	7.200	Jan 15, 2011	103.143	6.606	187	10	76,419
Goldman Sachs Group (GS)	5.150	Jan 15, 2014	95.140	5.814	108	10	74,871
General Motors Acceptance (GMAC)	5.850	Jan 14, 2009	100.876	5.631	179	5	70,711
Sprint Capital (FON)	7.625	Jan 30, 2011	110.421	5.726	100	10	69,156
Credit Suisse First Boston (USA) (CRDSUI)	6.125	Nov 15, 2011	104.639	5.364	63	10	68,727
Ford Motor Credit (F)	6.875	Feb 01, 2006	105.160	3.701	117	2	65,011
General Motors Acceptance (GMAC)	6.125	Aug 28, 2007	104.390	4.659	154	3	64,253
Ford Motor (F)	7.450	Jul 16, 2031	93.146	8.075	263	30	63,092
General Motors Acceptance (GMAC)	7.250	Mar 02, 2011	104.135	6.484	175	10	60,122
General Motors Acceptance (GMAC)	4.500	Jul 15, 2006	101.384	3.821	130	2	59,458
Alcoa (AA)	5.375	Jan 15, 2013	100.291	5.331	61	10	57,850
Lehman Brothers Holdings (LEH)	4.800	Mar 13, 2014	92.543	5.806	107	10	55,211
CIT Group (CIT)	3.375	Apr 01, 2009	94.357	4.686	81	5	54,721
General Motors Acceptance (GMAC)	6.125	Sep 15, 2006	104.711	3.973	145	2	53,886
Verizon Global Funding (VZ)	7.375	Sep 01, 2012	112.386	5.491	76	10	51,828
Bank of America (BAC)	6.625	Jun 15, 2004	100.367	1.085	n.a.	n.a.	51,718
Wisconsin Public Service (WPS)	4.875	Dec 01, 2012	97.930	5.178	44	10	51,628

Source: Wall Street Journal, May 19, 2004, p. C12.

assumes that the bond is purchased on the given day at the "Last Price" and held to the stated "Maturity" date.

The fifth column gives the "Est(imated) Spread" in *basis points* (100 basis points is one percentage point) over a U.S. Treasury security of similar maturity. The maturity of the Treasury issue used to find the estimated spread is given in the next column. For the GM bond, its spread above a 10-year U.S. Treasury issue is 187 basis points (1.87%).

The final column in the bond quote gives the dollar value (in $000) of the bond traded on the given day. GM's "Est(imated) $ Vol(ume)" on May 18, 2004, was $76,419,000.

Bond Ratings

Independent agencies such as Moody's and Standard & Poor's assess the riskiness of publicly traded bond issues. These agencies derive their ratings by using financial ratio and cash flow analyses to assess the likely payment of bond interest and

In Practice FOCUS ON ETHICS

CAN WE TRUST THE BOND RATERS?

Most investors have neither the time nor the expertise to do their own credit appraisals for potential bond investments, but assessing default risk still requires an evaluation of creditworthiness. Enter credit rating agencies, which offer a way to receive a third-party credit appraisal. But how reliable are their ratings? At least two of these agencies reportedly had "investment grade" ratings on Enron just a few weeks before its financial meltdown. Similar oversights occurred in the cases of WorldCom and Italian corporate giant Parmalat. The rating agencies, which are registered and approved by the SEC, command significant market power, but they have recently come under fire for questionable ethics in two areas: conflict of interest and timeliness of rating changes.

Most bond ratings are paid for by the bond issuer as a way to broaden the market appeal of its bonds. Companies want to be rated because the market for publicly traded unrated issues is much smaller and relatively illiquid. The lower a bond's rating, the higher the perceived default risk, and the higher the interest rate required by bond investors. A conflict of interest may arise because it is not in the best interest of the rater to downgrade the bonds of the corporate customer paying for the rating. A Senate Governmental Affairs Committee found that raters should have asked more and better questions in the raters' private discussions with companies such as Enron and Xerox.

The Sarbanes-Oxley Act enacted in 2002 dictated that the SEC conduct a review of credit-rating agencies. When the SEC asked for comments from the corporate community, the Association for Financial Professionals (AFP) conducted a survey of its membership of treasury and finance professionals. The survey responses were clear: Even though the raters say they serve the interests of debt investors first and foremost, only 22 percent of respondents believed that investors' interests are favored. In addition, of the respondents whose companies have rated debt, only 40 percent believed that changes in their companies' ratings are made on a timely basis. More than 70 percent of the finance professionals agreed that the SEC should evaluate registration of the credit agencies periodically.

One rating agency responded to these charges by asserting that it must balance investor and corporate issuer interests. Investors want faster rating changes, but corporate issuers want slower and more deliberate adjustments to ratings. The fact remains that it is the investors' interests that should be kept primary in the ratings process, however. Doing risk–return analysis in the bond markets depends on having trustworthy, accurate, timely information. No doubt the increased scrutiny from the SEC, regardless of any registration process that might or might not be added in the future, will add to the value of the ratings received by the investing public.

Sources: Association for Financial Professionals, "Rating Agencies Survey: Accuracy, Timeliness, and Regulation," November 2002, www.afponline.org/pub/pdf/ratings_survey.pdf.(Accessed June 14, 2004); and Lisa Yoon, "Downgrade Possible? SEC Looking at Credit Raters," June 9, 2003, www.cfo.com (Accessed June 13, 2004).

■ *Which of the AFP's findings would present the most serious ethics problems for the raters?*

principal. Table 6.2 summarizes these ratings. For discussion of ethical issues related to the bond-rating agencies, see the *In Practice* box above.

Normally an inverse relationship exists between the quality of a bond and the rate of return that it must provide bondholders: High-quality (high-rated) bonds provide lower returns than lower-quality (low-rated) bonds. This reflects the lender's risk–return trade-off. When considering bond financing, the financial manager must be concerned with the expected ratings of the bond issue, because these ratings affect salability and cost.

Hint Note that Moody's has 9 major ratings; Standard & Poor's has 10.

TABLE 6.2

Moody's and Standard & Poor's Bond Ratings[a]

Moody's	Interpretation	Standard & Poor's	Interpretation
Aaa	Prime quality	AAA	Bank investment quality
Aa	High grade	AA	
A	Upper medium grade	A	
Baa	Medium grade	BBB	
Ba	Lower medium grade	BB	Speculative
	or speculative	B	
B	Speculative		
Caa	From very speculative	CCC	
Ca	to near or in default	CC	
C	Lowest grade	C	Income bond
		D	In default

[a]Some ratings may be modified to show relative standing within a major rating category; for example, Moody's uses numerical modifiers (1, 2, 3), whereas Standard & Poor's uses plus (+) and minus (−) signs.

Sources: Moody's Investors Service, Inc. and Standard & Poor's Corporation.

Popular Types of Bonds

debentures
subordinated debentures
income bonds
mortgage bonds
collateral trust bonds
equipment trust certificates
See Table 6.3 on page 294.

zero- (or low-) coupon bonds
junk bonds
floating-rate bonds
extendible notes
putable bonds
See Table 6.4 on page 295.

Bonds can be classified in a variety of ways. Here we break them into traditional bonds (the basic types that have been around for years) and contemporary bonds (newer, more innovative types). The traditional types of bonds are summarized in terms of their key characteristics and priority of lender's claim in Table 6.3 (see page 294). Note that the first three types—**debentures, subordinated debentures,** and **income bonds**—are unsecured, whereas the last three—**mortgage bonds, collateral trust bonds,** and **equipment trust certificates**—are secured.

Table 6.4 (see page 295) describes the key characteristics of five contemporary types of bonds: **zero- (or low-) coupon bonds, junk bonds, floating-rate bonds, extendible notes,** and **putable bonds.** These bonds can be either unsecured or secured. Changing capital market conditions and investor preferences have spurred further innovations in bond financing in recent years and will probably continue to do so.

International Bond Issues

Companies and governments borrow internationally by issuing bonds in two principal financial markets: the Eurobond market and the foreign bond market. Both give borrowers the opportunity to obtain large amounts of long-term debt financing quickly, in the currency of their choice and with flexible repayment terms.

TABLE 6.3

Characteristics and Priority of Lender's Claim of Traditional Types of Bonds

Bond type	Characteristics	Priority of lender's claim
Unsecured Bonds		
Debentures	Unsecured bonds that only creditworthy firms can issue. Convertible bonds are normally debentures.	Claims are the same as those of any general creditor. May have other unsecured bonds subordinated to them.
Subordinated debentures	Claims are not satisfied until those of the creditors holding certain (senior) debts have been fully satisfied.	Claim is that of a general creditor but not as good as a senior debt claim.
Income bonds	Payment of interest is required only when earnings are available. Commonly issued in reorganization of a failing firm.	Claim is that of a general creditor. Are not in default when interest payments are missed, because they are contingent only on earnings being available.
Secured Bonds		
Mortgage bonds	Secured by real estate or buildings.	Claim is on proceeds from sale of mortgaged assets; if not fully satisfied, the lender becomes a general creditor. The *first-mortgage* claim must be fully satisfied before distribution of proceeds to *second-mortgage* holders, and so on. A number of mortgages can be issued against the same collateral.
Collateral trust bonds	Secured by stock and (or) bonds that are owned by the issuer. Collateral value is generally 25% to 35% greater than bond value.	Claim is on proceeds from stock and (or) bond collateral; if not fully satisfied, the lender becomes a general creditor.
Equipment trust certificates	Used to finance "rolling stock"—airplanes, trucks, boats, railroad cars. A trustee buys such an asset with funds raised through the sale of trust certificates and then leases it to the firm, which, after making the final scheduled lease payment, receives title to the asset. A type of leasing.	Claim is on proceeds from the sale of the asset; if proceeds do not satisfy outstanding debt, trust certificate lenders become general creditors.

Eurobond
A bond issued by an international borrower and sold to investors in countries with currencies other than the currency in which the bond is denominated.

A **Eurobond** is issued by an international borrower and sold to investors in countries with currencies other than the currency in which the bond is denominated. An example is a dollar-denominated bond issued by a U.S. corporation and sold to Belgian investors. From the founding of the Eurobond market in the 1960s until the mid-1980s, "blue chip" U.S. corporations were the largest single class of Eurobond issuers. Some of these companies were able to borrow in this market at interest rates below those the U.S. government paid on Treasury bonds. As the market matured, issuers became able to choose the currency in which they borrowed, and European and Japanese borrowers rose to prominence. In more recent years, the Eurobond market has become much more balanced in terms of the mix of borrowers, total issue volume, and currency of denomination.

foreign bond
A bond issued in a host country's financial market, in the host country's currency, by a foreign borrower.

In contrast, a **foreign bond** is issued in a host country's financial market, in the host country's currency, by a foreign borrower. A Swiss-franc–denominated bond issued in Switzerland by a U.S. company is an example of a foreign bond. The three largest foreign-bond markets are Japan, Switzerland, and the United States.

TABLE 6.4

Characteristics of Contemporary Types of Bonds

Bond type	Characteristics[a]
Zero- (or low-) coupon bonds	Issued with no (zero) or a very low coupon (stated interest) rate and sold at a large discount from par. A significant portion (or all) of the investor's return comes from gain in value (i.e., par value minus purchase price). Generally callable at par value. Because the issuer can annually deduct the current year's interest accrual without having to pay the interest until the bond matures (or is called), its cash flow each year is increased by the amount of the tax shield provided by the interest deduction.
Junk bonds	Debt rated Ba or lower by Moody's or BB or lower by Standard & Poor's. Commonly used during the 1980s by rapidly growing firms to obtain growth capital, most often as a way to finance mergers and takeovers. High-risk bonds with high yields—often yielding 2% to 3% more than the best-quality corporate debt.
Floating-rate bonds	Stated interest rate is adjusted periodically within stated limits in response to changes in specified money market or capital market rates. Popular when future inflation and interest rates are uncertain. Tend to sell at close to par because of the automatic adjustment to changing market conditions. Some issues provide for annual redemption at par at the option of the bondholder.
Extendible notes	Short maturities, typically 1 to 5 years, that can be renewed for a similar period at the option of holders. Similar to a floating-rate bond. An issue might be a series of 3-year renewable notes over a period of 15 years; every 3 years, the notes could be extended for another 3 years, at a new rate competitive with market interest rates at the time of renewal.
Putable bonds	Bonds that can be redeemed at par (typically, $1,000) at the option of their holder either at specific dates after the date of issue and every 1 to 5 years thereafter or when and if the firm takes specified actions, such as being acquired, acquiring another company, or issuing a large amount of additional debt. In return for its conferring the right to "put the bond" at specified times or when the firm takes certain actions, the bond's yield is lower than that of a nonputable bond.

[a]The claims of lenders (i.e., bondholders) against issuers of each of these types of bonds vary, depending on the bonds' other features. Each of these bonds can be unsecured or secured.

REVIEW QUESTIONS

6–6   What are typical maturities, denominations, and interest payments of a corporate bond? What mechanisms protect bondholders?

6–7   Differentiate between *standard debt provisions* and *restrictive covenants* included in a bond indenture. What are the consequences of violation of them by the bond issuer?

6–8   How is the cost of bond financing typically related to the cost of short-term borrowing? In addition to a bond's maturity, what other major factors affect its cost to the issuer?

6–9   What is a *conversion feature?* A *call feature? Stock purchase warrants?*

6–10   What information is found in a bond *quotation?* How are bonds rated, and why?

6–11   Compare the basic characteristics of *Eurobonds* and *foreign bonds*.

6.3 | # Valuation Fundamentals

valuation
The process that links risk and return to determine the worth of an asset.

Valuation is the process that links risk and return to determine the worth of an asset. It is a relatively simple process that can be applied to *expected* streams of benefits from bonds, stocks, income properties, oil wells, and so on. To determine an asset's worth at a given point in time, a financial manager uses the time-value-of-money techniques presented in Chapter 4 and the concepts of risk and return developed in Chapter 5.

Key Inputs

There are three key inputs to the valuation process: (1) cash flows (returns), (2) timing, and (3) a measure of risk, which determines the required return. Each is described below.

Cash Flows (Returns)

The value of any asset depends on the cash flow(s) it is *expected* to provide over the ownership period. To have value, an asset does not have to provide an annual cash flow; it can provide an intermittent cash flow or even a single cash flow over the period.

EXAMPLE Celia Sargent, financial analyst for Groton Corporation, a diversified holding company, wishes to estimate the value of three of its assets: common stock in Michaels Enterprises, an interest in an oil well, and an original painting by a well-known artist. Her cash flow estimates for each are as follows:

> **Stock in Michaels Enterprises** *Expect* to receive cash dividends of $300 per year indefinitely.

> **Oil well** *Expect* to receive cash flow of $2,000 at the end of year 1, $4,000 at the end of year 2, and $10,000 at the end of year 4, when the well is to be sold.

> **Original painting** *Expect* to be able to sell the painting in 5 years for $85,000.

With these cash flow estimates, Celia has taken the first step toward placing a value on each of the assets. ■

Timing

In addition to making cash flow estimates, we must know the timing of the cash flows.[10] For example, Celia expects the cash flows of $2,000, $4,000, and $10,000 for the oil well to occur at the ends of years 1, 2, and 4, respectively. The combination of the cash flow and its timing fully defines the return expected from the asset.

---

10. Although cash flows can occur at any time during a year, for computational convenience as well as custom, we will assume they occur at the *end of the year* unless otherwise noted.

Risk and Required Return

Hint The required rate of return is the result of investors being risk-averse. For the risk-averse investor to purchase a given asset, the investor *must expect* at least enough return to compensate for the asset's perceived risk.

The level of risk associated with a given cash flow can significantly affect its value. In general, the greater the risk of (or the less certain) a cash flow, the lower its value. Greater risk can be incorporated into a valuation analysis by using a higher required return or discount rate. As in the previous chapter, the higher the risk, the greater the required return, and the lower the risk, the less the required return.

EXAMPLE

Let's return to Celia Sargent's task of placing a value on Groton Corporation's original painting and consider two scenarios.

Scenario 1—Certainty A major art gallery has contracted to buy the painting for $85,000 at the end of 5 years. Because this is considered a certain situation, Celia views this asset as "money in the bank." She thus would use the prevailing risk-free rate of 9% as the required return when calculating the value of the painting.

Scenario 2—High Risk The values of original paintings by this artist have fluctuated widely over the past 10 years. Although Celia expects to be able to get $85,000 for the painting, she realizes that its sale price in 5 years could range between $30,000 and $140,000. Because of the high uncertainty surrounding the painting's value, Celia believes that a 15% required return is appropriate.

These two estimates of the appropriate required return illustrate how this rate captures risk. The often subjective nature of such estimates is also clear. ■

The Basic Valuation Model

Simply stated, the value of any asset is *the present value of all future cash flows it is expected to provide over the relevant time period*. The time period can be any length, even infinity. The value of an asset is therefore determined by discounting the expected cash flows back to their present value, using the required return commensurate with the asset's risk as the appropriate discount rate. Utilizing the present value techniques explained in Chapter 4, we can express the value of any asset at time zero, V_0, as

$$V_0 = \frac{CF_1}{(1+k)^1} + \frac{CF_2}{(1+k)^2} + \cdots + \frac{CF_n}{(1+k)^n} \qquad (6.5)$$

where

$$V_0 = \text{value of the asset at time zero}$$
$$CF_t = \text{cash flow } expected \text{ at the end of year } t$$
$$k = \text{appropriate required return (discount rate)}$$
$$n = \text{relevant time period}$$

Using present value interest factor notation, $PVIF_{k,n}$ from Chapter 4, Equation 6.5 can be rewritten as

$$V_0 = [CF_1 \times (PVIF_{k,1})] + [CF_2 \times (PVIF_{k,2})] + \cdots + [CF_n \times (PVIF_{k,n})] \qquad (6.6)$$

We can use Equation 6.6 to determine the value of any asset.

TABLE 6.5

Valuation of Groton Corporation's Assets by Celia Sargent

Asset	Cash flow, CF		Appropriate required return	Valuation[a]
Michaels Enterprises stock[b]	$300/year indefinitely		12%	$V_0 = \$300 \times (PVIFA_{12\%,\infty})$
				$= \$300 \times \dfrac{1}{0.12} = \underline{\underline{\$2,500}}$
Oil well[c]	Year (t)	CF_t	20%	$V_0 = [\$2,000 \times (PVIF_{20\%,1})]$
	1	$ 2,000		$+ [\$4,000 \times (PVIF_{20\%,2})]$
	2	4,000		$+ [\$0 \times (PVIF_{20\%,3})]$
	3	0		$+ [\$10,000 \times (PVIF_{20\%,4})]$
	4	10,000		$= [\$2,000 \times (0.833)]$
				$+ [\$4,000 \times (0.694)]$
				$+ [\$0 \times (0.579)]$
				$+ [\$10,000 \times (0.482)]$
				$= \$1,666 + \$2,776$
				$+ \$0 + \$4,820$
				$= \underline{\underline{\$9,262}}$
Original painting[d]	$85,000 at end of year 5		15%	$V_0 = \$85,000 \times (PVIF_{15\%,5})$
				$= \$85,000 \times (0.497)$
				$= \underline{\underline{\$42,245}}$

[a]Based on *PVIF* interest factors from Table A–2. If calculated using a calculator, the values of the oil well and original painting would have been $9,266.98 and $42,260.03, respectively.

[b]This is a perpetuity (infinite-lived annuity), and therefore the present value interest factor given in Equation 4.19 is applied.

[c]This is a mixed stream of cash flows and therefore requires a number of *PVIF*s, as noted.

[d]This is a single-amount cash flow and therefore requires a single *PVIF*.

EXAMPLE Celia Sargent used Equation 6.6 to calculate the value of each asset (using present value interest factors from Table A–2), as shown in Table 6.5. Michaels Enterprises stock has a value of $2,500, the oil well's value is $9,262, and the original painting has a value of $42,245. Note that regardless of the pattern of the expected cash flow from an asset, the basic valuation equation can be used to determine its value. ■

REVIEW QUESTIONS

6–12 Why is it important for financial managers to understand the valuation process?

6–13 What are the three key inputs to the valuation process?

6–14 Does the valuation process apply only to assets that provide an annual cash flow? Explain.

6–15 Define and specify the general equation for the value of any asset, V_0.

LG5   LG6   6.4 | Bond Valuation

The basic valuation equation can be customized for use in valuing specific securities: bonds, common stock, and preferred stock. Bond valuation is described in this chapter, and valuation of common stock and preferred stock is discussed in Chapter 7.

Bond Fundamentals

Hint A bondholder receives two cash flows from a bond if it is held to maturity—interest and the bond's face value. For valuation purposes, the interest is an annuity and the face value is a single payment received at a specified future date.

As noted earlier in this chapter, *bonds* are long-term debt instruments used by business and government to raise large sums of money, typically from a diverse group of lenders. Most corporate bonds pay interest *semiannually* (every 6 months) at a stated *coupon interest rate,* have an initial *maturity* of 10 to 30 years, and have a *par value,* or *face value,* of $1,000 that must be repaid at maturity.[11]

EXAMPLE

Mills Company, a large defense contractor, on January 1, 2007, issued a 10% coupon interest rate, 10-year bond with a $1,000 par value that pays interest semiannually. Investors who buy this bond receive the contractual right to two cash flows: (1) $100 annual interest (10% coupon interest rate × $1,000 par value) distributed as $50 (1/2 × $100) at the end of each 6 months, and (2) the $1,000 par value at the end of the tenth year. ◼

We will use data for Mills's bond issue to look at basic bond valuation.

Basic Bond Valuation

The value of a bond is the present value of the payments its issuer is contractually obligated to make, from the current time until it matures. The basic model for the value, B_0, of a bond is given by Equation 6.7:

$$B_0 = I \times \left[\sum_{t=1}^{n} \frac{1}{(1 + k_d)^t} \right] + M \times \left[\frac{1}{(1 + k_d)^n} \right] \qquad (6.7)$$

$$= I \times (PVIFA_{k_d,n}) + M \times (PVIF_{k_d,n}) \qquad (6.7a)$$

where

B_0 = value of the bond at time zero
I = *annual* interest paid in dollars[12]
n = number of years to maturity
M = par value in dollars
k_d = required return on a bond

---

11. Bonds often have features that allow them to be retired by the issuer prior to maturity; these *conversion* and *call* features were presented earlier in this chapter. For the purpose of the current discussion, these features are ignored.

12. The payment of annual rather than semiannual bond interest is assumed throughout the following discussion. This assumption simplifies the calculations involved, while maintaining the conceptual accuracy of the valuation procedures presented.

We can calculate bond value using Equation 6.7a and the appropriate financial tables (Tables A–2 and A–4) or by using a financial calculator.

EXAMPLE

Assuming that interest on the Mills Company bond issue is paid annually and that the required return is equal to the bond's coupon interest rate, $I = \$100$, $k_d = 10\%$, $M = \$1,000$, and $n = 10$ years.

The computations involved in finding the bond value are depicted graphically on the following time line.

Time line for bond valuation (Mills Company's 10% coupon interest rate, 10-year maturity, $1,000 par, January 1, 2007, issue paying annual interest; required return = 10%)

Table Use   Substituting the values noted above into Equation 6.7a yields

$$B_0 = \$100 \times (PVIFA_{10\%,10\text{yrs}}) + \$1,000 \times (PVIF_{10\%,10\text{yrs}})$$
$$= \$100 \times (6.145) + \$1,000 \times (0.386)$$
$$= \$614.50 + \$386.00 = \underline{\underline{\$1,000.50}}$$

The bond therefore has a value of approximately $1,000.[13]

Calculator Use   Using the Mills Company's inputs shown at the left, you should find the bond value to be exactly $1,000. Note that *the calculated bond value is equal to its par value; this will always be the case when the required return is equal to the coupon interest rate.*[14]

Spreadsheet Use   The value of the Mills Company bond also can be calculated as shown in the following Excel spreadsheet. (For another spreadsheet model

Input	Function
10	N
10	I
100	PMT
1000	FV
	CPT
	PV

Solution
1,000

---

13. Note that a slight rounding error ($0.50) results here from the use of the table factors, which are rounded to the nearest thousandth.

14. Note that because bonds pay interest in arrears, the prices at which they are quoted and traded reflect their value *plus* any accrued interest. For example, a $1,000 par value, 10% coupon bond paying interest semiannually and having a calculated value of $900 would pay interest of $50 at the end of each 6-month period. If it is now 3 months since the beginning of the interest period, three-sixths of the $50 interest, or $25 (i.e., 3/6 × $50), would be accrued. The bond would therefore be quoted at $925—its $900 value plus the $25 in accrued interest. For convenience, *throughout this book, bond values will always be assumed to be calculated at the beginning of the interest period,* thereby avoiding the need to consider accrued interest.

that computes the value of the Mills Company bond, see the book's Web site, www.aw-bc.com/gitman, Chapter 6.)

	A	B
1	**BOND VALUE, ANNUAL INTEREST, REQUIRED RETURN = COUPON INTEREST RATE**	
2	Annual interest payment	$100
3	Coupon interest rate	10%
4	Number of years to maturity	10
5	Par value	$1,000
6	Bond value	$1,000.00

Entry in Cell B6 is
(B2 * (1-(1/(1+B3)^B4))/B3) + (B6 * (1/(1+B3)^B4))

The expression 1-(1/(1+B3)^B4))/B3) calculates the Present Value Interest Factor for an Annuity.
The expression 1/(1+B3)^B4 calculates the Present Value Interest Factor for a Single Amount

Bond Value Behavior

In practice, the value of a bond in the marketplace is rarely equal to its par value. In bond quotations (see Figure 6.4 on page 291), the last prices of bonds often differ from their par values of 100 (100 percent of par). Some bonds are valued below par (quoted below 100), and others are valued above par (quoted above 100). A variety of forces in the economy, as well as the passage of time, tend to affect value. Although these external forces are in no way controlled by bond issuers or investors, it is useful to understand the impact that required return and time to maturity have on bond value.

Required Returns and Bond Values

Whenever the required return on a bond differs from the bond's coupon interest rate, the bond's value will differ from its par value. The required return is likely to differ from the coupon interest rate because either (1) economic conditions have changed, causing a shift in the basic cost of long-term funds, or (2) the firm's risk has changed. Increases in the basic cost of long-term funds or in risk will raise the required return; decreases in the cost of funds or in risk will lower the required return.

Regardless of the exact cause, what is important is the relationship between the required return and the coupon interest rate: When the required return is greater than the coupon interest rate, the bond value, B_0, will be less than its par value, M. In this case, the bond is said to sell at a **discount**, which will equal $M - B_0$. When the required return falls below the coupon interest rate, the bond value will be greater than par. In this situation, the bond is said to sell at a **premium**, which will equal $B_0 - M$.

discount
The amount by which a bond sells at a value that is less than its par value.

premium
The amount by which a bond sells at a value that is greater than its par value.

EXAMPLE

The preceding example showed that when the required return equaled the coupon interest rate, the bond's value equaled its $1,000 par value. If for the same bond the required return were to rise or fall, its value would be found as follows (using Equation 6.7a):

TABLE 6.6

Bond Values for Various Required Returns
(Mills Company's 10% Coupon Interest Rate, 10-Year Maturity,
$1,000 Par, January 1, 2007, Issue Paying Annual Interest)

Required return, k_d	Bond value, B_0	Status
12%	$ 887.00	Discount
10	1,000.00	Par value
8	1,134.00	Premium

Table Use

Required Return $= 12\%$	Required Return $= 8\%$
$B_0 = \$100 \times (PVIFA_{12\%,10\text{yrs}}) + \$1,000$ $\times (PVIF_{12\%,10\text{yrs}})$	$B_0 = \$100 \times (PVIFA_{8\%,10\text{yrs}}) + \$1,000$ $\times (PVIF_{8\%,10\text{yrs}})$
$= \underline{\$887.00}$	$= \underline{\$1,134.00}$

Input	Function
10	N
12	I
100	PMT
1000	FV
	CPT
	PV

Solution
887.00

Input	Function
10	N
8	I
100	PMT
1000	FV
	CPT
	PV

Solution
1,134.20

Calculator Use Using the inputs shown at the left for the two different required returns, you will find the value of the bond to be below or above par. At a 12% required return, the bond would sell at a *discount* of $113.00 ($1,000 par value − $887.00 value). At the 8% required return, the bond would sell for a *premium* of about $134.00 ($1,134.00 value − $1,000 par value). The results of this and earlier calculations for Mills Company's bond values are summarized in Table 6.6 and graphically depicted in Figure 6.5. The inverse relationship between bond value and required return is clearly shown in the figure.

FIGURE 6.5

Bond Values and Required Returns
Bond values and required returns (Mills Company's 10% coupon interest rate, 10-year maturity, $1,000 par, January 1, 2007, issue paying annual interest)

Spreadsheet Use   The values for the Mills Company bond at required returns of 12% and 8% also can be calculated as shown in the following Excel spreadsheet. (See the book's Web site, www.aw-bc.com/gitman, Chapter 6, for another spreadsheet model that computes the values of the Mills Company bond at a discount and a premium.)

	A	B	C
1	**BOND VALUE, ANNUAL INTEREST, REQUIRED RETURN NOT EQUAL TO COUPON INTEREST RATE**		
2	Annual interest payment	$100	$100
3	Coupon interest rate	10%	10%
4	Required return	12%	8%
5	Number of years to maturity	10	10
6	Par value	$1,000	$1,000
7	Bond value	$887.00	$1,134.20

Entry in Cell B7, a **bond discount**, is
(B2*(1-(1/(1+B4)^B5))/B4) + (B6*(1/(1+B4)^B5))
The expression 1-(1/(1+B4)^B5))/B4 calculates the Present Value Interest Factor for an Annuity.
The expression 1/(1+B4)^B5 calculates the Present Value Interest Factor for a Single Amount.

Entry in Cell C7, a **bond premium**, is
(C2*(1-(1/(1+C4)^C5))/C4) + (C6*(1/(1+C4)^C5))
The expression 1-(1/(1+C4)^C5))/C4 calculates the Present Value Interest Factor for an Annuity.
The expression 1/(1+C4)^C5 calculates the Present Value Interest Factor for a Single Amount.

Time to Maturity and Bond Values

Whenever the required return is different from the coupon interest rate, the amount of time to maturity affects bond value. An additional factor is whether required returns are constant or change over the life of the bond.

Constant Required Returns   When the required return is different from the coupon interest rate and is assumed to be *constant until maturity,* the value of the bond will approach its par value as the passage of time moves the bond's value closer to maturity. (Of course, when the required return *equals* the coupon interest rate, the bond's value will remain at par until it matures.)

EXAMPLE

interest rate risk
The chance that interest rates will change and thereby change the required return and bond value. Rising rates, which result in decreasing bond values, are of greatest concern.

Figure 6.6 (see page 304) depicts the behavior of the bond values calculated earlier and presented in Table 6.6 for Mills Company's 10% coupon interest rate bond paying annual interest and having 10 years to maturity. Each of the three required returns—12%, 10%, and 8%—is assumed to remain constant over the 10 years to the bond's maturity. The bond's value at both 12% and 8% approaches and ultimately equals the bond's $1,000 par value at its maturity, as the discount (at 12%) or premium (at 8%) declines with the passage of time. ■

Changing Required Returns   The chance that interest rates will change and thereby change the required return and bond value is called **interest rate risk.** (This was described as a shareholder-specific risk in Chapter 5, Table 5.1.)

FIGURE 6.6

**Time to Maturity
and Bond Values**
Relationship among time
to maturity, required
returns, and bond values
(Mills Company's 10%
coupon interest rate,
10-year maturity, $1,000
par, January 1, 2007, issue
paying annual interest)

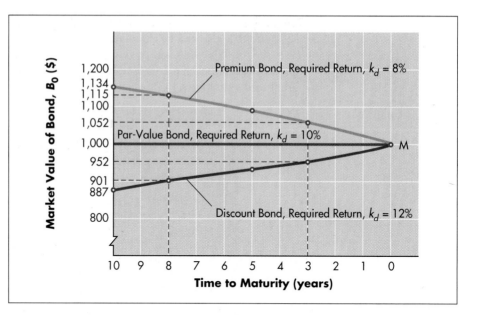

Bondholders are typically more concerned with rising interest rates because a rise in interest rates, and therefore in the required return, causes a decrease in bond value. The shorter the amount of time until a bond's maturity, the less responsive its market value to a given change in the required return. In other words, *short maturities have less interest rate risk than long maturities when all other features (coupon interest rate, par value, and interest payment frequency) are the same.* This is because of the mathematics of time value; the present values of short-term cash flows change far less than the present values of longer-term cash flows in response to a given change in the discount rate (required return).

EXAMPLE   The effect of changing required returns on bonds with differing maturities can be illustrated by using Mills Company's bond and Figure 6.6. If the required return rises from 10% to 12% when the bond has 8 years to maturity (see the dashed line at 8 years), the bond's value decreases from $1,000 to $901—a 9.9% decrease. If the same change in required return had occurred with only 3 years to maturity (see the dashed line at 3 years), the bond's value would have dropped to just $952—only a 4.8% decrease. Similar types of responses can be seen for the change in bond value associated with decreases in required returns. The shorter the time to maturity, the less the impact on bond value caused by a given change in the required return. ■

Yield to Maturity (YTM)

yield to maturity (YTM)
The rate of return that investors earn if they buy a bond at a specific price and hold it until maturity. (Assumes that the issuer makes all scheduled interest and principal payments as promised.)

When investors evaluate bonds, they commonly consider **yield to maturity (YTM)**. This is the rate of return that investors earn if they buy the bond at a specific price and hold it until maturity. (The measure assumes, of course, that the issuer makes all scheduled interest and principal payments as promised.) The yield to maturity on a bond with a current price equal to its par value (that is, $B_0 = M$) will always equal the coupon interest rate. When the bond value differs from par, the yield to maturity will differ from the coupon interest rate.

Assuming that interest is paid annually, the yield to maturity on a bond can be found by solving Equation 6.7 for k_d. In other words, the current value, the annual interest, the par value, and the years to maturity are known, and the required return must be found. The required return is the bond's yield to maturity. The YTM can be found by trial and error, by using a financial calculator, or by using an Excel spreadsheet. The calculator provides accurate YTM values with minimum effort.

EXAMPLE

The Mills Company bond, which currently sells for $1,080, has a 10% coupon interest rate and $1,000 par value, pays interest annually, and has 10 years to maturity. Because $B_0 = \$1,080$, $I = \$100$ $(0.10 \times \$1,000)$, $M = \$1,000$, and $n = 10$ years, substituting into Equation 6.7a yields 1080 $PV = 1080$

$$\$1,080 = \$100 \times (PVIFA_{k_d,10\text{yrs}}) + \$1,000 \times (PVIF_{k_d,10\text{yrs}})$$

Our objective is to solve the equation for k_d, the YTM.

Trial and Error   Because we know that a required return, k_d, of 10% (which equals the bond's 10% coupon interest rate) would result in a value of $1,000, the discount rate that would result in $1,080 must be less than 10%. (Remember that the lower the discount rate, the higher the present value, and the higher the discount rate, the lower the present value.) Trying 9%, we get

$$\$100 \times (PVIFA_{9\%,10\text{yrs}}) + \$1,000 \times (PVIF_{9\%,10\text{yrs}})$$
$$= \$100 \times (6.418) + \$1,000 \times (0.422)$$
$$= \$641.80 + \$422.00$$
$$= \$1,063.80$$

Because the 9% rate is not quite low enough to bring the value up to $1,080, we next try 8% and get

$$\$100 \times (PVIFA_{8\%,10\text{yrs}}) + \$1,000 \times (PVIF_{8\%,10\text{yrs}})$$
$$= \$100 \times (6.710) + \$1,000 \times (0.463)$$
$$= \$671.00 + \$463.00$$
$$= \$1,134.00$$

Input	Function
10	N
−1080	PV
100	PMT
1000	FV
	CPT
	I

Solution
8.766

Because the value at the 8% rate is higher than $1,080 and the value at the 9% rate is lower than $1,080, the bond's yield to maturity must be between 8% and 9%. Because the $1,063.80 is closer to $1,080, the YTM to the nearest whole percent is 9%. (By using *interpolation*, we could eventually find the more precise YTM value to be 8.77%.)[15]

Calculator Use   [*Note:* Most calculators require *either* the present value (B_0 in this case) or the future values (I and M in this case) to be input as negative numbers to calculate yield to maturity. That approach is employed here.] Using the inputs shown at the left, you should find the YTM to be 8.766%.

Spreadsheet Use   The yield to maturity of the 10% coupon rate Mills Company bond also can be calculated as shown in the Excel spreadsheet on page 306. (See the book's Web site, www.aw-bc.com/gitman, Chapter 6, for another spreadsheet model that computes the yield to maturity of the Mills Company bond.)

---

15. For information on how to interpolate to get a more precise answer, see the book's home page at www.aw-bc .com/gitman.

	A	B
1	**YIELD TO MATURITY, ANNUAL INTEREST**	
2	Annual interest payment	$100
3	Coupon interest rate	10%
4	Number of years to maturity	10
5	Par value	$1,000
6	Current bond price	$1,080
7	Yield to maturity	8.77%
8	**Trial and error method:**	
9	Choose various required rates and place them in Cell A14	
10	The spreadsheet will recalculate each time. Continue the process	
11	until the value of the bond equals the current price of the bond	
12	(in this example, it is $1,080).	
13		
14	8.77%	
15	**Payments PVIFA PVIF**	**PV**
16	$100 6.4831	$ 648
17	$1,000 0.4314	$ 431
18	Bond Value	$ 1,080

Semiannual Interest and Bond Values

The procedure used to value bonds paying interest semiannually is similar to that shown in Chapter 4 for compounding interest more frequently than annually, except that here we need to find present value instead of future value. It involves

1. Converting annual interest, I, to semiannual interest by dividing I by 2.
2. Converting the number of years to maturity, n, to the number of 6-month periods to maturity by multiplying n by 2.
3. Converting the required stated (rather than effective)[16] annual return for similar-risk bonds that also pay semiannual interest from an annual rate, k_d, to a semiannual rate by dividing k_d by 2.

Substituting these three changes into Equation 6.7 yields

$$B_0 = \frac{I}{2} \times \left[\sum_{t=1}^{2n} \frac{1}{\left(1 + \frac{k_d}{2}\right)^t} \right] + M \times \left[\frac{1}{\left(1 + \frac{k_d}{2}\right)^{2n}} \right] \qquad (6.8)^{[17]}$$

$$= \frac{I}{2} \times (PVIFA_{k_d/2,2n}) + M \times (PVIF_{k_d/2,2n}) \qquad (6.8a)$$

---

16. As we noted in Chapter 4, the effective annual rate of interest, EAR, for stated interest rate i, when interest is paid semiannually ($m = 2$), can be found by using Equation 4.24:

$$EAR = \left(1 + \frac{i}{2}\right)^2 - 1$$

For example, a bond with a 12% required stated return, k_d, that pays semiannual interest would have an effective annual rate of

$$EAR = \left(1 + \frac{0.12}{2}\right)^2 - 1 = (1.06)^2 - 1 = 1.1236 - 1 = 0.1236 = \underline{12.36\%}$$

Because most bonds pay semiannual interest at semiannual rates equal to 50% of the stated annual rate, their effective annual rates are generally higher than their stated annual rates.

EXAMPLE

Assuming that the Mills Company bond pays interest semiannually and that the required stated annual return, k_d, is 12% for similar-risk bonds that also pay semiannual interest, substituting these values into Equation 6.8a yields

$$B_0 = \frac{\$100}{2} \times (PVIFA_{12\%/2,\,2 \times 10\text{yrs}}) + \$1,000 \times (PVIF_{12\%/2,\,2 \times 10\text{yrs}})$$

Table Use

$$B_0 = \$50 \times (PVIFA_{6\%,\,20\text{periods}}) + \$1,000 \times (PVIF_{6\%,\,20\text{periods}})$$

$$= \$50 \times (11.470) + \$1,000 \times (0.312) = \underline{\underline{\$885.50}}$$

Input	Function
20	N
6	I
50	PMT
1000	FV
	CPT
	PV

Solution
885.30

Calculator Use   In using a calculator to find bond value when interest is paid semiannually, we must double the number of periods and divide both the required stated annual return and the annual interest by 2. For the Mills Company bond, we would use 20 periods (2×10 years), a required return of 6% ($12\% \div 2$), and an interest payment of $50 ($\$100 \div 2$). Using these inputs, you should find the bond value with semiannual interest to be $885.30, as shown at the left. Note that this value is more precise than the value calculated using the rounded financial-table factors.

Spreadsheet Use   The value of the Mills Company bond paying semiannual interest at a required return of 12% also can be calculated as shown in the following Excel spreadsheet. (See the book's Web site, www.aw-bc.com/gitman, Chapter 6, for another spreadsheet model that computes the value of the Mills Company bond paying semiannual interest.)

	A	B
1	**BOND VALUE, SEMIANNUAL INTEREST**	
2	Annual interest payment	$100
3	Stated annual return	12%
4	Number of years to maturity	10
5	Par value	$1,000
6	Bond value	$885.30
	Entry in Cell B6 is B2/2*(1-(1/(1+B3/2)^(2*B4)))/(B3/2) + (B5*(1/(1+B3/2)^(2*B4))) The expression 1-(1/(1+B3/2)^(2*B4)))/(B3/2) calculates the Present Value Interest Factor for an Annuity (semiannual interest). The expression 1/(1+B3/2)^(2*B4) calculates the Present Value Interest Factor for a Single Amount (semiannual interest).	

Comparing this result with the $887.00 value found earlier for annual compounding (see Table 6.6 on page 302), we can see that the bond's value is lower when semiannual interest is paid. *This will always occur when the bond sells at a discount.* For bonds selling at a premium, the opposite will occur: The value with semiannual interest will be greater than with annual interest.

---

17. Although it may appear inappropriate to use the semiannual discounting procedure on the maturity value, M, this technique is necessary to find the correct bond value. One way to confirm the accuracy of this approach is to calculate the bond value for the case where the required stated annual return and coupon interest rate are equal; for B_0 to equal M, as would be expected in such a case, the maturity value must be discounted on a semiannual basis.

REVIEW QUESTIONS

6–16   What basic procedure is used to value a bond that pays annual interest? Semiannual interest?

6–17   What relationship between the required return and the coupon interest rate will cause a bond to sell at a *discount?* At a *premium?* At its *par value?*

6–18   If the required return on a bond differs from its coupon interest rate, describe the behavior of the bond value over time as the bond moves toward maturity.

6–19   As a risk-averse investor, would you prefer bonds with short or long periods until maturity? Why?

6–20   What is a bond's *yield to maturity (YTM)?* Briefly describe the trial-and-error approach, the use of a financial calculator, and the use of an Excel spreadsheet for finding YTM.

Summary

Focus on Value

Interest rates and required returns embody the real cost of money, inflationary expectations, and issuer and issue risk. They reflect the level of return required by market participants as compensation for the risk perceived in a specific security or asset investment. Because these returns are affected by economic expectations, they vary as a function of time, typically rising for longer-term maturities or transactions. The yield curve reflects such market expectations at any point in time.

The value of an asset can be found by calculating the present value of its expected cash flows, using the required return as the discount rate. Bonds are the easiest financial assets to value, because both the amounts and the timing of their cash flows are contractual and therefore known with certainty. The financial manager needs to understand how to apply valuation techniques to bonds, stocks, and tangible assets (as will be demonstrated in the following chapters) to make decisions that are consistent with the firm's **share price maximization goal.**

Review of Learning Goals

Key definitions and formulas for this chapter are summarized in Table 6.7.

LG1 **Describe interest rate fundamentals, the term structure of interest rates, and risk premiums.** The flow of funds between savers and investors is regulated by the interest rate or required return. In a perfect, inflation-free, certain world there would be one cost of money—the real rate of interest. The nominal or actual interest rate is the sum of the risk-free rate and a risk premium reflecting issuer and issue characteristics. (The risk-free rate is the real rate of interest plus an inflation premium.)

For any class of similar-risk securities, the term structure of interest rates reflects the relationship between the interest rate or rate of return and the time to maturity. Yield curves can be downward-sloping (inverted), upward-sloping (normal), or flat. The expectations theory, liquidity preference theory, and

TABLE 6.7

Summary of Key Valuation Definitions and Formulas for Any Asset and for Bonds

Definitions of variables

B_0 = bond value

CF_t = cash flow *expected* at the end of year t

I = annual interest on a bond

k = appropriate required return (discount rate)

k_d = required return on a bond

M = par, or face, value of a bond

n = relevant time period, or number of years to maturity

V_0 = value of the asset at time zero

Valuation formulas

Value of any asset:

$$V_0 = \frac{CF_1}{(1+k)^1} + \frac{CF_2}{(1+k)^2} + \cdots + \frac{CF_n}{(1+k)^n} \qquad \text{[Equation 6.5]}$$

$$= [CF_1 \times (PVIF_{k,1})] + [CF_2 \times (PVIF_{k,2})] + \cdots + [CF_n \times (PVIF_{k,n})] \qquad \text{[Equation 6.6]}$$

Bond value:

$$B_0 = I \times \left[\sum_{t=1}^{n} \frac{1}{(1+k_d)^t} \right] + M \times \left[\frac{1}{(1+k_d)^n} \right] \qquad \text{[Equation 6.7]}$$

$$= I \times (PVIFA_{k_d,n}) + M \times (PVIF_{k_d,n}) \qquad \text{[Equation 6.7a]}$$

market segmentation theory are cited to explain the shape of the yield curve. Risk premiums for non-Treasury debt issues result from business risk, financial risk, interest rate risk, liquidity risk, tax risk, default risk, maturity risk, and contractual provision risk.

LG2 **Review the legal aspects of bond financing and bond cost.** Corporate bonds are long-term debt instruments indicating that a corporation has borrowed an amount that it promises to repay in the future under clearly defined terms. Most bonds are issued with maturities of 10 to 30 years and a par value of $1,000. The bond indenture, enforced by a trustee, states all conditions of the bond issue. It contains both standard debt provisions and restrictive covenants, which may include a sinking-fund requirement and/or a security interest. The cost of a bond to an issuer depends on its maturity, offering size, and issuer risk and on the basic cost of money.

LG3 **Discuss the general features, quotations, ratings, popular types, and international issues of corporate bonds.** A bond issue may include a conversion feature, a call feature, or stock purchase warrants. Bond quotations provide information such as current price, yield, and volume data. Bond ratings by independent agencies indicate the risk of a bond issue. Various types of traditional and contemporary bonds are available. Eurobonds and foreign bonds enable established creditworthy companies and governments to borrow large amounts internationally.

LG4 **Understand the key inputs and basic model used in the valuation process.** Key inputs to the valuation process include cash flows (returns), timing, and risk and the required return. The value of any asset is equal to the present value of all future cash flows it is *expected* to provide over the relevant time period.

LG5 **Apply the basic valuation model to bonds and describe the impact of required return and time to maturity on bond values.** The value of a bond is the present value of its interest payments plus the present value of its par value. The discount rate used to determine bond value is the required return, which may differ from the bond's coupon interest rate. A bond can sell at a discount, at par, or at a premium, depending on whether the required return is greater than, equal to, or less than its coupon interest rate. The amount of time to maturity affects bond values. The value of a bond will approach its par value as the bond moves closer to maturity. The chance that interest rates will change and thereby change the required return and bond value is called interest rate risk. The shorter the amount of time until a bond's maturity, the less responsive its market value to a given change in the required return.

LG6 **Explain yield to maturity (YTM), its calculation, and the procedure used to value bonds that pay interest semiannually.** Yield to maturity is the rate of return investors earn if they buy a bond at a specific price and hold it until maturity. YTM can be calculated by trial and error, by using a financial calculator, or by using an Excel spreadsheet. Bonds that pay interest semiannually are valued by using the same procedure used to value bonds paying annual interest, except that the interest payments are one-half of the annual interest payments, the number of periods is twice the number of years to maturity, and the required return is one-half of the stated annual required return on similar-risk bonds.

Self-Test Problems (Solutions in Appendix B)

LG5 **LG6**   **ST6–1** **Bond valuation**   Lahey Industries has outstanding a $1,000 par-value bond with an 8% coupon interest rate. The bond has 12 years remaining to its maturity date.
 a. If interest is paid *annually*, find the value of the bond when the required return is (1) 7%, (2) 8%, and (3) 10%.
 b. Indicate for each case in part **a** whether the bond is selling at a discount, at a premium, or at its par value.
 c. Using the 10% required return, find the bond's value when interest is paid *semiannually*.

LG6   **ST6–2** **Yield to maturity**   Elliot Enterprises' bonds currently sell for $1,150, have an 11% coupon interest rate and a $1,000 par value, pay interest *annually*, and have 18 years to maturity.
 a. Calculate the bonds' *yield to maturity (YTM)*.
 b. Compare the YTM calculated in part **a** to the bonds' coupon interest rate, and use a comparison of the bonds' current price and their par value to explain this difference.

Warm-Up Exercises

LG1

E6–1   The risk-free rate on T-bills recently was 1.23%. If the real rate of interest is estimated to be 0.80%, what was the expected level of inflation?

LG1

E6–2   The yields for Treasuries with differing maturities on a recent day were as shown in the following table:

Maturity	Yield
3 months	1.41%
6 months	1.71
2 years	2.68
3 years	3.01
5 years	3.7
10 years	4.51
30 years	5.25

Use the information above to construct a *yield curve* for this date.

LG1

E6–3   The yields for Treasuries with differing maturities, including an estimate of the real rate of interest, on a recent day were as shown in the following table:

Maturity	Yield	Real rate of interest
3 months	1.41%	0.80%
6 months	1.71	0.80
2 years	2.68	0.80
3 years	3.01	0.80
5 years	3.7	0.80
10 years	4.51	0.80
30 years	5.25	0.80

Use the information above to calculate the *inflation expectation* for each maturity.

LG1

E6–4   Recently, the annual inflation rate measured by the Consumer Price Index (CPI) was forecast to be 3.3%. How could a T-bill have had a negative real rate of return over the same period? How could it have had a zero real rate of return? What minimum rate of return must the T-bill have earned to meet your requirement of a 2% real rate of return?

LG1

E6–5   Calculate the *risk premium* for each of the following rating classes of long-term securities, assuming that the yield to maturity (YTM) for comparable Treasuries is 4.51%.

Rating class	Nominal interest rate
AAA	5.12%
BBB	5.78
B	7.82

LG4

E6–6 You have two assets and must calculate their values today based on their different payment streams and appropriate required returns. Asset 1 has a required return of 15% and will produce a stream of $500 at the end of each year indefinitely. Asset 2 has a required return of 10% and will produce an end-of-year cash flow of $1,200 in the first year, $1,500 in the second year, and $850 in its third and final year.

LG5

E6–7 A bond with 5 years to maturity and a coupon rate of 6% has a face value of $20,000. Interest is paid annually. If you required a return of 8% on this bond, what is the value of this bond to you?

LG5

E6–8 Assume a 5-year Treasury bond has a coupon rate of 4.5%.
  a. Give examples of required rates of return that would make the bond sell at a discount, at a premium, and at par.
  b. If this bond's par value is $10,000, calculate the differing values for this bond given the required rates you chose in part **a**.

Problems

LG1

BASIC

P6–1 **Interest rate fundamentals: The real rate of return** Carl Foster, a trainee at an investment banking firm, is trying to get an idea of what real rate of return investors are expecting in today's marketplace. He has looked up the rate paid on 3-month U.S. Treasury bills and found it to be 5.5%. He has decided to use the rate of change in the Consumer Price Index as a proxy for the inflationary expectations of investors. That annualized rate now stands at 3%. On the basis of the information that Carl has collected, what estimate can he make of the real rate of return?

LG1

INTERMEDIATE

P6–2 **Real rate of interest** To estimate the real rate of interest, the economics division of Mountain Banks—a major bank holding company—has gathered the data summarized in the table at the top of the facing page. Because there is a high likelihood that new tax legislation will be passed in the near future, current data as well as data reflecting the probable impact of passage of the legislation on the demand for funds are also included in the table. (*Note:* The proposed legislation will not affect the supply schedule of funds. Assume a perfect world in which inflation is expected to be zero, funds suppliers and demanders have no liquidity preference, and all outcomes are certain.)
  a. Draw the supply curve and the demand curve for funds using the current data. (*Note:* Unlike the functions in Figure 6.1 on page 279, the functions here will not appear as straight lines.)
  b. Using your graph, label and note the real rate of interest using current data.
  c. Add to the graph drawn in part **a** the new demand curve expected in the event that the proposed tax legislation is passed.
  d. What is the new real rate of interest? Compare and analyze this finding in light of your analysis in part **b**.

| Amount of funds supplied/demanded ($ billion) | Currently | | With passage of tax legislation |
	Interest rate required by funds suppliers	Interest rate required by funds demanders	Interest rate required by funds demanders
$ 1	2%	7%	9%
5	3	6	8
10	4	4	7
20	6	3	6
50	7	2	4
100	9	1	3

LG1

INTERMEDIATE

P6–3 **Real and nominal rates interest**   Zane Perelli currently has $100 that he can spend today on polo shirts costing $25 each. Alternatively, he could invest the $100 in a risk-free U.S. Treasury security that is expected to earn a 9% nominal rate of interest. The consensus forecast of leading economists is a 5% rate of inflation over the coming year.

a. How many polo shirts can Zane purchase today?

b. How much money will Zane have at the end of 1 year if he forgoes purchasing the polo shirts today?

c. How much would you expect the polo shirts to cost at the end of 1 year in light of the expected inflation?

d. Use your findings in parts **b** and **c** to determine how many polo shirts (fractions are okay) Zane can purchase at the end of 1 year. In percentage terms, how many more or fewer polo shirts can Zane buy at the end of 1 year?

e. What is Zane's real rate of return over the year? How is it related to the percentage change in Zane's buying power found in part **d**? Explain.

LG1

INTERMEDIATE

P6–4 **Yield curve**   A firm wishing to evaluate interest rate behavior has gathered yield data on five U.S. Treasury securities, each having a different maturity and all measured at the same point in time. The summarized data follow.

U.S. Treasury security	Time to maturity	Yield
A	1 year	12.6%
B	10 years	11.2
C	6 months	13.0
D	20 years	11.0
E	5 years	11.4

a. Draw the yield curve associated with these data.

b. Describe the resulting yield curve in part **a**, and explain the general expectations embodied in it.

P6–5 **Nominal interest rates and yield curves** A recent study of inflationary expectations has revealed that the consensus among economic forecasters yields the following average annual rates of inflation expected over the periods noted. (*Note:* Assume that the risk that future interest rate movements will affect longer maturities more than shorter maturities is zero; that is, there is no *maturity risk.*)

Period	Average annual rate of inflation
3 months	5%
2 years	6
5 years	8
10 years	8.5
20 years	9

a. If the real rate of interest is currently 2.5%, find the nominal interest rate on each of the following U.S. Treasury issues: 20-year bond, 3-month bill, 2-year note, and 5-year bond.

b. If the real rate of interest suddenly dropped to 2% without any change in inflationary expectations, what effect, if any, would this have on your answers in part **a**? Explain.

c. Using your findings in part **a**, draw a yield curve for U.S. Treasury securities. Describe the general shape and expectations reflected by the curve.

d. What would a follower of the *liquidity preference theory* say about how the preferences of lenders and borrowers tend to affect the shape of the yield curve drawn in part **c**? Illustrate that effect by placing on your graph a dotted line that approximates the yield curve without the effect of liquidity preference.

e. What would a follower of the *market segmentation theory* say about the supply and demand for long-term loans versus the supply and demand for short-term loans given the yield curve constructed for part **c** of this problem?

P6–6 **Nominal and real rates and yield curves** A firm wishing to evaluate interest rate behavior has gathered data on the nominal rate of interest and on inflationary expectations for five U.S. Treasury securities, each having a different maturity and each measured at a different point in time during the year just ended. (*Note:* Assume that the risk that future interest rate movements will affect longer maturities more than shorter maturities is zero; that is, there is no *maturity risk.*) These data are summarized in the following table.

U.S. Treasury security	Point in time	Maturity	Nominal rate of interest	Inflationary expectation
A	Jan. 7	2 years	12.6%	9.5%
B	Mar. 12	10 years	11.2	8.2
C	May 30	6 months	13.0	10.0
D	Aug. 15	20 years	11.0	8.1
E	Dec. 30	5 years	11.4	8.3

a. Using the preceding data, find the real rate of interest at each point in time.
b. Describe the behavior of the real rate of interest over the year. What forces might be responsible for such behavior?
c. Draw the yield curve associated with these data, assuming that the nominal rates were measured at the same point in time.
d. Describe the resulting yield curve in part **c**, and explain the general expectations embodied in it.

P6–7 Term structure of interest rates   The following yield data for a number of highest-quality corporate bonds existed at each of the three points in time noted.

	Yield		
Time to maturity (years)	5 years ago	2 years ago	Today
1	9.1%	14.6%	9.3%
3	9.2	12.8	9.8
5	9.3	12.2	10.9
10	9.5	10.9	12.6
15	9.4	10.7	12.7
20	9.3	10.5	12.9
30	9.4	10.5	13.5

a. On the same set of axes, draw the yield curve at each of the three given times.
b. Label each curve in part **a** with its general shape (downward-sloping, upward-sloping, flat).
c. Describe the general inflationary and interest rate expectation existing at each of the three times.

P6–8 Risk-free rate and risk premiums   The real rate of interest is currently 3%; the inflation expectation and risk premiums for a number of securities follow.

Security	Inflation expectation premium	Risk premium
A	6%	3%
B	9	2
C	8	2
D	5	4
E	11	1

a. Find the risk-free rate of interest, R_F, that is applicable to each security.
b. Although not noted, what factor must be the cause of the differing risk-free rates found in part **a**?
c. Find the nominal rate of interest for each security.

P6–9 Risk premiums   Eleanor Burns is attempting to find the nominal rate of interest for each of two securities—A and B—issued by different firms at the same point in time. She has gathered the following data:

Characteristic	Security A	Security B
Time to maturity	3 years	15 years
Inflation expectation premium	9.0%	7.0%
Risk premium for:		
Liquidity risk	1.0%	1.0%
Default risk	1.0%	2.0%
Maturity risk	0.5%	1.5%
Other risk	0.5%	1.5%

a. If the real rate of interest is currently 2%, find the risk-free rate of interest applicable to each security.

b. Find the total risk premium attributable to each security's issuer and issue characteristics.

c. Calculate the nominal rate of interest for each security. Compare and discuss your findings.

P6–10 Bond interest payments before and after taxes   Charter Corp. has issued 2,500 debentures with a total principal value of $2,500,000. The bonds have a coupon interest rate of 7%.

a. What dollar amount of interest per bond can an investor expect to receive each year from Charter?

b. What is Charter's total interest expense per year associated with this bond issue?

c. Assuming that Charter is in a 35% corporate tax bracket, what is the company's net after-tax interest cost associated with this bond issue?

P6–11 Bond quotation   Assume that the following quote for the Financial Management Corporation's $1,000-par-value bond was found in the Wednesday, November 8, issue of the *Wall Street Journal*.

Financial Management (FM) 5.700   May 15, 2013   97.708   6.034   129   10   47,807

Given this information, answer the following questions.

a. On what day did the trading activity occur?

b. What was the last price at which the bond traded on November 7?

c. When does the bond mature?

d. What dollar value of these bonds was traded on the day quoted?

e. What is the bond's coupon interest rate?

f. What is the bond's *yield?* Explain what this value represents.

g. What was this bond's spread over a similar-maturity U.S. Treasury issue? What maturity Treasury issue is used in this comparison?

P6–12 Valuation fundamentals   Imagine that you are trying to evaluate the economics of purchasing an automobile. You expect the car to provide annual after-tax cash benefits of $1,200 at the end of each year, and assume that you can sell the car for after-tax proceeds of $5,000 at the end of the planned 5-year ownership period. All funds for purchasing the car will be drawn from your savings, which are currently earning 6% after taxes.

a. Identify the cash flows, their timing, and the required return applicable to valuing the car.

b. What is the maximum price you would be willing to pay to acquire the car? Explain.

P6–13 Valuation of assets Using the information provided in the following table, find the value of each asset.

Asset	Cash flow End of year	Amount	Appropriate required return
A	1	$ 5,000	18%
	2	5,000	
	3	5,000	
B	1 through ∞	$ 300	15%
C	1	$ 0	16%
	2	0	
	3	0	
	4	0	
	5	35,000	
D	1 through 5	$ 1,500	12%
	6	8,500	
E	1	$ 2,000	14%
	2	3,000	
	3	5,000	
	4	7,000	
	5	4,000	
	6	1,000	

P6–14 Asset valuation and risk Laura Drake wishes to estimate the value of an asset expected to provide cash inflows of $3,000 per year at the end of years 1 through 4 and $15,000 at the end of year 5. Her research indicates that she must earn 10% on low-risk assets, 15% on average-risk assets, and 22% on high-risk assets.

a. Determine what is the most Laura should pay for the asset if it is classified as (1) low-risk, (2) average-risk, and (3) high-risk.

b. Suppose Laura is unable to assess the risk of the asset and wants to be certain she's making a good deal. On the basis of your findings in part **a**, what is the most she should pay? Why?

c. All else being the same, what effect does increasing risk have on the value of an asset? Explain in light of your findings in part **a**.

P6–15 Basic bond valuation Complex Systems has an outstanding issue of $1,000-par-value bonds with a 12% coupon interest rate. The issue pays interest *annually* and has 16 years remaining to its maturity date.

a. If bonds of similar risk are currently earning a 10% rate of return, how much should the Complex Systems bond sell for today?

b. Describe the *two* possible reasons why similar-risk bonds are currently earning a return below the coupon interest rate on the Complex Systems bond.

c. If the required return were at 12% instead of 10%, what would the current value of Complex Systems' bond be? Contrast this finding with your findings in part a and discuss.

LG5

BASIC

P6–16 **Bond valuation—Annual interest** Calculate the value of each of the bonds shown in the following table, all of which pay interest *annually*.

Bond	Par value	Coupon interest rate	Years to maturity	Required return
A	$1,000	14%	20	12%
B	1,000	8	16	8
C	100	10	8	13
D	500	16	13	18
E	1,000	12	10	10

LG5

INTERMEDIATE

P6–17 **Bond value and changing required returns** Midland Utilities has outstanding a bond issue that will mature to its $1,000 par value in 12 years. The bond has a coupon interest rate of 11% and pays interest *annually*.
a. Find the value of the bond if the required return is (1) 11%, (2) 15%, and (3) 8%.
b. Plot your findings in part a on a set of "required return (x axis)–market value of bond (y axis)" axes.
c. Use your findings in parts a and b to discuss the relationship between the coupon interest rate on a bond and the required return and the market value of the bond relative to its par value.
d. What *two* possible reasons could cause the required return to differ from the coupon interest rate?

LG5

INTERMEDIATE

P6–18 **Bond value and time—Constant required returns** Pecos Manufacturing has just issued a 15-year, 12% coupon interest rate, $1,000-par bond that pays interest *annually*. The required return is currently 14%, and the company is certain it will remain at 14% until the bond matures in 15 years.
a. Assuming that the required return does remain at 14% until maturity, find the value of the bond with (1) 15 years, (2) 12 years, (3) 9 years, (4) 6 years, (5) 3 years, and (6) 1 year to maturity.
b. Plot your findings on a set of "time to maturity (x axis)–market value of bond (y axis)" axes constructed similarly to Figure 6.6 on page 304.
c. All else remaining the same, when the required return differs from the coupon interest rate and is assumed to be constant to maturity, what happens to the bond value as time moves toward maturity? Explain in light of the graph in part b.

LG5

CHALLENGE

P6–19 **Bond value and time—Changing required returns** Lynn Parsons is considering investing in either of two outstanding bonds. The bonds both have $1,000 par values and 11% coupon interest rates and pay *annual* interest. Bond A has exactly 5 years to maturity, and bond B has 15 years to maturity.
a. Calculate the value of bond A if the required return is (1) 8%, (2) 11%, and (3) 14%.
b. Calculate the value of bond B if the required return is (1) 8%, (2) 11%, and (3) 14%.

c. From your findings in parts **a** and **b,** complete the following table, and discuss the relationship between time to maturity and changing required returns.

Required return	Value of bond A	Value of bond B
8%	?	?
11	?	?
14	?	?

d. If Lynn wanted to minimize *interest rate risk,* which bond should she purchase? Why?

P6–20 Yield to maturity   The relationship between a bond's yield to maturity and coupon interest rate can be used to predict its pricing level. For each of the bonds listed, state whether the price of the bond will be at a premium to par, at par, or at a discount to par.

Bond	Coupon interest rate	Yield to maturity	Price
A	6%	10%	_____
B	8	8	_____
C	9	7	_____
D	7	9	_____
E	12	10	_____

P6–21 Yield to maturity   The Salem Company bond currently sells for $955, has a 12% coupon interest rate and a $1,000 par value, pays interest *annually,* and has 15 years to maturity.
a. Calculate the *yield to maturity (YTM)* on this bond.
b. Explain the relationship that exists between the coupon interest rate and yield to maturity and the par value and market value of a bond.

P6–22 Yield to maturity   Each of the bonds shown in the following table pays interest *annually.*

Bond	Par value	Coupon interest rate	Years to maturity	Current value
A	$1,000	9%	8	$ 820
B	1,000	12	16	1,000
C	500	12	12	560
D	1,000	15	10	1,120
E	1,000	5	3	900

a. Calculate the *yield to maturity (YTM)* for each bond.
b. What relationship exists between the coupon interest rate and yield to maturity and the par value and market value of a bond? Explain.

P6–23   **Bond valuation and yield to maturity**   Mark Goldsmith's broker has shown him two bonds. Each has a maturity of 5 years, a par value of $1,000, and a yield to maturity of 12%. Bond A has a coupon interest rate of 6% paid annually. Bond B has a coupon interest rate of 14% paid annually.

a. Calculate the selling price for each of the bonds.

b. Mark has $20,000 to invest. Judging on the basis of the price of the bonds, how many of either one could Mark purchase if he were to choose it over the other? (Mark cannot really purchase a fraction of a bond, but for purposes of this question, pretend that he can.)

c. Calculate the yearly interest income of each bond on the basis of its coupon rate and the number of bonds that Mark could buy with his $20,000.

d. Assume that Mark will reinvest the interest payments as they are paid (at the end of each year) and that his rate of return on the reinvestment is only 10%. For each bond, calculate the value of the principal payment plus the value of Mark's reinvestment account at the end of the 5 years.

e. Why are the two values calculated in part **d** different? If Mark were worried that he would earn less than the 12% yield to maturity on the reinvested interest payments, which of these two bonds would be a better choice?

P6–24   **Bond valuation—Semiannual interest**   Find the value of a bond maturing in 6 years, with a $1,000 par value and a coupon interest rate of 10% (5% paid semiannually) if the required return on similar-risk bonds is 14% annual interest (7% paid semiannually).

P6–25   **Bond valuation—Semiannual interest**   Calculate the value of each of the bonds shown in the following table, all of which pay interest *semiannually*.

Bond	Par value	Coupon interest rate	Years to maturity	Required stated annual return
A	$1,000	10%	12	8%
B	1,000	12	20	12
C	500	12	5	14
D	1,000	14	10	10
E	100	6	4	14

P6–26   **Bond valuation—Quarterly interest**   Calculate the value of a $5,000-par-value bond paying quarterly interest at an annual coupon interest rate of 10% and having 10 years until maturity if the required return on similar-risk bonds is currently a 12% annual rate paid *quarterly*.

P6–27   **ETHICS PROBLEM**   Bond rating agencies have invested significant sums of money in an effort to determine which quantitative and nonquantitative factors best predict bond defaults. Furthermore, some of the raters invest time and money to meet privately with corporate personnel to get nonpublic information that is used in assigning the issue's bond rating. (They are exempted from the Regulation FD requirements that were mentioned in the Chapter 3 ethics box on page 129.) Does this approach provide an acceptable defense against the ethics charges that are being made against bond raters, as described in the *In Practice* box on page 292?

Chapter 6 Case: Evaluating Annie Hegg's Proposed Investment in Atilier Industries Bonds

Annie Hegg has been considering investing in the bonds of Atilier Industries. The bonds were issued 5 years ago at their $1,000 par value and have exactly 25 years remaining until they mature. They have an 8% coupon interest rate, are convertible into 50 shares of common stock, and can be called any time at $1,080. The bond is rated Aa by Moody's. Atilier Industries, a manufacturer of sporting goods, recently acquired a small athletic-wear company that was in financial distress. As a result of the acquisition, Moody's and other rating agencies are considering a rating change for Atilier bonds. Recent economic data suggest that expected inflation, currently at 5% annually, is likely to increase to a 6% annual rate.

Annie remains interested in the Atilier bond but is concerned about inflation, a potential rating change, and maturity risk. To get a feel for the potential impact of these factors on the bond value, she decided to apply the valuation techniques she learned in her finance course.

TO DO

a. If the price of the common stock into which the bond is convertible rises to $30 per share after 5 years and the issuer calls the bonds at $1,080, should Annie let the bond be called away from her or should she convert it into common stock?

b. For each of the following required returns, calculate the bond's value, assuming annual interest. Indicate whether the bond will sell at a discount, at a premium, or at par value.
   (1) Required return is 6%.
   (2) Required return is 8%.
   (3) Required return is 10%.

c. Repeat the calculations in part **b,** assuming that interest is paid *semiannually* and that the semiannual required returns are one-half of those shown. Compare and discuss differences between the bond values for each required return calculated here and in part **b** under the annual versus semiannual payment assumptions.

d. If Annie strongly believes that expected inflation will rise by 1% during the next few months, what is the most she should pay for the bond, assuming annual interest?

e. If the Atilier bonds are downrated by Moody's from Aa to A, and if such a rating change will result in an increase in the required return from 8% to 8.75%, what impact will this have on the bond value, assuming annual interest?

f. If Annie buys the bond today at its $1,000 par value and holds it for exactly 3 years, at which time the required return is 7%, how much of a gain or loss will she experience in the value of the bond (ignoring interest already received and assuming annual interest)?

g. Rework part **f,** assuming that Annie holds the bond for 10 years and sells it when the required return is 7%. Compare your finding to that in part **f,** and comment on the bond's *maturity risk.*

h. Assume that Annie buys the bond at its last price of 98.380 and holds it until maturity. What will her *yield to maturity* (*YTM*) be, assuming annual interest?

i. After evaluating all of the issues raised above, what recommendation would you give Annie with regard to her proposed investment in the Atilier Industries bonds?

Spreadsheet Exercise

CSM Corporation has a bond issue outstanding at the end of 2006. The bond has 15 years remaining to maturity and carries a coupon interest rate of 6%. Interest on the bond is compounded on a semiannual basis. The par value of the CSM bond is $1,000 and it is currently selling for $874.42.

TO DO

Create a spreadsheet similar to the spreadsheets for yield to maturity and semi-annual interest that can be viewed at www.aw-bc.com/gitman, to model the following:

a. Using the trial and error method, determine the *annual* required rate of return (k_d). Find one interest rate that results in a bond value greater than the current bond price, and then find another rate that results in a bond value lower than the current bond price.

b. What is the time to maturity (n)?

c. What is the semiannual coupon payment (pmt)?

d. What is the semiannual required rate of return ($k_d/2$)?

Group Exercise

This chapter continued our discussion of valuation using the concept of risk. You will again use your shadow firm to investigate the issue of credit ratings.

TO DO

a. Retrieve current information on the most recent debt issuance by your shadow firm. Several sites are available, including Standard & Poor's home page. Although you can use this site free of charge, you are required to register. Alternatively, you can use the bond screener tool at Yahoo! Finance (bonds.yahoo.com/).

b. Conduct a search for ratings on your corporation. Most likely you will find several ratings if your firm has issued multiple debt instruments. Note not only the rating but also the interest rate and yield to maturity of the most recently issued debt.

c. Using the current rating on your shadow company's most recent debt and a current quote on comparable Treasuries, estimate the risk premium inherent in the difference between the rates on the most recently issued debt and the risk-free Treasury.

d. Let's use the debt rating on your shadow firm to borrow money for your fictitious firm. Beyond determining the rate, your group must decide on an appropriate use for the funds. In other, words you must design an investment project that makes sense in the context of your fictitious firm. What is the purpose of the investment? What are the returns expected from the investment? Essentially, you should design and defend this investment. Show how this bond's valuation will change given differing assumptions on required return. In other words, what is likely to happen to the bond's valuation if market rates rise (or fall) following the issuance of this debt?

Web Exercise

Although several Web sites offer bond quotes, a particularly user-friendly site is the bond page at Yahoo! Finance (bonds.yahoo.com/). One very useful page is the composite bond rates page.

TO DO

a. From the home page, direct your browser to Bonds and highlight Rates. This page will give you a screen with both Treasury yields and corporate yields, allowing the risk premium to be estimated directly from this page. The top of this page shows the latest yield curve for Treasuries. Note the pattern of the curve as discussed in your text.

b. Next, a table for Treasuries shows the yields for all maturities. This table gives yields for the specified day, the day before, one week earlier, and one month earlier. Note the changes in yield over this period.

c. The next table gives similar information for municipal securities. Note the difference in yields between Treasuries and munis (municipal bonds). The difference is driven in part by taxation issues.

d. The final table gives the information on corporates.
   (1) Note the differences between the Treasuries and the corporate bonds.
   (2) Note the shape of the yield curve as discussed in the chapter.
   (3) Note the changes in yield over this period.

Remember to check the book's Web site at

www.aw-bc.com/gitman

for additional resources, including additional Web exercises.

Chapter 7

Stock Valuation

LEARNING GOALS

 LG1 Differentiate between debt and equity capital.

LG2 Discuss the rights, characteristics, and features of both common and preferred stock.

LG3 Describe the process of issuing common stock, including venture capital, going public, and the investment banker, and interpreting stock quotations.

 LG4 Understand the concept of market efficiency and basic common stock valuation using zero-growth, constant-growth, and variable-growth models.

LG5 Discuss the free cash flow valuation model and the book value, liquidation value, and price/earnings (P/E) multiples approaches.

LG6 Explain the relationships among financial decisions, return, risk, and the firm's value.

ACROSS THE DISCIPLINES WHY THIS CHAPTER MATTERS TO YOU

Accounting: You need to understand the difference between debt and equity in terms of tax treatment; the ownership claims of capital providers, including venture capitalists and stockholders; and why book value per share is not a sophisticated basis for common stock valuation.

Information systems: You need to understand the procedures used to issue common stock; the sources and types of information that affect stock value; and how such information can be used in stock valuation models to link proposed actions to share price.

Management: You need to understand the difference between debt and equity capital; the rights and claims of stockholders; the process of raising funds from venture

capitalists and through initial public offerings; and the various stock valuation models used to value the firm's common stock.

Marketing: You need to understand that the firm's ideas for products and services will greatly affect the willingness of venture capitalists and stockholders to contribute capital to the firm and that a perceived increase in risk as a result of new projects may negatively affect the firm's stock value.

Operations: You need to understand that the amount of capital the firm has to invest in plant assets and inventory will depend on the evaluations of venture capitalists and would-be investors; the better the prospects look for growth, the more money the firm will have for operations.

DOMINO'S PIZZA, INC.

A SLICE OF THE COMPANY IS NOW AVAILABLE TO THE PUBLIC

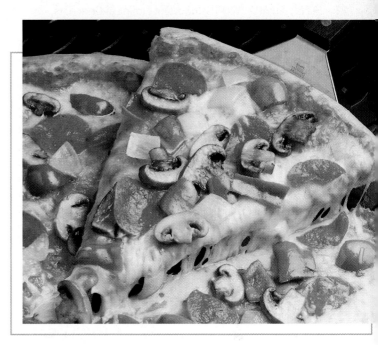

After the technology bubble burst in 2000, the market for initial public offerings (IPOs) of company stock quieted down considerably for several years. By 2004, the pace had picked up, with as many as 13 IPOs scheduled in one week in July 2004. Among the firms going public for the first time was **Domino's Pizza, Inc.** (www.dominos.com). Founded in 1960, Domino's is the second-largest pizza chain in the world, with 7,473 stores, including 2,553 international stores, in early 2004. With total annual sales exceeding $4 billion (a healthy slice of the $30 billion spent on pizza in 2003), Domino's Pizza stores are 90 percent franchisee owned.

In April 2004, Domino's announced that it would offer shares to the public. The initial plan was to issue 24.1 million shares—one of the largest restaurant offerings ever—at an estimated price of $15 to $17 per share. Ultimately, the shares were brought to market at the price of $14 per share and lost 3.8% of their value on the first day of trading. It is not unusual for shares of IPOs to trade in the secondary market at significantly higher or lower prices than the initial offering price.

Why did Domino's go public? The primary motivation was to offer liquidity to the private equity firm **Bain Capital,** which owned 65 percent of Domino's common stock before the offering. Of the 24.1 million privately held shares, existing stockholders sold 14.7 million shares. The remaining 9.4 million shares came from the company.

A secondary motivation for the IPO was to raise money so as to lower the company's debt. Before the offering, Domino's had some $942 million in long-term indebtedness. Adjusted for the $137 million raised in the IPO, long-term debt remains at over $800 million. After the IPO, Standard & Poor's revised its outlook for Domino's Pizza, Inc.'s debt rating from "stable" to "positive," citing the debt reduction from the recent IPO. This revision suggests that the company has a slightly higher chance of its ratings being upgraded over the next 24 months. Nevertheless, S&P's rating of Domino's long-term corporate credit was "B+," its fourth highest junk rating.

In this chapter you will learn about the differences between debt and equity capital, the characteristics of common and preferred stock, and several different valuation methods used to determine the value of common stock.

■ *How might the owners of a closely held company react to an initial public offering when the stock's value immediately rises significantly above its initial offering price?*

7.1 | Differences Between Debt and Equity Capital

capital
The long-term funds of a firm; all items on the right-hand side of the firm's balance sheet, *excluding current liabilities.*

debt capital
All long-term borrowing incurred by a firm, including bonds.

equity capital
The long-term funds provided by the firm's owners, the stockholders.

The term **capital** denotes the long-term funds of a firm. All items on the right-hand side of the firm's balance sheet, *excluding current liabilities,* are sources of capital. **Debt capital** includes all long-term borrowing incurred by a firm, including bonds, which were discussed in Chapter 6. **Equity capital** consists of long-term funds provided by the firm's owners, the stockholders. A firm can obtain equity capital either *internally,* by retaining earnings rather than paying them out as dividends to its stockholders, or *externally,* by selling common or preferred stock. The key differences between debt and equity capital are summarized in Table 7.1 and discussed below.

Voice in Management

Unlike creditors (lenders), holders of equity capital (common and preferred stockholders) are owners of the firm. Holders of common stock have voting rights that permit them to select the firm's directors and to vote on special issues. In contrast, debtholders and preferred stockholders may receive voting privileges only when the firm has violated its stated contractual obligations to them.

Claims on Income and Assets

Holders of equity have claims on both income and assets that are secondary to the claims of creditors. Their *claims on income* cannot be paid until the claims of all creditors (including both interest and scheduled principal payments) have been satisfied. After satisfying these claims, the firm's board of directors decides whether to distribute dividends to the owners.

The equity holders' *claims on assets* also are secondary to the claims of creditors. If the firm fails, its assets are sold, and the proceeds are distributed in this order: employees and customers, the government, creditors, and (finally) equity holders. Because equity holders are the last to receive any distribution of assets, they expect greater returns from dividends and/or increases in stock price.

As is explained in Chapter 11, the costs of equity financing are generally higher than debt costs. One reason is that the suppliers of equity capital take more

TABLE 7.1   Key Differences Between Debt and Equity Capital

| | Type of capital | |
Characteristic	Debt	Equity
Voice in management[a]	No	Yes
Claims on income and assets	Senior to equity	Subordinate to debt
Maturity	Stated	None
Tax treatment	Interest deduction	No deduction

[a]In the event that the issuer violates its stated contractual obligations to them, debtholders and preferred stockholders *may* receive a voice in management; otherwise, only common stockholders have voting rights.

risks because of their subordinate claims on income and assets. Despite being more costly, equity capital is necessary for a firm to grow. All corporations must initially be financed with some common stock equity.

Maturity

Unlike debt, equity capital is a *permanent form* of financing for the firm. It does not "mature" so repayment is not required. Because equity is liquidated only during bankruptcy proceedings, stockholders must recognize that although a ready market may exist for their shares, the price that can be realized may fluctuate. This fluctuation of the market price of equity makes the overall returns to a firm's stockholders even more risky.

Tax Treatment

Interest payments to debtholders are treated as tax-deductible expenses by the issuing firm, whereas dividend payments to a firm's common and preferred stockholders are not tax-deductible. The tax deductibility of interest lowers the corporation's cost of debt financing, further causing it to be lower than the cost of equity financing.

REVIEW QUESTION

7–1   What are the key differences between *debt capital* and *equity capital?*

LG2   LG3   7.2 | Common and Preferred Stock

A firm can obtain equity, or ownership, capital by selling either common or preferred stock. All corporations initially issue common stock to raise equity capital. Some of these firms later issue either additional common stock or preferred stock to raise more equity capital. Although both common and preferred stock are forms of equity capital, preferred stock has some similarities to debt capital that significantly differentiate it from common stock. Here we first consider the rights, characteristics, and features of both common and preferred stock and then describe the process of issuing common stock, including the use of venture capital.

Common Stock

The true owners of business firms are the common stockholders. Common stockholders are sometimes referred to as *residual owners* because they receive what is left—the residual—after all other claims on the firm's income and assets have been satisfied. They are assured of only one thing: that they cannot lose any more than they have invested in the firm. As a result of this generally uncertain position, common stockholders expect to be compensated with adequate dividends and, ultimately, capital gains.

Ownership

The common stock of a firm can be **privately owned** by a single individual, **closely owned** by a small group of investors (such as a family), or **publicly owned** by a broad group of unrelated individual or institutional investors. Typically, small corporations are privately or closely owned; if their shares are traded, this trading occurs infrequently and in small amounts. Large corporations, which are emphasized in the following discussions, are publicly owned, and their shares are generally actively traded on the major securities exchanges described in Chapter 1.

privately owned (stock)
All common stock of a firm owned by a single individual.

closely owned (stock)
All common stock of a firm owned by a small group of investors (such as a family).

publicly owned (stock)
Common stock of a firm owned by a broad group of unrelated individual or institutional investors.

Par Value

Unlike bonds, which always have a par value, common stock may be sold with or without a par value. The **par value** of a common stock is a relatively useless value established for legal purposes in the firm's corporate charter. It is generally quite low, about $1.

Firms often issue stock with no par value, in which case they may assign the stock a value or record it on the books at the price at which it is sold. A low par value may be advantageous in states where certain corporate taxes are based on the par value of stock; if a stock has no par value, the tax may be based on an arbitrarily determined per-share figure.

par value (stock)
A relatively useless value for a stock established for legal purposes in the firm's corporate charter.

Preemptive Rights

The **preemptive right** allows common stockholders to maintain their *proportionate* ownership in the corporation when new shares are issued. It allows existing shareholders to maintain voting control and protects them against the dilution of their ownership. **Dilution of ownership** usually results in the dilution of earnings, because each present shareholder has a claim on a *smaller* part of the firm's earnings than previously.

In a *rights offering*, the firm grants **rights** to its shareholders. These financial instruments allow stockholders to purchase additional shares at a price below the market price, in direct proportion to their number of owned shares. Rights are used primarily by smaller corporations whose shares are either *closely owned* or *publicly owned* and not actively traded. In these situations, rights are an important financing tool without which shareholders would run the risk of losing their proportionate control of the corporation. From the firm's viewpoint, the use of rights offerings to raise new equity capital may be less costly and may generate more interest than a public offering of stock.

preemptive right
Allows common stockholders to maintain their *proportionate* ownership in the corporation when new shares are issued.

dilution of ownership
Occurs when a new stock issue results in each present shareholder having a claim on a *smaller* part of the firm's earnings than previously.

rights
Financial instruments that allow stockholders to purchase additional shares at a price below the market price, in direct proportion to their number of owned shares.

Authorized, Outstanding, and Issued Shares

A firm's corporate charter indicates how many **authorized shares** it can issue. The firm cannot sell more shares than the charter authorizes without obtaining approval through a shareholder vote. To avoid later having to amend the charter, firms generally attempt to authorize more shares than they initially plan to issue.

Authorized shares become **outstanding shares** when they are held by the public. If the *firm* repurchases any of its outstanding shares, these shares are recorded as **treasury stock** and are no longer considered to be outstanding shares. **Issued shares** are the shares of common stock that have been put into circulation; they represent the sum of outstanding shares and treasury stock.

authorized shares
The number of shares of common stock that a firm's corporate charter allows it to issue.

outstanding shares
The number of shares of common stock held by the public.

treasury stock
The number of shares of outstanding stock that have been repurchased by the firm.

issued shares
The number of shares of common stock that have been put into circulation; the sum of outstanding shares and treasury stock.

EXAMPLE   Golden Enterprises, a producer of medical pumps, has the following stockholders' equity account on December 31:

Stockholders' Equity

Common stock—$0.80 par value:	
Authorized 35,000,000 shares; issued 15,000,000 shares	$ 12,000,000
Paid-in capital in excess of par	63,000,000
Retained earnings	31,000,000
	$106,000,000
Less: Cost of treasury stock (1,000,000 shares)	4,000,000
Total stockholders' equity	$102,000,000

How many shares of additional common stock can Golden sell without gaining approval from its shareholders? The firm has 35 million authorized shares, 15 million issued shares, and 1 million shares of treasury stock. Thus 14 million shares are outstanding (15 million issued shares − 1 million shares of treasury stock), and Golden can issue 21 million additional shares (35 million authorized shares − 14 million outstanding shares) without seeking shareholder approval. This total includes the treasury shares currently held, which the firm can reissue to the public without obtaining shareholder approval.   ▪

Voting Rights

Generally, each share of common stock entitles its holder to one vote in the election of directors and on special issues. Votes are generally assignable and may be cast at the annual stockholders' meeting.

In recent years, many firms have issued two or more classes of common stock; they differ mainly in having unequal voting rights. A firm can use different classes of stock as a defense against a *hostile takeover* in which an outside group, without management support, tries to gain voting control of the firm by buying its shares in the marketplace. **Supervoting shares** of stock give each owner multiple votes. When supervoting shares are issued to "insiders," an outside group, whose shares have only one vote each typically cannot obtain enough votes to gain control of the firm. At other times, a class of **nonvoting common stock** is issued when the firm wishes to raise capital through the sale of common stock but does not want to give up its voting control.

When different classes of common stock are issued on the basis of unequal voting rights, class A common is typically—but not universally—designated as nonvoting, and class B common has voting rights. Generally, higher classes of shares (class A, for example) are given preference in the distribution of earnings (dividends) and assets; lower-class shares, in exchange, receive voting rights. Treasury stock, which is held within the corporation, generally *does not* have voting rights, *does not* earn dividends, and *does not* have a claim on assets in liquidation.

Because most small stockholders do not attend the annual meeting to vote, they may sign a **proxy statement** transferring their votes to another party. The solicitation of proxies from shareholders is closely controlled by the Securities

supervoting shares
Stock that carries with it multiple votes per share rather than the single vote per share typically given on regular shares of common stock.

nonvoting common stock
Common stock that carries no voting rights; issued when the firm wishes to raise capital through the sale of common stock but does not want to give up its voting control.

proxy statement
A statement transferring the votes of a stockholder to another party.

and Exchange Commission to ensure that proxies are not being solicited on the basis of false or misleading information. Existing management generally receives the stockholders' proxies, because it is able to solicit them at company expense.

proxy battle
The attempt by a non-management group to gain control of the management of a firm by soliciting a sufficient number of proxy votes.

Occasionally, when the firm is widely owned, outsiders may wage a **proxy battle** to unseat the existing management and gain control. To win a corporate election, votes from a majority of the shares voted are required. However, the odds of a nonmanagement group winning a proxy battle are generally slim.

Dividends

The payment of dividends to the firm's shareholders is at the discretion of the corporation's board of directors. Most corporations pay dividends quarterly. Dividends may be paid in cash, stock, or merchandise. Cash dividends are the most common, merchandise dividends the least.

Common stockholders are not promised a dividend, but they come to expect certain payments on the basis of the historical dividend pattern of the firm. Before dividends are paid to common stockholders, the claims of the government, all creditors, and preferred stockholders must be satisfied. Since passage of the *Jobs and Growth Tax Relief Reconciliation Act of 2003*, many firms have begun to pay larger dividends to shareholders, who are subject to a maximum tax rate of 15 percent on dividends rather than the maximum tax rate of 39 percent in effect prior to passage of the act. Because of the importance of the dividend decision to the growth and valuation of the firm, dividends are discussed in greater detail in Chapter 13.

International Stock Issues

Although the international market for common stock is not as large as the international market for bonds, cross-border issuance and trading of common stock have increased dramatically in the past 25 years.

Some corporations *issue stock in foreign markets*. For example, the stock of General Electric trades in Frankfurt, London, Paris, and Tokyo; the stocks of Time Warner and Microsoft trade in Frankfurt and London; and the stock of McDonalds trades in Frankfurt, London, and Paris. The London, Frankfurt, and Tokyo markets are the most popular. Issuing stock internationally broadens the ownership base and helps a company to integrate itself into the local business scene. A listing on a foreign stock exchange both increases local business press coverage and serves as effective corporate advertising. Having locally traded stock can also facilitate corporate acquisitions, because shares can be used as an acceptable method of payment.

Foreign corporations have also discovered the benefits of trading their stock in the United States. The disclosure and reporting requirements mandated by the U.S. Securities and Exchange Commission have historically discouraged all but the largest foreign firms from directly listing their shares on the New York Stock Exchange or the American Stock Exchange. For example, in 1993, Daimler-Benz (now DaimlerChrysler) became the first large German company to be listed on the NYSE.

American depositary receipts (ADRs)
Claims issued by U.S. banks representing ownership of shares of a foreign company's stock held on deposit by the U.S. bank in the foreign market and issued in dollars to U.S. investors.

As an alternative, most foreign companies choose to tap the U.S. market through **American depositary receipts (ADRs)**. These are claims issued by U.S. banks representing ownership of shares of a foreign company's stock held on deposit by the U.S. bank in the foreign market. Because ADRs are issued, in dollars, by a U.S. bank to U.S. investors, they are subject to U.S. securities laws. At the same time, they give investors the opportunity to diversify their portfolios internationally.

Preferred Stock

Preferred stock gives its holders certain privileges that make them senior to common stockholders. Preferred stockholders are promised a fixed periodic dividend, which is stated either as a percentage or as a dollar amount. How the dividend is specified depends on whether the preferred stock has a *par value*, which, as in common stock, is a relatively useless stated value established for legal purposes. **Par-value preferred stock** has a stated face value, and its annual dividend is specified as a percentage of this value. **No-par preferred stock** has no stated face value, but its annual dividend is stated in dollars. Preferred stock is most often issued by public utilities, by acquiring firms in merger transactions, and by firms that are experiencing losses and need additional financing.

Basic Rights of Preferred Stockholders

The basic rights of preferred stockholders are somewhat more favorable than the rights of common stockholders. Preferred stock is often considered *quasi-debt* because, much like interest on debt, it specifies a fixed periodic payment (dividend). Of course, as ownership, preferred stock is unlike debt in that it has no maturity date. Because they have a fixed claim on the firm's income that takes precedence over the claim of common stockholders, preferred stockholders are exposed to less risk. They are consequently *not normally given a voting right.*

Preferred stockholders have *preference over common stockholders in the distribution of earnings.* If the stated preferred stock dividend is "passed" (not paid) by the board of directors, the payment of dividends to common stockholders is prohibited. It is this preference in dividend distribution that makes common stockholders the true risk takers.

Preferred stockholders are also usually given *preference over common stockholders in the liquidation of assets* in a legally bankrupt firm, although they must "stand in line" behind creditors. The amount of the claim of preferred stockholders in liquidation is normally equal to the par or stated value of the preferred stock.

Features of Preferred Stock

A number of features are generally included as part of a preferred stock issue. These features, along with the stock's par value, the amount of dividend payments, the dividend payment dates, and any restrictive covenants, are specified in an agreement similar to a *bond indenture.*

Restrictive Covenants   The restrictive covenants in a preferred stock issue are aimed at ensuring the firm's continued existence and regular payment of the dividend. These covenants include provisions about passing dividends, the sale of senior securities, mergers, sales of assets, minimum liquidity requirements, and repurchases of common stock. The violation of preferred stock covenants usually permits preferred stockholders either to obtain representation on the firm's board of directors or to force the retirement of their stock at or above its par or stated value.

cumulative (preferred stock)
Preferred stock for which all passed (unpaid) dividends in arrears, along with the current dividend, must be paid before dividends can be paid to common stockholders.

noncumulative (preferred stock)
Preferred stock for which passed (unpaid) dividends do not accumulate.

conversion feature (preferred stock)
A feature of *convertible preferred stock* that allows holders to change each share into a stated number of shares of common stock.

Cumulation   Most preferred stock is **cumulative** with respect to any dividends passed. That is, all dividends in arrears, along with the current dividend, must be paid before dividends can be paid to common stockholders. If preferred stock is **noncumulative,** passed (unpaid) dividends do not accumulate. In this case, only the current dividend must be paid before dividends can be paid to common stockholders. Because the common stockholders can receive dividends only after the dividend claims of preferred stockholders have been satisfied, it is in the firm's best interest to pay preferred dividends when they are due.[1]

Other Features   Preferred stock is generally *callable*—the issuer can retire outstanding stock within a certain period of time at a specified price. The call option generally cannot be exercised until after a specified date. The call price is normally set above the initial issuance price, but it may decrease as time passes. Making preferred stock callable provides the issuer with a way to bring the fixed-payment commitment of the preferred issue to an end if conditions in the financial markets make it desirable to do so.

Preferred stock quite often contains a **conversion feature** that allows *holders of convertible preferred stock* to change each share into a stated number of shares of common stock. Sometimes the number of shares of common stock that the preferred stock can be exchanged for changes according to a prespecified formula.

Issuing Common Stock

Because of the high risk associated with a business startup, a firm's initial financing typically comes from its founders in the form of a common stock investment. Until the founders have made an equity investment, it is highly unlikely that others will contribute either equity or debt capital. Early-stage investors in the firm's equity, as well as lenders who provide debt capital, want to be assured that they are taking no more risk than the founding owner(s). In addition, they want confirmation that the founders are confident enough in their vision for the firm that they are willing to risk their own money.

The initial nonfounder financing for business startups with attractive growth prospects comes from private equity investors. Then, as the firm establishes the viability of its product or service offering and begins to generate revenues, cash flow, and profits, it will often "go public" by issuing shares of common stock to a much broader group of investors.

Before we consider the initial *public* sales of equity, let's review some of the key aspects of early-stage equity financing in firms that have attractive growth prospects.

Venture Capital

venture capital
Privately raised external equity capital used to fund early-stage firms with attractive growth prospects.

The initial external equity financing privately raised by firms, typically early-stage firms with attractive growth prospects, is called **venture capital.** Those who pro-

---

1. Most preferred stock is cumulative, because it is difficult to sell noncumulative stock. Common stockholders obviously prefer issuance of noncumulative preferred stock, because it does not place them in quite so risky a position. But it is often in the best interest of the firm to sell cumulative preferred stock because of its lower cost.

Most preferred stock has a fixed dividend, but some firms issue *adjustable-rate (floating-rate) preferred stock (ARPS)* whose dividend rate is tied to interest rates on specific government securities. Rate adjustments are commonly made quarterly. ARPS offers investors protection against sharp rises in interest rates, which means that the issue can be sold at an initially lower dividend rate.

venture capitalists (VCs)
Providers of venture capital; typically, formal businesses that maintain strong oversight over the firms they invest in and that have clearly defined exit strategies.

angel capitalists (angels)
Wealthy individual investors who do not operate as a business but invest in promising early-stage companies in exchange for a portion of the firm's equity.

vide venture capital are known as **venture capitalists (VCs)**. They typically are formal business entities that maintain strong oversight over the firms they invest in and that have clearly defined exit strategies. Less visible early-stage investors called **angel capitalists** (or **angels**) tend to be investors who do not actually operate as a business; they are often wealthy individual investors who are willing to invest in promising early-stage companies in exchange for a portion of the firm's equity. Although angels play a major role in early-stage equity financing, we will focus on VCs because of their more formal structure and greater public visibility.

Organization and Investment Stages   Institutional venture capital investors tend to be organized in one of four basic ways, as described in Table 7.2. The *VC limited partnership* is by far the dominant structure. These funds have as their sole objective to earn high returns, rather than to obtain access to the companies in order to sell or buy other products or services.

VCs can invest in early-stage companies, later-stage companies, or buyouts and acquisitions. Generally, about 40 to 50 percent of VC investments are devoted to early-stage companies (for startup funding and expansion) and a similar percentage to later-stage companies (for marketing, production expansion, and preparation for public offering); the remaining 5 to 10 percent are devoted to the buyout or acquisition of other companies. Generally, VCs look for compound annual rates of return ranging from 20 to 50 percent or more, depending on both the development stage and the attributes of each company. Earlier-stage investments tend to demand higher returns than later-stage investments because of the higher risk associated with the earlier stages of a firm's growth.

Deal Structure and Pricing   Regardless of the development stage, venture capital investments are made under a legal contract that clearly allocates responsibilities and ownership interests between existing owners (founders) and the VC fund or limited partnership. The terms of the agreement will depend on numerous factors related to the founders; the business structure, stage of development, and outlook; and other market and timing issues. The specific financial terms will, of

TABLE 7.2

Organization of Institutional Venture Capital Investors

Organization	Description
Small business investment companies (SBICs)	Corporations chartered by the federal government that can borrow at attractive rates from the U.S. Treasury and use the funds to make venture capital investments in private companies.
Financial VC funds	Subsidiaries of financial institutions, particularly banks, set up to help young firms grow and, it is hoped, become major customers of the institution.
Corporate VC funds	Firms, sometimes subsidiaries, established by nonfinancial firms, typically to gain access to new technologies that the corporation can access to further its own growth.
VC limited partnerships	Limited partnerships organized by professional VC firms, which serve as the general partner and organize, invest, and manage the partnership using the limited partners' funds; the professional VCs ultimately liquidate the partnership and distribute the proceeds to all partners.

course, depend on the value of the enterprise, the amount of funding, and the perceived risk. To control the VC's risk, various covenants are included in the agreement, and the actual funding may be pegged to the achievement of *measurable milestones*. The VC will negotiate numerous other provisions into the contract, both to ensure the firm's success and to control its risk exposure. The contract will have an explicit exit strategy for the VC that may be tied both to measurable milestones and to time.

The amount of equity to which the VC is entitled will, of course, depend on the value of the firm, the terms of the contract, the exit terms, and the minimum compound annual rate of return required by the VC on its investment. Although each VC investment is unique and no standard contract exists, the transaction will be structured to provide the VC with a high rate of return that is consistent with the typically high risk of such transactions. The exit strategy of most VC investments is to take the firm public through an initial public offering.

Going Public

When a firm wishes to sell its stock in the primary market, it has three alternatives. It can make (1) a *public offering,* in which it offers its shares for sale to the general public; (2) a *rights offering,* in which new shares are sold to existing stockholders; or (3) a *private placement,* in which the firm sells new securities directly to an investor or group of investors. Here we focus on public offerings, particularly the **initial public offering (IPO)**, which is the first public sale of a firm's stock. IPOs are typically made by small, rapidly growing companies that either require additional capital to continue expanding or have met a milestone for going public that was established in a contract signed earlier in order to obtain VC funding.

initial public offering (IPO)
The first public sale of a firm's stock.

To go public, the firm must first obtain the approval of its current shareholders, the investors who own its privately issued stock. Next, the company's auditors and lawyers must certify that all documents for the company are legitimate. The company then finds an investment bank willing to *underwrite* the offering. This underwriter is responsible for promoting the stock and facilitating the sale of the company's IPO shares. The underwriter often brings in other investment banking firms as participants. We'll discuss the role of the investment banker in more detail in the next section.

prospectus
A portion of a security registration statement that describes the key aspects of the issue, the issuer, and its management and financial position.

The company files a registration statement with the SEC. One portion of the registration statement is called the **prospectus**. It describes the key aspects of the issue, the issuer, and its management and financial position. During the waiting period between the statement's filing and its approval, prospective investors can receive a preliminary prospectus. This preliminary version is called a **red herring**, because a notice printed in red on the front cover indicates the tentative nature of the offer. The cover of the preliminary prospectus describing the 2004 stock issue of Genworth Financial, Inc., is shown in Figure 7.1. Note the red herring printed vertically on its left edge.

red herring
A preliminary prospectus made available to prospective investors during the waiting period between the registration statement's filing with the SEC and its approval.

After the SEC approves the registration statement, the investment community can begin analyzing the company's prospects. However, from the time it files until at least one month after the IPO is complete, the company must observe a *quiet period,* during which there are restrictions on what company officials may say about the company. The purpose of the quiet period is to make sure that all potential investors have access to the same information about the company—the

FIGURE 7.1

Cover of a Preliminary Prospectus for a Stock Issue
Some of the key factors related to the 2004 common stock issue by Genworth Financial, Inc., are summarized on the cover of the prospectus. The type printed vertically on the left edge is normally red, which explains its name "red herring." (*Source:* Genworth Financial, Inc., April 28, 2004, p. 1.)

The information in this preliminary prospectus is not complete and may be changed. This preliminary prospectus is not an offer to sell nor does it seek an offer to buy these securities in any jurisdiction where the offer or sale is not permitted. These securities may not be sold until the registration statement filed with the Securities and Exchange Commission is effective.

PROSPECTUS   (Subject to Completion)
Issued April 28, 2004

145,000,000 Shares

Genworth
Financial
Built on GE Heritage

Class A Common Stock

GE Financial Assurance Holdings, Inc., the selling stockholder and an indirect subsidiary of General Electric Company, is offering all the 145,000,000 shares of Class A Common Stock to be sold in this offering. This is our initial public offering, and no public market currently exists for our shares. We anticipate that the initial public offering price of the shares will be between $21.00 and $23.00 per share.

The selling stockholder has granted the underwriters the right to purchase up to an additional 21,750,000 shares of Class A Common Stock to cover over-allotments.

The Class A Common Stock has been approved for listing on The New York Stock Exchange under the symbol "GNW."

Concurrently with this offering, the selling stockholder is offering, by means of a separate prospectus, $600 million of our   % Equity Units. Each Equity Unit will have a stated amount of $25 and will initially consist of a contract to purchase shares of our Class A Common Stock and an interest in a   % senior note due 2009 issued by us. Concurrently with this offering, the selling stockholder also is offering, by means of a separate prospectus, $100 million of our   % Series A Cumulative Preferred Stock.

We will not receive any proceeds from the sale by the selling stockholder of Class A Common Stock in this offering or the Equity Units or Series A Cumulative Preferred Stock in the concurrent offerings.

Investing in our Class A Common Stock involves risks. See "Risk Factors" beginning on page 20.

PRICE $ A SHARE

	Per Share	Total
Price to public	$	$
Underwriting discounts and commissions	$	$
Proceeds to selling stockholder	$	$

Neither the Securities and Exchange Commission nor any other regulatory body has approved or disapproved of these securities or passed upon the adequacy or accuracy of this prospectus. Any representation to the contrary is a criminal offense.

The underwriters expect to deliver the shares of Class A Common Stock to purchasers on   , 2004.

Morgan Stanley   Goldman, Sachs & Co.

Banc of America Securities LLC   Citigroup   Credit Suisse First Boston
Deutsche Bank Securities   JPMorgan   Lehman Brothers
Merrill Lynch & Co.   UBS Investment Bank

Blaylock & Partners, L.P.   Cochran, Caronia & Co.   Dowling & Partners Securities
Edward D. Jones & Co., L.P.   Fox-Pitt, Kelton   Keefe, Bruyette & Woods
KeyBanc Capital Markets   Legg Mason Wood Walker   Raymond James
Stephens Inc.   Incorporated   The Williams Capital Group, L.P.

, 2004

information presented in the preliminary prospectus—and not to any unpublished data that might give them an unfair advantage.

The investment bankers and company executives promote the company's stock offering through a *road show*, a series of presentations to potential investors around the country and sometimes overseas. In addition to providing investors with information about the new issue, road show sessions help the investment bankers gauge the demand for the offering and set an expected pricing range. After the underwriter sets terms and prices the issue, the SEC must approve the offering.

The Investment Banker's Role

Most public offerings are made with the assistance of an **investment banker.** The investment banker is a financial intermediary (such as Salomon Brothers or Goldman, Sachs) that specializes in selling new security issues and advising firms with regard to major financial transactions. The main activity of the investment banker is **underwriting.** This process involves purchasing the security issue from the issuing corporation at an agreed-on price and bearing the risk of reselling it to the public at a profit. The investment banker also provides the issuer with advice about pricing and other important aspects of the issue.

In the case of very large security issues, the investment banker brings in other bankers as partners to form an **underwriting syndicate.** The syndicate shares the financial risk associated with buying the entire issue from the issuer and reselling the new securities to the public. The originating investment banker and the syndicate members put together a **selling group,** normally made up of themselves and a large number of brokerage firms. Each member of the selling group accepts the responsibility for selling a certain portion of the issue and is paid a commission on the securities it sells. The selling process for a large security issue is depicted in Figure 7.2.

Compensation for underwriting and selling services typically comes in the form of a discount on the sale price of the securities. For example, an investment banker may pay the issuing firm $24 per share for stock that will be sold for $26 per share. The investment banker may then sell the shares to members of the selling group for $25.25 per share. In this case, the original investment banker earns $1.25 per share ($25.25 sale price − $24 purchase price). The members of the selling group earn 75 cents for each share they sell ($26 sale price − $25.25 purchase price). Although some primary security offerings are directly placed by the issuer, the majority of new issues are sold through public offering via the mechanism just described.

FIGURE 7.2

The Selling Process for a Large Security Issue
The investment banker hired by the issuing corporation may form an underwriting syndicate. The underwriting syndicate buys the entire security issue from the issuing corporation at an agreed-on price. The underwriter then has the opportunity (and bears the risk) of reselling the issue to the public at a profit. Both the originating investment banker and the other syndicate members put together a selling group to sell the issue on a commission basis to investors.

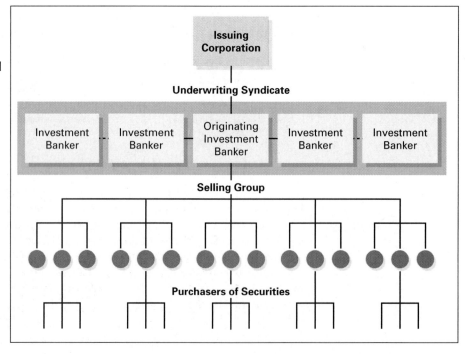

Interpreting Stock Quotations

The financial manager needs to stay abreast of the market values of the firm's outstanding stock, whether it is traded on an organized exchange, over the counter, or in international markets. Similarly, existing and prospective stockholders need to monitor the prices of the securities they own because these prices represent the current value of their investments. Price *quotations,* which include current price data along with statistics on recent price behavior, are readily available for actively traded stocks. The most up-to-date "quotes" can be obtained electronically, via a personal computer. Price information is available from stockbrokers and is widely published in news media. Popular sources of daily security price quotations include financial newspapers, such as the *Wall Street Journal* and *Investor's Business Daily,* and the business sections of daily general newspapers.

Figure 7.3 includes an excerpt from the NYSE quotations, reported in the *Wall Street Journal* of May 19, 2004, for transactions through the close of trading on Tuesday, May 18, 2004. We'll look at the quotations for the common stock of McDonalds, highlighted in the figure. The quotations show that stock prices are quoted in dollars and cents.

The first column gives the percent change in the stock's closing price for the calendar year to date. You can see that McDonalds' price has increased 3.9 percent (+3.9) since the start of 2004. The next two columns, labeled "HI" and "LO," show the highest and lowest prices at which the stock sold during the

Hint Preferred stock quotations are listed separately and include only four data items: dividend, dividend yield, closing price, and change in closing price from the previous day.

FIGURE 7.3

Stock Quotations
Selected stock quotations for May 18, 2004

YTD % CHG	52-WEEK HI	52-WEEK LO	STOCK (SYM)	DIV	YLD %	PE	VOL 100S	CLOSE	NET CHG	
-8.6	29	18	MasoniteIntl MHM	...		12	159	24.37	-0.17	
10.4	26.90	10.80	MasseyEngy MEE	.16	.7	dd	10453	22.97	0.67	
-72.3	16.50	3.15	MasTec MTZ	...		dd	2991	4.10	-0.01	
5.3	23.34	15.74	Matav MTA	2.05e	10.4	...	140	19.70	0.83	
-10.8	13.09	8.38	MaterlScl MSC	.01e	.1	dd	1109	9.02	0.21	
-6.0	15.80	8.32	MatsuElec MC	.12e	.9	...	1004	13.10	0.38	
-11.3	22.33	16.74	Mattel MAT	.40f	2.3	15	17320	17.10	0.12	
10.4	27.99	14.29♣	MavrckTube MVK	...		17	5765	21.25	0.29	
-12.6	41.24	23.90	Maximus MMS	...		20	304	34.19	0.28	
-38.6	15.38	6.09	Maxtor MXO	...		20	13340	6.82	0.05	
-0.9	36.48	20.02	MayDeptStrs MAY	.97	3.4	21	19416	28.82	0.43	
-10.0	32.21	21.06	Maytag MYG	.72	2.9	16	8786	25.07	0.18	
1.7	74.38	55.58	McClatchy A MNI	.48f	.7	21	464	69.95	0.75	
↓ 17.6	34.85	25.13	McCrmkCo Vtg MKCV	.56	1.6	...	1	35.10	0.90	
↓ 17.5	35.38	25.12	McCrmkCo MKC	.56	1.6	23	6527	35.38	0.27	
-41.8	12.56	3.70	McDermInt MDR	...		dd	9512	6.95	-0.12	
3.9	29.98	16.58	McDonalds MCD	.40f	1.6	20	35174	25.79	-0.08	◄——McDonalds
10.3	81.34	58.60	McGrawH MHP	1.20	1.6	22	6055	77.12	0.56	
4.5	37.14	27.01	McKesson MCK	.24	.7	15	17423	33.61	-0.13	
-30.4	20	10.35	McMoRanExpl MMR	.63e	4.8	dd	731	13.05	-0.30	
24.3	5.86	2.75♣	MdwbrkInsGp MIG	...		15	1934	5.26	-0.04	
-12.5	30.19	23.50	MeadWVaco MWV	.92	3.5	77	6065	26.03	0.18	
8.2	39.25	20.20	MedcoHlthSol MHS n	...		23	10822	36.77	0.32	
4.6	72.48	53.67	MediaGen A MEG	.80	1.2	23	547	68.10	0.15	
↑ -48.2	12.31	5.79	MedStaffNtwk MRN	...		dd	1029	5.67	-0.13	
20.0	45.26	26.03	MedicisPhrm MRX s	.10	.2	cc	8099	42.79	-0.28	
1.0	52.92	42.90	Medtronic MDT	.29	.6	32	44221	49.10	-0.20	
-12.6	34.13	25.30	MellonFnl MEL	.72f	2.6	15	15806	28.08	0.41	
-4.3	31.25	17.20	MensWearhs MW	...		18	2632	23.93	0.69	
25.4	33.12	18.66	MentorCp MNT	.60	2.0	27	2642	30.18	0.38	
1.4	60.10	40.57	Merck MRK	1.48	3.2	16	37488	46.85	0.21	
4.6	53.40	42.05♣	MercuryGen MCY	1.48f	3.0	13	634	48.70	0.18	
5.5	53.47	41.59	Meredith MDP	.48	.9	26	771	51.49	0.33	
-18.1	15.72	8.95♣	MeridnGld MDG	...		31	6926	11.96	0.38	

Source: Wall Street Journal, May 19, 2004, p. C6.

preceding 52 weeks. McDonalds common stock, for example, traded between $16.58 and $29.98 during the 52-week period that ended May 18, 2004. Listed to the right of the company's name is its *stock symbol;* McDonalds goes by "MCD." The figure listed right after the stock symbol under "DIV" is the annual cash dividend paid on each share of stock. The dividend for McDonalds was $0.40 per share. The next item, labeled "YLD%," is the *dividend yield,* which is found by dividing the stated dividend by the closing share price. The dividend yield for McDonalds is 1.6 percent ($0.40 \div 25.79 = 0.0155 = 1.6\%$).

The *price/earnings (P/E) ratio,* labeled "PE," is next. It is calculated by dividing the closing market price by the firm's most recent annual earnings per share (EPS). The price/earnings (P/E) ratio, as noted in Chapter 2, measures the amount investors are willing to pay for each dollar of the firm's earnings. McDonalds' P/E ratio was 20—the stock was trading at 20 times its earnings. The P/E ratio is believed to reflect investor expectations concerning the firm's future prospects: Higher P/E ratios reflect investor optimism and confidence; lower P/E ratios reflect investor pessimism and concern.

The daily volume, labeled "VOL 100s," follows the P/E ratio. Here the day's sales are quoted in lots of 100 shares. The value 35174 for McDonalds indicates that 3,517,400 shares of its common stock were traded on May 18, 2004. The next column, labeled "CLOSE," contains the closing (last) price at which the stock sold on the given day. The value for McDonalds was $25.79. The final column, "NET CHG," indicates the change in the closing price from that on the prior trading day. McDonalds closed down $0.08 from May 17, 2004, which means the closing price on that day was $25.87.

Similar quotations systems are used for stocks that trade on other exchanges such as the American Stock Exchange (AMEX) and for the over-the-counter (OTC) exchange's Nasdaq National Market Issues. Also note that when a stock (or bond) issue is not traded on a given day, it generally is not quoted in the financial and business press.

REVIEW QUESTIONS

7–2   What risks do common stockholders take that other suppliers of long-term capital do not?

7–3   How does a *rights offering* protect a firm's stockholders against the *dilution of ownership?*

7–4   Explain the relationships among authorized shares, outstanding shares, treasury stock, and issued shares.

7–5   What are the advantages to both U.S.-based and foreign corporations of issuing stock outside their home markets? What are *American depositary receipts (ADRs)?*

7–6   What claims do preferred stockholders have with respect to distribution of earnings (dividends) and assets?

7–7   Explain the *cumulative feature* of preferred stock. What is the purpose of a *call feature* in a preferred stock issue?

7–8   What is the difference between a *venture capitalist* (VC) and an *angel capitalist* (*angel*)?

7–9   Into what bodies are institutional VCs most commonly organized? How are their deals structured and priced?

7–10   What general procedures must a private firm follow to go public via an *initial public offering* (IPO)?

7–11   What role does an *investment banker* play in a public offering? Explain the sequence of events in the issuing of stock.

7–12   Describe the key items of information included in a stock *quotation*. What information does the stock's *price/earnings (P/E) ratio* provide?

LG4   **LG5**   # 7.3 | Common Stock Valuation

Common stockholders expect to be rewarded through periodic cash dividends and an increasing—or at least nondeclining—share value. Like current owners, prospective owners and security analysts frequently estimate the firm's value. Investors purchase the stock when they believe that it is *undervalued*—when its true value is greater than its market price. They sell the stock when they feel that it is *overvalued*—when its market price is greater than its true value.

In this section, we will describe specific stock valuation techniques. First, though, we will look at the concept of an efficient market, which questions whether the prices of actively traded stocks can differ from their true values.

Market Efficiency[2]

Hint Be sure to clarify in your own mind the difference between the required return and the expected return. *Required return* is what an investor *has to have* to invest in a specific asset, and *expected return* is the return an investor *thinks he or she will get* if the asset is purchased.

Economically rational buyers and sellers use their assessment of an asset's risk and return to determine its value. To a buyer, the asset's value represents the maximum price that he or she would pay to acquire it; a seller views the asset's value as a minimum sale price. In competitive markets with many active participants, such as the New York Stock Exchange, the interactions of many buyers and sellers result in an equilibrium price—the *market value*—for each security. This price reflects the collective actions that buyers and sellers take on the basis of all available information. Buyers and sellers are assumed to digest new information immediately as it becomes available and, through their purchase and sale activities, to create a new market equilibrium price quickly.

Market Adjustment to New Information

expected return, $\hat{k}$
The return that is expected to be earned on a given asset each period over an infinite time horizon.

The process of market adjustment to new information can be viewed in terms of rates of return. From Chapter 5, we know that for a given level of risk, investors require a specified periodic return—the *required return, k*—which can be estimated by using beta and CAPM. At each point in time, investors estimate the **expected return, $\hat{k}$**—the return that is expected to be earned on a given asset each period over an infinite time horizon. The expected return can be estimated by using a simplified form of Equation 5.1:

$$\hat{k} = \frac{\text{Expected benefit during each period}}{\text{Current price of asset}} \tag{7.1}$$

2. A great deal of theoretical and empirical research has been performed in the area of market efficiency. For purposes of this discussion, generally accepted beliefs about market efficiency are described, rather than the technical aspects of the various forms of market efficiency and their theoretical implications. For a good discussion of the theory and evidence relative to market efficiency, see Scott B. Smart, William L. Megginson, and Lawrence J. Gitman, *Corporate Finance* (Mason, OH: South-Western, 2004), Chapter 10.

Hint **Hint** This relationship between the expected return and the required return can be seen in Equation 7.1, where a decrease in asset price will result in an increase in the expected return.

Whenever investors find that the expected return is not equal to the required return ($\hat{k} \neq k$), a market price adjustment occurs. If the expected return is less than the required return ($\hat{k} < k$), investors sell the asset, because they do not expect it to earn a return commensurate with its risk. Such action drives the asset's price down, which (assuming no change in expected benefits) causes its expected return to rise to the level of its required return. If the expected return were above the required return ($\hat{k} > k$), investors would buy the asset, driving its price up and its expected return down to the point where it equals the required return.

EXAMPLE

The common stock of Alton Industries (AI) is currently selling for $50 per share, and market participants expect it to generate benefits of $6.50 per share during each coming period. In addition, the risk-free rate, R_F, is currently 7%; the market return, k_m, is 12%; and the stock's beta, b_{AI}, is 1.20. When the appropriate values are substituted into Equation 7.1, the firm's current expected return, $\hat{k}_0$, is

$$\hat{k}_0 = \frac{\$6.50}{\$50.00} = \underline{\underline{13\%}}$$

When the appropriate values are substituted into the CAPM (Equation 5.8), the current required return, k_0, is

$$k_0 = 7\% + [1.20 \times (12\% - 7\%)] = 7\% + 6\% = \underline{\underline{13\%}}$$

Because $\hat{k}_0 = k_0$, the market is currently in equilibrium, and the stock is fairly priced at $50 per share.

Assume that a press release announces that a major product liability suit has been filed against Alton Industries. As a result, investors immediately adjust their risk assessment upward, raising the firm's beta from 1.20 to 1.40. The new required return, k_1, becomes

$$k_1 = 7\% + [1.40 \times (12\% - 7\%)] = 7\% + 7\% = \underline{\underline{14\%}}$$

Because the expected return of 13% is now below the required return of 14%, many investors sell the stock—driving its price down to about $46.43—the price that will result in a 14% expected return, $\hat{k}_1$.

$$\hat{k}_1 = \frac{\$6.50}{\$46.43} = \underline{\underline{14\%}}$$

The new price of $46.43 brings the market back into equilibrium, because the expected return now equals the required return. ■

Another possible market adjustment, a "credibility premium," is discussed in the *In Practice* box on the facing page.

The Efficient-Market Hypothesis

efficient-market hypothesis (EMH)
Theory describing the behavior of an assumed "perfect" market in which (1) securities are typically in equilibrium, (2) security prices fully reflect all public information available and react swiftly to new information, and, (3) because stocks are fully and fairly priced, investors need not waste time looking for mispriced securities.

As noted in Chapter 1, active markets such as the New York Stock Exchange are *efficient*—they are made up of many rational investors who react quickly and objectively to new information. The **efficient-market hypothesis (EMH)**, which is the basic theory describing the behavior of such a "perfect" market, specifically states that

1. Securities are typically in equilibrium, which means that they are fairly priced and that their expected returns equal their required returns.

DO INVESTORS NOW REQUIRE A "CREDIBILITY PREMIUM"?

Possibly following the "moral" advice of actor Michael Douglas in the movie *Wall Street* that "Greed is good," numerous public companies have published inaccurate and misleading financial reports in recent years. Stock brokerages further muddied the investment information waters by overrating the prospects of companies whose securities they helped bring to the market. These ethical lapses have serious implications for investors and for the value of the stocks they hold.

A March 2004 survey of finance executives by *CFO* magazine asked these managers to put themselves in the role of investing their own money. Their responses were highly revealing: A mere 27 percent would feel "very confident" that they were getting high-quality and complete information from public companies (with 65 percent feeling somewhat

confident and 8 percent feeling not confident). Lynn Turner, former SEC chief accountant, believes stock investors lost $100 billion over the past 6 years due to restatements of financial reports. Warren Buffett said it best: "Situational ethics has reared its ugly head."

Information put out by securities analysts working for stock brokerages has been equally flawed—or worse. According to *Kiplinger's Magazine*, N.Y. state attorney general Eliot Spitzer levied a $1.4 billion fine on ten Wall Street firms, documenting ratings that were routinely inflated, bribes to other firms' analysts to get them to write glowing reports, and pressure on individual analysts to reverse negative ratings.

Why should the analyst doing valuation care about the public attitude? Because when people don't trust the numbers, they price

assets to reflect both a risk premium (for business and financial risks) and what Robert Arnott calls "a credibility premium." As a result, stock prices are lower than they should be, and honest companies may get penalized along with the dishonest ones. The good news is that the heightened scrutiny and Sarbanes-Oxley Act are having a positive effect: 77 percent of CFOs surveyed said that the new law makes it easier for them to resist pressure to misstate financials. Many corporate executives are hopeful that investor confidence will be restored as a result.

Sources: Fred Frailey, "How About Real Remorse?" *Kiplinger's,* July 2003; Andy Serwer, "Dirty Rotten Numbers," *Fortune,* February 18, 2002.

■ *If you were a professor in a business school, what might you tell students about the effects of dishonesty and greed?*

2. At any point in time, security prices fully reflect all public information available about the firm and its securities,[3] and these prices react swiftly to new information.
3. Because stocks are fully and fairly priced, investors need not waste their time trying to find and capitalize on mispriced (undervalued or overvalued) securities.

Not all market participants are believers in the efficient-market hypothesis. Some feel that it is worthwhile to search for undervalued or overvalued securities and to trade them to profit from market inefficiencies. Others argue that it is

---

3. Those market participants who have nonpublic—*inside*—information may have an unfair advantage that enables them to earn an excess return. Since the mid-1980s disclosure of the insider-trading activities of a number of well-known financiers and investors, major national attention has been focused on the "problem" of insider trading and its resolution. Clearly, those who trade securities on the basis of inside information have an unfair and illegal advantage. Empirical research has confirmed that those with inside information do indeed have an opportunity to earn an excess return. Here we ignore this possibility, given its illegality and the fact that enhanced surveillance and enforcement by the securities industry and the government have in recent years (it appears) significantly reduced insider trading. We, in effect, assume that all relevant information is public and that therefore the market is efficient.

mere luck that would allow market participants to anticipate new information correctly and as a result earn *excess returns*—that is, actual returns greater than required returns. They believe it is unlikely that market participants can *over the long run* earn excess returns. Contrary to this belief, some well-known investors such as Warren Buffett and Peter Lynch *have* over the long run consistently earned excess returns on their portfolios. It is unclear whether their success is the result of their superior ability to anticipate new information or of some form of market inefficiency.

The Behavioral Finance Challenge

Although considerable evidence supports the concept of market efficiency, a growing body of academic evidence has begun to cast doubt on the validity of this notion. The research documents various *anomalies*—deviations from accepted beliefs—in stock returns. A number of academics as well as practitioners have also recognized that emotions and other subjective factors play a role in investment decisions.

behavioral finance
A growing body of research that focuses on investor behavior and its impact on investment decisions and stock prices. Advocates are commonly referred to as "behaviorists."

This focus on investor behavior has resulted in a significant body of research, which is collectively referred to as **behavioral finance.** Advocates of behavioral finance are commonly referred to as "behaviorists." One notable event that acknowledged the importance of the field of behavioral finance was the awarding of the 2002 Nobel Prize in economics to Daniel Kahneman for his work in integrating insights from psychology and economics. Ongoing research into the psychological factors that can affect investor behavior and the resulting effects on stock prices will likely result in growing acceptance of behavioral finance. The *In Practice* box on the facing page discusses more about the opposing views of the efficient-market hypothesis and behavioral finance.

Throughout this text we ignore both disbelievers and behaviorists and continue to assume market efficiency. This means that *the terms "expected return" and "required return" are used interchangeably,* because they should be equal in an efficient market. This also means that stock prices accurately reflect true value based on risk and return. In other words, we will operate under the assumption that the market price at any point in time is the best estimate of value. We're now ready to look closely at the mechanics of common stock valuation.

The Basic Common Stock Valuation Equation

Like the value of a bond, which we discussed in Chapter 6, *the value of a share of common stock is equal to the present value of all future cash flows (dividends) that it is expected to provide over an infinite time horizon.*[4] Although a stockholder can earn capital gains by selling stock at a price above that originally paid, what is really sold is the right to all future dividends. What about stocks that are not expected to pay dividends in the foreseeable future? Such stocks have a value attributable to a distant dividend expected to result from sale of the company or liquidation of its assets. Therefore, *from a valuation viewpoint, only dividends are relevant.*

---

4. The need to consider an infinite time horizon is not critical, because a sufficiently long period—say, 50 years—will result in about the same present value as an infinite period for moderate-sized required returns. For example, at 15%, a dollar to be received 50 years from now, $PVIF_{15\%,50yrs}$, is worth only about $0.001 today.

In Practice FOCUS ON PRACTICE

SHOWDOWN AT THE EMH CORRAL

Investors, get ready for the big showdown! At one end of town, Eugene Fama—University of Chicago professor and co-author of the *efficient-market hypothesis (EMH)*. The EMH says that investors are rational, the markets are always right, and relevant new information is immediately reflected in stock prices. In this view, most investors can't beat the market and should invest in index funds that try to match the performance of major indexes.

At the other end of town, representing behavioral finance, is Nobel Prize winner Daniel Kahneman of Princeton University. According to the behaviorist view, investors are not rational but are motivated by greed, fear, and other emotions. Says Robert Shiller, Yale University professor and author of *Irrational Exuberance,* "[The emotional state of investors was] no doubt one of the most important factors causing the bull market" that peaked in early 2000—and its collapse.

Fortunately, no shots need to be fired. In fact, *both* EMH and behavioral finance may have played a role in the formation of the tech bubble and its subsequent collapse. Proponents of EMH

explain that since markets are rational, rocketing stock prices were in line with investors' soaring expectations. Buoyed by their success with blue-chip stocks, investors gravitated to the cutting-edge dot-coms. But as behaviorists will tell you, many investors then let their emotions overrule rational analysis. They became overconfident in their ability to pick winners, ignored risks, reacted too slowly to unexpected news, and held on to losing stocks, hoping the prices would once again rise to former levels.

A recent study (Ackert et al., 2003) that examined investor behavior also found some common middle ground. Emotional investors, say the study's authors, listen to their gut instincts, which helps them focus on broader issues. Rational investors fully analyze each situation (though they may sometimes get too caught up in the details). Even the most rational investor, however, cannot totally eliminate emotion—and shouldn't. The authors conclude, "We believe that emotion is an important aspect of the human condition that can actually enhance decision-making."

Interestingly, experts on both sides offer similar advice to

investors. Princeton's Burton Malkiel, author of the classic *A Random Walk Down Wall Street,* recommends acting as though markets are efficient, even if they aren't. Build well-diversified portfolios with low expenses using index funds, he says. Although behavioral theory says that investors can beat the market, behaviorist Richard Thaler of the University of Chicago cautions that individual investors probably don't have the skills to do so (and neither, he says, do many active mutual fund managers). He, too, encourages individual investors to buy index funds and accept average market returns.

Sources: Adapted from Lucy F. Ackert et al., "Emotion and Financial Markets," *Economic Review,* Federal Reserve Bank of Atlanta, Second Quarter 2003, pp. 33–41; Justin Fox, "Is the Market Rational?" *Fortune,* December 9, 2002, pp. 117–126; Chern Yeh Kwok, "Beating the Market Isn't for the Likes of Individual Investors," *St. Louis Post-Dispatch,* July 6, 2003, p. C.1; Seth Lubove, "Analyze This," *Forbes,* November 11, 2002, p. 162+; and Tom Walker, "Be Like Kirk, Not Like Spock, on Wall Street," *Houston Chronicle,* August 11, 2003, p. B-1.

■ *Would you consider yourself a rational or an emotional investor? Why?*

By redefining terms, the basic valuation model in Equation 6.5 can be specified for common stock, as given in Equation 7.2:

$$P_0 = \frac{D_1}{(1+k_s)^1} + \frac{D_2}{(1+k_s)^2} + \cdots + \frac{D_\infty}{(1+k_s)^\infty} \tag{7.2}$$

where

P_0 = value of common stock

D_t = per-share dividend *expected* at the end of year t

k_s = required return on common stock

in the cash flows they are entitled to receive from now to infinity. The present value of those expected cash flows is the firm's share value.

To determine this present value, forecast cash flows are discounted at a rate that reflects their risk. Riskier cash flows are discounted at higher rates, resulting in lower present values than less risky expected cash flows, which are discounted at lower rates. The value of the firm's common stock is therefore driven by its expected cash flows (returns) and risk (certainty of the expected cash flows).

In pursuing the firm's goal of **maximizing the stock price,** the financial manager must carefully consider the balance of return and risk associated with each proposal and must undertake only those actions that create value for owners—that is, increase share price. By focusing on value creation and by managing and monitoring the firm's cash flows and risk, the financial manager should be able to achieve the firm's goal of share price maximization.

Review of Learning Goals

Key definitions and formulas for this chapter are summarized in Table 7.6.

LG1 **Differentiate between debt and equity capital.** Holders of equity capital (common and preferred stock) are owners of the firm. Typically, only common stockholders have a voice in management. Equity holders' claims on income and assets are secondary to creditors' claims, there is no maturity date, and dividends paid to stockholders are not tax-deductible, as is interest paid to debtholders.

LG2 **Discuss the rights, characteristics, and features of both common and preferred stock.** The common stock of a firm can be privately owned, closely owned, or publicly owned. It can be sold with or without a par value. Preemptive rights allow common stockholders to avoid dilution of ownership when new shares are issued. Not all shares authorized in the corporate charter are outstanding. If a firm has treasury stock, it will have issued more shares than are outstanding. Some firms have two or more classes of common stock that differ mainly in having unequal voting rights. Proxies transfer voting rights from one party to another. The decision to pay dividends to common stockholders is made by the firm's board of directors. Firms can issue stock in foreign markets. The stock of many foreign corporations is traded in the form of American depositary receipts (ADRs) in U.S. markets.

Preferred stockholders have preference over common stockholders with respect to the distribution of earnings and assets. They do not normally have voting privileges. Preferred stock issues may have certain restrictive covenants, cumulative dividends, a call feature, and a conversion feature.

LG3 **Describe the process of issuing common stock, including venture capital, going public, and the investment banker, and interpreting stock quotations.** The initial nonfounder financing for business startups with attractive growth prospects typically comes from private equity investors. These investors can be either angel capitalists or venture capitalists (VCs). VCs usually invest in both early-stage and later-stage companies that they hope to take public so as to cash out their investments.

TABLE 7.6

Summary of Key Valuation Definitions and Formulas for Common Stock

Definitions of variables

D_t = per-share dividend *expected* at the end of year t

FCF_t = free cash flow *expected* at the end of year t

g = constant rate of growth in dividends

g_1 = initial dividend growth rate (in variable-growth model)

g_2 = subsequent dividend growth rate (in variable-growth model)

k_a = weighted average cost of capital

k_s = required return on common stock

N = last year of initial growth period (in variable-growth model)

P_0 = value of common stock

V_C = value of the entire company

V_D = market value of all the firm's debt

V_P = market value of preferred stock

V_S = value of common stock

Valuation formulas

Basic stock value:

$$P_0 = \frac{D_1}{(1 + k_s)^1} + \frac{D_2}{(1 + k_s)^2} + \cdots + \frac{D_\infty}{(1 + k_s)^\infty} \qquad \text{[Equation 7.2]}$$

Common stock value:

Zero-growth:

$$P_0 = \frac{D_1}{k_s} \text{ (also used to value preferred stock)} \qquad \text{[Equation 7.3]}$$

Constant-growth:

$$P_0 = \frac{D_1}{k_s - g} \qquad \text{[Equation 7.5]}$$

Variable-growth:

$$P_0 = \sum_{t=1}^{N} \frac{D_0 \times (1 + g_1)^t}{(1 + k_s)^t} + \left[\frac{1}{(1 + k_s)^N} \times \frac{D_{N+1}}{k_s - g_2} \right] \qquad \text{[Equation 7.6]}$$

FCF value of entire company:

$$V_C = \frac{FCF_1}{(1 + k_a)^1} + \frac{FCF_2}{(1 + k_a)^2} + \cdots + \frac{FCF_\infty}{(1 + k_a)^\infty} \qquad \text{[Equation 7.7]}$$

FCF common stock value:

$$V_S = V_C - V_D - V_P \qquad \text{[Equation 7.8]}$$

The first public issue of a firm's stock is called an initial public offering (IPO). The company selects an investment banker to advise it and to sell the securities. The lead investment banker may form a selling syndicate with other investment bankers. The IPO process includes getting SEC approval, promoting the offering to investors, and pricing the issue.

Stock quotations provide information on calendar-year change in price, 52-week high and low, dividend, dividend yield, P/E ratio, volume, closing price, and net price change from the prior trading day.

LG4 **Understand the concept of market efficiency and basic common stock valuation using zero-growth, constant-growth, and variable-growth models.** Market efficiency assumes that the quick reactions of rational investors to new information cause the market value of common stock to adjust upward or downward quickly. The efficient-market hypothesis (EMH) suggests that securities are fairly priced, that they reflect fully all publicly available information, and that investors should therefore not waste time trying to find and capitalize on mispriced securities. Behavioral finance advocates challenge this hypothesis by arguing that emotion and other factors play a role in investment decisions.

The value of a share of common stock is the present value of all future dividends it is expected to provide over an infinite time horizon. Three dividend growth models—zero-growth, constant-growth, and variable-growth—can be considered in common stock valuation. The most widely cited model is the constant-growth model.

LG5 **Discuss the free cash flow valuation model and the book value, liquidation value, and price/earnings (P/E) multiples approaches.** The free cash flow valuation model values startups, firms that have no dividend history, or operating units of a larger public company. The model finds the value of the entire company by discounting the firm's expected free cash flow at its weighted average cost of capital. The common stock value is found by subtracting the market values of the firm's debt and preferred stock from the value of the entire company.

Book value per share is the amount per share of common stock that would be received if all of the firm's assets were *sold for their exact book (accounting) value* and the proceeds remaining after paying all liabilities (including preferred stock) were divided among the common stockholders. Liquidation value per share is the *actual amount* per share of common stock that would be received if all of the firm's assets were *sold for their market value,* liabilities (including preferred stock) were paid, and the remaining money were divided among the common stockholders. The price/earnings (P/E) multiples approach estimates stock value by multiplying the firm's expected earnings per share (EPS) by the average price/earnings (P/E) ratio for the industry.

LG6 **Explain the relationships among financial decisions, return, risk, and the firm's value.** In a stable economy, any action of the financial manager that increases the level of expected return without changing risk should increase share value; any action that reduces the level of expected return without changing risk should reduce share value. Similarly, any action that increases risk (required return) will reduce share value; any action that reduces risk will increase share value. An assessment of the combined effect of return and risk on stock value must be part of the financial decision-making process.

Self-Test Problems (Solutions in Appendix B)

LG4

ST7–1 Common stock valuation   Perry Motors' common stock currently pays an annual dividend of $1.80 per share. The required return on the common stock is 12%. Estimate the value of the common stock under each of the following assumptions about the dividend.
  a. Dividends are expected to grow at an annual rate of 0% to infinity.
  b. Dividends are expected to grow at a constant annual rate of 5% to infinity.
  c. Dividends are expected to grow at an annual rate of 5% for each of the next 3 years, followed by a constant annual growth rate of 4% in years 4 to infinity.

LG5

ST7–2 Free cash flow valuation   Erwin Footwear wishes to assess the value of its Active Shoe Division. This division has debt with a market value of $12,500,000 and no preferred stock. Its weighted average cost of capital is 10%. The Active Shoe Division's estimated free cash flow each year from 2007 through 2010 is given in the following table. Beyond 2010 to infinity, the firm expects its free cash flow to grow at 4% annually.

Year (t)	Free cash flow (FCF_t)
2007	$ 800,000
2008	1,200,000
2009	1,400,000
2010	1,500,000

  a. Use the *free cash flow valuation model* to estimate the value of Erwin's entire Active Shoe Division.
  b. Use your finding in part **a** along with the data provided above to find this division's common stock value.
  c. If the Active Shoe Division as a public company will have 500,000 shares outstanding, use your finding in part **b** to calculate its value per share.

Warm-Up Exercises

LG1

E7–1 A balance sheet balances assets with their sources of debt and equity financing. If a corporation has assets equal to $5.2 million and a debt ratio of 75.0%, how much debt does the corporation have on its books?

LG2

E7–2 Angina, Inc., has 5 million shares outstanding. The firm is considering issuing an additional 1 million shares. After selling these shares at their $20 per share offering price and netting 95% of the sale proceeds, the firm is obligated by an earlier agreement to sell an additional 250,000 shares at 90% of the offering price. In total, how much cash will the firm net from these stock sales?

LG2

E7–3 Figurate Industries has 750,000 shares of cumulative preferred stock outstanding. It has passed the last three quarterly dividends of $2.50 per share and now wishes to distribute a total of $12 million to its shareholders. If Figurate has

3 million shares of common stock outstanding, how large a per-share common stock dividend will it be able to pay?

LG3

E7–4 Today the common stock of Gresham Technology closed at $24.60 per share, down $0.35 from yesterday. If the company has 4.6 million shares outstanding and annual earnings of $11.2 million, what is its P/E ratio today? What was its P/E ratio yesterday?

LG4

E7–5 Stacker Weight Loss currently pays an annual year-end dividend of $1.20 per share. It plans to increase this dividend by 5% next year and maintain it at the new level for the foreseeable future. If the required return on this firm's stock is 8%, what is the value of Stacker's stock?

LG6

E7–6 Brash Corporation initiated a new corporate strategy that fixes its annual dividend at $2.25 per share. Currently the risk-free rate is 4.5%, and Brash has a beta of 1.8. If the market return is 10.5%, what is the value of Brash's stock?

Problems

LG2

BASIC

P7–1 **Authorized and available shares**   Aspin Corporation's charter authorizes issuance of 2,000,000 shares of common stock. Currently, 1,400,000 shares are outstanding and 100,000 shares are being held as treasury stock. The firm wishes to raise $48,000,000 for a plant expansion. Discussions with its investment bankers indicate that the sale of new common stock will net the firm $60 per share.
a. What is the maximum number of new shares of common stock that the firm can sell without receiving further authorization from shareholders?
b. Judging on the basis of the data given and your finding in part **a**, will the firm be able to raise the needed funds without receiving further authorization?
c. What must the firm do to obtain authorization to issue more than the number of shares found in part **a**?

LG2

INTERMEDIATE

P7–2 **Preferred dividends**   Slater Lamp Manufacturing has an outstanding issue of preferred stock with an $80 par value and an 11% annual dividend.
a. What is the annual dollar dividend? If it is paid quarterly, how much will be paid each quarter?
b. If the preferred stock is *noncumulative* and the board of directors has passed the preferred dividend for the last 3 quarters, how much must be paid to preferred stockholders before dividends are paid to common stockholders?
c. If the preferred stock is *cumulative* and the board of directors has passed the preferred dividend for the last 3 quarters, how much must be paid to preferred stockholders before dividends are paid to common stockholders?

LG2

INTERMEDIATE

P7–3 **Preferred dividends**   In each case in the table on the facing page, how many dollars of preferred dividends per share must be paid to preferred stockholders before common stock dividends are paid?

Case	Type	Par value	Dividend per share per period	Periods of dividends passed
A	Cumulative	$ 80	$ 5	2
B	Noncumulative	110	8%	3
C	Noncumulative	100	$11	1
D	Cumulative	60	8.5%	4
E	Cumulative	90	9%	0

LG2

CHALLENGE

P7–4 Convertible preferred stock Valerian Corp. convertible preferred stock has a fixed conversion ratio of 5 common shares per 1 share of preferred stock. The preferred stock pays a dividend of $10.00 per share per year. The common stock currently sells for $20.00 per share and pays a dividend of $1.00 per share per year.

    a. Judging on the basis of the conversion ratio and the price of the common shares, what is the current conversion value of each preferred share?

    b. If the preferred shares are selling at $96.00 each, should an investor convert the preferred shares to common shares?

    c. What factors might cause an investor not to convert from preferred to common stock?

LG2

BASIC

P7–5 Stock quotation Assume that the following quote for the Advanced Business Machines stock (traded on the NYSE) was found in the Thursday, December 14, issue of the *Wall Street Journal*.

+3.2   84.13   51.25   AdvBusMach   ABM   1.32   1.6   23   12432   81.75   +1.63

Given this information, answer the following questions:

    a. On what day did the trading activity occur?

    b. At what price did the stock sell at the end of the day on Wednesday, December 13?

    c. What percentage change has occurred in the stock's closing price since the beginning of the calendar year?

    d. What is the firm's price/earnings ratio? What does it indicate?

    e. What is the last price at which the stock traded on the day quoted?

    f. How large a dividend is expected in the current year?

    g. What are the highest and the lowest price at which the stock traded during the latest 52-week period?

    h. How many shares of stock were traded on the day quoted?

    i. How much, if any, of a change in stock price took place between the day quoted and the day before? At what price did the stock close on the day before?

LG4

BASIC

P7–6 Common stock valuation—Zero growth Scotto Manufacturing is a mature firm in the machine tool component industry. The firm's most recent common stock dividend was $2.40 per share. Because of its maturity as well as its stable sales and earnings, the firm's management feels that dividends will remain at the current level for the foreseeable future.

    a. If the required return is 12%, what will be the value of Scotto's common stock?

    b. If the firm's risk as perceived by market participants suddenly increases, causing the required return to rise to 20%, what will be the common stock value?

c. Judging on the basis of your findings in parts **a** and **b**, what impact does risk have on value? Explain.

P7–7   Common stock value—Zero growth   Kelsey Drums, Inc., is a well-established supplier of fine percussion instruments to orchestras all over the United States. The company's class A common stock has paid a dividend of $5.00 per share per year for the last 15 years. Management expects to continue to pay at that rate for the foreseeable future. Sally Talbot purchased 100 shares of Kelsey class A common 10 years ago at a time when the required rate of return for the stock was 16%. She wants to sell her shares today. The current required rate of return for the stock is 12%. How much capital gain or loss will Sally have on her shares?

P7–8   Preferred stock valuation   Jones Design wishes to estimate the value of its outstanding preferred stock. The preferred issue has an $80 par value and pays an annual dividend of $6.40 per share. Similar-risk preferred stocks are currently earning a 9.3% annual rate of return.
a. What is the market value of the outstanding preferred stock?
b. If an investor purchases the preferred stock at the value calculated in part **a**, how much does she gain or lose per share if she sells the stock when the required return on similar-risk preferreds has risen to 10.5%? Explain.

P7–9   Common stock value—Constant growth   Use the constant-growth model (Gordon model) to find the value of each firm shown in the following table.

Firm	Dividend expected next year	Dividend growth rate	Required return
A	$1.20	8%	13%
B	4.00	5	15
C	0.65	10	14
D	6.00	8	9
E	2.25	8	20

P7–10   Common stock value—Constant growth   McCracken Roofing, Inc., common stock paid a dividend of $1.20 per share last year. The company expects earnings and dividends to grow at a rate of 5% per year for the foreseeable future.
a. What required rate of return for this stock would result in a price per share of $28?
b. If McCracken expects both earnings and dividends to grow at an annual rate of 10%, what required rate of return would result in a price per share of $28?

P7–11   Common stock value—Constant growth   Elk County Telephone has paid the dividends shown in the following table over the past 6 years.

Year	Dividend per share
2006	$2.87
2005	2.76
2004	2.60
2003	2.46
2002	2.37
2001	2.25

The firm's dividend per share next year is expected to be $3.02.

a. If you can earn 13% on similar-risk investments, what is the most you would be willing to pay per share?

b. If you can earn only 10% on similar-risk investments, what is the most you would be willing to pay per share?

c. Compare and contrast your findings in parts **a** and **b,** and discuss the impact of changing risk on share value.

P7–12 Common stock value—Variable growth   Newman Manufacturing is considering a cash purchase of the stock of Grips Tool. During the year just completed, Grips earned $4.25 per share and paid cash dividends of $2.55 per share ($D_0 = \$2.55$). Grips' earnings and dividends are expected to grow at 25% per year for the next 3 years, after which they are expected to grow at 10% per year to infinity. What is the maximum price per share that Newman should pay for Grips if it has a required return of 15% on investments with risk characteristics similar to those of Grips?

P7–13 Common stock value—Variable growth   Home Place Hotels, Inc., is entering into a 3-year remodeling and expansion project. The construction will have a limiting effect on earnings during that time, but when it is complete, it should allow the company to enjoy much improved growth in earnings and dividends. Last year, the company paid a dividend of $3.40. It expects zero growth in the next year. In years 2 and 3, 5% growth is expected, and in year 4, 15% growth. In year 5 and thereafter, growth should be a constant 10% per year. What is the maximum price per share that an investor who requires a return of 14% should pay for Home Place Hotels common stock?

P7–14 Common stock value—Variable growth   Lawrence Industries' most recent annual dividend was $1.80 per share ($D_0 = \$1.80$), and the firm's required return is 11%. Find the market value of Lawrence's shares when:

a. Dividends are expected to grow at 8% annually for 3 years, followed by a 5% constant annual growth rate in years 4 to infinity.

b. Dividends are expected to grow at 8% annually for 3 years, followed by a 0% constant annual growth rate in years 4 to infinity.

c. Dividends are expected to grow at 8% annually for 3 years, followed by a 10% constant annual growth rate in years 4 to infinity.

P7–15 Common stock value—All growth models   You are evaluating the potential purchase of a small business currently generating $42,500 of after-tax cash flow ($D_0 = \$42,500$). On the basis of a review of similar-risk investment opportunities, you must earn an 18% rate of return on the proposed purchase. Because you are relatively uncertain about future cash flows, you decide to estimate the firm's value using several possible assumptions about the growth rate of cash flows.

a. What is the firm's value if cash flows are expected to grow at an annual rate of 0% from now to infinity?

b. What is the firm's value if cash flows are expected to grow at a constant annual rate of 7% from now to infinity?

c. What is the firm's value if cash flows are expected to grow at an annual rate of 12% for the first 2 years, followed by a constant annual rate of 7% from year 3 to infinity?

LG5

CHALLENGE

P7–16   Free cash flow valuation   Nabor Industries is considering going public but is unsure of a fair offering price for the company. Before hiring an investment banker to assist in making the public offering, managers at Nabor have decided to make their own estimate of the firm's common stock value. The firm's CFO has gathered data for performing the valuation using the free cash flow valuation model.

The firm's weighted average cost of capital is 11%, and it has $1,500,000 of debt at market value and $400,000 of preferred stock at its assumed market value. The estimated free cash flows over the next 5 years, 2007 through 2011, are given below. Beyond 2011 to infinity, the firm expects its free cash flow to grow by 3% annually.

Year (t)	Free cash flow (FCF_t)
2007	$200,000
2008	250,000
2009	310,000
2010	350,000
2011	390,000

a. Estimate the value of Nabor Industries' entire company by using the *free cash flow valuation model*.
b. Use your finding in part **a**, along with the data provided above, to find Nabor Industries' common stock value.
c. If the firm plans to issue 200,000 shares of common sock, what is its estimated value per share?

LG5

CHALLENGE

P7–17   Using the free cash flow valuation model to price an IPO   Assume that you have an opportunity to buy the stock of CoolTech, Inc., an IPO being offered for $12.50 per share. Although you are very much interested in owning the company, you are concerned about whether it is fairly priced. To determine the value of the shares, you have decided to apply the free cash flow valuation model to the firm's financial data that you've developed from a variety of data sources. The key values you have compiled are summarized in the following table.

Free cash flow		
Year (t)	FCF_t	Other data
2007	$ 700,000	Growth rate of FCF, beyond 2010 to infinity = 2%
2008	800,000	Weighted average cost of capital = 8%
2009	950,000	Market value of all debt = $2,700,000
2010	1,100,000	Market value of preferred stock = $1,000,000
		Number of shares of common stock outstanding = 1,100,000

a. Use the *free cash flow valuation model* to estimate CoolTech's common stock value per share.
b. Judging on the basis of your finding in part **a** and the stock's offering price, should you buy the stock?

c. Upon further analysis, you find that the growth rate in FCF beyond 2010 will be 3% rather than 2%. What effect would this finding have on your responses in parts **a** and **b?**

P7–18   Book and liquidation value   The balance sheet for Gallinas Industries is as follows.

Gallinas Industries
Balance Sheet
December 31

Assets		Liabilities and Stockholders' Equity	
Cash	$ 40,000	Accounts payable	$100,000
Marketable securities	60,000	Notes payable	30,000
Accounts receivable	120,000	Accrued wages	30,000
Inventories	160,000	Total current liabilities	$160,000
Total current assets	$380,000	Long-term debt	$180,000
Land and buildings (net)	$150,000	Preferred stock	$ 80,000
Machinery and equipment	250,000	Common stock (10,000 shares)	360,000
Total fixed assets (net)	$400,000	Total liabilities and stockholders' equity	$780,000
Total assets	$780,000		

Additional information with respect to the firm is available:
(1) Preferred stock can be liquidated at book value.
(2) Accounts receivable and inventories can be liquidated at 90% of book value.
(3) The firm has 10,000 shares of common stock outstanding.
(4) All interest and dividends are currently paid up.
(5) Land and buildings can be liquidated at 130% of book value.
(6) Machinery and equipment can be liquidated at 70% of book value.
(7) Cash and marketable securities can be liquidated at book value.

Given this information, answer the following:
a. What is Gallinas Industries' book value per share?
b. What is its liquidation value per share?
c. Compare, contrast, and discuss the values found in parts **a** and **b**.

P7–19   Valuation with price/earnings multiples   For each of the firms shown in the following table, use the data given to estimate its common stock value employing price/earnings (P/E) multiples.

Firm	Expected EPS	Price/earnings multiple
A	$3.00	6.2
B	4.50	10.0
C	1.80	12.6
D	2.40	8.9
E	5.10	15.0

P7–20 Management action and stock value   REH Corporation's most recent dividend was $3 per share, its expected annual rate of dividend growth is 5%, and the required return is now 15%. A variety of proposals are being considered by management to redirect the firm's activities. Determine the impact on share price for each of the following proposed actions, and indicate the best alternative.

a. Do nothing, which will leave the key financial variables unchanged.

b. Invest in a new machine that will increase the dividend growth rate to 6% and lower the required return to 14%.

c. Eliminate an unprofitable product line, which will increase the dividend growth rate to 7% and raise the required return to 17%.

d. Merge with another firm, which will reduce the growth rate to 4% and raise the required return to 16%.

e. Acquire a subsidiary operation from another manufacturer. The acquisition should increase the dividend growth rate to 8% and increase the required return to 17%.

P7–21 Integrative—Valuation and CAPM formulas   Given the following information for the stock of Foster Company, calculate its beta.

Current price per share of common	$50.00
Expected dividend per share next year	$ 3.00
Constant annual dividend growth rate	9%
Risk-free rate of return	7%
Return on market portfolio	10%

P7–22 Integrative—Risk and valuation   Giant Enterprises has a beta of 1.20, the risk-free rate of return is currently 10%, and the market return is 14%. The company, which plans to pay a dividend of $2.60 per share in the coming year, anticipates that its future dividends will increase at an annual rate consistent with that experienced over the 2000–2006 period, when the following dividends were paid:

Year	Dividend per share
2006	$2.45
2005	2.28
2004	2.10
2003	1.95
2002	1.82
2001	1.80
2000	1.73

a. Use the capital asset pricing model (CAPM) to determine the required return on Giant's stock.

b. Using the constant-growth model and your finding in part **a**, estimate the value of Giant's stock.

c. Explain what effect, if any, a decrease in beta would have on the value of Giant's stock.

P7–23   Integrative—Valuation and CAPM   Hamlin Steel Company wishes to determine the value of Craft Foundry, a firm that it is considering acquiring for cash. Hamlin wishes to use the capital asset pricing model (CAPM) to determine the applicable discount rate to use as an input to the constant-growth valuation model. Craft's stock is not publicly traded. After studying the betas of firms similar to Craft that are publicly traded, Hamlin believes that an appropriate beta for Craft's stock would be 1.25. The risk-free rate is currently 9%, and the market return is 13%. Craft's dividend per share for each of the past 6 years is shown in the following table.

Year	Dividend per share
2006	$3.44
2005	3.28
2004	3.15
2003	2.90
2002	2.75
2001	2.45

a. Given that Craft is expected to pay a dividend of $3.68 next year, determine the maximum cash price that Hamlin should pay for each share of Craft.
b. Discuss the use of the CAPM for estimating the value of common stock, and describe the effect on the resulting value of Craft of:
  (1) A decrease in its dividend growth rate of 2% from that exhibited over the 2001–2006 period.
  (2) A decrease in its beta to 1.

P7–24   ETHICS PROBLEM   Melissa is trying to value Generic Utility, Inc.'s stock, which is clearly not growing at all. Generic declared and paid a $5 dividend last year. The required rate of return for utility stocks is 11%, but Melissa is unsure about the financial reporting integrity of Generic's finance team. She decides to add an extra 1% "credibility" risk premium to the required return as part of her valuation analysis.
a. What is the value of Generic's stock, assuming that the financials are trustworthy?
b. What is the value of Generic's stock, assuming that Melissa includes the extra 1% "credibility" risk premium?
c. What is the difference between the values found in parts **a** and **b**, and how might one interpret that difference?

Chapter 7 Case: Assessing the Impact of Suarez Manufacturing's Proposed Risky Investment on Its Stock Value

Early in 2007, Inez Marcus, the chief financial officer for Suarez Manufacturing, was given the task of assessing the impact of a proposed risky investment on the firm's stock value. To perform the necessary analysis, Inez gathered the following information on the firm's stock.

During the immediate past 5 years (2002–2006), the annual dividends paid on the firm's common stock were as follows:

Year	Dividend per share
2006	$1.90
2005	1.70
2004	1.55
2003	1.40
2002	1.30

The firm expects that without the proposed investment, the dividend in 2007 will be $2.09 per share and the historical annual rate of growth (rounded to the nearest whole percent) will continue in the future. Currently, the required return on the common stock is 14%. Inez's research indicates that if the proposed investment is undertaken, the 2007 dividend will rise to $2.15 per share and the annual rate of dividend growth will increase to 13%. She feels that in the *best case,* the dividend would continue to grow at this rate each year into the future and that in the *worst case,* the 13% annual rate of growth in dividends would continue only through 2009, and then, at the beginning of 2010, would return to the rate that was experienced between 2002 and 2006. As a result of the increased risk associated with the proposed risky investment, the required return on the common stock is expected to increase by 2% to an annual rate of 16%, regardless of which dividend growth outcome occurs.

Armed with the preceding information, Inez must now assess the impact of the proposed risky investment on the market value of Suarez's stock. To simplify her calculations, she plans to round the historical growth rate in common stock dividends to the nearest whole percent.

TO DO

a. Find the *current* value per share of Suarez Manufacturing's common stock.
b. Find the value of Suarez's common stock in the event that it *undertakes the proposed risky investment* and assuming that the dividend growth rate stays at 13% forever. Compare this value to that found in part **a.** What effect would the proposed investment have on the firm's stockholders? Explain.
c. On the basis of your findings in part **b,** do the stockholders win or lose as a result of undertaking the proposed risky investment? Should the firm do it? Why?
d. Rework parts **b** and **c** assuming that at the beginning of 2010 the annual dividend growth rate returns to the rate experienced between 2002 and 2006.

Spreadsheet Exercise

You are interested in purchasing the common stock of Azure Corporation. The firm recently paid a dividend of $3 per share. It expects its earnings—and hence its dividends—to grow at a rate of 7% for the foreseeable future. Currently, similar-risk stocks have required returns of 10%.

TO DO

a. Given the data above, calculate the present value of this security. Use the constant-growth model (Equation 7.5) to find the stock value.

b. One year later, your broker offers to sell you additional shares of Azure at $73. The most recent dividend paid was $3.21, and the expected growth rate for earnings remains at 7%. To determine the required rate of return, you decide to use the capital asset pricing model (CAPM). The risk-free rate, R_F, is currently 5.25%; the market return, k_m, is 11.55%; and the stock's beta, b_{Azure}, is 1.07. Substitute the appropriate values into the CAPM (Equation 5.8) to determine the firm's current required return, k_{Azure}.

c. Applying Equation 7.5, determine the value of the stock using the new dividend and required return from part **b.**

d. Given your calculation in part **c,** would you buy the additional shares from your broker at $73 per share? Explain.

e. Given your calculation in part **c,** would you sell your old shares for $73? Explain.

Group Exercise

This chapter discussed the basics of equity financing, including the specifics of the IPO process. We began this semester with your fictitious firm going public; here, we will revisit that process. We will also consider some recent real-world IPOs, and will look at recent quotes for your shadow firm.

TO DO

LG3   a. Your first task is to develop a preliminary prospectus for your firm following closely the sample prospectus in Figure 7.1 on page 335 of the text. Specify the number of shares issued and the price per share at issuance.

LG3   b. Look up recent IPO activity. Familiarize yourself with a particular offering, and summarize its details. A Google search will provide you with several Web sites that can be used for this task.

LG3   c. Look up the current quotation and recent market information on your shadow firm. Several Web sites have up-to-date information; one suggestion is the Web site moneycentral.msn.com/investor/home.asp (as suggested in the following Web Exercise). Report all the market numbers and concentrate on the recent news and analyses regarding your firm. The information should include ratings for your shadow firm.

Web Exercise

Stock market investing has become increasingly popular. Many Web sites provide detailed information relating to the topics covered in this chapter.

TO DO

Go to moneycentral.msn.com/investor/home.asp, the Web site jointly hosted by CNBC and MSN. Investigate this site and report your findings. Look up current quotations for three stocks in which you are interested and report the specifics of the quotes. They should include the following information:

a. Information on price, including the current price, recent changes in the price, and the high and low over the past 52 weeks.

b. Information on valuation, by reporting the P/E ratio, market capitalization, earnings per share, and dividend yield.

c. Other topics of interest, including trading volume.

Remember to check the book's Web site at

www.aw-bc.com/gitman

for additional resources, including additional Web exercises.

Integrative Case

2

Encore International

In the world of trendsetting fashion, instinct and marketing savvy are prerequisites to success. Jordan Ellis had both. During 2006, his international casual-wear company, Encore, rocketed to $300 million in sales after 10 years in business. His fashion line covered the young woman from head to toe with hats, sweaters, dresses, blouses, skirts, pants, sweatshirts, socks, and shoes. In Manhattan, there was an Encore shop every five or six blocks, each featuring a different color. Some shops showed the entire line in mauve, and others featured it in canary yellow.

Encore had made it. The company's historical growth was so spectacular that no one could have predicted it. However, securities analysts speculated that Encore could not keep up the pace. They warned that competition is fierce in the fashion industry and that the firm might encounter little or no growth in the future. They estimated that stockholders also should expect no growth in future dividends.

Contrary to the conservative securities analysts, Jordan Ellis felt that the company could maintain a constant annual growth rate in dividends per share of 6% in the future, or possibly 8% for the next 2 years and 6% thereafter. Ellis based his estimates on an established long-term expansion plan into European and Latin American markets. Venturing into these markets was expected to cause the risk of the firm, as measured by beta, to increase immediately from 1.10 to 1.25.

In preparing the long-term financial plan, Encore's chief financial officer has assigned a junior financial analyst, Marc Scott, to evaluate the firm's current stock price. He has asked Marc to consider the conservative predictions of the securities analysts and the aggressive predictions of the company founder, Jordan Ellis.

Marc has compiled these 2006 financial data to aid his analysis:

Data item	2006 value
Earnings per share (EPS)	$6.25
Price per share of common stock	$40.00
Book value of common stock equity	$60,000,000
Total common shares outstanding	2,500,000
Common stock dividend per share	$4.00

Figure 1

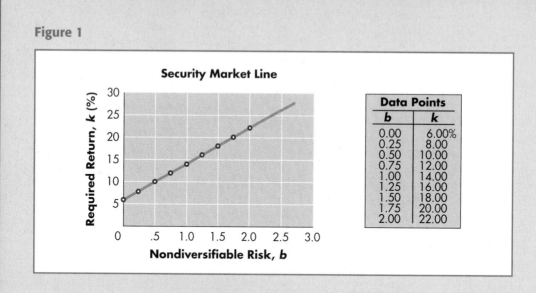

Security Market Line

Data Points	
b	**k**
0.00	6.00%
0.25	8.00
0.50	10.00
0.75	12.00
1.00	14.00
1.25	16.00
1.50	18.00
1.75	20.00
2.00	22.00

TO DO

a. What is the firm's current book value per share?

b. What is the firm's current P/E ratio?

c. (1) What are the required return and risk premium for Encore stock using the capital asset pricing model, assuming a beta of 1.10? (*Hint:* Use the security market line—with data points noted—given in Figure 1 to find the market return.)

(2) What are the required return and risk premium for Encore stock using the capital asset pricing model, assuming a beta of 1.25?

(3) What will be the effect on the required return if the beta rises as expected?

d. If the securities analysts are correct and there is no growth in future dividends, what will be the value per share of the Encore stock? (*Note:* Beta = 1.25.)

e. (1) If Jordan Ellis's predictions are correct, what will be the value per share of Encore stock if the firm maintains a constant annual 6% growth rate in future dividends? (*Note:* Beta = 1.25.)

(2) If Jordan Ellis's predictions are correct, what will be the value per share of Encore stock if the firm maintains a constant annual 8% growth rate in dividends per share over the next 2 years and 6% thereafter? (*Note:* Beta = 1.25.)

f. Compare the current (2006) price of the stock and the stock values found in parts **a, d,** and **e.** Discuss why these values may differ. Which valuation method do you believe most clearly represents the true value of the Encore stock?

PART THREE

Long-Term Investment Decisions

Chapter 8

Capital Budgeting Cash Flows

LEARNING GOALS

LG1 Understand the key motives for capital expenditure and the steps in the capital budgeting process.

LG2 Define basic capital budgeting terminology.

LG3 Discuss relevant cash flows, expansion versus replacement decisions, sunk costs and opportunity costs, and international capital budgeting.

LG4 Calculate the initial investment associated with a proposed capital expenditure.

LG5 Find the relevant operating cash inflows associated with a proposed capital expenditure.

LG6 Determine the terminal cash flow associated with a proposed capital expenditure.

ACROSS THE DISCIPLINES WHY THIS CHAPTER MATTERS TO YOU

Accounting: You need to understand capital budgeting cash flows to provide revenue, cost, depreciation, and tax data for use both in monitoring existing projects and in developing cash flows for proposed projects.

Information systems: You need to understand capital budgeting cash flows to maintain and facilitate the retrieval of cash flow data for both completed and existing projects.

Management: You need to understand capital budgeting cash flows so that you will understand which cash flows are relevant in making decisions about proposals for acquiring

additional production facilities, for new products, and for the expansion of existing product lines.

Marketing: You need to understand capital budgeting cash flows so that you can make revenue and cost estimates for proposals for new marketing programs, for new products, and for the expansion of existing product lines.

Operations: You need to understand capital budgeting cash flows so that you can make revenue and cost estimates for proposals for the acquisition of new equipment and production facilities.

FedEx Corp.

Calculating a Terminal's Value

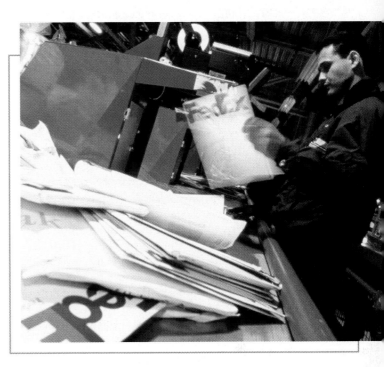

FedEx Express, a subsidiary of **FedEx Corp.** (www.fedex.com), announced in July 2004 the opening of its newest facility—the Miami Gateway Hub. The Memphis, Tennessee–based provider of transportation, e-commerce, and supply chain management services built the new $50 million facility to serve the growing South Florida market and to significantly enhance the company's connectivity to Latin America and the Caribbean.

Located on 23 acres of land at the Miami International Airport, the Miami Gateway Hub is expected to sort as many as 6,000 packages per hour (40,000 packages per day). The hub will also have a 1,000-square-foot cooler system to provide refrigerated storage space for agricultural products such as produce and flowers. Miami receives nearly 80 percent of U.S. air imports from Latin America and the Caribbean, and it is emerging as a crossroads for Asian and European trade routes as well, with more than 1,200 multinational corporations operating in the area. According to the Beacon Council, Miami-Dade County's official economic development partnership, 54 percent of all U.S. trade with Central America flows through Miami, 40 percent of the Caribbean trade, and 34 percent of U.S. trade with South America.

Before approving the construction of the 145,000-square-foot facility, FedEx Corp. had to identify all of the relevant cash flows for the project. In addition to the initial investment of $50 million for the new facility, financial managers had to determine estimated revenue, expected operating expenses, and probable terminal (final-year) cash flows. These calculations evidently convinced the company that the facility would be a valuable investment.

Like FedEx Corp., every firm must evaluate the costs and returns of projects for expansion, asset replacement or renewal, research and development, advertising, and other areas that require long-term commitment of funds in expectation of future returns. Chapter 8 introduces this process, called *capital budgeting,* and explains how to identify the relevant cash outflows and inflows that must be considered in making capital budgeting decisions.

Source: Adapted from "FedEx Express Opens New Gateway Hub in Miami to Facilitate Global Trade," downloaded from www.businesswire.com on July 21, 2004.

■ *Where might financial managers find the type of information they need to evaluate the cost-effectiveness of a new project?*

LG1 LG2   ## 8.1 | The Capital Budgeting Decision Process

Long-term investments represent sizable outlays of funds that commit a firm to some course of action. Consequently, the firm needs procedures to analyze and properly select its long-term investments. It must be able to measure cash flows and apply appropriate decision techniques. As time passes, fixed assets may become obsolete or may require an overhaul; at these points, too, financial decisions may be required. **Capital budgeting** is the process of evaluating and selecting long-term investments that are consistent with the firm's goal of maximizing owner wealth. Firms typically make a variety of long-term investments, but the most common for the manufacturing firm is in *fixed assets,* which include property (land), plant, and equipment. These assets, often referred to as *earning assets,* generally provide the basis for the firm's earning power and value.

capital budgeting
The process of evaluating and selecting long-term investments that are consistent with the firm's goal of maximizing owner wealth.

Because firms treat capital budgeting (investment) and financing decisions *separately,* Chapters 8 through 10 concentrate on fixed-asset acquisition without regard to the specific method of financing used. We begin by discussing the motives for capital expenditure.

Motives for Capital Expenditure

capital expenditure
An outlay of funds by the firm that is expected to produce benefits over a period of time *greater than* 1 year.

A **capital expenditure** is an outlay of funds by the firm that is expected to produce benefits over a period of time *greater than* 1 year. An **operating expenditure** is an outlay resulting in benefits received *within* 1 year. Fixed-asset outlays are capital expenditures, but not all capital expenditures are classified as fixed assets. A $60,000 outlay for a new machine with a usable life of 15 years is a capital expenditure that would appear as a fixed asset on the firm's balance sheet. A $60,000 outlay for an advertising campaign that is expected to produce benefits over a long period is also a capital expenditure, but would rarely be shown as a fixed asset.[1]

operating expenditure
An outlay of funds by the firm resulting in benefits received *within* 1 year.

Capital expenditures are made for many reasons. The basic motives for capital expenditures are to expand, replace, or renew fixed assets or to obtain some other, less tangible benefit over a long period. Table 8.1 briefly describes the key motives for making capital expenditures.

Steps in the Process

capital budgeting process
Five distinct but interrelated steps: *proposal generation, review and analysis, decision making, implementation,* and *follow-up.*

The **capital budgeting process** consists of five distinct but interrelated steps.

1. *Proposal generation.* Proposals are made at all levels within a business organization and are reviewed by finance personnel. Proposals that require large outlays are more carefully scrutinized than less costly ones.
2. *Review and analysis.* Formal review and analysis is performed to assess the appropriateness of proposals and evaluate their economic viability. Once the analysis is complete, a summary report is submitted to decision makers.

---

1. Some firms do, in effect, capitalize advertising outlays if there is reason to believe that the benefit of the outlay will be received at some future date. The capitalized advertising may appear as a deferred charge such as "deferred advertising expense," which is then amortized over the future. Expenses of this type are often deferred for reporting purposes to increase reported earnings, whereas for tax purposes, the entire amount is expensed to reduce tax liability.

TABLE 8.1

Key Motives for Making Capital Expenditures

Motive	Description
Expansion	The most common motive for a capital expenditure is to expand the level of operations—usually through acquisition of fixed assets. A growing firm often needs to acquire new fixed assets rapidly, as in the purchase of property and plant facilities.
Replacement	As a firm's growth slows and it reaches maturity, most capital expenditures will be made to replace or renew obsolete or worn-out assets. Each time a machine requires a major repair, the outlay for the repair should be compared to the outlay to replace the machine and the benefits of replacement.
Renewal	Renewal, an alternative to replacement, may involve rebuilding, overhauling, or retrofitting an existing fixed asset. For example, an existing drill press could be renewed by replacing its motor and adding a computer control system, or a physical facility could be renewed by rewiring and adding air conditioning. To improve efficiency, both replacement and renewal of existing machinery may be suitable solutions.
Other purposes	Some capital expenditures do not result in the acquisition or transformation of tangible fixed assets. Instead, they involve a long-term commitment of funds in expectation of a future return. These expenditures include outlays for advertising campaigns, research and development, management consulting, and new products.

3. *Decision making.* Firms typically delegate capital expenditure decision making on the basis of dollar limits. Generally, the board of directors must authorize expenditures beyond a certain amount. Often plant managers are given authority to make decisions necessary to keep the production line moving.
4. *Implementation.* Following approval, expenditures are made and projects implemented. Expenditures for a large project often occur in phases.
5. *Follow-up.* Results are monitored, and actual costs and benefits are compared with those that were expected. Action may be required if actual outcomes differ from projected ones.

Each step in the process is important. Review and analysis and decision making (Steps 2 and 3) consume the majority of time and effort, however. Follow-up (Step 5) is an important but often ignored step aimed at allowing the firm to improve the accuracy of its cash flow estimates continuously. Because of their fundamental importance, this and the following chapters give primary consideration to review and analysis and to decision making.

Basic Terminology

Before we develop the concepts, techniques, and practices related to the capital budgeting process, we need to explain some basic terminology. In addition, we will present some key assumptions that are used to simplify the discussion in the remainder of this chapter and in Chapters 9 and 10.

Independent Versus Mutually Exclusive Projects

independent projects
Projects whose cash flows are unrelated or independent of one another; the acceptance of one *does not eliminate* the others from further consideration.

mutually exclusive projects
Projects that compete with one another, so that the acceptance of one *eliminates* from further consideration all other projects that serve a similar function.

The two most common types of projects are (1) independent projects and (2) mutually exclusive projects. **Independent projects** are those whose cash flows are unrelated or independent of one another; the acceptance of one *does not eliminate* the others from further consideration. **Mutually exclusive projects** are those that have the same function and therefore compete with one another. The acceptance of one *eliminates* from further consideration all other projects that serve a similar function. For example, a firm in need of increased production capacity could obtain it by (1) expanding its plant, (2) acquiring another company, or (3) contracting with another company for production. Clearly, accepting any one option eliminates the need for either of the others.

Unlimited Funds Versus Capital Rationing

unlimited funds
The financial situation in which a firm is able to accept all independent projects that provide an acceptable return.

capital rationing
The financial situation in which a firm has only a fixed number of dollars available for capital expenditures, and numerous projects compete for these dollars.

The availability of funds for capital expenditures affects the firm's decisions. If a firm has **unlimited funds** for investment, making capital budgeting decisions is quite simple: All independent projects that will provide an acceptable return can be accepted. Typically, though, firms operate under **capital rationing** instead. This means that they have only a fixed number of dollars available for capital expenditures and that numerous projects will compete for these dollars. Procedures for dealing with capital rationing are presented in Chapter 10. The discussions that follow here and in the following chapter assume unlimited funds.

Accept–Reject Versus Ranking Approaches

accept–reject approach
The evaluation of capital expenditure proposals to determine whether they meet the firm's minimum acceptance criterion.

ranking approach
The ranking of capital expenditure projects on the basis of some predetermined measure, such as the rate of return.

Two basic approaches to capital budgeting decisions are available. The **accept–reject approach** involves evaluating capital expenditure proposals to determine whether they meet the firm's minimum acceptance criterion. This approach can be used when the firm has unlimited funds, as a preliminary step when evaluating mutually exclusive projects, or in a situation in which capital must be rationed. In these cases, only acceptable projects should be considered.

The second method, the **ranking approach,** involves ranking projects on the basis of some predetermined measure, such as the rate of return. The project with the highest return is ranked first, and the project with the lowest return is ranked last. Only acceptable projects should be ranked. Ranking is useful in selecting the "best" of a group of mutually exclusive projects and in evaluating projects with a view to capital rationing.

Conventional Versus Nonconventional Cash Flow Patterns

conventional cash flow pattern
An initial outflow followed only by a series of inflows.

Cash flow patterns associated with capital investment projects can be classified as *conventional* or *nonconventional*. A **conventional cash flow pattern** consists of an initial outflow followed only by a series of inflows. For example, a firm may spend $10,000 today and as a result expect to receive equal annual cash inflows (an annuity) of $2,000 each year for the next 8 years, as depicted on the timeline in Figure 8.1.[2] A conventional cash flow pattern that provides a mixed stream of cash inflows is depicted in Figure 8.3 on page 381.

---

2. Arrows rather than plus or minus signs are frequently used on time lines to distinguish between cash inflows and cash outflows. Upward-pointing arrows represent cash inflows (positive cash flows), and downward-pointing arrows represent cash outflows (negative cash flows).

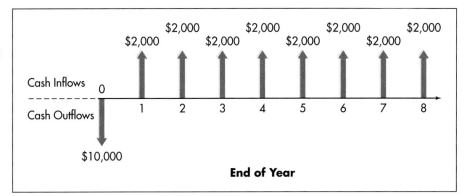

FIGURE 8.1

Conventional Cash Flow
Time line for a conventional
cash flow pattern

nonconventional cash flow
pattern
An initial outflow followed
by a series of inflows *and*
outflows.

A **nonconventional cash flow pattern** is one in which an initial outflow is followed by a series of inflows *and* outflows. For example, the purchase of a
machine may require an initial cash outflow of $20,000 and may generate cash
inflows of $5,000 each year for 4 years. In the fifth year after purchase, an out-
flow of $8,000 may be required to overhaul the machine, after which it generates
inflows of $5,000 each year for 5 more years. This nonconventional pattern is
illustrated on the time line in Figure 8.2.

Difficulties often arise in evaluating projects with nonconventional patterns
of cash flow. *The discussions in the remainder of this chapter and in Chapters 9
and 10 are therefore limited to the evaluation of conventional cash flow patterns.*

FIGURE 8.2

**Nonconventional
Cash Flow**
Time line for a
nonconventional
cash flow pattern

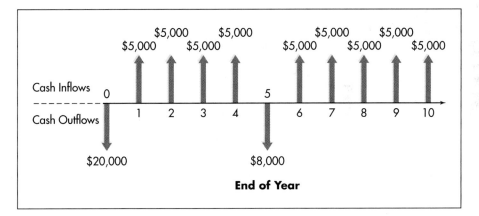

REVIEW QUESTIONS

8–1   What is *capital budgeting?* Do all capital expenditures involve fixed
assets? Explain.

8–2   What are the key motives for making capital expenditures? Discuss, compare, and contrast them.

8–3   What are the five steps involved in the capital budgeting process?

8–4   Differentiate between the members of each of the following pairs of capital budgeting terms: (a) independent versus mutually exclusive projects;
(b) unlimited funds versus capital rationing; (c) accept–reject versus ranking approaches; and (d) conventional versus nonconventional cash flow
patterns.

8.2 | The Relevant Cash Flows

relevant cash flows
The *incremental cash outflow (investment) and resulting subsequent inflows* associated with a proposed capital expenditure.

incremental cash flows
The *additional* cash flows—outflows or inflows—expected to result from a proposed capital expenditure.

To evaluate capital expenditure alternatives, the firm must determine the **relevant cash flows.** These are the *incremental cash outflow (investment) and resulting subsequent inflows.* The **incremental cash flows** represent the *additional* cash flows—outflows or inflows—expected to result from a proposed capital expenditure. As noted in Chapter 3, cash flows rather than accounting figures are used, because cash flows directly affect the firm's ability to pay bills and purchase assets. The *In Practice* box below takes a look at the accuracy of cash flow estimates in practice.

The remainder of this chapter is devoted to the procedures for measuring the relevant cash flows associated with proposed capital expenditures.

In Practice FOCUS ON ETHICS

HOW ACCURATE ARE CASH FLOWS?

The process of capital budgeting based on calculating various decision measures from projected cash flows has been a part of the investment decision process for more than 40 years. This procedure for evaluating investment opportunities works well when cash flows can be estimated with certainty, but in real-world corporate practice many investment decisions involve a high degree of uncertainty.

Because estimates of the cash flows from an investment project involve making assumptions about the future, they may be subject to considerable error. The problem becomes more complicated as the period of time under consideration becomes longer and when the project is unique in nature with no comparables. Other complications may arise involving accounting for additional (extraordinary) cash flows beyond the project's operating cash flows—for example, the cost of litigation, compliance with tougher environmental stan-

dards, or the costs of disposal or recycling of an asset at the completion of the project.

Examples of how cash flow estimates may differ from reality can readily be found. When financial analysts tried several years ago to value Internet startup companies with little or no revenues, negative earnings and operating cash flows, and no history of performance, they encountered many difficulties in forecasting most of the relevant financial information. For example, in the case of online retailer **Amazon.com,** according to forecasts made in early 2000, analysts expected revenues of $5.6 billion in 2001, $9.8 billion in 2002, and $14.7 billion in 2003. These projections proved to be completely off the mark, as the actual revenues were $3.1 billion, $3.9 billion, and $5.2 billion, respectively, when revenue growth slowed considerably as a result of the bursting of the Internet bubble and subsequent recession. Estimates of free cash flow proved equally wrong. In fact,

Amazon.com started generating positive cash flows 4 years earlier than forecast, despite the fact that revenues were about only 40 percent of those predicted.

The preceding example indicates how crucial calculations of cash flows from the project are for capital budgeting decisions. Consequently, capital budgeting decisions can only be as accurate as cash flow projections. The temptation to "shade" cash flow projections in an effort to "make the numbers work," especially when projected benefits are inaccurate in some way, can exist. Financial managers need to take a hard look at cash flow projections, to be sure that they are realistic and based on more than just wishful thinking.

Source: Aswath Damodaran, "The Dark Side of Valuations: Firms with No Earnings, No History, and No Comparables. Can Amazon.com Be Valued?" *Stern School of Business,* NYU, March 2000.

■ *As a company manager, should you focus on net income rather than cash flows? If so, why?*

Major Cash Flow Components

The cash flows of any project having the *conventional pattern* can include three basic components: (1) an initial investment, (2) operating cash inflows, and (3) terminal cash flow. All projects—whether for expansion, replacement, renewal, or some other purpose—have the first two components. Some, however, lack the final component, terminal cash flow.

Figure 8.3 depicts on a time line the cash flows for a project. The **initial investment** for the proposed project is $50,000. This is the relevant cash outflow at time zero. The **operating cash inflows,** which are the incremental after-tax cash inflows resulting from implementation of the project during its life, gradually increase from $4,000 in its first year to $10,000 in its tenth and final year. The **terminal cash flow** is the after-tax nonoperating cash flow occurring in the final year of the project. It is usually attributable to liquidation of the project. In this case it is $25,000, received at the end of the project's 10-year life. Note that the terminal cash flow does *not* include the $10,000 operating cash inflow for year 10.

Expansion Versus Replacement Decisions

Developing relevant cash flow estimates is most straightforward in the case of *expansion decisions.* In this case, the initial investment, operating cash inflows, and terminal cash flow are merely the after-tax cash outflow and inflows associated with the proposed capital expenditure.

Identifying relevant cash flows for *replacement decisions* is more complicated, because the firm must identify the *incremental* cash outflow and inflows that would result from the proposed replacement. The initial investment in the case of replacement is the difference between the initial investment needed to

In Practice GLOBAL FOCUS

EMERGING FROM GANGSTER CAPITALISM

In the wild and woolly days of the 1990s, privatization schemes allowed a handful of Russian supertycoons to heist the former Soviet economy's crown jewels through insider trading, fixed auctions, and corrupt Kremlin ties. More recently, a measure of stability has emerged. Russia has taken steps to attract foreign investors by improving general foreign direct investment laws, streamlining tax administration, adopting the Organization for Economic Co-operation and Development's (OECD) Principles of Corporate Governance, and reforming land law, its customs codes, and foreign exchange regulation.

Nevertheless, some barriers to foreign capital investments in Russia continue to make investing there a risky proposition. In June 2004, senior officials from the Russian Federation and from OECD countries met to discuss recommendations designed to boost foreign direct investment in Russia. Recommendations included

phasing out ceilings for foreign ownership in certain sectors (e.g., financial services and national energy companies), improving opportunities for foreign participation in privatization by increasing transparency in bidding procedures and dispute resolution, ensuring greater local compliance with regulations relating to investment, and intensifying efforts in support of corporate and public sector integrity.

Despite the reforms, some projects may simply not be worth the investment on purely economic grounds. According to the American Chamber of Commerce in Russia, the city of Moscow plans to triple its number of hotel rooms by the year 2010. The need, according to city officials, is to accommodate an expected 5 million tourists by 2010 and 10 million visitors by 2015. As it turns out, though, the $300 per person cost of a visa to visit the country makes it unlikely that international tourists will drop into Moscow for a weekend's getaway.

In addition, good building sites in the center of Moscow are rare and extremely expensive. On the face of it, the economic wisdom of an investment to improve hotel capacity seems dubious.

Yet for all of its problems, Russia is making progress. It recorded healthy GDP growth rates of 5.1 percent in 2001, 4.7 percent in 2002, and 7 percent in 2003. The country has a wealth of mineral sources and cheap power, low labor expenses, and highly skilled workers, and its citizens are just starting to improve their purchasing power. For any company willing to navigate the complex political environment and commit capital for the long term, the rewards may be worthwhile.

Sources: www.amcham.ru and www.oecd.org.

■ *The need to improve corporate and public sector integrity is not a problem confined to Russia. Can you think of examples of corporate impropriety in the United States?*

8–7   What effect do *sunk costs* and *opportunity costs* have on a project's incremental cash flows?

8–8   How can *currency risk* and *political risk* be minimized when one is making *foreign direct investment?*

LG4 8.3 | Finding the Initial Investment

The term *initial investment* as used here refers to the relevant cash outflows to be considered when evaluating a prospective capital expenditure. Because our discussion of capital budgeting is concerned only with investments that exhibit conventional cash flows, the initial investment occurs at *time zero*—the time at which the expenditure is made. The initial investment is calculated by subtracting all cash inflows occurring at time zero from all cash outflows occurring at time zero.

TABLE 8.2

The Basic Format for Determining Initial Investment

Installed cost of new asset =
Cost of new asset
+ Installation costs
− **After-tax proceeds from sale of old asset =**
Proceeds from sale of old asset
∓ Tax on sale of old asset
± **Change in net working capital**
Initial investment

The basic format for determining the initial investment is given in Table 8.2. The cash flows that must be considered when determining the initial investment associated with a capital expenditure are the installed cost of the new asset, the after-tax proceeds (if any) from the sale of an old asset, and the change (if any) in net working capital. Note that if there are no installation costs and the firm is not replacing an existing asset, then the purchase price of the asset, adjusted for any change in net working capital, is equal to the initial investment.

Installed Cost of New Asset

cost of new asset
The net outflow necessary to acquire a new asset.

installation costs
Any added costs that are necessary to place an asset into operation.

installed cost of new asset
The *cost of new asset* plus its *installation costs;* equals the asset's depreciable value.

As shown in Table 8.2, the installed cost of the new asset is found by adding the cost of the new asset to its installation costs. The **cost of new asset** is the net outflow that its acquisition requires. Usually, we are concerned with the acquisition of a fixed asset for which a definite purchase price is paid. **Installation costs** are any added costs that are necessary to place an asset into operation. The Internal Revenue Service (IRS) requires the firm to add installation costs to the purchase price of an asset to determine its depreciable value, which is expensed over a period of years. The **installed cost of new asset,** calculated by adding the *cost of new asset* to its *installation costs,* equals its depreciable value.

After-Tax Proceeds from Sale of Old Asset

after-tax proceeds from sale of old asset
The difference between the old asset's sale proceeds and any applicable taxes or tax refunds related to its sale.

proceeds from sale of old asset
The cash inflows, net of any *removal* or *cleanup costs,* resulting from the sale of an existing asset.

tax on sale of old asset
Tax that depends on the relationship between the old asset's sale price and *book value,* and on existing government tax rules.

Table 8.2 shows that the **after-tax proceeds from sale of old asset** decrease the firm's initial investment in the new asset. These proceeds are the difference between the old asset's sale proceeds and any applicable taxes or tax refunds related to its sale. The **proceeds from sale of old asset** are the net cash inflows it provides. This amount is net of any costs incurred in the process of removing the asset. Included in these *removal costs* are *cleanup costs,* such as those related to removal and disposal of chemical and nuclear wastes. These costs may not be trivial.

The proceeds from the sale of an old asset are normally subject to some type of tax.[3] This **tax on sale of old asset** depends on the relationship between its sale price and *book value,* and on existing government tax rules.

---

3. A brief discussion of the tax treatment of ordinary and capital gains income was presented in Chapter 1. Because corporate capital gains and ordinary income are taxed at the same rate, for convenience, we do not differ between them in the following discussions.

as ordinary income. Because the firm is assumed to be in the 40% tax bracket, the taxes on the $22,000 gain are $8,800 (0.40 × $22,000). This amount in taxes should be used in calculating the initial investment in the new asset.

The sale of the asset for its book value   If the asset is sold for $48,000, its book value, the firm breaks even. There is no gain or loss, as shown under the $48,000 sale price in Figure 8.5. Because *no tax results from selling an asset for its book value,* there is no tax effect on the initial investment in the new asset.

The sale of the asset for less than its book value   If Hudson sells the asset for $30,000, it experiences a loss of $18,000 ($48,000 − $30,000), as shown under the $30,000 sale price in Figure 8.5. If this is a depreciable asset used in the business, the loss may be used to offset ordinary operating income. If the asset is *not* depreciable or is *not* used in the business, the loss can be used only to offset capital gains. In either case, the loss will save the firm $7,200 (0.40 × $18,000) in taxes. And, if current operating earnings or capital gains are not sufficient to offset the loss, the firm may be able to apply these losses to prior or future years' taxes.[6]

Change in Net Working Capital[7]

net working capital
The amount by which a firm's current assets exceed its current liabilities.

Net working capital is the amount by which a firm's current assets exceed its current liabilities. This topic is treated in depth in Chapter 14, but at this point it is important to note that changes in net working capital often accompany capital expenditure decisions. If a firm acquires new machinery to expand its level of operations, it will experience an increase in levels of cash, accounts receivable, inventories, accounts payable, and accruals. These increases result from the need for more cash to support expanded operations, more accounts receivable and inventories to support increased sales, and more accounts payable and accruals to support increased outlays made to meet expanded product demand. As noted in Chapter 3, increases in cash, accounts receivable, and inventories are *outflows of cash,* whereas increases in accounts payable and accruals are *inflows of cash.*

change in net working capital
The difference between a change in current assets and a change in current liabilities.

The difference between the change in current assets and the change in current liabilities is the **change in net working capital.** Generally, current assets increase by more than current liabilities, resulting in an increased investment in net working capital. This increased investment is treated as an initial outflow.[8] If the change in net working capital were negative, it would be shown as an initial inflow. The change in net working capital—regardless of whether it is an increase or a decrease—*is not taxable* because it merely involves a net buildup or net reduction of current accounts.

---

6. The tax law provides detailed procedures for using *tax loss carrybacks/carryforwards.* Application of such procedures to capital budgeting is beyond the scope of this text, and they are therefore ignored in subsequent discussions.

7. Occasionally, this cash outflow is intentionally ignored to enhance the attractiveness of a proposed investment and thereby improve its likelihood of acceptance. Similar intentional omissions and/or overly optimistic estimates are sometimes made to enhance project acceptance. The presence of formal review and analysis procedures should help the firm to ensure that capital budgeting cash flow estimates are realistic and unbiased and that the "best" projects—those that make the maximum contribution to owner wealth—are accepted.

8. When changes in net working capital apply to the initial investment associated with a proposed capital expenditure, they are for convenience assumed to be instantaneous and thereby occurring at time zero. In practice, the change in net working capital will frequently occur over a period of months as the capital expenditure is implemented.

TABLE 8.4

Calculation of Change in Net Working Capital
for Danson Company

Current account		Change in balance
Cash		+ $ 4,000
Accounts receivable		+ 10,000
Inventories		+ 8,000
(1) Current assets		+$22,000
Accounts payable	+$ 7,000	
Accruals	+ 2,000	
(2) Current liabilities		+ 9,000
Change in net working capital [(1) − (2)]		+$13,000

EXAMPLE

Danson Company, a metal products manufacturer, is contemplating expanding its operations. Financial analysts expect that the changes in current accounts summarized in Table 8.4 will occur and will be maintained over the life of the expansion. Current assets are expected to increase by $22,000, and current liabilities are expected to increase by $9,000, resulting in a $13,000 increase in net working capital. In this case, the increase will represent an increased net working capital investment and will be treated as a cash outflow in calculating the initial investment. ■

Calculating the Initial Investment

A variety of tax and other considerations enter into the initial investment calculation. The following example illustrates calculation of the initial investment according to the format in Table 8.2.[9]

EXAMPLE

Powell Corporation, a large, diversified manufacturer of aircraft components, is trying to determine the initial investment required to replace an old machine with a new, more sophisticated model. The proposed machine's purchase price is $380,000, and an additional $20,000 will be necessary to install it. It will be depreciated under MACRS using a 5-year recovery period. The present (old) machine was purchased 3 years ago at a cost of $240,000 and was being depreciated under MACRS using a 5-year recovery period. The firm has found a buyer willing to pay $280,000 for the present machine and to remove it at the buyer's expense. The firm expects that a $35,000 increase in current assets and an $18,000 increase in current liabilities will accompany the replacement; these changes will result in a $17,000 ($35,000 − $18,000) *increase* in net working capital. The firm pays taxes at a rate of 40%.

---

9. Throughout the discussions of capital budgeting, all assets evaluated as candidates for replacement are assumed to be depreciable assets that are directly used in the business, so any losses on the sale of these assets can be applied against ordinary operating income. The decisions are also structured to ensure that the usable life remaining on the old asset is just equal to the life of the new asset; this assumption enables us to avoid the problem of unequal lives, which is discussed in Chapter 10.

P8–24 **Integrative—Determining relevant cash flows** Lombard Company is contemplating the purchase of a new high-speed widget grinder to replace the existing grinder. The existing grinder was purchased 2 years ago at an installed cost of $60,000; it was being depreciated under MACRS using a 5-year recovery period. The existing grinder is expected to have a usable life of 5 more years. The new grinder costs $105,000 and requires $5,000 in installation costs; it has a 5-year usable life and would be depreciated under MACRS using a 5-year recovery period. Lombard can currently sell the existing grinder for $70,000 without incurring any removal or cleanup costs. To support the increased business resulting from purchase of the new grinder, accounts receivable would increase by $40,000, inventories by $30,000, and accounts payable by $58,000. At the end of 5 years, the existing grinder is expected to have a market value of zero; the new grinder would be sold to net $29,000 after removal and cleanup costs and before taxes. The firm is subject a 40% tax rate. The estimated *earnings before depreciation, interest, and taxes* over the 5 years for both the new and the existing grinder are shown in the following table. (Table 3.2 on page 106 contains the applicable MACRS depreciation percentages.)

	Earnings before depreciation, interest, and taxes	
Year	New grinder	Existing grinder
1	$43,000	$26,000
2	43,000	24,000
3	43,000	22,000
4	43,000	20,000
5	43,000	18,000

a. Calculate the *initial investment* associated with the replacement of the existing grinder by the new one.
b. Determine the *incremental operating cash inflows* associated with the proposed grinder replacement. (*Note:* Be sure to consider the depreciation in year 6.)
c. Determine the *terminal cash flow* expected at the end of year 5 from the proposed grinder replacement.
d. Depict on a time line the *relevant cash flows* associated with the proposed grinder replacement decision.

P8–25 **Integrative—Determining relevant cash flows** Atlantic Drydock is considering replacing an existing hoist with one of two newer, more efficient pieces of equipment. The existing hoist is 3 years old, cost $32,000, and is being depreciated under MACRS using a 5-year recovery period. Although the existing hoist has only 3 years (years 4, 5, and 6) of depreciation remaining under MACRS, it has a remaining usable life of 5 years. Hoist A, one of the two possible replacement hoists, costs $40,000 to purchase and $8,000 to install. It has a 5-year usable life and will be depreciated under MACRS using a 5-year recovery period. Hoist B costs $54,000 to purchase and $6,000 to install. It also has a 5-year usable life and will be depreciated under MACRS using a 5-year recovery period.

Increased investments in net working capital will accompany the decision to acquire hoist A or hoist B. Purchase of hoist A would result in a $4,000 increase in net working capital; hoist B would result in a $6,000 increase in net working capital. The projected *earnings before depreciation, interest, and taxes* with each alternative hoist and the existing hoist are given in the following table.

	Earnings before depreciation, interest, and taxes		
Year	With hoist A	With hoist B	With existing hoist
1	$21,000	$22,000	$14,000
2	21,000	24,000	14,000
3	21,000	26,000	14,000
4	21,000	26,000	14,000
5	21,000	26,000	14,000

The existing hoist can currently be sold for $18,000 and will not incur any removal or cleanup costs. At the end of 5 years, the existing hoist can be sold to net $1,000 before taxes. Hoists A and B can be sold to net $12,000 and $20,000 before taxes, respectively, at the end of the 5-year period. The firm is subject to a 40% tax rate. (Table 3.2 on page 106 contains the applicable MACRS depreciation percentages.)

a. Calculate the *initial investment* associated with each alternative.
b. Calculate the *incremental operating cash inflows* associated with each alternative. (*Note:* Be sure to consider the depreciation in year 6.)
c. Calculate the *terminal cash flow* at the end of year 5 associated with each alternative.
d. Depict on a time line the *relevant cash flows* associated with each alternative.

P8–26 **ETHICS PROBLEM**   According to academic research, capital budgeting cash flow projections are used rarely in practice by small firms, which often use accounting projections instead. What is the most likely explanation of this behavior?

Chapter 8 Case: Developing Relevant Cash Flows for Clark Upholstery Company's Machine Renewal or Replacement Decision

Bo Humphries, chief financial officer of Clark Upholstery Company, expects the firm's *net operating profit after taxes* for the next 5 years to be as shown in the following table.

Year	Net operating profit after taxes
1	$100,000
2	150,000
3	200,000
4	250,000
5	320,000

c. Create a spreadsheet to calculate the *operating cash inflows* for Damon Corporation for both the proposed and the present machine.

d. Create a spreadsheet to calculate the *terminal cash flow* associated with the project.

Group Exercise

This chapter is the first of a three-chapter set on long-term investment decisions. In this group exercise, your firm will begin analyzing a capital investment decision that you will refine in Chapters 9 and 10. Keep this in mind as you develop a potential investment for your firm. This assignment may appear to be shorter than previous exercises, but spending time to adequately design possible capital investment projects will make the next chapters' work much easier.

TO DO

a. Your firm, like most firms, is constantly evaluating potential capital investments. For your first task, you are to design two mutually exclusive capital investment proposals. As part of the design process, you should spend a good deal of time developing the motivation for these projects. You need to fully answer the question of *why* your firm should consider these projects.

b. The next step is to begin reviewing and analyzing these two proposals. This activity will include estimating the relevant cash flows for each of the proposals. Begin with the initial investment and then flesh out the operating cash inflows and any terminal cash flow. As in the text, these cash flows should be organized on an annual basis. Each project should have a minimum useful life of 5 years.

c. To complete the assignment for this chapter, summarize all relevant cash flows on a time line as done in the text.

Web Exercise

For this exercise, you are to go to a Web site of your choosing where you can investigate the recent past of two corporations (also of your own choosing). You. will need access to annual reports for the two firms so that you can assess their levels of capital expenditures.

TO DO

a. For each corporation, report the amount of capital spending. Go back 3 years and compare the levels within each firm. Has the amount been roughly constant, or were there big fluctuations? Describe the purposes of the capital expenditures made by each firm.

b. Compare the level of capital spending across the two firms. Are they greatly different, particularly in comparison to their relative sizes?

Remember to check the book's Web site at

www.aw-bc.com/gitman

for additional resources, including additional Web exercises.

TABLE 9.2

	Relevant Cash Flows and Payback Periods for DeYarman Enterprises' Projects	
	Project Gold	Project Silver
Initial investment	$50,000	$50,000
Year	Operating cash inflows	
1	$ 5,000	$40,000
2	5,000	2,000
3	40,000	8,000
4	10,000	10,000
5	10,000	10,000
Payback period	3 years	3 years

$50,000 invested in project Silver is recovered, whereas only $5,000 of the $50,000 investment in project Gold is recovered. Given the time value of money, project Silver would clearly be preferred over project Gold, in spite of the fact that both have identical 3-year payback periods. The payback approach does not fully account for the time value of money, which, if recognized, would cause project Silver to be preferred over project Gold. ◼

A third weakness of payback is its failure to recognize cash flows that occur *after* the payback period.

EXAMPLE   Rashid Company, a software developer, has two investment opportunities, X and Y. Data for X and Y are given in Table 9.3. The payback period for project X is 2 years; for project Y it is 3 years. Strict adherence to the payback approach suggests that project X is preferable to project Y. However, if we look beyond the payback period, we see that project X returns only an additional $1,200 ($1,000 in year 3 + $100 in year 4 + $100 in year 5), whereas project Y returns an additional $7,000 ($4,000 in year 4 + $3,000 in year 5). On the basis of this informa-

p. 424
ex.

TABLE 9.3

	Calculation of the Payback Period for Rashid Company's Two Alternative Investment Projects	
	Project X	Project Y
Initial investment	$10,000	$10,000
Year	Operating cash inflows	
1	$5,000	$3,000
2	5,000	4,000
3	1,000	3,000
4	100	4,000
5	100	3,000
Payback period	2 years	3 years

tion, project Y appears preferable to X. The payback approach ignored the cash inflows occurring after the end of the payback period.[4]   ■

REVIEW QUESTIONS

9–2   What is the *payback period?* How is it calculated?
9–3   What weaknesses are commonly associated with the use of the payback period to evaluate a proposed investment?

LG3   # 9.3 | Net Present Value (NPV)

net present value (NPV)
A sophisticated capital budgeting technique; found by subtracting a project's initial investment from the present value of its cash inflows discounted at a rate equal to the firm's cost of capital.

Because *net present value (NPV)* gives explicit consideration to the time value of money, it is considered a *sophisticated capital budgeting technique.* All such techniques in one way or another discount the firm's cash flows at a specified rate. This rate—often called the *discount rate, required return, cost of capital,* or *opportunity cost*—is the minimum return that must be earned on a project to leave the firm's market value unchanged. In this chapter, we take this rate as a "given." In Chapter 11 we will explore how it is determined.

The **net present value (NPV)** is found by subtracting a project's initial investment (CF_0) from the present value of its cash inflows (CF_t) discounted at a rate equal to the firm's cost of capital (k).

$$NPV = \text{Present value of cash inflows} - \text{Initial investment}$$

$$NPV = \sum_{t=1}^{n} \frac{CF_t}{(1+k)^t} - CF_0 \tag{9.1}$$

$$= \sum_{t=1}^{n} (CF_t \times PVIF_{k,t}) - CF_0 \tag{9.1a}$$

When NPV is used, both inflows and outflows are measured in terms of present dollars. Because we are dealing only with investments that have *conventional cash flow patterns,* the initial investment is automatically stated in terms of today's dollars. If it were not, the present value of a project would be found by subtracting the present value of outflows from the present value of inflows.

The Decision Criteria

When NPV is used to make accept–reject decisions, the decision criteria are as follows:

- If the NPV is *greater than* $0, *accept* the project.
- If the NPV is *less than* $0, *reject* the project.

---

4. To get around this weakness, some analysts add a desired dollar return to the initial investment and then calculate the payback period for the increased amount. For example, if the analyst wished to pay back the initial investment plus 20% for projects X and Y in Table 9.3, the amount to be recovered would be $12,000 [$10,000 + (0.20 × $10,000)]. For project X, the payback period would be infinite because the $12,000 would never be recovered; for project Y, the payback period would be 3.5 years [3 years + ($2,000 ÷ $4,000) years]. Clearly, project Y would be preferred.

If the NPV is greater than $0, the firm will earn a return greater than its cost of capital. Such action should increase the market value of the firm, and therefore the wealth of its owners by an amount equal to the NPV.

EXAMPLE

Project A

Input	Function
−42000	CF₀
14000	CF₁
5	N
10	I
	NPV

Solution
11,071.01

We can illustrate the net present value (NPV) approach by using the Bennett Company data presented in Table 9.1. If the firm has a 10% cost of capital, the net present values for projects A (an annuity) and B (a mixed stream) can be calculated as shown on the time lines in Figure 9.2. These calculations result in net present values for projects A and B of $11,071 and $10,924, respectively. Both projects are acceptable, because the net present value of each is greater than $0. If the projects were being ranked, however, project A would be considered superior to B, because it has a higher net present value than that of B ($11,071 versus $10,924).

Calculator Use   The preprogrammed NPV function in a financial calculator can be used to simplify the NPV calculation. The keystrokes for project A—the annuity—typically are as shown at left. Note that because project A is an annuity, only its first cash inflow, $CF_1 = 14000$, is input, followed by its frequency, $N = 5$.

FIGURE 9.2   **Calculation of NPVs for Bennett Company's Capital Expenditure Alternatives**
Time lines depicting the cash flows and NPV calculations for projects A and B

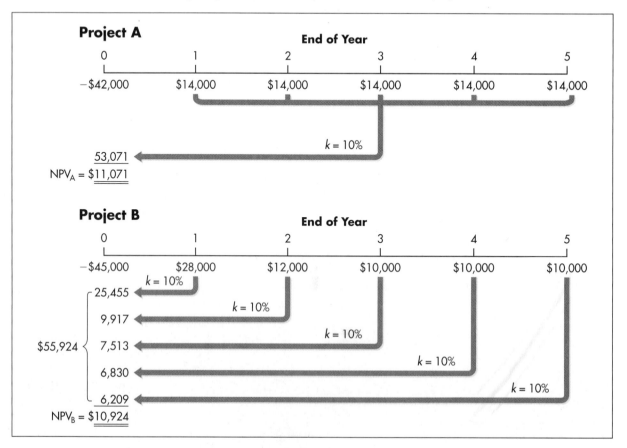

Project B

Input	Function
-45000	CF₀
28000	CF₁
12000	CF₂
10000	CF₃
3	N
10	I
	NPV

Solution
10,924.40

The keystrokes for project B—the mixed stream—are as shown at left. Because the last three cash inflows for project B are the same ($CF_3 = CF_4 = CF_5 = 10000$), after inputting the first of these cash inflows, CF_3, we merely input its frequency, $N = 3$.

The calculated NPVs for projects A and B of $11,071 and $10,924, respectively, agree with the NPVs cited above.

Spreadsheet Use   The NPVs can be calculated as shown on the following Excel spreadsheet.

	A	B	C
1	DETERMINING THE NET PRESENT VALUE		
2	Firm's cost of capital		10%
3		Year-End Cash Flow	
4	Year	Project A	Project B
5	0	$ (42,000)	$ (45,000)
6	1	$ 14,000	$ 28,000
7	2	$ 14,000	$ 12,000
8	3	$ 14,000	$ 10,000
9	4	$ 14,000	$ 10,000
10	5	$ 14,000	$ 10,000
11	NPV	$ 11,071	$ 10,924
12	Choice of project		Project A

Entry in Cell B11 is
=NPV(C2,B6:B10)+B5
Copy the entry in Cell B11 to Cell C11.
Entry in Cell C12 is IF(B11>C11,B4,C4).

REVIEW QUESTIONS

9–4   How is the *net present value (NPV)* calculated for a project with a *conventional cash flow pattern?*

9–5   What are the acceptance criteria for NPV? How are they related to the firm's market value?

LG4   9.4 | Internal Rate of Return (IRR)

internal rate of return (IRR)
A sophisticated capital budgeting technique; the discount rate that equates the NPV of an investment opportunity with $0 (because the present value of cash inflows equals the initial investment); it is the compound annual rate of return that the firm will earn if it invests in the project and receives the given cash inflows.

The *internal rate of return (IRR)* is probably the most widely used *sophisticated capital budgeting technique*. However, it is considerably more difficult than NPV to calculate by hand. The **internal rate of return (IRR)** is the discount rate that equates the NPV of an investment opportunity with $0 (because the present value of cash inflows equals the initial investment). It is the compound annual rate of return that the firm will earn if it invests in the project and receives the given cash inflows. Mathematically, the IRR is the value of k in Equation 9.1 that causes NPV to equal $0.

$$\$0 = \sum_{t=1}^{n} \frac{CF_t}{(1 + IRR)^t} - CF_0 \qquad (9.2)$$

Problems

P9–1   Payback period   Jordan Enterprises is considering a capital expenditure that requires an initial investment of $42,000 and returns after-tax cash inflows of $7,000 per year for 10 years. The firm has a maximum acceptable payback period of 8 years.

a. Determine the *payback period* for this project.
b. Should the company accept the project? Why or why not?

P9–2   Payback comparisons   Nova Products has a 5-year maximum acceptable payback period. The firm is considering the purchase of a new machine and must choose between two alternative ones. The first machine requires an initial investment of $14,000 and generates annual after-tax cash inflows of $3,000 for each of the next 7 years. The second machine requires an initial investment of $21,000 and provides an annual cash inflow after taxes of $4,000 for 20 years.

a. Determine the *payback period* for each machine.
b. Comment on the acceptability of the machines, assuming that they are independent projects.
c. Which machine should the firm accept? Why?
d. Do the machines in this problem illustrate any of the weaknesses of using payback? Discuss.

P9–3   Choosing between two projects with acceptable payback periods   Shell Camping Gear, Inc., is considering two mutually exclusive projects. Each requires an initial investment of $100,000. John Shell, president of the company, has set a maximum payback period of 4 years. The after-tax cash inflows associated with each project are as follows:

	Cash inflows (CF_t)	
Year	Project A	Project B
1	$10,000	$40,000
2	20,000	30,000
3	30,000	20,000
4	40,000	10,000
5	20,000	20,000

a. Determine the *payback period* of each project.
b. Because they are mutually exclusive, Shell must choose one. Which should the company invest in?
c. Explain why one of the projects is a better choice than the other.

P9–4   NPV   Calculate the *net present value (NPV)* for the following 20-year projects. Comment on the acceptability of each. Assume that the firm has an opportunity cost of 14%.

a. Initial investment is $10,000; cash inflows are $2,000 per year.
b. Initial investment is $25,000; cash inflows are $3,000 per year.
c. Initial investment is $30,000; cash inflows are $5,000 per year.

LG3

BASIC

P9–5 NPV for varying costs of capital   Dane Cosmetics is evaluating a new fragrance-mixing machine. The machine requires an initial investment of $24,000 and will generate after-tax cash inflows of $5,000 per year for 8 years. For each of the costs of capital listed, (1) calculate the *net present value (NPV)*, (2) indicate whether to accept or reject the machine, and (3) explain your decision.
  a. The cost of capital is 10%.
  b. The cost of capital is 12%.
  c. The cost of capital is 14%.

LG3

INTERMEDIATE

P9–6 Net present value—Independent projects   Using a 14% cost of capital, calculate the *net present value* for each of the independent projects shown in the following table, and indicate whether each is acceptable.

	Project A	Project B	Project C	Project D	Project E
Initial investment (CF_0)	$26,000	$500,000	$170,000	$950,000	$80,000
Year (t)			Cash inflows (CF_t)		
1	$4,000	$100,000	$20,000	$230,000	$ 0
2	4,000	120,000	19,000	230,000	0
3	4,000	140,000	18,000	230,000	0
4	4,000	160,000	17,000	230,000	20,000
5	4,000	180,000	16,000	230,000	30,000
6	4,000	200,000	15,000	230,000	0
7	4,000		14,000	230,000	50,000
8	4,000		13,000	230,000	60,000
9	4,000		12,000		70,000
10	4,000		11,000		

LG3

CHALLENGE

P9–7 NPV   Simes Innovations, Inc., is negotiating to purchase exclusive rights to manufacture and market a solar-powered toy car. The car's inventor has offered Simes the choice of either a one-time payment of $1,500,000 today or a series of 5 year-end payments of $385,000.
  a. If Simes has a cost of capital of 9%, which form of payment should the company choose?
  b. What yearly payment would make the two offers identical in value at a cost of capital of 9%?
  c. Would your answer to part **a** of this problem be different if the yearly payments were made at the beginning of each year? Show what difference, if any, that change in timing would make to the present value calculation.
  d. The after-tax cash inflows associated with this purchase are projected to amount to $250,000 per year for 15 years. Will this factor change the firm's decision about how to fund the initial investment?

LG3

CHALLENGE

P9–8 NPV and maximum return   A firm can purchase a fixed asset for a $13,000 initial investment. The asset generates an annual after-tax cash inflow of $4,000 for 4 years.
  a. Determine the *net present value (NPV)* of the asset, assuming that the firm has a 10% cost of capital. Is the project acceptable?

b. Determine the maximum required rate of return (closest whole-percentage rate) that the firm can have and still accept the asset. Discuss this finding in light of your response in part **a.**

P9–9 NPV—Mutually exclusive projects   Hook Industries is considering the replacement of one of its old drill presses. Three alternative replacement presses are under consideration. The relevant cash flows associated with each are shown in the following table. The firm's cost of capital is 15%.

	Press A	Press B	Press C
Initial investment (CF_0)	$85,000	$60,000	$130,000
Year (t)		Cash inflows (CF_t)	
1	$18,000	$12,000	$50,000
2	18,000	14,000	30,000
3	18,000	16,000	20,000
4	18,000	18,000	20,000
5	18,000	20,000	20,000
6	18,000	25,000	30,000
7	18,000	—	40,000
8	18,000	—	50,000

a. Calculate the *net present value (NPV)* of each press.
b. Using NPV, evaluate the acceptability of each press.
c. Rank the presses from best to worst using NPV.

P9–10 Payback and NPV   Neil Corporation has three projects under consideration. The cash flows for each project are shown in the following table. The firm has a 16% cost of capital.

	Project A	Project B	Project C
Initial investment (CF_0)	$40,000	$40,000	$40,000
Year (t)		Cash inflows (CF_t)	
1	$13,000	$ 7,000	$19,000
2	13,000	10,000	16,000
3	13,000	13,000	13,000
4	13,000	16,000	10,000
5	13,000	19,000	7,000

a. Calculate each project's *payback period*. Which project is preferred according to this method?
b. Calculate each project's *net present value (NPV)*. Which project is preferred according to this method?
c. Comment on your findings in parts **a** and **b,** and recommend the best project. Explain your recommendation.

P9–11 **Internal rate of return** For each of the projects shown in the following table, calculate the *internal rate of return (IRR)*. Then indicate, for each project, the maximum cost of capital that the firm could have and still find the IRR acceptable.

	Project A	Project B	Project C	Project D
Initial investment (CF_0)	$90,000	$490,000	$20,000	$240,000
Year (*t*)		Cash inflows (CF_t)		
1	$20,000	$150,000	$7,500	$120,000
2	25,000	150,000	7,500	100,000
3	30,000	150,000	7,500	80,000
4	35,000	150,000	7,500	60,000
5	40,000	—	7,500	—

P9–12 **IRR—Mutually exclusive projects** Bell Manufacturing is attempting to choose the better of two mutually exclusive projects for expanding the firm's warehouse capacity. The relevant cash flows for the projects are shown in the following table. The firm's cost of capital is 15%.

	Project X	Project Y
Initial investment (CF_0)	$500,000	$325,000
Year (*t*)	Cash inflows (CF_t)	
1	$100,000	$140,000
2	120,000	120,000
3	150,000	95,000
4	190,000	70,000
5	250,000	50,000

a. Calculate the IRR to the nearest whole percent for each of the projects.
b. Assess the acceptability of each project on the basis of the IRRs found in part **a.**
c. Which project, on this basis, is preferred?

P9–13 **IRR, investment life, and cash inflows** Oak Enterprises accepts projects earning more than the firm's 15% cost of capital. Oak is currently considering a 10-year project that provides annual cash inflows of $10,000 and requires an initial investment of $61,450. (*Note:* All amounts are after taxes.)
a. Determine the IRR of this project. Is it acceptable?
b. Assuming that the cash inflows continue to be $10,000 per year, how many *additional years* would the flows have to continue to make the project acceptable (that is, to make it have an IRR of 15%)?
c. With the given life, initial investment, and cost of capital, what is the minimum annual cash inflow that the firm should accept?

P9–14 NPV and IRR Benson Designs has prepared the following estimates for a long-term project it is considering. The initial investment is $18,250, and the project is expected to yield after-tax cash inflows of $4,000 per year for 7 years. The firm has a 10% cost of capital.

a. Determine the *net present value (NPV)* for the project.
b. Determine the *internal rate of return (IRR)* for the project.
c. Would you recommend that the firm accept or reject the project? Explain your answer.

P9–15 NPV, with rankings Botany Bay, Inc., a maker of casual clothing, is considering four projects. Because of past financial difficulties, the company has a high cost of capital at 15%. Which of these projects would be acceptable under those cost circumstances?

	Project A	Project B	Project C	Project D
Initial investment (CF_0)	$50,000	$100,000	$80,000	$180,000
Year (t)		Cash inflows (CF_t)		
1	$20,000	$35,000	$20,000	$100,000
2	20,000	50,000	40,000	80,000
3	20,000	50,000	60,000	60,000

a. Calculate the NPV of each project, using a cost of capital of 15%.
b. Rank acceptable projects by NPV.
c. Calculate the IRR of each project and use it to determine the highest cost of capital at which all of the projects would be acceptable.

P9–16 All techniques, conflicting rankings Nicholson Roofing Materials, Inc., is considering two mutually exclusive projects, each with an initial investment of $150,000. The company's board of directors has set a maximum 4-year payback requirement and has set its cost of capital at 9%. The cash inflows associated with the two projects are as follows:

	Cash inflows (CF_t)	
Year	Project A	Project B
1	$45,000	$75,000
2	45,000	60,000
3	45,000	30,000
4	45,000	30,000
5	45,000	30,000
6	45,000	30,000

a. Calculate the *payback period* for each project.
b. Calculate the NPV of each project at 0%.
c. Calculate the NPV of each project at 9%.
d. Derive the IRR of each project.
e. Rank the projects by each of the techniques used. Make and justify a recommendation.

P9–17 **Payback, NPV, and IRR**   Rieger International is attempting to evaluate the feasibility of investing $95,000 in a piece of equipment that has a 5-year life. The firm has estimated the *cash inflows* associated with the proposal as shown in the following table. The firm has a 12% cost of capital.

Year (t)	Cash inflows (CF_t)
1	$20,000
2	25,000
3	30,000
4	35,000
5	40,000

a. Calculate the *payback period* for the proposed investment.
b. Calculate the *net present value (NPV)* for the proposed investment.
c. Calculate the *internal rate of return (IRR)*, rounded to the nearest whole percent, for the proposed investment.
d. Evaluate the acceptability of the proposed investment using NPV and IRR. What recommendation would you make relative to implementation of the project? Why?

P9–18 **NPV, IRR, and NPV profiles**   Thomas Company is considering two mutually exclusive projects. The firm, which has a 12% cost of capital, has estimated its cash flows as shown in the following table.

	Project A	Project B
Initial investment (CF_0)	$130,000	$85,000
Year (t)	Cash inflows (CF_t)	
1	$25,000	$40,000
2	35,000	35,000
3	45,000	30,000
4	50,000	10,000
5	55,000	5,000

a. Calculate the NPV of each project, and assess its acceptability.
b. Calculate the IRR for each project, and assess its acceptability.
c. Draw the *NPV profiles* for both projects on the same set of axes.
d. Evaluate and discuss the rankings of the two projects on the basis of your findings in parts **a, b,** and **c.**
e. Explain your findings in part **d** in light of the pattern of cash inflows associated with each project.

P9–19 **All techniques—Decision among mutually exclusive investments**   Pound Industries is attempting to select the best of three mutually exclusive projects. The initial investment and after-tax cash inflows associated with these projects are shown in the table at the top of page 444.

Cash flows	Project A	Project B	Project C
Initial investment (CF_0)	$60,000	$100,000	$110,000
Cash inflows (CF_t), $t = 1$ to 5	$20,000	$ 31,500	$ 32,500

a. Calculate the *payback period* for each project.
b. Calculate the *net present value (NPV)* of each project, assuming that the firm has a cost of capital equal to 13%.
c. Calculate the *internal rate of return (IRR)* for each project.
d. Draw the *net present value profiles* for both projects on the same set of axes, and discuss any conflict in ranking that may exist between NPV and IRR.
e. Summarize the preferences dictated by each measure, and indicate which project you would recommend. Explain why.

P9–20 **All techniques with NPV profile—Mutually exclusive projects**   Projects A and B, of equal risk, are alternatives for expanding Rosa Company's capacity. The firm's cost of capital is 13%. The cash flows for each project are shown in the following table.

	Project A	Project B
Initial investment (CF_0)	$80,000	$50,000
Year (t)	Cash inflows (CF_t)	
1	$15,000	$15,000
2	20,000	15,000
3	25,000	15,000
4	30,000	15,000
5	35,000	15,000

a. Calculate each project's *payback period*.
b. Calculate the *net present value (NPV)* for each project.
c. Calculate the *internal rate of return (IRR)* for each project.
d. Draw the *net present value profiles* for both projects on the same set of axes, and discuss any conflict in ranking that may exist between NPV and IRR.
e. Summarize the preferences dictated by each measure, and indicate which project you would recommend. Explain why.

P9–21 **Integrative—Complete investment decision**   Wells Printing is considering the purchase of a new printing press. The total installed cost of the press is $2.2 million. This outlay would be partially offset by the sale of an existing press. The old press has zero book value, cost $1 million 10 years ago, and can be sold currently for $1.2 million before taxes. As a result of acquisition of the new press, sales in each of the next 5 years are expected to be $1.6 million higher than with the existing press, but product costs (excluding depreciation) will represent 50% of sales. The new press will not affect the firm's net working capital requirements. The new press will be depreciated under MACRS using a 5-year recovery period (see Table 3.2 on page 106). The firm is subject to a 40% tax rate. Wells Printing's cost of capital is 11%. (*Note:* Assume that both the old and the new press will have terminal values of $0 at the end of year 6.)

a. Determine the *initial investment* required by the new press.

b. Determine the *operating cash inflows* attributable to the new press. (*Note:* Be sure to consider the depreciation in year 6.)

c. Determine the *payback period*.

d. Determine the *net present value (NPV)* and the *internal rate of return (IRR)* related to the proposed new press.

e. Make a recommendation to accept or reject the new press, and justify your answer.

P9–22   Integrative—Investment decision   Holliday Manufacturing is considering the replacement of an existing machine. The new machine costs $1.2 million and requires installation costs of $150,000. The existing machine can be sold currently for $185,000 before taxes. It is 2 years old, cost $800,000 new, and has a $384,000 book value and a remaining useful life of 5 years. It was being depreciated under MACRS using a 5-year recovery period (see Table 3.2 on page 106) and therefore has the final 4 years of depreciation remaining. If it is held for 5 more years, the machine's market value at the end of year 5 will be $0. Over its 5-year life, the new machine should reduce operating costs by $350,000 per year. The new machine will be depreciated under MACRS using a 5-year recovery period (see Table 3.2 on page 106). The new machine can be sold for $200,000 net of removal and cleanup costs at the end of 5 years. An increased investment in net working capital of $25,000 will be needed to support operations if the new machine is acquired. Assume that the firm has adequate operating income against which to deduct any loss experienced on the sale of the existing machine. The firm has a 9% cost of capital and is subject to a 40% tax rate.

a. Develop the *relevant cash flows* needed to analyze the proposed replacement.

b. Determine the *net present value (NPV)* of the proposal.

c. Determine the *internal rate of return (IRR)* of the proposal.

d. Make a recommendation to accept or reject the replacement proposal, and justify your answer.

e. What is the highest cost of capital that the firm could have and still accept the proposal? Explain.

P9–23   ETHICS PROBLEM   Gap, Inc., is trying to incorporate human resource and supplier considerations into its management decision making. Here is Gap's report of findings from its most recent Social Responsibility Report:

> Because factory owners sometimes try to hide violations, Gap emphasizes training for factory managers. However, due to regional differences, the training varies from one site to another. The report notes that 10 to 25 percent of workers in China, Taiwan, and Saipan have been harassed and humiliated. Less than half of the factories in sub-Saharan Africa have adequate worker safety regulations and infrastructure. In Mexico, Latin America, and the Caribbean, 25 to 50 percent of the suppliers fail to pay even the minimum wage.

Calvert Group, Ltd., a mutual fund family that focuses on "socially responsible investing," had this to say about the impact of Gap's report:

> With revenues of $15.9 billion and over 300,000 employees worldwide, Gap leads the U.S. apparel sector and has contracts with over 3,000 factories globally. Calvert has been in dialogue with Gap for about five years, the last two as part of the Working Group.
>
> Gap's supplier monitoring program focuses on remediation, because its suppliers produce for multiple apparel companies and would likely move their capacity to different clients rather than adopt conditions deemed too demanding. About one-third of the factories Gap examined comfortably met Gap's criteria, another third had barely acceptable conditions, and the final third missed the minimum standards. Gap terminated contracts with 136 factories where it found conditions to be beyond remediation.
>
> Increased transparency and disclosure are crucial in measuring a company's commitment to raising human rights standards and improving the lives of workers. Gap's report is an important first step in the direction of a model format that other companies can adapt.
>
> *Source:* www.calvert.com/news_newsArticle.asp?article=4612&image=cn .gif&keepleftnav= Calvert+News

If Gap were to aggressively pursue renegotiations with suppliers, based on this report, what is the likely effect on Gap's expenses in the next 5 years? In your opinion, what would be the impact on its stock price in the immediate future? After 10 years?

Chapter 9 Case: Making Norwich Tool's Lathe Investment Decision

Norwich Tool, a large machine shop, is considering replacing one of its lathes with either of two new lathes—lathe A or lathe B. Lathe A is a highly automated, computer-controlled lathe; lathe B is a less expensive lathe that uses standard technology. To analyze these alternatives, Mario Jackson, a financial analyst, prepared estimates of the initial investment and incremental (relevant) cash inflows associated with each lathe. These are shown in the following table.

	Lathe A	Lathe B
Initial investment (CF_0)	$660,000	$360,000
Year (t)	Cash inflows (CF_t)	
1	$128,000	$ 88,000
2	182,000	120,000
3	166,000	96,000
4	168,000	86,000
5	450,000	207,000

Note that Mario plans to analyze both lathes over a 5-year period. At the end of that time, the lathes would be sold, thus accounting for the large fifth-year cash inflows.

Mario believes that the two lathes are equally risky and that the acceptance of either of them will not change the firm's overall risk. He therefore decides to apply the firm's 13% cost of capital when analyzing the lathes. Norwich Tool requires all projects to have a maximum payback period of 4.0 years.

TO DO

a. Use the *payback period* to assess the acceptability and relative ranking of each lathe.
b. Assuming equal risk, use the following sophisticated capital budgeting techniques to assess the acceptability and relative ranking of each lathe:
(1) Net present value (NPV).
(2) Internal rate of return (IRR).
c. Summarize the preferences indicated by the techniques used in parts **a** and **b**. Do the projects have conflicting rankings?
d. Draw the *net present value profiles* for both projects on the same set of axes, and discuss any conflict in rankings that may exist between NPV and IRR. Explain any observed conflict in terms of the relative differences in the magnitude and timing of each project's cash flows.
e. Use your findings in parts **a** through **d** to indicate, on both (1) a theoretical basis and (2) a practical basis, which lathe would be preferred. Explain any difference in recommendations.

Spreadsheet Exercise

The Drillago Company is involved in searching for locations in which to drill for oil. The firm's current project requires an initial investment of $15 million and has an estimated life of 10 years. The expected future cash inflows for the project are as follows:

Year	Cash inflows
1	$ 600,000
2	1,000,000
3	1,000,000
4	2,000,000
5	3,000,000
6	3,500,000
7	4,000,000
8	6,000,000
9	8,000,000
10	12,000,000

The firm's current cost of capital is 13%.

TO DO

Create a spreadsheet to answer the following:

a. Calculate the project's *net present value (NPV)*. Is the project acceptable under the NPV technique? Explain.

b. Calculate the project's *internal rate of return (IRR)*. Is the project acceptable under the IRR technique? Explain.

c. In this case, did the two methods produce the same results? Generally, is there a preference between the NPV and IRR techniques? Explain.

d. Calculate the *payback period* for the project. If the firm usually accepts projects that have payback periods between 1 and 7 years, is this project acceptable?

Group Exercise

This assignment continues the work begun in Chapter 8 by taking a closer look at the numbers initially estimated for capital projects. Your work for this exercise will follow a similar pattern. You will take the two projects you designed in the previous chapter and begin to choose which will be implemented according to several criteria. Some of the cash flow numbers you developed in Chapter 8 may have to be modified to allow for adequate analysis. This alteration is permitted, but your group should try to retain the flavor of the examples you designed previously.

TO DO

LG2 a. Begin the analysis of the competing projects by calculating the *payback period* for each project. (You must have two projects that both have positive payback periods, so a slight adjustment of the cash flows may be required here.)

LG3 b. Calculate the NPV for both projects. (Again, both projects should have a NPV that is greater than zero.) The crucial step in this part of the exercise is to apply an accurate discount rate. Your group should choose this rate (typically, the cost of capital) and, more important, defend its use. In other words, explain why you used the given discount rate to calculate the NPVs of the projects and why it makes sense given the current interest rate environment. Completion of this task must include a simple *NPV profile*.

LG4 c. Calculate the IRR for both projects.

LG6 d. Choose the project to be implemented based on all three techniques from parts **a, b,** and **c.** Your analysis must include an interpretation and evaluation of all three techniques. (This choice will be revisited in Chapter 10, which will provide more complete information.)

Web Exercise

Many Web sites offer financial calculators and tutorials with varying degrees of detail. In this exercise, you will evaluate a Web site in terms of its focus on NPV and IRR.

TO DO

a. Direct your browser to www.investopedia.com/default.asp. The best way to begin is to search for NPV in this Web site's dedicated search engine. Follow the links to the definition and then tutorials. Next, do the same for IRR.

b. Summarize how each topic was handled on this Web site, and compare and contrast how this site handled these topics relative to how this textbook covers the same material. What aspects of the Web site did you like, and why? What didn't you like?

that would result in unused production capacity that could be used to perform contract manufacturing for another firm, and (2) the project's computerized control system could, with some modification, control two other machines, thereby reducing labor cost, without affecting operation of the new project.

Bennett's management estimated the NPV of the contract manufacturing over the 2 years following implementation of project B to be $1,500 and the NPV of the computer control sharing to be $2,000. Management felt there was a 60% chance that the contract manufacturing option would be exercised and only a 30% chance that the computer control sharing option would be exercised. The combined value of these two real options would be the sum of their expected values.

$$\text{Value of real options for project B} = (0.60 \times \$1,500) + (0.30 \times \$2,000)$$
$$= \$900 + \$600 = \$1,500$$

Substituting the $1,500 real options value along with the traditional NPV of $10,924 for project B (from Table 10.1) into Equation 10.7, we get the strategic NPV for project B.

$$\text{NPV}_{\text{strategic}} = \$10,924 + \$1,500 = \underline{\$12,424}$$

Bennett Company's project B therefore has a strategic NPV of $12,424, which is above its traditional NPV and now exceeds project A's NPV of $11,071. Clearly, recognition of project B's real options improved its NPV (from $10,924 to $12,424) and causes it to be preferred over project A (NPV of $12,424 for B > NPV of $11,071 for A), which has no real options embedded in it.   ■

It is important to realize that the recognition of attractive real options when determining NPV could cause an otherwise unacceptable project ($\text{NPV}_{\text{traditional}} <$ $0) to become acceptable ($\text{NPV}_{\text{strategic}} > \$0$). The failure to recognize the value of real options could therefore cause management to reject projects that are acceptable. Although doing so requires more strategic thinking and analysis, it is important for the financial manager to identify and incorporate real options in the NPV process. The procedures for doing this efficiently are emerging, and the use of the strategic NPV that incorporates real options is expected to become more commonplace in the future.

Capital Rationing

Hint Because everyone in the firm knows that long-term funds are rationed and they want a portion of them, there is *intense competition* for those funds. This competition increases the need for the firm to be objective and proficient in its analysis. Knowing how to use the techniques discussed in this chapter to justify your needs will help you get your share of the available long-term funds.

Firms commonly operate under *capital rationing*—they have more acceptable independent projects than they can fund. *In theory,* capital rationing should not exist. Firms should accept all projects that have positive NPVs (or IRRs > the cost of capital). However, *in practice,* most firms operate under capital rationing. Generally, firms attempt to isolate and select the best acceptable projects subject to a capital expenditure budget set by management. Research has found that management internally imposes capital expenditure constraints to avoid what it deems to be "excessive" levels of new financing, particularly debt. Although failing to fund all acceptable independent projects is theoretically inconsistent with the goal of maximizing owner wealth, here we will discuss capital rationing procedures because they are widely used in practice.

The objective of *capital rationing* is to select the group of projects that provides the *highest overall net present value* and does not require more dollars than are budgeted. As a prerequisite to capital rationing, the best of any mutually exclusive projects must be chosen and placed in the group of independent projects. Two basic approaches to project selection under capital rationing are discussed here.

Internal Rate of Return Approach

internal rate of return approach
An approach to capital rationing that involves graphing project IRRs in descending order against the total dollar investment to determine the group of acceptable projects.

investment opportunities schedule (IOS)
The graph that plots project IRRs in descending order against the total dollar investment.

The **internal rate of return approach** involves graphing project IRRs in descending order against the total dollar investment. This graph, which is discussed in more detail in Chapter 11, is called the **investment opportunities schedule (IOS)**. By drawing the cost-of-capital line and then imposing a budget constraint, the financial manager can determine the group of acceptable projects. The problem with this technique is that it does not guarantee the maximum dollar return to the firm. It merely provides a satisfactory solution to capital-rationing problems.

EXAMPLE

Tate Company, a fast-growing plastics company, is confronted with six projects competing for its fixed budget of $250,000. The initial investment and IRR for each project are as follows:

Project	Initial investment	IRR
A	$ 80,000	12%
B	70,000	20
C	100,000	16
D	40,000	8
E	60,000	15
F	110,000	11

The firm has a cost of capital of 10%. Figure 10.4 (see page 474) presents the IOS that results from ranking the six projects in descending order on the basis of their IRRs. According to the schedule, only projects B, C, and E should be accepted. Together they will absorb $230,000 of the $250,000 budget. Projects A and F are acceptable but cannot be chosen because of the budget constraint. Project D is not worthy of consideration; its IRR is less than the firm's 10% cost of capital.

The drawback of this approach is that there is no guarantee that the acceptance of projects B, C, and E will maximize *total dollar returns* and therefore owners' wealth. ■

Net Present Value Approach

net present value approach
An approach to capital rationing that is based on the use of present values to determine the group of projects that will maximize owners' wealth.

The **net present value approach** is based on the use of present values to determine the group of projects that will maximize owners' wealth. It is implemented by ranking projects on the basis of IRRs and then evaluating the present value of the benefits from each potential project to determine *the combination of projects with the highest overall present value*. This is the same as maximizing net present value, because the entire budget is viewed as the total initial investment. Any portion of the firm's budget that is not used does not increase the firm's value. At

FIGURE 10.4

Investment Opportunities Schedule
Investment opportunities schedule (IOS) for Tate Company projects

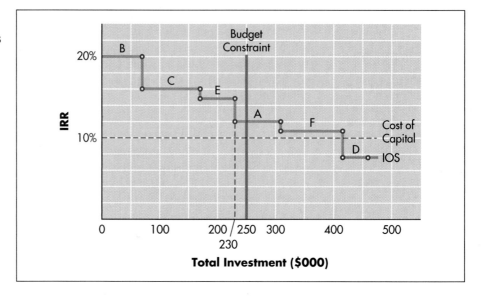

best, the unused money can be invested in marketable securities or returned to the owners in the form of cash dividends. In either case, the wealth of the owners is not likely to be enhanced.

EXAMPLE
The group of projects described in the preceding example is ranked in Table 10.5 on the basis of IRRs. The present value of the cash inflows associated with the projects is also included in the table. Projects B, C, and E, which together require $230,000, yield a present value of $336,000. However, if projects B, C, and A were implemented, the total budget of $250,000 would be used, and the present value of the cash inflows would be $357,000. This is greater than the return expected from selecting the projects on the basis of the highest IRRs. Implementing B, C, and A is preferable, because they maximize the present value for the given budget. *The firm's objective is to use its budget to generate the highest present value of inflows.* Assuming that any unused portion of the budget does not gain or lose money, the total NPV for projects B, C, and E would be $106,000 ($336,000 − $230,000), whereas the total NPV for projects B, C, and A would be $107,000 ($357,000 − $250,000). Selection of projects B, C, and A will therefore maximize NPV. ■

TABLE 10.5

Rankings for Tate Company Projects

Project	Initial investment	IRR	Present value of inflows at 10%	
B	$ 70,000	20%	$112,000	
C	100,000	16	145,000	
E	60,000	15	79,000	
A	80,000	12	100,000	
F	110,000	11	126,500	Cutoff point
D	40,000	8	36,000	(IRR < 10%)

REVIEW QUESTIONS

10–8   Explain why a mere comparison of the NPVs of unequal-lived, ongoing, mutually exclusive projects is inappropriate. Describe the *annualized net present value (ANPV) approach* for comparing unequal-lived, mutually exclusive projects.

10–9   What are *real options?* What are some major types of real options?

10–10 What is the difference between the *strategic NPV* and the *traditional NPV?* Do they always result in the same accept–reject decisions?

10–11 What is *capital rationing?* In theory, should capital rationing exist? Why does it frequently occur in practice?

10–12 Compare and contrast the *internal rate of return approach* and the *net present value approach* to capital rationing. Which is better? Why?

Summary

Focus on Value

Not all capital budgeting projects have the same level of risk as the firm's existing portfolio of projects. In addition, mutually exclusive projects often possess differing levels of risk. The financial manager must therefore adjust projects for differences in risk when evaluating their acceptability. Without such adjustment, management could mistakenly accept projects that destroy shareholder value or could reject projects that create shareholder value. To ensure that neither of these outcomes occurs, the financial manager must make sure that only those projects that create shareholder value are recommended.

Risk-adjusted discount rates (RADRs) provide a mechanism for adjusting the discount rate so that it is consistent with the risk–return preferences of market participants and thereby with accepting only value-creating projects. Procedures for comparing projects with unequal lives, procedures for explicitly recognizing real options embedded in capital projects, and procedures for selecting projects under capital rationing enable the financial manager to refine the capital budgeting process further. These procedures, along with risk-adjustment techniques, should enable the financial manager to make capital budgeting decisions that are consistent with the firm's goal of **maximizing stock price.**

Review of Learning Goals

LG1 Understand the importance of recognizing risk in the analysis of capital budgeting projects. The cash flows associated with capital budgeting projects typically have different levels of risk, and the acceptance of a project generally affects the firm's overall risk. Thus it is important to incorporate risk considerations in capital budgeting. Various behavioral approaches can be used to get a "feel" for the level of project risk, whereas other approaches explicitly recognize project risk in the analysis of capital budgeting projects.

LG2 Discuss breakeven cash inflow, sensitivity and scenario analysis, and simulation as behavioral approaches for dealing with risk. Risk in capital budgeting is the degree of variability of cash flows. Finding the breakeven cash inflow and estimating the probability that it will be realized make up one behavioral approach for assessing capital budgeting risk. Sensitivity analysis and scenario analysis are also behavioral approaches for capturing the variability of cash inflows and NPVs. Simulation is a statistically based approach that results in a probability distribution of project returns.

LG3 **Review the unique risks that multinational companies face.** Although the basic capital budgeting techniques are the same for multinational and purely domestic companies, firms that operate in several countries must also deal with exchange rate and political risks, tax law differences, transfer pricing, and strategic issues.

LG4 **Describe the determination and use of risk-adjusted discount rates (RADRs), portfolio effects, and the practical aspects of RADRs.** The risk of a project whose initial investment is known with certainty is embodied in the present value of its cash inflows, using NPV. Two opportunities to adjust the present value of cash inflows for risk exist—adjust the cash inflows or adjust the discount rate. Because adjusting the cash inflows is highly subjective, adjusting discount rates is more popular. The RADRs use a market-based adjustment of the discount rate to calculate NPV. The RADR is closely linked to CAPM, but because real corporate assets are generally not traded in an efficient market, the CAPM cannot be applied directly to capital budgeting. Instead, firms develop some CAPM-type relationship to link a project's risk to its required return, which is used as the discount rate. Often, for convenience, firms will rely on total risk as an approximation for relevant risk when estimating required project returns. RADRs are commonly used in practice, because decision makers prefer rates of return and find them easy to estimate and apply.

LG5 **Select the best of a group of unequal-lived, mutually exclusive projects using annualized net present values (ANPVs).** The ANPV approach is the most efficient method of comparing ongoing, mutually exclusive projects that have unequal usable lives. It converts the NPV of each unequal-lived project into an equivalent annual amount—its ANPV. The ANPV can be calculated using financial tables, a financial calculator, or a spreadsheet. The project with the highest ANPV is best.

LG6 **Explain the role of real options and the objective and procedures for selecting projects under capital rationing.** Real options are opportunities that are embedded in capital projects and that allow managers to alter their cash flow and risk in a way that affects project acceptability (NPV). By explicitly recognizing real options, the financial manager can find a project's strategic NPV. Some of the more common types of real options are abandonment, flexibility, growth, and timing options. The strategic NPV improves the quality of the capital budgeting decision.

Capital rationing exists when firms have more acceptable independent projects than they can fund. Although, in theory, capital rationing should not exist, in practice it commonly occurs. Its objective is to select from all acceptable projects the group that provides the highest overall net present value and does not require more dollars than are budgeted. The two basic approaches for choosing projects under capital rationing are the internal rate of return approach and the net present value approach. The NPV approach better achieves the objective of using the budget to generate the highest present value of inflows.

Self-Test Problem (Solution in Appendix B)

LG4

ST10–1 **Risk-adjusted discount rates**   CBA Company is considering two mutually exclusive projects, A and B. The following table shows the CAPM-type relationship between a risk index and the required return (RADR) applicable to CBA Company.

Risk index	Required return (RADR)
0.0	7.0% (risk-free rate, R_F)
0.2	8.0
0.4	9.0
0.6	10.0
0.8	11.0
1.0	12.0
1.2	13.0
1.4	14.0
1.6	15.0
1.8	16.0
2.0	17.0

Project data are shown as follows:

	Project A	Project B
Initial investment (CF_0)	$15,000	$20,000
Project life	3 years	3 years
Annual cash inflow (CF)	$7,000	$10,000
Risk index	0.4	1.8

a. Ignoring any differences in risk and assuming that the firm's cost of capital is 10%, calculate the *net present value (NPV)* of each project.
b. Use NPV to evaluate the projects, using *risk-adjusted discount rates (RADRs)* to account for risk.
c. Compare, contrast, and explain your findings in parts **a** and **b**.

Warm-Up Exercises

LG2

E10–1 Birkenstock's is considering an investment in a nylon-knitting machine. The machine requires an initial investment of $25,000, has a 5-year life, and has no residual value at the end of the 5 years. The company's cost of capital is 12%.

Known with less certainty are the actual after-tax cash inflows for each of the 5 years. The company has estimated expected cash inflows for three "states of nature": pessimistic, most likely, and optimistic. These expected cash inflows are listed below. Calculate the range for the NPV given each state of nature.

	Expected cash inflows		
Year	Pessimistic	Most likely	Optimistic
1	$5,500	$ 8,000	$10,500
2	6,000	9,000	12,000
3	7,500	10,500	14,500
4	6,500	9,500	11,500
5	4,500	6,500	7,500

LG2

E10–2 You wish to evaluate a project requiring an initial investment of $45,000 and having a useful life of 5 years. What minimum amount of annual cash inflow do you need if your firm has an 8% cost of capital? If the project is forecast to earn $12,500 per year over the 5 years, what is its IRR? Is the project acceptable?

LG4

E10–3 Like most firms in its industry, Yeastime Bakeries uses a subjective risk assessment tool of its own design. The tool is a simple index by which projects are ranked by level of perceived risk on a scale of 0–10. The scale is recreated below.

Risk	Required Return
0	4.0% (current risk-free rate)
1	4.5
2	5.0
3	5.5
4	6.0
5	6.5 (current IRR)
6	7.0
7	7.5
8	8.0
9	8.5
10	9.0

The firm is analyzing two projects based on their RADRs. Project Sourdough requires an initial investment of $12,500 and is assigned a risk index of 6.0. Project Greek Salad requires an initial investment of $7,500 and is assigned a risk index of 8.0. The two projects have 7-year lives. Sourdough is projected to generate cash inflows of $5,500 per year. Greek Salad is projected to generate cash inflows of $4,000 per year. Use each project's RADR to select the best project.

LG5

E10–4 Outcast, Inc., has hired you to advise the firm on a capital budgeting issue involving two unequal-lived, mutually exclusive projects, M and N. The cash flows for each project are presented in the table at the top of the facing page. Calculate the NPV and the *annualized net present value (ANPV)* for each project using the firm's cost of capital of 8%. Which project would you recommend?

	Project M	Project N
Initial investment	$35,000	$55,000
Year	Cash inflows	
1	$12,000	$18,000
2	25,000	15,000
3	30,000	25,000
4	—	10,000
5	—	8,000
6	—	5,000
7	—	5,000

LG6

E10–5   Longchamps Electric is faced with a capital budget of $150,000 for the coming year. It is considering six investment projects and has a cost of capital of 7%. The six projects are listed below, along with their initial investments and their IRRs. Using the data given, prepare an *investment opportunities schedule (IOS)*. Which projects does the IOS suggest should be funded? Does this group of projects maximize NPV? Explain.

Project	Initial investment	IRR
1	$75,000	8%
2	40,000	10
3	35,000	7
4	50,000	11
5	45,000	9
6	20,000	6

Problems

LG1

BASIC

P10–1   **Recognizing risk**   Caradine Corp., a media services firm with net earnings of $3,200,000 in the last year, is considering several projects.

Project	Initial investment	Details
A	$ 35,000	Replace existing office furnishings.
B	500,000	Purchase digital film-editing equipment for use with several existing accounts.
C	450,000	Develop proposal to bid for a $2,000,000 per year 10-year contract with the U.S. Navy, not now an account.
D	685,000	Purchase the exclusive rights to market a quality educational television program in syndication to local markets in the European Union, a part of the firm's existing business activities.

The media services business is cyclical and highly competitive. The board of directors has asked you, as chief financial officer, to do the following:

P10–6   Simulation   Ogden Corporation has compiled the following information on a capital expenditure proposal:

(1) The projected cash *inflows* are normally distributed with a mean of $36,000 and a standard deviation of $9,000.
(2) The projected cash *outflows* are normally distributed with a mean of $30,000 and a standard deviation of $6,000.
(3) The firm has an 11% cost of capital.
(4) The probability distributions of cash inflows and cash outflows are not expected to change over the project's 10-year life.

a. Describe how the foregoing data can be used to develop a simulation model for finding the net present value of the project.
b. Discuss the advantages of using a simulation to evaluate the proposed project.

P10–7   Risk-adjusted discount rates—Basic   Country Wallpapers is considering investing in one of three mutually exclusive projects, E, F, and G. The firm's cost of capital, k, is 15%, and the risk-free rate, R_F, is 10%. The firm has gathered the following basic cash flow and risk index data for each project.

	Project (j)		
	E	F	G
Initial investment (CF_0)	$15,000	$11,000	$19,000
Year (t)	Cash inflows (CF_t)		
1	$ 6,000	$ 6,000	$ 4,000
2	6,000	4,000	6,000
3	6,000	5,000	8,000
4	6,000	2,000	12,000
Risk index (RI_j)	1.80	1.00	0.60

a. Find the *net present value (NPV)* of each project using the firm's cost of capital. Which project is preferred in this situation?
b. The firm uses the following equation to determine the risk-adjusted discount rate, $RADR_j$, for each project j:

$$RADR_j = R_F + [RI_j \times (k - R_F)]$$

where

R_F = risk-free rate of return
RI_j = risk index for project j
k = cost of capital

Substitute each project's risk index into this equation to determine its RADR.

c. Use the RADR for each project to determine its *risk-adjusted NPV*. Which project is preferable in this situation?
d. Compare and discuss your findings in parts **a** and **c**. Which project do you recommend that the firm accept?

P10–8   Risk-adjusted discount rates—Tabular   After a careful evaluation of investment alternatives and opportunities, Masters School Supplies has developed a CAPM-type relationship linking a risk index to the required return (RADR), as shown in the following table.

Risk index	Required return (RADR)
0.0	7.0% (risk-free rate, R_F)
0.2	8.0
0.4	9.0
0.6	10.0
0.8	11.0
1.0	12.0
1.2	13.0
1.4	14.0
1.6	15.0
1.8	16.0
2.0	17.0

The firm is considering two mutually exclusive projects, A and B. Following are the data the firm has been able to gather about the projects.

	Project A	Project B
Initial investment (CF_0)	$20,000	$30,000
Project life	5 years	5 years
Annual cash inflow (CF)	$7,000	$10,000
Risk index	0.2	1.4

All the firm's cash inflows have already been adjusted for taxes.
a. Evaluate the projects using *risk-adjusted discount rates*.
b. Discuss your findings in part **a,** and recommend the preferred project.

P10–9   Risk-adjusted rates of return using CAPM   Centennial Catering, Inc., is considering two mutually exclusive investments. The company wishes to use a risk-adjusted rate of return in its analysis. Centennial's cost of capital (similar to the market return in CAPM) is 12%, and the current risk-free rate of return is 7%. Cash flows associated with the two projects are as follows:

	Project X	Project Y
Initial investment (CF_0)	$70,000	$78,000
Year (t)	Cash inflows (CF_t)	
1	$30,000	$22,000
2	30,000	32,000
3	30,000	38,000
4	30,000	46,000

a. Use a risk-adjusted rate of return approach to calculate the net present value of each project, given that project X has a RADR factor of 1.20 and project Y has a RADR factor of 1.40. The RADR factors are similar to project betas. (Use Equation 10.5 to calculate the required project return for each.)

b. Discuss your findings in part a, and recommend the preferred project.

LG4

BASIC

P10–10 Risk classes and RADR Moses Manufacturing is attempting to select the best of three mutually exclusive projects, X, Y, and Z. Although all the projects have 5-year lives, they possess differing degrees of risk. Project X is in class V, the highest-risk class; project Y is in class II, the below-average-risk class; and project Z is in class III, the average-risk class. The basic cash flow data for each project and the risk classes and risk-adjusted discount rates (RADRs) used by the firm are shown in the following tables.

	Project X	Project Y	Project Z
Initial investment (CF_0)	$180,000	$235,000	$310,000
Year (t)	Cash inflows (CF_t)		
1	$80,000	$50,000	$90,000
2	70,000	60,000	90,000
3	60,000	70,000	90,000
4	60,000	80,000	90,000
5	60,000	90,000	90,000

Risk Classes and RADRs		
Risk Class	Description	Risk-adjusted discount rate (RADR)
I	Lowest risk	10%
II	Below-average risk	13
III	Average risk	15
IV	Above-average risk	19
V	Highest risk	22

a. Find the risk-adjusted NPV for each project.

b. Which project, if any, would you recommend that the firm undertake?

LG5

INTERMEDIATE

P10–11 Unequal lives—ANPV approach Evans Industries wishes to select the best of three possible machines, each of which is expected to satisfy the firm's ongoing need for additional aluminum-extrusion capacity. The three machines—A, B, and C—are equally risky. The firm plans to use a 12% cost of capital to evaluate each of them. The initial investment and annual cash inflows over the life of each machine are shown in the table at the top of the facing page.

	Machine A	Machine B	Machine C
Initial investment (CF_0)	$92,000	$65,000	$100,500
Year (t)		Cash inflows (CF_t)	
1	$12,000	$10,000	$30,000
2	12,000	20,000	30,000
3	12,000	30,000	30,000
4	12,000	40,000	30,000
5	12,000	—	30,000
6	12,000	—	—

a. Calculate the NPV for each machine over its life. Rank the machines in descending order on the basis of NPV.
b. Use the *annualized net present value (ANPV)* approach to evaluate and rank the machines in descending order on the basis of ANPV.
c. Compare and contrast your findings in parts **a** and **b**. Which machine would you recommend that the firm acquire? Why?

P10–12 **Unequal lives—ANPV approach**   Portland Products is considering the purchase of one of three mutually exclusive projects for increasing production efficiency. The firm plans to use a 14% cost of capital to evaluate these equal-risk projects. The initial investment and annual cash inflows over the life of each project are shown in the following table.

	Project X	Project Y	Project Z
Initial investment (CF_0)	$78,000	$52,000	$66,000
Year (t)		Cash inflows (CF_t)	
1	$17,000	$28,000	$15,000
2	25,000	38,000	15,000
3	33,000	—	15,000
4	41,000	—	15,000
5	—	—	15,000
6	—	—	15,000
7	—	—	15,000
8	—	—	15,000

a. Calculate the NPV for each project over its life. Rank the projects in descending order on the basis of NPV.
b. Use the *annualized net present value (ANPV)* approach to evaluate and rank the projects in descending order on the basis of ANPV.
c. Compare and contrast your findings in parts **a** and **b**. Which project would you recommend that the firm purchase? Why?

and project Beta has an estimated life of 9 years. The following cash flow data have been prepared.

	Cash flows	
	Project Alpha	Project Beta
CF_0	−$5,500,000	−$6,500,000
CF_1	300,000	400,000
CF_2	500,000	600,000
CF_3	500,000	800,000
CF_4	550,000	1,100,000
CF_5	700,000	1,400,000
CF_6	800,000	2,000,000
CF_7	950,000	2,500,000
CF_8	1,000,000	2,000,000
CF_9	1,250,000	1,000,000
CF_{10}	1,500,000	
CF_{11}	2,000,000	
CF_{12}	2,500,000	

TO DO

Create a spreadsheet to answer the following questions.

a. Calculate the NPV for each project over its respective life. Rank the projects in descending order on the basis of NPV. Which one would you choose?
b. Use the *annualized net present value (ANPV) approach* to evaluate and rank the projects in descending order on the basis of ANPV. Which one would you choose?
c. Compare and contrast your findings in parts **a** and **b**. Which project would you recommend that the firm choose? Explain.

Group Exercise

This chapter refined the budgeting techniques of previous chapters to include the concept of risk in the analysis of capital investment proposals. Your firm will now revisit the work done in Chapters 8 and 9 and apply a measurement of risk to the previously computed cash flows.

TO DO

a. Create a variable or set of variables that will introduce risk—and therefore a lack of certainty regarding the estimated cash flows—for each of the two investment projects.
b. Using the variable(s) selected in part **a**, take each annual cash flow and assign three possible dollar amounts given three "states of the world": pessimistic, most likely, and optimistic. Let the dollar value you originally chose be the most likely amount, the pessimistic value be less than this amount, and the optimistic value be greater than this amount.

LG2   c. Calculate the *ranges* of the NPVs between the pessimistic and optimistic outcomes, and determine which of the two projects is riskier.

LG4   d. Develop a simplified RADR by adjusting the discount rate originally chosen for the different levels of risk calculated in part **c**, and calculate the *risk-adjusted NPV* for each project.

LG4   e. Using all of the analysis from Chapters 8, 9, and 10, and concentrating on the new risk-based information, choose which project your firm will implement and explain why. Be mindful that the reasons for the decision are as important as the choice of investment made by your group. View your final decision as an opportunity to defend your choice to a broader audience, perhaps the firm's board of directors.

Web Exercise

The concept of risk can have different meanings depending on the context. For example, *Webster's Dictionary* defines "risk" as the chance of injury, damage, or loss. In finance we define risk more generally to refer to a lack of certainty. This exercise will help you better understand different views of risk and how the science of risk analysis is used.

TO DO

a. Point your browser to www.hcra.harvard.edu/, the home page of the Harvard Center for Risk Analysis. Begin by scrolling down the list called Risk Quiz.

b. Read and summarize the About Us section. Note the continuation of the risk quiz ranked by states, with the most and fewest causes of death by states.

c. Click on the link for Risk in Perspective. The risk quiz continues.

d. Scroll down the page to the links of listed articles. Visit one and briefly summarize its contents. (These articles are brief and are meant to be applicable for a mainstream audience, so don't be intimidated by the connection to Harvard!)

Remember to check the book's Web site at

www.aw-bc.com/gitman

for additional resources, including additional Web exercises.

Integrative Case
3

Lasting Impressions Company

Lasting Impressions (LI) Company is a medium-sized commercial printer of promotional advertising brochures, booklets, and other direct-mail pieces. The firm's major clients are ad agencies based in New York and Chicago. The typical job is characterized by high quality and production runs of more than 50,000 units. LI has not been able to compete effectively with larger printers because of its existing older, inefficient presses. The firm is currently having problems cost-effectively meeting run length requirements as well as meeting quality standards.

The general manager has proposed the purchase of one of two large, six-color presses designed for long, high-quality runs. The purchase of a new press would enable LI to reduce its cost of labor and therefore the price to the client, putting the firm in a more competitive position. The key financial characteristics of the old press and of the two proposed presses are summarized in what follows.

Old press Originally purchased 3 years ago at an installed cost of $400,000, it is being depreciated under MACRS using a 5-year recovery period. The old press has a remaining economic life of 5 years. It can be sold today to net $420,000 before taxes; if it is retained, it can be sold to net $150,000 before taxes at the end of 5 years.

Press A This highly automated press can be purchased for $830,000 and will require $40,000 in installation costs. It will be depreciated under MACRS using a 5-year recovery period. At the end of the 5 years, the machine could be sold to net $400,000 before taxes. If this machine is acquired, it is anticipated that the following current account changes would result:

Cash	+ $ 25,400
Accounts receivable	+ 120,000
Inventories	− 20,000
Accounts payable	+ 35,000

Press B This press is not as sophisticated as press A. It costs $640,000 and requires $20,000 in installation costs. It will be depreciated under MACRS using a 5-year recovery period. At the end of 5 years, it can be sold to net $330,000 before taxes. Acquisition of this press will have no effect on the firm's net working capital investment.

Table 1

Earnings Before Depreciation, Interest, and Taxes for Lasting Impressions Company's Presses

Year	Old press	Press A	Press B
1	$120,000	$250,000	$210,000
2	120,000	270,000	210,000
3	120,000	300,000	210,000
4	120,000	330,000	210,000
5	120,000	370,000	210,000

The firm estimates that its earnings before depreciation, interest, and taxes with the old press and with press A or press B for each of the 5 years would be as shown in Table 1. The firm is subject to a 40% tax rate. The firm's cost of capital, k, applicable to the proposed replacement is 14%.

TO DO

a. For each of the two proposed replacement presses, determine:
   (1) Initial investment.
   (2) Operating cash inflows. (*Note:* Be sure to consider the depreciation in year 6.)
   (3) Terminal cash flow. (*Note:* This is at the end of year 5.)
b. Using the data developed in part **a,** find and depict on a time line the relevant cash flow stream associated with each of the two proposed replacement presses, assuming that each is terminated at the end of 5 years.
c. Using the data developed in part **b,** apply each of the following decision techniques:
   (1) Payback period. (*Note:* For year 5, use only the operating cash inflows—that is, exclude terminal cash flow—when making this calculation.)
   (2) Net present value (NPV).
   (3) Internal rate of return (IRR).
d. Draw *net present value profiles* for the two replacement presses on the same set of axes, and discuss conflicting rankings of the two presses, if any, resulting from use of NPV and IRR decision techniques.
e. Recommend which, if either, of the presses the firm should acquire if the firm has (1) unlimited funds or (2) capital rationing.
f. What is the impact on your recommendation of the fact that the operating cash inflows associated with press A are characterized as very risky in contrast to the low-risk operating cash inflows of press B?

PART FOUR

Long-Term Financial Decisions

11.1 | An Overview of the Cost of Capital

cost of capital
The rate of return that a firm must earn on the projects in which it invests to maintain its market value and attract funds.

The **cost of capital** is the rate of return that a firm must earn on the projects in which it invests to maintain the market value of its stock. It can also be thought of as the rate of return required by the market suppliers of capital to attract their funds to the firm. If risk is held constant, projects with a rate of return above the cost of capital will increase the value of the firm, and projects with a rate of return below the cost of capital will decrease the value of the firm.

The cost of capital is an extremely important financial concept. It acts as a major link between the firm's long-term investment decisions (discussed in Part 3) and the wealth of the owners as determined by investors in the marketplace. It is, in effect, the "magic number" that is used to decide whether a proposed corporate investment will increase or decrease the firm's stock price. Clearly, only those investments that are expected to increase stock price (NPV > $0, or IRR > cost of capital) would be recommended. Because of its key role in financial decision making, the importance of the cost of capital cannot be overemphasized.

Some Key Assumptions

The cost of capital is a dynamic concept affected by a variety of economic and firm-specific factors. To isolate the basic structure of the cost of capital, we make some key assumptions relative to risk and taxes:

business risk
The risk to the firm of being unable to cover operating costs.

financial risk
The risk to the firm of being unable to cover required financial obligations (interest, lease payments, preferred stock dividends).

1. **Business risk**—the risk to the firm of being unable to cover operating costs—*is assumed to be unchanged.* This assumption means that the firm's acceptance of a given project does not affect its ability to meet operating costs.
2. **Financial risk**—the risk to the firm of being unable to cover required financial obligations (interest, lease payments, preferred stock dividends)—*is assumed to be unchanged.* This assumption means that projects are financed in such a way that the firm's ability to meet required financing costs is unchanged. For an example of the catastrophic effect that inability to manage financial risk had on one company, WorldCom, see the *In Practice* box on the facing page.
3. After-tax costs are considered relevant. In other words, *the cost of capital is measured on an after-tax basis.* This assumption is consistent with the after-tax framework used to make capital budgeting decisions.

Hint Because of the positive relationship between risk and return, a firm's financing cost (cost of capital) will change if the acceptance of a project changes the firm's business or financial risk. The cost of capital can therefore be more easily measured by assuming that new projects do not change these risks.

The Basic Concept

target capital structure
The desired optimal mix of debt and equity financing that most firms attempt to maintain.

The cost of capital is estimated at a given point in time. It reflects the *expected average future cost of funds over the long run.* Although firms typically raise money in lumps, the cost of capital should reflect the interrelatedness of financing activities. For example, if a firm raises funds with debt (borrowing) today, it is likely that some form of equity, such as common stock, will have to be used the next time it needs funds. Most firms attempt to maintain a desired optimal mix of debt and equity financing. This mix is commonly called a **target capital structure**—a topic that will be addressed in Chapter 12. Here, it is sufficient to

In Practice FOCUS ON ETHICS

CREATIVE ACCOUNTING AND COST OF CAPITAL AT WORLDCOM

Cost of capital is the minimum rate of return on invested funds that a firm must earn in order to stay in business. However, this widely accepted definition of cost of capital was not what some executives at **WorldCom** had in mind when they embarked on the $11 billion accounting fraud that brought the $185 billion telecommunications giant to its knees in the summer of 2002.

The spectacular implosion of WorldCom has been by far the largest fraud and the biggest bankruptcy in corporate history. In the complaint filed in November 2002, the Securities and Exchange Commission alleged that several accounting executives at WorldCom from early 1999 until the spring of 2002 fraudulently manipulated its financial results by improperly reducing its operating expenses.

Many of the improper accounting entries were related to fees WorldCom paid to third-party telecommunication carriers to maintain sufficient network capacity. Anticipating fast growth in telecommunications services due to the expansion of the Internet, WorldCom entered into a number of long-term lease agreements with various third-party carriers to have the right to

access their networks. Many of these leases required WorldCom to make fixed monthly payments to the contracted company over the full term of the lease, regardless of whether WorldCom used all or only some of the capacity of the leased networks. These fees were properly recorded as operating expenses and reported as operating expenses on WorldCom's income statement.

However, these fixed payments became an increasingly large percentage of company revenues, cutting into operating margins and resulting in a decline in WorldCom's net income. Company management, including the CFO David Sullivan, knew that this decline in income could fail to meet the expectations of Wall Street analysts and result in a substantial decline of WorldCom's stock price.

Under increasing pressure from the management, accountants at WorldCom concealed the true magnitude of the lease costs: first, by improperly reducing loss reserves held against these costs, and then, after exhausting all reserves, by booking lease fees as capital expenditures. Accounting rules require that operating expenses are reported on a company's income statement and

subtracted from revenues in the period in which the expense is incurred or paid, thus affecting net income. Capital expenditures, on the other hand, are reported as capital assets on a company's balance sheet.

As a result of accounting gimmicks, WorldCom falsely portrayed itself as a profitable business and concealed the large losses it suffered. Because it kept its investment-grade credit rating, WorldCom was able to borrow large amounts of money at relatively low interest rates in the months preceding bankruptcy.

The SEC first estimated that fraudulent accounting at WorldCom resulted in inflating the pretax earnings by $3.8 billion during five quarters. More recent estimates indicate that accounting fraud was closer to $11 billion. By concealing its dire financial situation, the company, for a while, created the illusion of solvency, by which it lowered its cost of financing.

Source: SEC Amended Complaint Against Worldcom—Litigation Release: www.sec. gov/litigation/litreleases/lr17829.htm

■ *How did "creative accounting" at WorldCom affect its cost of capital?*

---

say that although firms raise money in lumps, they tend toward some desired *mix of financing*.

To capture the interrelatedness of financing assuming the presence of a target capital structure, we need to look at the *overall cost of capital* rather than the cost of the specific source of funds used to finance a given expenditure.

EXAMPLE   A firm is *currently* faced with an investment opportunity. Assume the following:

Best project available today

$$\text{Cost} = \$100,000$$
$$\text{Life} = 20 \text{ years}$$
$$\text{IRR} = 7\%$$

Cost of least-cost financing source available

$$\text{Debt} = 6\%$$

Because it can earn 7% on the investment of funds costing only 6%, the firm undertakes the opportunity. Imagine that *1 week later* a new investment opportunity is available:

Best project available 1 week later

$$\text{Cost} = \$100,000$$
$$\text{Life} = 20 \text{ years}$$
$$\text{IRR} = 12\%$$

Cost of least-cost financing source available

$$\text{Equity} = 14\%$$

In this instance, the firm rejects the opportunity, because the 14% financing cost is greater than the 12% expected return.

Were the firm's actions in the best interests of its owners? No; it accepted a project yielding a 7% return and rejected one with a 12% return. Clearly, there should be a better way, and there is: The firm can use a combined cost, which over the long run will yield better decisions. By weighting the cost of each source of financing by its *target proportion* in the firm's capital structure, the firm can obtain a *weighted average cost* that reflects the interrelationship of financing decisions. Assuming that a 50–50 mix of debt and equity is targeted, the weighted average cost here would be 10% [(0.50 × 6% debt) + (0.50 × 14% equity)]. With this cost, the first opportunity would have been rejected (7% IRR < 10% weighted average cost), and the second would have been accepted (12% IRR > 10% weighted average cost). Such an outcome would clearly be more desirable. ■

Specific Sources of Capital

This chapter focuses on finding the costs of specific sources of capital and combining them to determine the weighted average cost of capital. Our concern is only with the *long-term* sources of funds available to a business firm, because these sources supply the permanent financing. Long-term financing supports the firm's fixed-asset investments.[1] We assume throughout the chapter that such investments are selected by using appropriate capital budgeting techniques.

There are four basic sources of long-term funds for the business firm: long-term debt, preferred stock, common stock, and retained earnings. The right-hand side of the balance sheet on the facing page can be used to illustrate these sources:

---

1. The role of both long-term and short-term financing in supporting both fixed- and current-asset investments is addressed in Chapter 14. Suffice it to say that long-term funds are at minimum used to finance fixed assets.

Although not every firm will use all of these methods of financing, each firm is expected to have funds from some of these sources in its capital structure.

The *specific cost* of each source of financing is the *after-tax* cost of obtaining the financing *today*, not the historically based cost reflected by the existing financing on the firm's books. Techniques for determining the specific cost of each source of long-term funds are presented on the following pages. Although these techniques tend to develop precisely calculated values, the resulting values are at best *rough approximations* because of the numerous assumptions and forecasts that underlie them. Although we round calculated costs to the nearest 0.1 percent throughout this chapter, it is not unusual for practicing financial managers to use costs rounded to the nearest 1 percent because these values are merely estimates.

REVIEW QUESTIONS

11–1   What is the *cost of capital?* What role does it play in long-term investment decisions?

11–2   Why do we assume that *business risk* and *financial risk* are unchanged when evaluating the cost of capital? Discuss the implications of these assumptions on the acceptance and financing of new projects.

11–3   Why is the cost of capital measured on an *after-tax basis?* Why is use of a weighted average cost of capital rather than the cost of the specific source of funds recommended?

11–4   You have just been told, "Because we are going to finance this project with debt, its required rate of return must exceed the cost of debt." Do you agree or disagree? Explain.

LG2   11.2 | The Cost of Long-Term Debt

cost of long-term debt, k_i
The after-tax cost today of raising long-term funds through borrowing.

The **cost of long-term debt**, k_i, is the after-tax cost today of raising long-term funds through borrowing. For convenience, we typically assume that the funds are raised through the sale of bonds. In addition, as we did in Chapter 6, we assume that the bonds pay *annual* (rather than *semiannual*) interest.

Net Proceeds

net proceeds
Funds actually received from the sale of a security.

flotation costs
The total costs of issuing and selling a security.

Most corporate long-term debts are incurred through the sale of bonds. The **net proceeds** from the sale of a bond, or any security, are the funds that are actually received from the sale. **Flotation costs**—the total costs of issuing and selling a security—reduce the net proceeds from the sale. These costs apply to all public offerings of securities—debt, preferred stock, and common stock. They include two components: (1) *underwriting costs*—compensation earned by investment bankers for selling the security, and (2) *administrative costs*—issuer expenses such as legal, accounting, printing, and other expenses.

EXAMPLE

Duchess Corporation, a major hardware manufacturer, is contemplating selling $10 million worth of 20-year, 9% coupon (stated *annual* interest rate) bonds, each with a par value of $1,000. Because similar-risk bonds earn returns greater than 9%, the firm must sell the bonds for $980 to compensate for the lower coupon interest rate. The flotation costs are 2% of the par value of the bond ($0.02 \times \$1,000$), or $20. The *net proceeds* to the firm from the sale of each bond are therefore $960 ($980 − $20). ■

Before-Tax Cost of Debt

The before-tax cost of debt, k_d, for a bond can be obtained in any of three ways: quotation, calculation, or approximation.

Using Cost Quotations

Hint From the issuer's perspective, the IRR on a bond's cash flows is its *cost to maturity;* from the investor's perspective, the IRR on a bond's cash flows is its *yield to maturity* (YTM), as explained in Chapter 6. These two measures are conceptually similar, although their point of view is different.

When the net proceeds from sale of a bond equal its par value, the before-tax cost just equals the coupon interest rate. For example, a bond with a 10 percent coupon interest rate that nets proceeds equal to the bond's $1,000 par value would have a before-tax cost, k_d, of 10 percent.

A second quotation that is sometimes used is the *yield to maturity* (YTM) on a similar-risk bond[2] (see Chapter 6). For example, if a similar-risk bond has a YTM of 9.7 percent, this value can be used as the before-tax cost of debt, k_d.

Calculating the Cost

This approach finds the before-tax cost of debt by calculating the *internal rate of return (IRR)* on the bond cash flows. From the issuer's point of view, this value is the *cost to maturity* of the cash flows associated with the debt. The cost to maturity can be calculated by using a trial-and-error technique[3], a financial calculator, or an electronic spreadsheet. It represents the annual before-tax percentage cost of the debt.

EXAMPLE

In the preceding example, the net proceeds of a $1,000, 9% coupon interest rate, 20-year bond were found to be $960. The calculation of the annual cost is quite simple. The cash flow pattern is exactly the opposite of a conventional pattern; it

2. Generally, the yield to maturity of bonds with a similar "rating" is used. Bond ratings, which are published by independent agencies, were discussed in Chapter 6.

3. The trial-and-error technique is presented at the book's Web site www.aw-bc.com/gitman.

consists of an initial inflow (the net proceeds) followed by a series of annual out-lays (the interest payments). In the final year, when the debt is retired, an outlay representing the repayment of the principal also occurs. The cash flows associ-ated with Duchess Corporation's bond issue are as follows:

End of year(s)	Cash flow
0	$ 960
1–20	−$ 90
20	−$1,000

The initial $960 inflow is followed by annual interest outflows of $90 (9% coupon interest rate × $1,000 par value) over the 20-year life of the bond. In year 20, an outflow of $1,000 (the repayment of the principal) occurs. We can deter-mine the cost of debt by finding the IRR, which is the discount rate that equates the present value of the outflows to the initial inflow.

Input	Function
20	N
960	PV
−90	PMT
−1000	FV
	CPT
	I

Solution
9.452

Calculator Use   [*Note:* Most calculators require either the present (net proceeds) or the future (annual interest payments and repayment of principal) values to be input as negative numbers when we calculate cost to maturity. That approach is used here.] Using the calculator and the inputs shown at the left, you should find the before-tax cost (cost to maturity) to be 9.452%.

Spreadsheet Use   The before-tax cost of debt on the Duchess Corporation bond also can be calculated as shown in the Excel spreadsheet starting below and con-tinued at the top of the next page. (See the book's Web site, www.aw-bc.com/gitman, Chapter 11, for another spreadsheet model that computes the bond's before-tax cost of debt.)

	A	B	C	D
1	FINDING THE IRR ON A 20-YEAR BOND			
2	Net Proceeds from sale of bond	$960		
3	(coupon payment)	$90		
4	Years to maturity	20		
5	Par value (principal)	$1,000		
6	Before taxes	9.452%		
7				
8	Trial and Error method:			
9	Choose various required rates and place them in Cell C12			
10	The spreadsheet will recalculate each time. Continue the process until			
11	the sum of the NPV (Cell D36) is $0			
12			9.452%	
13	End of Year(s)	Cash Flow	PVIF	PV
14	0	$ 960	1.0000	$ 960
15	1	$ (90)	0.9136	(82)
16	2	$ (90)	0.8347	(75)
17	3	$ (90)	0.7627	(69)
18	4	$ (90)	0.6968	(63)
19	5	$ (90)	0.6366	(57)

20	6	$	(90)	0.5816	(52)
21	7	$	(90)	0.5314	(48)
22	8	$	(90)	0.4855	(44)
23	9	$	(90)	0.4436	(40)
24	10	$	(90)	0.4053	(36)
25	11	$	(90)	0.3703	(33)
26	12	$	(90)	0.3383	(30)
27	13	$	(90)	0.3091	(28)
28	14	$	(90)	0.2824	(25)
29	15	$	(90)	0.2580	(23)
30	16	$	(90)	0.2357	(21)
31	17	$	(90)	0.2154	(19)
32	18	$	(90)	0.1968	(18)
33	19	$	(90)	0.1798	(16)
34	20	$	(90)	0.1643	(15)
35	20	$	(1,000)	0.1643	(16.4)
36	(The rate of 9.452% equates the NPV to zero)			$	(0)

Approximating the Cost

The before-tax cost of debt, k_d, for a bond with a $1,000 par value can be approximated by using the following equation:

$$k_d = \frac{I + \dfrac{\$1,000 - N_d}{n}}{\dfrac{N_d + \$1,000}{2}} \tag{11.1}$$

where

I = annual interest in dollars

N_d = net proceeds from the sale of debt (bond)

n = number of years to the bond's maturity

EXAMPLE   Substituting the appropriate values from the Duchess Corporation example into the approximation formula given in Equation 11.1, we get

$$k_d = \frac{\$90 + \dfrac{\$1,000 - \$960}{20}}{\dfrac{\$960 + \$1,000}{2}} = \frac{\$90 + \$2}{\$980}$$

$$= \frac{\$92}{\$980} = \underline{\underline{9.4\%}}$$

This approximate before-tax cost of debt is close to the 9.452% value calculated precisely in the preceding example.

After-Tax Cost of Debt

As indicated earlier, the *specific cost* of financing must be stated on an after-tax basis. Because interest on debt is tax deductible, it reduces the firm's taxable income. The after-tax cost of debt, k_i, can be found by multiplying the before-tax cost, k_d, by 1 minus the tax rate, T, as stated in the following equation:

$$k_i = k_d \times (1 - T) \tag{11.2}$$

EXAMPLE   Duchess Corporation has a 40% tax rate. Using the 9.4% before-tax debt cost calculated above, and applying Equation 11.2, we find an after-tax cost of debt of 5.6% [9.4% $\times$ (1 − 0.40)]. Typically, the cost of long-term debt is less than the cost of any of the alternative forms of long-term financing, primarily because of the tax deductibility of interest. ■

REVIEW QUESTIONS

11–5   What are the *net proceeds* from the sale of a bond? What are *flotation costs* and how do they affect a bond's net proceeds?

11–6   What three methods can be used to find the before-tax cost of debt?

11–7   How is the before-tax cost of debt converted into the after-tax cost?

LG2   11.3 | The Cost of Preferred Stock

Preferred stock represents a special type of ownership interest in the firm. It gives preferred stockholders the right to receive their *stated* dividends before any earnings can be distributed to common stockholders. Because preferred stock is a form of ownership, the proceeds from its sale are expected to be held for an infinite period of time. The key characteristics of preferred stock were described in Chapter 7. However, the one aspect of preferred stock that requires review is dividends.

Preferred Stock Dividends

Most preferred stock dividends are stated as a *dollar amount:* "*x* dollars per year." When dividends are stated this way, the stock is often referred to as "*x*-dollar preferred stock." Thus a "$4 preferred stock" is expected to pay preferred stockholders $4 in dividends each year on each share of preferred stock owned.

Sometimes preferred stock dividends are stated as an *annual percentage rate.* This rate represents the percentage of the stock's par, or face, value that equals the annual dividend. For instance, an 8 percent preferred stock with a $50 par value would be expected to pay an annual dividend of $4 per share ($0.08 \times \$50$ par = $4). Before the cost of preferred stock is calculated, any dividends stated as percentages should be converted to annual dollar dividends.

Calculating the Cost of Preferred Stock

cost of preferred stock, k_p
The ratio of the preferred stock dividend to the firm's net proceeds from the sale of preferred stock; calculated by dividing the annual dividend, D_p, by the net proceeds from the sale of the preferred stock, N_p.

The **cost of preferred stock, k_p**, is the ratio of the preferred stock dividend to the firm's net proceeds from the sale of the preferred stock. The net proceeds represents the amount of money to be received minus any flotation costs. Equation 11.3 gives the cost of preferred stock, k_p, in terms of the annual dollar dividend, D_p, and the net proceeds from the sale of the stock, N_p:

$$k_p = \frac{D_p}{N_p}$$

(11.3)

Because preferred stock dividends are paid out of the firm's *after-tax* cash flows, a tax adjustment is not required.

EXAMPLE Duchess Corporation is contemplating issuance of a 10% preferred stock that is expected to sell for its $87-per-share par value.[4] The cost of issuing and selling the stock is expected to be $5 per share. The first step in finding the cost of the stock is to calculate the dollar amount of the annual preferred dividend, which is $8.70 ($0.10 \times \$87$). The net proceeds per share from the proposed sale of stock equals the sale price minus the flotation costs ($87 - \$5 = \$82$). Substituting the annual dividend, D_p, of $8.70 and the net proceeds, N_p, of $82 into Equation 11.3 gives the cost of preferred stock, 10.6% ($8.70 \div \$82$). ■

The cost of Duchess's preferred stock (10.6%) is much greater than the cost of its long-term debt (5.6%). This difference exists primarily because the cost of long-term debt (the interest) is tax deductible.

REVIEW QUESTION

11–8 How would you calculate the cost of preferred stock?

LG3 11.4 | The Cost of Common Stock

The *cost of common stock* is the return required on the stock by investors in the marketplace. There are two forms of common stock financing: (1) retained earnings and (2) new issues of common stock. As a first step in finding each of these costs, we must estimate the cost of common stock equity.

---

4. For simplicity, the preferred stock in this example is assumed to be sold for its par value. In practice, particularly for subsequent issues of already outstanding preferred stock, it is typically sold at a price that differs from its par value.

Finding the Cost of Common Stock Equity

cost of common stock equity, k_s
The rate at which investors discount the expected dividends of the firm to determine its share value.

The **cost of common stock equity, k_s,** is the rate at which investors discount the expected dividends of the firm to determine its share value. Two techniques are used to measure the cost of common stock equity.[5] One relies on the constant-growth valuation model, the other on the capital asset pricing model (CAPM).

Using the Constant-Growth Valuation (Gordon) Model

constant-growth valuation (Gordon) model
Assumes that the value of a share of stock equals the present value of all future dividends (assumed to grow at a constant rate) that it is expected to provide over an infinite time horizon.

In Chapter 7 we found the value of a share of stock to be equal to the present value of all future dividends, which in one model were assumed to grow at a constant annual rate over an infinite time horizon. This is the **constant-growth valuation model,** also known as the **Gordon model.** The key expression derived for this model was presented as Equation 7.5 and is restated here:

$$P_0 = \frac{D_1}{k_s - g} \tag{11.4}$$

where

P_0 = value of common stock
D_1 = per-share dividend *expected* at the end of year 1
k_s = required return on common stock
g = constant rate of growth in dividends

Solving Equation 11.4 for k_s results in the following expression for the *cost of common stock equity:*

$$k_s = \frac{D_1}{P_0} + g \tag{11.5}$$

Equation 11.5 indicates that the cost of common stock equity can be found by dividing the dividend expected at the end of year 1 by the current price of the stock and adding the expected growth rate. Because common stock dividends are paid from *after-tax* income, no tax adjustment is required.

EXAMPLE   Duchess Corporation wishes to determine its cost of common stock equity, k_s. The market price, P_0, of its common stock is $50 per share. The firm expects to pay a dividend, D_1, of $4 at the end of the coming year, 2007. The dividends paid on the outstanding stock over the past 6 years (2001–2006) were as follows:

Year	Dividend
2006	$3.80
2005	3.62
2004	3.47
2003	3.33
2002	3.12
2001	2.97

5. Other, more subjective techniques are available for estimating the cost of common stock equity. One popular technique is the *bond yield plus a premium;* it estimates the cost of common stock equity by adding a premium, typically between 3% and 5%, to the firm's current cost of long-term debt. Another, even more subjective technique uses the firm's *expected return on equity (ROE)* as a measure of its cost of common stock equity. Here we focus only on the more theoretically based techniques.

Using the table for the present value interest factors, *PVIF* (Table A–2), or a financial calculator or electronic spreadsheet in conjunction with the technique described for finding growth rates in Chapter 4, we can calculate the annual growth rate of dividends, *g*. It turns out to be approximately 5% (more precisely, it is 5.05%). Substituting $D_1 = \$4$, $P_0 = \$50$, and $g = 5\%$ into Equation 11.5 yields the cost of common stock equity:

$$k_s = \frac{\$4}{\$50} + 0.05 = 0.08 + 0.05 = 0.130, \text{ or } \underline{\underline{13.0\%}}$$

The 13.0% cost of common stock equity represents the return required by *existing* shareholders on their investment. If the actual return is less than that, shareholders are likely to begin selling their stock.   ■

Using the Capital Asset Pricing Model (CAPM)

capital asset pricing model (CAPM)
Describes the relationship between the required return, k_s, and the nondiversifiable risk of the firm as measured by the beta coefficient, *b*.

Recall from Chapter 5 that the **capital asset pricing model (CAPM)** describes the relationship between the required return, k_s, and the nondiversifiable risk of the firm as measured by the beta coefficient, *b*. The basic CAPM is

$$k_s = R_F + [b \times (k_m - R_F)] \tag{11.6}$$

where

R_F = risk-free rate of return

k_m = market return; return on the market portfolio of assets

Using CAPM indicates that the cost of common stock equity is the return required by investors as compensation for the firm's nondiversifiable risk, measured by beta.

EXAMPLE   Duchess Corporation now wishes to calculate its cost of common stock equity, k_s, by using the capital asset pricing model. The firm's investment advisors and its own analyses indicate that the risk-free rate, R_F, equals 7%; the firm's beta, *b*, equals 1.5; and the market return, k_m, equals 11%. Substituting these values into Equation 11.6, the company estimates the cost of common stock equity, k_s, to be

$$k_s = 7.0\% + [1.5 \times (11.0\% - 7.0\%)] = 7.0\% + 6.0\% = \underline{\underline{13.0\%}}$$

The 13.0% cost of common stock equity represents the required return of investors in Duchess Corporation common stock. It is the same as that found by using the constant-growth valuation model.   ■

Comparing the Constant-Growth and CAPM Techniques

The CAPM technique differs from the constant-growth valuation model in that it directly considers the firm's risk, as reflected by beta, in determining the *required* return or cost of common stock equity. The constant-growth model does not look at risk; it uses the market price, P_0, as a reflection of the *expected* risk–return preference of investors in the marketplace. The constant-growth valuation and CAPM techniques for finding k_s are theoretically equivalent. It is difficult to demonstrate that equivalency, however, because of measurement problems associated with growth, beta, the risk-free rate (what maturity of government security to use), and the market return. The use of the constant-growth valuation model is often preferred because the data required are more readily available.

Another difference is that when the constant-growth valuation model is used to find the cost of common stock equity, it can easily be adjusted for flotation costs to find the cost of new common stock; the CAPM does not provide a simple adjustment mechanism. The difficulty in adjusting the cost of common stock equity calculated by using CAPM occurs because in its common form the model does not include the market price, P_0, a variable needed to make such an adjustment. Although CAPM has a stronger theoretical foundation, the computational appeal of the traditional constant-growth valuation model justifies its use throughout this text to measure common stock costs.

The Cost of Retained Earnings

cost of retained earnings, k_r
The same as the cost of an *equivalent fully subscribed issue of additional common stock,* which is equal to the cost of common stock equity, k_s.

As you know, dividends are paid out of a firm's earnings. Their payment, made in cash to common stockholders, reduces the firm's retained earnings. Suppose a firm needs common stock equity financing of a certain amount. It has two choices relative to retained earnings: It can issue additional common stock in that amount and still pay dividends to stockholders out of retained earnings, or it can increase common stock equity by retaining the earnings (not paying the cash dividends) in the needed amount. In a strict accounting sense, the retention of earnings increases common stock equity in the same way that the sale of additional shares of common stock does. Thus the **cost of retained earnings, k_r,** to the firm is the same as the cost of an *equivalent fully subscribed issue of additional common stock.* Stockholders find the firm's retention of earnings acceptable only if they expect that it will earn at least their required return on the reinvested funds.

Hint Using retained earnings as a major source of financing for capital expenditures does not give away control of the firm and does not dilute present earnings per share, as would occur if new common stock were issued. However, the firm must effectively manage retained earnings to produce profits that increase future retained earnings.

Viewing retained earnings as a fully subscribed issue of additional common stock, we can set the firm's cost of retained earnings, k_r, equal to the cost of common stock equity as given by Equations 11.5 and 11.6.[6]

$$k_r = k_s \qquad (11.7)$$

It is not necessary to adjust the cost of retained earnings for flotation costs, because by retaining earnings, the firm "raises" equity capital without incurring these costs.

EXAMPLE

The cost of retained earnings for Duchess Corporation was actually calculated in the preceding examples: It is equal to the cost of common stock equity. Thus k_r equals 13.0%. As we will show in the next section, the cost of retained earnings is always lower than the cost of a new issue of common stock, because it entails no flotation costs.

---

6. Technically, if a stockholder received dividends and wished to invest them in additional shares of the firm's stock, he or she would first have to pay personal taxes at capital gains rates on the dividends and then pay brokerage fees before acquiring additional shares. By using pt as the average stockholder's capital gains tax rate and bf as the average brokerage fees stated as a percentage, we can specify the cost of retained earnings, k_r, as $k_r = k_s \times (1 - pt) \times (1 - bf)$. Because of the difficulty in estimating pt and bf, only the simpler definition of k_r given in Equation 11.7 is used here.

In Practice FOCUS ON PRACTICE

EVALUE CREATION

Answering the question "Does the company use investors' money wisely?" is one of the financial manager's chief responsibilities and greatest challenges. At many organizations—from *Fortune* 500 companies and investment firms to community hospitals—economic value added (EVA®) is the measurement tool of choice for making investment decisions, measuring overall financial performance, and motivating management.

Developed in 1983 by financial consultants **Stern Stewart & Co.** and protected by trademark, EVA® is the difference between an investment's net operating profit after taxes and the cost of the funds used to finance that investment (the amount of capital multiplied by the company's cost of capital). An investment with a positive EVA® earns more than the firm's cost of capital and therefore creates wealth. The EVA® calculation is similar to calculating internal rate of return (IRR), except that the result is stated *in dollars* rather than as a percentage. It can be applied to the company as a whole as well as to specific long-term investments such as new facilities and acquisitions.

According to its proponents, EVA® represents "real" profits and provides a more accurate measure than accounting profits. Over time, it also has a better correlation with stock prices than do earnings per share (EPS). Income calculations include only the cost of debt (interest expense), whereas EVA® uses the total cost of capital, both debt and equity (an expensive form of capital). In addition, EVA® treats research and development (R&D) outlays as investments in future products or processes and capitalizes (rather than expenses) them. A growing EVA® can signal future increases in stock prices.

Companies use EVA® because they believe doing so leads to better overall performance. Managers who apply it focus on allocating and managing assets, not just accounting profits. They will accelerate the development of a hot new product, even if that effort reduces earnings in the near term. Likewise, EVA®-driven companies will expense rather than capitalize the cost of a new venture. Although earnings will drop for a few quarters, so will taxes—and cash flow will eventually increase.

EVA® is not a panacea for all firms' shortcomings, however. Its critics say it's just another accounting measure and may not be the right one for many companies. They claim that because it favors big projects in big companies, it doesn't do a good job on capital allocation.

Each year *Fortune* and Stern Stewart & Co. publish a list that answers a critical question: Is the company creating or destroying wealth for its shareholders? This list uses both EVA® and market value added (MVA®)—the difference between what investors can now take out of a company and what they put in—to rank companies. **General Electric** again topped the 2003 list, followed by **Wal-Mart, Altria Group, Home Depot, Microsoft, ExxonMobil, IBM,** and **Johnson & Johnson,** with **Pfizer** and **Dell** rounding out the top ten.

Sources: Geoffrey Colvin, "Earnings Aren't Everything," *Fortune* (September 17, 2001), p. 58; Randy Meyers, "Measure for Measure," *CFO* (November 1997), downloaded from www.cfonet.com; G. Bennett Stewart III, "Champions of Profitable Growth," *Harvard Business Review* (July–August 2004); and the Stern Stewart and Co. Web site, www.sternstewart.com.

■ *Why might a company use EVA® as a measure of its performance in addition to the standard accounting measures?*

REVIEW QUESTIONS

11–11 What is the *weighted average cost of capital (WACC)*, and how is it calculated?

11–12 Describe the logic underlying the use of *target capital structure weights*, and compare and contrast this approach with the use of *historical weights*. What is the preferred weighting scheme?

11–13 What is *economic value added (EVA®)?* How is the *weighted average cost of capital (WACC)* used in calculating EVA®?

LG5 LG6 11.6 | The Marginal Cost and Investment Decisions

The firm's weighted average cost of capital is a key input to the investment decision-making process. As demonstrated earlier in the chapter, the firm should make only those investments for which the expected return is greater than the weighted average cost of capital. Of course, at any given time, the firm's financing costs and investment returns will be affected by the volume of financing and investment undertaken. The *weighted marginal cost of capital* and the *investment opportunities schedule* are mechanisms whereby financing and investment decisions can be made simultaneously.

The Weighted Marginal Cost of Capital (WMCC)

weighted marginal cost of capital (WMCC)
The firm's weighted average cost of capital (WACC) associated with its *next dollar* of total new financing.

The weighted average cost of capital may vary over time, depending on the volume of financing that the firm plans to raise. *As the volume of financing increases, the costs of the various types of financing will increase, raising the firm's weighted average cost of capital.* Therefore, it is useful to calculate the **weighted marginal cost of capital (WMCC)** , which is simply the firm's weighted average cost of capital (WACC) associated with its *next dollar* of total new financing. This marginal cost is relevant to current decisions.

The costs of the financing components (debt, preferred stock, and common stock) rise as larger amounts are raised. Suppliers of funds require greater returns in the form of interest, dividends, or growth as compensation for the increased risk introduced by larger volumes of *new* financing. The WMCC is therefore an increasing function of the level of total new financing.

Another factor that causes the weighted average cost of capital to increase is the use of common stock equity financing. New financing provided by common stock equity will be provided by retaining earnings until this supply is exhausted and then will be obtained through new common stock financing. Because retained earnings are a less expensive form of common stock equity financing than the sale of new common stock, the weighted average cost of capital will rise with the addition of new common stock.

Finding Break Points

break point
The level of *total* new financing at which the cost of one of the financing components rises, thereby causing an upward shift in the *weighted marginal cost of capital (WMCC).*

To calculate the WMCC, we must calculate **break points,** which reflect the level of *total* new financing at which the cost of one of the financing components rises. The following general equation can be used to find break points:

$$BP_j = \frac{AF_j}{w_j} \tag{11.10}$$

where

BP_j = break point for financing source j

AF_j = amount of funds available from financing source j at a given cost

w_j = capital structure weight (stated in decimal form) for financing source j

EXAMPLE   When Duchess Corporation exhausts its $300,000 of available retained earnings (at $k_r = 13.0\%$), it must use the more expensive new common stock financing (at $k_n = 14.0\%$) to meet its common stock equity needs. In addition, the firm expects that it can borrow only $400,000 of debt at the 5.6% cost; additional debt will have an after-tax cost (k_i) of 8.4%. Two break points therefore exist: (1) when the $300,000 of retained earnings costing 13.0% is exhausted, and (2) when the $400,000 of long-term debt costing 5.6% is exhausted.

The break points can be found by substituting these values and the corresponding capital structure weights given earlier into Equation 11.10. We get the dollar amounts of *total* new financing at which the costs of the given financing sources rise:

$$BP_{\text{common equity}} = \frac{\$300,000}{0.50} = \$600,000$$

$$BP_{\text{long-term debt}} = \frac{\$400,000}{0.40} = \$1,000,000$$

Calculating the WMCC

Once the break points have been determined, the next step is to calculate the weighted average cost of capital over the range of total new financing between break points. First, we find the WACC for a level of total new financing between zero and the first break point. Next, we find the WACC for a level of total new financing between the first and second break points, and so on. By definition, for each of the ranges of total new financing between break points, certain component capital costs (such as debt or common equity) will increase. This will cause the weighted average cost of capital to increase to a higher level than that over the preceding range.

Together, these data can be used to prepare a **weighted marginal cost of capital (WMCC) schedule**. This graph relates the firm's weighted average cost of capital to the level of total new financing.

weighted marginal cost of capital (WMCC) schedule
Graph that relates the firm's weighted average cost of capital to the level of total new financing.

EXAMPLE

Table 11.2 summarizes the calculation of the WACC for Duchess Corporation over the three ranges of total new financing created by the two break points—$600,000 and $1,000,000. Comparing the costs in column 3 of the table for each of the three ranges, we can see that the costs in the first range ($0 to $600,000) are those calculated in earlier examples and used in Table 11.1. The second range ($600,000 to $1,000,000) reflects the increase in the common stock equity cost to 14.0%. In the final range, the increase in the long-term debt cost to 8.4% is introduced.

The weighted average costs of capital (WACC) for the three ranges are summarized in the table shown at the bottom of Figure 11.1. These data describe the weighted marginal cost of capital (WMCC), which increases as levels of total new financing increase. Figure 11.1 presents the WMCC schedule. Again, it is clear that the WMCC is an increasing function of the amount of total new financing raised.

The Investment Opportunities Schedule (IOS)

At any given time, a firm has certain investment opportunities available to it. These opportunities differ with respect to the size of investment, risk, and return.[9]

---

9. Because the calculated weighted average cost of capital does not apply to risk-changing investments, we assume that all opportunities have equal risk similar to the firm's risk.

TABLE 11.2

Weighted Average Cost of Capital for Ranges of
Total New Financing for Duchess Corporation

Range of total new financing	Source of capital (1)	Weight (2)	Cost (3)	Weighted cost [(2) × (3)] (4)
$0 to $600,000	Debt	.40	5.6%	2.2%
	Preferred	.10	10.6	1.1
	Common	.50	13.0	6.5
			Weighted average cost of capital	9.8%
$600,000 to $1,000,000	Debt	.40	5.6%	2.2%
	Preferred	.10	10.6	1.1
	Common	.50	14.0	7.0
			Weighted average cost of capital	10.3%
$1,000,000 and above	Debt	.40	8.4%	3.4%
	Preferred	.10	10.6	1.1
	Common	.50	14.0	7.0
			Weighted average cost of capital	11.5%

investment opportunities schedule (IOS)
A ranking of investment possibilities from best (highest return) to worst (lowest return).

The firm's **investment opportunities schedule (IOS)** is a ranking of investment possibilities from best (highest return) to worst (lowest return). Generally, the first project selected will have the highest return, the next project the second highest, and so on. The return on investments will *decrease* as the firm accepts additional projects.

FIGURE 11.1

WMCC Schedule
Weighted marginal cost of capital (WMCC) schedule for Duchess Corporation

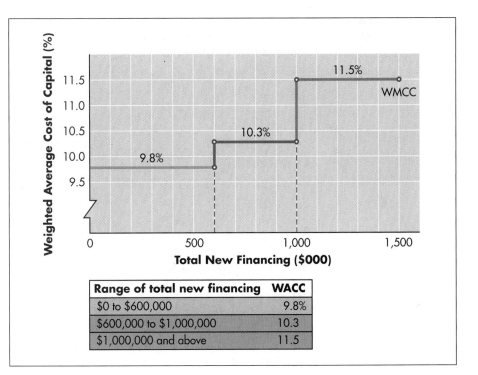

Range of total new financing	WACC
$0 to $600,000	9.8%
$600,000 to $1,000,000	10.3
$1,000,000 and above	11.5

TABLE 11.3

Investment Opportunities Schedule (IOS) for Duchess Corporation

Investment opportunity	Internal rate of return (IRR) (1)	Initial investment (2)	Cumulative investment[a] (3)
A	15.0%	$100,000	$ 100,000
B	14.5	200,000	300,000
C	14.0	400,000	700,000
D	13.0	100,000	800,000
E	12.0	300,000	1,100,000
F	11.0	200,000	1,300,000
G	10.0	100,000	1,400,000

[a]The cumulative investment represents the total amount invested in projects with higher returns plus the investment required for the corresponding investment opportunity.

EXAMPLE   Column 1 of Table 11.3 shows Duchess Corporation's current investment opportunities schedule (IOS) listing the investment possibilities from best (highest return) to worst (lowest return). Column 2 of the table shows the initial investment required by each project. Column 3 shows the cumulative total invested funds necessary to finance all projects better than and including the corresponding investment opportunity. Plotting the project returns against the cumulative investment (column 1 against column 3) results in the firm's investment opportunities schedule (IOS). A graph of the IOS for Duchess Corporation is given in Figure 11.2. ■

FIGURE 11.2

IOS and WMCC Schedules
Using the IOS and WMCC to select projects for Duchess Corporation

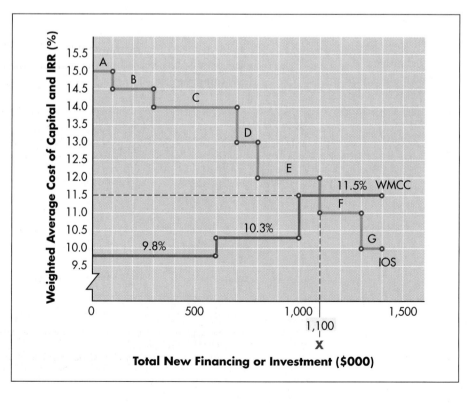

Using the WMCC and IOS to Make Financing/Investment Decisions

As long as a project's internal rate of return is greater than the weighted marginal cost of new financing, the firm should accept the project.[10] The return will decrease with the acceptance of more projects, and the weighted marginal cost of capital will increase because greater amounts of financing will be required. The decision rule therefore would be: *Accept projects up to the point at which the marginal return on an investment equals its weighted marginal cost of capital.* Beyond that point, its investment return will be less than its capital cost.[11]

This approach is consistent with the maximization of net present value (NPV) for conventional projects for two reasons: (1) The NPV is positive as long as the IRR exceeds the weighted average cost of capital, k_a. (2) The larger the difference between the IRR and k_a, the larger the resulting NPV. Therefore, the acceptance of projects beginning with those that have the greatest positive difference between IRR and k_a, down to the point at which IRR just equals k_a, should result in the maximum total NPV for all independent projects accepted. Such an outcome is completely consistent with the firm's goal of maximizing owner wealth.

EXAMPLE   Figure 11.2 shows Duchess Corporation's WMCC schedule and IOS on the same set of axes. By raising $1,100,000 of new financing and investing these funds in projects A, B, C, D, and E, the firm should maximize the wealth of its owners, because these projects result in the maximum total net present value. Note that the 12.0% return on the last dollar invested (in project E) *exceeds* its 11.5% weighted average cost. Investment in project F is not feasible, because its 11.0% return is *less than* the 11.5% cost of funds available for investment. ■

The firm's optimal capital budget of $1,100,000 is marked with an X in Figure 11.2. At that point, the IRR equals the weighted average cost of capital, and the firm's size as well as its shareholder value will be optimized. In a sense, the size of the firm is determined by the market—the availability of and returns on investment opportunities, and the availability and cost of financing.

In practice, most firms operate under *capital rationing*. That is, management imposes constraints that keep the capital expenditure budget below optimal (where IRR $= k_a$). Because of this, a gap frequently exists between the theoretically optimal capital budget and the firm's actual level of financing/investment.

REVIEW QUESTIONS

11–14 What is the *weighted marginal cost of capital (WMCC)?* What does the WMCC *schedule* represent? Why does this schedule increase?

11–15 What is the *investment opportunities schedule (IOS)?* Is it typically depicted as an increasing or a decreasing function? Why?

---

10. Although net present value could be used to make these decisions, the internal rate of return is used here because of the ease of comparison it offers.

11. So as not to confuse the discussion presented here, the fact that using the IRR for selecting projects may not yield optimal decisions is ignored. The problems associated with the use of IRR in capital rationing were discussed in greater detail in Chapter 10.

11–16 How can the WMCC schedule and the IOS be used to find the level of financing/investment that maximizes owner wealth? Why do many firms finance/invest at a level below this optimum?

Summary

Focus on Value

The cost of capital is an extremely important rate of return used by the firm in the long-term decision process, particularly in capital budgeting decisions. It is the expected average future cost to the firm of funds over the long run. Because the cost of capital is the pivotal rate of return used in the investment decision process, its accuracy can significantly affect the quality of these decisions.

Even with good estimates of project cash flows, the application of NPV and IRR decision techniques, and adequate consideration of project risk, a poorly estimated cost of capital can result in the destruction of shareholder value. Underestimation of the cost of capital can result in the mistaken acceptance of poor projects, whereas overestimation can cause good projects to be rejected. In either situation, the firm's action could be detrimental to the firm's value. By applying the techniques presented in this chapter to estimate the firm's cost of capital, the financial manager will improve the likelihood that the firm's long-term decisions will be consistent with the firm's overall goal of **maximizing stock price (owner wealth)**.

Review of Learning Goals

Key definitions and formulas for this chapter are summarized in Table 11.4.

LG1 **Understand the key assumptions, the basic concept, and the specific sources of capital associated with the cost of capital.** The cost of capital is the rate of return that a firm must earn on its investments to maintain its market value and attract needed funds. It is affected by business and financial risks, and is measured on an after-tax basis. A weighted average cost of capital should be used to find the expected average future cost of funds over the long run. The specific costs of the basic sources of capital (long-term debt, preferred stock, retained earnings, and common stock) can be calculated individually.

LG2 **Determine the cost of long-term debt and the cost of preferred stock.** The cost of long-term debt is the after-tax cost today of raising long-term funds through borrowing. Cost quotations, calculation, or an approximation can be used to find the before-tax cost of debt, which must then be tax-adjusted. The cost of preferred stock is the ratio of the preferred stock dividend to the firm's net proceeds from the sale of preferred stock.

LG3 **Calculate the cost of common stock equity and convert it into the cost of retained earnings and the cost of new issues of common stock.** The cost of common stock equity can be calculated by using the constant-growth valuation (Gordon) model or the CAPM. The cost of retained earnings is equal to the cost of common stock equity. An adjustment in the cost of common stock equity to reflect underpricing and flotation costs is necessary to find the cost of new issues of common stock.

TABLE 11.4

Summary of Key Definitions and Formulas for Cost of Capital

Definitions of variables

AF_j = amount of funds available from financing source j at a given cost

b = beta coefficient or measure of nondiversifiable risk

BP_j = break point for financing source j

D_1 = per-share dividend *expected* at the end of year 1

D_p = annual preferred stock dividend (in dollars)

g = constant rate of growth in dividends

I = annual interest in dollars

k_a = weighted average cost of capital

k_d = before-tax cost of debt

k_i = after-tax cost of debt

k_m = required return on the market portfolio

k_n = cost of a new issue of common stock

k_p = cost of preferred stock

k_r = cost of retained earnings

k_s = required return on common stock

n = number of years to the bond's maturity

N_d = net proceeds from the sale of debt (bond)

N_n = net proceeds from the sale of new common stock

N_p = net proceeds from the sale of preferred stock

P_0 = value of common stock

R_F = risk-free rate of return

T = firm's tax rate

w_i = proportion of long-term debt in capital structure

w_j = capital structure proportion (historical or target, stated in decimal form) for financing source j

w_p = proportion of preferred stock in capital structure

w_s = proportion of common stock equity in capital structure

Cost of capital formulas

Before-tax cost of debt (approximation):

$$k_d = \frac{I + \dfrac{\$1{,}000 - N_d}{n}}{\dfrac{N_d + \$1{,}000}{2}} \qquad \text{[Equation 11.1]}$$

After-tax cost of debt: $k_i = k_d \times (1 - T)$ [Equation 11.2]

Cost of preferred stock: $k_p = \dfrac{D_p}{N_p}$ [Equation 11.3]

Cost of common stock equity:

Using constant-growth valuation model: $k_s = \dfrac{D_1}{P_0} + g$ [Equation 11.5]

Using CAPM: $k_s = R_F + [b \times (k_m - R_F)]$ [Equation 11.6]

Cost of retained earnings: $k_r = k_s$ [Equation 11.7]

Cost of new issues of common stock: $k_n = \dfrac{D_1}{N_n} + g$ [Equation 11.8]

Weighted average cost of capital (WACC): $k_a = (w_i \times k_i) + (w_p \times k_p) + (w_s \times k_{r\,or\,n})$ [Equation 11.9]

Break point: $BP_j = \dfrac{AF_j}{w_j}$ [Equation 11.10]

Calculate the weighted average cost of capital (WACC) and discuss alternative weighting schemes and economic value added (EVA®). The firm's WACC reflects the expected average future cost of funds over the long run. It combines the costs of specific types of capital after weighting each of them by its proportion. The theoretically preferred approach uses target weights based on market values. Economic value added (EVA®) is a popular measure that uses the WACC to determine whether a proposed investment is expected to make a positive contribution to the owners' wealth.

LG5 Describe the procedures used to determine break points and the weighted marginal cost of capital (WMCC). As total new financing increases, the costs of the various types of financing will increase, raising the firm's WACC. The WMCC is the firm's WACC associated with its next dollar of total new financing. Break points represent the level of total new financing at which the cost of one of the financing components rises, causing an upward shift in the WMCC. The WMCC schedule relates the WACC to each level of total new financing.

LG6 Explain the weighted marginal cost of capital (WMCC) and its use with the investment opportunities schedule (IOS) to make financing/investment decisions. The IOS ranks currently available investments from best to worst. It is used with the WMCC to find the level of financing/investment that maximizes owner wealth. The firm accepts projects up to the point at which the marginal return on its investment equals its weighted marginal cost of capital.

Self-Test Problem (Solution in Appendix B)

LG2 LG3 LG4
LG5 LG6

ST11–1   Specific costs, WACC, WMCC, and IOS   Humble Manufacturing is interested in measuring its overall cost of capital. The firm is in the 40% tax bracket. Current investigation has gathered the following data:

Debt   The firm can raise an unlimited amount of debt by selling $1,000-par-value, 10% coupon interest rate, 10-year bonds on which *annual interest* payments will be made. To sell the issue, an average discount of $30 per bond must be given. The firm must also pay flotation costs of $20 per bond.

Preferred stock   The firm can sell 11% (annual dividend) preferred stock at its $100-per-share par value. The cost of issuing and selling the preferred stock is expected to be $4 per share. An unlimited amount of preferred stock can be sold under these terms.

Common stock   The firm's common stock is currently selling for $80 per share. The firm expects to pay cash dividends of $6 per share next year. The firm's dividends have been growing at an annual rate of 6%, and this rate is expected to continue in the future. The stock will have to be underpriced by $4 per share, and flotation costs are expected to amount to $4 per share. The firm can sell an unlimited amount of new common stock under these terms.

Retained earnings   The firm expects to have $225,000 of retained earnings available in the coming year. Once these retained earnings are exhausted, the firm will use new common stock as the form of common stock equity financing.

a. Calculate the specific cost of each source of financing. (Round to the nearest 0.1%.)
b. The firm uses the weights shown in the following table, which are based on target capital structure proportions, to calculate its weighted average cost of capital. (Round to the nearest 0.1%.)

Source of capital	Weight
Long-term debt	40%
Preferred stock	15
Common stock equity	45
Total	100%

(1) Calculate the single *break point* associated with the firm's financial situation. (*Hint:* This point results from the exhaustion of the firm's retained earnings.)
(2) Calculate the weighted average cost of capital associated with total new financing *below* the break point calculated in part (1).
(3) Calculate the weighted average cost of capital associated with total new financing *above* the break point calculated in part (1).
c. Using the results of part **b** along with the information shown in the following table on the available investment opportunities, draw the firm's weighted marginal cost of capital (WMCC) schedule and investment opportunities schedule (IOS) on the same set of axes (total new financing or investment on the *x* axis and weighted average cost of capital and IRR on the *y* axis).

Investment opportunity	Internal rate of return (IRR)	Initial investment
A	11.2%	$100,000
B	9.7	500,000
C	12.9	150,000
D	16.5	200,000
E	11.8	450,000
F	10.1	600,000
G	10.5	300,000

d. Which, if any, of the available investments do you recommend that the firm accept? Explain your answer. How much total new financing is required?

Warm-Up Exercises

E11–1 Weekend Warriors, Inc., has a 35% debt and 65% equity in its capital structure. The firm's estimated cost of debt is 8% and its estimated cost of equity is 13%. Determine the firm's *weighted average cost of capital (WACC)*.

E11–2 A firm raises capital by selling $20,000 worth of debt with flotation costs equal to 2% of its par value. If the debt matures in 10 years and has a coupon interest rate of 8%, what is the bond's IRR?

LG2   E11–3   Your firm, People's Consulting Group, has been asked to consult on a potential preferred stock offering by Brave New World. This 15% preferred stock issue would be sold at its par value of $35 per share. Flotation costs would total $3 per share. Calculate the cost of this preferred stock.

LG3   E11–4   Duke Energy has been paying dividends steadily for 20 years. During that time, dividends have grown at a compound annual rate of 7%. If Duke Energy's current stock price is $78 and the firm plans to pay a dividend of $6.50 next year, what is Duke's *cost of common stock equity*?

LG4   E11–5   Oxy Corporation uses debt, preferred stock, and common stock to raise capital. The firm's capital structure targets the following proportions: debt, 55%; preferred stock, 10%; and common stock, 35%. If the cost of debt is 6.7%, preferred stock costs 9.2%, and common stock costs 10.6%, what is Oxy's *weighted average cost of capital (WACC)*?

Problems

LG1

BASIC

P11–1   **Concept of cost of capital**   Wren Manufacturing is in the process of analyzing its investment decision-making procedures. The two projects evaluated by the firm during the past month were projects 263 and 264. The basic variables surrounding each project analysis, using the IRR decision technique, and the resulting decision actions are summarized in the following table.

Basic variables	Project 263	Project 264
Cost	$64,000	$58,000
Life	15 years	15 years
IRR	8%	15%
Least-cost financing		
Source	Debt	Equity
Cost (after-tax)	7%	16%
Decision		
Action	Accept	Reject
Reason	8% IRR > 7% cost	15% IRR < 16% cost

a. Evaluate the firm's decision-making procedures, and explain why the acceptance of project 263 and rejection of project 264 may not be in the owners' best interest.
b. If the firm maintains a capital structure containing 40% debt and 60% equity, find its weighted average cost using the data in the table.
c. If the firm had used the weighted average cost calculated in part **b**, what actions would have been indicated relative to projects 263 and 264?
d. Compare and contrast the firm's actions with your findings in part **c**. Which decision method seems more appropriate? Explain why.

LG2

INTERMEDIATE

P11–2   Cost of debt using both methods   Currently, Warren Industries can sell 15-year, $1,000-par-value bonds paying *annual interest* at a 12% coupon rate. As a result of current interest rates, the bonds can be sold for $1,010 each; flotation costs of $30 per bond will be incurred in this process. The firm is in the 40% tax bracket.
  a. Find the net proceeds from sale of the bond, N_d.
  b. Show the cash flows from the firm's point of view over the maturity of the bond.
  c. Use the *IRR approach* to calculate the before-tax and after-tax costs of debt.
  d. Use the *approximation formula* to estimate the before-tax and after-tax costs of debt.
  e. Compare and contrast the costs of debt calculated in parts c and d. Which approach do you prefer? Why?

LG2

BASIC

P11–3   Cost of debt using the approximation formula   For each of the following $1,000-par-value bonds, assuming *annual interest* payment and a 40% tax rate, calculate the *after-tax* cost to maturity using the *approximation formula*.

Bond	Life	Underwriting fee	Discount (−) or premium (+)	Coupon interest rate
A	20 years	$25	−$20	9%
B	16	40	+ 10	10
C	15	30	− 15	12
D	25	15	Par	9
E	22	20	− 60	11

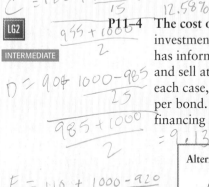

LG2

INTERMEDIATE

P11–4   The cost of debt   Gronseth Drywall Systems, Inc., is in discussions with its investment bankers regarding the issuance of new bonds. The investment banker has informed the firm that different maturities will carry different coupon rates and sell at different prices. The firm must choose among several alternatives. In each case, the bonds will have a $1,000 par value and flotation costs will be $30 per bond. The company is taxed at a rate of 40%. Calculate the after-tax cost of financing with each of the following alternatives.

Alternative	Coupon rate	Time to maturity	Premium or discount
A	9%	16 years	$250
B	7	5	50
C	6	7	par
D	5	10	− 75

LG2

BASIC

P11–5   Cost of preferred stock   Taylor Systems has just issued preferred stock. The stock has a 12% annual dividend and a $100 par value and was sold at $97.50 per share. In addition, flotation costs of $2.50 per share must be paid.
  a. Calculate the *cost of the preferred stock*.
  b. If the firm sells the preferred stock with a 10% annual dividend and nets $90.00 after flotation costs, what is its cost?

P11–6 Cost of preferred stock Determine the cost for each of the following preferred stocks.

Preferred stock	Par value	Sale price	Flotation cost	Annual dividend
A 11.96%	$100	$101	$9.00	11%
B 9.28%	40	38	$3.50	8%
C 15.15%	35	37	$4.00	$5.00
D 12.24%	30	26	5% of par	$3.00
E 10.29%	20	20	$2.50	9%

P11–7 Cost of common stock equity—CAPM J&M Corporation common stock has a beta, b, of 1.2. The risk-free rate is 6%, and the market return is 11%.
a. Determine the risk premium on J&M common stock.
b. Determine the required return that J&M common stock should provide.
c. Determine J&M's *cost of common stock equity* using the CAPM.

P11–8 Cost of common stock equity Ross Textiles wishes to measure its cost of common stock equity. The firm's stock is currently selling for $57.50. The firm expects to pay a $3.40 dividend at the end of the year (2007). The dividends for the past 5 years are shown in the following table.

Year	Dividend
2006	$3.10
2005	2.92
2004	2.60
2003	2.30
2002	2.12

After underpricing and flotation costs, the firm expects to net $52 per share on a new issue.
a. Determine the growth rate of dividends.
b. Determine the net proceeds, N_n, that the firm will actually receive.
c. Using the constant-growth valuation model, determine the *cost of retained earnings, k_r.*
d. Using the constant-growth valuation model, determine the *cost of new common stock, k_n.*

P11–9 Retained earnings versus new common stock Using the data for each firm shown in the following table, calculate the *cost of retained earnings* and the *cost of new common stock* using the constant-growth valuation model.

Firm	Current market price per share	Dividend growth rate	Projected dividend per share next year	Underpricing per share	Flotation cost per share
A	$50.00	8%	$2.25	$2.00	$1.00
B	20.00	4	1.00	0.50	1.50
C	42.50	6	2.00	1.00	2.00
D	19.00	2	2.10	1.30	1.70

P11–10 **The effect of tax rate on WACC**   Equity Lighting Corp. wishes to explore the effect on its cost of capital of the rate at which the company pays taxes. The firm wishes to maintain a capital structure of 30% debt, 10% preferred stock, and 60% common stock. The cost of financing with retained earnings is 14%, the cost of preferred stock financing is 9%, and the before-tax cost of debt financing is 11%. Calculate the weighted average cost of capital (WACC) given the tax rate assumptions in parts **a** to **c**.

a. Tax rate = 40%
b. Tax rate = 35%
c. Tax rate = 25%
d. Describe the relationship between changes in the rate of taxation and the weighted average cost of capital.

P11–11 **WACC—Book weights**   Ridge Tool has on its books the amounts and specific (after-tax) costs shown in the following table for each source of capital.

Source of capital	Book value	Specific cost
Long-term debt	$700,000	5.3%
Preferred stock	50,000	12.0
Common stock equity	650,000	16.0

a. Calculate the firm's weighted average cost of capital using book value weights.
b. Explain how the firm can use this cost in the investment decision-making process.

P11–12 **WACC—Book weights and market weights**   Webster Company has compiled the information shown in the following table.

Source of capital	Book value	Market value	After-tax cost
Long-term debt	$4,000,000	$3,840,000	6.0%
Preferred stock	40,000	60,000	13.0
Common stock equity	1,060,000	3,000,000	17.0
Totals	$5,100,000	$6,900,000	

a. Calculate the weighted average cost of capital using *book value weights*.
b. Calculate the weighted average cost of capital using *market value weights*.
c. Compare the answers obtained in parts **a** and **b**. Explain the differences.

P11–13 **WACC and target weights**   After careful analysis, Dexter Brothers has determined that its optimal capital structure is composed of the sources and target market value weights shown in the following table.

Source of capital	Target market value weight
Long-term debt	30%
Preferred stock	15
Common stock equity	55
Total	100%

The cost of debt is estimated to be 7.2%; the cost of preferred stock is estimated to be 13.5%; the cost of retained earnings is estimated to be 16.0%; and the cost of new common stock is estimated to be 18.0%. All of these are after-tax rates. The company's debt represents 25%, the preferred stock represents 10%, and the common stock equity represents 65% of total capital on the basis of the market values of the three components. The company expects to have a significant amount of retained earnings available and does not expect to sell any new common stock.

a. Calculate the weighted average cost of capital on the basis of *historical market value weights.*

b. Calculate the weighted average cost of capital on the basis of *target market value weights.*

c. Compare the answers obtained in parts **a** and **b**. Explain the differences.

P11–14 **Cost of capital and break point** Edna Recording Studios, Inc., reported earnings available to common stock of $4,200,000 last year. From those earnings, the company paid a dividend of $1.26 on each of its 1,000,000 common shares outstanding. The capital structure of the company includes 40% debt, 10% preferred stock, and 50% common stock. It is taxed at a rate of 40%.

a. If the market price of the common stock is $40 and dividends are expected to grow at a rate of 6% per year for the foreseeable future, what is the company's cost of financing with retained earnings?

b. If underpricing and flotation costs on new shares of common stock amount to $7.00 per share, what is the company's cost of new common stock financing?

c. The company can issue $2.00 dividend preferred stock for a market price of $25.00 per share. Flotation costs would amount to $3.00 per share. What is the cost of preferred stock financing?

d. The company can issue $1,000-par-value, 10% coupon, 5-year bonds that can be sold for $1,200 each. Flotation costs would amount to $25.00 per bond. Use the estimation formula to figure the approximate cost of new debt financing.

e. What is the maximum investment that Edna Recording Studios can make in new projects before it must issue new common stock?

f. What is the WACC for projects with a cost at or below the amount calculated in part e?

g. What is the WACC for projects with a cost above the amount calculated in part e (assuming that debt across all ranges remains at the percentage cost calculated in part d)?

P11–15 **Calculation of specific costs, WACC, and WMCC** Dillon Labs has asked its financial manager to measure the cost of each specific type of capital as well as the weighted average cost of capital. The weighted average cost is to be measured by using the following weights: 40% long-term debt, 10% preferred stock, and 50% common stock equity (retained earnings, new common stock, or both). The firm's tax rate is 40%.

Debt The firm can sell for $980 a 10-year, $1,000-par-value bond paying *annual interest* at a 10% coupon rate. A flotation cost of 3% of the par value is required in addition to the discount of $20 per bond.

Preferred stock   Eight percent (annual dividend) preferred stock having a par value of $100 can be sold for $65. An additional fee of $2 per share must be paid to the underwriters.

Common stock   The firm's common stock is currently selling for $50 per share. The dividend expected to be paid at the end of the coming year (2007) is $4. Its dividend payments, which have been approximately 60% of earnings per share in each of the past 5 years, were as shown in the following table.

Year	Dividend
2006	$3.75
2005	3.50
2004	3.30
2003	3.15
2002	2.85

It is expected that to attract buyers, new common stock must be underpriced $5 per share, and the firm must also pay $3 per share in flotation costs. Dividend payments are expected to continue at 60% of earnings.
a. Calculate the specific cost of each source of financing. (Assume that $k_r = k_s$.)
b. If earnings available to common shareholders are expected to be $7 million, what is the *break point* associated with the exhaustion of retained earnings?
c. Determine the weighted average cost of capital between zero and the break point calculated in part **b**.
d. Determine the weighted average cost of capital just beyond the break point calculated in part **b**.

P11–16   **Calculation of specific costs, WACC, and WMCC**   Lang Enterprises is interested in measuring its overall cost of capital. Current investigation has gathered the following data. The firm is in the 40% tax bracket.

Debt   The firm can raise an unlimited amount of debt by selling $1,000-par-value, 8% coupon interest rate, 20-year bonds on which *annual interest* payments will be made. To sell the issue, an average discount of $30 per bond would have to be given. The firm also must pay flotation costs of $30 per bond.

Preferred stock   The firm can sell 8% preferred stock at its $95-per-share par value. The cost of issuing and selling the preferred stock is expected to be $5 per share. An unlimited amount of preferred stock can be sold under these terms.

Common stock   The firm's common stock is currently selling for $90 per share. The firm expects to pay cash dividends of $7 per share next year. The firm's dividends have been growing at an annual rate of 6%, and this growth is expected to continue into the future. The stock must be underpriced by $7 per share, and flotation costs are expected to amount to $5 per share. The firm can sell an unlimited amount of new common stock under these terms.

Retained earnings   When measuring this cost, the firm does not concern itself with the tax bracket or brokerage fees of owners. It expects to have available $100,000 of retained earnings in the coming year; once these retained earnings are exhausted, the firm will use new common stock as the form of common stock equity financing.

a. Calculate the specific cost of each source of financing. (Round answers to the nearest 0.1%.)

Source of capital	Weight
Long-term debt	30%
Preferred stock	20
Common stock equity	50
Total	100%

b. The firm's capital structure weights used in calculating its weighted average cost of capital are shown in the table above. (Round answer to the nearest 0.1%.)
   (1) Calculate the single *break point* associated with the firm's financial situation. (*Hint:* This point results from exhaustion of the firm's retained earnings.)
   (2) Calculate the weighted average cost of capital associated with total new financing below the break point calculated in part (1).
   (3) Calculate the weighted average cost of capital associated with total new financing above the break point calculated in part (1).

P11–17 **Integrative—WACC, WMCC, and IOS**   Cartwell Products has compiled the data shown in the following table for the current costs of its three basic sources of capital—long-term debt, preferred stock, and common stock equity—for various ranges of new financing.

Source of capital	Range of new financing	After-tax cost
Long-term debt	$0 to $320,000	6%
	$320,000 and above	8
Preferred stock	$0 and above	17%
Common stock equity	$0 to $200,000	20%
	$200,000 and above	24

The company's capital structure weights used in calculating its weighted average cost of capital are shown in the following table.

Source of capital	Weight
Long-term debt	40%
Preferred stock	20
Common stock equity	40
Total	100%

a. Determine the *break points* and ranges of *total* new financing associated with each source of capital.
b. Using the data developed in part **a**, determine the break points (levels of *total* new financing) at which the firm's weighted average cost of capital will change.

c. Calculate the weighted average cost of capital for each range of total new financing found in part **b.** (*Hint:* There are three ranges.)

d. Using the results of part **c,** along with the following information on the available investment opportunities, draw the firm's weighted marginal cost of capital (WMCC) schedule and investment opportunities schedule (IOS) on the same set of axes (total new financing or investment on the *x* axis and weighted average cost of capital and IRR on the *y* axis).

Investment opportunity	Internal rate of return (IRR)	Initial investment
A	19%	$200,000
B	15	300,000
C	22	100,000
D	14	600,000
E	23	200,000
F	13	100,000
G	21	300,000
H	17	100,000
I	16	400,000

e. Which, if any, of the available investments do you recommend that the firm accept? Explain your answer.

P11–18 **Integrative—WACC, WMCC, and IOC** Grainger Corp., a supplier of fitness equipment, is trying to decide whether to undertake any or all of the proposed projects in its investment opportunities schedule (IOS). The firm's cost-of-capital schedule and investment opportunities schedules follow.

Cost-of-Capital Schedule			
Range of new financing	Source	Weight	After-tax cost
0–$600,000	Debt	.50	6.3%
	Preferred stock	.10	12.5
	Common stock	.40	15.3
$600,000–$1,000,000	Debt	.50	6.3%
	Preferred stock	.10	12.5
	Common stock	.40	16.4
$1,000,000 and above	Debt	.50	7.8%
	Preferred stock	.10	12.5
	Common stock	.40	16.4

Investment Opportunities Schedule		
Investment opportunity	Internal rate of return	Cost
Project H	14.5%	$200,000
Project G	13.0	700,000
Project K	12.8	500,000
Project M	11.4	600,000

a. Complete the cost-of-capital schedule by calculating the WACC and the WMCC schedule for the various ranges of new financing.
b. Identify those projects that you recommend that Grainger Corp. undertake in the next year.
c. Illustrate your recommendations by drawing a graph of Grainger's weighted average costs and investment opportunities similar to Figure 11.2.
d. Explain why certain projects are recommended and other(s) are not.

P11–19 ETHICS PROBLEM   Why did the implosion of the communication giant WorldCom happen so rapidly despite its large size—assets estimated to be close to $105 billion and stockholders' equity of $58 billion—reported just a few months before the bankruptcy?

Chapter 11 Case: Making Star Products' Financing/Investment Decision

Star Products Company is a growing manufacturer of automobile accessories whose stock is actively traded on the over-the-counter (OTC) exchange. During 2006, the Dallas-based company experienced sharp increases in both sales and earnings. Because of this recent growth, Melissa Jen, the company's treasurer, wants to make sure that available funds are being used to their fullest. Management policy is to maintain the current capital structure proportions of 30% long-term debt, 10% preferred stock, and 60% common stock equity for at least the next 3 years. The firm is in the 40% tax bracket.

Star's division and product managers have presented several competing investment opportunities to Jen. However, because funds are limited, choices of which projects to accept must be made. The investment opportunities schedule (IOS) is shown in the following table.

Investment opportunity	Internal rate of return (IRR)	Initial investment
A	15%	$400,000
B	22	200,000
C	25	700,000
D	23	400,000
E	17	500,000
F	19	600,000
G	14	500,000

Investment Opportunities Schedule (IOS) for Star Products Company

To estimate the firm's weighted average cost of capital (WACC), Jen contacted a leading investment banking firm, which provided the financing cost data shown in the table at the top of the facing page.

Financing Cost Data
Star Products Company

Long-term debt: The firm can raise $450,000 of additional debt by selling 15-year, $1,000-par-value, 9% coupon interest rate bonds that pay *annual interest*. It expects to net $960 per bond after flotation costs. Any debt in excess of $450,000 will have a before-tax cost, k_d, of 13%.

Preferred stock: Preferred stock, regardless of the amount sold, can be issued with a $70 par value and a 14% annual dividend rate and will net $65 per share after flotation costs.

Common stock equity: The firm expects dividends and earnings per share to be $0.96 and $3.20, respectively, in 2007 and to continue to grow at a constant rate of 11% per year. The firm's stock currently sells for $12 per share. Star expects to have $1,500,000 of retained earnings available in the coming year. Once the retained earnings have been exhausted, the firm can raise additional funds by selling new common stock, netting $9 per share after underpricing and flotation costs.

TO DO

a. Calculate the cost of each source of financing, as specified:
   (1) Long-term debt, first $450,000.
   (2) Long-term debt, greater than $450,000.
   (3) Preferred stock, all amounts.
   (4) Common stock equity, first $1,500,000.
   (5) Common stock equity, greater than $1,500,000.
b. Find the *break points* associated with each source of capital, and use them to specify each of the ranges of total new financing over which the firm's weighted average cost of capital (WACC) remains constant.
c. Calculate the weighted average cost of capital (WACC) over each of the ranges of total new financing specified in part **b.**
d. Using your findings in part **c** along with the investment opportunities schedule (IOS), draw the firm's weighted marginal cost of capital (WMCC) and IOS on the same set of axes (total new financing or investment on the *x* axis and weighted average cost of capital and IRR on the *y* axis).
e. Which, if any, of the available investments would you recommend that the firm accept? Explain your answer.

Spreadsheet Exercise

Nova Corporation is interested in measuring the cost of each specific type of capital as well as the weighted average cost of capital. Historically, the firm has raised capital in the following manner:

Source of capital	Weight
Long-term debt	35%
Preferred stock	12
Common stock equity	53

The tax rate of the firm is currently 40%. The needed financial information and data are as follows:

Debt   Nova can raise an unlimited amount of debt by selling $1,000-par-value, 6.5% coupon interest rate, 10-year bonds on which *annual interest payments* will be made. To sell the issue, an average discount of $20 per bond needs to be given. There is an associated flotation cost of 2% of par value.

Preferred stock   An unlimited amount of preferred stock can be sold under the following terms: The security has a par value of $100 per share, the annual dividend rate is 6% of the par value, and the floatation cost is expected to be $4 per share. The preferred stock is expected to sell for $102 before cost considerations.

Common stock   The current price of Nova's common stock is $35 per share. The cash dividend is expected to be $3.25 per share next year. The firm's dividends have grown at an annual rate of 5%, and it is expected that the dividend will continue at this rate for the foreseeable future. The flotation costs are expected to be approximately $2 per share. Nova can sell an unlimited amount of new common stock under these terms.

Retained earnings   The firm expects to have available $100,000 of retained earnings in the coming year. Once these retained earnings are exhausted, the firm will use new common stock as the form of common stock equity financing. (*Note:* When measuring this cost, the firm does not concern itself with the tax bracket or brokerage fees of owners.)

TO DO

Create a spreadsheet to answer the following questions:

a. Calculate the specific cost of *each source of financing*. (Round answers to the nearest 0.1%.)
b. Calculate the single *break point* associated with the firm's financial situation. This point results from exhaustion of the firm's retained earnings.
c. Calculate the weighted average cost of capital (WACC) associated with total financing *below* the break point calculated in part **b**.
d. Calculate the weighted average cost of capital (WACC) associated with total financing *above* the break point calculated in part **b**.

Group Exercise

By this time, you should be well aware of the linkages between theory and practice as shown throughout the text and previous exercises. The topic covered in this chapter is a good example of practice catching up with theory. U.S. corporations increasingly are using the tools discussed in the text to more accurately measure the cost of capital and therefore make better capital budgeting decisions. This exercise likewise attempts to bridge the gap between textbook theory and actual management practice.

TO DO

LG1   **a.** By looking at the balance sheet of your shadow firm, investigate how the firm has raised capital for investment opportunities. Begin by describing the mix of debt and equity, and calculate the proportions for each source of long-term funds.

LG1   **b.** Return to your group's fictitious firm. Design a balance sheet that approximates the sources and uses of financing of your shadow firm.

LG2 **LG3** **LG4**   **c.** Assign rough cost estimates, rounding where necessary, and calculate the weighted average cost of capital for your fictitious firm.

LG4   **d.** Apply the EVA® tool by designing a new investment opportunity and calculating NOPAT for the investment. Use the cost estimates from part **c** and make a decision with regard to the investment opportunity.

Web Exercise

This chapter uses the cost of capital to introduce the topic of long-term financial decisions. The place to begin any of this analysis is the applicable rate of interest. In that vein, we will again review different market rates of interest.

TO DO

a. Point your browser to www.bankrate.com/brm/default.asp. This Web site provides a myriad of current interest rates for all types of financing decisions. Your assignment is simply to wade through the information and retrieve the recent rates for several types of borrowing. Report the recent rates across as many types of loans as you can find.

b. Describe the recent trend you observe in rates.

Remember to check the book's Web site at

www.aw-bc.com/gitman

for additional resources, including additional Web exercises.

Chapter 12

Leverage and Capital Structure

LEARNING GOALS

LG1 Discuss leverage, capital structure, breakeven analysis, the operating breakeven point, and the effect of changing costs on it.

LG2 Understand operating, financial, and total leverage and the relationships among them.

LG3 Describe the types of capital, external assessment of capital structure, the capital structure of non-U.S. firms, and capital structure theory.

LG4 Explain the optimal capital structure using a graphical view of the firm's cost-of-capital functions and a zero-growth valuation model.

LG5 Discuss the EBIT–EPS approach to capital structure.

LG6 Review the return and risk of alternative capital structures, their linkage to market value, and other important considerations related to capital structure.

ACROSS THE DISCIPLINES WHY THIS CHAPTER MATTERS TO YOU

Accounting: You need to understand how to calculate and analyze operating and financial leverage and to be familiar with the tax and earnings effects of various capital structures.

Information systems: You need to understand the types of capital and what capital structure is, because you will provide much of the information needed in management's determination of the best capital structure for the firm.

Management: You need to understand leverage so that you can control risk and magnify returns for the firm's owners

and to understand capital structure theory so that you can make decisions about the firm's optimal capital structure.

Marketing: You need to understand breakeven analysis, which you will use in pricing and product feasibility decisions.

Operations: You need to understand the impact of fixed and variable operating costs on the firm's breakeven point and its operating leverage, because these costs will have a major impact on the firm's risk and return.

KRISPY KREME

INVESTORS EAT UP
KRISPY KREME STOCK

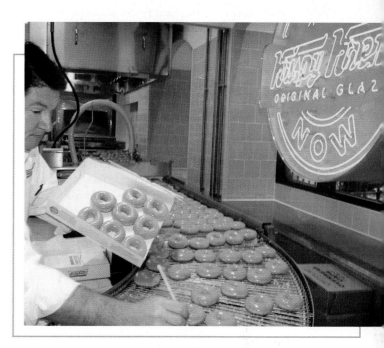

In April 2000, **Krispy Kreme Doughnuts** (www.krispykreme.com) went public at $21 per share. Investors gobbled up the 3,450,000 shares as fast as consumers did its hot-from-the-oven glazed doughnuts. In 2001, the company did a secondary offering of 2,600,000 shares at $67 per share. Shortly thereafter, the stock split twice, reducing the per-share issuing prices to $5.25 and $16.75, respectively, while quadrupling the number of shares outstanding. Krispy Kreme used the proceeds of its equity issues to fund an aggressive expansion campaign to build stores in new U.S. and international markets. Its timing was particularly good: Investors were looking for an alternative to dot-com high fliers, and the company's popular brand and product appealed to many different types of consumers. The stock soared and reached a high of $49.74 in August 2003.

Krispy Kreme's capital structure (the mix of debt and equity used to fund the company) at October 31, 2001, consisted of $9.7 million in long-term debt and $175.8 million in stockholders' equity. With a debt-to-equity ratio of just 5.5 percent (extremely low compared to the industry average of 92 percent) and a times interest earned ratio of 22, Krispy Kreme had plenty of flexibility in its capital structure.

Following its stock offerings, Krispy Kreme turned to debt to further its expansion. By August 2004, its debt-to-equity ratio had climbed to 32.27 percent. At the same time, its stock price was tumbling into the mid-teens, partially due to an SEC inquiry into Krispy Kreme's May 2004 announcement that it was lowering its guidance (expectations of future performance), a move that the company blamed on the low-carb diet phenomenon.

Is a capital structure consisting mostly of equity better than one with a higher percentage of debt? Not necessarily. Capital structure varies among companies in the same industry and across industry groups.

Each type of long-term capital has its advantages. As we learned in Chapter 11, debt costs less than equity. Adding debt, with its fixed rate, to the capital structure creates *financial leverage,* the use of fixed financial costs to magnify returns. Of course, leverage also increases risk. This chapter will show that financial leverage and capital structure are closely related concepts that can minimize the cost of capital and maximize owners' wealth.

Source: Krispy Kreme press releases downloaded August 9, 2004, from www.krispykreme.com.

■ *What other factors may have led to the 2004 decline in the Krispy Kreme stock price?*

12.1 | Leverage

leverage
Results from the use of fixed-cost assets or funds to magnify returns to the firm's owners.

capital structure
The mix of long-term debt and equity maintained by the firm.

Leverage results from the use of fixed-cost assets or funds to magnify returns to the firm's owners. Generally, increases in leverage result in increased return and risk, whereas decreases in leverage result in decreased return and risk. The amount of leverage in the firm's **capital structure**—the mix of long-term debt and equity maintained by the firm—can significantly affect its value by affecting return and risk. Unlike some causes of risk, management has almost complete control over the risk introduced through the use of leverage. Because of its effect on value, the financial manager must understand how to measure and evaluate leverage, particularly when making capital structure decisions.

The three basic types of leverage can best be defined with reference to the firm's income statement, as shown in the general income statement format in Table 12.1.

- *Operating leverage* is concerned with the relationship between the firm's sales revenue and its earnings before interest and taxes, or EBIT. (EBIT is a descriptive label for *operating profits.*)
- *Financial leverage* is concerned with the relationship between the firm's EBIT and its common stock earnings per share (EPS).
- *Total leverage* is concerned with the relationship between the firm's sales revenue and EPS.

We will examine the three types of leverage concepts in detail in sections that follow. First, though, we will look at breakeven analysis, which lays the foundation for leverage concepts by demonstrating the effects of fixed costs on the firm's operations.

TABLE 12.1

General Income Statement Format and Types of Leverage

	Sales revenue
	Less: Cost of goods sold
Operating leverage	Gross profits
	Less: Operating expenses
	Earnings before interest and taxes (EBIT)
	Less: Interest
	Net profits before taxes
	Less: Taxes
Financial leverage	Net profits after taxes
	Less: Preferred stock dividends
	Earnings available for common stockholders
	Earnings per share (EPS)

Total leverage

Breakeven Analysis

breakeven analysis
Indicates the level of operations necessary to cover all costs and the profitability associated with various levels of sales.

operating breakeven point
The level of sales necessary to cover all *operating costs;* the point at which EBIT = $0.

Breakeven analysis, sometimes called *cost-volume-profit analysis,* is used by the firm (1) to determine the level of operations necessary to cover all costs and (2) to evaluate the profitability associated with various levels of sales. The firm's **operating breakeven point** is the level of sales necessary to cover all *operating costs.* At that point, earnings before interest and taxes equals $0.[1]

The first step in finding the operating breakeven point is to divide the cost of goods sold and operating expenses into fixed and variable operating costs. *Fixed costs* are a function of time, not sales volume, and are typically contractual; rent, for example, is a fixed cost. *Variable costs* vary directly with sales and are a function of volume, not time; shipping costs, for example, are a variable cost.[2]

The Algebraic Approach

Using the following variables, we can recast the operating portion of the firm's income statement given in Table 12.1 into the algebraic representation shown in Table 12.2.

P = sale price per unit

Q = sales quantity in units

FC = fixed *operating* cost per period

VC = variable *operating* cost per unit

Rewriting the algebraic calculations in Table 12.2 as a formula for earnings before interest and taxes yields Equation 12.1:

$$EBIT = (P \times Q) - FC - (VC \times Q) \tag{12.1}$$

Simplifying Equation 12.1 yields

$$EBIT = Q \times (P - VC) - FC \tag{12.2}$$

TABLE 12.2

Operating Leverage, Costs, and Breakeven Analysis

	Item	Algebraic representation
Operating leverage	Sales revenue	$(P \times Q)$
	Less: Fixed operating costs	$- \quad FC$
	Less: Variable operating costs	$-(VC \times Q)$
	Earnings before interest and taxes	EBIT

---

1. Quite often, the breakeven point is calculated so that it represents the point at which *all costs—both operating and financial*—are covered. Our concern in this chapter is not with this overall breakeven point.

2. Some costs, commonly called *semifixed* or *semivariable,* are partly fixed and partly variable. An example is sales commissions that are fixed for a certain volume of sales and then increase to higher levels for higher volumes. For convenience and clarity, we assume that all costs can be classified as either fixed or variable.

As noted above, the operating breakeven point is the level of sales at which all fixed and variable *operating costs* are covered—the level at which EBIT equals $0. Setting EBIT equal to $0 and solving Equation 12.2 for Q yield

$$Q = \frac{FC}{P - VC} \quad (12.3)$$

Q is the firm's operating breakeven point.[3]

EXAMPLE

Assume that Cheryl's Posters, a small poster retailer, has fixed operating costs of $2,500, its sale price per unit (poster) is $10, and its variable operating cost per unit is $5. Applying Equation 12.3 to these data yields

$$Q = \frac{\$2,500}{\$10 - \$5} = \frac{\$2,500}{\$5} = 500 \text{ units}$$

At sales of 500 units, the firm's EBIT should just equal $0. The firm will have positive EBIT for sales greater than 500 units and negative EBIT, or a loss, for sales less than 500 units. We can confirm this by substituting values above and below 500 units, along with the other values given, into Equation 12.1. ■

The Graphical Approach

Figure 12.1 presents in graphical form the breakeven analysis of the data in the preceding example. The firm's operating breakeven point is the point at which its *total operating cost*—the sum of its fixed and variable operating costs—equals sales revenue. At this point, EBIT equals $0. The figure shows that for sales *below* 500 units, total operating cost exceeds sales revenue, and EBIT is less than $0 (a loss). For sales *above* the breakeven point of 500 units, sales revenue exceeds total operating cost, and EBIT is greater than $0.

Changing Costs and the Operating Breakeven Point

A firm's operating breakeven point is sensitive to a number of variables: fixed operating cost (FC), the sale price per unit (P), and the variable operating cost per unit (VC). The effects of increases or decreases in these variables can be readily seen by referring to Equation 12.3. The sensitivity of the breakeven sales volume (Q) to an *increase* in each of these variables is summarized in Table 12.3. As might be expected, an increase in cost (FC or VC) tends to increase the operating breakeven point, whereas an increase in the sale price per unit (P) decreases the operating breakeven point.

EXAMPLE

Assume that Cheryl's Posters wishes to evaluate the impact of several options: (1) increasing fixed operating costs to $3,000, (2) increasing the sale price per unit to $12.50, (3) increasing the variable operating cost per unit to $7.50, and

---

3. Because the firm is assumed to be a single-product firm, its operating breakeven point is found in terms of unit sales, Q. For multiproduct firms, the operating breakeven point is generally found in terms of dollar sales, S. This is done by substituting the contribution margin, which is 100% minus total variable operating costs as a percentage of total sales, denoted VC%, into the denominator of Equation 12.3. The result is Equation 12.3a:

$$S = \frac{FC}{1 - VC\%} \quad (12.3a)$$

This multiproduct-firm breakeven point assumes that the firm's product mix remains the same at all levels of sales.

FIGURE 12.1

Breakeven Analysis
Graphical operating
breakeven analysis

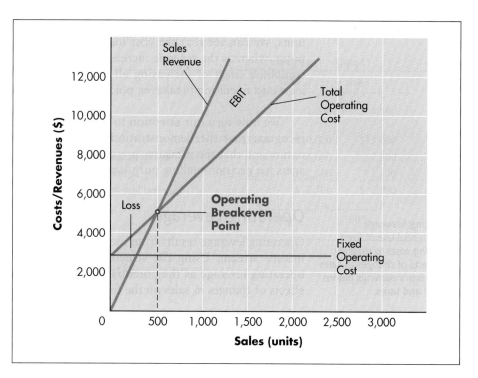

(4) simultaneously implementing all three of these changes. Substituting the appropriate data into Equation 12.3 yields the following results:

$$(1)\ \text{Operating breakeven point} = \frac{\$3,000}{\$10 - \$5} = 600 \text{ units}$$

$$(2)\ \text{Operating breakeven point} = \frac{\$2,500}{\$12.50 - \$5} = 333\tfrac{1}{3} \text{ units}$$

$$(3)\ \text{Operating breakeven point} = \frac{\$2,500}{\$10 - \$7.50} = 1,000 \text{ units}$$

$$(4)\ \text{Operating breakeven point} = \frac{\$3,000}{\$12.50 - \$7.50} = 600 \text{ units}$$

TABLE 12.3

**Sensitivity of Operating Breakeven Point
to Increases in Key Breakeven Variables**

Increase in variable	Effect on operating breakeven point
Fixed operating cost *(FC)*	Increase
Sale price per unit *(P)*	Decrease
Variable operating cost per unit *(VC)*	Increase

Note: Decreases in each of the variables shown would have the opposite effect from their effect on operating breakeven point.

EXAMPLE

Applying Equation 12.4 to cases 1 and 2 in Table 12.4 yields the following results:[5]

$$\text{Case 1:} \quad \frac{+100\%}{+50\%} = 2.0$$

$$\text{Case 2:} \quad \frac{-100\%}{-50\%} = 2.0$$

Because the result is greater than 1, operating leverage exists. For a given base level of sales, the higher the value resulting from applying Equation 12.4, the greater the degree of operating leverage. ■

A more direct formula for calculating the degree of operating leverage at a base sales level, Q, is shown in Equation 12.5.[6]

$$\text{DOL at base sales level } Q = \frac{Q \times (P - VC)}{Q \times (P - VC) - FC} \tag{12.5}$$

EXAMPLE

Substituting $Q = 1,000$, $P = \$10$, $VC = \$5$, and $FC = \$2,500$ into Equation 12.5 yields the following result:

$$\text{DOL at 1,000 units} = \frac{1,000 \times (\$10 - \$5)}{1,000 \times (\$10 - \$5) - \$2,500} = \frac{\$5,000}{\$2,500} = 2.0$$

The use of the formula results in the same value for DOL (2.0) as that found by using Table 12.4 and Equation 12.4.[7] ■

See the *In Practice* box on the facing page for discussion of operating leverage at software maker Adobe.

Fixed Costs and Operating Leverage

Changes in fixed operating costs affect operating leverage significantly. Firms sometimes can incur fixed operating costs rather than variable operating costs and at other times may be able to substitute one type of cost for the other. For example, a firm could make fixed-dollar lease payments rather than payments equal to a specified percentage of sales. Or it could compensate sales representatives with a fixed salary and bonus rather than on a pure percent-of-sales commis-

---

5. Because the concept of leverage is *linear,* positive and negative changes of equal magnitude will always result in equal degrees of leverage when the same base sales level is used as a point of reference. This relationship holds for all types of leverage discussed in this chapter.

6. Technically, the formula for DOL given in Equation 12.5 should include absolute value signs because it is possible to get a negative DOL when the EBIT for the base sales level is negative. Because we assume that the EBIT for the base level of sales is positive, we do not use the absolute value signs.

7. When total revenue in dollars from sales—instead of unit sales—is available, the following equation, in which TR = total revenue in dollars at a base level of sales and TVC = total variable operating costs in dollars, can be used:

$$\text{DOL at base dollar sales } TR = \frac{TR - TVC}{TR - TVC - FC}$$

This formula is especially useful for finding the DOL for multiproduct firms. It should be clear that because in the case of a single-product firm, $TR = P \times Q$ and $TVC = VC \times Q$, substitution of these values into Equation 12.5 results in the equation given here.

ADOBE'S OPERATING LEVERAGE

Adobe Systems, the second largest PC software company in the United States, dominates the markets for graphic design, imaging, dynamic media, and authoring-tool software. Web site designers prefer its Photoshop and Illustrator software applications, and Adobe's Acrobat software has become a standard for sharing documents online.

Despite a sales slowdown in 2001–2002, the company continued to meet its earnings targets. Its ability to manage discretionary expenses helped to keep its bottom line strong. As a software company, Adobe has an additional advantage: *operating leverage,* the use of fixed operating costs to magnify the effects of changes in sales on earnings before interest and taxes (EBIT).

Adobe and its peers in the software industry incur the bulk of their costs early in a product's life cycle, during the research and development (R&D) and initial marketing stages. The up-front development costs are fixed, regardless of how many copies of a program the company sells, and subse-

quent production costs are practically zero. The economies of scale are huge. Indeed, once a company sells enough copies to cover its fixed costs, incremental dollars go primarily to profit.

As demonstrated in the table below, operating leverage magnified the *increase* in Adobe's EBIT in 2000 and 2003 while magnifying the *decrease* in EBIT in 2001 and 2002. A 2.8 percent drop in 2001 sales resulted in an EBIT reduction of 7.3 percent. In 2002, an additional drop in sales of 5.3 percent resulted in a 24.1 percent decrease in EBIT. In 2003, a modest increase in sales—just over 11 percent—turned into a 32 percent increase in EBIT. Because the company has no long-term debt in its capital struc-

ture, its total leverage is derived only from fixed operating costs. (It's important to remember that this example represents only 4 years of data and that Adobe's degree of operating leverage may change in the future.)

The table below demonstrates the impact of operating leverage on Adobe Systems in fiscal years (FYs) 2000–2003.

Sources: Adapted from Zeke Ashton, "The Software Advantage," *Motley Fool* (March 31, 2000); and "Operating Leverage Helps Adobe," *Motley Fool* (March 16, 2001), both downloaded from www.motley.fool.com; updated using data from Adobe's 2003 *Annual Report.*

■ *What events might have accelerated the degree of operating leverage for Adobe in 2002?*

Item	FY1999	FY2000	FY2001	FY2002	FY2003
Sales revenue (millions)	$1,015	$1,266	$1,230	$1,165	$1,295
EBIT (millions)	$260	$408	$378	$287	$379
(1) Percent change in sales		24.7%	−2.8%	−5.3%	11.2%
(2) Percent change in EBIT		56.9%	−7.3%	−24.1%	32.0%
DOL [(2) ÷ (1)]		2.3	2.6	4.5	2.6

sion basis. The effects of changes in fixed operating costs on operating leverage can best be illustrated by continuing our example.

EXAMPLE Assume that Cheryl's Posters exchanges a portion of its variable operating costs for fixed operating costs by eliminating sales commissions and increasing sales salaries. This exchange results in a reduction in the variable operating cost per unit from $5 to $4.50 and an increase in the fixed operating costs from $2,500 to $3,000. Table 12.5 (see page 546) presents an analysis like that in Table 12.4, but using the new costs. Although the EBIT of $2,500 at the 1,000-unit sales level is the same as before the shift in operating cost structure, Table 12.5 shows that the firm has increased its operating leverage by shifting to greater fixed operating costs.

TABLE 12.5

Operating Leverage and Increased Fixed Costs

		Case 2		Case 1
		−50%		+50%
Sales (in units)		500	1,000	1,500
Sales revenue[a]		$5,000	$10,000	$15,000
Less: Variable operating costs[b]		2,250	4,500	6,750
Less: Fixed operating costs		3,000	3,000	3,000
Earnings before interest and taxes (EBIT)		−$ 250	$ 2,500	$ 5,250
			−110%	+110%

[a]Sales revenue was calculated as indicated in Table 12.4.
[b]Variable operating costs = $4.50/unit × sales in units.

With the substitution of the appropriate values into Equation 12.5, the degree of operating leverage at the 1,000-unit base level of sales becomes

$$\text{DOL at 1,000 units} = \frac{1,000 \times (\$10 - \$4.50)}{1,000 \times (\$10 - \$4.50) - \$3,000} = \frac{\$5,500}{\$2,500} = 2.2$$

Comparing this value to the DOL of 2.0 before the shift to more fixed costs makes it is clear that the higher the firm's fixed operating costs relative to variable operating costs, the greater the degree of operating leverage.

Financial Leverage

financial leverage
The potential use of *fixed financial costs* to magnify the effects of changes in earnings before interest and taxes on the firm's earnings per share.

Financial leverage results from the presence of *fixed financial costs* in the firm's income stream. Using the framework in Table 12.1, we can define **financial leverage** as the potential use of *fixed financial costs* to magnify the effects of changes in earnings before interest and taxes on the firm's earnings per share. The two fixed financial costs that may be found on the firm's income statement are (1) interest on debt and (2) preferred stock dividends. These charges must be paid regardless of the amount of EBIT available to pay them.[8]

EXAMPLE

Chen Foods, a small Asian food company, expects EBIT of $10,000 in the current year. It has a $20,000 bond with a 10% (annual) coupon rate of interest and an issue of 600 shares of $4 (annual dividend per share) preferred stock outstanding. It also has 1,000 shares of common stock outstanding. The annual interest on the bond issue is $2,000 (0.10 × $20,000). The annual dividends on the preferred

---

8. As noted in Chapter 7, although preferred stock dividends can be "passed" (not paid) at the option of the firm's directors, it is generally believed that payment of such dividends is necessary. *This text treats the preferred stock dividend as a contractual obligation, not only to be paid as a fixed amount, but also to be paid as scheduled.* Although failure to pay preferred dividends cannot force the firm into bankruptcy, it increases the common stockholders' risk because they cannot be paid dividends until the claims of preferred stockholders are satisfied.

TABLE 12.6

The EPS for Various EBIT Levels[a]

		Case 2		Case 1
		−40%		+40%
EBIT	$6,000	$10,000		$14,000
Less: Interest (I)	2,000	2,000		2,000
Net profits before taxes	$4,000	$ 8,000		$12,000
Less: Taxes (T = 0.40)	1,600	3,200		4,800
Net profits after taxes	$2,400	$ 4,800		$ 7,200
Less: Preferred stock dividends (PD)	2,400	2,400		2,400
Earnings available for common (EAC)	$ 0	$ 2,400		$ 4,800
Earnings per share (EPS)	$\frac{\$0}{1,000}=\$0$	$\frac{\$2,400}{1,000}=\$2.40$		$\frac{\$4,800}{1,000}=\$4.80$
		−100%		+100%

[a]As noted in Chapter 1, for accounting and tax purposes, interest is a *tax-deductible expense*, whereas dividends must be paid from after-tax cash flows.

stock are $2,400 ($4.00/share × 600 shares). Table 12.6 presents the EPS corresponding to levels of EBIT of $6,000, $10,000, and $14,000, assuming that the firm is in the 40% tax bracket. Two situations are shown:

Case 1   A 40% *increase* in EBIT (from $10,000 to $14,000) results in a 100% *increase* in earnings per share (from $2.40 to $4.80).

Case 2   A 40% *decrease* in EBIT (from $10,000 to $6,000) results in a 100% *decrease* in earnings per share (from $2.40 to $0).

The effect of financial leverage is such that an increase in the firm's EBIT results in a more-than-proportional increase in the firm's earnings per share, whereas a decrease in the firm's EBIT results in a more-than-proportional decrease in EPS.

Measuring the Degree of Financial Leverage (DFL)

degree of financial leverage (DFL)
The numerical measure of the firm's financial leverage.

The **degree of financial leverage (DFL)** is the numerical measure of the firm's financial leverage. Computing it is much like computing the degree of operating leverage. The following equation presents one approach for obtaining the DFL.[9]

$$DFL = \frac{\text{Percentage change in EPS}}{\text{Percentage change in EBIT}} \quad (12.6)$$

Whenever the percentage change in EPS resulting from a given percentage change in EBIT is greater than the percentage change in EBIT, financial leverage exists. This means that whenever DFL is greater than 1, there is financial leverage.

9. This approach is valid only when the same base level of EBIT is used to calculate and compare these values. In other words, *the base level of EBIT must be held constant to compare the financial leverage associated with different levels of fixed financial costs.*

EXAMPLE Applying Equation 12.6 to cases 1 and 2 in Table 12.6 yields

$$\text{Case 1:} \quad \frac{+100\%}{+40\%} = 2.5$$

$$\text{Case 2:} \quad \frac{-100\%}{-40\%} = 2.5$$

In both cases, the quotient is greater than 1, so financial leverage exists. The higher this value, the greater the degree of financial leverage. ■

A more direct formula for calculating the degree of financial leverage at a base level of EBIT is given by Equation 12.7, where the notation from Table 12.6 is used.[10] Note that in the denominator, the term $1/(1 - T)$ converts the after-tax preferred stock dividend to a before-tax amount for consistency with the other terms in the equation.

$$\text{DFL at base level EBIT} = \frac{\text{EBIT}}{\text{EBIT} - I - \left(PD \times \dfrac{1}{1 - T}\right)} \tag{12.7}$$

EXAMPLE Substituting EBIT = $10,000, I = $2,000, PD = $2,400, and the tax rate (T = 0.40) into Equation 12.7 yields the following result:

$$\text{DFL at \$10,000 EBIT} = \frac{\$10,000}{\$10,000 - \$2,000 - \left(\$2,400 \times \dfrac{1}{1 - 0.40}\right)}$$

$$= \frac{\$10,000}{\$4,000} = 2.5$$ ■

Note that the formula given in Equation 12.7 provides a more direct method for calculating the degree of financial leverage than the approach illustrated using Table 12.6 and Equation 12.6.

Total Leverage

We also can assess the combined effect of operating and financial leverage on the firm's risk by using a framework similar to that used to develop the individual concepts of leverage. This combined effect, or **total leverage,** can be defined as the potential use of *fixed costs, both operating and financial,* to magnify the effects of changes in sales on the firm's earnings per share. Total leverage can therefore be viewed as the *total impact of the fixed costs* in the firm's operating and financial structure.

total leverage
The potential use of *fixed costs, both operating and financial,* to magnify the effects of changes in sales on the firm's earnings per share.

EXAMPLE Cables Inc., a computer cable manufacturer, expects sales of 20,000 units at $5 per unit in the coming year and must meet the following obligations: variable operating costs of $2 per unit, fixed operating costs of $10,000, interest of

10. By using the formula for DFL in Equation 12.7, it is possible to get a negative value for the DFL if the EPS for the base level of EBIT is negative. Rather than show absolute value signs in the equation, we instead assume that the base-level EPS is positive.

TABLE 12.7

The Total Leverage Effect

	+50%	
Sales (in units)	20,000	30,000
Sales revenue[a]	$100,000	$150,000
Less: Variable operating costs[b]	40,000	60,000
Less: Fixed operating costs	10,000	10,000
Earnings before interest and taxes (EBIT)	$ 50,000	$ 80,000

$$\text{DOL} = \frac{+60\%}{+50\%} = 1.2$$

+60%

Less: Interest	20,000	20,000
Net profits before taxes	$ 30,000	$ 60,000
Less: Taxes (T = 0.40)	12,000	24,000
Net profits after taxes	$ 18,000	$ 36,000
Less: Preferred stock dividends	12,000	12,000
Earnings available for common	$ 6,000	$ 24,000
Earnings per share (EPS)	$\frac{\$6,000}{5,000} = \$1.20$	$\frac{\$24,000}{5,000} = \$4.80$

$$\text{DFL} = \frac{+300\%}{+60\%} = 5.0$$

$$\text{DTL} = \frac{+300\%}{+50\%} = 6.0$$

+300%

[a]Sales revenue = $5/unit × sales in units.

[b]Variable operating costs = $2/unit × sales in units.

$20,000, and preferred stock dividends of $12,000. The firm is in the 40% tax bracket and has 5,000 shares of common stock outstanding. Table 12.7 presents the levels of earnings per share associated with the expected sales of 20,000 units and with sales of 30,000 units.

The table illustrates that as a result of a 50% increase in sales (from 20,000 to 30,000 units), the firm would experience a 300% increase in earnings per share (from $1.20 to $4.80). Although it is not shown in the table, a 50% decrease in sales would, conversely, result in a 300% decrease in earnings per share. The linear nature of the leverage relationship accounts for the fact that sales changes of equal magnitude in opposite directions result in EPS changes of equal magnitude in the corresponding direction. At this point, it should be clear that whenever a firm has fixed costs—operating or financial—in its structure, total leverage will exist.

Measuring the Degree of Total Leverage (DTL)

degree of total leverage (DTL)
The numerical measure of the firm's total leverage.

The **degree of total leverage (DTL)** is the numerical measure of the firm's total leverage. It can be computed much as operating and financial leverage are computed. The following equation presents one approach for measuring DTL:[11]

$$\text{DTL} = \frac{\text{Percentage change in EPS}}{\text{Percentage change in sales}} \tag{12.8}$$

11. This approach is valid only when the same base level of sales is used to calculate and compare these values. In other words, *the base level of sales must be held constant if we are to compare the total leverage associated with different levels of fixed costs.*

REVIEW QUESTIONS

12–1 What is meant by the term *leverage?* How are operating leverage, financial leverage, and total leverage related to the income statement?

12–2 What is the *operating breakeven point?* How do changes in fixed operating costs, the sale price per unit, and the variable operating cost per unit affect it?

12–3 What is *operating leverage?* What causes it? How is the *degree of operating leverage (DOL)* measured?

12–4 What is *financial leverage?* What causes it? How is the *degree of financial leverage (DFL)* measured?

12–5 What is the general relationship among operating leverage, financial leverage, and the total leverage of the firm? Do these types of leverage complement one another? Why or why not?

LG3 LG4 12.2 | The Firm's Capital Structure

Capital structure is one of the most complex areas of financial decision making because of its interrelationship with other financial decision variables.[13] Poor capital structure decisions can result in a high cost of capital, thereby lowering the NPVs of projects and making more of them unacceptable. Effective capital structure decisions can lower the cost of capital, resulting in higher NPVs and more acceptable projects—and thereby increasing the value of the firm. This section links together many of the concepts presented in Chapters 4, 5, 6, 7, and 11 and the discussion of leverage in this chapter.

Types of Capital

All of the items on the right-hand side of the firm's balance sheet, excluding current liabilities, are sources of capital. The following simplified balance sheet illustrates the basic breakdown of total capital into its two components, *debt capital* and *equity capital.*

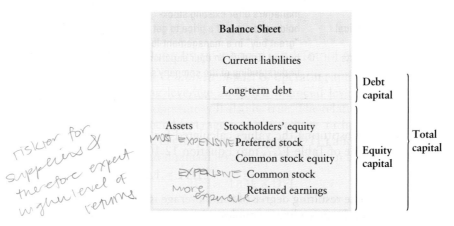

13. Of course, although capital structure is financially important, it—like many business decisions—is generally not so important as the firm's products or services. In a practical sense, a firm can probably more readily increase its value by improving quality and reducing costs than by fine-tuning its capital structure.

The various types and characteristics of *corporate bonds,* a major source of *debt capital,* were discussed in detail in Chapter 6. The cost of debt is lower than the cost of other forms of financing. Lenders demand relatively lower returns because they take the least risk of any long-term contributors of capital: (1) They have a higher priority of claim against any earnings or assets available for payment. (2) They can exert far greater legal pressure against the company to make payment than can owners of preferred or common stock. (3) The tax deductibility of interest payments lowers the debt cost to the firm substantially.

Unlike debt capital, which must be repaid at some future date, *equity capital* is expected to remain in the firm for an indefinite period of time. The two basic sources of equity capital are (1) preferred stock and (2) common stock equity, which includes common stock and retained earnings. Common stock is typically the most expensive form of equity, followed by retained earnings and then preferred stock. Our concern here is the relationship between debt and equity capital. Key differences between these two types of capital, relative to voice in management, claims on income and assets, maturity, and tax treatment, were summarized in Chapter 7, Table 7.1. Because of equity's secondary position relative to debt, suppliers of equity capital take greater risk than suppliers of debt capital and therefore must be compensated with higher expected returns.

External Assessment of Capital Structure

We saw earlier that *financial leverage* results from the use of fixed-cost financing, such as debt and preferred stock, to magnify return and risk. The amount of leverage in the firm's capital structure can affect its value by affecting return and risk. Those outside the firm can make a rough assessment of capital structure by using measures found in the firm's financial statements. Some of these important debt ratios were presented in Chapter 2. For example, a direct measure of the degree of indebtedness is the *debt ratio.* The higher this ratio, the greater the relative amount of debt (or financial leverage) in the firm's capital structure. Measures of the firm's ability to meet contractual payments associated with debt include the *times interest earned ratio* and the *fixed-payment coverage ratio.* These ratios provide indirect information on financial leverage. Generally, the smaller these ratios, the greater the firm's financial leverage and the less able it is to meet payments as they come due.

The level of debt (financial leverage) that is acceptable for one industry or line of business can be highly risky in another, because different industries and lines of business have different operating characteristics. Table 12.8 (see page 554) presents the debt and times interest earned ratios for selected industries and lines of business. Significant industry differences can be seen in these data. Differences in debt positions are also likely to exist *within* an industry or line of business.

 ## Capital Structure of Non-U.S. Firms

In general, non-U.S. companies have much higher degrees of indebtedness than their U.S. counterparts. Most of the reasons for this are related to the fact that U.S. capital markets are much more developed than those elsewhere and have played a greater role in corporate financing than has been the case in other countries. In most European countries and especially in Japan and other Pacific Rim nations, large commercial banks are more actively involved in the financing of corporate activity than has been true in the United States. Furthermore, in many

TABLE 12.8

Debt Ratios for Selected Industries and Lines of Business (Fiscal Years Ended 4/1/02 Through 3/31/03)

Industry or line of business	Debt ratio	Times interest earned ratio
Manufacturing industries		
Books	75.1%	3.4
Dairy products	73.8	4.1
Electronic computers	59.2	2.1
Iron and steel forgings	70.0	1.9
Machine tools, metal cutting types	65.4	1.3
Wines and distilled alcoholic beverages	65.7	4.8
Women's and girls' dresses	66.0	4.2
Wholesaling industries		
Furniture	67.2	2.3
General groceries	68.3	3.5
Men's and boys' clothing	63.0	4.4
Retailing industries		
Department stores	57.6	4.4
New car dealers	80.1	3.0
Supermarkets and grocery stores	75.6	2.9
Service industries		
Advertising agencies	87.9	4.3
General automotive repair	75.8	2.6
Insurance agencies and brokerages	85.1	4.8
Offices of Certified Public Accountants	70.4	7.2

Source: RMA Annual Statement Studies, 2003–2004 (fiscal years ended 4/1/02 through 3/31/03) (Philadelphia: Risk Management Association, 2003). Copyright © 2003 by Risk Management Association.

Note: The Risk Management Association recommends that these ratios be regarded only as general guidelines and not as absolute industry norms. No claim is made as to the representativeness of these figures.

of these countries, banks are allowed to make large equity investments in nonfinancial corporations—a practice that is prohibited for U.S. banks. Finally, share ownership tends to be more tightly controlled among founding-family, institutional, and even public investors in Europe and Asia than it is for most large U.S. corporations. Tight ownership enables owners to understand the firm's financial condition better, resulting in their willingness to tolerate a higher degree of indebtedness.

On the other hand, similarities do exist between U.S. corporations and corporations in other countries. First, the same industry patterns of capital structure tend to be found all around the world. For example, in nearly all countries, pharmaceutical and other high-growth industrial firms tend to have lower debt ratios than do steel companies, airlines, and electric utility companies. Second, the capital structures of the largest U.S.-based multinational companies, which have access to many different capital markets around the world, typically resemble the capital structures of multinational companies from other countries more than they resemble those of smaller U.S. companies. Finally, the worldwide trend is away from reliance on banks for corporate financing and toward greater reliance on security issuance. Over time, the differences in the capital structures of U.S. and non-U.S. firms will probably lessen.

Capital Structure Theory

Scholarly research suggests that there is an optimal capital structure range. *It is not yet possible to provide financial managers with a specified methodology for use in determining a firm's optimal capital structure.* Nevertheless, financial theory does offer help in understanding how a firm's chosen financing mix affects the firm's value.

In 1958, Franco Modigliani and Merton H. Miller[14] (commonly known as "M and M") demonstrated algebraically that, assuming perfect markets,[15] the capital structure that a firm chooses does not affect its value. Many researchers, including M and M, have examined the effects of less restrictive assumptions on the relationship between capital structure and the firm's value. The result is a theoretical *optimal* capital structure based on balancing the benefits and costs of debt financing. The major benefit of debt financing is the tax shield, which allows interest payments to be deducted in calculating taxable income. The cost of debt financing results from (1) the increased probability of bankruptcy caused by debt obligations, (2) the *agency costs* of the lender's constraining the firm's actions, and (3) the costs associated with managers having more information about the firm's prospects than do investors.

Tax Benefits

Allowing firms to deduct interest payments on debt when calculating taxable income reduces the amount of the firm's earnings paid in taxes, thereby making more earnings available for bondholders and stockholders. The deductibility of interest means the cost of debt, k_i, to the firm is subsidized by the government. Letting k_d equal the before-tax cost of debt and letting T equal the tax rate, from Chapter 11 (Equation 11.2), we have $k_i = k_d \times (1 - T)$.

Probability of Bankruptcy

The chance that a firm will become bankrupt because of an inability to meet its obligations as they come due depends largely on its level of both business risk and financial risk.

Business Risk   In Chapter 11, we defined *business risk* as the risk to the firm of being unable to cover its operating costs. In general, the greater the firm's *operating leverage*—the use of fixed operating costs—the higher its business risk. Although operating leverage is an important factor affecting business risk, two other factors—revenue stability and cost stability—also affect it. *Revenue stability* reflects the relative variability of the firm's sales revenues. Firms with reasonably

---

14. Franco Modigliani and Merton H. Miller, "The Cost of Capital, Corporation Finance, and the Theory of Investment," *American Economic Review* (June 1958), pp. 261–297.

15. Perfect-market assumptions include (1) no taxes, (2) no brokerage or flotation costs for securities, (3) symmetrical information—investors and managers have the same information about the firm's investment prospects, and (4) investor ability to borrow at the same rate as corporations.

stable levels of demand and with products that have stable prices have stable revenues. The result is low levels of business risk. Firms with highly volatile product demand and prices have unstable revenues that result in high levels of business risk. *Cost stability* reflects the relative predictability of input prices such as those for labor and materials. The more predictable and stable these input prices are, the lower the business risk; the less predictable and stable they are, the higher the business risk.

Business risk varies among firms, regardless of their lines of business, and is not affected by capital structure decisions. The level of business risk must be taken as a "given." The higher a firm's business risk, the more cautious the firm must be in establishing its capital structure. Firms with high business risk therefore tend toward less highly leveraged capital structures, and firms with low business risk tend toward more highly leveraged capital structures. We will hold business risk constant throughout the discussions that follow.

EXAMPLE

Cooke Company, a soft drink manufacturer, is preparing to make a capital structure decision. It has obtained estimates of sales and the associated levels of earnings before interest and taxes (EBIT) from its forecasting group: There is a 25% chance that sales will total $400,000, a 50% chance that sales will total $600,000, and a 25% chance that sales will total $800,000. Fixed operating costs total $200,000, and variable operating costs equal 50% of sales. These data are summarized, and the resulting EBIT calculated, in Table 12.9.

The table shows that there is a 25% chance that the EBIT will be $0, a 50% chance that it will be $100,000, and a 25% chance that it will be $200,000. When developing the firm's capital structure, the financial manager must accept as given these levels of EBIT and their associated probabilities. These EBIT data effectively reflect a certain level of business risk that captures the firm's operating leverage, sales revenue variability, and cost predictability. ∎

Hint The cash flows to investors from bonds are less risky than the dividends from preferred stock, which are ess risky than dividends from common stock. Only with bonds is the issuer contractually obligated to pay the scheduled interest, and the amounts due to bondholders and preferred stockholders are usually fixed. Therefore, the required return for bonds is generally lower than that for preferred stock, which is lower than that for common stock.

Financial Risk   The firm's capital structure directly affects its *financial risk*, which is the risk to the firm of being unable to cover required financial obligations. The penalty for not meeting financial obligations is bankruptcy. The more fixed-cost financing—debt (including financial leases) and preferred stock—a firm has in its capital structure, the greater its financial leverage and risk. Financial risk depends on the capital structure decision made by the management, and that decision is affected by the business risk the firm faces.

The *total risk* of a firm—business and financial risk combined—determines its probability of bankruptcy. Financial risk, its relationship to business risk, and their combined impact can be demonstrated by continuing the Cooke Company example.

TABLE 12.9

Sales and Associated EBIT Calculations for Cooke Company ($000)

Probability of sales	.25	.50	.25
Sales revenue	$400	$600	$800
Less: Fixed operating costs	200	200	200
Less: Variable operating costs (50% of sales)	200	300	400
Earnings before interest and taxes (EBIT)	$ 0	$100	$200

EXAMPLE   Cooke Company's current capital structure is as follows:

Current capital structure	
Long-term debt	$ 0
Common stock equity (25,000 shares at $20)	500,000
Total capital (assets)	$500,000

Hint As you learned in Chapter 2, the debt ratio is equal to the amount of total debt divided by the total assets. The higher this ratio, the more financial leverage a firm is using.

Let us assume that the firm is considering seven alternative capital structures. If we measure these structures using the debt ratio, they are associated with ratios of 0%, 10%, 20%, 30%, 40%, 50%, and 60%. Assuming that (1) the firm has no current liabilities, (2) its capital structure currently contains all equity as shown, and (3) the total amount of capital remains constant[16] at $500,000, the mix of debt and equity associated with the seven debt ratios would be as shown in Table 12.10. Also shown in the table is the number of shares of common stock outstanding under each alternative.

Associated with each of the debt levels in column 3 of Table 12.10 would be an interest rate that would be expected to increase with increases in financial leverage. The level of debt, the associated interest rate (assumed to apply to *all* debt), and the dollar amount of annual interest associated with each of the alternative capital structures are summarized in Table 12.11 (see page 558). Because both the level of debt and the interest rate increase with increasing financial leverage (debt ratios), the annual interest increases as well.

TABLE 12.10   Capital Structures Associated with Alternative Debt Ratios for Cooke Company

	Capital structure ($000)			Shares of common stock outstanding (000)
Debt ratio (1)	Total assets[a] (2)	Debt [(1) × (2)] (3)	Equity [(2) − (3)] (4)	[(4) ÷ $20][b] (5)
0%	$500	$ 0	$500	25.00
10	500	50	450	22.50
20	500	100	400	20.00
30	500	150	350	17.50
40	500	200	300	15.00
50	500	250	250	12.50
60	500	300	200	10.00

[a]Because the firm, for convenience, is assumed to have no current liabilities, its total assets equal its total capital of $500,000.

[b]The $20 value represents the book value per share of common stock equity noted earlier.

---

16. This assumption is needed so that we can assess alternative capital structures without having to consider the returns associated with the investment of additional funds raised. Attention here is given only to the *mix* of capital, not to its investment.

TABLE 12.11

Level of Debt, Interest Rate, and Dollar Amount of Annual Interest Associated with Cooke Company's Alternative Capital Structures

Capital structure debt ratio	Debt ($000) (1)	Interest rate on *all* debt (2)	Interest ($000) [(1) × (2)] (3)
0%	$ 0	0.0%	$ 0.00
10	50	9.0	4.50
20	100	9.5	9.50
30	150	10.0	15.00
40	200	11.0	22.00
50	250	13.5	33.75
60	300	16.5	49.50

Table 12.12 on the facing page uses the levels of EBIT and associated probabilities developed in Table 12.9, the number of shares of common stock found in column 5 of Table 12.10, and the annual interest values calculated in column 3 of Table 12.11 to calculate the earnings per share (EPS) for debt ratios of 0%, 30%, and 60%. A 40% tax rate is assumed. Also shown are the resulting expected EPS, the standard deviation of EPS, and the coefficient of variation of EPS associated with each debt ratio.[17]

Table 12.13 (see page 560) summarizes the pertinent data for the seven alternative capital structures. The values shown for 0%, 30%, and 60% debt ratios were developed in Table 12.12, whereas calculations of similar values for the other debt ratios (10%, 20%, 40%, and 50%) are not shown. Because the coefficient of variation measures the risk relative to the expected EPS, it is the preferred risk measure for use in comparing capital structures. As the firm's financial leverage increases, so does its coefficient of variation of EPS. As expected, an increasing level of risk is associated with increased levels of financial leverage.

The relative risks of the two extremes of the capital structures evaluated in Table 12.12 (debt ratios = 0% and 60%) can be illustrated by showing the probability distribution of EPS associated with each of them. Figure 12.3 (see page 560) shows these two distributions. The expected level of EPS increases with increasing financial leverage, and so does risk, as reflected in the relative dispersion of each of the distributions. Clearly, the uncertainty of the expected EPS, as well as the chance of experiencing negative EPS, is greater when higher degrees of financial leverage are employed.

Further, the nature of the risk–return tradeoff associated with the seven capital structures under consideration can be clearly observed by plotting the expected EPS and coefficient of variation relative to the debt ratio. Plotting the data from Table 12.13 results in Figure 12.4 (see page 561). The figure shows that as debt is substituted for equity (as the debt ratio increases), the level of EPS rises and then

---

17. For explanatory convenience, the *coefficient of variation of EPS*, which measures total (nondiversifiable and diversifiable) risk, is used throughout this chapter as a proxy for beta, which measures the relevant nondiversifiable risk.

TABLE 12.12 Calculation of EPS for Selected Debt Ratios ($000) for Cooke Company

Probability of EBIT	.25	.50	.25
Debt ratio = 0%			
EBIT (Table 12.9)	$ 0.00	$100.00	$200.00
Less: Interest (Table 12.11)	0.00	0.00	0.00
Net profits before taxes	$ 0.00	$100.00	$200.00
Less: Taxes ($T = 0.40$)	0.00	40.00	80.00
Net profits after taxes	$ 0.00	$ 60.00	$120.00
EPS (25.0 shares, Table 12.10)	$ 0.00	$ 2.40	$ 4.80
Expected EPS[a]		$ 2.40	
Standard deviation of EPS[a]		$ 1.70	
Coefficient of variation of EPS[a]		0.71	
Debt ratio = 30%			
EBIT (Table 12.9)	$ 0.00	$100.00	$200.00
Less: Interest (Table 12.11)	15.00	15.00	15.00
Net profits before taxes	($15.00)	$ 85.00	$185.00
Less: Taxes ($T = 0.40$)	(6.00)[b]	34.00	74.00
Net profits after taxes	($ 9.00)	$ 51.00	$111.00
EPS (17.50 shares, Table 12.10)	($ 0.51)	$ 2.91	$ 6.34
Expected EPS[a]		$ 2.91	
Standard deviation of EPS[a]		$ 2.42	
Coefficient of variation of EPS[a]		0.83	
Debt ratio = 60%			
EBIT (Table 12.9)	$ 0.00	$100.00	$200.00
Less: Interest (Table 12.11)	49.50	49.50	49.50
Net profits before taxes	($49.50)	$ 50.50	$150.50
Less: Taxes ($T = 0.40$)	(19.80)[b]	20.20	60.20
Net profits after taxes	($29.70)	$ 30.30	$ 90.30
EPS (10.00 shares, Table 12.10)	($ 2.97)	$ 3.03	$ 9.03
Expected EPS[a]		$ 3.03	
Standard deviation of EPS[a]		$ 4.24	
Coefficient of variation of EPS[a]		1.40	

[a]The procedures used to calculate the expected value, standard deviation, and coefficient of variation were presented in Equations 5.2, 5.3, and 5.4, respectively, in Chapter 5.

[b]It is assumed that the firm receives the tax benefit from its loss in the current period as a result of applying the *tax loss carryback* procedures specified in the tax law but not discussed in this text.

Cost Functions and Value
Capital costs and the
optimal capital structure

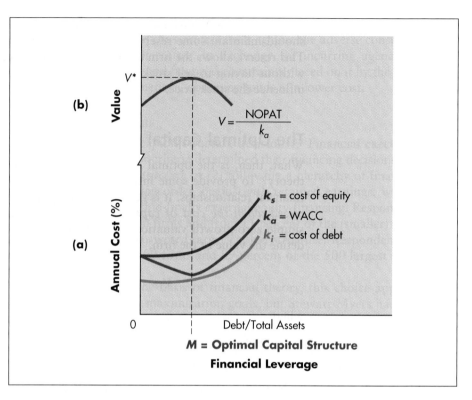

M = **Optimal Capital Structure**
Financial Leverage

A Graphical View of the Optimal Structure

optimal capital structure
The capital structure at which
the weighted average cost of
capital is minimized, thereby
maximizing the firm's value.

Because the maximization of value, *V*, is achieved when the overall cost of capital, k_a, is at a minimum (see Equation 12.11), the **optimal capital structure** is that at which the weighted average cost of capital, k_a, is minimized. In Figure 12.5(*a*), point *M* represents the *minimum weighted average cost of capital*—the point of optimal financial leverage and hence of optimal capital structure for the firm. Figure 12.5(*b*) plots the value of the firm that results from substitution of k_a in Figure 12.5(*a*) for various levels of financial leverage into the zero-growth valuation model in Equation 12.11. As shown in Figure 12.5(*b*), at the optimal capital structure, point *M*, the value of the firm is maximized at V^*.

Generally, the lower the firm's weighted average cost of capital, the greater the difference between the return on a project and the WACC, and therefore the greater the owners' return. Simply stated, minimizing the weighted average cost of capital allows management to undertake a larger number of profitable projects, thereby further increasing the value of the firm.

As a practical matter, there is no way to calculate the optimal capital structure implied by Figure 12.5. Because it is impossible either to know or to remain at the precise optimal capital structure, firms generally try to operate in a *range* that places them near what they believe to be the optimal capital structure.

REVIEW QUESTIONS

12–6   What is a firm's *capital structure?* What ratios assess the degree of financial leverage in a firm's capital structure?

12–7   In what ways are the capital structures of U.S. and non-U.S. firms different? How are they similar?

12–8   What is the major benefit of debt financing? How does it affect the firm's cost of debt?

12–9   What are *business risk* and *financial risk?* How does each of them influence the firm's capital structure decisions?

12–10 Briefly describe the *agency problem* that exists between owners and lenders. How do lenders cause firms to incur *agency costs* to resolve this problem?

12–11 How does *asymmetric information* affect the firm's capital structure decisions? How do the firm's financing actions give investors *signals* that reflect management's view of stock value?

12–12 How do the cost of debt, the cost of equity, and the weighted average cost of capital (WACC) behave as the firm's financial leverage increases from zero? Where is the *optimal capital structure?* What is its relationship to the firm's value at that point?

LG5 12.3 | The EBIT–EPS Approach to Capital Structure

EBIT–EPS approach
An approach for selecting the capital structure that maximizes earnings per share (EPS) over the expected range of earnings before interest and taxes (EBIT).

It should be clear from earlier chapters that the goal of the financial manager is to maximize owner wealth—that is, the firm's stock price. One of the widely followed variables affecting the firm's stock price is its earnings, which represents the returns earned on behalf of owners. In spite of the fact that focusing on earnings ignores risk—the other key variable affecting the firm's stock price—earnings per share (EPS) can be conveniently used to analyze alternative capital structures. The **EBIT–EPS approach** to capital structure involves selecting the capital structure that maximizes EPS over the expected range of earnings before interest and taxes (EBIT).

Presenting a Financing Plan Graphically

To analyze the effects of a firm's capital structure on the owners' returns, we consider the relationship between earnings before interest and taxes (EBIT) and earnings per share (EPS). A constant level of EBIT—constant *business risk*—is assumed, to isolate the effect on returns of the financing costs associated with alternative capital structures. EPS is used to measure the owners' returns, which are expected to be closely related to share price.[20]

The Data Required

To graph a financing plan, we need to know at least two EBIT–EPS coordinates. The approach for obtaining coordinates can be illustrated by an example.

---

20. The relationship that is expected to exist between EPS and owner wealth is not one of cause and effect. As indicated in Chapter 1, the maximization of profits does not necessarily ensure that owners' wealth is also maximized. Nevertheless, it is expected that the movement of earnings per share will have some effect on owners' wealth, because EPS data constitute one of the few pieces of information investors receive, and they often bid the firm's share price up or down in response to the level of these earnings.

TABLE 12.16

Important Factors to Consider in Making Capital Structure Decisions

Concern	Factor	Description
Business risk	Revenue stability	Firms that have stable and predictable revenues can more safely undertake highly leveraged capital structures than can firms with volatile patterns of sales revenue. Firms with growing sales tend to benefit from added debt because they can reap the positive benefits of financial leverage, which magnifies the effect of these increases.
	Cash flow	When considering a new capital structure, the firm must focus on its ability to generate the cash flows necessary to meet obligations. Cash forecasts reflecting an ability to service debts (and preferred stock) must support any shift in capital structure.
Agency costs	Contractual obligations	A firm may be contractually constrained with respect to the type of funds that it can raise. For example, a firm might be prohibited from selling additional debt except when the claims of holders of such debt are made subordinate to the existing debt. Contractual constraints on the sale of additional stock, as well as on the ability to distribute dividends on stock, might also exist.
	Management preferences	Occasionally, a firm will impose an internal constraint on the use of debt to limit its risk exposure to a level deemed acceptable to management. In other words, because of risk aversion, the firm's management constrains the firm's capital structure at a level that may or may not be the true optimum.
	Control	A management group concerned about control may prefer to issue debt rather than (voting) common stock. Under favorable market conditions, a firm that wanted to sell equity could make a *preemptive offering* or issue *nonvoting shares* (see Chapter 7), allowing each shareholder to maintain proportionate ownership. Generally, only in closely held firms or firms threatened by takeover does control become a major concern in the capital structure decision.
Asymmetric information	External risk assessment	The firm's ability to raise funds quickly and at favorable rates depends on the external risk assessments of lenders and bond raters. The firm must therefore consider the impact of capital structure decisions both on share value and on published financial statements from which lenders and raters assess the firm's risk.
	Timing	At times when the general level of interest rates is low, debt financing might be more attractive; when interest rates are high, the sale of stock may be more appealing. Sometimes both debt and equity capital become unavailable at what would be viewed as reasonable terms. General economic conditions—especially those of the capital market—can thus significantly affect capital structure decisions.

therefore carefully consider the types of operating and financial costs it incurs, recognizing that with greater fixed costs comes higher risk. Major decisions with regard to both operating cost structure and capital structure must therefore focus on their impact on the firm's value. Only those leverage and capital structure decisions that are consistent with the firm's goal of **maximizing its stock price** should be implemented.

Review of Learning Goals

LG1 Discuss leverage, capital structure, breakeven analysis, the operating breakeven point, and the effect of changing costs on it. Leverage results from the use of fixed costs to magnify returns to a firm's owners. Capital structure, the firm's mix of long-term debt and equity, affects leverage and therefore the firm's value. Breakeven analysis measures the level of sales necessary to cover total operating costs. The operating breakeven point may be calculated algebraically, by dividing fixed operating costs by the difference between the sale price per unit and variable operating cost per unit, or it may be determined graphically. The operating breakeven point increases with increased fixed and variable operating costs and decreases with an increase in sale price, and vice versa.

LG2 Understand operating, financial, and total leverage and the relationships among them. Operating leverage is the use of fixed operating costs by the firm to magnify the effects of changes in sales on EBIT. The higher the fixed operating costs, the greater the operating leverage. Financial leverage is the use of fixed financial costs by the firm to magnify the effects of changes in EBIT on EPS. The higher the fixed financial costs, the greater the financial leverage. The total leverage of the firm is the use of fixed costs—both operating and financial—to magnify the effects of changes in sales on EPS.

LG3 Describe the types of capital, external assessment of capital structure, the capital structure of non-U.S. firms, and capital structure theory. Debt capital and equity capital make up a firm's capital structure. Capital structure can be externally assessed by using financial ratios—debt ratio, times interest earned ratio, and fixed-payment coverage ratio. Non-U.S. companies tend to have much higher degrees of indebtedness than do their U.S. counterparts, primarily because U.S. capital markets are much more developed.

Research suggests that there is an optimal capital structure that balances the firm's benefits and costs of debt financing. The major benefit of debt financing is the tax shield. The costs of debt financing include the probability of bankruptcy; agency costs imposed by lenders; and asymmetric information, which typically causes firms to raise funds in a pecking order so as to send positive signals to the market and thereby enhance shareholder wealth.

LG4 Explain the optimal capital structure using a graphical view of the firm's cost-of-capital functions and a zero-growth valuation model. The zero-growth valuation model defines the firm's value as its net operating profits after taxes (NOPAT), or after-tax EBIT, divided by its weighted average cost of capital. Assuming that NOPAT is constant, the value of the firm is maximized by minimizing its weighted average cost of capital (WACC). The optimal capital structure is the one that minimizes the WACC. Graphically, the firm's WACC exhibits a U-shape, whose minimum value defines the optimal capital structure that maximizes owner wealth.

LG5 Discuss the EBIT–EPS approach to capital structure. The EBIT–EPS approach evaluates capital structures in light of the returns they provide the firm's owners and their degree of financial risk. Under the EBIT–EPS approach, the preferred capital structure is the one that is expected to provide maximum EPS over the firm's expected range of EBIT. Graphically, this approach reflects risk in terms of the financial breakeven point and the slope of the capital structure line. The major shortcoming of EBIT–EPS analysis is that it concentrates on maximizing earnings (returns) rather than owners' wealth, which considers risk as well as return.

LG6 **Review the return and risk of alternative capital structures, their linkage to market value, and other important considerations related to capital structure.** The best capital structure can be selected by using a valuation model to link return and risk factors. The preferred capital structure is the one that results in the highest estimated share value, not the highest EPS. Other important non-quantitative factors must also be considered when making capital structure decisions.

Self-Test Problems (Solutions in Appendix B)

LG1 **LG2**   **ST12–1 Breakeven point and all forms of leverage** TOR most recently sold 100,000 units at $7.50 each; its variable operating costs are $3.00 per unit, and its fixed operating costs are $250,000. Annual interest charges total $80,000, and the firm has 8,000 shares of $5 (annual dividend) preferred stock outstanding. It currently has 20,000 shares of common stock outstanding. Assume that the firm is subject to a 40% tax rate.
   a. At what level of sales (in units) would the firm break even on operations (that is, EBIT = $0)?
   b. Calculate the firm's *earnings per share (EPS)* in tabular form at (1) the current level of sales and (2) a 120,000-unit sales level.
   c. Using the current *$750,000 level of sales as a base*, calculate the firm's degree of operating leverage (DOL).
   d. Using the EBIT *associated with the $750,000 level of sales as a base*, calculate the firm's degree of financial leverage (DFL).
   e. Use the degree of total leverage (DTL) concept to determine the effect (in percentage terms) of a 50% increase in TOR's sales *from the $750,000 base level* on its earnings per share.

LG5   **ST12–2 EBIT–EPS analysis** Newlin Electronics is considering additional financing of $10,000. It currently has $50,000 of 12% (annual interest) bonds and 10,000 shares of common stock outstanding. The firm can obtain the financing through a 12% (annual interest) bond issue or through the sale of 1,000 shares of common stock. The firm has a 40% tax rate.
   a. Calculate two EBIT–EPS coordinates for each plan by selecting any two EBIT values and finding their associated EPS values.
   b. Plot the two financing plans on a set of EBIT–EPS axes.
   c. On the basis of your graph in part **b**, at what level of EBIT does the bond plan become superior to the stock plan?

ST12–3 **Optimal capital structure**   Hawaiian Macadamia Nut Company has collected the following data with respect to its capital structure, expected earnings per share, and required return.

Capital structure debt ratio	Expected earnings per share	Required return, k_s
0%	$3.12	13%
10	3.90	15
20	4.80	16
30	5.44	17
40	5.51	19
50	5.00	20
60	4.40	22

a. Compute the *estimated share value* associated with each of the capital structures, using the simplified method described in this chapter (see Equation 12.12).

b. Determine the optimal capital structure on the basis of (1) maximization of expected earnings per share and (2) maximization of share value.

c. Which capital structure do you recommend? Why?

Warm-Up Exercises

E12–1 Canvas Reproductions has fixed operating costs of $12,500, variable operating costs of $10 per unit, and sells its paintings for $25 each. At what level of unit sales will the company breakeven in terms of EBIT?

E12–2 The Great Fish Taco Corporation currently has fixed operating costs of $15,000, sells its pre-made tacos for $6 per box, and incurs variable operating costs of $2.50 per box. If the firm has a potential investment that would simultaneously raise its fixed costs to $16,500 and allow it to charge a per-box sale price of $6.50 due to better-textured tacos, what will the impact be on its operating breakeven point in boxes?

E12–3 Chico's has sales of 15,000 units at a price of $20 per unit. The firm incurs fixed operating costs of $30,000 and variable operating costs of $12 per unit. What is Chico's *degree of operating leverage (DOL)* at a base level of sales of 15,000 units?

E12–4 Parker Investments has EBIT of $20,000, interest expense of $3,000, and preferred dividends of $4,000. If it pays taxes at a rate of 38%, what is Parker's *degree of financial leverage (DFL)* at a base level of EBIT of $20,000?

E12–5 Cobalt Industries had sales of 150,000 units at a price of $10 per unit. It faced fixed operating costs of $250,000 and variable operating costs of $5 per unit. The company is subject to a tax rate of 38% and has a weighted average cost of capital of 8.5%. Calculate Cobalt's *net operating profits after taxes (NOPAT)*, and use it to estimate the value of the firm.

Problems

LG1
BASIC

P12–1 **Breakeven point—Algebraic** Kate Rowland wishes to estimate the number of flower arrangements she must sell at $24.95 to break even. She has estimated fixed operating costs of $12,350 per year and variable operating costs of $15.45 per arrangement. How many flower arrangements must Kate sell to break even on operating costs?

LG1
BASIC

P12–2 **Breakeven comparisons—Algebraic** Given the price and cost data shown in the accompanying table for each of the three firms, F, G, and H, answer the following questions.

Firm	F	G	H
Sale price per unit	$ 18.00	$ 21.00	$ 30.00
Variable operating cost per unit	6.75	13.50	12.00
Fixed operating cost	45,000	30,000	90,000

  a. What is the *operating breakeven point* in units for each firm?
  b. How would you rank these firms in terms of their risk?

LG1
INTERMEDIATE

P12–3 **Breakeven point—Algebraic and graphical** Fine Leather Enterprises sells its single product for $129.00 per unit. The firm's fixed operating costs are $473,000 annually, and its variable operating costs are $86.00 per unit.
  a. Find the firm's *operating breakeven point* in units.
  b. Label the *x* axis "Sales (units)" and the *y* axis "Costs/Revenues ($)," and then graph the firm's sales revenue, total operating cost, and fixed operating cost functions on these axes. In addition, label the operating breakeven point and the areas of loss and profit (EBIT).

LG1
INTERMEDIATE

P12–4 **Breakeven analysis** Barry Carter is considering opening a music store. He wants to estimate the number of CDs he must sell to break even. The CDs will be sold for $13.98 each, variable operating costs are $10.48 per CD, and annual fixed operating costs are $73,500.
  a. Find the *operating breakeven point* in number of CDs.
  b. Calculate the total operating costs at the breakeven volume found in part **a.**
  c. If Barry estimates that at a minimum he can sell 2,000 CDs *per month*, should he go into the music business?
  d. How much EBIT will Barry realize if he sells the minimum 2,000 CDs per month noted in part **c?**

LG1
INTERMEDIATE

P12–5 **Breakeven point—Changing costs/revenues** JWG Company publishes *Creative Crosswords*. Last year the book of puzzles sold for $10 with variable operating cost per book of $8 and fixed operating costs of $40,000. How many books must JWG sell this year to achieve the breakeven point for the stated operating costs, given the following different circumstances?
  a. All figures remain the same as for last year.
  b. Fixed operating costs increase to $44,000; all other figures remain the same.
  c. The selling price increases to $10.50; all costs remain the same as for last year.

    d. Variable operating cost per book increases to $8.50; all other figures remain the same.

    e. What conclusions about the operating breakeven point can be drawn from your answers?

P12–6 **Breakeven analysis** Molly Jasper and her sister, Caitlin Peters, got into the novelties business almost by accident. Molly, a talented sculptor, often made little figurines as gifts for friends. Occasionally, she and Caitlin would set up a booth at a crafts fair and sell a few of the figurines along with jewelry that Caitlin made. Little by little, demand for the figurines, now called Mollycaits, grew, and the sisters began to reproduce some of the favorites in resin, using molds of the originals. The day came when a buyer for a major department store offered them a contract to produce 1,500 figurines of various designs for $10,000. Molly and Caitlin realized that it was time to get down to business. To make bookkeeping simpler, Molly had priced all of the figurines at $8.00. Variable operating costs amounted to an average of $6.00 per unit. To produce the order, Molly and Caitlin would have to rent industrial facilities for a month, which would cost them $4,000.

    a. Calculate Mollycaits' *operating breakeven point.*

    b. Calculate Mollycaits' EBIT on the department store order.

    c. If Molly renegotiates the contract at a price of $10.00 per figurine, what will the EBIT be?

    d. If the store refuses to pay more than $8.00 per unit but is willing to negotiate quantity, what quantity of figurines will result in an EBIT of $4,000?

    e. At this time, Mollycaits come in 15 different varieties. Whereas the average variable cost per unit is $6.00, the actual cost varies from unit to unit. What recommendation would you have for Molly and Caitlin with regard to pricing and/or the numbers and types of units that they offer for sale?

P12–7 **EBIT sensitivity** Stewart Industries sells its finished product for $9 per unit. Its fixed operating costs are $20,000, and the variable operating cost per unit is $5.

    a. Calculate the firm's earnings before interest and taxes (EBIT) for sales of 10,000 units.

    b. Calculate the firm's EBIT for sales of 8,000 and 12,000 units, respectively.

    c. Calculate the percentage changes in sales (from the 10,000-unit base level) and associated percentage changes in EBIT for the shifts in sales indicated in part **b.**

    d. On the basis of your findings in part **c,** comment on the sensitivity of changes in EBIT in response to changes in sales.

P12–8 **Degree of operating leverage** Grey Products has fixed operating costs of $380,000, variable operating costs of $16 per unit, and a selling price of $63.50 per unit.

    a. Calculate the *operating breakeven point* in units.

    b. Calculate the firm's EBIT at 9,000, 10,000, and 11,000 units, respectively.

    c. With 10,000 units as a base, what are the percentage changes in units sold and EBIT as sales move from the base to the other sales levels used in part **b?**

    d. Use the percentages computed in part **c** to determine the degree of operating leverage (DOL).

    e. Use the formula for degree of operating leverage to determine the DOL at 10,000 units.

P12–9 **Degree of operating leverage—Graphical**   Levin Corporation has fixed operating costs of $72,000, variable operating costs of $6.75 per unit, and a selling price of $9.75 per unit.
  a. Calculate the *operating breakeven point* in units.
  b. Compute the degree of operating leverage (DOL) for the following unit sales levels: 25,000, 30,000, 40,000. Use the formula given in the chapter.
  c. Graph the DOL figures that you computed in part **b** (on the *y* axis) against sales levels (on the *x* axis).
  d. Compute the degree of operating leverage at 24,000 units; add this point to your graph.
  e. What principle do your graph and figures illustrate?

P12–10 **EPS calculations**   Southland Industries has $60,000 of 16% (annual interest) bonds outstanding, 1,500 shares of preferred stock paying an annual dividend of $5 per share, and 4,000 shares of common stock outstanding. Assuming that the firm has a 40% tax rate, compute earnings per share (EPS) for the following levels of EBIT:
  a. $24,600
  b. $30,600
  c. $35,000

P12–11 **Degree of financial leverage**   Northwestern Savings and Loan has a current capital structure consisting of $250,000 of 16% (annual interest) debt and 2,000 shares of common stock. The firm pays taxes at the rate of 40%.
  a. Using EBIT values of $80,000 and $120,000, determine the associated earnings per share (EPS).
  b. Using $80,000 of EBIT as a base, calculate the degree of financial leverage (DFL).
  c. Rework parts **a** and **b** assuming that the firm has $100,000 of 16% (annual interest) debt and 3,000 shares of common stock.

P12–12 **DFL and graphical display of financing plans**   Wells and Associates has EBIT of $67,500. Interest costs are $22,500, and the firm has 15,000 shares of common stock outstanding. Assume a 40% tax rate.
  a. Use the degree of financial leverage (DFL) formula to calculate the DFL for the firm.
  b. Using a set of EBIT–EPS axes, plot Wells and Associates' financing plan.
  c. If the firm also has 1,000 shares of preferred stock paying a $6.00 annual dividend per share, what is the DFL?
  d. Plot the financing plan, including the 1,000 shares of $6.00 preferred stock, on the axes used in part **b**.
  e. Briefly discuss the graph of the two financing plans.

P12–13 **Integrative—Multiple leverage measures**   Play-More Toys produces inflatable beach balls, selling 400,000 balls per year. Each ball produced has a variable operating cost of $0.84 and sells for $1.00. Fixed operating costs are $28,000. The firm has annual interest charges of $6,000, preferred dividends of $2,000, and a 40% tax rate.
  a. Calculate the *operating breakeven point* in units.
  b. Use the degree of operating leverage (DOL) formula to calculate DOL.
  c. Use the degree of financial leverage (DFL) formula to calculate DFL.

d. Use the degree of total leverage (DTL) formula to calculate DTL. Compare this to the product of DOL and DFL calculated in parts **b** and **c.**

P12–14   Integrative—Leverage and risk   Firm R has sales of 100,000 units at $2.00 per unit, variable operating costs of $1.70 per unit, and fixed operating costs of $6,000. Interest is $10,000 per year. Firm W has sales of 100,000 units at $2.50 per unit, variable operating costs of $1.00 per unit, and fixed operating costs of $62,500. Interest is $17,500 per year. Assume that both firms are in the 40% tax bracket.

a. Compute the degree of operating, financial, and total leverage for firm R.
b. Compute the degree of operating, financial, and total leverage for firm W.
c. Compare the relative risks of the two firms.
d. Discuss the principles of leverage that your answers illustrate.

P12–15   Integrative—Multiple leverage measures and prediction   Carolina Fastener, Inc., makes a patented marine bulkhead latch that wholesales for $6.00. Each latch has variable operating costs of $3.50. Fixed operating costs are $50,000 per year. The firm pays $13,000 interest and preferred dividends of $7,000 per year. At this point, the firm is selling 30,000 latches per year and is taxed at a rate of 40%.

a. Calculate Carolina Fastener's *operating breakeven point.*
b. On the basis of the firm's current sales of 30,000 units per year and its interest and preferred dividend costs, calculate its EBIT and net profits.
c. Calculate the firm's degree of operating leverage (DOL).
d. Calculate the firm's degree of financial leverage (DFL).
e. Calculate the firm's degree of total leverage (DTL).
f. Carolina Fastener has entered into a contract to produce and sell an additional 15,000 latches in the coming year. Use the DOL, DFL, and DTL to predict and calculate the changes in EBIT and net profit. Check your work by a simple calculation of Carolina Fastener's EBIT and net profit, using the basic information given.

P12–16   Various capital structures   Charter Enterprises currently has $1 million in total assets and is totally equity-financed. It is contemplating a change in its capital structure. Compute the amount of debt and equity that would be outstanding if the firm were to shift to each of the following debt ratios: 10%, 20%, 30%, 40%, 50%, 60%, and 90%. (*Note:* The amount of total assets would not change.) Is there a limit to the debt ratio's value?

P12–17   Debt and financial risk   Tower Interiors has made the forecast of sales shown in the following table. Also given is the probability of each level of sales.

Sales	Probability
$200,000	.20
300,000	.60
400,000	.20

The firm has fixed operating costs of $75,000 and variable operating costs equal to 70% of the sales level. The company pays $12,000 in interest per period. The tax rate is 40%.

a. Compute the earnings before interest and taxes (EBIT) for each level of sales.

b. Compute the earnings per share (EPS) for each level of sales, the expected EPS, the standard deviation of the EPS, and the coefficient of variation of EPS, assuming that there are 10,000 shares of common stock outstanding.

c. Tower has the opportunity to reduce its leverage to zero and pay no interest. This will require that the number of shares outstanding be increased to 15,000. Repeat part **b** under this assumption.

d. Compare your findings in parts **b** and **c**, and comment on the effect of the reduction of debt to zero on the firm's financial risk.

P12–18   EPS and optimal debt ratio   Williams Glassware has estimated, at various debt ratios, the expected earnings per share and the standard deviation of the earnings per share as shown in the following table.

Debt ratio	Earnings per share (EPS)	Standard deviation of EPS
0%	$2.30	$1.15
20	3.00	1.80
40	3.50	2.80
60	3.95	3.95
80	3.80	5.53

a. Estimate the *optimal debt ratio* on the basis of the relationship between earnings per share and the debt ratio. You will probably find it helpful to graph the relationship.

b. Graph the relationship between the *coefficient of variation* and the debt ratio. Label the areas associated with business risk and financial risk.

P12–19   EBIT–EPS and capital structure   Data-Check is considering two capital structures. The key information is shown in the following table. Assume a 40% tax rate.

Source of capital	Structure A	Structure B
Long-term debt	$100,000 at 16% coupon rate	$200,000 at 17% coupon rate
Common stock	4,000 shares	2,000 shares

a. Calculate two *EBIT–EPS coordinates* for each of the structures by selecting any two EBIT values and finding their associated EPS values.

b. Plot the two capital structures on a set of EBIT–EPS axes.

c. Indicate over what EBIT range, if any, each structure is preferred.

d. Discuss the leverage and risk aspects of each structure.

e. If the firm is fairly certain that its EBIT will exceed $75,000, which structure would you recommend? Why?

P12–20   EBIT–EPS and preferred stock   Litho-Print is considering two possible capital structures, A and B, shown in the table at the top of the facing page. Assume a 40% tax rate.

Source of capital	Structure A	Structure B
Long-term debt	$75,000 at 16% coupon rate	$50,000 at 15% coupon rate
Preferred stock	$10,000 with an 18% annual dividend	$15,000 with an 18% annual dividend
Common stock	8,000 shares	10,000 shares

a. Calculate two *EBIT–EPS coordinates* for each of the structures by selecting any two EBIT values and finding their associated EPS values.
b. Graph the two capital structures on the same set of EBIT–EPS axes.
c. Discuss the leverage and risk associated with each of the structures.
d. Over what range of EBIT is each structure preferred?
e. Which structure do you recommend if the firm expects its EBIT to be $35,000? Explain.

 P12–21 **Integrative—Optimal capital structure**   Medallion Cooling Systems, Inc., has total assets of $10,000,000, EBIT of $2,000,000, and preferred dividends of $200,000 and is taxed at a rate of 40%. In an effort to determine the optimal capital structure, the firm has assembled data on the cost of debt, the number of shares of common stock for various levels of indebtedness, and the overall required return on investment:

Capital structure debt ratio	Cost of debt, k_d	No. of common stock shares	Required return, k_s
0%	0%	200,000	12%
15	8	170,000	13
30	9	140,000	14
45	12	110,000	16
60	15	80,000	20

a. Calculate *earnings per share* for each level of indebtedness.
b. Use Equation 12.12 and the earnings per share calculated in part **a** to calculate a price per share for each level of indebtedness.
c. Choose the optimal capital structure. Justify your choice.

P12–22 **Integrative—Optimal capital structure**   Nelson Corporation has made the following forecast of sales, with the associated probabilities of occurrence noted.

Sales	Probability
$200,000	.20
300,000	.60
400,000	.20

The company has fixed operating costs of $100,000 per year, and variable operating costs represent 40% of sales. The existing capital structure consists of 25,000 shares of common stock that have a $10 per share book value. No other capital items are outstanding. The marketplace has assigned the following required returns to risky earnings per share.

Coefficient of variation of EPS	Estimated required return, k_s
0.43	15%
0.47	16
0.51	17
0.56	18
0.60	22
0.64	24

The company is contemplating *shifting its capital structure* by substituting debt in the capital structure for common stock. The three different debt ratios under consideration are shown in the following table, along with an estimate, for each ratio, of the corresponding required interest rate on *all* debt.

Debt ratio	Interest rate on *all* debt
20%	10%
40	12
60	14

The tax rate is 40%. The market value of the equity for a leveraged firm can be found by using the simplified method (see Equation 12.12).

a. Calculate the expected earnings per share (EPS), the standard deviation of EPS, and the coefficient of variation of EPS for the three proposed capital structures.

b. Determine the optimal capital structure, assuming (1) maximization of earnings per share and (2) maximization of share value.

c. Construct a graph (similar to Figure 12.7) showing the relationships in part **b**. (*Note:* You will probably have to sketch the lines, because you have only three data points.)

P12–23   **Integrative—Optimal capital structure**   The board of directors of Morales Publishing, Inc., has commissioned a capital structure study. The company has total assets of $40,000,000. It has earnings before interest and taxes of $8,000,000 and is taxed at a rate of 40%.

a. Create a spreadsheet like the one in Table 12.10 showing values of debt and equity as well as the total number of shares, assuming a book value of $25 per share.

% Debt	Total assets	$ Debt	$ Equity	No. of shares @ $25
0%	$40,000,000	$_____	$_____	_____
10	40,000,000	_____	_____	_____
20	40,000,000	_____	_____	_____
30	40,000,000	_____	_____	_____
40	40,000,000	_____	_____	_____
50	40,000,000	_____	_____	_____
60	40,000,000	_____	_____	_____

b. Given the before-tax cost of debt at various levels of indebtedness, calculate the yearly interest expenses.

% Debt	$ Total debt	Before-tax cost of debt, k_d	$ Interest expense
0%	$_____	0.0%	$_____
10	_____	7.5	_____
20	_____	8.0	_____
30	_____	9.0	_____
40	_____	11.0	_____
50	_____	12.5	_____
60	_____	15.5	_____

c. Using EBIT of $8,000,000, a 40% tax rate, and the information developed in parts **a** and **b,** calculate the most likely earnings per share for the firm at various levels of indebtedness. Mark the level of indebtedness that maximizes EPS.

% Debt	EBIT	Interest expense	EBT	Taxes	Net income	No. of shares	EPS
0%	$8,000,000	_____	_____	_____	_____	_____	_____
10	8,000,000	_____	_____	_____	_____	_____	_____
20	8,000,000	_____	_____	_____	_____	_____	_____
30	8,000,000	_____	_____	_____	_____	_____	_____
40	8,000,000	_____	_____	_____	_____	_____	_____
50	8,000,000	_____	_____	_____	_____	_____	_____
60	8,000,000	_____	_____	_____	_____	_____	_____

d. Using the EPS developed in part **c,** the estimates of required return, k_s, and Equation 12.12, estimate the value per share at various levels of indebtedness. Mark the level of indebtedness that results in the maximum price per share, P_0.

Debt	EPS	k_s	P_0
0%	_____	10.0%	_____
10	_____	10.3	_____
20	_____	10.9	_____
30	_____	11.4	_____
40	_____	12.6	_____
50	_____	14.8	_____
60	_____	17.5	_____

e. Prepare a recommendation to the board of directors of Morales Publishing that specifies the degree of indebtedness that will accomplish the firm's goal of optimizing shareholder wealth. Use your findings in parts **a** through **d** to justify your recommendation.

P12–24 Integrative—Optimal capital structure   Country Textiles, which has fixed operating costs of $300,000 and variable operating costs equal to 40% of sales, has made the following three sales estimates, with their probabilities noted.

Sales	Probability
$ 600,000	.30
900,000	.40
1,200,000	.30

The firm wishes to analyze five possible capital structures—0%, 15%, 30%, 45%, and 60% debt ratios. The firm's total assets of $1 million are assumed to be constant. Its common stock has a book value of $25 per share, and the firm is in the 40% tax bracket. The following additional data have been gathered for use in analyzing the five capital structures under consideration.

Capital structure debt ratio	Before-tax cost of debt, k_d	Required return, k_s
0%	0.0%	10.0%
15	8.0	10.5
30	10.0	11.6
45	13.0	14.0
60	17.0	20.0

a. Calculate the level of EBIT associated with each of the three levels of sales.
b. Calculate the amount of debt, the amount of equity, and the number of shares of common stock outstanding for each of the capital structures being considered.
c. Calculate the annual interest on the debt under each of the capital structures being considered. (*Note:* The before-tax cost of debt, k_d, is the interest rate applicable to *all* debt associated with the corresponding debt ratio.)
d. Calculate the EPS associated with each of the three levels of EBIT calculated in part a for each of the five capital structures being considered.
e. Calculate (1) the expected EPS, (2) the standard deviation of EPS, and (3) the coefficient of variation of EPS for each of the capital structures, using your findings in part d.
f. Plot the expected EPS and coefficient of variation of EPS against the capital structures (*x* axis) on separate sets of axes, and comment on the return and risk relative to capital structure.
g. Using the EBIT–EPS data developed in part d, plot the 0%, 30%, and 60% capital structures on the same set of EBIT–EPS axes, and discuss the ranges over which each is preferred. What is the major problem with the use of this approach?
h. Using the valuation model given in Equation 12.12 and your findings in part e, estimate the share value for each of the capital structures being considered.
i. Compare and contrast your findings in parts f and h. Which structure is preferred if the goal is to *maximize EPS*? Which structure is preferred if the goal is to *maximize share value*? Which capital structure do you recommend? Explain.

P12–25   **ETHICS PROBLEM**   "Information asymmetry lies at the heart of the ethical dilemma that managers, stockholders, and bondholders confront when companies initiate management buyouts or swap debt for equity." Comment on this statement. What steps might a board of directors take to ensure that the company's actions are ethical to all parties?

Chapter 12 Case: Evaluating Tampa Manufacturing's Capital Structure

Tampa Manufacturing, an established producer of printing equipment, expects its sales to remain flat for the next 3 to 5 years because of both a weak economic outlook and an expectation of little new printing technology development over that period. On the basis of this scenario, the firm's management has been instructed by its board to institute programs that will allow it to operate more efficiently, earn higher profits, and, most important, maximize share value. In this regard, the firm's chief financial officer (CFO), Jon Lawson, has been charged with evaluating the firm's capital structure. Lawson believes that the current capital structure, which contains 10% debt and 90% equity, may lack adequate financial leverage. To evaluate the firm's capital structure, Lawson has gathered the data summarized in the following table on the current capital structure (10% debt ratio) and two alternative capital structures—A (30% debt ratio) and B (50% debt ratio)—that he would like to consider.

| | Capital structure[a] | | |
Source of capital	Current (10% debt)	A (30% debt)	B (50% debt)
Long-term debt	$1,000,000	$3,000,000	$5,000,000
Coupon interest rate[b]	9%	10%	12%
Common stock	100,000 shares	70,000 shares	40,000 shares
Required return on equity, k_s[c]	12%	13%	18%

[a]These structures are based on maintaining the firm's current level of $10,000,000 of total financing.
[b]Interest rate applicable to *all* debt.
[c]Market-based return for the given level of risk.

Lawson expects the firm's earnings before interest and taxes (EBIT) to remain at its current level of $1,200,000. The firm has a 40% tax rate.

TO DO

a. Use the current level of EBIT to calculate the times interest earned ratio for each capital structure. Evaluate the current and two alternative capital structures using the times interest earned and debt ratios.

b. Prepare a single EBIT–EPS graph showing the current and two alternative capital structures.

c. On the basis of the graph in part **b,** which capital structure will maximize Tampa's earnings per share (EPS) at its expected level of EBIT of $1,200,000? Why might this *not* be the best capital structure?

d. Using the zero-growth valuation model given in Equation 12.12, find the market value of Tampa's equity under each of the three capital structures at the $1,200,000 level of expected EBIT.

e. On the basis of your findings in parts c and d, which capital structure would you recommend? Why?

Spreadsheet Exercise

Starstruck Company would like to determine its optimal capital structure. Several of its managers believe that the best method is to rely on the estimated earnings per share (EPS) of the firm, because they feel that profits and stock price are closely related. The financial managers have suggested another method that depends on the estimated required returns of the firm. The following financial data are available.

Capital structure debt ratio	Estimated EPS	Estimated required return
0%	$1.75	11.40%
10	1.90	11.80
20	2.25	12.50
30	2.55	13.25
40	3.18	18.00
50	3.06	19.00
60	3.10	25.00

TO DO

a. Based upon the given financial data, create a spreadsheet to calculate the estimated share values associated with the seven alternative capital structures. Refer to Table 12.15 in the text (or view it at www.aw-bc.com/gitman).

b. Use Excel to graph the relationship between capital structure and the estimated EPS of the firm. What is the optimal debt ratio? Refer to Figure 12.7 in the text (or view it at www.aw-bc.com/gitman).

c. Use Excel to graph the relationship between capital structure and the estimated share value of the firm. What is the optimal debt ratio? Refer to Figure 12.7 in the text (or view it at www.aw-bc.com/gitman).

d. Do both methods lead to the same *optimal capital structure?* Which method do you favor? Explain.

e. What is the major difference between the EPS and required return methods?

Group Exercise

This chapter continues the valuation process of the firm by investigating different types of leverage in conjunction with the capital structure. Here the analysis begins by bringing in the income statement to broaden the methodology introduced in Chapter 11. Your group will continue to combine data for your shadow and fictitious firm.

TO DO

LG1   a. Return to your shadow firm and view its most recent income statement. Identify the important measures used in reporting leverage including EBIT and fixed and variable operating costs.

LG1 **LG2**   b. Use your shadow firm's information to design a similar set of numbers for your fictitious firm. Assign a simple per-unit price for your product.

LG1   c. Calculate the *operating breakeven point* for your firm. Create a simple graph for sales revenue and total operating costs, highlighting the breakeven sales level in units.

LG2   d. Calculate the degree of operating leverage for your fictitious firm at a base sales level.

LG5   e. Return to your shadow firm and calculate its degree of financial leverage at its current levels of EPS and EBIT. Likewise, calculate your shadow firm's degree of total leverage at current sales and EPS levels.

LG5   f. Use Equation 12.11 to value your shadow firm. Use estimates for your firm's weighted average cost of capital. Do the same for your fictitious firm, using the numbers you assigned in Chapter 11's exercise.

Web Exercise

In this assignment, you will revisit the Web sites with which you have become familiar in your previous work. Your goal is to use the tools of leverage analysis to describe a publicly traded firm.

TO DO

a. Go to a company Web site of your own choosing. Find the firm's EBIT and EPS for the last two periods and graph this information.

b. Connect the dots on your graph in part **a**, and make statements about the value of the firm.

c. Discuss the capital structure of your chosen firm. What has happened recently to your firm's debt ratio?

Remember to check the book's Web site at

www.aw-bc.com/gitman

for additional resources, including additional Web exercises.

Chapter 13

Dividend Policy

LEARNING GOALS

LG1 Understand cash dividend payment procedures, the tax treatment of dividends, and the role of dividend reinvestment plans.

LG2 Describe the residual theory of dividends and the key arguments with regard to dividend irrelevance and relevance.

LG3 Discuss the key factors involved in establishing a dividend policy.

LG4 Review and evaluate the three basic types of dividend policies.

LG5 Evaluate stock dividends from accounting, shareholder, and company points of view.

LG6 Explain stock splits and stock repurchases and the firm's motivation for undertaking each of them.

ACROSS THE DISCIPLINES WHY THIS CHAPTER MATTERS TO YOU

Accounting: You need to understand the types of dividends and payment procedures for them because you will need to record and report the declaration and payment of dividends; you also will provide the financial data that management must have to make dividend decisions.

Information systems: You need to understand types of dividends, payment procedures, and the financial data that the firm must have to make and implement dividend decisions.

Management: To make appropriate dividend decisions for the firm, you need to understand types of dividends, the

factors that affect dividend policy, types of dividend policies, and arguments about the relevance of dividends.

Marketing: You need to understand factors affecting dividend policy because you may want to argue that the firm would be better off retaining funds for use in new marketing programs or products, rather than paying them out as dividends.

Operations: You need to understand factors affecting dividend policy because you may find that the firm's dividend policy imposes limitations on planned replacement, modernization, or expansion projects.

MICROSOFT CORPORATION

GIVING BACK TO THE SHAREHOLDERS

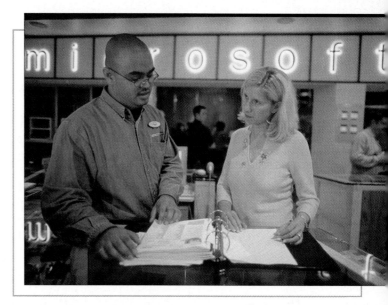

On July 20, 2004, **Microsoft Corporation** (www.microsoft.com) announced that its board of directors approved an $0.08 per share quarterly dividend; a 4-year, $30 billion stock buyback; and a one-time special dividend of $3 per share. Under this plan the company would change its $0.16 per share annual dividend to a quarterly dividend of $0.08 per share, essentially doubling the annual dividend payout to $3.5 billion. The cost of the $3 special dividend would be about $32 billion given the nearly 10.8 billion shares outstanding in mid-2004.

With Microsoft's assets in the form of cash and marketable securities rising from $17 billion in 1999 to more than $49 billion in 2003, the company was faced with a decision of how to deploy that capital. "As we looked at our cash management choices, our priorities were to increase our regular payments to shareholders, increase our stock buyback efforts given our confidence in the company's growth prospects, and distribute additional resources in the form of a special one-time dividend," said Steve Ballmer, Microsoft's chief executive officer.

In the prior 2 years, Microsoft had made significant progress in resolving many of the legal issues facing the company—including a U.S. Court of Appeals decision reaffirming its settlement of antitrust charges, most of the state class-action lawsuits, and the **America Online** and **Sun Microsystems** cases—along with some patent claims litigation. Resolving those issues marked an important step forward in clarifying Microsoft's legal and related business risk.

Despite its 2004 dividend payout, Microsoft's stated dividend policy is that "the Board will continue to evaluate whether to pay a larger or smaller dividend on an ongoing basis and will continue to base its decisions on the Company's potential future long-term capital requirements."

This chapter addresses the issue of whether dividends matter to stockholders. Some stockholders want and expect to receive dividends, whereas others would rather see those funds reinvested in the company. We'll also describe the key factors involved in setting a firm's dividend policy, the different types of dividend policies, and other forms of dividends such as stock dividends and stock repurchases.

Source: Microsoft press release dated July 20, 2004, downloaded from www.microsoft.com on August 9, 2004.

■ *Microsoft's press release says that it will return as much as $75 billion to shareholders over a 4-year period, including $14 billion in regular dividends ($3.5 billion per year), $32 billion for the special dividend, and $30 billion in stock buybacks. As you read this chapter, ponder this question: From the shareholders' viewpoint, what value would they receive from each of the three planned cash disbursements?*

589

[LG1] 13.1 | Dividend Fundamentals

Expected cash dividends are the key return variable from which owners and investors determine share value. They represent a source of cash flow to stockholders and provide information about the firm's current and future performance. Because **retained earnings,** earnings not distributed to owners as dividends, are a form of *internal* financing, the dividend decision can significantly affect the firm's *external* financing requirements. In other words, if the firm needs financing, the larger the cash dividend paid, the greater the amount of financing that must be raised externally through borrowing or through the sale of common or preferred stock. (Remember that although dividends are charged to retained earnings, they are actually paid out of cash.) The first thing to know about cash dividends is the procedures for paying them.

retained earnings
Earnings not distributed to owners as dividends; a form of *internal* financing.

Cash Dividend Payment Procedures

Whether and in what amount to pay cash dividends to corporate stockholders is decided by the firm's board of directors at quarterly or semiannual meetings. The past period's financial performance and future outlook, as well as recent dividends paid, are key inputs to the dividend decision. The payment date of the cash dividend, if one is declared, must also be established.

Amount of Dividends

Whether dividends should be paid, and if so, in what amount, are important decisions that depend primarily on the firm's dividend policy. Most firms have a set policy with respect to the periodic dividend, but the firm's directors can change this amount, largely on the basis of significant increases or decreases in earnings.

Relevant Dates

If the directors of the firm declare a dividend, they also typically issue a statement indicating the dividend decision, the record date, and the payment date. This statement is generally quoted in the *Wall Street Journal* and other financial news media.

date of record (dividends)
Set by the firm's directors, the date on which all persons whose names are recorded as stockholders receive a declared dividend at a specified future time.

Record Date All persons whose names are recorded as stockholders on the **date of record** set by the directors receive a declared dividend at a specified future time. These stockholders are often referred to as *holders of record.*

Because of the time needed to make bookkeeping entries when a stock is traded, the stock begins selling **ex dividend** 2 *business days* prior to the date of record. Purchasers of a stock selling ex dividend do not receive the current dividend. A simple way to determine the first day on which the stock sells ex dividend is to subtract 2 days from the date of record; if a weekend intervenes, subtract 4 days. Ignoring general market fluctuations, the stock's price is expected to drop by the amount of the declared dividend on the ex dividend date.

ex dividend
Period, beginning 2 *business days* prior to the date of record, during which a stock is sold without the right to receive the current dividend.

payment date
Set by the firm's directors, the actual date on which the firm mails the dividend payment to the holders of record.

Payment Date The **payment date,** also set by the directors, is the actual date on which the firm mails the dividend payment to the holders of record. It is generally a few weeks after the record date. An example will clarify the various dates and the accounting effects.

EXAMPLE   At the quarterly dividend meeting of Rudolf Company, a distributor of office products, held on June 10, the directors declared an $0.80-per-share cash dividend for holders of record on Friday, July 2. The firm had 100,000 shares of common stock outstanding. The payment date for the dividend was Monday, August 2. A time line depicting the key dates relative to the Rudolf Company's dividend is given in Figure 13.1. Before the dividend was declared, the key accounts of the firm were as follows:

Cash	$200,000	Dividends payable	$ 0
		Retained earnings	1,000,000

When the dividend was announced by the directors, $80,000 of the retained earnings ($0.80 per share $\times$ 100,000 shares) was transferred to the dividends payable account. The key accounts thus became

Cash	$200,000	Dividends payable	$ 80,000
		Retained earnings	920,000

Rudolf Company's stock began selling ex dividend 2 *business days* prior to the date of record, which was Wednesday, June 30. This date was found by subtracting 2 days from the July 2 date of record. Purchasers of Rudolf's stock on Tuesday, June 29 or earlier received the rights to the dividends; those who purchased the stock on or after June 30 did not. Assuming a stable market, Rudolf's stock price was expected to drop by approximately $0.80 per share when it began selling ex dividend on June 30. On August 2 the firm mailed dividend checks to the holders of record as of July 2. This produced the following balances in the key accounts of the firm:

Cash	$120,000	Dividends payable	$ 0
		Retained earnings	920,000

The net effect of declaring and paying the dividend was to reduce the firm's total assets (and stockholders' equity) by $80,000. ■

FIGURE 13.1

Dividend Payment Time Line
Time line for the announcement and payment of a cash dividend for Rudolf Company

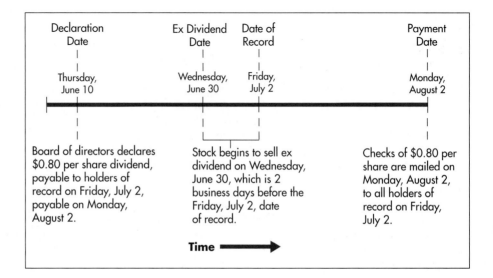

Tax Treatment of Dividends

The *Jobs and Growth Tax Relief Reconciliation Act of 2003* significantly changed the tax treatment of corporate dividends for most taxpayers. Prior to passage of the 2003 law, dividends received by investors were taxed as ordinary income at rates as high as 35 percent. The 2003 act reduced the tax rate on corporate dividends for most taxpayers to the tax rate applicable to capital gains, which is a maximum rate of 15 percent. This change significantly diminishes the degree of

In Practice FOCUS ON PRACTICE

TAX LAW CHANGE LEADS TO INCREASED DIVIDEND PAYOUTS

In 1980, the percentage of firms paying monthly, quarterly, semi-annual, or annual dividends stood at 60 percent. By the fourth quarter of 2002, this percentage had declined to 20 percent. In May 2003, President George W. Bush signed into law the *Jobs and Growth Tax Relief Reconciliation Act of 2003 (JGTRRA)*. Prior to the signing of this tax cut legislation, dividends were taxed once as part of corporate earnings at a 35 percent rate, and again as the personal income of the investor with a potential top rate of 35 percent, resulting in an effective tax rate of 57.75 percent on some dividends. The high rate of double taxation was a major factor in the 20-year decline of companies paying a dividend.

The JGTRRA cut individual tax rates on dividend income. Taxpayers in tax brackets above 15 percent are subject to a 15 percent rate of tax on dividends paid between January 1, 2003, and December 31, 2008. For taxpayers with a marginal tax rate of 15 percent or lower, the dividend tax rate is 5 percent until December 31, 2007, and zero percent in 2008. *Pre-JGTRRA taxation of dividends will reappear in 2009.* Long-term

capital gains tax rates were reduced to the same rates as the new dividend tax rates; pre-JGTRRA capital gains rates will reappear in 2009, unless further legislation makes the current law permanent.

While the 2003 tax law did not completely eliminate the double taxation of dividends, it reduced the maximum possible effect of the double taxation of dividends to 44.75 percent from its previous maximum effect of 57.75 percent. For taxpayers in the lower tax brackets, the combined effect is a maximum tax rate of 38.25 percent on dividends.

The reduction of the tax burden on dividends has several potential benefits. First, the equalization of the tax treatment of dividends and capital gains allows corporations to base their payout policies on the *economic value* of a decision, not the tax consequences. Previously, due to tax considerations, companies disproportionately favored generating capital gains through stock repurchases over paying dividends. A second benefit of the reduction of the double-taxation burden is that if corporations increase their dividend payouts, lower cash reserves

will force managers to undertake only the most productive internal investments. In addition, the regular payment of quarterly dividends can be made only out of earnings or cash reserves that actually exist, which promotes honest accounting practices.

The new tax treatment of dividends appears to have had the expected effect on the dividend payout policies. A 2004 study conducted by Chetty and Saez, examining data from the Center for Research in Security Prices, found that the proportion of firms issuing dividends had rebounded from the 2002 low of 20 percent to 25 percent by the end of 2003.

Sources: Daniel Clifton, "Incentives Matter: A Lesson," *Tech Central Station* (July 23, 2004), www.techcentralstation.org (August 9, 2004); Carlos Lozada, "Lower Tax Rates Spurred Dividend Growth," www.nber.org (August 9, 2004); and Raj Chetty and Emmanuel Saez, "Do Dividend Payments Respond to Taxes? Preliminary Evidence from the 2003 Dividend Tax Cut," *NBER Working Paper No. 10572,* as cited in "Lower Tax Rates Spurred Dividend Growth," www.nber.org/digest/aug04/w10572.html (August 9, 2004).

■ *How might the scheduled reappearance (in 2009) of higher tax rates on individuals receiving dividends affect corporate dividend payout policies?*

"double taxation" of dividends that results from the corporation first being taxed on its income and then the investor who receives the dividend also being taxed on it. (For more details on the new law, see the *In Practice* box on the previous page.)

Immediately after passage of the act in 2003, many firms either initiated or increased dividends paid to their stockholders. Clearly, the fact that the after-tax cash flow to dividend recipients is much greater at the lower applicable tax rate has resulted in noticeably higher dividend payouts by corporations today than prior to passage of the 2003 legislation. The reduction in the degree of double taxation is expected to continue to result in higher dividend payouts and an increase in the appeal of common stocks to investors, particularly those in need of income rather than capital gains.

Dividend Reinvestment Plans

dividend reinvestment plans (DRIPs)
Plans that enable stockholders to use dividends received on the firm's stock to acquire additional shares—even fractional shares—at little or no transaction cost.

Today many firms offer **dividend reinvestment plans** (**DRIPs**), which enable stockholders to use dividends received on the firm's stock to acquire additional shares—even fractional shares—at little or no transaction cost. Some companies even allow investors to make their *initial purchases* of the firm's stock directly from the company without going through a broker. With DRIPs, plan participants typically can acquire shares at about 5 percent below the prevailing market price. From its point of view, the firm can issue new shares to participants more economically, avoiding the underpricing and flotation costs that would accompany the public sale of new shares. Clearly, the existence of a DRIP may enhance the market appeal of a firm's shares.

REVIEW QUESTIONS

13–1 Who are *holders of record?* When does a stock sell *ex dividend?*

13–2 What effect did the *Jobs and Growth Tax Relief Reconciliation Act of 2003* have on the taxation of corporate dividends? On corporate dividend payouts?

13–3 What benefit is available to participants in a *dividend reinvestment plan?* How might the firm benefit?

LG2 13.2 | The Relevance of Dividend Policy

Numerous theories and empirical findings concerning dividend policy have been reported in the financial literature. Although this research provides some interesting insights about dividend policy, capital budgeting and capital structure decisions are generally considered far more important than dividend decisions. In other words, good investment and financing decisions should not be sacrificed for a dividend policy of questionable importance.

A number of key questions have yet to be resolved: Does dividend policy matter? What effect does dividend policy have on share price? Is there a model that can be used to evaluate alternative dividend policies in view of share value?

Here we begin by describing the residual theory of dividends, which is used as a backdrop for discussion of the key arguments in support of dividend irrelevance and then those in support of dividend relevance.

The Residual Theory of Dividends

residual theory of dividends
A school of thought that suggests that the dividend paid by a firm should be viewed as a *residual*—the amount left over after all acceptable investment opportunities have been undertaken.

The **residual theory of dividends** is a school of thought that suggests that the dividend paid by a firm should be viewed as a *residual*—the amount left over after all acceptable investment opportunities have been undertaken. Using this approach, the firm would treat the dividend decision in three steps, as follows:

Step 1 Determine its optimal level of capital expenditures, which would be the level generated by the point of intersection of the investment opportunities schedule (IOS) and weighted marginal cost of capital (WMCC) schedule (see Chapter 11).

Step 2 Using the optimal capital structure proportions (see Chapter 12), estimate the total amount of equity financing needed to support the expenditures generated in Step 1.

Step 3 Because the cost of retained earnings, k_r, is less than the cost of new common stock, k_n, use retained earnings to meet the equity requirement determined in Step 2. If retained earnings are inadequate to meet this need, sell new common stock. If the available retained earnings are in excess of this need, distribute the surplus amount—the residual—as dividends.

According to this approach, as long as the firm's equity need exceeds the amount of retained earnings, no cash dividend is paid. The argument for this approach is that it is sound management to be certain that the company has the money it needs to compete effectively. This view of dividends suggests that the required return of investors, k_s, is *not* influenced by the firm's dividend policy—a premise that in turn implies that dividend policy is irrelevant.

EXAMPLE Overbrook Industries, a manufacturer of canoes and other small watercraft, has available from the current period's operations $1.8 million that can be retained or paid out in dividends. The firm's optimal capital structure is at a debt ratio of 30%, which represents 30% debt and 70% equity. Figure 13.2 depicts the firm's weighted marginal cost of capital (WMCC) schedule along with three investment opportunities schedules. For each IOS, the level of total new financing or investment determined by the point of intersection of the IOS and the WMCC has been noted. For IOS_1, it is $1.5 million, for IOS_2 $2.4 million, and for IOS_3 $3.2 million. Although only one IOS will exist in practice, it is useful to look at the possible dividend decisions generated by applying the residual theory in each of the three cases. Table 13.1 summarizes this analysis.

Table 13.1 shows that if IOS_1 exists, the firm will pay out $750,000 in dividends, because only $1,050,000 of the $1,800,000 of available earnings is needed. A 41.7% payout ratio results. For IOS_2, dividends of $120,000 (a payout ratio of 6.7%) result. Should IOS_3 exist, the firm would pay no dividends (a 0% payout ratio), because its retained earnings of $1,800,000 would be less than the $2,240,000 of equity needed. In this case, the firm would have to obtain addi-

FIGURE 13.2

WMCC and IOSs
WMCC and IOSs for
Overbrook Industries

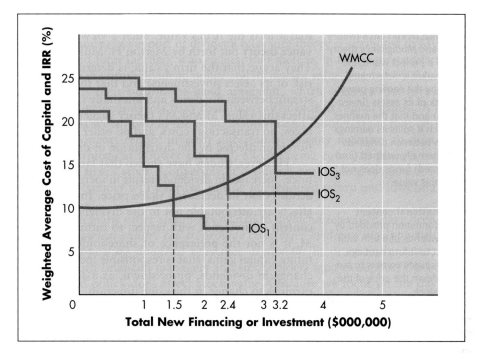

TABLE 13.1

Applying the Residual Theory of Dividends to Overbrook Industries for Each of Three IOSs (Shown in Figure 13.2)

Item	Investment opportunities schedules		
	IOS₁	IOS₂	IOS₃
(1) New financing or investment (Fig. 13.2)	$1,500,000	$2,400,000	$3,200,000
(2) Retained earnings available (given)	$1,800,000	$1,800,000	$1,800,000
(3) Equity needed [70% × (1)]	1,050,000	1,680,000	2,240,000
(4) Dividends [(2) − (3)]	$ 750,000	$ 120,000	$ 0ᵃ
(5) Dividend payout ratio [(4) ÷ (2)]	41.7%	6.7%	0%

ᵃIn this case, additional new common stock in the amount of $440,000 ($2,240,000 needed − $1,800,000 available) would have to be sold; no dividends would be paid.

tional new common stock financing to meet the new requirements generated by the intersection of the IOS₃ and WMCC. Depending on which IOS exists, the firm's dividend would in effect be the residual, if any, remaining after all acceptable investments had been financed. ■

Arguments for Dividend Irrelevance

The residual theory of dividends implies that if the firm cannot invest its earnings to earn a return (IRR) that is in excess of cost (WMCC), it should distribute the earnings by paying dividends to stockholders. This approach suggests that

dividend payout ratio
Indicates the percentage of each dollar earned that is distributed to the owners in the form of cash. It is calculated by dividing the firm's cash dividend per share by its earnings per share.

constant-payout-ratio dividend policy
A dividend policy based on the payment of a certain percentage of earnings to owners in each dividend period.

Constant-Payout-Ratio Dividend Policy

One type of dividend policy involves use of a constant payout ratio. The **dividend payout ratio** indicates the percentage of each dollar earned that is distributed to the owners in the form of cash. It is calculated by dividing the firm's cash dividend per share by its earnings per share. With a **constant-payout-ratio dividend policy,** the firm establishes that a certain percentage of earnings is paid to owners in each dividend period.

The problem with this policy is that if the firm's earnings drop or if a loss occurs in a given period, the dividends may be low or even nonexistent. Because dividends are often considered an indicator of the firm's future condition and status, the firm's stock price may be adversely affected.

EXAMPLE

Peachtree Industries, a miner of potassium, has a policy of paying out 40% of earnings in cash dividends. In periods when a loss occurs, the firm's policy is to pay no cash dividends. Data on Peachtree's earnings, dividends, and average stock prices for the past 6 years follow.

Year	Earnings/share	Dividends/share	Average price/share
2006	−$0.50	$0.00	$42.00
2005	3.00	1.20	52.00
2004	1.75	0.70	48.00
2003	−1.50	0.00	38.00
2002	2.00	0.80	46.00
2001	4.50	1.80	50.00

Dividends increased in 2004 and in 2005 but decreased in the other years. In years of decreasing dividends, the firm's stock price dropped; when dividends increased, the price of the stock increased. Peachtree's sporadic dividend payments appear to make its owners uncertain about the returns they can expect. ■

Hint Regulated utilities in low-growth areas can use a constant-payout-ratio dividend policy. Their capital requirements are usually low and their earnings are more stable than those of most firms.

Although some firms use a constant-payout-ratio dividend policy, it is *not* recommended.

regular dividend policy
A dividend policy based on the payment of a fixed-dollar dividend in each period.

Regular Dividend Policy

The **regular dividend policy** is based on the payment of a fixed-dollar dividend in each period. This policy provides the owners with generally positive information, thereby minimizing their uncertainty. Often, firms that use this policy increase the regular dividend once a *proven* increase in earnings has occurred. Under this policy, dividends are almost never decreased.

EXAMPLE

The dividend policy of Woodward Laboratories, a producer of a popular artificial sweetener, is to pay annual dividends of $1.00 per share until per-share earnings have exceeded $4.00 for three consecutive years. At that point, the annual dividend is raised to $1.50 per share, and a new earnings plateau is established. The firm does not anticipate decreasing its dividend unless its liquidity is in jeopardy. Data for Woodward's earnings, dividends, and average stock prices for the past 12 years follow.

Year	Earnings/share	Dividends/share	Average price/share
2006	$4.50	$1.50	$47.50
2005	3.90	1.50	46.50
2004	4.60	1.50	45.00
2003	4.20	1.00	43.00
2002	5.00	1.00	42.00
2001	2.00	1.00	38.50
2000	6.00	1.00	38.00
1999	3.00	1.00	36.00
1998	0.75	1.00	33.00
1997	0.50	1.00	33.00
1996	2.70	1.00	33.50
1995	2.85	1.00	35.00

Whatever the level of earnings, Woodward Laboratories paid dividends of $1.00 per share through 2003. In 2004, the dividend increased to $1.50 per share because earnings in excess of $4.00 per share had been achieved for 3 years. In 2004, the firm also had to establish a new earnings plateau for further dividend increases. Woodward Laboratories' average price per share exhibited a stable, increasing behavior in spite of a somewhat volatile pattern of earnings. ∎

target dividend-payout ratio
A dividend policy under which the firm attempts to pay out a certain *percentage* of earnings as a stated dollar dividend and adjusts that dividend toward a target payout as proven earnings increases occur.

Often a regular dividend policy is built around a **target dividend-payout ratio.** Under this policy, the firm attempts to pay out a certain *percentage* of earnings, but rather than let dividends fluctuate, it pays a stated dollar dividend and adjusts that dividend toward the target payout as proven earnings increases occur. For instance, Woodward Laboratories appears to have a target payout ratio of around 35 percent. The payout was about 35 percent ($1.00 ÷ $2.85) when the dividend policy was set in 1995, and when the dividend was raised to $1.50 in 2004, the payout ratio was about 33 percent ($1.50 ÷ $4.60).

Low-Regular-and-Extra Dividend Policy

low-regular-and-extra dividend policy
A dividend policy based on paying a low regular dividend, supplemented by an additional dividend when earnings are higher than normal in a given period.

extra dividend
An additional dividend optionally paid by the firm if earnings are higher than normal in a given period.

Some firms establish a **low-regular-and-extra dividend policy,** paying a low regular dividend, supplemented by an additional dividend when earnings are higher than normal in a given period. By calling the additional dividend an **extra dividend,** the firm avoids giving shareholders false hopes. This policy is especially common among companies that experience cyclical shifts in earnings.

By establishing a low regular dividend that is paid each period, the firm gives investors the stable income necessary to build confidence in the firm, and the extra dividend permits them to share in the earnings from an especially good period. Firms using this policy must raise the level of the regular dividend once proven increases in earnings have been achieved. The extra dividend should not be a regular event; otherwise, it becomes meaningless. The use of a target dividend-payout ratio in establishing the regular dividend level is advisable.

REVIEW QUESTION

13–7   Describe a constant-payout-ratio dividend policy, a regular dividend policy, and a low-regular-and-extra dividend policy. What are the effects of these policies?

| LG5 | LG6 | 13.5 | Other Forms of Dividends |

Dividends can be paid in forms other than cash. Here we discuss two other methods of paying dividends—stock dividends and stock repurchases—as well as a closely related topic, stock splits.

Stock Dividends

stock dividend
The payment, to existing owners, of a dividend in the form of stock.

A **stock dividend** is the payment, to existing owners, of a dividend in the form of stock. Often firms pay stock dividends as a replacement for or a supplement to cash dividends. Although stock dividends do not have a real value, stockholders may perceive them to represent something they did not have before.

Accounting Aspects

small (ordinary) stock dividend
A stock dividend representing less than 20 to 25 percent of the common stock outstanding when the dividend is declared.

In an accounting sense, the payment of a stock dividend is a shifting of funds between stockholders' equity accounts rather than an outflow of funds. When a firm declares a stock dividend, the procedures for announcement and distribution are the same as those described earlier for a cash dividend. The accounting entries associated with the payment of a stock dividend vary depending on its size. A **small (ordinary) stock dividend** is a stock dividend that represents less than 20 to 25 percent of the common stock outstanding when the dividend is declared. Small stock dividends are most common.

EXAMPLE   The current stockholders' equity on the balance sheet of Garrison Corporation, a distributor of prefabricated cabinets, is as shown in the following accounts.

Preferred stock	$ 300,000
Common stock (100,000 shares at $4 par)	400,000
Paid-in capital in excess of par	600,000
Retained earnings	700,000
Total stockholders' equity	$2,000,000

Garrison, which has 100,000 shares outstanding, declares a 10% stock dividend when the market price of its stock is $15 per share. Because 10,000 new shares (10% of 100,000) are issued at the prevailing market price of $15 per share, $150,000 ($15 per share × 10,000 shares) is shifted from retained earnings to the common stock and paid-in capital accounts. A total of $40,000 ($4 par × 10,000 shares) is added to common stock, and the remaining $110,000 [($15 − $4) × 10,000 shares] is added to the paid-in capital in excess of par. The resulting account balances are as follows:

Preferred stock	$ 300,000
Common stock (110,000 shares at $4 par)	440,000
Paid-in capital in excess of par	710,000
Retained earnings	550,000
Total stockholders' equity	$2,000,000

The firm's total stockholders' equity has not changed; funds have merely been *shifted* among stockholders' equity accounts. ■

The Shareholder's Viewpoint

The shareholder receiving a stock dividend typically receives nothing of value. After the dividend is paid, the per-share value of the shareholder's stock decreases in proportion to the dividend in such a way that the market value of his or her total holdings in the firm remains unchanged. The shareholder's proportion of ownership in the firm also remains the same, and *as long as the firm's earnings remain unchanged,* so does his or her share of total earnings. (However, if the firm's earnings and cash dividends increase when the stock dividend is issued, an increase in share value is likely to result.)

EXAMPLE   Ms. X owned 10,000 shares of Garrison Corporation's stock. The company's most recent earnings were $220,000, and earnings are not expected to change in the near future. Before the stock dividend, Ms. X owned 10% (10,000 shares ÷ 100,000 shares) of the firm's stock, which was selling for $15 per share. Earnings per share were $2.20 ($220,000 ÷ 100,000 shares). Because Ms. X owned 10,000 shares, her earnings were $22,000 ($2.20 per share × 10,000 shares). After receiving the 10% stock dividend, Ms. X has 11,000 shares, which again is 10% of the ownership (11,000 shares ÷ 110,000 shares). The market price of the stock can be expected to drop to $13.64 per share [$15 × (1.00 ÷ 1.10)], which means that the market value of Ms. X's holdings is $150,000 (11,000 shares × $13.64 per share). This is the same as the initial value of her holdings (10,000 shares × $15 per share). The future earnings per share drops to $2 ($220,000 ÷ 110,000 shares) because the same $220,000 in earnings must now be divided among 110,000 shares. Because Ms. X still owns 10% of the stock, her share of total earnings is still $22,000 ($2 per share × 11,000 shares). ■

In summary, if the firm's earnings remain constant and total cash dividends do not increase, a stock dividend results in a lower per-share market value for the firm's stock.

The Company's Viewpoint

Stock dividends are more costly to issue than cash dividends, but certain advantages may outweigh these costs. Firms find the stock dividend to be a way to give owners something without having to use cash. Generally, when a firm needs to preserve cash to finance rapid growth, a stock dividend is used. When the stockholders recognize that the firm is reinvesting the cash flow so as to maximize future earnings, the market value of the firm should at least remain unchanged. However, if the stock dividend is paid so that cash can be retained to satisfy past-due bills, a decline in market value may result.

LG5

E13-5 The current stockholders' equity account for Hilo Farms is as follows:

Common stock (50,000 shares at $3 par)	$150,000
Paid-in capital in excess of par	250,000
Retained earnings	450,000
Total stockholders' equity	$850,000

Hilo has announced plans to issue an additional 5,000 shares of common stock as part of its stock dividend plan. The current market price of Hilo's common stock is $20 per share. Show how the proposed *stock dividend* would affect the stockholder's equity account.

Problems

LG1

BASIC

P13-1 Dividend payment procedures   At the quarterly dividend meeting, Wood Shoes declared a cash dividend of $1.10 per share for holders of record on Monday, July 10. The firm has 300,000 shares of common stock outstanding and has set a payment date of July 31. Prior to the dividend declaration, the firm's key accounts were as follows:

Cash	$500,000	Dividends payable	$ 0
		Retained earnings	2,500,000

a. Show the entries after the meeting adjourned.
b. When is the *ex dividend* date?
c. What values would the key accounts have after the July 31 payment date?
d. What effect, if any, will the dividend have on the firm's total assets?
e. Ignoring general market fluctuations, what effect, if any, will the dividend have on the firm's stock price on the ex dividend date?

LG1

INTERMEDIATE

P13-2 Dividend payment   Kathy Snow wishes to purchase shares of Countdown Computing, Inc. The company's board of directors has declared a cash dividend of $0.80 to be paid to holders of record on Wednesday, May 12.
a. What is the last day that Kathy can purchase the stock (trade date) and still receive the dividend?
b. What day does this stock begin trading "ex dividend"?
c. What change, if any, would you expect in the price per share when the stock begins trading on the ex dividend day?
d. If Kathy held the stock for less than one quarter and then sold it for $39 per share, would she achieve a higher investment return by (1) buying the stock *prior to* the ex dividend date at $35 per share and collecting the $0.80 dividend, or (2) buying it *on* the ex dividend date at $34.20 per share but not receiving the dividend?

LG2

INTERMEDIATE

P13-3 Residual dividend policy   As president of Young's of California, a large clothing chain, you have just received a letter from a major stockholder. The stockholder asks about the company's dividend policy. In fact, the stockholder has asked you to estimate the amount of the dividend that you are likely to pay

next year. You have not yet collected all the information about the expected dividend payment, but you do know the following:
(1) The company follows a residual dividend policy.
(2) The total capital budget for next year is likely to be one of three amounts, depending on the results of capital budgeting studies that are currently under way. The capital expenditure amounts are $2 million, $3 million, and $4 million.
(3) The forecasted level of potential retained earnings next year is $2 million.
(4) The target or optimal capital structure is a debt ratio of 40%.

You have decided to respond by sending the stockholder the best information available to you.
a. Describe a *residual dividend policy*.
b. Compute the amount of the dividend (or the amount of new common stock needed) and the dividend payout ratio for each of the three capital expenditure amounts.
c. Compare, contrast, and discuss the amount of dividends (calculated in part **b**) associated with each of the three capital expenditure amounts.

P13–4   **Dividend constraints**   The Howe Company's stockholders' equity account is as follows:

Common stock (400,000 shares at $4 par)	$1,600,000
Paid-in capital in excess of par	1,000,000
Retained earnings	1,900,000
Total stockholders' equity	$4,500,000

The earnings available for common stockholders from this period's operations are $100,000, which have been included as part of the $1.9 million retained earnings.
a. What is the maximum dividend per share that the firm can pay? (Assume that legal capital includes *all* paid-in capital.)
b. If the firm has $160,000 in cash, what is the largest per-share dividend it can pay without borrowing?
c. Indicate the accounts and changes, if any, that will result if the firm pays the dividends indicated in parts **a** and **b**.
d. Indicate the effects of an $80,000 cash dividend on stockholders' equity.

P13–5   **Dividend constraints**   A firm has $800,000 in paid-in capital, retained earnings of $40,000 (including the current year's earnings), and 25,000 shares of common stock outstanding. In the current year, it has $29,000 of earnings available for the common stockholders.
a. What is the most the firm can pay in cash dividends to each common stockholder? (Assume that legal capital includes *all* paid-in capital.)
b. What effect would a cash dividend of $0.80 per share have on the firm's balance sheet entries?
c. If the firm cannot raise any new funds from external sources, what do you consider the key constraint with respect to the magnitude of the firm's dividend payments? Why?

P13–6 **Low-regular-and-extra dividend policy**   Bennett Farm Equipment Sales, Inc., is in a highly cyclic business. Although the firm has a target payout ratio of 25%, its board realizes that strict adherence to that ratio would result in a fluctuating dividend and create uncertainty for the firm's stockholders. Therefore, the firm has declared a regular dividend of $0.50 per share per year with extra cash dividends to be paid when earnings justify them. Earnings per share for the last several years are as follows:

Year	EPS
2006	$3.00
2005	2.40
2004	2.20
2003	2.80
2002	2.15
2001	1.97

a. Calculate the *payout ratio* for each year on the basis of the regular $0.50 dividend and the cited EPS.
b. Calculate the difference between the regular $0.50 dividend and a 25% payout for each year.
c. Bennett has established a policy of paying an extra dividend of $0.25 only when the difference between the regular dividend and a 25% payout amounts to $1.00 or more. Show the regular and extra dividends in those years when an extra dividend would be paid. What would be done with the "extra" earnings that are not paid out?
d. The firm expects that future earnings per share will continue to cycle but will remain above $2.20 per share in most years. What factors should be considered in making a revision to the amount paid as a regular dividend? If the firm revises the regular dividend, what new amount should it pay?

P13–7 **Alternative dividend policies**   Over the last 10 years, a firm has had the earnings per share shown in the following table.

Year	Earnings per share
2006	$4.00
2005	3.80
2004	3.20
2003	2.80
2002	3.20
2001	2.40
2000	1.20
1999	1.80
1998	− 0.50
1997	0.25

a. If the firm's dividend policy were based on a *constant payout ratio* of 40% for all years with positive earnings and 0% otherwise, what would be the annual dividend for each year?

b. If the firm had a dividend payout of $1.00 per share, increasing by $0.10 per share whenever the dividend payout fell below 50% for two consecutive years, what annual dividend would the firm pay each year?

c. If the firm's policy were to pay $0.50 per share each period except when earnings per share exceed $3.00, when an extra dividend equal to 80% of earnings beyond $3.00 would be paid, what annual dividend would the firm pay each year?

d. Discuss the pros and cons of each dividend policy described in parts **a** through **c**.

P13–8 **Alternative dividend policies**   Given the earnings per share over the period 1999–2006 shown in the following table, determine the annual dividend per share under each of the policies set forth in parts **a** through **d**.

Year	Earnings per share
2006	$1.40
2005	1.56
2004	1.20
2003	− 0.85
2002	1.05
2001	0.60
2000	1.00
1999	0.44

a. Pay out 50% of earnings in all years with positive earnings.

b. Pay $0.50 per share and increase to $0.60 per share whenever earnings per share rise above $0.90 per share for two consecutive years.

c. Pay $0.50 per share except when earnings exceed $1.00 per share, in which case pay an extra dividend of 60% of earnings above $1.00 per share.

d. Combine the policies described in parts **b** and **c**. When the dividend is raised (in part **b**), raise the excess dividend base (in part **c**) from $1.00 to $1.10 per share.

e. Compare and contrast each of the dividend policies described in parts **a** through **d**.

P13–9 **Stock dividend—Firm**   Columbia Paper has the following stockholders' equity account. The firm's common stock has a current market price of $30 per share.

Preferred stock	$100,000
Common stock (10,000 shares at $2 par)	20,000
Paid-in capital in excess of par	280,000
Retained earnings	100,000
Total stockholders' equity	$500,000

a. Show the effects on Columbia of a 5% stock dividend.

b. Show the effects of (1) a 10% and (2) a 20% stock dividend.

c. In light of your answers to parts **a** and **b**, discuss the effects of stock dividends on stockholders' equity.

After much discussion, McNeely and Rook agreed that she would recommend to the board one of the following types of dividend policies:

1. Constant-payout-ratio dividend policy
2. Regular dividend policy
3. Low-regular-and-extra dividend policy

McNeely realizes that her dividend proposal would significantly affect future financing opportunities and costs and the firm's share price. She also knows that she must be sure that her proposal is complete and that it fully educates the board with regard to the long-term implications of each policy.

TO DO

a. Analyze each of the three dividend policies in light of GAC's financial position.
b. Which dividend policy would you recommend? Justify your recommendation.
c. What are the key factors to consider when setting the amount of a firm's initial annual dividend?
d. How should Ms. McNeely go about deciding what initial annual dividend she will recommend to the board?
e. In view of your dividend policy recommendation in part **b**, how large an initial dividend would you recommend? Justify your recommendation.

Spreadsheet Exercise

One way to lower the market price of a firm's stock is via a stock split. Rock-O Corporation finds itself in a different situation: Its stock has been selling at relatively low prices. To increase the market price of the stock, the company chooses to use a *reverse stock split* of 2-for-3.

The company currently has 700,000 common shares outstanding and no preferred stock. The common stock carries a par value of $1. At this time, the paid-in capital in excess of par is $7,000,000, and the firm's retained earnings is $3,500,000.

TO DO

Create a spreadsheet to determine the following:

a. The stockholders' equity section of the balance sheet *before* the reverse stock split.
b. The stockholders' equity section of the balance sheet *after* the reverse stock split.

Group Exercise

Dividends have been drawn into the spotlight of late because of scandal and "fictitious" earnings. Dividends have also attained greater prominence as a result of tax law changes and increased shareholder activism. This chapter looked at dividend policy in the context of a firm's long-term financing decisions. This exercise continues to combine data for your shadow firm and your group's fictitious firm in considering some dividend issues.

TO DO

LG1   **a.** Return to your shadow firm's financials. Describe the extent to which dividends are used by your shadow firm, both currently and in the recent past. Compare this information to the matching measures of EPS for each of the recent years.

LG1   **b.** Apply similar numbers for your fictitious firm. (If your shadow firm doesn't currently pay dividends, simulate numbers that make sense in the context of your previous work.)

LG1 LG2 LG3   **c.** Describe a change in dividends that has been approved by your fictitious firm's board. You must specify the amount of the dividend, its frequency, and the relevant dates for payment. Explain and defend the change.

LG3   **d.** Return to your shadow firm and describe its stockholders' equity account.

LG3   **e.** Use similar numbers in designing your fictitious firm's equity account.

LG4 LG6   **f.** Describe any recent events related to your shadow firm's equity financing, including dividend changes and stock repurchases or splits.

Web Exercise

Dividends have consequences for both firms and shareholders. This assignment combines an investigation of both the dividend payment history of several firms and the increasing availability of *dividend reinvestment plans (DRIPs)* for shareholders.

TO DO

a. Begin by investigating the dividend policies of several firms. Report concisely on the pattern exhibited in the recent history of dividend payments for each firm.

b. Point your browser to www.dripcentral.com/. This Web site is a good source of information about DRIP plans for various firms. Begin by reading about DRIP basics, and then report on the various firms and programs described at this Web site.

> **Remember to check the book's Web site at**
>
> **www.aw-bc.com/gitman**
>
> **for additional resources, including additional Web exercises.**

Integrative Case

4

O'Grady Apparel Company

O'Grady Apparel Company was founded nearly 160 years ago when an Irish merchant named Garrett O'Grady landed in Los Angeles with an inventory of heavy canvas, which he hoped to sell for tents and wagon covers to miners headed for the California goldfields. Instead, he turned to the sale of harder-wearing clothing.

Today, O'Grady Apparel Company is a small manufacturer of fabrics and clothing whose stock is traded on the over-the-counter exchange. In 2006, the Los Angeles–based company experienced sharp increases in both domestic and European markets resulting in record earnings. Sales rose from $15.9 million in 2005 to $18.3 million in 2006 with earnings per share of $3.28 and $3.84, respectively.

European sales represented 29% of total sales in 2006, up from 24% the year before and only 3% in 2001, 1 year after foreign operations were launched. Although foreign sales represent nearly one-third of total sales, the growth in the domestic market is expected to affect the company most markedly. Management expects sales to surpass $21 million in 2007, and earnings per share are expected to rise to $4.40. (Selected income statement items are presented in Table 1.)

Because of the recent growth, Margaret Jennings, the corporate treasurer, is concerned that available funds are not being used to their fullest potential. The projected $1,300,000 of internally generated 2007 funds is expected to be insufficient to meet the company's expan-

Table 1

Selected Income Statement Items

	2004	2005	2006	Projected 2007
Net sales	$13,860,000	$15,940,000	$18,330,000	$21,080,000
Net profits after taxes	1,520,000	1,750,000	2,020,000	2,323,000
Earnings per share (EPS)	2.88	3.28	3.84	4.40
Dividends per share	1.15	1.31	1.54	1.76

sion needs. Management has set a policy of maintaining the current capital structure proportions of 25% long-term debt, 10% preferred stock, and 65% common stock equity for at least the next 3 years. In addition, it plans to continue paying out 40% of its earnings as dividends. Total capital expenditures are yet to be determined.

Jennings has been presented with several competing investment opportunities by division and product managers. However, because funds are limited, choices of which projects to accept must be made. The investment opportunities schedule (IOS) is shown in Table 2. To analyze the effect of the increased financing requirements on the weighted average cost of capital (WACC), Jennings contacted a leading investment banking firm that provided the financing cost data given in Table 3. O'Grady is in the 40% tax bracket.

Table 2

Investment Opportunities Schedule (IOS)

Investment opportunity	Internal rate of return (IRR)	Initial investment
A	21%	$400,000
B	19	200,000
C	24	700,000
D	27	500,000
E	18	300,000
F	22	600,000
G	17	500,000

Table 3

Financing Cost Data

Long-term debt: The firm can raise $700,000 of additional debt by selling 10-year, $1,000, 12% annual interest rate bonds to net $970 after flotation costs. Any debt in excess of $700,000 will have a before-tax cost, k_d, of 18%.

Preferred stock: Preferred stock, regardless of the amount sold, can be issued with a $60 par value and a 17% annual dividend rate. It will net $57 per share after flotation costs.

Common stock equity: The firm expects its dividends and earnings to continue to grow at a constant rate of 15% per year. The firm's stock is currently selling for $20 per share. The firm expects to have $1,300,000 of available retained earnings. Once the retained earnings has been exhausted, the firm can raise additional funds by selling new common stock, netting $16 per share after underpricing and flotation costs.

a. Over the relevant ranges noted in the following table, calculate the after-tax cost of each source of financing needed to complete the table.

Source of capital	Range of new financing	After-tax cost (%)
Long-term debt	$0–$700,000	_____
	$700,000 and above	_____
Preferred stock	$0 and above	_____
Common stock equity	$0–$1,300,000	_____
	$1,300,000 and above	_____

b. (1) Determine the *break points* associated with each source of capital.

    (2) Using the break points developed in part (1), determine each of the ranges of *total new financing* over which the firm's weighted average cost of capital (WACC) remains constant.

    (3) Calculate the weighted average cost of capital for each range of total new financing.

c. (1) Using your findings in part **b**(3) with the investment opportunities schedule (IOS), draw the firm's weighted marginal cost of capital (WMCC) schedule and the IOS on the same set of axes, with total new financing or investment on the *x* axis and weighted average cost of capital and IRR on the *y* axis.

    (2) Which, if any, of the available investments would you recommend that the firm accept? Explain your answer.

d. (1) Assuming that the specific financing costs do not change, what effect would a shift to a more highly leveraged *capital structure* consisting of 50% long-term debt, 10% preferred stock, and 40% common stock have on your previous findings? (*Note:* Rework parts **b** and **c** using these capital structure weights.)

    (2) Which capital structure—the original one or this one—seems better? Why?

e. (1) What type of *dividend policy* does the firm appear to employ? Does it seem appropriate given the firm's recent growth in sales and profits and given its current investment opportunities?

    (2) Would you recommend an alternative dividend policy? Explain. How would this policy affect the investments recommended in part **c**(2)?

PART FIVE

Short-Term Financial Decisions

Chapter 14

Working Capital and Current Assets Management

LEARNING GOALS

LG1 Understand short-term financial management, net working capital, and the related tradeoff between profitability and risk.

LG2 Describe the cash conversion cycle, its funding requirements, and the key strategies for managing it.

LG3 Discuss inventory management: differing views, common techniques, and international concerns.

LG4 Explain the credit selection process and the quantitative procedure for evaluating changes in credit standards.

LG5 Review the procedures for quantitatively considering cash discount changes, other aspects of credit terms, and credit monitoring.

LG6 Understand the management of receipts and disbursements, including float, speeding up collections, slowing down payments, cash concentration, zero-balance accounts, and investing in marketable securities.

 ACROSS THE DISCIPLINES WHY THIS CHAPTER MATTERS TO YOU

Accounting: You need to understand the cash conversion cycle and the management of inventory, accounts receivable, and receipts and disbursements of cash.

Information systems: You need to understand the cash conversion cycle, inventory, accounts receivable, and receipts and disbursements of cash to design financial information systems that facilitate effective short-term financial management.

Management: You need to understand the management of working capital so that you can efficiently manage cur-

rent assets and decide whether to finance the firm's funds requirements aggressively or conservatively.

Marketing: You need to understand credit selection and monitoring because sales will be affected by the availability of credit to purchasers; sales will also be affected by inventory management.

Operations: You need to understand the cash conversion cycle because you will be responsible for reducing the cycle through the efficient management of production, inventory, and costs.

AT&T

OUTSOURCING IS IN THE CARDS

AT&T (www.att.com) is among the world's premiere voice, video, and data communications companies, serving consumers, businesses, and government. Backed by the research and development capabilities of AT&T Labs, the company runs the world's largest, most sophisticated communications network and is a leading supplier of data and Internet services for businesses.

One of AT&T's services consists of prepaid phone cards. The company, which is highly skilled at delivering telecommunications services, had minimal experience in the supply chain management processes needed to bring tangible, packaged goods to channels such as convenience stores and mass merchants. AT&T made a strategic business decision to outsource its PrePaid Card end-to-end supply chain management functions. AT&T chose **Accenture**, a global management-consulting, technology services, and outsourcing company, to solve its problem.

Accenture teamed with AT&T to develop a customer-focused supply chain operating model for the prepaid phone cards. This model integrated all of the supply chain business processes, including sourcing, production, scheduling, account service, warehousing, fulfillment, inventory, billing, and systems management. Accenture organized purchasing and inventory decision-making processes and substantially reduced inventory levels and cost.

Together, AT&T and Accenture transformed and accelerated the delivery of bottom-line business results, including reducing PrePaid Card production costs by 15 percent, improving warehouse productivity by 25 percent, and reducing raw materials inventory by 25 percent.

Reducing raw materials inventory through outsourcing or by converting to just-in-time manufacturing can lower net working capital requirements, the difference between a firm's current assets (including inventory) and a firm's current liabilities. Because long-term assets provide a better return than short-term assets, reducing short-term assets can free up capital, which can then be better employed by the company.

In this chapter we look at techniques and strategies for managing working capital and current assets. We first discuss the fundamentals of net working capital and then demonstrate the cash conversion cycle. The balance of the chapter considers the management of inventory, accounts receivable, and receipts and disbursements in the context of the cash conversion cycle.

Source: www.accenture.com.

■ *What are the possible benefits of outsourcing finance and accounting activities?*

627

14.1 | Net Working Capital Fundamentals

[LG1]

The firm's balance sheet provides information about the structure of the firm's investments on the one hand and the structure of its financing sources on the other hand. The structures chosen should consistently lead to the maximization of the value of the owners' investment in the firm.

Important components of the firm's financial structure include the level of investment in current assets and the extent of current liability financing. In U.S. manufacturing firms, current assets account for about 40 percent of total assets; current liabilities represent about 26 percent of total financing. Therefore, it should not be surprising to learn that **short-term financial management**—managing current assets and current liabilities—is one of the financial manager's most important and time-consuming activities. A study of *Fortune* 1000 firms found that more than one-third of financial management time is spent managing current assets and about one-fourth of financial management time is spent managing current liabilities.[1]

The goal of short-term financial management is to manage each of the firm's current assets (inventory, accounts receivable, cash, and marketable securities) and current liabilities (accounts payable, accruals, and notes payable) to achieve a balance between profitability and risk that contributes positively to the firm's value. This chapter does not discuss the optimal level of current assets and current liabilities that a firm should have. That issue is unresolved in the financial literature. Here we first use net working capital to consider the basic relationship between current assets and current liabilities and then use the cash conversion cycle to consider the key aspects of current asset management. In the following chapter, we consider current liability management.

short-term financial management
Management of current assets and current liabilities.

Net Working Capital

working capital
Current assets, which represent the portion of investment that circulates from one form to another in the ordinary conduct of business.

Current assets, commonly called **working capital,** represent the portion of investment that circulates from one form to another in the ordinary conduct of business. This idea embraces the recurring transition from cash to inventories to receivables and back to cash. As cash substitutes, *marketable securities* are considered part of working capital.

Current liabilities represent the firm's short-term financing, because they include all debts of the firm that come due (must be paid) in 1 year or less. These debts usually include amounts owed to suppliers (accounts payable), employees and governments (accruals), and banks (notes payable), among others.

net working capital
The difference between the firm's current assets and its current liabilities; can be *positive* or *negative*.

As noted in Chapter 8, **net working capital** is commonly defined as the difference between the firm's current assets and its current liabilities. When the current assets exceed the current liabilities, the firm has *positive net working capital.* When current assets are less than current liabilities, the firm has *negative net working capital.*

---

1. Lawrence J. Gitman and Charles E. Maxwell, "Financial Activities of Major U.S. Firms: Survey and Analysis of Fortune's 1000," *Financial Management* (Winter 1985), pp. 57–65.

The conversion of current assets from inventory to receivables to cash provides the cash used to pay the current liabilities. The cash outlays for current liabilities are relatively predictable. When an obligation is incurred, the firm generally knows when the corresponding payment will be due. What is difficult to predict are the cash inflows—the conversion of the current assets to more liquid forms. The more predictable its cash inflows, the less net working capital a firm needs. Because most firms are unable to match cash inflows to outflows with certainty, current assets that more than cover outflows for current liabilities are usually necessary. In general, the greater the margin by which a firm's current assets cover its current liabilities, the better able it will be to pay its bills as they come due.

Hint Stated differently, some portion of current assets is usually held to provide liquidity in case it is unexpectedly needed.

The Tradeoff Between Profitability and Risk

profitability
The relationship between revenues and costs generated by using the firm's assets—both current and fixed—in productive activities.

A tradeoff exists between a firm's profitability and its risk. **Profitability,** in this context, is the relationship between revenues and costs generated by using the firm's assets—both current and fixed—in productive activities. A firm's profits can be increased by (1) increasing revenues or (2) decreasing costs. **Risk,** in the context of short-term financial management, is the probability that a firm will be unable to pay its bills as they come due. A firm that cannot pay its bills as they come due is said to be **technically insolvent.** It is generally assumed that the greater the firm's net working capital, the lower its risk. In other words, the more net working capital, the more liquid the firm and therefore the lower its risk of becoming technically insolvent. Using these definitions of profitability and risk, we can demonstrate the tradeoff between them by considering changes in current assets and current liabilities separately.

risk (of technical insolvency)
The probability that a firm will be unable to pay its bills as they come due.

technically insolvent
Describes a firm that is unable to pay its bills as they come due.

Changes in Current Assets

How changing the level of the firm's current assets affects its profitability–risk tradeoff can be demonstrated using the ratio of current assets to total assets. This ratio indicates the *percentage of total assets* that is current. For purposes of illustration, we will assume that the level of total assets remains unchanged.[2] The effects on both profitability and risk of an increase or decrease in this ratio are summarized in the upper portion of Table 14.1 (on page 630). When the ratio increases—that is, when current assets increase—profitability decreases. Why? Because current assets are less profitable than fixed assets. Fixed assets are more profitable because they add more value to the product than that provided by current assets. Without fixed assets, the firm could not produce the product.

The risk effect, however, decreases as the ratio of current assets to total assets increases. The increase in current assets increases net working capital, thereby reducing the risk of technical insolvency. In addition, as you go down the asset side of the balance sheet, the risk associated with the assets increases: Investment in cash and marketable securities is less risky than investment in accounts receivable, inventories, and fixed assets. Accounts receivable investment is less risky

Hint It is generally easier to turn receivables into the more liquid asset cash than it is to turn inventory into cash. As we will learn in Chapter 15, the firm can sell its receivables for cash. Often inventory is sold on credit and is therefore converted to a receivable before it becomes cash.

---

2. To isolate the effect of changing asset and financing mixes on the firm's profitability and risk, we assume the level of total assets to be *constant* in this and the following discussion.

TABLE 14.1

Effects of Changing Ratios on Profits and Risk

Ratio	Change in ratio	Effect on profit	Effect on risk
Current assets / Total assets	Increase	Decrease	Decrease
	Decrease	Increase	Increase
Current liabilities / Total assets	Increase	Increase	Increase
	Decrease	Decrease	Decrease

than investment in inventories and fixed assets. Investment in inventories is less risky than investment in fixed assets. The nearer an asset is to cash, the less risky it is. The opposite effects on profit and risk result from a decrease in the ratio of current assets to total assets.

Changes in Current Liabilities

How changing the level of the firm's current liabilities affects its profitability–risk tradeoff can be demonstrated by using the ratio of current liabilities to total assets. This ratio indicates the percentage of total assets that has been financed with current liabilities. Again, assuming that total assets remain unchanged, the effects on both profitability and risk of an increase or decrease in the ratio are summarized in the lower portion of Table 14.1. When the ratio increases, profitability increases. Why? Because the firm uses more of the less expensive current liabilities financing and less long-term financing. Current liabilities are less expensive because only notes payable, which represent about 20 percent of the typical manufacturer's current liabilities, have a cost. The other current liabilities are basically debts on which the firm pays no charge or interest. However, when the ratio of current liabilities to total assets increases, the risk of technical insolvency also increases, because the increase in current liabilities in turn decreases net working capital. The opposite effects on profit and risk result from a decrease in the ratio of current liabilities to total assets.

REVIEW QUESTIONS

14–1 Why is *short-term financial management* one of the most important and time-consuming activities of the financial manager? What is *net working capital?*

14–2 What is the relationship between the predictability of a firm's cash inflows and its required level of net working capital? How are net working capital, liquidity, and *risk of technical insolvency* related?

14–3 Why does an increase in the ratio of current to total assets decrease both profits and risk as measured by net working capital? How do changes in the ratio of current liabilities to total assets affect profitability and risk?

LG2 14.2 | The Cash Conversion Cycle

Central to short-term financial management is an understanding of the firm's cash conversion cycle.[3] This cycle frames discussion of the management of the firm's current assets in this chapter and that of the management of current liabilities in Chapter 15. Here, we begin by demonstrating the calculation and application of the cash conversion cycle.

Calculating the Cash Conversion Cycle

operating cycle (OC)
The time from the beginning of the production process to the collection of cash from the sale of the finished product.

A firm's **operating cycle (OC)** is the time from the beginning of the production process to collection of cash from the sale of the finished product. The operating cycle encompasses two major short-term asset categories: inventory and accounts receivable. It is measured in elapsed time by summing the *average age of inventory (AAI)* and the *average collection period (ACP)*.

$$OC = AAI + ACP \tag{14.1}$$

Hint A firm can lower its working capital if it can speed up its operating cycle. For example, if a firm accepts bank credit (like a Visa card), it will receive cash sooner after the sale is transacted than if it has to wait until the customer pays its accounts receivable.

However, the process of producing and selling a product also includes the purchase of production inputs (raw materials) on account, which results in accounts payable. Accounts payable reduce the number of days a firm's resources are tied up in the operating cycle. The time it takes to pay the accounts payable, measured in days, is the *average payment period (APP)*. The operating cycle less the average payment period is referred to as the **cash conversion cycle (CCC)**. It represents the amount of time the firm's resources are tied up. The formula for the cash conversion cycle is

cash conversion cycle (CCC)
The amount of time a firm's resources are tied up; calculated by subtracting the average payment period from the *operating cycle.*

$$CCC = OC - APP \tag{14.2}$$

Substituting the relationship in Equation 14.1 into Equation 14.2, we can see that the cash conversion cycle has three main components, as shown in Equation 14.3: (1) average age of the inventory, (2) average collection period, and (3) average payment period.

$$CCC = AAI + ACP - APP \tag{14.3}$$

Clearly, if a firm changes any of these time periods, it changes the amount of resources tied up in the day-to-day operation of the firm.

EXAMPLE   MAX Company, a producer of paper dinnerware, has annual sales of $10 million, a cost of goods sold of 75% of sales, and purchases that are 65% of cost of goods sold. MAX has an average age of inventory (AAI) of 60 days, an average collection period (ACP) of 40 days, and an average payment period (APP) of 35 days. Thus the cash conversion cycle for MAX is 65 days (60 + 40 − 35). Figure 14.1 (on page 632) presents MAX Company's cash conversion cycle as a time line.

---

3. The conceptual model that is used in this section to demonstrate basic short-term financial management strategies was developed by Lawrence J. Gitman in "Estimating Corporate Liquidity Requirements: A Simplified Approach," *The Financial Review* (1974), pp. 79–88, and refined and operationalized by Lawrence J. Gitman and Kanwal S. Sachdeva in "A Framework for Estimating and Analyzing the Required Working Capital Investment," *Review of Business and Economic Research* (Spring 1982), pp. 35–44.

aggressive funding strategy
A funding strategy under which the firm funds its seasonal requirements with short-term debt and its permanent requirements with long-term debt.

conservative funding strategy
A funding strategy under which the firm funds both its seasonal and its permanent requirements with long-term debt.

Aggressive Versus Conservative Seasonal Funding Strategies

Short-term funds are typically less expensive than long-term funds. (The yield curve is typically upward-sloping.) However, long-term funds allow the firm to lock in its cost of funds over a period of time and thus avoid the risk of increases in short-term interest rates. Also, long-term funding ensures that the required funds are available to the firm when needed. Short-term funding exposes the firm to the risk that it may not be able to obtain the funds needed to cover its seasonal peaks. Under an **aggressive funding strategy,** the firm funds its seasonal requirements with short-term debt and its permanent requirements with long-term debt. Under a **conservative funding strategy,** the firm funds both its seasonal and its permanent requirements with long-term debt.

EXAMPLE

Semper Pump Company has a permanent funding requirement of $135,000 in operating assets and seasonal funding requirements that vary between $0 and $990,000 and average $101,250 (calculated from data not shown). If Semper can borrow short-term funds at 6.25% and long-term funds at 8%, and if it can earn 5% on the investment of any surplus balances, then the annual cost of an aggressive strategy for seasonal funding will be

Cost of short-term financing	= 0.0625 ×	$101,250 =	$ 6,328.13
+ Cost of long-term financing	= 0.0800 ×	135,000 =	10,800.00
− Earnings on surplus balances[4]	= 0.0500 ×	0 =	0
Total cost of aggressive strategy			$17,128.13

Alternatively, Semper can choose a conservative strategy, under which surplus cash balances are fully invested. (In Figure 14.2, this surplus will be the difference between the peak need of $1,125,000 and the total need, which varies between $135,000 and $1,125,000 during the year.) The cost of the conservative strategy will be

Cost of short-term financing	= 0.0625 × $	0 = $	0
+ Cost of long-term financing	= 0.0800 ×	1,125,000 =	90,000.00
− Earnings on surplus balances[5]	= 0.0500 ×	888,750 =	44,437.50
Total cost of conservative strategy			$45,562.50

It is clear from these calculations that for Semper, the aggressive strategy is far less expensive than the conservative strategy. However, it is equally clear that Semper has substantial peak-season operating-asset needs and that it must have adequate funding available to meet the peak needs and ensure ongoing operations. ■

Clearly, the aggressive strategy's heavy reliance on short-term financing makes it riskier than the conservative strategy because of interest rate swings and possible difficulties in obtaining needed short-term financing quickly when sea-

---

4. Because under this strategy the amount of financing exactly equals the estimated funding need, no surplus balances exist.

5. The average surplus balance would be calculated by subtracting the sum of the permanent need ($135,000) and the average seasonal need ($101,250) from the seasonal peak need ($1,125,000) to get $888,750 ($1,125,000 − $135,000 − $101,250). This represents the surplus amount of financing that on average could be invested in short-term vehicles that earn a 5% annual return.

sonal peaks occur. The conservative strategy avoids these risks through the locked-in interest rate and long-term financing, but it is more costly because of the negative spread between the earnings rate on surplus funds (5% in the example) and the cost of the long-term funds that create the surplus (8% in the example). Where the firm operates, between the extremes of the aggressive and conservative seasonal funding strategies, depends on management's disposition toward risk and the strength of its banking relationships.

Strategies for Managing the Cash Conversion Cycle

A positive cash conversion cycle, as we saw for MAX Company in the earlier example, means the firm must use negotiated liabilities (such as bank loans) to support its operating assets. Negotiated liabilities carry an explicit cost, so the firm benefits by minimizing their use in supporting operating assets. Simply stated, the goal is to *minimize the length of the cash conversion cycle*, which minimizes negotiated liabilities. This goal can be realized through application of the following strategies:

1. *Turn over inventory as quickly as possible* without stockouts that result in lost sales.
2. *Collect accounts receivable as quickly as possible* without losing sales from high-pressure collection techniques.
3. *Manage mail, processing, and clearing time* to reduce them when collecting from customers and to increase them when paying suppliers.
4. *Pay accounts payable as slowly as possible* without damaging the firm's credit rating.

Techniques for implementing these four strategies are the focus of the remainder of this chapter and the following chapter.

REVIEW QUESTIONS

14–4   What is the difference between the firm's *operating cycle* and its *cash conversion cycle?*

14–5   Why is it helpful to divide the funding needs of a seasonal business into its permanent and seasonal funding requirements when developing a funding strategy?

14–6   What are the benefits, costs, and risks of an *aggressive funding strategy* and of a *conservative funding strategy?* Under which strategy is the borrowing often in excess of the actual need?

14–7   Why is it important for a firm to minimize the length of its cash conversion cycle?

LG3 14.3 | Inventory Management

The first component of the cash conversion cycle is the average age of inventory. The objective for managing inventory, as noted earlier, is to turn over inventory as quickly as possible without losing sales from stockouts. The financial manager

In Practice FOCUS ON PRACTICE

RFID: THE WAVE OF THE FUTURE

Wal-Mart Stores, Inc., the world's #1 retailer, has more than 4,800 stores, including some 1,475 discount stores, 1,750 combination discount and grocery stores, and 540 warehouse stores. With 2003 sales of $256 billion, Wal-Mart is able to exert tremendous pressure on its suppliers. So when Wal-Mart announced in April 2004 that it was beginning a pilot program to test *radio frequency identification (RFID)* technology to improve its inventory and supply chain management, suppliers and competitors alike sat up and took notice.

Radio frequency identification is not new technology—it's been around since the 1940s. Anyone unlocking a car door using a keyless remote or using a tollbooth transponder is already using RFID. In their inventory control capacity, passive RFID chips with small antennae are attached to cases and pallets. A tag reader activates the chip, and its unique product identifier code is transmitted back to an inventory control system.

One of the first companies to introduce bar codes in the early

1980s, Wal-Mart plans to require its top 100 suppliers to put RFID tags on shipping crates and pallets by January 2005, with the next 200 largest suppliers using the technology by January 2006. Wal-Mart's goal is to have all of its 86,000-plus suppliers on board using electronic product codes (EPC) with RFID technology.

Several hurdles must be dealt with before full implementation can be achieved. Currently, capacity for manufacturing the new chips is insufficient to produce chips in the quantity needed for full implementation of Wal-Mart's plans. Wal-Mart's move is expected to require nearly 1 billion RFID tags. **Texas Instruments,** a producer of RFID tags, has shipped a total of 200 million RFID tags to date. With the expected increase in demand for more chips, Texas Instruments is considering a potential investment in a new production facility to increase its RFID manufacturing capacity. Such a facility would cost more than $1 billion. A second issue is per-chip cost. Each chip currently

sells for 30 to 50 cents; Wal-Mart has requested a price of 5 cents per tag. With a substantial increase in demand for chips, it expects economies of scale to push the price down.

Initially, Wal-Mart plans to use RFID technology to improve its inventory management. One of the company's measures of efficiency is inventory growth at a rate of less than half of sales growth. For 2003, Wal-Mart's inventories grew at 9.1 percent while sales increased 11.6 percent. Using RFID technology, Wal-Mart will attempt to improve this number and reduce its net working capital requirements.

Sources: Wal-Mart press releases, www.walmartstores.com (accessed August 25, 2004); and Jaikumar Vijayan and Bob Brewin, "Wal-Mart's Plan Poses Challenges for Chip Makers" (June 16, 2003), www.computerworld.com (accessed August 25, 2004).

■ *What problem might occur with the full implementation of RFID technology in retail industries? Specifically, consider the amount of data that might be collected.*

---

by including information about suppliers and customers. ERP electronically integrates all of a firm's departments so that, for example, production can call up sales information and immediately know how much must be produced to fill customer orders. Because all available resources—human and material—are known, the system can eliminate production delays and control costs. ERP systems automatically note changes, such as a supplier's inability to meet a scheduled delivery date, so that necessary adjustments can be made.

International Inventory Management

International inventory management is typically much more complicated for exporters in general, and for multinational companies in particular, than for purely domestic firms. The production and manufacturing economies of scale that might be expected from selling products globally may prove elusive if products must be tailored for individual local markets, as very frequently happens, or if actual production takes place in factories around the world. When raw materials, intermediate goods, or finished products must be transported over long distances—particularly by ocean shipping—there will inevitably be more delays, confusion, damage, theft, and other difficulties than occur in a one-country operation. The international inventory manager therefore puts a premium on flexibility. He or she is usually less concerned about ordering the economically optimal quantity of inventory than about making sure that sufficient quantities of inventory are delivered where they are needed, when they are needed, and in a condition to be used as planned.

REVIEW QUESTIONS

14–8   What are likely to be the viewpoints of each of the following managers about the levels of the various types of inventory: finance, marketing, manufacturing, and purchasing? Why is inventory an investment?

14–9   Briefly describe each of the following techniques for managing inventory: ABC system, economic order quantity (EOQ) model, just-in-time (JIT) system, and computerized systems for resource control—MRP, MRP II, and ERP.

14–10 What factors make managing inventory more difficult for exporters and multinational companies?

`LG4` `LG5` 14.4 | # Accounts Receivable Management

The second component of the cash conversion cycle is the average collection period. This period is the average length of time from a sale on credit until the payment becomes usable funds for the firm. The average collection period has two parts. The first part is the time from the sale until the customer mails the payment. The second part is the time from when the payment is mailed until the firm has the collected funds in its bank account. The first part of the average collection period involves managing the credit available to the firm's customers, and the second part involves collecting and processing payments. This section of the chapter discusses the firm's accounts receivable credit management.

Hint Some small businesses resolve these problems by selling their accounts receivable to a third party at a discount. Though expensive, this strategy overcomes the problem of not having adequate personnel. It also creates a buffer between the small business and those customers who need a little prodding to stay current.

The objective for managing accounts receivable is to collect accounts receivable as quickly as possible without losing sales from high-pressure collection techniques. Accomplishing this goal encompasses three topics: (1) credit selection and standards, (2) credit terms, and (3) credit monitoring.

Credit Selection and Standards

credit standards
The firm's minimum requirements for extending credit to a customer.

Credit selection involves application of techniques for determining which customers should receive credit. This process involves evaluating the customer's creditworthiness and comparing it to the firm's **credit standards,** its minimum requirements for extending credit to a customer.

Five C's of Credit

One popular credit selection technique is the **five C's of credit,** which provides a framework for in-depth credit analysis. Because of the time and expense involved, this credit selection method is used for large-dollar credit requests. The five C's are

1. *Character:* The applicant's record of meeting past obligations.
2. *Capacity:* The applicant's ability to repay the requested credit, as judged in terms of financial statement analysis focused on cash flows available to repay debt obligations.
3. *Capital:* The applicant's debt relative to equity.
4. *Collateral:* The amount of assets the applicant has available for use in securing the credit. The larger the amount of available assets, the greater the chance that a firm will recover funds if the applicant defaults.
5. *Conditions:* Current general and industry-specific economic conditions, and any unique conditions surrounding a specific transaction.

Analysis via the five C's of credit does not yield a specific accept/reject decision, so its use requires an analyst experienced in reviewing and granting credit requests. Application of this framework tends to ensure that the firm's credit customers will pay, without being pressured, within the stated credit terms.

Credit Scoring

Credit scoring is a method of credit selection that is commonly used with high-volume/small-dollar credit requests. **Credit scoring** applies statistically derived weights to a credit applicant's scores on key financial and credit characteristics to predict whether he or she will pay the requested credit in a timely fashion. Simply stated, the procedure results in a score that measures the applicant's overall credit strength, and the score is used to make the accept/reject decision for granting the applicant credit. Credit scoring is most commonly used by large credit card operations, such as those of banks, oil companies, and department stores. The purpose of credit scoring is to make a relatively informed credit decision quickly and inexpensively, recognizing that the cost of a single bad scoring decision is small. However, if bad debts from scoring decisions increase, then the scoring system must be reevaluated. For a demonstration of credit scoring, including use of a spreadsheet for that purpose, see the book's Web site at www.aw-bc.com/gitman.

Changing Credit Standards

The firm sometimes will contemplate changing its credit standards in an effort to improve its returns and create greater value for its owners. To demonstrate, consider the following changes and effects on profits expected to result from the *relaxation* of credit standards.

Effects of Relaxation of Credit Standards		
Variable	Direction of change	Effect on profits
Sales volume	Increase	Positive
Investment in accounts receivable	Increase	Negative
Bad-debt expenses	Increase	Negative

If credit standards were tightened, the opposite effects would be expected.

EXAMPLE   Dodd Tool, a manufacturer of lathe tools, is currently selling a product for $10 per unit. Sales (all on credit) for last year were 60,000 units. The variable cost per unit is $6. The firm's total fixed costs are $120,000.

The firm is currently contemplating a *relaxation of credit standards* that is expected to result in the following: a 5% increase in unit sales to 63,000 units; an increase in the average collection period from 30 days (the current level) to 45 days; an increase in bad-debt expenses from 1% of sales (the current level) to 2%. The firm's required return on equal-risk investments, which is the opportunity cost of tying up funds in accounts receivable, is 15%.

To determine whether to relax its credit standards, Dodd Tool must calculate its effect on the firm's additional profit contribution from sales, the cost of the marginal investment in accounts receivable, and the cost of marginal bad debts.

Additional Profit Contribution from Sales   Because fixed costs are "sunk" and therefore are unaffected by a change in the sales level, the only cost relevant to a change in sales is variable costs. Sales are expected to increase by 5%, or 3,000 units. The profit contribution per unit will equal the difference between the sale price per unit ($10) and the variable cost per unit ($6). The profit contribution per unit therefore will be $4. The total additional profit contribution from sales will be $12,000 (3,000 units × $4 per unit).

Cost of the Marginal Investment in Accounts Receivable   To determine the cost of the marginal investment in accounts receivable, Dodd must find the difference between the cost of carrying receivables under the two credit standards. Because its concern is only with the out-of-pocket costs, *the relevant cost is the variable cost.* The average investment in accounts receivable can be calculated by using the following formula:

$$\frac{\text{Average investment}}{\text{in accounts receivable}} = \frac{\text{Total variable cost of annual sales}}{\text{Turnover of accounts receivable}} \qquad (14.9)$$

where

$$\text{Turnover of accounts receivable} = \frac{365}{\text{Average collection period}}$$

The total variable cost of annual sales under the present and proposed plans can be found as follows, using the variable cost per unit of $6.

Total variable cost of annual sales

Under present plan: ($6 × 60,000 units) = $360,000
Under proposed plan: ($6 × 63,000 units) = $378,000

The turnover of accounts receivable is the number of times each year that the firm's accounts receivable are actually turned into cash. It is found by dividing the average collection period into 365 (the number of days assumed in a year).

Turnover of accounts receivable

$$\text{Under present plan: } \frac{365}{30} = 12.2$$

$$\text{Under present plan: } \frac{365}{45} = 8.1$$

By substituting the cost and turnover data just calculated into Equation 14.9 for each case, we get the following average investments in accounts receivable:

Average investment in accounts receivable

$$\text{Under present plan: } \frac{\$360,000}{12.2} = \$29,508$$

$$\text{Under proposed plan: } \frac{\$378,000}{8.1} = \$46,667$$

The marginal investment in accounts receivable and its cost are calculated as follows:

Cost of marginal investment in accounts receivable

Average investment under proposed plan	$46,667
− Average investment under present plan	29,508
Marginal investment in accounts receivable	$17,159
× Required return on investment	0.15
Cost of marginal investment in A/R	$ 2,574

The resulting value of $2,574 is considered a cost because it represents the maximum amount that could have been earned on the $17,159 had it been placed in the best equal-risk investment alternative available at the firm's required return on investment of 15%.

Cost of Marginal Bad Debts   The cost of marginal bad debts is found by taking the difference between the levels of bad debts before and after the proposed relaxation of credit standards.

Cost of marginal bad debts

Under proposed plan: $(0.02 \times \$10/\text{unit} \times 63,000 \text{ units})$	=	$12,600
Under present plan: $(0.01 \times \$10/\text{unit} \times 60,000 \text{ units})$	=	6,000
Cost of marginal bad debts		$ 6,600

Note that the bad-debt costs are calculated by using the sale price per unit ($10) to deduct not just the true loss of variable cost ($6) that results when a customer fails to pay its account, but also the profit contribution per unit (in this case $4) that is included in the "additional profit contribution from sales." Thus the resulting cost of marginal bad debts is $6,600.   ■

Making the Credit Standard Decision   To decide whether to relax its credit standards, the firm must compare the additional profit contribution from sales to the added costs of the marginal investment in accounts receivable and marginal bad debts. If the additional profit contribution is greater than marginal costs, credit standards should be relaxed.

EXAMPLE   The results and key calculations related to Dodd Tool's decision whether to relax its credit standards are summarized in Table 14.2 on the facing page. The net addition to total profits resulting from such an action will be $2,826 per year. Therefore, the firm *should* relax its credit standards as proposed.   ■

TABLE 14.2		
The Effects on Dodd Tool of a Relaxation of Credit Standards		

Additional profit contribution from sales

$[3,000 \text{ units} \times (\$10 - \$6)]$ · $12,000

Cost of marginal investment in A/R[a]

Average investment under proposed plan:

$$\frac{\$6 \times 63,000}{8.1} = \frac{\$378,000}{8.1} \qquad \$46,667$$

Average investment under present plan:

$$\frac{\$6 \times 60,000}{12.2} = \frac{\$360,000}{12.2} \qquad \underline{29,508}$$

Marginal investment in A/R · $17,159

   Cost of marginal investment in A/R $(0.15 \times \$17,159)$ · ($ 2,574)

Cost of marginal bad debts

   Bad debts under proposed plan $(0.02 \times \$10 \times 63,000)$ · · · · · · $12,600

   Bad debts under present plan $(0.01 \times \$10 \times 60,000)$ · · · · · · · · · · · · · · · · $\underline{6,000}$

   Cost of marginal bad debts · ($ 6,600)

Net profit from implementation of proposed plan · $ 2,826

[a]The denominators 8.1 and 12.2 in the calculation of the average investment in accounts receivable under the proposed and present plans are the accounts receivable turnovers for each of these plans $(365/45 = 8.1$ and $365/30 = 12.2)$.

The procedure described here for evaluating a proposed change in credit standards is also commonly used to evaluate other changes in the management of accounts receivable. If Dodd Tool had been contemplating tightening its credit standards, for example, the cost would have been a reduction in the profit contribution from sales, and the return would have been from reductions in the cost of the investment in accounts receivable and in the cost of bad debts. Another application of this procedure is demonstrated later in the chapter.

Managing International Credit

Credit management is difficult enough for managers of purely domestic companies, and these tasks become much more complex for companies that operate internationally. This is partly because (as we have seen before) international operations typically expose a firm to *exchange rate risk*. It is also due to the dangers and delays involved in shipping goods long distances and in having to cross at least two international borders.

Exports of finished goods are usually priced in the currency of the importer's local market; most commodities, on the other hand, are priced in dollars. Therefore, a U.S. company that sells a product in Japan, for example, would have to price that product in Japanese yen and extend credit to a Japanese wholesaler in the local currency (yen). If the yen *depreciates* against the dollar before the U.S. exporter collects on its account receivable, the U.S. company experiences an exchange rate loss; the yen collected are worth fewer dollars than expected at the time the sale was made. Of course, the dollar could just as easily depreciate against

c. Determine the *reorder point*.

d. Indicate which of the following variables change if the firm does not hold the safety stock: (1) order cost, (2) carrying cost, (3) total inventory cost, (4) reorder point, (5) economic order quantity. Explain.

P14–7   Accounts receivable changes without bad debts   Tara's Textiles currently has credit sales of $360 million per year and an average collection period of 60 days. Assume that the price of Tara's products is $60 per unit and that the variable costs are $55 per unit. The firm is considering an accounts receivable change that will result in a 20% increase in sales and a 20% increase in the average collection period. No change in bad debts is expected. The firm's equal-risk opportunity cost on its investment in accounts receivable is 14%. (*Note:* Use a 365-day year.)

a. Calculate the *additional profit contribution from new sales* that the firm will realize if it makes the proposed change.

b. What *marginal investment in accounts receivable* will result?

c. Calculate the *cost of the marginal investment in accounts receivable*.

d. Should the firm implement the proposed change? What other information would be helpful in your analysis?

P14–8   Accounts receivable changes with bad debts   A firm is evaluating an accounts receivable change that would increase bad debts from 2% to 4% of sales. Sales are currently 50,000 units, the selling price is $20 per unit, and the variable cost per unit is $15. As a result of the proposed change, sales are forecast to increase to 60,000 units.

a. What are bad debts in dollars currently and under the proposed change?

b. Calculate the *cost of the marginal bad debts* to the firm.

c. Ignoring the additional profit contribution from increased sales, if the proposed change saves $3,500 and causes no change in the average investment in accounts receivable, would you recommend it? Explain.

d. Considering *all* changes in costs and benefits, would you recommend the proposed change? Explain.

e. Compare and discuss your answers in parts **c** and **d**.

P14–9   Relaxation of credit standards   Lewis Enterprises is considering relaxing its credit standards to increase its currently sagging sales. As a result of the proposed relaxation, sales are expected to increase by 10% from 10,000 to 11,000 units during the coming year; the average collection period is expected to increase from 45 to 60 days; and bad debts are expected to increase from 1% to 3% of sales. The sale price per unit is $40, and the variable cost per unit is $31. The firm's required return on equal-risk investments is 25%. Evaluate the proposed relaxation, and make a recommendation to the firm. (*Note:* Assume a 365-day year.)

P14–10   Initiating a cash discount   Gardner Company currently makes all sales on credit and offers no cash discount. The firm is considering offering a 2% cash discount for payment within 15 days. The firm's current average collection period is 60 days, sales are 40,000 units, selling price is $45 per unit, and variable cost per unit is $36. The firm expects that the change in credit terms will result in an increase in sales to 42,000 units, that 70% of the sales will take the discount, and that the average collection period will fall to 30 days. If the firm's required rate of return on equal-risk investments is 25%, should the proposed discount be offered? (*Note:* Assume a 365-day year.)

P14–11   Shortening the credit period   A firm is contemplating *shortening* its credit period from 40 to 30 days and believes that as a result of this change, its average collection period will decline from 45 to 36 days. Bad-debt expenses are expected to decrease from 1.5% to 1% of sales. The firm is currently selling 12,000 units but believes that as a result of the proposed change, sales will decline to 10,000 units. The sale price per unit is $56, and the variable cost per unit is $45. The firm has a required return on equal-risk investments of 25%. Evaluate this decision, and make a recommendation to the firm. (*Note:* Assume a 365-day year.)

P14–12   Lengthening the credit period   Parker Tool is considering lengthening its credit period from 30 to 60 days. All customers will continue to pay on the net date. The firm currently bills $450,000 for sales and has $345,000 in variable costs. The change in credit terms is expected to increase sales to $510,000. Bad-debt expenses will increase from 1% to 1.5% of sales. The firm has a required rate of return on equal-risk investments of 20%. (*Note:* Assume a 365-day year.)

a. What *additional profit contribution from sales* will be realized from the proposed change?
b. What is the *cost of the marginal investment in accounts receivable?*
c. What is the *cost of the marginal bad debts?*
d. Do you recommend this change in credit terms? Why or why not?

P14–13   Float   Simon Corporation has daily cash receipts of $65,000. A recent analysis of its collections indicated that customers' payments were in the mail an average of 2.5 days. Once received, the payments are processed in 1.5 days. After payments are deposited, it takes an average of 3 days for these receipts to clear the banking system.

a. How much *collection float (in days)* does the firm currently have?
b. If the firm's opportunity cost is 11%, would it be economically advisable for the firm to pay an annual fee of $16,500 to reduce collection float by 3 days? Explain why or why not.

P14–14   Lockbox system   Eagle Industries feels that a lockbox system can shorten its accounts receivable collection period by 3 days. Credit sales are $3,240,000 per year, billed on a continuous basis. The firm has other equally risky investments with a return of 15%. The cost of the lockbox system is $9,000 per year. (*Note:* Assume a 365-day year.)

a. What amount of cash will be made available for other uses under the lockbox system?
b. What net benefit (cost) will the firm realize if it adopts the lockbox system? Should it adopt the proposed lockbox system?

P14–15   Zero-balance account   Union Company is considering establishment of a zero-balance account. The firm currently maintains an average balance of $420,000 in its disbursement account. As compensation to the bank for maintaining the zero-balance account, the firm will have to pay a monthly fee of $1,000 and maintain a $300,000 non–interest-earning deposit in the bank. The firm currently has no other deposits in the bank. Evaluate the proposed zero-balance account, and make a recommendation to the firm, assuming that it has a 12% opportunity cost.

P14–16 **ETHICS PROBLEM** Controlled disbursing is defined as an information product—that is, the bank on which the company's checks are drawn provides an early-morning notification of the total dollar amount of checks that will clear the account that day. Based on that notification, the company may then fund the account for that amount by the close of business that afternoon. How might controlled disbursing still be viewed as a form of "remote disbursing," and therefore be considered unethical?

LG6

INTERMEDIATE

Chapter 14 Case: Assessing Roche Publishing Company's Cash Management Efficiency

Lisa Pinto, vice president of finance at Roche Publishing Company, a rapidly growing publisher of college texts, is concerned about the firm's high level of short-term resource investment. She believes that the firm can improve the management of its cash and, as a result, reduce this investment. In this regard, she charged Arlene Bessenoff, the treasurer, with assessing the firm's cash management efficiency. Arlene decided to begin her investigation by studying the firm's operating and cash conversion cycles.

Arlene found that Roche's average payment period was 25 days. She consulted industry data, which showed that the average payment period for the industry was 40 days. Investigation of three similar publishing companies revealed that their average payment period was also 40 days. She estimated the annual cost of achieving a 40-day payment period to be $53,000.

Next, Arlene studied the production cycle and inventory policies. The average age of inventory was 120 days. She determined that the industry standard as reported in a survey done by *Publishing World,* the trade association journal, was 85 days. She estimated the annual cost of achieving an 85-day average age of inventory to be $150,000.

Further analysis showed Arlene that the firm's average collection period was 60 days. The industry average, derived from the trade association data and information on three similar publishing companies, was found to be 42 days—30% lower than Roche's. Arlene estimated that if Roche initiated a 2% cash discount for payment within 10 days of the beginning of the credit period, the firm's average collection period would drop from 60 days to the 42-day industry average. She also expected the following to occur as a result of the discount: Annual sales would increase from $13,750,000 to $15,000,000; bad debts would remain unchanged; and the 2% cash discount would be applied to 75% of the firm's sales. The firm's variable costs equal 80% of sales.

Roche Publishing Company is currently spending $12,000,000 per year on its operating-cycle investment, but it expects that initiating a cash discount will increase its operating-cycle investment to $13,100,000 per year. (*Note:* The operating-cycle investment per dollar of inventory, receivables, and payables is assumed to be the same.) Arlene's concern was whether the firm's cash management was as efficient as it could be. Arlene knew that the company paid 12% annual interest for its resource investment and therefore viewed this value as the firm's required return. For this reason, she was concerned about the resource investment cost resulting from any inefficiencies in the management of Roche's cash conversion cycle. (*Note:* Assume a 365-day year.)

TO DO

a. Assuming a constant rate for purchases, production, and sales throughout the year, what are Roche's existing *operating cycle (OC), cash conversion cycle (CCC)*, and *resource investment* need?

b. If Roche can optimize operations according to industry standards, what would its *operating cycle (OC), cash conversion cycle (CCC)*, and *resource investment* need be under these more efficient conditions?

c. In terms of resource investment requirements, what is the annual cost of Roche's operational inefficiency?

d. Evaluate whether Roche's strategy for speeding its collection of accounts receivable would be acceptable. What annual net profit or loss would result from implementation of the cash discount?

e. Use your finding in part **d,** along with the payables and inventory costs given, to determine the total annual cost the firm would incur to achieve the industry level of operational efficiency.

f. Judging on the basis of your findings in parts **c** and **e,** should the firm incur the annual cost to achieve the industry level of operational efficiency? Explain why or why not.

Spreadsheet Exercise

The current balance in accounts receivable for Eboy Corporation is $443,000. This level was achieved with annual (365 days) credit sales of $3,544,000. The firm offers its customers credit terms of *net 30.* However, in an effort to help its cash flow position and to follow the actions of its rivals, the firm is considering changing its credit terms from net 30 to *2/10 net 30.* The objective is to speed up the receivable collections and thereby improve the firm's cash flows. Eboy would like to increase its accounts receivable turnover to 12.0.

The firm works with a raw material whose current annual usage is 1,450 units. Each finished product requires 1 unit of this raw material at a variable cost of $2,600 per unit and sells for $4,200 on terms of net 30. It is estimated that 70% of the firm's customers will take the 2% cash discount and that with the discount, sales of the finished product will increase by 50 units per year. The firm's opportunity cost of funds invested in accounts receivable is 12.5%

In analyzing the investment in accounts receivable, use the variable cost of the product sold instead of the sale price, because the variable cost is a better indicator of the firm's investment.

TO DO

Create a spreadsheet similar to Table 14.3 (or to one that can be viewed at www.aw-bc.com/gitman) to analyze whether the firm should initiate the proposed cash discount. What is your advice? Make sure you calculate the following:

a. Additional profit contribution from sales.
b. Average investment in accounts receivable at present (without cash discount).
c. Average investment in accounts receivable with the proposed cash discount.
d. Reduction in investment in accounts receivable.
e. Cost savings from reduced investment in accounts receivable.
f. Cost of the cash discount.
g. Net profit (loss) from initiation of proposed cash discount.

Group Exercise

This chapter covers several short-term financial management topics that are vital to any business's success. These topics are often overlooked by the inexperienced manager/owner. Many businesses fail not because of a lack of sales but because of an inability to adequately manage current assets and current liabilities. With this point in mind, your group will "get its hands dirty" as it establishes proper controls meant to better manage short-term finances.

TO DO

Your group's fictitious firm, like all firms, needs to develop proper controls to ensure that short-term needs are met and that the firm gets the most out of its limited funds. To that end your group should do the following:

`LG2` a. Establish your firm's operating cycle by determining its AAI and ACP as well as its CCC based on its OC and its APP.
`LG2` b. Discuss the funding requirements, and state whether there is any seasonality to your required resource investment.
`LG3` c. Choose a method for managing inventory, and discuss how this method applies to your business.
`LG5` d. Establish the specific credit terms by which you will be selling your firm's good/service.

Web Exercise

As this chapter points out, cash management is not only important, but it is also challenging. Many small businesses simply do not have the managerial expertise needed to properly manage working capital and current assets. As a result of this knowledge vacuum, many banks have stepped in to offer small business services.

TO DO

Point your browser to www.bankofamerica.com/, the home page for the Bank of America (BoA). Click on the small business tab and investigate the types of services BoA offers. Report on those services offered by BoA and how they relate to the topics covered in this chapter.

Remember to check the book's Web site at

www.aw-bc.com/gitman

for additional resources, including additional Web exercises.

Chapter 15

Current Liabilities Management

LEARNING GOALS

 LG1 Review accounts payable, the key components of credit terms, and the procedures for analyzing those terms.

LG2 Understand the effects of stretching accounts payable on their cost, and the use of accruals.

LG3 Describe interest rates and the basic types of unsecured bank sources of short-term loans.

LG4 Discuss the basic features of commercial paper and the key aspects of international short-term loans.

LG5 Explain the characteristics of secured short-term loans and the use of accounts receivable as short-term-loan collateral.

LG6 Describe the various ways in which inventory can be used as short-term-loan collateral.

ACROSS THE DISCIPLINES | WHY THIS CHAPTER MATTERS TO YOU

Accounting: You need to understand how to analyze supplier credit terms to decide whether the firm should take or give up cash discounts; you also need to understand the various types of short-term loans, both unsecured and secured, that you will be required to record and report.

Information systems: You need to understand what data the firm will need to process accounts payable, track accruals, and meet bank loans and other short-term debt obligations in a timely manner.

Management: You need to know the sources of short-term loans so that if short-term financing is needed, you will understand its availability and cost.

Marketing: You need to understand how accounts receivable and inventory can be used as loan collateral; the procedures used by the firm to secure short-term loans with such collateral could affect customer relationships.

Operations: You need to understand the use of accounts payable as a form of short-term financing and the effect on one's suppliers of stretching payables; you also need to understand the process by which a firm uses inventory as collateral.

TURNER INDUSTRIES
CONSTRUCTING A MORE EFFICIENT ACCOUNTS PAYABLE SYSTEM

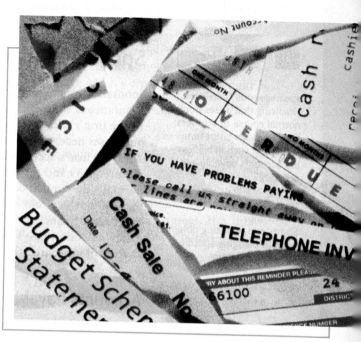

Turner Industries, (www.turner-industries.com), the largest privately owned industrial construction and maintenance company in Louisiana, offers a range of services to the petrochemical industry including construction, scaffolding, equipment rental, maintenance, and tank cleaning. With sales growing from $310 million to more than $800 million over the last 10 years, the company decided in 2003 to centralize its accounting process so as to provide a quicker turnaround on customer billing and corporate payables. To achieve this goal, the company implemented an electronic data-capture solution from **Kofax Image Products, Inc.**

"Turner needed faster and more complete access to vendor invoices, purchase orders, and support documentation," noted Andy Naquin, a business systems analyst at Turner. The company's primary goal was to reduce the time, effort, and cost required for document processing and invoicing. Reducing accounts payable expenses is one method of improving management of current liabilities.

The Kofax-based system makes it easy for Turner to quickly move information into its accounts payable system. Each month, the company captures and processes as many as 15,000 vendor invoices, each with an average of 10 pages of support documentation. Previously, this work was performed using a strictly paper-based system spread across the company's various offices. Turner estimates that the new information-capture system is saving the company about $270,000 each year by ensuring that all documents are readable and available when needed by accounts payable personnel.

For the first time, Turner can aggregate vendor invoices and support documents, invoice its clients, and in many cases get paid by them before the company has to pay its vendors. Controlling accounts payable expenses and improving its management of accounts receivable have allowed Turner to reduce its short-term liabilities.

As firms grow, so too do their needs for capital to fund the buildup of inventory and accounts receivable. Firms employ a variety of strategies to pay for these current assets. In this chapter you will learn how some companies use current liabilities including accounts payable, accruals, lines of credit, commercial paper issues, and short-term loans to finance current assets.

Source: Business Editors/High-Tech Writers, "Kofax Technology Centralizes Accounts Payable Processes for Turner Industries" *Business Wire* (December 19, 2003), www.findarticles.com (accessed August 31, 2004).

■ *As you read this chapter, ponder this question: Of the techniques used to fund current assets, which method is a small business more likely to use?*

Casa de Diseño sells to all of its customers on a net-60 basis, in line with the industry trend to grant such credit terms on specialty furniture. Leal discovered, by aging the accounts receivable, that the average collection period for the firm was 75 days. Investigation of the trade association's and California manufacturers' averages showed that the same collection period existed where net-60 credit terms were given. Where cash discounts were offered, the collection period was significantly shortened. Leal believed that if Casa de Diseño were to offer credit terms of 3/10 net 60, the average collection period could be reduced by 40 percent.

Casa de Diseño was spending an estimated $26,500,000 per year on operating-cycle investments. Leal considered this expenditure level to be the minimum she could expect the firm to disburse during 2007. Her concern was whether the firm's cash management was as efficient as it could be. She knew that the company paid 15 percent annual interest for its resource investment. For this reason, she was concerned about the financing cost resulting from any inefficiencies in the management of Casa de Diseño's cash conversion cycle. (*Note:* Assume a 365-day year and that the operating-cycle investment per dollar of payables, inventory, and receivables is the same.)

TO DO

a. Assuming a constant rate for purchases, production, and sales throughout the year, what are Casa de Diseño's existing operating cycle (OC), cash conversion cycle (CCC), and resource investment need?

b. If Leal can optimize Casa de Diseño's operations according to industry standards, what will Casa de Diseño's operating cycle (OC), cash conversion cycle (CCC), and resource investment need to be under these more efficient conditions?

c. In terms of resource investment requirements, what is the cost of Casa de Diseño's operational inefficiency?

d. (1) If in addition to achieving industry standards for payables and inventory, the firm can reduce the average collection period by offering credit terms of 3/10 net 60, what additional savings in resource investment costs will result from the shortened cash conversion cycle, assuming that the level of sales remains constant?

   (2) If the firm's sales (all on credit) are $40,000,000 and 45% of the customers are expected to take the cash discount, by how much will the firm's annual revenues be reduced as a result of the discount?

   (3) If the firm's variable cost of the $40,000,000 in sales is 80%, determine the reduction in the average investment in accounts receivable and the annual savings that will result from this reduced investment, assuming that sales remain constant.

   (4) If the firm's bad-debts expenses decline from 2% to 1.5% of sales, what annual savings will result, assuming that sales remain constant?

   (5) Use your findings in parts (2) through (4) to assess whether offering the cash discount can be justified financially. Explain why or why not.

e. On the basis of your analysis in parts **a** through **d,** what recommendations would you offer Teresa Leal?

f. Review for Teresa Leal the key sources of short-term financing, other than accounts payable, that she may consider to finance Casa de Diseño's resource investment need calculated in part **b.** Be sure to mention both unsecured and secured sources.

PART SIX

Special Topics in Managerial Finance

Chapter 16

Hybrid and Derivative Securities

LEARNING GOALS

LG1 Differentiate between hybrid and derivative securities and their roles in the corporation.

LG2 Review the types of leases, leasing arrangements, the lease-versus-purchase decision, the effects of leasing on future financing, and the advantages and disadvantages of leasing.

LG3 Describe the types of convertible securities, their general features, and financing with convertibles.

LG4 Demonstrate the procedures for determining the straight bond value, the conversion (or stock) value, and the market value of a convertible bond.

LG5 Explain the key characteristics of stock purchase warrants, the implied price of an attached warrant, and the values of warrants.

LG6 Define options and discuss calls and puts, options markets, options trading, the role of call and put options in fund raising, and hedging foreign-currency exposures with options.

ACROSS THE DISCIPLINES WHY THIS CHAPTER MATTERS TO YOU

Accounting: You need to understand the types of leasing arrangements and the general features of convertible securities, stock purchase warrants, and options, which you will be required to record and report.

Information systems: You need to understand types of leasing arrangements and of convertible securities to design systems that will track data used to make lease-or-purchase and conversion decisions.

Management: You need to understand when and why it may make better sense to lease assets rather than to purchase them. You need to understand how convertible secu-

rities and stock purchase warrants work to decide when the firm would benefit from their use. You also need to understand the impact of call and put options on the firm.

Marketing: You need to understand leasing as a way to finance a new project proposal. You also should understand how hybrid securities can be used to raise funds for new projects.

Operations: You need to understand the role of leasing in financing new equipment. You also need to understand the maintenance obligations associated with leased equipment.

WALT DISNEY CO.

LEASES TO UNITED AIRLINES ARE NOT VERY ENTERTAINING

Walt Disney Company (www.disney.go.com) is in the business of providing entertainment based on its rich legacy of creative content and exceptional storytelling. From theme parks and resorts to motion pictures and cartoons, Disney presents tales in which many Disney characters live happily ever after. However, one Disney tale that may not have a happy ending is its investment in aircraft leases.

Using a structure known as a *leveraged lease,* cash-rich Disney purchased airplanes in the early 1990s and leased them out to air carriers. The deals, which featured iron-clad terms, were seen as safe and offered tax advantages. Since the 1980s, large corporations have been leasing out planes to take advantage of tax rules that allow for accelerated depreciation of large equipment. Under a typical leveraged lease, Disney put up 20 percent of the purchase price. The rest was borrowed under a loan using the plane as collateral. None of Disney's other assets were put at risk.

During the 1990s, leveraged leases were attractive investments that boosted a company's return on investment. However, the events of September 11, 2001, and the ensuing reaction to potential terrorist threats crippled air travel and put U.S. air carriers under tremendous financial pressure. The result for several airlines was bankruptcy. Under bankruptcy protection, **United Airlines** was allowed to renegotiate its leases, lowering its lease payments to market rates. If no deal were reached, United was able to walk away from the leases. The $114 million book value that Disney had assigned to its investment in two Boeing 747s and two 767s leased to United had to be written down entirely.

With aircraft leased out to two other carriers, **Delta Air Lines** (five aircraft, $119 million) and **FedEx Corporation** (two aircraft, $56 million), the final scenes of the Disney tale of leveraged leases have not yet played out. The FedEx leases seem to be safe, but Delta Air Lines could be headed for bankruptcy. Given the current status of the airline industry, some doubts have been raised about the recoverability of Disney's remaining lease investments.

In this chapter, we'll demonstrate how to analyze lease financing, a hybrid financing technique that incorporates elements of debt and equity. You will also learn about other hybrids, including convertible securities, stock purchase warrants, and derivative securities such as stock options.

Source: Anthony Palazzo, "Once Seen as Wise Investment, Disney Jets Burden Bottom Line," *Los Angeles Business Journal,* downloaded from www.findarticles.com (accessed September 2, 2004).

■ *As you read this chapter, consider this question: Were the Disney leases of aircraft to United Airlines* operating leases *or* financial leases?

[LG1] 16.1 | An Overview of Hybrids and Derivatives

Chapters 6 and 7 described the characteristics of the key securities—corporate bonds, common stock, and preferred stock—used by corporations to raise long-term funds. In their simplest form, bonds are pure debt and common stock is pure equity. Preferred stock, on the other hand, is a form of equity that promises to pay fixed periodic dividends that are similar to the fixed contractual interest payments on bonds. Because it blends the characteristics of *both* debt (a fixed dividend payment) and equity (ownership), preferred stock is considered a **hybrid security.** Other popular hybrid securities include financial leases, convertible securities, and stock purchase warrants. Each of these hybrid securities is described in the following pages.

hybrid security
A form of debt or equity financing that possesses characteristics of *both* debt and equity financing.

The final section of this chapter focuses on *options*, a popular **derivative security**—a security that is neither debt nor equity but derives its value from an underlying asset that is often another security. As you'll learn, *derivatives* are not used by corporations to raise funds, but rather serve as a useful tool for managing certain aspects of the firm's risk.

derivative security
A security that is neither debt nor equity but derives its value from an underlying asset that is often another security; called "derivatives," for short.

REVIEW QUESTION

16–1   Differentiate between a *hybrid security* and a *derivative security*. How do their uses by the corporation differ?

[LG2] 16.2 | Leasing

Leasing enables the firm to obtain the use of certain fixed assets for which it must make a series of contractual, periodic, tax-deductible payments. The **lessee** is the receiver of the services of the assets under the lease contract; the **lessor** is the owner of the assets. Leasing can take a number of forms.

leasing
The process by which a firm can obtain the use of certain fixed assets for which it must make a series of contractual, periodic, tax-deductible payments.

Types of Leases

The two basic types of leases that are available to a business are *operating leases* and *financial leases* (often called *capital leases* by accountants).

lessee
The receiver of the services of the assets under a lease contract.

lessor
The owner of assets that are being leased.

Operating Leases

An **operating lease** is normally a contractual arrangement whereby the lessee agrees to make periodic payments to the lessor, often for 5 or fewer years, to obtain an asset's services. Such leases are generally *cancelable* at the option of the lessee, who may be required to pay a penalty for cancellation. Assets that are leased under operating leases have a usable life that is *longer* than the term of the lease. Usually, however, they would become less efficient and technologically obsolete if leased for a longer period. Computer systems are prime examples of assets whose relative efficiency is expected to diminish as the technology changes. The operating lease is therefore a common arrangement for obtaining such systems, as well as for other relatively short-lived assets such as automobiles.

operating lease
A *cancelable* contractual arrangement whereby the lessee agrees to make periodic payments to the lessor, often for 5 or fewer years, to obtain an asset's services; generally, the total payments over the term of the lease are *less* than the lessor's initial cost of the leased asset.

If an operating lease is held to maturity, the lessee at that time returns the leased asset to the lessor, who may lease it again or sell the asset. Normally, the asset still has a positive market value at the termination of the lease. In some instances, the lease contract gives the lessee the opportunity to purchase the leased asset. Generally, the total payments made by the lessee to the lessor are *less* than the lessor's initial cost of the leased asset.

Financial (or Capital) Leases

financial (or capital) lease
A *longer-term* lease than an operating lease that is *noncancelable* and obligates the lessee to make payments for the use of an asset over a predefined period of time; the total payments over the term of the lease are *greater* than the lessor's initial cost of the leased asset.

A **financial (or capital) lease** is a *longer-term* lease than an operating lease. Financial leases are *noncancelable* and obligate the lessee to make payments for the use of an asset over a predefined period of time. Financial leases are commonly used for leasing land, buildings, and large pieces of equipment. The noncancelable feature of the financial lease makes it similar to certain types of long-term debt. The lease payment becomes a fixed, tax-deductible expenditure that must be paid at predefined dates. As with debt, failure to make the contractual lease payments can result in bankruptcy for the lessee.

With a financial lease, the total payments over the lease period are *greater* than the lessor's initial cost of the leased asset. In other words, the lessor must receive more than the asset's purchase price to earn its required return on the investment. Technically, under Financial Accounting Standards Board (FASB) Standard No. 13, "Accounting for Leases," a financial (or capital) lease is defined as one that has *any* of the following elements:

1. The lease transfers ownership of the property to the lessee by the end of the lease term.
2. The lease contains an option to purchase the property at a "bargain price." Such an option must be exercisable at a "fair market value."
3. The lease term is equal to 75 percent or more of the estimated economic life of the property (exceptions exist for property leased toward the end of its usable economic life).
4. At the beginning of the lease, the present value of the lease payments is equal to 90 percent or more of the fair market value of the leased property.

The emphasis in this chapter is on financial leases, because they result in inescapable long-term financial commitments by the firm.

Leasing Arrangements

direct lease
A lease under which a lessor owns or acquires the assets that are leased to a given lessee.

sale–leaseback arrangement
A lease under which the lessee sells an asset for cash to a prospective lessor and then *leases back* the same asset, making fixed periodic payments for its use.

Lessors use three primary techniques for obtaining assets to be leased. The method depends largely on the desires of the prospective lessee.

1. A **direct lease** results when a lessor owns or acquires the assets that are leased to a given lessee. In other words, the lessee did not previously own the assets that it is leasing.
2. In a **sale–leaseback arrangement,** lessors acquire leased assets by purchasing assets already owned by the lessee and leasing them back. This technique is normally initiated by a firm that needs funds for operations. By selling an existing asset to a lessor and then *leasing it back*, the lessee receives cash for the asset immediately, while obligating itself to make fixed periodic payments for use of the leased asset.

leveraged lease
A lease under which the lessor acts as an equity participant, supplying only about 20 percent of the cost of the asset, while a lender supplies the balance.

maintenance clauses
Provisions normally included in an operating lease that require the lessor to maintain the assets and to make insurance and tax payments.

renewal options
Provisions especially common in operating leases that grant the lessee the right to re-lease assets at the expiration of the lease.

purchase options
Provisions frequently included in both operating and financial leases that allow the lessee to purchase the leased asset at maturity, typically for a prespecified price.

lease-versus-purchase (or lease-versus-buy) decision
The decision facing firms needing to acquire new fixed assets: whether to lease the assets or to purchase them, using borrowed funds or available liquid resources.

Hint Although, for clarity, the approach demonstrated here compares the present values of the cash flows for the lease and the purchase, a more direct approach would calculate the NPV of the *incremental* cash flows.

3. Leasing arrangements that include one or more third-party lenders are **leveraged leases.** Under a leveraged lease, the lessor acts as an equity participant, supplying only about 20 percent of the cost of the asset, and a lender supplies the balance. Leveraged leases have become especially popular in structuring leases of very expensive assets.

A lease agreement typically specifies whether the lessee is responsible for maintenance of the leased assets. Operating leases normally include **maintenance clauses** requiring the lessor to maintain the assets and to make insurance and tax payments. Financial leases nearly always require the lessee to pay maintenance and other costs.

The lessee is usually given the option to renew a lease at its expiration. **Renewal options,** which grant lessees the right to re-lease assets at expiration, are especially common in operating leases, because their term is generally shorter than the usable life of the leased assets. **Purchase options** allowing the lessee to purchase the leased asset at maturity, typically for a prespecified price, are frequently included in both operating and financial leases.

The lessor can be one of a number of parties. In operating leases, the lessor is likely to be the manufacturer's leasing subsidiary or an independent leasing company. Financial leases are frequently handled by independent leasing companies or by the leasing subsidiaries of large financial institutions such as commercial banks and life insurance companies. Life insurance companies are especially active in real estate leasing. Pension funds, like commercial banks, have also been increasing their leasing activities. The *In Practice* box on the facing page discusses a leasing arrangement called a "triple net lease."

The Lease-Versus-Purchase Decision

Firms that are contemplating the acquisition of new fixed assets commonly confront the **lease-versus-purchase (or lease-versus-buy) decision.** The alternatives available are (1) lease the assets, (2) borrow funds to purchase the assets, or (3) purchase the assets using available liquid resources. Alternatives 2 and 3, although they differ, are analyzed in a similar fashion; even if the firm has the liquid resources with which to purchase the assets, the use of these funds is viewed as equivalent to borrowing. Therefore, we need to compare only the leasing and purchasing alternatives.

The lease-versus-purchase decision involves application of the capital budgeting methods presented in Chapters 8 through 10. First, we determine the relevant cash flows and then apply present value techniques. The following steps are involved in the analysis:

Step 1 Find the *after-tax cash outflows for each year under the lease alternative.* This step generally involves a fairly simple tax adjustment of the annual lease payments. In addition, the cost of exercising a purchase option in the final year of the lease term must frequently be included.[1]

---

1. Including the cost of exercising a purchase option in the cash flows for the lease alternative ensures that under both lease and purchase alternatives the firm owns the asset at the end of the relevant time horizon. The other approach would be to include the cash flows from sale of the asset in the cash flows for the purchase alternative at the end of the lease term. These strategies guarantee avoidance of unequal lives, which were discussed in Chapter 10. In addition, they make any subsequent cash flows irrelevant because these would be either identical or nonexistent, respectively, under each alternative.

In Practice FOCUS ON PRACTICE

TRIPLE NET LEASE: BUYING A SMALL PART OF A BIG DEAL

The next time you walk into an **Arby's**, an **Applebee's Neighborhood Grill and Bar** restaurant, or a **Tractor Supply Company** retail store, you might wonder who actually owns the building. In many cases, the buildings are not owned by the operators, but rather by an assortment of individual investors or corporate investors that lease the properties to the retailers via a *triple net lease.* With a triple net lease, the tenant pays rent to the property owner and is responsible for all taxes, insurance, and maintenance expenses that arise from the use of the property.

How does an individual become the owner of a property leased by a well-known retail chain? Most often the process begins when the individual decides to dispose of a piece of commercial real estate—perhaps residential real estate property, a piece of farmland, a section of undeveloped land, or commercial income property. One concern that a property owner has when disposing of commercial property is paying taxes on accumulated capital gains or recaptured depreciation. However, the tax consequences associated with disposing of commercial property can be delayed through a process known as a *Section 1031 exchange.*

In a Section 1031 exchange, commercial property can be exchanged, tax-free, for "like kind" property. The process requires the use of a "qualified intermediary," such as **AEI Fund Management,** a company specializing in providing sale–leaseback property financing for chain restaurants and retail properties throughout the United States. The seller of the commercial property has a limited amount of time to find replacement property, or else face the tax consequences. This point is where a firm such as AEI steps in, to identify an appropriate replacement property.

Once the Section 1031 exchange is completed, the owner of the new property can sit back while the intermediary collects the rent and ensures that the tenant upholds the provisions of the triple net lease. A rent escalation clause protects the owner from the effects of inflation. Corporations also use the Section 1031 exchange to make tax-free property transfers. IRS rules require the exchanger to have a net worth of $1 million or an annual income of $200,000 (single) or $300,000 (joint).

Source: www.aeifunds.com.

■ *What effect might the recent lowering of capital gains tax rates have on the volume of Section 1031 property exchanges?*

Step 2   Find the *after-tax cash outflows for each year under the purchase alternative.* This step involves adjusting the sum of the scheduled loan payment and maintenance cost outlay for the tax shields resulting from the tax deductions attributable to maintenance, depreciation, and interest.

Step 3   Calculate the *present value of the cash outflows* associated with the lease (from Step 1) and purchase (from Step 2) alternatives using the *after-tax cost of debt* as the discount rate. The after-tax cost of debt is used to evaluate the lease-versus-purchase decision because the decision itself involves the choice between two *financing* techniques—leasing and borrowing—that have very low risk.

Step 4   Choose the alternative with the *lower present value* of cash outflows from Step 3. It will be the *least-cost* financing alternative.

The application of each of these steps is demonstrated in the following example.

| EXAMPLE | Roberts Company, a small machine shop, is contemplating acquiring a new machine that costs $24,000. Arrangements can be made to lease or purchase the machine. The firm is in the 40% tax bracket. |

Lease The firm would obtain a 5-year lease requiring annual end-of-year lease payments of $6,000.[2] All maintenance costs would be paid by the lessor, and insurance and other costs would be borne by the lessee. The lessee would exercise its option to purchase the machine for $4,000 at termination of the lease.

Purchase The firm would finance the purchase of the machine with a 9%, 5-year loan requiring end-of-year installment payments of $6,170.[3] The machine would be depreciated under MACRS using a 5-year recovery period. The firm would pay $1,500 per year for a service contract that covers all maintenance costs; insurance and other costs would be borne by the firm. The firm plans to keep the machine and use it beyond its 5-year recovery period.

Using these data, we can apply the steps presented earlier.

Step 1 The after-tax cash outflow from the lease payments can be found by multiplying the before-tax payment of $6,000 by 1 minus the tax rate, T, of 40%.

$$\text{After-tax cash outflow from lease} = \$6,000 \times (1 - T)$$
$$= \$6,000 \times (1 - 0.40) = \$3,600$$

Therefore, the lease alternative results in annual cash outflows over the 5-year lease of $3,600. In the final year, the $4,000 cost of the purchase option would be added to the $3,600 lease outflow to get a total cash outflow in year 5 of $7,600 ($3,600 + $4,000).

Step 2 The after-tax cash outflow from the purchase alternative is a bit more difficult to find. First, the interest component of each annual loan payment must be determined, because the Internal Revenue Service allows the deduction of interest only—not principal—from income for tax purposes.[4] Table 16.1 presents the calculations necessary to split the loan payments into their interest and principal components. Columns 3 and 4 show the annual interest and principal paid.

In Table 16.2, the annual loan payment is shown in column 1, and the annual maintenance cost, which is a tax-deductible expense, is shown in column 2. Next, we find the annual depreciation write-off resulting

---

2. Lease payments are generally made at the beginning of the year. To simplify the following discussions, *end-of-year lease payments are assumed.*

3. The annual loan payment on the 9%, 5-year loan of $24,000 is calculated by using the loan amortization technique described in Chapter 4. Dividing the present value interest factor for an annuity, *PVIFA*, from Table A–4 at 9% for 5 years (3.890) into the loan principal of $24,000 results in the annual loan payment of $6,170. (*Note:* If a financial calculator were used, the annual loan payment would be $6,170.22.) For a more detailed discussion of loan amortization, see Chapter 4.

4. When the rate of interest on the loan used to finance the purchase just equals the cost of debt, the present value of the after-tax loan payments (annual loan payments − interest tax shields) discounted at the after-tax cost of debt just equals the initial loan principal. In such a case, it is unnecessary to amortize the loan to determine the payment amount and the amounts of interest when finding after-tax cash outflows. The loan payments and interest payments (columns 1 and 3 in Table 16.2) can be ignored, and in their place, the initial loan principal ($24,000) is shown as an outflow occurring at time zero. To allow for a loan interest rate that is different from the firm's cost of debt and for easier understanding, here we isolate the loan payments and interest payments rather than use this computationally more efficient approach.

TABLE 16.1

Determining the Interest and Principal Components of the Roberts Company Loan Payments

End of year	Loan payments (1)	Beginning-of-year principal (2)	Payments Interest $[0.09 \times (2)]$ (3)	Payments Principal $[(1) - (3)]$ (4)	End-of-year principal $[(2) - (4)]$ (5)
1	$6,170	$24,000	$2,160	$4,010	$19,990
2	6,170	19,990	1,799	4,371	15,619
3	6,170	15,619	1,406	4,764	10,855
4	6,170	10,855	977	5,193	5,662
5	6,170	5,662	510	5,660	—[a]

[a]The values in this table have been rounded to the nearest dollar, which results in a slight difference ($2) between the beginning-of-year-5 principal (in column 2) and the year-5 principal payment (in column 4).

from the $24,000 machine. Using the applicable MACRS 5-year recovery period depreciation percentages—20% in year 1, 32% in year 2, 19% in year 3, and 12% in years 4 and 5—given in Table 3.2 on page 106 results in the annual depreciation for years 1 through 5 given in column 3 of Table 16.2.[5]

Table 16.2 presents the calculations required to determine the cash outflows[6] associated with borrowing to purchase the new machine. Column 7 of the table presents the after-tax cash outflows associated with the purchase alternative. A few points should be clarified with

TABLE 16.2

After-Tax Cash Outflows Associated with Purchasing for Roberts Company

End of year	Loan payments (1)	Maintenance costs (2)	Depreciation (3)	Interest[a] (4)	Total deductions $[(2) + (3) + (4)]$ (5)	Tax shields $[(0.40 \times (5)]$ (6)	After-tax cash outflows $[(1) + (2) - (6)]$ (7)
1	$6,170	$1,500	$4,800	$2,160	$ 8,460	$3,384	$4,286
2	6,170	1,500	7,680	1,799	10,979	4,392	3,278
3	6,170	1,500	4,560	1,406	7,466	2,986	4,684
4	6,170	1,500	2,880	977	5,357	2,143	5,527
5	6,170	1,500	2,880	510	4,890	1,956	5,714

[a]From Table 16.1, column 3.

5. The year-6 depreciation is ignored, because we are considering the cash flows solely over a 5-year time horizon. Similarly, depreciation on the leased asset, when it is purchased at the end of the lease for $4,000, is ignored. The tax benefits resulting from this depreciation would make the lease alternative even more attractive. Clearly, the analysis would become both more precise and more complex if we chose to look beyond the 5-year time horizon.

6. Although other cash outflows such as insurance and operating expenses may be relevant here, they would be the same under the lease and purchase alternatives and therefore would cancel out in the final analysis.

TABLE 16.3

A Comparison of the Cash Outflows Associated with Leasing Versus Purchasing for Roberts Company

	Leasing			Purchasing		
End of Year	After-tax cash outflows (1)	Present value factors^a (2)	Present value of outflows [(1) × (2)] (3)	After-tax cash outflows^b (4)	Present value factors^a (5)	Present value of outflows [(4) × (5)] (6)
1	$3,600	0.943	$ 3,395	$4,286	0.943	$ 4,042
2	3,600	0.890	3,204	3,278	0.890	2,917
3	3,600	0.840	3,024	4,684	0.840	3,935
4	3,600	0.792	2,851	5,527	0.792	4,377
5	7,600^c	0.747	5,677	5,714	0.747	4,268
		PV of cash outflows	$18,151		PV of cash outflows	$19,539

^{a}From Table A–2, *PVIF*, for 6% and the corresponding year.
^{b}From column 7 of Table 16.2.
^{c}After-tax lease payment outflow of $3,600 plus the $4,000 cost of exercising the purchase option.

respect to the calculations in Table 16.2. The major cash outflows are the total loan payment for each year given in column 1 and the annual maintenance cost in column 2. The sum of these two outflows is reduced by the tax savings from writing off the maintenance, depreciation, and interest expenses associated with the new machine and its financing. The resulting cash outflows are the after-tax cash outflows associated with the purchase alternative.

Step 3   The present values of the cash outflows associated with the lease (from Step 1) and purchase (from Step 2) alternatives are calculated in Table 16.3 using the firm's 6% after-tax cost of debt.[7] Applying the appropriate present value interest factors given in columns 2 and 5 to the after-tax cash outflows in columns 1 and 4 results in the present values of lease and purchase cash outflows in columns 3 and 6, respectively. The sum of the present values of the cash outflows for the leasing alternative is given in column 3 of Table 16.3, and the sum of those for the purchasing alternative is given in column 6.

Step 4   Because the present value of cash outflows for leasing ($18,151) is lower than that for purchasing ($19,539), *the leasing alternative is preferred.* Leasing results in an incremental savings of $1,388 ($19,539 − $18,151) and is therefore the less costly alternative.[8]   ■

The techniques described here for comparing lease and purchase alternatives may be applied in different ways. The approach illustrated by the Roberts Com-

---

7. If we ignore any flotation costs, the firm's after-tax cost of debt would be 5.4% [9% debt cost × (1 − 0.40 tax rate)]. To reflect both the flotation costs associated with selling new debt and the possible need to sell the debt at a discount, we use an after-tax debt cost of 6% as the applicable discount rate. A more detailed discussion of techniques for calculating the after-tax cost of debt is found in Chapter 11.

8. Using a financial calculator would reveal the present value of the cash outflows for the lease to be $18,154, and that for the purchase to be $19,541, resulting in an incremental savings of $1,387.

pany data is one of the most straightforward. It is important to recognize that the lower cost of one alternative over the other results from factors such as the differing tax brackets of the lessor and lessee, different tax treatments of leases versus purchases, and differing risks and borrowing costs for lessor and lessee. Therefore, when making a lease-versus-purchase decision, the firm will find that inexpensive borrowing opportunities, high required lessor returns, and a low risk of obsolescence increase the attractiveness of purchasing. Subjective factors must also be included in the decision-making process. Like most financial decisions, the lease-versus-purchase decision requires some judgment or intuition.

Effects of Leasing on Future Financing

Because leasing is considered a type of financing, it affects the firm's future financing. Lease payments are shown as a tax-deductible expense on the firm's income statement. Anyone analyzing the firm's income statement would probably recognize that an asset is being leased, although the amount and term of the lease would be unclear.

capitalized lease
A *financial (capital) lease* that has the present value of all its payments included as an asset and corresponding liability on the firm's balance sheet, as required by Financial Accounting Standards Board (FASB) Standard No. 13.

The Financial Accounting Standards Board (FASB), in Standard No. 13, "Accounting for Leases," requires explicit disclosure of *financial (capital) lease* obligations on the firm's balance sheet. Such a lease must be shown as a **capitalized lease,** meaning that the present value of all its payments is included as an asset and corresponding liability on the firm's balance sheet. An *operating lease,* on the other hand, need not be capitalized, but its basic features must be disclosed in a footnote to the financial statements. Standard No. 13, of course, establishes detailed guidelines to be used in capitalizing leases. Subsequent standards have further refined lease capitalization and disclosure procedures.

EXAMPLE Jeffrey Company, a manufacturer of water purifiers, is leasing an asset under a 10-year lease requiring annual end-of-year payments of $15,000. The lease can be capitalized merely by calculating the present value of the lease payments over the life of the lease. However, the rate at which the payments should be discounted is difficult to determine.[9] If 10% were used, the present, or capitalized, value of the lease would be $92,175 ($15,000 × 6.145). (The value calculated by using a financial calculator is $92,169.) This value would be shown as an asset and corresponding liability on the firm's balance sheet, which should result in an accurate reflection of the firm's true financial position.

Because the consequences of missing a financial lease payment are the same as those of missing an interest or principal payment on debt, a financial analyst must view the lease as a long-term financial commitment of the lessee. With FASB Standard No. 13, the inclusion of each financial (capital) lease as an asset and corresponding liability (i.e., long-term debt) provides for a balance sheet that more accurately reflects the firm's financial status. It thereby permits various types of financial ratio analyses to be performed directly on the statement by any interested party.

9. The Financial Accounting Standards Board in Standard No. 13 established certain guidelines for the appropriate discount rate to use when capitalizing leases. Most commonly, the rate that the lessee would have incurred to borrow the funds to buy the asset with a secured loan under terms similar to the lease repayment schedule is used. This simply represents the *before-tax cost of a secured debt.*

Advantages and Disadvantages of Leasing

Leasing has a number of commonly cited advantages and disadvantages that managers should consider when making a lease-versus-purchase decision. It is not unusual for a number of them to apply in a given situation.

Advantages

The commonly cited advantages of leasing are as follows:

1. In a lease arrangement, the firm may *avoid the cost of obsolescence* if the lessor fails to anticipate accurately the obsolescence of assets and sets the lease payment too low. This is especially true in the case of operating leases, which generally have relatively short lives.
2. A lessee *avoids many of the restrictive covenants* that are normally included as part of a long-term loan. Requirements with respect to minimum liquidity, subsequent borrowing, cash dividend payments, and so on are *not* normally found in a lease agreement.
3. In the case of low-cost assets that are infrequently acquired, leasing—especially operating leases—may provide the firm with needed *financing flexibility*. That is, the firm does not have to arrange other financing for these assets.
4. Sale–leaseback arrangements may permit the firm to *increase its liquidity* by converting an *existing* asset into cash, which can then be used as working capital. This can be advantageous for a firm that is short of working capital or in a liquidity bind.
5. Leasing allows the lessee, in effect, to *depreciate land,* which is prohibited if the land were purchased. Because the lessee who leases land is permitted to deduct the *total lease payment* as an expense for tax purposes, the effect is the same as though the firm had purchased the land and then depreciated it.
6. Because it results in the receipt of service from an asset possibly without increasing the assets or liabilities on the firm's balance sheet, leasing may result in misleading *financial ratios*. Understating assets and liabilities can cause certain ratios, such as the total asset turnover, to look better than they might be. With the adoption of FASB Standard No. 13, this advantage no longer applies to financial leases, although in the case of operating leases, it remains a potential advantage.
7. Leasing provides *100 percent financing*. Most loan agreements for the purchase of fixed assets require the borrower to pay a portion of the purchase price as a down payment. As a result, the borrower is able to borrow only 90 to 95 percent of the purchase price of the asset.
8. When a *firm becomes bankrupt* or is reorganized, the maximum claim of lessors against the corporation is 3 years of lease payments, and the lessor of course gets the asset back. If debt is used to purchase an asset, the creditors have a claim that is equal to the total outstanding loan balance.

Disadvantages

The commonly cited disadvantages of leasing are as follows:

1. A lease does not have a stated interest cost. Thus, in many leases the *return to the lessor is quite high,* so the firm might be better off borrowing to purchase the asset.

2. At the end of the term of the lease agreement, the *salvage value* of an asset, if any, is realized by the lessor. If the lessee had purchased the asset, it could have claimed its salvage value. Of course, an expected salvage value when recognized by the lessor results in lower lease payments.

3. Under a lease, the lessee is generally *prohibited from making improvements* on the leased property or asset without the approval of the lessor. If the property were owned outright, this difficulty would not arise. Of course, lessors generally encourage leasehold improvements when these are expected to enhance the asset's salvage value.

4. If a lessee leases an *asset that subsequently becomes obsolete*, it still must make lease payments over the remaining term of the lease. This is true even if the asset is unusable.

REVIEW QUESTIONS

16–2 What is *leasing?* Define, compare, and contrast *operating leases* and *financial (or capital) leases.* How does the Financial Accounting Standards Board (FASB) Standard No. 13 define a financial (or capital) lease? Describe three methods used by lessors to acquire assets to be leased.

16–3 Describe the four basic steps involved in the *lease-versus-purchase decision* process. How are capital budgeting methods applied in this process?

16–4 What type of lease must be treated as a *capitalized lease* on the balance sheet? How does the financial manager capitalize a lease?

16–5 List and discuss the commonly cited advantages and disadvantages that should be considered when deciding whether to lease or purchase.

LG3 LG4 16.3 | Convertible Securities

conversion feature
An option that is included as part of a bond or a preferred stock issue and allows its holder to change the security into a stated number of shares of common stock.

A **conversion feature** is an option that is included as part of a bond or a preferred stock issue and allows its holder to change the security into a stated number of shares of common stock. The conversion feature typically enhances the marketability of an issue.

Types of Convertible Securities

Corporate bonds and preferred stocks may be convertible into common stock. The most common type of convertible security is the bond. Convertibles normally have an accompanying *call feature.* This feature permits the issuer to retire or encourage conversion of outstanding convertibles when appropriate.

Convertible Bonds

convertible bond
A bond that can be changed into a specified number of shares of common stock.

A **convertible bond** can be changed into a specified number of shares of common stock. It is nearly always a *debenture*—an unsecured bond—with a call feature. Because the conversion feature provides the purchaser with the possibility of becoming a stockholder on favorable terms, convertible bonds are generally a less

straight bond
A bond that is nonconvertible, having no conversion feature.

expensive form of financing than similar-risk nonconvertible or **straight bonds.** The conversion feature adds a degree of speculation to a bond issue, although the issue still maintains its value as a bond.

Convertible Preferred Stock

convertible preferred stock
Preferred stock that can be changed into a specified number of shares of common stock.

straight preferred stock
Preferred stock that is nonconvertible, having no conversion feature.

Convertible preferred stock is preferred stock that can be changed into a specified number of shares of common stock. It can normally be sold with a lower stated dividend than a similar-risk nonconvertible or **straight preferred stock.** The reason is that the convertible preferred holder is assured of the fixed dividend payment associated with a preferred stock and also may receive the appreciation resulting from increases in the market price of the underlying common stock. Convertible preferred stock behaves much like convertible bonds. The following discussions will concentrate on the more popular convertible bonds.

General Features of Convertibles

Convertible securities are nearly always convertible at any time during the life of the security. Occasionally, conversion is permitted only for a limited number of years—say, for 5 or 10 years after issuance of the convertible.

conversion ratio
The ratio at which a convertible security can be exchanged for common stock.

conversion price
The per-share price that is effectively paid for common stock as the result of conversion of a convertible security.

Conversion Ratio

The **conversion ratio** is the ratio at which a convertible security can be exchanged for common stock. The conversion ratio can be stated in two ways.

1. Sometimes the conversion ratio is stated in terms of a given number of shares of common stock. To find the **conversion price,** which is the per-share price that is effectively paid for common stock as the result of conversion, divide the *par value* (not the market value) of the convertible security by the conversion ratio.

> **EXAMPLE**   Western Wear Company, a manufacturer of denim products, has outstanding a bond that has a $1,000 par value and is convertible into 25 shares of common stock. The bond's conversion ratio is 25. The conversion price for the bond is $40 per share ($1,000 ÷ 25). ■

2. Sometimes, instead of the conversion ratio, the conversion price is given. The conversion ratio can be obtained by dividing the *par value* of the convertible by the conversion price.

> **EXAMPLE**   Mosher Company, a franchiser of seafood restaurants, has outstanding a convertible 20-year bond with a par value of $1,000. The bond is convertible at $50 per share into common stock. The conversion ratio is 20 ($1,000 ÷ $50). ■

The issuer of a convertible security normally establishes a conversion ratio or conversion price that *sets the conversion price per share at the time of issuance above the current market price of the firm's stock.* If the prospective purchasers do not expect conversion ever to be feasible, they will purchase a straight security or some other convertible issue.

conversion (or stock) value
The value of a convertible security measured in terms of the market price of the common stock into which it can be converted.

Conversion (or Stock) Value

The **conversion (or stock) value** is the value of the convertible measured in terms of the market price of the common stock into which it can be converted. The conversion value can be found simply by multiplying the conversion ratio by the current market price of the firm's common stock.

EXAMPLE McNamara Industries, a petroleum processor, has outstanding a $1,000 bond that is convertible into common stock at $62.50 per share. The conversion ratio is therefore 16 ($1,000 ÷ $62.50). Because the current market price of the common stock is $65 per share, the conversion value is $1,040 (16 × $65). Because the conversion value is above the bond value of $1,000, conversion is a viable option for the owner of the convertible security. ∎

Effect on Earnings

contingent securities
Convertibles, warrants, and stock options. Their presence affects the reporting of a firm's earnings per share (EPS).

The presence of **contingent securities,** which include convertibles as well as warrants (described later in this chapter) and stock options (described in Chapter 1 and later in this chapter), affects the reporting of the firm's earnings per share (EPS). Firms with contingent securities that if converted or exercised would dilute (that is, lower) earnings per share are required to report earnings in two ways—*basic EPS* and *diluted EPS.*

basic EPS
Earnings per share (EPS) calculated without regard to any contingent securities.

Basic EPS are calculated without regard to any contingent securities. They are found by dividing earnings available for common stockholders by the number of shares of common stock outstanding. This is the standard method of calculating EPS that has been used throughout this textbook.

diluted EPS
Earnings per share (EPS) calculated under the assumption that *all* contingent securities that would have dilutive effects are converted and exercised and are therefore common stock.

Diluted EPS are calculated under the assumption that *all* contingent securities that would have dilutive effects are converted and exercised and are therefore common stock. They are found by adjusting basic EPS for the impact of converting all convertibles and exercising all warrants and options that would have dilutive effects on the firm's earnings. This approach treats as common stock *all* contingent securities. It is calculated by dividing earnings available for common stockholders (adjusted for interest and preferred stock dividends that would *not* be paid, given assumed conversion of *all* outstanding contingent securities that would have dilutive effects) by the number of shares of common stock that would be outstanding if *all* contingent securities that would have dilutive effects were converted and exercised. Rather than demonstrate these accounting calculations,[10] suffice it to say that firms with outstanding convertibles, warrants, and/or stock options must report basic and diluted EPS on their income statements.

Financing with Convertibles

Using convertible securities to raise long-term funds can help the firm achieve its cost-of-capital and capital structure goals. There also are a number of more specific motives and considerations involved in evaluating convertible financing.

10. For excellent discussions and demonstrations of the two methods of reporting EPS, see Donald A. Kieso, Jerry J. Weygandt, and Terry D. Warfield, *Intermediate Accounting,* 11th ed. (New York: John Wiley, 2003), pp. 143–144, 794–797, 810–814.

Motives for Convertible Financing

Convertibles can be used for a variety of reasons. One popular motive is their use as a form of *deferred common stock financing*. When a convertible security is issued, both issuer and purchaser expect the security to be converted into common stock at some future point. Because the security is first sold with a conversion price above the current market price of the firm's stock, conversion is initially not attractive. The issuer of a convertible could alternatively sell common stock, but only at or below its current market price. By selling the convertible, the issuer in effect makes a *deferred sale* of common stock. As the market price of the firm's common stock rises to a higher level, conversion may occur. Deferring the issuance of new common stock until the market price of the stock has increased means that fewer shares will have to be issued, thereby decreasing the dilution of both ownership and earnings.

Hint Convertible securities are advantageous to both the issuer and the holder. The issuer does not have to give up immediate control as it would have to if it were issuing common stock. The holder of a convertible security has the possibility of a future speculative gain.

Another motive for convertible financing is its *use as a "sweetener" for financing*. Because the purchaser of the convertible is given the opportunity to become a common stockholder and share in the firm's future success, *convertibles can be normally sold with lower interest rates than nonconvertibles*. Therefore, from the firm's viewpoint, including a conversion feature reduces the interest cost of debt. The purchaser of the issue sacrifices a portion of interest return for the potential opportunity to become a common stockholder. Another important motive for issuing convertibles is that, generally speaking, *convertible securities can be issued with far fewer restrictive covenants than nonconvertibles*. Because many investors view convertibles as equity, the covenant issue is not important to them.

A final motive for using convertibles is to *raise cheap funds temporarily*. By using convertible bonds, the firm can temporarily raise debt, which is typically less expensive than common stock, to finance projects. Once such projects are under way, the firm may wish to shift its capital structure to a less highly levered position. A conversion feature gives the issuer the opportunity, through actions of convertible holders, to shift its capital structure at a future time.

Other Considerations

When the price of the firm's common stock rises above the conversion price, the market price of the convertible security will normally rise to a level close to its conversion value. When this happens, many convertible holders will not convert, because they already have the market price benefit obtainable from conversion and can still receive fixed periodic interest payments. Because of this behavior, virtually all convertible securities have a *call feature* that enables the issuer to encourage or *"force"* conversion. The call price of the security generally exceeds the security's par value by an amount equal to 1 year's stated interest on the security. Although the issuer must pay a premium for calling a security, the call privilege is generally not exercised until the conversion value of the security is 10 to 15 percent *above the call price*. This type of premium above the call price helps to assure the issuer that the holders of the convertible will convert it when the call is made, instead of accepting the call price.

overhanging issue
A convertible security that cannot be forced into conversion by using the call feature.

Unfortunately, there are instances when the market price of a security does not reach a level sufficient to stimulate the conversion of associated convertibles. A convertible security that cannot be forced into conversion by using the call feature is called an **overhanging issue.** An overhanging issue can be quite detrimental to a firm. If the firm were to call the issue, the bondholders would accept the call price rather than convert the bonds. In this case, the firm not only would have to pay the call premium but would also require additional financing to pay off the bonds at their par value. If the firm raised these funds through the sale of equity, a large number of shares would have to be issued because of their low market price. This, in turn, could result in the dilution of existing ownership. Another means of financing the call would be the use of debt or preferred stock, but this use would leave the firm's capital structure no less levered than before the call.

Determining the Value of a Convertible Bond

The key characteristic of convertible securities that enhances their marketability is their ability to minimize the possibility of a loss while providing a possibility of capital gains. Here we discuss the three values of a convertible bond: (1) the straight bond value, (2) the conversion value, and (3) the market value.

Straight Bond Value

straight bond value
The price at which a convertible bond would sell in the market without the conversion feature.

The **straight bond value** of a convertible bond is the price at which it would sell in the market without the conversion feature. This value is found by determining the value of a nonconvertible bond with similar payments issued by a firm with the same risk. The straight bond value is typically the *floor*, or minimum, price at which the convertible bond would be traded. The straight bond value equals the present value of the bond's interest and principal payments discounted at the interest rate the firm would have to pay on a nonconvertible bond.

EXAMPLE   Duncan Company, a Southeastern discount store chain, has just sold a $1,000-par-value, 20-year convertible bond with a 12% coupon interest rate. The bond interest will be paid at the end of each year, and the principal will be repaid at maturity.[11] A straight bond could have been sold with a 14% coupon interest rate, but the conversion feature compensates for the lower rate on the convertible. The straight bond value of the convertible is calculated as shown:

Year(s)	Payments (1)	Present value interest factor at 14% (2)	Present value [(1) × (2)] (3)
1–20	$ 120[a]	6.623[b]	$794.76
20	1,000	0.073[c]	73.00
		Straight bond value	$867.76

[a]$1,000 at 12% = $120 interest per year.
[b]Present value interest factor for an annuity, *PVIFA*, discounted at 14% for 20 years, from Table A–4.
[c]Present value interest factor for $1, *PVIF*, discounted at 14% for year 20, from Table A–2.

---

11. Just as we did in Chapter 6, we continue to assume the payment of annual rather than semiannual bond interest. This assumption simplifies the calculations involved, while maintaining the conceptual accuracy of the procedures presented.

This value, $867.76, is the minimum price at which the convertible bond is expected to sell. (The value calculated using a financial calculator is $867.54.) Generally, only in certain instances in which the stock's market price is below the conversion price will the bond be expected to sell at this level.   ■

Conversion (or Stock) Value

Recall that the *conversion (or stock) value* of a convertible security is the value of the convertible measured in terms of the market price of the common stock into which the security can be converted. When the market price of the common stock exceeds the conversion price, the conversion (or stock) value exceeds the par value. An example will clarify the point.

EXAMPLE   Duncan Company's convertible bond described earlier is convertible at $50 per share. Each bond can be converted into 20 shares, because each bond has a $1,000 par value. The conversion values of the bond when the stock is selling at $30, $40, $50, $60, $70, and $80 per share are shown in the following table.

Market price of stock	Conversion value
$30	$ 600
40	800
50 (conversion price)	1,000 (par value)
60	1,200
70	1,400
80	1,600

When the market price of the common stock exceeds the $50 conversion price, the conversion value exceeds the $1,000 par value. Because the straight bond value (calculated in the preceding example) is $867.76, the bond will, in a stable environment, never sell for less than this amount, regardless of how low its conversion value is. If the market price per share were $30, the bond would still sell for $867.76—not $600—because its value as a bond would dominate.   ■

Market Value

market premium
The amount by which the market value exceeds the straight or conversion value of a convertible security.

The market value of a convertible is likely to be greater than its straight value or its conversion value. The amount by which the market value exceeds its straight or conversion value is called the **market premium.** The general relationships among the straight bond value, conversion value, market value, and market premium for Duncan Company's convertible bond are shown in Figure 16.1. The straight bond value acts as a floor for the security's value up to the point X, where the stock price is high enough to cause the conversion value to exceed the straight bond value. The market premium is attributed to the fact that the convertible gives investors a chance to experience attractive capital gains from increases in the stock price, while taking less risk. The floor (straight bond value) provides protection against losses resulting from a decline in the stock price caused by falling profits or other factors. The market premium tends to be greatest when the straight bond value and conversion (or stock) value are nearly

FIGURE 16.1

Values and Market Premium

The values and market premium for Duncan Company's convertible bond

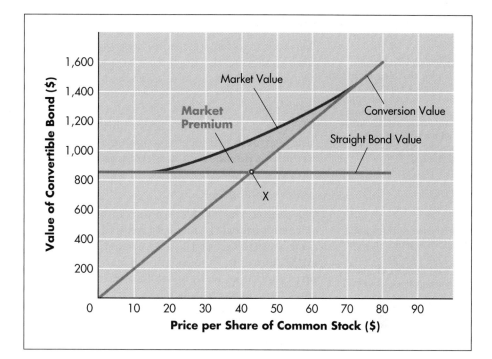

equal. Investors perceive the benefits of these two sources of value to be greatest at this point.

REVIEW QUESTIONS

16–6 What is the *conversion feature?* What is a *conversion ratio?* How do convertibles and other *contingent securities* affect EPS? Briefly describe the motives for convertible financing.

16–7 When the market price of the stock rises above the conversion price, why may a convertible security *not* be converted? How can the *call feature* be used to force conversion in this situation? What is an *overhanging issue?*

16–8 Define the *straight bond value, conversion (or stock) value, market value,* and *market premium* associated with a convertible bond, and describe the general relationships among them.

LG5 16.4 | Stock Purchase Warrants

stock purchase warrant
An instrument that gives its holder the right to purchase a certain number of shares of common stock at a specified price over a certain period of time.

Stock purchase warrants are similar to stock *rights,* which were briefly described in Chapter 7. A **stock purchase warrant** gives the holder the right to purchase a certain number of shares of common stock at a specified price over a certain period of time. (Of course, holders of warrants earn no income from them until the warrants are exercised or sold.) Warrants also bear some similarity to convertibles in that they provide for the injection of additional equity capital into the firm at some future date.

Key Characteristics

Warrants are often attached to debt issues as "sweeteners." When a firm makes a large bond issue, the attachment of stock purchase warrants may add to the marketability of the issue and lower the required interest rate. As sweeteners, warrants are similar to conversion features. Often, when a new firm is raising its initial capital, suppliers of debt will require warrants to permit them to share in whatever success the firm achieves. In addition, established companies sometimes offer warrants with debt to compensate for risk and thereby lower the interest rate and/or provide for fewer *restrictive covenants*.

Exercise Prices

exercise (or option) price
The price at which holders of warrants can purchase a specified number of shares of common stock.

The price at which holders of warrants can purchase a specified number of shares of common stock is normally referred to as the **exercise (or option) price**. This price is usually set at 10 to 20 percent above the market price of the firm's stock at the time of issuance. Until the market price of the stock exceeds the exercise price, holders of warrants will not exercise them, because they can purchase the stock more inexpensively in the marketplace.

Warrants normally have a life of no more than 10 years, although some have infinite lives. Although, unlike convertible securities, warrants cannot be called, their limited life stimulates holders to exercise them when the exercise price is below the market price of the firm's stock.

Warrant Trading

A warrant is usually *detachable,* which means that the bondholder may sell the warrant without selling the security to which it is attached. Many detachable warrants are listed and actively traded on organized securities exchanges and on the over-the-counter exchange. The majority of actively traded warrants are listed on the American Stock Exchange. Warrants often provide investors with better opportunities for gain (with increased risk) than the underlying common stock.

Comparison of Warrants to Rights and Convertibles

The similarity between a warrant and a right should be clear. Both result in new equity capital, although the warrant provides for *deferred* equity financing. The life of a right is typically not more than a few months; a warrant is generally exercisable for a period of years. Rights are issued at a subscription price *below* the prevailing market price of the stock; warrants are generally issued at an exercise price 10 to 20 percent *above* the prevailing market price.

Warrants and convertibles also have similarities. The exercise of a warrant shifts the firm's capital structure to a less highly levered position because new common stock is issued without any change in debt. If a convertible bond were converted, the reduction in leverage would be even more pronounced, because common stock would be issued in exchange for a reduction in debt. In addition, the exercise of a warrant provides an influx of new capital; with convertibles, the new capital is raised when the securities are originally issued rather than when they are converted. The influx of new equity capital resulting from the exercise of a warrant does not occur until the firm has achieved a certain degree of success that is reflected in an increased price for its stock. In this case, the firm conveniently obtains needed funds.

The Implied Price of an Attached Warrant

implied price of a warrant
The price effectively paid for each warrant attached to a bond.

When warrants are attached to a bond, the **implied price of a warrant**—the price that is effectively paid for each attached warrant—can be found by first using Equation 16.1:

$$\text{Implied price of } \textit{all} \text{ warrants} = \text{Price of bond with warrants attached} - \text{Straight bond value} \quad (16.1)$$

The straight bond value is found in a fashion similar to that used in valuing convertible bonds. Dividing the implied price of *all* warrants by the number of warrants attached to each bond results in the implied price of *each* warrant.

EXAMPLE

Martin Marine Products, a manufacturer of marine drive shafts and propellers, just issued a 10.5%-coupon-interest-rate, $1,000-par, 20-year bond paying annual interest and having 20 warrants attached for the purchase of the firm's stock. The bonds were initially sold for their $1,000 par value. When issued, similar-risk straight bonds were selling to yield a 12% rate of return. The straight value of the bond would be the present value of its payments discounted at the 12% yield on similar-risk straight bonds.

Year(s)	Payments (1)	Present value interest factor at 12% (2)	Present value[a] [(1) × (2)] (3)
1–20	$ 105[b]	7.469[c]	$784
20	1,000	0.104[d]	104
		Straight bond value[e]	$888

[a]For convenience, these values have been rounded to the nearest $1.
[b]$1,000 at 10.5% = $105 interest per year.
[c]Present value interest factor for an annuity, *PVIFA*, discounted at 12% for 20 years, from Table A–4.
[d]Present value interest factor for $1, *PVIF*, discounted at 12% for year 20, from Table A–2.
[e]The value calculated by using a financial calculator and rounding to the nearest $1 is also $888.

Substituting the $1,000 price of the bond with warrants attached and the $888 straight bond value into Equation 16.1, we get an implied price of *all* warrants of $112:

$$\text{Implied price of } \textit{all} \text{ warrants} = \$1,000 - \$888 = \underline{\$112}$$

Dividing the implied price of *all* warrants by the number of warrants attached to each bond—20 in this case—we find the implied price of *each* warrant:

$$\text{Implied price of } \textit{each} \text{ warrant} = \frac{\$112}{20} = \$5.60$$

Therefore, by purchasing Martin Marine Products' bond with warrants attached for $1,000, one is effectively paying $5.60 for each warrant. ▪

The implied price of each warrant is meaningful only when compared to the specific features of the warrant—the number of shares that can be purchased and the specified exercise price. These features can be analyzed in light of the prevailing common stock price to estimate the true *market value* of each warrant. Clearly, if the implied price is above the estimated market value, the price of the bond with warrants attached may be too high. If the implied price is below the estimated market value, the bond may be quite attractive. Firms must therefore price their bonds with warrants attached in a way that causes the implied price of its warrants to fall slightly below their estimated market value. Such an approach allows the firm to sell the bonds more easily at a lower coupon interest rate than would apply to straight debt, thereby reducing its debt service costs.

The Value of Warrants

warrant premium
The difference between the market value and the theoretical value of a warrant.

Like a convertible security, a warrant has both a market value and a theoretical value. The difference between these values, or the **warrant premium**, depends largely on investor expectations and on the ability of investors to get more leverage from the warrants than from the underlying stock.

Theoretical Value of a Warrant

The *theoretical value* of a stock purchase warrant is the amount one would expect the warrant to sell for in the marketplace. Equation 16.2 gives the theoretical value of a warrant:

$$TVW = (P_0 - E) \times N \tag{16.2}$$

where

TVW = theoretical value of a warrant

P_0 = current market price of a share of common stock

E = exercise price of the warrant

N = number of shares of common stock obtainable with one warrant

The use of Equation 16.2 can be illustrated by the following example.

EXAMPLE Dustin Electronics, a major producer of transistors, has outstanding warrants that are exercisable at $40 per share and entitle holders to purchase three shares of common stock. The warrants were initially attached to a bond issue to sweeten the bond. The common stock of the firm is currently selling for $45 per share. Substituting $P_0 = \$45$, $E = \$40$, and $N = 3$ into Equation 16.2 yields a theoretical warrant value of $15 [($45 − $40) × 3]. Therefore, Dustin's warrants should sell for $15 in the marketplace. ■

Market Value of a Warrant

The market value of a stock purchase warrant is generally above the theoretical value of the warrant. Only when the theoretical value of the warrant is very high or the warrant is near its expiration date are the market and theoretical values close. The general relationship between the theoretical and market values of Dustin Electronics' warrants is presented graphically in Figure 16.2. The market value of warrants generally exceeds the theoretical value by the greatest amount when the stock's market price is close to the warrant exercise price per share. The

FIGURE 16.2

Values and Warrant Premium

The values and warrant premium for Dustin Electronics' stock purchase warrants

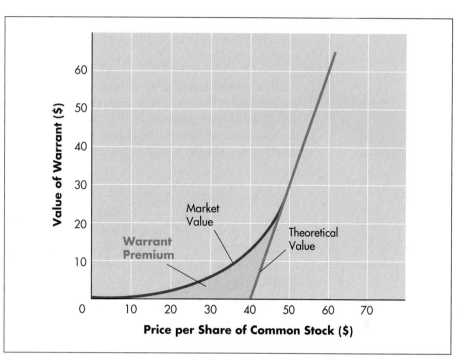

amount of time until expiration also affects the market value of the warrant. Generally speaking, the closer the warrant is to its expiration date, the more likely that its market value will equal its theoretical value.

Warrant Premium

The *warrant premium,* or the amount by which the market value of Dustin Electronics' warrants exceeds the theoretical value of these warrants, is also shown in Figure 16.2. This premium results from a combination of positive investor expectations and the ability of the investor with a fixed sum to invest to obtain much larger potential returns (and risk) by trading in warrants rather than the underlying stock.

EXAMPLE   Stan Buyer has $2,430, which he is interested in investing in Dustin Electronics. The firm's stock is currently selling for $45 per share, and its warrants are selling for $18 per warrant. Each warrant entitles the holder to purchase three shares of Dustin's common stock at $40 per share. Because the stock is selling for $45 per share, the theoretical warrant value, calculated in the preceding example, is $15 [($45 − $40) × 3].

The warrant premium results from positive investor expectations and leverage opportunities. Stan Buyer could spend his $2,430 in either of two ways: He could purchase 54 shares of common stock at $45 per share, or 135 warrants at $18 per warrant, ignoring brokerage fees. If Mr. Buyer purchases the stock and its price rises to $48, he will gain $162 ($3 per share × 54 shares) by selling the stock. If instead he purchases the 135 warrants and the stock price increases by $3 per share, Mr. Buyer will gain approximately $1,215. Because the price of a share of stock rises by $3, the price of each warrant can be expected to rise by $9 (because each warrant can be used to purchase three shares of common stock). A gain of $9 per warrant on 135 warrants means a total goal gain of $1,215 on the warrants.

The greater leverage associated with trading warrants should be clear from the example. Of course, because leverage works both ways, it results in greater risk. If the market price fell by $3, the loss on the stock would be $162, whereas the loss on the warrants would be close to $1,215. Clearly, investing in warrants is more risky than investing in the underlying stock.

REVIEW QUESTIONS

16–9   What are *stock purchase warrants?* What are the similarities and key differences between the effects of warrants and those of convertibles on the firm's capital structure and its ability to raise new capital?

16–10   What is the *implied price of a warrant?* How is it estimated? To be effective, how should it be related to the estimated *market value* of a warrant?

16–11   What is the general relationship between the theoretical and market values of a warrant? In what circumstances are these values quite close? What is a *warrant premium?*

LG6 16.5 | Options

option
An instrument that provides its holder with an opportunity to purchase or sell a specified asset at a stated price on or before a set *expiration date.*

In the most general sense, an **option** can be viewed as an instrument that provides its holder with an opportunity to purchase or sell a specified asset at a stated price on or before a set *expiration date.* Options are probably the most popular type of *derivative security.* Today, the interest in options centers on options on common stock.[12] The development of organized options exchanges has created markets in which to trade these options, which themselves are securities. Three basic forms of options are rights, warrants, and calls and puts. Rights are discussed in Chapter 7, and warrants were described in the preceding section.

call option
An option to *purchase* a specified number of shares of a stock (typically 100) on or before a specified future date at a stated price.

Calls and Puts

striking price
The price at which the holder of a call option can buy (or the holder of a put option can sell) a specified amount of stock at any time prior to the option's expiration date.

The two most common types of options are calls and puts. A **call option** is an option to *purchase* a specified number of shares of a stock (typically 100) on or before a specified future date at a stated price. Call options usually have initial lives of 1 to 9 months, occasionally 1 year. The **striking price** is the price at which the holder of the option can buy the stock at any time prior to the option's expiration date; it is generally set at or near the prevailing market price of the stock at

---

12. *Real* options—opportunities embedded in capital projects that enable management to alter their cash flows and risk—were discussed in Chapter 10. The *options* described here differ from real options; they are a type of derivative security that derives its value from an underlying financial asset, typically common stock. Although some of the analytical tools used to value both types of options are similar, the focus here is merely on the definitional aspects of options. The models used to value these options are typically discussed in more advanced financial management textbooks.

the time the option is issued. For example, if a firm's stock is currently selling for $50 per share, a call option on the stock initiated today will probably have a striking price set at $50 per share. One must pay a specified price (normally a few hundred dollars) to purchase a call option.

A **put option** is an option to *sell* a specified number of shares of a stock (typically 100) on or before a specified future date at a stated striking price. Like the call option, the striking price of the put is set close to the market price of the underlying stock at the time of issuance. The lives and costs of puts are similar to those of calls.

put option
An option to *sell* a specified number of shares of a stock (typically 100) on or before a specified future date at a stated price.

Options Markets

There are two ways of making options transactions. The first involves making a transaction through one of 20 or so call and put options dealers with the help of a stockbroker. The other, more popular mechanism is the organized options exchanges. The dominant exchange is the *Chicago Board Options Exchange (CBOE),* which was established in 1973. Other exchanges on which options are traded include the American Stock Exchange, the Philadelphia Stock Exchange, and the Pacific Stock Exchange. The options traded on these exchanges are standardized and thus are considered registered securities. Each option is for 100 shares of the underlying stock. The price at which options transactions can be made is determined by the forces of supply and demand.

Options Trading

The most common motive for purchasing call options is the expectation that the market price of the underlying stock will *rise* by more than enough to cover the cost of the option, thereby allowing the purchaser of the call to profit.

EXAMPLE   Assume that Cindy Peters pays $250 for a 3-month *call option* on Wing Enterprises, a maker of aircraft components, at a striking price of $50. This means that by paying $250, Cindy is guaranteed that she can purchase 100 shares of Wing at $50 per share at any time during the next 3 months. The stock price must climb $2.50 per share ($250 ÷ 100 shares) to $52.50 per share to cover the cost of the option (ignoring any brokerage fees or dividends). If the stock price were to rise to $60 per share during the period, Cindy's net profit would be $750 [(100 shares × $60/share) − (100 shares × $50/share) − $250].

Because this return would be earned on a $250 investment, it illustrates the high potential return on investment that options offer. Of course, had the stock price not risen above $50 per share, Cindy would have lost the $250 she invested, because there would have been no reason to exercise the option. Had the stock price risen to between $50 and $52.50 per share, Cindy probably would have exercised the option to reduce her loss to an amount less than $250. ■

Hint Put and call options are created by individuals and other firms. The firm itself has nothing to do with the creation of these options. Convertibles and warrants, by contrast, are created by the issuing firm.

Put options are purchased in the expectation that the share price of a given security will *decline* over the life of the option. Purchasers of puts commonly own the shares and wish to protect a gain they have realized since their initial purchase. Buying a put locks in the gain because it enables them to sell their shares at a known price during the life of the option. Investors gain from put options when the price of the underlying stock declines by more than the per-share cost of the option. The logic underlying the purchase of a put is exactly the opposite of that underlying the use of call options.

| EXAMPLE | Assume that Don Kelly pays $325 for a 6-month *put option* on Dante United, a baked goods manufacturer, at a striking price of $40. Don purchased the put option in expectation that the stock price would drop because of the introduction of a new product line by Dante's chief competitor. By paying $325, Don is assured that he can sell 100 shares of Dante at $40 per share at any time during the next 6 months. The stock price must drop by $3.25 per share ($325 ÷ 100 shares) to $36.75 per share to cover the cost of the option (ignoring any brokerage fees or dividends). If the stock price were to drop to $30 per share during the period, Don's net profit would be $675 [(100 shares × $40/share) − (100 shares × $30/share) − $325].

Because the return would be earned on a $325 investment, it again illustrates the high potential return on investment that options offer. Of course, had the stock price risen above $40 per share, Don would have lost the $325 he invested, because there would have been no reason to exercise the option. Had the stock price fallen to between $36.75 and $40.00 per share, Don probably would have exercised the option to reduce his loss to an amount less than $325. ∎

The Role of Call and Put Options in Fund Raising

Although call and put options are extremely popular investment vehicles, they play *no* direct role in the fund-raising activities of the financial manager. These options are issued by investors, not businesses. *They are not a source of financing to the firm.* Corporate pension managers, whose job it is to invest and manage corporate pension funds, may use call and put options as part of their investment activities to earn a return or to protect or lock in returns already earned on securities. The presence of options trading in the firm's stock could—by increasing trading activity—stabilize the firm's share price in the marketplace, but the financial manager has no direct control over this. Buyers of options have neither any say in the firm's management nor any voting rights; only stockholders are given these privileges. Despite the popularity of call and put options as an investment vehicle, the financial manager has very little need to deal with them, especially as part of fund-raising activities.

Employee stock options are a form of call options. As the *In Practice* box on the facing page describes, these options, very much in the news, can have a large financial impact on the firm.

Hedging Foreign-Currency Exposures with Options

The Chicago Mercantile Exchange (CME) and the Philadelphia Stock Exchange (PHLX) offer exchange-traded options contracts on the Canadian dollar, the euro, the Japanese yen, the Swiss franc, and several other important currencies. *Currency options* are used by a wide range of traders—from the largest multinational companies to small exporters and importers, as well as by individual investors and speculators. Unlike futures and forward contracts, options offer the

In Practice FOCUS ON ETHICS

VALUATION OF DERIVATIVES: THE POLITICS OF ACCOUNTING

Hybrid securities are issued for the purpose of raising capital; derivative securities are issued for the purpose of speculation or hedging risk. Both share a similar problem: how to determine the fair price. For liquid securities, price determination is quite straightforward: One can check the prices assigned by the market and verified by reliable quote services. For illiquid securities, price is often determined by complicated theoretical models.

When it comes to practice in the real world, however, the problems of valuation often seem more complicated than academic models. Consider employee stock options, for example. *Employee stock options (ESOs)* are essentially long-term calls, whose purpose is to compensate employees. They allow company executives and ordinary employees to purchase company stock at a predetermined exercise price (generally below the current market price) during a specified period of time. At the time that the option is exercised, the difference between the market price and the exercise price (known as the *option spread*) constitutes profit to the option holder. Because compensation from stock options can reach hundreds of millions of dollars per year without affecting the firm's bottom line, ESOs have become a popular compensation tool for senior management and rank-and-file employees alike.

Until recently, under the existing accounting rules firms were not required to expense stock options on their income statements. As Joseph Stiglitz, the 2001 Nobel Laureate in economics explained, by means of stock options, "corporate officers could ensure that they were extremely well paid, without at the same time taking out anything from the corporation's bottom line. It was almost too good to be true: While executives were receiving millions, no one seemed to be bearing the cost. It was a mirage: Shareholder value was being diluted."

Traditional put and call options, both short-term and long-term, used for hedging or for speculation, can easily be valued. When the identical instruments are used to reward employees, their value is not so easy to determine. Here's why: Many proposals have been made to include the cost of options in financial statements, but the technology-based industries have managed to block legislative efforts. The case for ESO expensing has been strengthened by recent accounting scandals at **Enron, WorldCom,** and **Global Crossing,** where top executives reaped billions of dollars from stock options. In spring 2003, the Financial Accounting Standards Board (FASB) voted to mandate the expensing of employee stock options. It recommended that option valuation should be based on the fair value principle. The FASB ruling was supported by a large number of individual and institutional investors and voluntarily implemented by hundreds of U.S. companies, including **General Electric, Wal-Mart, Coca-Cola, General Motors,** and **Dow Chemical,** among many others. In addition, some companies, such as **Microsoft,** stopped issuing ESOs altogether and replaced them with restricted stock. Fed Chairman Alan Greenspan and SEC chairman William Donaldson also support expensing of options.

Bowing to pressure from lobbyists representing deep-pocketed high-tech companies, such as **Dell, Intel,** and **Cisco,** and trade groups, including the **Business Roundtable** and the **American Electronic Association,** the U.S. Congress stepped in to kill the FASB proposal. In a rare bipartisan show of unity, the House passed the Baker-Eshoo bill requiring that firms need to expense only those options awarded to the top five executives of an organization. This legislation would also allow newly public companies to delay expensing for top executives in the first three years. Approval of the legislation by the Senate, however, appears very problematic.

Source: Joseph E. Stiglitz, "Corporate Corruption," *The Guardian* (July 4, 2002); *H.R. 3574.EH,* thomas.loc.gov/.

■ *The high- tech industry adamantly opposes the expensing of stock options and tries to block any FASB initiative to mandate this practice. What arguments would you use if you were hired as the industry spokesperson?*

hedging
Offsetting or protecting against the risk of adverse price movements.

key benefit of **hedging**, which involves offsetting or protecting against the risk of adverse price movements, while simultaneously preserving the possibility of profiting from favorable price movements. The key drawback to using options to hedge foreign-currency exposures is their high cost relative to using more traditional futures or forward contracts.

EXAMPLE   Assume that a U.S. exporter just booked a sale denominated in Swiss francs with payment due upon delivery in 3 months. The company could hedge the risk of depreciation in the dollar by purchasing a Swiss franc put option. This would give the company the right to sell Swiss francs at a fixed price (say, $0.75/Sf). This option would become valuable if the Swiss franc were to depreciate from today's $0.78/Sf to, say, $0.70/Sf before the exporter receives payment in Swiss francs. On the other hand, if the Swiss franc were to appreciate from $0.78/Sf to, say, $0.85/Sf, the U.S. exporter would allow the put option to expire unexercised and would instead convert the Swiss francs received in payment into dollars at the new, higher dollar price. The exporter would be protected from adverse price risk but would still be able to profit from favorable price movements. ▪

REVIEW QUESTIONS

16–12 What is an *option?* Define *calls* and *puts*. What role, if any, do call and put options play in the fund-raising activities of the financial manager?

16–13 How can the firm use currency options to *hedge* foreign-currency exposures resulting from international transactions? Describe the key benefit and the key drawback of using currency options rather than futures and forward contracts.

Summary

Focus on Value

In addition to the basic corporate securities, the firm can use various types of hybrid securities to improve its fund-raising activities. These securities, which possess characteristics of both debt and equity, enable the firm to raise funds more inexpensively or to provide for desired future changes in the firm's capital structure.

Leasing, particularly financial (capital) leases, may enable the firm to use the lease as a substitute for the debt-financed purchase of a given asset. Leasing may provide more attractive risk–return tradeoffs to the firm than would result from using debt financing to purchase a given asset. Similarly, by issuing convertible rather than straight debt or by attaching stock purchase warrants to a bond issue or debt financing, the firm may provide lenders with the potential to benefit from stock price movements in exchange for being charged a lower interest rate or including less restrictive covenants in the bond or debt agreement. Although options are not a source of financing to the firm, the presence of this derivative security can help stabilize the firm's share price. Currency options can be used to hedge, or protect against, adverse currency movements in international transactions.

Clearly, the financial manager should use hybrid and derivative securities to increase return (often by lowering financing costs) and reduce risk. By taking only those actions believed to result in attractive risk–return tradeoffs, the financial manager can positively contribute to the firm's goal of **maximizing the stock price.**

Review of Learning Goals

LG1 **Differentiate between hybrid and derivative securities and their roles in the corporation.** Hybrid securities are forms of debt or equity financing that possess characteristics of both debt and equity financing. Popular hybrid securities include preferred stock, financial leases, convertible securities, and stock purchase warrants. Derivative securities are neither debt nor equity and derive their value from an underlying asset that is often another security. Options are a popular derivative security.

LG2 **Review the types of leases, leasing arrangements, the lease-versus-purchase decision, the effects of leasing on future financing, and the advantages and disadvantages of leasing.** A lease enables the firm to make contractual, tax-deductible payments to obtain the use of fixed assets. Operating leases are generally 5 or fewer years in term, cancelable, and renewable, and they provide for maintenance by the lessor. Financial leases are longer-term, noncancelable, and not renewable, and they require the lessee to maintain the asset. FASB Standard No. 13 provides specific guidelines for defining a financial (or capital) lease. A lessor can obtain assets to be leased through a direct lease, a sale–leaseback arrangement, or a leveraged lease. The lease-versus-purchase decision can be evaluated by calculating the after-tax cash outflows associated with the leasing and purchasing alternatives. The more desirable alternative is the one that has the lower present value of after-tax cash outflows. FASB Standard No. 13 requires firms to show financial (or capital) leases as assets and corresponding liabilities on their balance sheets; operating leases must be shown in footnotes to the financial statements. A number of commonly cited advantages and disadvantages should be considered when making lease-versus-purchase decisions.

LG3 **Describe the types of convertible securities, their general features, and financing with convertibles.** Corporate bonds and preferred stock may both be convertible into common stock. The conversion ratio indicates the number of shares for which a convertible can be exchanged and determines the conversion price. A conversion privilege is nearly always available at any time in the life of the security. The conversion (or stock) value is the value of the convertible measured in terms of the market price of the common stock into which it can be converted. The presence of convertibles and other contingent securities (warrants and stock options) often requires the firm to report both basic and diluted earnings per share (EPS). Convertibles are used to obtain deferred common stock financing, to "sweeten" bond issues, to minimize restrictive covenants, and to raise cheap funds temporarily. The call feature is sometimes used to encourage or "force" conversion; occasionally, an overhanging issue results.

LG4 **Demonstrate the procedures for determining the straight bond value, the conversion (or stock) value, and the market value of a convertible bond.** The straight bond value of a convertible is the price at which it would sell in the market without the conversion feature. It typically represents the minimum value at which a convertible bond trades. The conversion value of the convertible is found by multiplying the conversion ratio by the current market price of the underlying common stock. The market value of a convertible generally exceeds both its straight and conversion values, resulting in a market premium. The premium is largest when the straight and conversion values are nearly equal.

LG5 **Explain the key characteristics of stock purchase warrants, the implied price of an attached warrant, and the values of warrants.** Stock purchase warrants enable their holders to purchase a certain number of shares of common stock at the specified exercise price. Warrants are often attached to debt issues as "sweeteners," generally have limited lives, are detachable, and may be traded on securities exchanges. Warrants are similar to stock rights, except that the exercise price of a warrant is initially set above the underlying stock's current market price. Warrants are similar to convertibles, but exercising them has a less pronounced effect on the firm's leverage and brings in new funds. The implied price of an attached warrant can be found by dividing the difference between the bond price with warrants attached and the straight bond value by the number of warrants attached to each bond. The market value of a warrant usually exceeds its theoretical value, creating a warrant premium. Investors generally get more leverage from trading warrants than from trading the underlying stock.

LG6 **Define options and discuss calls and puts, options markets, options trading, the role of call and put options in fund raising, and hedging foreign-currency exposures with options.** An option provides its holder with an opportunity to purchase or sell a specified asset at a stated price on or before a set expiration date. Rights, warrants, and calls and puts are all options. Calls are options to purchase common stock, and puts are options to sell common stock. Options exchanges provide organized marketplaces in which purchases and sales of call and put options can be made. The options traded on the exchanges are standardized, and the prices at which they trade are determined by the forces of supply and demand. Call and put options do not play a direct role in the fund-raising activities of the financial manager. Currency options can be used to hedge the firm's foreign-currency exposures resulting from international transactions.

Self-Test Problems (Solutions in Appendix B)

LG2

ST16–1 **Lease versus purchase** The Hot Bagel Shop wishes to evaluate two plans, leasing and borrowing to purchase, for financing an oven. The firm is in the 40% tax bracket.

Lease The shop can lease the oven under a 5-year lease requiring annual end-of-year payments of $5,000. All maintenance costs will be paid by the lessor, and insurance and other costs will be borne by the lessee. The lessee will exercise its option to purchase the asset for $4,000 at termination of the lease.

Purchase   The oven costs $20,000 and will have a 5-year life. It will be depreciated under MACRS using a 5-year recovery period. (See Table 3.2 on page 106 for the applicable depreciation percentages.) The total purchase price will be financed by a 5-year, 15% loan requiring equal annual end-of-year payments of $5,967. The firm will pay $1,000 per year for a service contract that covers all maintenance costs; insurance and other costs will be borne by the firm. The firm plans to keep the equipment and use it beyond its 5-year recovery period.

a. For the leasing plan, calculate the following:
   (1) The after-tax cash outflow each year.
   (2) The present value of the cash outflows, using a 9% *discount rate.*
b. For the purchasing plan, calculate the following:
   (1) The annual interest expense deductible for tax purposes for each of the 5 years.
   (2) The after-tax cash outflow resulting from the purchase for each of the 5 years.
   (3) The present value of the cash outflows, using a 9% *discount rate.*
c. Compare the present values of the cash outflow streams for these two plans, and determine which plan would be preferable. Explain your answer.

LG4   **ST16–2   Finding convertible bond values**   Mountain Mining Company has an outstanding issue of convertible bonds with a $1,000 par value. These bonds are convertible into 40 shares of common stock. They have an 11% annual coupon interest rate and a 25-year maturity. The interest rate on a straight bond of similar risk is currently 13%.

a. Calculate the *straight bond value* of the bond.
b. Calculate the *conversion (or stock) value* of the bond when the market price of the common stock is $20, $25, $28, $35, and $50 per share.
c. For each of the stock prices given in part **b,** at what price would you expect the bond to sell? Why?
d. What is the least you would expect the bond to sell for, regardless of the common stock price behavior?

Warm-Up Exercises

LG2   **E16–1**   N and M Corp. is considering leasing a new machine for $25,000 per year. The lease arrangement calls for a 5-year lease with an option to purchase the machine at the end of the lease for $3,500. The firm is in the 34% tax bracket. What is the present value of the lease outflows, including the purchase option, if lease payments are made at the end of each year and if the after-tax cost of debt is 7%?

LG3   **E16–2**   During the past 2 years Meacham Industries issued three separate convertible bonds. For each of them, calculate the *conversion price.*
a. A $1,000-par-value bond that is convertible into 10 shares of common stock.
b. A $2,000-par-value bond that is convertible into 20 shares of common stock.
c. A $1,500-par-value bond that is convertible into 30 shares of common stock.

LG3   E16–3   Newcomb Company has a bond outstanding with a $1,500 par value and convertible at $30 per share. What is the bond's *conversion ratio?* If the underlying stock currently trades at $25 per share, what is the bond's *conversion value?* Would it be advisable for a bondholder to exercise the conversion option?

LG4   E16–4   Crystal Cafes recently sold a $2,000-par-value, 10-year convertible bond with an 8% coupon interest rate. The interest payments will be paid annually at the end of each year and the principal will be repaid at maturity. A similar bond without a conversion feature would have sold with a 9% coupon interest rate. What is the minimum price that the Crystal Cafes' convertible bond should sell for?

LG6   E16–5   A 6-month call option on 100 shares of SRS Corp. stock is selling for $300. The striking price for the option is $40. The stock is currently selling at $38 per share. Ignoring brokerage fees, what price must the stock achieve to just cover the expense of the option? If the stock price rises to $45, what will the net profit on the option contract be?

Problems

LG2

BASIC

P16–1   **Lease cash flows**   Given the lease payments and terms shown in the following table, determine the *yearly after-tax cash outflows* for each firm, assuming that lease payments are made at the end of each year and that the firm is in the 40% tax bracket. Assume that no purchase option exists.

Firm	Annual lease payment	Term of lease
A	$100,000	4 years
B	80,000	14
C	150,000	8
D	60,000	25
E	20,000	10

LG2

INTERMEDIATE

P16–2   **Loan interest**   For each of the loan amounts, interest rates, annual payments, and loan terms shown in the following table, calculate the *annual interest paid* each year over the term of the loan, assuming that the payments are made at the end of each year.

Loan	Amount	Interest rate	Annual payment	Term
A	$14,000	10%	$ 4,416	4 years
B	17,500	12	10,355	2
C	2,400	13	1,017	3
D	49,000	14	14,273	5
E	26,500	16	7,191	6

LG2

INTERMEDIATE

P16–3 **Loan payments and interest** Schuyler Company wishes to purchase an asset costing $117,000. The full amount needed to finance the asset can be borrowed at 14% interest. The terms of the loan require equal end-of-year payments for the next 6 years. Determine the total annual loan payment, and break it into the amount of interest and the amount of principal paid for each year. (*Hint:* Use the techniques presented in Chapter 4 to find the loan payment.)

LG2

CHALLENGE

P16–4 **Lease versus purchase** JLB Corporation is attempting to determine whether to lease or purchase research equipment. The firm is in the 40% tax bracket, and its after-tax cost of debt is currently 8%. The terms of the lease and of the purchase are as follows:

Lease Annual end-of-year lease payments of $25,200 are required over the 3-year life of the lease. All maintenance costs will be paid by the lessor; insurance and other costs will be borne by the lessee. The lessee will exercise its option to purchase the asset for $5,000 at termination of the lease.

Purchase The research equipment, costing $60,000, can be financed entirely with a 14% loan requiring annual end-of-year payments of $25,844 for 3 years. The firm in this case will depreciate the equipment under MACRS using a 3-year recovery period. (See Table 3.2 on page 106 for the applicable depreciation percentages.) The firm will pay $1,800 per year for a service contract that covers all maintenance costs; insurance and other costs will be borne by the firm. The firm plans to keep the equipment and use it beyond its 3-year recovery period.

a. Calculate the *after-tax cash outflows* associated with each alternative.
b. Calculate the present value of each cash outflow stream, using the after-tax cost of debt.
c. Which alternative—lease or purchase—would you recommend? Why?

LG2

CHALLENGE

P16–5 **Lease versus purchase** Northwest Lumber Company needs to expand its facilities. To do so, the firm must acquire a machine costing $80,000. The machine can be leased or purchased. The firm is in the 40% tax bracket, and its after-tax cost of debt is 9%. The terms of the lease and purchase plans are as follows:

Lease The leasing arrangement requires end-of-year payments of $19,800 over 5 years. All maintenance costs will be paid by the lessor; insurance and other costs will be borne by the lessee. The lessee will exercise its option to purchase the asset for $24,000 at termination of the lease.

Purchase If the firm purchases the machine, its cost of $80,000 will be financed with a 5-year, 14% loan requiring equal end-of-year payments of $23,302. The machine will be depreciated under MACRS using a 5-year recovery period. (See Table 3.2 on page 106 for the applicable depreciation percentages.) The firm will pay $2,000 per year for a service contract that covers all maintenance costs; insurance and other costs will be borne by the firm. The firm plans to keep the equipment and use it beyond its 5-year recovery period.

a. Determine the *after-tax cash outflows* of Northwest Lumber under each alternative.

   b. Find the present value of each after-tax cash outflow stream, using the after-tax cost of debt.
   c. Which alternative—lease or purchase—would you recommend? Why?

P16-6 Capitalized lease values   Given the lease payments, terms remaining until the leases expire, and discount rates shown in the following table, calculate the *capitalized value* of each lease, assuming that lease payments are made annually at the end of each year.

Lease	Lease payment	Remaining term	Discount rate
A	$ 40,000	12 years	10%
B	120,000	8	12
C	9,000	18	14
D	16,000	3	9
E	47,000	20	11

P16-7 Conversion price   Calculate the *conversion price* for each of the following convertible bonds:
   a. A $1,000-par-value bond that is convertible into 20 shares of common stock.
   b. A $500-par-value bond that is convertible into 25 shares of common stock.
   c. A $1,000-par-value bond that is convertible into 50 shares of common stock.

P16-8 Conversion ratio   What is the *conversion ratio* for each of the following bonds?
   a. A $1,000-par-value bond that is convertible into common stock at $43.75 per share.
   b. A $1,000-par-value bond that is convertible into common stock at $25 per share.
   c. A $600-par-value bond that is convertible into common stock at $30 per share.

P16-9 Conversion (or stock) value   What is the *conversion (or stock) value* of each of the following convertible bonds?
   a. A $1,000-par-value bond that is convertible into 25 shares of common stock. The common stock is currently selling for $50 per share.
   b. A $1,000-par-value bond that is convertible into 12.5 shares of common stock. The common stock is currently selling for $42 per share.
   c. A $1,000-par-value bond that is convertible into 100 shares of common stock. The common stock is currently selling for $10.50 per share.

P16-10 Conversion (or stock) value   Find the *conversion (or stock) value* for each of the convertible bonds described in the following table.

Convertible	Conversion ratio	Current market price of stock
A	25	$42.25
B	16	50.00
C	20	44.00
D	5	19.50

P16–11 **Straight bond value**   Calculate the *straight bond value* for each of the bonds shown in the following table.

Bond	Par value	Coupon interest rate (paid annually)	Interest rate on equal-risk straight bond	Years to maturity
A	$1,000	10%	14%	20
B	800	12	15	14
C	1,000	13	16	30
D	1,000	14	17	25

P16–12 **Determining values—Convertible bond**   Eastern Clock Company has an outstanding issue of convertible bonds with a $1,000 par value. These bonds are convertible into 50 shares of common stock. They have a 10% annual coupon interest rate and a 20-year maturity. The interest rate on a straight bond of similar risk is currently 12%.

a. Calculate the *straight bond value* of the bond.

b. Calculate the *conversion (or stock) value* of the bond when the market price of the common stock is $15, $20, $23, $30, and $45 per share.

c. For each of the stock prices given in part **b,** at what price would you expect the bond to sell? Why?

d. What is the least you would expect the bond to sell for, regardless of the common stock price behavior?

P16–13 **Determining values—Convertible bond**   Craig's Cake Company has an outstanding issue of 15-year convertible bonds with a $1,000 par value. These bonds are convertible into 80 shares of common stock. They have a 13% annual coupon interest rate, whereas the interest rate on straight bonds of similar risk is 16%.

a. Calculate the *straight bond value* of this bond.

b. Calculate the *conversion (or stock) value* of the bond when the market price is $9, $12, $13, $15, and $20 per share of common stock.

c. For each of the common stock prices given in part **b,** at what price would you expect the bond to sell? Why?

d. Graph the straight value and conversion value of the bond for each common stock price given. Plot the per-share common stock prices on the *x* axis and the bond values on the *y* axis. Use this graph to indicate the minimum market value of the bond associated with each common stock price.

P16–14 **Implied prices of attached warrants**   Calculate the implied price of *each* warrant for each of the bonds shown in the following table.

Bond	Price of bond with warrants attached	Par value	Coupon interest rate (paid annually)	Interest rate on equal-risk straight bond	Years to maturity	Number of warrants attached to bond
A	$1,000	$1,000	12 %	13%	15	10
B	1,100	1,000	9.5	12	10	30
C	500	500	10	11	20	5
D	1,000	1,000	11	12	20	20

b. How much will Carol earn on the option transaction if the underlying stock price rises to $70?

c. How high must the stock price rise for Carol to break even on the option transaction?

d. Compare, contrast, and discuss the relative profit and risk associated with the stock and the option transactions.

LG6

INTERMEDIATE

P16–21 Put option Ed Martin, the pension fund manager for Stark Corporation, is considering purchase of a put option in anticipation of a price decline in the stock of Carlisle, Inc. The option to sell 100 shares of Carlisle, Inc., at any time during the next 90 days at a striking price of $45 can be purchased for $380. The stock of Carlisle is currently selling for $46 per share.

a. Ignoring any brokerage fees or dividends, what profit or loss will Ed make if he buys the option and the lowest price of Carlisle stock during the 90 days is $46, $44, $40, and $35?

b. What effect would the fact that the price of Carlisle's stock slowly rose from its initial $46 level to $55 at the end of 90 days have on Ed's purchase?

c. In light of your findings, discuss the potential risks and returns from using put options to attempt to profit from an anticipated decline in share price.

LG6

CHALLENGE

P16–22 ETHICS PROBLEM Many economists and accountants argue that expensing of options is not necessary because the dilutive impact of options is accounted for by the increased number of shares. Do you agree with them?

Chapter 16 Case: Financing L. Rashid Company's Chemical Waste Disposal System

L. Rashid Company, a rapidly growing chemical processor, needs to raise $3 million in external funds to finance the acquisition of a new chemical waste disposal system. After carefully analyzing alternative financing sources, Denise McMahon, the firm's vice president of finance, reduced the financing possibilities to three alternatives: (1) debt, (2) debt with warrants, and (3) a financial lease. The key terms of each of these financing alternatives follow.

Debt The firm can borrow the full $3 million from First Shreveport Bank. The bank will charge 12% annual interest and require annual end-of-year payments of $1,249,050 over the next 3 years. The disposal system will be depreciated under MACRS using a 3-year recovery period. (See Table 3.2 on page 106 for the applicable depreciation percentages.) The firm will pay $45,000 at the end of each year for a service contract that covers all maintenance costs; insurance and other costs will be borne by the firm. The firm plans to keep the equipment and use it beyond its 3-year recovery period.

Debt with Warrants The firm can borrow the full $3 million from Southern National Bank. The bank will charge 10% annual interest and will, in addition, require a grant of 50,000 warrants, each allowing the purchase of two shares of the firm's stock for $30 per share at any time during the next 10 years. The stock is currently selling for $28 per share, and the warrants are estimated to have a market value of $1 each. The price (market value) of the debt with the warrants attached is estimated to equal the $3 million initial loan principal. The annual end-of-year payments on this loan will be $1,206,345 over the next 3 years. Depreciation, maintenance, insurance, and other costs will have the same costs and treatments under this alternative as those described before for the straight debt financing alternative.

Financial Lease   The waste disposal system can be leased from First International Capital. The lease will require annual end-of-year payments of $1,200,000 over the next 3 years. All maintenance costs will be paid by the lessor; insurance and other costs will be borne by the lessee. The lessee will exercise its option to purchase the system for $220,000 at termination of the lease at the end of 3 years.

Denise decided first to determine which of the debt financing alternatives—debt or debt with warrants—would least burden the firm's cash flows over the next 3 years. In this regard, she felt that very few, if any, warrants would be exercised during this period. Once the better debt financing alternative was found, Denise planned to use lease-versus-purchase analysis to evaluate it in light of the lease alternative. The firm is in the 40% tax bracket, and its after-tax cost of debt would be 7% under the debt alternative and 6% under the debt with warrants alternative.

TO DO

a. Under the debt with warrants, find the following:
   (1) Straight debt value.
   (2) Implied price of *all* warrants.
   (3) Implied price of *each* warrant.
   (4) Theoretical value of a warrant.
b. On the basis of your findings in part **a,** do you think the price of the debt with warrants is too high or too low? Explain.
c. Assuming that the firm can raise the needed funds under the specified terms, which debt financing alternative—debt or debt with warrants—would you recommend in view of your findings above? Explain.
d. For the purchase alternative, financed as recommended in part **c,** calculate the following:
   (1) The annual interest expense deductible for tax purposes for each of the next 3 years.
   (2) The after-tax cash outflow for each of the next 3 years.
   (3) The present value of the cash outflows using the appropriate discount rate.
e. For the lease alternative, calculate the following:
   (1) The after-tax cash outflow for each of the next 3 years.
   (2) The present value of the cash outflows using the appropriate discount rate applied in part **d**(3).
f. Compare the present values of the cash outflow streams for the purchase [in part **d**(3)] and lease [in part **e**(2)] alternatives, and determine which would be preferable. Explain and discuss your recommendation.

Spreadsheet Exercise

Morris Company, a small manufacturing firm, wants to acquire a new machine that costs $30,000. Arrangements can be made to lease or purchase the machine. The firm is in the 40% tax bracket. The firm has gathered the following information about the two alternatives.

Lease Morris would obtain a 5-year lease requiring annual end-of-year lease payments of $10,000. The lessor would pay all maintenance costs; insurance and other costs would be borne by the lessee. Morris would be given the right to exercise its option to purchase the machine for $3,000 at the end of the lease term.

Purchase Morris can finance the purchase of the machine with an 8.5%, 5-year loan requiring annual end-of-year installment payments. The machine would be depreciated under MACRS using a 5-year recovery period. The exact depreciation rates over the next six periods would be 20%, 32%, 19%, 12%, 12%, and 5%, respectively. Morris would pay $1,200 per year for a service contract that covers all maintenance costs. The firm plans to keep the machine and use it beyond its 5-year recovery period.

TO DO

Create a spreadsheet similar to Tables 16.1, 16.2, and 16.3 (or view them at www.aw-bc.com/gitman) to answer the following:

a. Calculate the after-tax cash outflow from the lease for Morris Company.
b. Calculate the annual loan payment.
c. Determine the interest and principal components of the loan payments.
d. Calculate the after-tax cash outflows associated with the purchasing option.
e. Compare the cash outflows associated with both the leasing and purchasing options.
f. Which alternative is preferable? Explain.

Group Exercise

This chapter is the first of three chapters focusing on special topics in managerial finance. The hybrid and derivative securities covered in Chapter 16 (leases, convertible securities, warrants, and options) show creative solutions to financing needs. In that vein, this assignment will require your group to be creative as we near the end of your fictitious firm's story.

TO DO

For many weeks your group has been creating all of the financials necessary to tell the story of your fictitious firm. At this point you can almost see the firm as a real entity. Given your familiarity with the specifics of your firm's financials, you will now add your own touches to the story. To complete this assignment your group will use several types of the hybrid and derivative securities described in this chapter. Specifically, you are to do the following:

LG2   **a.** Design a leasing arrangement for your firm.

LG3 **LG4**   **b.** Describe the issuance of a convertible security, either a bond or preferred stock, by your firm.

LG5 **LG6**   **c.** Choose a third type of creative financing—for example, warrants or options—that your firm could use to meet its needs.

Web Exercise

One topic covered in this chapter is leasing. Many firms choose to lease rather than purchase equipment. Due to the high demand for leasing, numerous manufacturers and financial institutions specialize in leasing equipment to businesses. One such company is Unistar Leasing.

TO DO

a. Point your browser to www.unistarleasing.com/, Unistar's home page. Investigate the leasing services offered by Unistar.

b. Unistar's Web site also offers a calculator and explains the differences between leasing and taking out loans. Investigate and report on the information provided at this Web site.

Remember to check the book's Web site at

www.aw-bc.com/gitman

for additional resources, including additional Web exercises.

Chapter 17

Mergers, LBOs, Divestitures, and Business Failure

LEARNING GOALS

LG1 Understand merger fundamentals, including terminology, motives for merging, and types of mergers.

LG2 Describe the objectives and procedures used in leveraged buyouts (LBOs) and divestitures.

LG3 Demonstrate the procedures used to value the target company, and discuss the effect of stock swap transactions on earnings per share.

LG4 Discuss the merger negotiation process, holding companies, and international mergers.

LG5 Understand the types and major causes of business failure and the use of voluntary settlements to sustain or liquidate the failed firm.

LG6 Explain bankruptcy legislation and the procedures involved in reorganizing or liquidating a bankrupt firm.

 ACROSS THE DISCIPLINES WHY THIS CHAPTER MATTERS TO YOU

Accounting: You need to understand mergers, leveraged buyouts, and divestitures of assets to record and report these organizational changes; you also need to understand bankruptcy procedures because you will play a large part in any reorganization or liquidation.

Information systems: You need to understand what data need to be tracked in the case of mergers, leveraged buyouts, divestitures of assets, or bankruptcy, to devise the systems needed to effect these organizational changes.

Management: You need to understand the motives for mergers so that you will know when and why a merger is a good idea. Also, you may need to know how to fend off an unwelcome takeover attempt, when to divest the firm of

assets for strategic reasons, and what options are available in the case of business failure.

Marketing: You need to understand mergers and divestitures, which may enable the firm to grow, diversify, or achieve synergy and therefore require changes in the firm's marketing organization, plans, and goals.

Operations: You need to understand mergers and divestitures because ongoing operations will be significantly affected by these organizational changes. Also, you should know that business failure may result in reorganization of the firm to provide adequate financing for ongoing operations.

746

JCPENNEY COMPANY, INC.

GETTING BACK TO BASICS—AGAIN

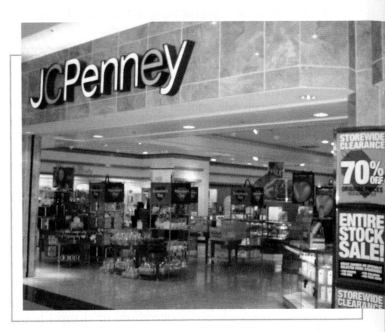

For decades, **JCPenney Company** (www.JCPenney.com), the general merchandise company founded in 1902 by James Cash Penney, pursued a strategy of nationwide expansion. Along the way, the company dabbled in noncore businesses such as restaurants, hard-line appliances, portrait studios, auto parts and services, banking, and life, health, auto, and homeowner's insurance. JCPenney's largest effort at diversification was its foray into the drugstore business, which began in 1969 with the purchase of **Thrift Drug** and climaxed in 1996 with the acquisition of **Eckerd Corporation.** Altogether, JCPenney accumulated more than 2,800 drugstores.

From time to time over its more than 100 years of business life, JCPenney announced major corporate restructurings in an attempt to refocus its business. In 1982, the company announced its intention to focus primarily on its core business as a department store. Several regional realignments followed in 1988 and 1996. Over the years, the company divested itself of several lines of business, including its supermarkets in 1977; The Treasury discount stores in 1980; auto service, paint, and hardware in 1982; the JCPenney Casualty Insurance Company in 1989; and the JCPenney National Bank in 1997.

In late 2003, the company announced that it was evaluating strategic alternatives regarding its 2,735 Eckerd drugstores, including retention, merger, spin-off, or sale, and had retained Credit Suisse First Boston to help evaluate the various alternatives. On April 5, 2004, JCPenney announced the sale of its Eckerd drugstore operations for $4.525 billion in cash. **The Jean Contu Group** acquired the stores in 13 Northeast and mid-Atlantic states, and **CVS Corporation** bought the remainder, located primarily in the South. In announcing the divestiture of Eckerd, Allen Questrom, Chairman and CEO of JCPenney, said, "This sale will allow JCPenney to focus entirely on our core department store and catalog/Internet business."

Whether JCPenney remains focused on its core business remains to be seen. If the past is any indication of the future, it may be tempted to once again stray into noncore businesses. This chapter looks at several types of corporate restructuring—mergers, leveraged buyouts, and divestitures—as well as restructuring due to business failure. Whether growing or shrinking, organizational changes are a way of life for many corporations.

Source: JCPenney press releases and company history from www.JCPenney.com (accessed August 30, 2004).

■ *What options does JCPenney have for the use of its after-tax cash proceeds from the sale of the Eckerd drugstores?*

747

P17–13   **Voluntary settlements**   For a firm with outstanding debt of $125,000, classify each of the following voluntary settlements as an extension, a composition, or a combination of the two.

    a. Paying a group of creditors in full in four periodic installments and paying the remaining creditors in full immediately.

    b. Paying a group of creditors 90 cents on the dollar immediately and paying the remaining creditors 80 cents on the dollar in two periodic installments.

    c. Paying all creditors 15 cents on the dollar.

    d. Paying all creditors in full in 180 days.

P17–14   **Voluntary settlements—Payments**   Jacobi Supply Company recently ran into certain financial difficulties that have resulted in the initiation of voluntary settlement procedures. The firm currently has $150,000 in outstanding debts and approximately $75,000 in liquidatable short-term assets. Indicate, for each of the following plans, whether the plan is an extension, a composition, or a combination of the two. Also indicate the cash payments and timing of the payments required of the firm under each plan.

    a. Each creditor will be paid 50 cents on the dollar immediately, and the debts will be considered fully satisfied.

    b. Each creditor will be paid 80 cents on the dollar in two quarterly installments of 50 cents and 30 cents. The first installment is to be paid in 90 days.

    c. Each creditor will be paid the full amount of its claims in three installments of 50 cents, 25 cents, and 25 cents on the dollar. The installments will be made in 60-day intervals, beginning in 60 days.

    d. A group of creditors with claims of $50,000 will be immediately paid in full; the rest will be paid 85 cents on the dollar, payable in 90 days.

P17–15   **ETHICS PROBLEM**   Why might employees and suppliers support management in a Chapter 11 bankruptcy declaration if they will have to wait to be paid, and may never get paid? How can a CEO act ethically toward these two groups of stakeholders in the time before, during, and after the bankruptcy period?

Chapter 17 Case: Deciding Whether to Acquire or Liquidate Procras Corporation

Sharon Scotia, CFO of Rome Industries, must decide what to do about Procras Corporation, a major customer that is bankrupt. Rome Industries is a large plastic-injection-molding firm that produces plastic products to customer order. Procras Corporation is a major customer of Rome Industries that designs and markets a variety of plastic toys. As a result of mismanagement and inventory problems, Procras has become bankrupt. Among its unsecured debts are total past-due accounts of $1.9 million owed to Rome Industries.

Recognizing that it probably cannot recover the full $1.9 million that Procras Corporation owes it, the management of Rome Industries has isolated two mutually exclusive alternative actions: (1) acquire Procras through an exchange of stock or (2) let Procras be liquidated and recover Rome Industries' proportionate claim against any funds available for unsecured creditors. Rome's management feels that acquisition of Procras would have appeal in that it would allow Rome to integrate vertically and expand its business from strictly industrial manufacturing to include product development and marketing. Of course, the firm wants to select the alternative that will create the most value for its shareholders. Charged with making a recommendation as to whether Rome should acquire Procras Corporation or allow it to be liquidated, Ms. Scotia gathered the following data.

Acquire Procras Corporation   Negotiations with Procras management have resulted in a planned ratio of exchange of 0.6 share of Rome Industries for each share of Procras Corporation common stock. The following table reflects current data for Rome Industries and Rome's expectations of the data values for Procras Corporation with proper management in place.

Item	Rome Industries	Procras Corporation
Earnings available for common stock	$640,000	$180,000
Number of shares of common stock outstanding	400,000	60,000
Market price per share	$32	$30

Rome Industries estimates that after the proposed acquisition of Procras Corporation, its price/earnings (P/E) ratio will be 18.5.

Liquidation of Procras Corporation   Procras Corporation was denied its petition for reorganization, and the court-appointed trustee was expected to charge $150,000 for his services in liquidating the firm. In addition, $100,000 in unpaid bills were expected to be incurred between the time of filing the bankruptcy petition and formal action by the court. The firm's preliquidation balance sheet is shown below. Use the liquidation example on the text's Web site at www.aw-bc .com/gitman as a guide in analyzing this alternative.

Procras Corporation Balance Sheet			
Assets		**Liabilities and Stockholders' Equity**	
Cash	$ 20,000	Accounts payable	$2,700,000
Marketable securities	1,000	Notes payable—bank	1,300,000
Accounts receivable	1,800,000	Accrued wages[a]	120,000
Inventories	3,000,000	Unsecured customer deposits[b]	60,000
Prepaid expenses	14,000	Taxes payable	70,000
Total current assets	$4,835,000	Total current liabilities	$4,250,000
Land	$ 415,000	First mortgage[c]	$ 300,000
Net plant	200,000	Second mortgage[c]	200,000
Net equipment	350,000	Unsecured bonds	400,000
Total fixed assets	$ 965,000	Total long-term debt	$ 900,000
Total	$5,800,000	Common stock (60,000 shares)	$ 120,000
		Paid-in capital in excess of par	480,000
		Retained earnings	50,000
		Total stockholders' equity	$ 650,000
		Total	$5,800,000

[a]Represents wages of $600 per employee earned within 90 days of filing bankruptcy for 200 of the firm's employees.
[b]Unsecured customer deposits not exceeding $900 each.
[c]The first and second mortgages are on the firm's total fixed assets.

The trustee expects to liquidate the assets for $3.2 million—$2.5 million from current assets and $700,000 from fixed assets.

TO DO

a. Calculate (1) the *ratio of exchange in market price* and (2) the *earnings per share (EPS)* and *price/earnings (P/E) ratio* for each company on the basis of the data given in the table that accompanies discussion of the acquisition alternative.
b. Find the *postmerger earnings per share (EPS)* for Rome Industries, assuming that it acquires Procras Corporation under the terms given.
c. Use the estimated postmerger price/earnings (P/E) ratio and your finding in part **b** to find the postmerger share price.
d. Use your finding in part **c** to determine how much, if any, the *total market value* of Rome Industries will change as a result of acquiring Procras Corporation.
e. Determine how much each claimant will receive if Procras Corporation is liquidated under the terms given.
f. How much, if any, of its $1.9 million balance due from Procras Corporation will Rome Industries recover as a result of liquidation of Procras?
g. Compare your findings in parts **d** and **f**, and make a recommendation for Rome Industries with regard to its best action—acquisition of Procras or the liquidation of Procras.
h. Which alternative would the shareholders of Procras Corporation prefer? Why?

Spreadsheet Exercise

Ram Electric Company is being considered for acquisition by Cavalier Electric. Cavalier expects the combination to increase its cash flows by $100,000 for each of the next 5 years and by $125,000 for each of the following 5 years. Ram Electric has relatively high financial leverage; Cavalier expects its cost of capital to be 12% for the first 5 years and estimates that it will increase to 16% for the following 5 years if the merger is undertaken. The cash price of Ram Electric is $325,000.

TO DO

Create a spreadsheet similar to Table 17.3 (or view a similar one at www.aw-bc .com/gitman) to answer the following questions.

a. Determine the *present value of the expected future cash inflows* over the next 10 years.
b. Calculate the *net present value (NPV)* for the Ram Electric acquisition.
c. All else being equal, would you recommend the acquisition of Ram Electric by Cavalier Electric? Explain.

Group Exercise

This chapter described several types of corporate restructurings, including expansions, contractions, and changes in financial structures. As pointed out in the text, firms undergo such changes for a variety of reasons. The ultimate goal, however, should always be to increase the value of the firm. Keep this simple fact in mind as your group experiences restructurings of your own design.

TO DO

Your fictitious firm is looking to acquire a competitor in hopes of improving its own value. This acquisition will be financed with a stock swap. Your assignment is to do following:

a. Establish the basics of the target firm, including its current stock price.
b. Defend your firm's motive(s) for making this acquisition.
c. Use the stock prices of the target and of your own firm to calculate the *ratio of exchange* and the *ratio of exchange in market price*.
d. Develop simple numbers that show how the *postmerger firm's earnings per share* are enhanced.

Web Exercise

Mergers and acquisitions occur all the time, whether in good economic times or bad. Each merger has its own characteristics, which are determined by the specifics of the firms involved.

TO DO

To get an understanding of how mergers vary, point your browser to www .maadvisor.com/maadvisor/, the home page of the mergers and acquisitions advisor. Scroll down Today's M and A news. Read and summarize some of the different stories regarding recent mergers and acquisitions.

Remember to check the book's Web site at

www.aw-bc.com/gitman

for additional resources, including additional Web exercises.

Chapter 18

International Managerial Finance

LEARNING GOALS

LG1 Understand the major factors that influence the financial operations of multinational companies (MNCs).

LG2 Describe the key differences between purely domestic and international financial statements—consolidation, translation of individual accounts, and international profits.

LG3 Discuss exchange rate risk and political risk, and explain how MNCs manage them.

LG4 Describe foreign direct investment, investment cash flows and decisions, the MNCs' capital structure, and the international debt and equity instruments available to MNCs.

LG5 Discuss the role of the Eurocurrency market in short-term borrowing and investing (lending) and the basics of international cash, credit, and inventory management.

LG6 Review recent trends in international mergers and joint ventures.

ACROSS THE DISCIPLINES WHY THIS CHAPTER MATTERS TO YOU

Accounting: You need to understand the tax rules for multinational companies, how to prepare consolidated financial statements for subsidiary companies, and how to account for international items in financial statements.

Information systems: You need to understand that if the firm undertakes foreign operations, it will need systems that track investments and operations in another currency and their fluctuations against the domestic currency.

Management: You need to understand both the opportunities and the risks involved in international operations; the possible role of international financial markets in raising capital; and the basic hedging strategies that multinational companies can use to protect themselves against exchange rate risk.

Marketing: You need to understand the potential for expanding into international markets and the ways of doing so (exports, foreign direct investment, mergers, and joint ventures); also, you should know how investment cash flows in foreign projects will be measured.

Operations: You need to understand the costs and benefits of moving operations offshore and/or buying equipment, parts, and inventory in foreign markets. Such an understanding will allow you to participate in the firm's decisions with regard to international operations.

GENERAL ELECTRIC COMPANY

GROWING IN AN UNCERTAIN WORLD

The world's largest firm, **General Electric Company** (www.ge.com), with a market capitalization of more than $343 billion, considers globalization one of its core competencies. GE has manufactured and sold products outside the United States for 100 years, and a third of its leadership team is global. With global revenues of $61 billion (45 percent of its total revenues in 2003), the company expects its international sales to grow 15 percent in 2004. GE believes that global growth requires more than simply shipping products. A company must be equally committed to developing capabilities and relationships in the markets where it wants to succeed.

One of GE's markets is China, where its revenues totaled $2.6 billion in 2003. China will invest $300 billion for infrastructure—energy, aviation, water, and health care—in this decade. The 2008 Olympics in Beijing will be one of its massive infrastructure projects. With its superior infrastructure technology, GE expects to be a major participant in helping China prepare for the 2008 summer games. To support its Chinese customers, GE has more than 1,700 sales and service people on the ground. It has built a Global Research Center in Shanghai to develop the capabilities of its Chinese suppliers, and the company is training its own Chinese business leaders and customers in GE management techniques. In other words, it is treating China exactly as it does developed markets such as the United States, Japan, and Europe.

This approach is working in other developing markets. The firm's revenues in Eastern Europe, Russia, and Iraq are expected to grow from $1.2 billion in 2003 to $5 billion in 2005. GE recently signed a $700 million agreement to modernize the rail system in Russia and has an additional $2 billion of power project opportunities. GE's Consumer and Commercial Finance profits in Eastern Europe are growing 30 percent annually. With more than half of Iraq's power grid based on GE technology, the company has the capabilities that Iraq will need as it rebuilds. GE received $450 million of orders in Iraq in 2003 and believes that it could receive $3 billion more over the next few years.

Like GE, many companies are looking beyond their home countries' borders for new market opportunities. While globalization can bring controversy, companies such as GE believe that future growth requires that U.S. companies view the world as their market. This chapter will explain the additional considerations they must take into account as they apply the principles of managerial finance in the international setting.

Source: 2003 Annual Report, www.ge.com (accessed August 16, 2004).

■ *When countries or regions experience currency and/or economic stress, how might it affect a company that does business in that area of the world?*

LG3

LG5

LG3 LG5

LG5

Proble

LG1

INTERMEDIATE

LG3

INTERMEDIATE

Chapter 18 Case: Assessing a Direct Investment in Chile by U.S. Computer Corporation

David Smith is chief financial officer for U.S. Computer Corporation (USCC), a successful and rapidly growing manufacturer of personal computers. He has been asked to evaluate an investment project calling for USCC to build a factory in Chile to assemble the company's most popular computer for sale in the Chilean market. David knows that Chile has been a real business success story in recent years—having achieved economic growth rates averaging over 7% per year from 1990 through 2004, even as it made the transition from military dictatorship to democracy—and USCC is eager to invest in this developing economy if an attractive opportunity arises. David's job is to use the information below to see whether this particular proposal meets the company's investment standards.

On the basis of the current Chilean peso (Ps)-to-dollar exchange rate of Ps 700/US$ (assumed value), David calculates that the factory would cost Ps 7 billion ($10 million) to build (including working capital) and would generate sales of Ps 14 billion ($20 million) per year for the first several years. Initially, the factory would import key components from the United States and assemble the computers in Chile using local labor. Smith estimates that half the company's costs will be dollar-denominated components and half will be local currency (peso) costs, but all USCC's revenues will be in pesos. As long as the peso/dollar exchange rate is stable, the company's operating cash flow is expected to equal 20% of sales. If, however, the peso were to depreciate relative to the dollar, the company's peso cost of acquiring dollar-denominated components would increase, and its profit margin would shrink because the peso sale prices of its computers would not change.

If USCC made this investment, it would set up a subsidiary in Chile and structure the factory investment so that the subsidiary's capital structure was 60% debt and 40% equity. Therefore, to finance the Ps 7 billion factory cost, USCC must obtain Ps 4.2 billion ($6 million) in debt and Ps 2.8 billion ($4 million) in equity. The debt can be obtained either by issuing $6 million of dollar-denominated bonds in the Eurobond market at a 6% annual rate and then converting the proceeds into pesos or by borrowing the Ps 4.2 billion in the Chilean market at a 14% annual interest rate. If borrowing is done in dollars, however, the parent company must also service and repay the debt in dollars, even though all project revenues will be in pesos.

For simplicity, assume the parent company decides to contribute the equity capital for the project itself. USCC would do this by contributing $4 million to the subsidiary from its existing resources or from the proceeds of newly issued stock. This equity financing would then be converted to pesos. (Alternatively, the subsidiary could sell Ps 2.8 billion of stock to Chilean investors by listing shares on the Santiago Stock Exchange.) USCC has a 12% required return on equity on its dollar-denominated investments.

TO DO

a. Compute the *weighted average cost of capital* for this project, assuming that the long-term debt financing is in dollars.

b. Assuming that the peso/dollar exchange rate remains unchanged, compute the present value of the first 5 years of the project's cash flows, using the weighted average cost of capital computed in part **a.** (*Note:* Round off your answer in part **a** to the nearest 1% prior to making this calculation.) What happens to the present value if the dollar appreciates against the peso?

c. Identify the exchange rate risks involved in this project. Given that no forward, futures, or options market exists for the Chilean peso, how might USCC minimize the exchange rate risk of this project via changes in production, sourcing, and sales? (*Hint:* Exchange rate risk can be minimized by decreasing dollar-denominated costs, by increasing dollar-denominated revenue, or by doing both.)

d. What are the risks involved in financing this project as much as possible with local funds (pesos)? Which financing strategy—dollar versus peso—would minimize the project's exchange rate risk? Would your answer change if Chile began to experience political instability? What would happen to the attractiveness of the project if Chile joined NAFTA or signed a bilateral trade pact with the United States?

Spreadsheet Exercise

As the financial manager for a large multinational corporation (MNC), you have been asked to assess the firm's *economic exposure*. The two major currencies, other than the U.S. dollar, that affect the company are the Mexican peso (MP) and the British pound (£). You have been given the projected future cash flows for next year:

Currency	Total inflow	Total outflow
British pounds	£17,000,000	£11,000,000
Mexican pesos	MP 100,000,000	MP 25,000,000

The current expected exchange rate in U.S. dollars with respect to the two currencies is as follows:

Currency	Exchange rate
British pounds	$1.66
Mexican pesos	$0.10

TO DO

Assume that the movements in the Mexican peso and the British pound are highly correlated. Create a spreadsheet to answer the following questions.

a. Determine the net cash flows for both the Mexican peso and the British pound.

b. Determine the net cash flow as measured in U.S. dollars. It will represent the value of the *economic exposure.*

c. Provide your assessment as to the company's degree of economic exposure. In other words, is it high or low based on your findings in part **b?**

Group Exercise

This is the final chapter in this text and the final group assignment for your fictitious firm. In this chapter the author has "gone international" and your firm has now developed to a point where it is time to look for opportunities abroad.

TO DO

LG2 LG3 LG4 LG5

The first objective for your firm is to decide whether you are looking abroad for a new supplier or to expand your sales. You will then have to choose which country to investigate. Once these choices have been made and defended, you must address exchange rate risk. Up until now we have assumed that all costs and revenues were in dollars and therefore we avoided this issue. Accordingly, you have to find the recent exchange rate for this country in relation to the dollar and also look at the recent exchange rate history, say the last 5 years, to get a sense of its volatility. Now look up this country's inflation rate and compare it to the US CPI. If we expect the current inflation rates to continue over the following year, this information can be used to form expectations of changing exchange rates during the year. Compare your analysis of exchange rates using the respective inflation rates to the recent historical pattern of the exchange rate for your country. Lastly, explain what your firm perceives as the risk/reward tradeoff of going international.

Web Exercise

International trade continues to grow, shrinking the "size" of the world. This trend will continue as more nations open their markets. A major arbiter of rules regarding international trade is the World Trade Organization (WTO). Although referenced in the text, obviously there is much more to this organization which resolves trade disputes between nations. Your assignment is to investigate what the WTO does.

TO DO

Point your browser to www.wto.org/, the home page of the WTO. Explore and report on what the WTO does. One suggestion is to follow the Trade Topics link on the left side of the Web site. This link provides information about the different types of rulings made by the WTO.

> **Remember to check the book's Web site at**
>
> **www.aw-bc.com/gitman**
>
> **for additional resources, including additional Web exercises.**

Integrative Case

6

Organic Solutions

Organic Solutions (OS), one of the nation's largest plant wholesalers in the southeastern United States, was poised for expansion. Through strong profitability, a conservative dividend policy, and some recent realized gains in real estate, OS had a strong cash position and was searching for a target company to acquire. The executive members on the acquisition search committee had agreed that they preferred to find a firm in a similar line of business rather than one that would provide broad diversification. This would be their first acquisition, and they preferred to stay in a familiar line of business. Jennifer Morgan, director of marketing, had identified the targeted lines of business through exhaustive market research.

Ms. Morgan had determined that the servicing of plants in large commercial offices, hotels, zoos, and theme parks would complement the existing wholesale distribution business. Frequently, OS was requested by its large clients to bid on a service contract. However, the company was neither staffed nor equipped to enter this market. Ms. Morgan was familiar with the major plant service companies in the Southeast and had suggested Green Thumbs, Inc. (GTI), as an acquisition target because of its significant market share and excellent reputation.

GTI had successfully commercialized a market that had been dominated by small local contractors and in-house landscaping departments. By its first winning a contract from one of the largest theme parks in the United States, GTI's growth in sales had compounded remarkably over its 8-year history.

GTI had also been selected because of its large portfolio of long-term service contracts with several major *Fortune* 500 companies. These contracted clients would provide a captive customer base for the wholesale distribution of OS's plant products.

At the National Horticultural meeting in Los Angeles this past March, Ms. Morgan and OS's chief financial officer, Jack Levine, had approached the owner of GTI (a closely held corporation) to determine whether a merger offer would be welcomed. GTI's majority owner and president, Herb Merrell, had reacted favorably and subsequently provided financial data including GTI's earnings record and current balance sheet. This data is presented in Tables 1 and 2 on the next page.

Jack Levine had estimated that the incremental cash flow after taxes from the acquisition would be $18,750,000 for years 1 and 2; $20,500,000 for year 3; $21,750,000 for year 4;

$24,000,000 for year 5; and $25,000,000 for years 6 through 30. He also estimated that the company should earn a rate of return of at least 16% on an investment of this type. Additional financial data for 2006 are given in Table 3.

Table 1

Green Thumbs, Inc.
Earning Record

Year	EPS	Year	EPS
1999	$2.20	2003	$2.85
2000	2.35	2004	3.00
2001	2.45	2005	3.10
2002	2.60	2006	3.30

Table 2

Green Thumbs, Inc.
Balance Sheet (December 31, 2006)

Assets		Liabilities and Equity	
Cash	$ 2,500,000	Current liabilities	$ 5,250,000
Accounts receivable	1,500,000	Mortgage payable	3,125,000
Inventories	7,625,000	Common stock	15,625,000
Land	7,475,000	Retained earnings	9,000,000
Fixed assets (net)	13,900,000	Total liabilities and equity	$33,000,000
Total assets	$33,000,000		

Table 3

OS and GTI Financial Data
(December 31, 2006)

Item	OS	GTI
Earnings available for common stock	$35,000,000	$15,246,000
Number of shares of common stock	10,000,000	4,620,000
Market price per share	$50	$30[a]

[a]Estimated by Organic Solutions.

TO DO

a. What is the maximum price that Organic Solutions should offer GTI for a cash acquisition? (*Note:* Assume the relevant time horizon for analysis is 30 years.)

b. If OS planned to sell bonds to finance 80% of the cash acquisition price found in part **a,** how might issuance of each of the following bonds affect the firm? Describe the characteristics and pros and cons of each bond.
   (1) Straight bonds.
   (2) Convertible bonds.
   (3) Bonds with stock purchase warrants attached.

c. (1) What is the *ratio of exchange* in a stock swap acquisition if OS pays $30 per share for GTI? Explain why.
   (2) What effect will this swap of stock have on the EPS of the original shareholders of (i) Organic Solutions and (ii) Green Thumbs, Inc.? Explain why.
   (3) If the earnings attributed to GTI's assets grow at a much slower rate than those attributed to OS's premerger assets, what effect might this have on the EPS of the merged firm over the long run?

d. What other merger proposals could OS make to GTI's owners?

e. What impact would the fact that GTI is actually a foreign-based company have on the foregoing analysis? Describe the added regulations, costs, benefits, and risks that are likely to be associated with such an international merger.

Chapter 2

ST2–1

Ratio	Too high	Too low
Current ratio = current assets/ current liabilities	May indicate that the firm is holding excessive cash, accounts receivable, or inventory.	May indicate poor ability to satisfy short-term obligations.
Inventory turnover = CGS/inventory	May indicate lower level of inventory, which may cause stockouts and lost sales.	May indicate poor inventory management, excessive inventory, or obsolete inventory.
Times interest earned = earnings before interest and taxes/interest		May indicate poor ability to pay contractual interest payments.
Gross profit margin = gross profits/sales	Indicates the low cost of merchandise sold relative to the sales price; may indicate noncompetitive pricing and potential lost sales.	Indicates the high cost of the merchandise sold relative to the sales price; may indicate either a low sales price or a high cost of goods sold.
Return on total assets = net profits after taxes/total assets		Indicates ineffective management in generating profits with the available assets.
Price/earnings (P/E) ratio = market price per share of common stock/earnings per share	Investors may have an excessive degree of confidence in the firm's future and underestimate its risk.	Investors lack confidence in the firm's future outcomes and feel that the firm has an excessive level of risk.

ST2–2

O'Keefe Industries
Balance Sheet
December 31, 2006

Assets		Liabilities and Stockholders' Equity	
Cash	$ 32,720	Accounts payable	$ 120,000
Marketable securities	25,000	Notes payable	160,000[e]
Accounts receivable	197,280[a]	Accruals	20,000
Inventories	225,000[b]	Total current liabilities	$ 300,000[d]
Total current assets	$ 480,000	Long-term debt	$ 600,000[f]
Net fixed assets	$1,020,000[c]	Stockholders' equity	$ 600,000
Total assets	$1,500,000	Total liabilities and stockholders' equity	$1,500,000

[a]Average collection period (ACP) = 40 days
ACP = Accounts receivable/Average sales per day
40 = Accounts receivable/($1,800,000/365)
40 = Accounts receivable/$4,932
$197,280 = Accounts receivable

[b]Inventory turnover = 6.0
Inventory turnover = Cost of goods sold/Inventory
6.0 = [Sales × (1 = Gross profit margin)]/Inventory
6.0 = [$1,800,000 × (1 = 0.25)]/Inventory
$225,000 = Inventory

[c]Total asset turnover = 1.20
Total asset turnover = Sales/Total assets
1.20 = $1,800,000/Total assets
$1,500,000 = Total assets
Total assets = Current assets + Net fixed assets
$1,500,000 = $480,000 + Net fixed assets
$1,020,000 = Net fixed assets

[d]Current ratio = 1.60
Current ratio = Current assets/Current liabilities
1.60 = $480,000/Current liabilities
$300,000 = Current liabilities

[e]Notes payable = Total current liabilities − Accounts payable − Accruals
= $300,000 − $120,000 − $20,000
= $160,000

[f]Debt ratio = 0.60
Debt ratio = Total liabilities/Total assets
0.60 = Total liabilities/$1,500,000
$900,000 = Total liabilities

Total liabilities = Current liabilities + Long-term debt
$900,000 = $300,000 + Long-term debt
$600,000 = Long-term debt

Chapter 3

ST3-1 **a.** Depreciation Schedule

Year	Cost[a] (1)	Percentages (from Table 3.2) (2)	Depreciation [(1) × (2)] (3)
1	$150,000	20%	$ 30,000
2	150,000	32	48,000
3	150,000	19	28,500
4	150,000	12	18,000
5	150,000	12	18,000
6	150,000	5	7,500
	Totals	100%	$150,000

[a]$140,000 asset cost + $10,000 installation cost.

b. Accounting definition:

Year	EBIT (1)	Interest (2)	Net profits before taxes [(1) − (2)] (3)	Taxes [0.40 × (3)] (4)	Net profits after taxes [(3) − (4)] (5)	Depreciation (from part a, col. 3) (6)	Cash flows from operations [(5) + (6)] (7)
1	$160,000	$15,000	$145,000	$58,000	$87,000	$30,000	$117,000
2	160,000	15,000	145,000	58,000	87,000	48,000	135,000
3	160,000	15,000	145,500	58,000	87,000	28,500	115,500
4	160,000	15,000	145,000	58,000	87,000	18,000	105,000
5	160,000	15,000	145,000	58,000	87,000	18,000	105,000
6	160,000	15,000	145,500	58,000	87,000	7,500	94,500

Financial definition:

Year	EBIT (1)	NOPAT [(1) × (1 − 0.40)] (2)	Depreciation (3)	Operating cash flows [(2) + (3)] (4)
1	$160,000	$96,000	$30,000	$126,000
2	160,000	96,000	48,000	144,000
3	160,000	96,000	28,500	124,500
4	160,000	96,000	18,000	114,000
5	160,000	96,000	18,000	114,000
6	160,000	96,000	7,500	103,500

c. Change in net fixed assets in year 6 = $0 − $7,500 = −$7,500

NFAI in year 6 = −$7,500 + $7,500 = $0

Change in current assets in year 6 = $110,000 − $90,000 = $20,000

Change in (Accounts payable + Accruals) in year 6 = ($45,000 + $7,000) − ($40,000 + $8,000) = $52,000 − $48,000 = $4,000

NCAI in year 6 = $20,000 - $4,000 = $16,000

For year 6

FCF = OCF − NFAI − NCAI

= $103,500* − $0 − $16,000 = $87,500

*From part **b** financial definition, column 4 value for year 6.

d. In part **b** we can see that in each of the six years, the operating cash flow is greater when viewed from a financial perspective than when viewed from a strict accounting point of view. This difference results from the fact that the accounting definition includes interest as an operating flow, whereas the financial definition excludes it. This causes (in this case) each year's accounting flow to be $9,000 below the financial flow; $9,000 is equal to the after-tax cost of the $15,000 annual interest, $15,000 × (1 − 0.40). The free cash flow (FCF) calculated in part **c** for year 6 represents the cash flow available to investors—providers of debt and equity—after covering all operating needs and paying for net fixed asset investment (NFAI) and net current asset investment (NCAI) that occurred during the year.

ST3–2   a.

	Caroll Company Cash Budget April–June					Accounts receivable at end of June	
	February	March	April	May	June	July	August
Forecast sales	$500	$600	$400	$200	$200		
Cash sales (0.30)	$150	$180	$120	$ 60	$ 60		
Collections of A/R							
Lagged 1 month [(0.7 × 0.7) = 0.49]		245	294	196	98	$ 98	
Lagged 2 months [(0.3 × 0.7) = 0.21]			105	126	84	42	$42
						$140 + $42 = $182	
Total cash receipts			$519	$382	$242		
Less: Total cash disbursements			600	500	200		
Net cash flow			($ 81)	($118)	$ 42		
Add: Beginning cash			115	34	(84)		
Ending cash			$ 34	($ 84)	($ 42)		
Less: Minimum cash balance			25	25	25		
Required total financing (notes payable)			—	$109	$ 67		
Excess cash balance (marketable securities)			$ 9	—	—		

b. Caroll Company would need a maximum of $109 in financing over the 3-month period.

c.

Account	Amount	Source of amount
Cash	$ 25	Minimum cash balance—June
Notes payable	67	Required total financing—June
Marketable securities	0	Excess cash balance—June
Accounts receivable	182	Calculation at right of cash budget statement

ST3–3   a.

Euro Designs, Inc., Pro Forma Income Statement for the Year Ended December 31, 2007	
Sales revenue (given)	$3,900,000
Less: Cost of goods sold (0.55)[a]	2,145,000
Gross profits	$1,755,000
Less: Operating expenses (0.12)[b]	468,000
Operating profits	$1,287,000
Less: Interest expense (given)	325,000
Net profits before taxes	$ 962,000
Less: Taxes (0.40 × $962,000)	384,800
Net profits after taxes	$ 577,200
Less: Cash dividends (given)	320,000
To retained earnings	$ 257,200

[a]From 2006: CGS/Sales = $1,925,000/$3,500,000 = 0.55.
[b]From 2006: Oper. Exp./Sales = $420,000/$3,500,000 = 0.12.

b. The percent-of-sales method may underestimate actual 2007 pro forma income by assuming that all costs are variable. If the firm has fixed costs, which by definition would not increase with increasing sales, the 2007 pro forma income would probably be underestimated.

Chapter 4

ST4–1   a. *Bank A:*

$$FV_3 = \$10,000 \times FVIF_{4\%/3yrs} = \$10,000 \times 1.125 = \underline{\$11,250}$$

(Calculator solution = $11,248.64)

Bank B:

$$FV_3 = \$10,000 \times FVIF_{4\%/2,2 \times 3yrs} = \$10,000 \times FVIF_{2\%,6yrs}$$
$$= \$10,000 \times 1.126 = \underline{\$11,260}$$

(Calculator solution = $11,261.62)

Bank C:

$$FV_3 = \$10,000 \times FVIF_{4\%/4,4 \times 3yrs} = \$10,000 \times FVIF_{1\%,12yrs}$$
$$= \$10,000 \times 1.127 = \underline{\$11,270}$$

(Calculator solution = $11,268.25)

b. *Bank A:*

$$EAR = (1 + 4\%/1)^1 - 1 = (1 + 0.04)^1 - 1 = 1.04 - 1 = 0.04 = \underline{4\%}$$

Bank B:

$$EAR = (1 + 4\%/2)^2 - 1 = (1 + 0.02)^2 - 1 = 1.0404 - 1 = 0.0404 = \underline{4.04\%}$$

Bank C:

$$EAR = (1 + 4\%/4)^4 - 1 = (1 + 0.01)^4 - 1 = 1.0406 - 1 = 0.0406 = \underline{4.06\%}$$

   c. Ms. Martin should deal with Bank C: The quarterly compounding of interest at the given 4% rate results in the highest future value as a result of the corresponding highest effective annual rate.

   d. *Bank D:*

$$FV_3 = \$10,000 \times FVIF_{4\%,3yrs} \text{ (continuous compounding)}$$
$$= \$10,000 \times e^{0.04 \times 3} = \$10,000 \times e^{0.12}$$
$$= \$10,000 \times 1.127497$$
$$= \underline{\underline{\$11,274.97}}$$

This alternative is better than Bank C; it results in a higher future value because of the use of continuous compounding, which with otherwise identical cash flows always results in the highest future value of any compounding period.

ST4–2 **a.** On a purely subjective basis, annuity Y looks more attractive than annuity X because it provides $1,000 more each year than does annuity X. Of course, the fact that X is an annuity due means that the $9,000 would be received at the beginning of the first year, unlike the $10,000 at the end of the year, and this makes annuity X awfully tempting.

  b. *Annuity X:*

$$FVA_6 = \$9,000 \times FVIFA_{15\%,6yrs} \times (1 + 0.15)$$
$$= \$9,000 \times 8.754 \times 1.15 = \underline{\$90,603.90}$$

(Calculator solution = $90,601.19)

Annuity Y:

$$FVA_6 = \$10,000 \times FVIFA_{15\%,6yrs}$$
$$= \$10,000 \times 8.754 = \underline{\$87,540.00}$$

(Calculator solution = $87,537.38)

  c. Annuity X is more attractive, because its future value at the end of year 6, FVA_6, of $90,603.90 is greater than annuity Y's end-of-year-6 future value, FVA_6, of $87,540.00. The subjective assessment in part **a** was incorrect. The benefit of receiving annuity X's cash inflows at the beginning of each year appears to have outweighed the fact that annuity Y's annual cash inflow, which occurs at the end of each year, is $1,000 larger ($10,000 vs. $9,000) than annuity X's.

ST4–3 *Alternative A:*

Cash flow stream:

$$PVA_5 = \$700 \times PVIFA_{9\%,5yrs}$$
$$= \$700 \times 3.890 = \underline{\$2,723}$$

(Calculator solution = $2,722.76)

Single amount: $\underline{\$2,825}$

Alternative B:

Cash flow stream:

Year (n)	Cash flow (1)	$PVIF_{9\%,n}$ (2)	Present value [(1) × (2)] (3)
1	$1,100	0.917	$1,008.70
2	900	0.842	757.80
3	700	0.772	540.40
4	500	0.708	354.00
5	300	0.650	195.00
		Present value	$2,855.90

(Calculator solution = $2,856.41)

Single amount: $2,800

Conclusion: Alternative B in the form of a cash flow stream is preferred because its present value of $2,855.90 is greater than the other three values.

ST4–4 $FVA_5 = \$8,000$; $FVIFA_{7\%,5yrs} = 5.751$; $PMT = ?$

$FVA_n = PMT \times (FVIFA_{k,n})$ [Equation 4.14 or 4.24]

$\$8,000 = PMT \times 5.751$

$PMT = \$8,000/5.751 = \underline{\$1,391.06}$

(Calculator solution = $1,391.13)

Judi should deposit $1,391.06 at the end of each of the 5 years to meet her goal of accumulating $8,000 at the end of the fifth year.

Chapter 5

ST5–1 a. Expected return, $\bar{k} = \dfrac{\Sigma \text{Returns}}{3}$ *(Equation 5.2a in footnote 9)*

$$\bar{k}_A = \frac{12\% + 14\% + 16\%}{3} = \frac{42\%}{3} = \underline{\underline{14\%}}$$

$$\bar{k}_B = \frac{16\% + 14\% + 12\%}{3} = \frac{42\%}{3} = \underline{\underline{14\%}}$$

$$\bar{k}_C = \frac{12\% + 14\% + 16\%}{3} = \frac{42\%}{3} = \underline{\underline{14\%}}$$

b. Standard deviation, $\sigma_k = \sqrt{\dfrac{\sum_{j=1}^{n}(k_i - \bar{k})^2}{n-1}}$ *(Equation 5.3a in footnote 10)*

$$\sigma_{k_A} = \sqrt{\frac{(12\% - 14\%)^2 + (14\% - 14\%)^2 + (16\% - 14\%)^2}{3-1}}$$

$$= \sqrt{\frac{4\% + 0\% + 4\%}{2}} = \sqrt{\frac{8\%}{2}} = \underline{\underline{2\%}}$$

$$\sigma_{k_B} = \sqrt{\frac{(16\% - 14\%)^2 + (14\% - 14\%)^2 + (12\% - 14\%)^2}{3 - 1}}$$

$$= \sqrt{\frac{4\% + 0\% + 4\%}{2}} = \sqrt{\frac{8\%}{2}} = \underline{\underline{2\%}}$$

$$\sigma_{k_C} = \sqrt{\frac{(12\% - 14\%)^2 + (14\% - 14\%)^2 + (16\% - 14\%)^2}{3 - 1}}$$

$$= \sqrt{\frac{4\% + 0\% + 4\%}{2}} = \sqrt{\frac{8\%}{2}} = \underline{\underline{2\%}}$$

c.

		Annual expected returns	
Year	Portfolio AB		Portfolio AC
2007	$(0.50 \times 12\%) + (0.50 \times 16\%) = 14\%$		$(0.50 \times 12\%) + (0.50 \times 12\%) = 12\%$
2008	$(0.50 \times 14\%) + (0.50 \times 14\%) = 14\%$		$(0.50 \times 14\%) + (0.50 \times 14\%) = 14\%$
2009	$(0.50 \times 16\%) + (0.50 \times 12\%) = 14\%$		$(0.50 \times 16\%) + (0.50 \times 16\%) = 16\%$

Over the 3-year period:

$$\bar{k}_{AB} = \frac{14\% + 14\% + 14\%}{3} = \frac{42\%}{3} = \underline{\underline{14\%}}$$

$$\bar{k}_{AC} = \frac{12\% + 14\% + 16\%}{3} = \frac{42\%}{3} = \underline{\underline{14\%}}$$

d. AB is perfectly negatively correlated.

AC is perfectly positively correlated.

e. Standard deviation of the portfolios

$$\sigma_{k_{AB}} = \sqrt{\frac{(14\% - 14\%)^2 + (14\% - 14\%)^2 + (14\% - 14\%)^2}{3 - 1}}$$

$$= \sqrt{\frac{(0\% + 0\% + 0\%)}{2}} = \sqrt{\frac{0\%}{2}} = \underline{\underline{0\%}}$$

$$\sigma_{k_{AC}} = \sqrt{\frac{(12\% - 14\%)^2 + (14\% - 14\%)^2 + (16\% - 14\%)^2}{3 - 1}}$$

$$= \sqrt{\frac{4\% + 0\% + 4\%}{2}} = \sqrt{\frac{8\%}{2}} = \underline{\underline{2\%}}$$

f. Portfolio AB is preferred, because it provides the same return (14%) as AC but with less risk $[(\sigma_{k_{AB}} = 0\%) < (\sigma_{k_{AC}} = 2\%)]$.

ST5–2 a. When the market return increases by 10%, the project's required return would be expected to increase by 15% ($1.50 \times 10\%$). When the market return decreases by 10%, the project's required return would be expected to decrease by 15% $[1.50 \times (-10\%)]$.

b. $k_j = R_F + [b_j \times (k_m - R_F)]$

$= 7\% + [1.50 \times (10\% - 7\%)]$

$= 7\% + 4.5\% = \underline{\underline{11.5\%}}$

c. No, the project should be rejected, because its *expected* return of 11% is less than the 11.5% return *required* from the project.

d. $k_j = 7\% + [1.50 \times (9\% - 7\%)]$

$= 7\% + 3\% = \underline{\underline{10\%}}$

The project would now be acceptable, because its *expected* return of 11% is now in excess of the *required* return, which has declined to 10% as a result of investors in the marketplace becoming less risk-averse.

Chapter 6

ST6–1 **a.** $B_0 = I \times (PVIFA_{k_d,n}) + M \times (PVIF_{k_d,n})$

$I = 0.08 \times \$1,000 = \$80$

$M = \$1,000$

$n = 12$ yrs

(1) $k_d = 7\%$

$B_0 = \$80 \times (PVIFA_{7\%,12\text{yrs}}) + \$1,000 \times (PVIF_{7\%,12\text{yrs}})$

$= (\$80 \times 7.943) + (\$1,000 \times 0.444)$

$= \$635.44 + \$444.00 = \underline{\underline{\$1,079.44}}$

(Calculator solution = $1,079.43)

(2) $k_d = 8\%$

$B_0 = \$80 \times (PVIFA_{8\%,12\text{yrs}}) + \$1,000 \times (PVIF_{8\%,12\text{yrs}})$

$= (\$80 \times 7.536) + (\$1,000 \times 0.397)$

$= \$602.88 + \$397.00 = \underline{\underline{\$999.88}}$

(Calculator solution = $1,000)

(3) $k_d = 10\%$

$B_0 = \$80 \times (PVIFA_{10\%,12\text{yrs}}) + \$1,000 \times (PVIF_{10\%,12\text{yrs}})$

$= (\$80 \times 6.814) + (\$1,000 \times 0.319)$

$= \$545.12 + \$319.00 = \underline{\underline{\$864.12}}$

(Calculator solution = $863.73)

b. (1) $k_d = 7\%$, $B_0 = \$1,079.44$; sells at a *premium*

(2) $k_d = 8\%$, $B_0 = \$999.88 \approx \$1,000.00$; sells at its *par value*

(3) $k_d = 10\%$, $B_0 = \$864.12$; sells at a *discount*

c. $B_0 = \dfrac{I}{2} \times (PVIFA_{k_d/2,2n}) + M \times (PVIF_{k_d/2,2n})$

$= \dfrac{\$80}{2} \times (PVIFA_{10\%/2,2\times12\text{periods}}) + \$1,000 \times (PVIF_{10\%/2,2\times12\text{periods}})$

$= \$40 \times (PVIFA_{5\%,24\text{periods}}) + \$1,000 \times (PVIF_{5\%,24\text{periods}})$

$= (\$40 \times 13.799) + (\$1,000 \times 0.310)$

$= \$551.96 + \$310.00 = \underline{\underline{\$861.96}}$

(Calculator solution = $862.01)

ST6–2 **a.** $B_0 = \$1,150$

$I = 0.11 \times \$1,000 = \$110$

$M = \$1,000$

$n = 18$ yrs

$\$1,150 = \$110 \times (PVIFA_{k_d,18\text{yrs}}) + \$1,000 \times (PVIF_{k_d,18\text{yrs}})$

Because if $k_d = 11\%$, $B_0 = \$1,000 = M$, try $k_d = 10\%$.

$B_0 = \$110 \times (PVIFA_{10\%,18\text{yrs}}) + \$1,000 \times (PVIF_{10\%,18\text{yrs}})$

$= (\$110 \times 8.201) + (\$1,000 \times 0.180)$

$= \$902.11 + \$180.00 = \$1,082.11$

Because $\$1,082.11 < \$1,150$, try $k_d = 9\%$.

$B_0 = \$110 \times (PVIFA_{9\%,18\text{yrs}}) + \$1,000 \times (PVIF_{9\%,18\text{yrs}})$

$= (\$110 \times 8.756) + (\$1,000 \times 0.212)$

$= \$963.16 + \$212.00 = \$1,175.16$

Because the $\$1,175.16$ value at 9% is higher than $\$1,150$, and the $\$1,082.11$ value at 10% rate is lower than $\$1,150$, the bond's yield to maturity must be between 9% and 10%. Because the $\$1,175.16$ value is closer to $\$1,150$, rounding to the nearest whole percent, the YTM is 9%. (By using interpolation, the more precise YTM value is 9.27%.)

(Calculator solution = 9.26%)

b. The calculated YTM of 9+% is below the bond's 11% coupon interest rate, because the bond's market value of $\$1,150$ is above its $\$1,000$ par value. Whenever a bond's market value is above its par value (it sells at a *premium*), its YTM will be below its coupon interest rate; when a bond sells at *par*, the YTM will equal its coupon interest rate; and when the bond sells for less than par (at a *discount*), its YTM will be greater than its coupon interest rate.

Chapter 7

ST7–1 $D_0 = \$1.80$/share

$k_s = 12\%$

a. *Zero growth:*

$$P_0 = \frac{D_1}{k_s} = \frac{D_1 = D_0 = \$1.80}{0.12} = \underline{\underline{\$15\text{/share}}}$$

b. *Constant growth, g = 5%:*

$D_1 = D_0 \times (1 + g) = \$1.80 = (1 + 0.05) = \$1.89$/share

$$P_0 = \frac{D_1}{k_s - g} = \frac{\$1.89}{0.12 - 0.05} = \frac{\$1.89}{0.07} = \underline{\underline{\$27\text{/share}}}$$

c. *Variable growth, N = 3, $g_1 = 5\%$ for years 1 to 3 and $g_2 = 4\%$ for years 4 to ∞:*

$D_1 = D_0 \times (1 + g_1)^1 = \$1.80 \times (1 + 0.05)^1 = \$1.89$/share

$D_2 = D_0 \times (1 + g_1)^2 = \$1.80 \times (1 + 0.05)^2 = \$1.98$/share

$D_3 = D_0 \times (1 + g_1)^3 = \$1.80 \times (1 + 0.05)^3 = \$2.08$/share

$D_4 = D_3 \times (1 + g_2) = \$2.08 \times (1 + 0.04) = \$2.16$/share

$$P_0 = \sum_{t=1}^{N} \frac{D_0 \times (1 + g_1)^t}{(1 + k_s)^t} + \left(\frac{1}{(1 + k_s)^N} \times \frac{D_{N+1}}{k_s - g_2} \right)$$

$$\sum_{t=1}^{N} \frac{D_0 \times (1 + g_1)^t}{(1 + k_s)^t} + \frac{1.89}{(1 + 0.12)^1} + \frac{1.98}{(1 + 0.12)^2} + \frac{2.08}{(1 + 0.12)^3}$$

$$= [\$1.89 \times (PVIF_{12\%,1yr})] + [\$1.98 \times (PVIF_{12\%,2yrs})]$$
$$+ [\$2.08 \times (PVIF_{12\%,3yrs})]$$

$$= (\$1.89 \times 0.893) + (\$1.98 \times 0.797) + (\$2.08 \times 0.712)$$

$$= \$1.69 + \$1.58 + \$1.48 = \$4.75$$

$$\left[\frac{1}{(1 + k_s)^N} \times \frac{D_{N+1}}{k_s - g_2} \right] = \frac{1}{(1 + 0.12)^3} \times \frac{D_4 = \$2.16}{0.12 - 0.04}$$

$$= (PVIF_{12\%,3yrs}) \times \frac{\$2.16}{0.08}$$

$$= 0.712 \times \$27.00 = \$19.22$$

$$P_0 = \sum_{t=1}^{N} \frac{D_0 \times (1 + g_1)^t}{(1 + k_s)^t} + \left[\frac{1}{(1 + k_s)^N} \times \frac{D_{N+1}}{k_s - g_2} \right] = \$4.75 + \$19.22$$

$$= \underline{\$23.97/\text{share}}$$

ST7–2   **a.** **Step 1:** Present value of free cash flow from end of 2011 to infinity measured at the end of 2010.

$$FCF_{2011} = \$1,500,000 \times (1 + 0.04) = \$1,560,000$$

$$\text{Value of } FCF_{2011 \to \infty} = \frac{\$1,560,000}{0.10 - 0.04} = \frac{\$1,560,000}{0.06} = \underline{\$26,000,000}$$

Step 2: Add the value found in Step 1 to the 2010 FCF.

Total $FCF_{2010} = \$1,500,000 + \$26,000,000 = \underline{\$27,500,000}$

Step 3: Find the sum of the present values of the FCFs for 2007 through 2010 to determine company value, V_C.

Year (t)	FCF_t (1)	$PVIF_{10\%,t}$ (2)	Present value of FCF_t [(1) × (2)] (3)
2007	$ 800,000	0.909	$ 727,200
2008	1,200,000	0.826	991,200
2009	1,400,000	0.751	1,051,400
2010	27,500,000	0.683	18,782,500
		Value of entire company, $V_C =$	$\underline{\$21,552,300}$

(Calculator solution = $21,553,719)

b. Common Stock value, $V_S = V_C - V_D - V_P$

$V_C = \$21,552,300$ (calculated in part **a**)

$V_D = \$12,500,000$ (given)

$V_P = \$0$ (given)

$V_S = \$21,552,300 - \$12,500,000 - \$0 = \underline{\$9,052,300}$

(Calculator solution = $9,053,719)

c. Price per share $= \dfrac{\$9,052,300}{500,000} = \underline{\underline{\$18.10/\text{share}}}$

(Calculator solution = $18.11/share)

Chapter 8

ST8–1 **a.** Book value = Installed cost − Accumulated depreciation
Installed cost = $50,000
Accumulated depreciation $= \$50,000 \times (0.20 + 0.32 + 0.19 + 0.12)$
$= \$50,000 \times 0.83 = \$41,500$
Book value $= \$50,000 - \$41,500 = \underline{\underline{\$8,500}}$

b. Taxes on sale of old equipment:
Gain on sale = Sale price − Book value
$= \$55,000 - \$8,500 = \$46,500$
Taxes $= 0.40 \times \$46,500 = \underline{\underline{\$18,600}}$

c. Initial investment:

Installed cost of new equipment		
Cost of new equipment	$75,000	
+ Installation costs	5,000	
Total installed cost—new		$80,000
− After-tax proceeds from sale of old equipment		
Proceeds from sale of old equipment	$55,000	
− Taxes on sale of old equipment	18,600	
Total after-tax proceeds—old		36,400
+ Change in net working capital		15,000
Initial investment		$58,600

ST8–2 **a.** Initial investment:

Installed cost of new machine		
Cost of new machine	$140,000	
+ Installation costs	10,000	
Total installed cost—new		
(depreciable value)		$150,000
− After-tax proceeds from sale of old machine		
Proceeds from sale of old machine	$ 42,000	
− Taxes on sale of old machine[1]	9,120	
Total after-tax proceeds—old		32,880
+ Change in net working capital[2]		20,000
Initial investment		$137,120

---

[1]Book value of old machine $= \$40,000 - [(0.20 + 0.32) \times \$40,000]$
$= \$40,000 - (0.52 \times \$40,000)$
$= \$40,000 - \$20,800 = \$19,200$
Gain on sale $= \$42,000 - \$19,200 = \$22,800$
Taxes $= .40 \times \$22,800 = \underline{\underline{\$9,120}}$

[2]Change in net working capital $= +\$10,000 + \$25,000 - \$15,000$
$= \$35,000 - \$15,000 = \underline{\underline{\$20,000}}$

b. Incremental operating cash inflows:

Calculation of Depreciation Expense

Year	Cost (1)	Applicable MACRS depreciation percentages (from Table 3.2) (2)	Depreciation [(1) × (2)] (3)
With new machine			
1	$150,000	33%	$ 49,500
2	150,000	45	67,500
3	150,000	15	22,500
4	150,000	7	10,500
		Totals 100%	$150,000
With old machine			
2	$ 40,000	19% (year-3 depreciation)	$ 7,600
2	40,000	12 (year-4 depreciation)	4,800
3	40,000	12 (year-5 depreciation)	4,800
4	40,000	5 (year-6 depreciation)	2,000
		Total	$19,200[a]

[a]The total of $19,200 represents the book value of the old machine at the end of the second year, which was calculated in part **a.**

Calculation of Operating Cash Inflows

	Year			
	1	2	3	4
With new machine				
Earnings before depr., int., and taxes[a]	$120,000	$130,000	$130,000	$ 0
− Depreciation[b]	49,500	67,500	22,500	10,500
Earnings before int. and taxes	$ 70,500	$ 62,500	$107,500	−$10,500
− Taxes (rate, $T = 40\%$)	28,200	25,000	43,000	− 4,200
Net operating profit after taxes	$ 42,300	$ 37,500	$ 64,500	−$ 6,300
+ Depreciation[b]	49,500	67,500	22,500	10,500
Operating cash inflows	$ 91,800	$105,000	$ 87,000	$ 4,200
With old machine				
Earnings before depr., int., and taxes[a]	$ 70,000	$ 70,000	$ 70,000	$ 0
− Depreciation[c]	7,600	4,800	4,800	2,000
Earnings before int. and taxes	$ 62,400	$ 65,200	$ 65,200	−$ 2,000
− Taxes (rate, $T = 40\%$)	24,960	26,080	26,080	− 800
Net operating profit after taxes	$ 37,440	$ 39,120	$ 39,120	−$ 1,200
+ Depreciation	7,600	4,800	4,800	2,000
Operating cash inflows	$ 45,040	$ 43,920	$ 43,920	$ 800

[a]Given in the problem.

[b]From column 3 of the preceding table, top.

[c]From column 3 of the preceding table, bottom.

	Calculation of Incremental Operating Cash Inflows		
	Operating cash inflows		
Year	New machine[a] (1)	Old machine[a] (2)	Incremental (relevant) [(1) − (2)] (3)
1	$ 91,800	$45,040	$46,760
2	105,000	43,920	61,080
3	87,000	43,920	43,080
4	4,200	800	3,400

[a]From the final row for the respective machine in the preceding table.

c. Terminal cash flow (end of year 3):

    After-tax proceeds from sale of new machine

        Proceeds from sale of new machine $35,000

            Total after-tax proceeds—new[1]   9,800

            Total after-tax proceeds—new $25,200

   − After-tax proceeds from sale of old machine

        Proceeds from sale of old machine $ 0

      − Tax on sale of old machine[2]   − 800

            Total after-tax proceeds—old   800

  + Change in net working capital   20,000

            Terminal cash flow $44,400

[1]Book value of new machine at end of year 3
$$= \$150,000 - [(0.33 + 0.45 + 0.15) \times \$150,000] = \$150,000 - (0.93 \times \$150,000)$$
$$= \$15,000 - \$139,500 = \$10,500$$
Tax on sale $= 0.40 \times (\$35,000 \text{ sale price} - \$10,500 \text{ book value})$
$$= 0.40 \times \$24,500 = \underline{\$9,800}$$

[2]Book value of old machine at end of year 3
$$= \$40,000 - [(0.20 + 0.32 + 0.19 + 0.12 + 0.12) \times \$40,000] = \$40,000 - (0.95 \times \$40,000)$$
$$= \$40,000 - \$38,000 = \$2,000$$

Tax on sale $= 0.40 \times (\$0 \text{ sale price} - \$2,000 \text{ book value})$
$$= 0.40 \times (-\$2,500 = -\underline{\$800} \text{ (i.e., \$800 tax saving)}$$

d.

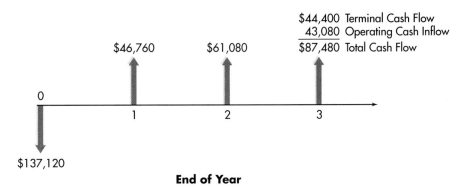

$44,400 Terminal Cash Flow
43,080 Operating Cash Inflow
$87,480 Total Cash Flow

$46,760 $61,080

0

1   2   3

$137,120

End of Year

Note: The year-4 incremental operating cash inflow of $3,400 is not directly included; it is instead reflected in the book values used to calculate the taxes on sale of the machines at the end of year 3 and is therefore part of the terminal cash flow.

Chapter 9

ST9–1 **a.** Payback period:

Project M: $\dfrac{\$28,500}{\$10,000} = \underline{\underline{2.85}}$ years

Project N:

Year (t)	Cash inflows (CF$_t$)	Cumulative cash inflows
1	$11,000	$11,000
2	10,000	21,000 ←
3	9,000	30,000
4	8,000	38,000

$$2 + \frac{\$27,000 - \$21,000}{\$9,000} \text{ years}$$

$$2 + \frac{\$6,000}{\$9,000} \text{ years} = \underline{\underline{2.67}} \text{ years}$$

b. Net present value (NPV):

Project M: NPV $= (\$10,000 \times PVIFA_{14\%,4\text{yrs}}) - \$28,500$
$= (\$10,000 \times 2.914) - \$28,500$
$= \$29,140 - \$28,500 = \underline{\underline{\$640}}$

(Calculator solution = $637.12)

Project N:

Year (t)	Cash inflows (CF$_t$) (1)	PVIF$_{14\%,t}$ (2)	Present value at 14% [(1) ÷ (2)] (3)
1	$11,000	0.877	$ 9,647
2	10,000	0.769	7,690
3	9,000	0.675	6,075
4	8,000	0.592	4,736
		Present value of cash inflows	$28,148
	− Initial investment		27,000
	Net present value (NPV)		$ 1,148

(Calculator solution = $1,155.18)

c. Internal rate of return (IRR):

Project M: $\dfrac{\$28,500}{\$10,000} = 2.850$

$PVIFA_{IRR,4yrs} = 2.850$

From Table A–4:

$PVIFA_{15\%,4yrs} = 2.855$

$PVIFA_{16\%,4yrs} = 2.798$

IRR = $\underline{\underline{15\%}}$ (2.850 is closest to 2.855)

(Calculator solution = 15.09%)

Project N:

Average annual cash inflow $= \dfrac{\$11,000 + \$10,000 + \$9,000 + \$8,000}{4}$

$= \dfrac{\$38,000}{4} = \$9,500$

$PVIFA_{k,4yrs} = \dfrac{\$27,000}{\$9,500} = 2.842$

$k \approx 15\%$

Try 16%, because there are more cash inflows in early years.

Year (t)	CF_t (1)	$PVIF_{16\%,t}$ (2)	Present value at 16% [(1) × (2)] (3)	$PVIF_{17\%,t}$ (4)	Present value at 17% [(1) × (4)] (5)
1	$11,000	0.862	$ 9,482	0.855	$ 9,405
2	10,000	0.743	7,430	0.731	7,310
3	9,000	0.641	5,769	0.624	5,616
4	8,000	0.552	4,416	0.534	4,272
	Present value of cash inflows		$27,097		$26,603
	− Initial investment		27,000		27,000
	NPV		$ 97		−$ 397

IRR = $\underline{\underline{16\%}}$ (rounding to nearest whole percent)

(Calculator solution = 16.19%)

d.

	Project M	Project N
Payback period	2.85 years	2.67 years[a]
NPV	$640	$1,148[a]
IRR	15%	16%[a]

[a]Preferred project.

Project N is recommended, because it has the shorter payback period and the higher NPV, which is greater than zero, and the larger IRR, which is greater than the 14% cost of capital.

e. Net present value profiles:

	Data	
		NPV
Discount rate	Project M	Project N
0%	$11,500[a]	$11,000[b]
14	640	1,148
15	0	—
16	—	0

[a]($10,000 + $10,000 + $10,000 + $10,000) − $28,500
 = $40,000 − $28,500
 = $11,500
[b]($11,000 + $10,000 + $9,000 + $8,000) − $27,000
 = $38,000 − $27,000
 = $11,000

From the NPV profile that follows, it can be seen that if the firm has a cost of capital below approximately 6% (exact value is 5.75%), conflicting rankings of the projects would exist using the NPV and IRR decision techniques. Because the firm's cost of capital is 14%, it can be seen in part **d** that no conflict exists.

Discount Rate (%)

Chapter 10

ST10–1 a. $NPV_A = (\$7,000 \times PVIFA_{10\%, 3yrs}) - \$15,000$

$= (\$7,000 \times 2.487) - \$15,000$

$= \$17,409 - \$15,000 = \underline{\$2,409}$

(Calculator solution = $2,407.96)

$$NPV_B = (\$10,000 \times PVIFA_{10\%,3yrs}) - \$20,000$$
$$= (\$10,000 - 2.487) - \$20,000$$
$$= \$24,870 - \$20,000 = \underline{\$4,870}^*$$

(Calculator solution = $4,868.52)

*Preferred project, because higher NPV.

b. From the CAPM-type relationship, the risk-adjusted discount rate ($RADR$) for project A, which has a risk index of 0.4, is 9%; for project B, with a risk index of 1.8, the $RADR$ is 16%.

$$NPV_A = (\$7,000 \times PVIFA_{9\%,3yrs}) - \$15,000$$
$$= (\$7,000 \times 2.531) - \$15,000$$
$$= \$17,717 - \$15,000 = \underline{\$2,717}^*$$

(Calculator solution = $2,719.06)

$$NPV_B = (\$10,000 \times PVIFA_{16\%,3yrs}) - \$20,000$$
$$= (\$10,000 \times 2.246) - \$20,000$$
$$= \$22,460 - \$20,000 = \underline{\$2,460}$$

(Calculator solution = $2,458.90)

*Preferred project, because higher NPV.

c. When the differences in risk were ignored in part **a,** project B was preferred over project A; but when the higher risk of project B is incorporated into the analysis using risk-adjusted discount rates in part **b,** *project A is preferred over project B.* Clearly, project A should be implemented.

Chapter 11

ST11–1 a. Cost of debt, k_i (using approximation formula)

$$k_d = \frac{I + \dfrac{\$1,000 - N_d}{n}}{\dfrac{N_d + \$1,000}{2}}$$

$$I = 0.10 \times \$1,000 = \$100$$
$$N_d = \$1,000 - \$30 \text{ discount} - \$20 \text{ flotation cost} = \$950$$
$$n = 10 \text{ years}$$

$$k_d = \frac{\$100 + \dfrac{\$1,000 - \$950}{10}}{\dfrac{\$950 + \$1,000}{2}} = \frac{\$100 + \$5}{\$975} = 10.8\%$$

(Calculator solution = 10.8%)
$$k_i = k_d \times (1 - T)$$
$$T = 0.40$$
$$k_i = 10.8\% \times (1 - 0.40) = \underline{\underline{6.5\%}}$$

Cost of preferred stock, k_p

$$k_p = \frac{D_p}{N_p}$$

$D_p = 0.11 \times \$100 = \$11$

$N_p = \$100 - \$4 \text{ flotation cost} = \$96$

$$k_p = \frac{\$11}{\$96} = \underline{\underline{11.5\%}}$$

Cost of retained earnings, k_r

$$k_r = k_s = \frac{D_1}{P_0} + g$$

$$= \frac{\$6}{\$80} + 6.0\% = 7.5\% + 6.0\% = \underline{\underline{13.5\%}}$$

Cost of new common stock, k_n

$$k_n = \frac{D_1}{N_n} + g$$

$D_1 = \$6$

$N_n = \$80 - \$4 \text{ underpricing} - \$4 \text{ flotation cost} = \$72$

$g = 6.0\%$

$$k_n = \frac{\$6}{\$72} + 6.0\% = 8.3\% + 6.0\% = \underline{\underline{14.3\%}}$$

b. (1) Break point, BP

$$BP_{\text{common equity}} = \frac{AF_{\text{common equity}}}{w_{\text{common equity}}}$$

$AF_{\text{common equity}} = \$225,000$

$w_{\text{common equity}} = 45\%$

$$BP_{\text{common equity}} = \frac{\$225,000}{0.45} = \$500,000$$

(2) WACC for total new financing $< \$500,000$

Source of capital	Weight (1)	Cost (2)	Weighted cost [(1) × (2)] (3)
Long-term debt	.40	6.5%	2.6%
Preferred stock	.15	11.5	1.7
Common stock equity	.45	13.5	6.1
Totals	1.00		10.4%

Weighted average cost of capital $= 10.4\%$

(3) WACC for total new financing > $500,000

Source of capital	Weight (1)	Cost (2)	Weighted cost [(1) × (2)] (3)
Long-term debt	.40	6.5%	2.6%
Preferred stock	.15	11.5	1.7
Common stock equity	.45	14.3	6.4
Totals	1.00		10.7%

Weighted average cost of capital = 10.7%

c. IOS data for graph

Investment opportunity	Internal rate of return (IRR)	Initial investment	Cumulative investment
D	16.5%	$200,000	$ 200,000
C	12.9	150,000	350,000
E	11.8	450,000	800,000
A	11.2	100,000	900,000
G	10.5	300,000	1,200,000
F	10.1	600,000	1,800,000
B	9.7	500,000	2,300,000

Total New Financing or Investment ($000)

d. Projects D, C, E, and A should be accepted because their respective IRRs exceed the WMCC. They will require $900,000 of total new financing.

Chapter 12

ST12–1 **a.** $Q = \dfrac{FC}{P - VC}$

$$= \frac{\$250,000}{\$7.50 - \$3.00} = \frac{\$250,000}{\$4.50} = \underline{\underline{55,556}} \text{ units}$$

b.

		+20%
Sales (in units)	100,000	120,000
Sales revenue (units × $7.50/unit)	$750,000	$900,000
Less: Variable operating costs (units × $3.00/unit)	300,000	360,000
Less: Fixed operating costs	250,000	250,000
Earnings before interest and taxes (EBIT)	$200,000	$290,000

+45%

Less: Interest	80,000	80,000
Net profits before taxes	$120,000	$210,000
Less: Taxes ($T = 0.40$)	48,000	84,000
Net profits after taxes	$ 72,000	$126,000
Less: Preferred dividends (8,000 shares × $5.00/share)	40,000	40,000
Earnings available for common	$132,000	$ 86,000
Earnings per share (EPS)	$32,000/20,000 = $1.60/share	$86,000/20,000 = $4.30/share

+169%

$$\textbf{c.} \quad \text{DOL} = \frac{\% \text{ change in EBIT}}{\% \text{ change in sales}} = \frac{+45\%}{+20\%} = \underline{\underline{2.25}}$$

$$\textbf{d.} \quad \text{DFL} = \frac{\% \text{ change in EPS}}{\% \text{ change in EBIT}} = \frac{+169\%}{+45} = \underline{\underline{3.76}}$$

e. DTL = DOL × DFL

$\qquad = 2.25 \times 3.76 = \underline{\underline{8.46}}$

Using the other DTL formula:

$$\text{DTL} = \frac{\% \text{ change in EPS}}{\% \text{ change in sales}}$$

$$8.46 = \frac{\% \text{ change in EPS}}{+50\%}$$

% change in EPS $= 8.46 \times 0.50 = 4.23 = \underline{\underline{+423\%}}$

ST12–2

Data summary for alternative plans		
Source of capital	**Plan A (bond)**	**Plan B (stock)**
Long-term debt	$60,000 at 12% annual interest	$50,000 at 12% annual interest
Annual interest =	0.12 = $60,000 = $7,200	0.12 × $50,000 = $6,000
Common stock	10,000 shares	11,000 shares

a.

	Plan A (bond)		Plan B (stock)	
EBIT[a]	$30,000	$40,000	$30,000	$40,000
Less: Interest	7,200	7,200	6,000	6,000
Net profits before taxes	$22,800	$32,800	$24,000	$34,000
Less: Taxes ($T = 0.40$)	9,120	13,120	9,600	13,600
Net profits after taxes	$13,680	$19,680	$14,400	$20,400
EPS (10,000 shares)	$1.37	$1.97		
(11,000 shares)			$1.31	$1.85

[a]Values were arbitrarily selected; other values could have been used.

Coordinates

	EBIT	
	$30,000	$40,000
Financing plan	Earnings per share (EPS)	
A (Bond)	$1.37	$1.97
B (Stock)	1.31	1.85

b.

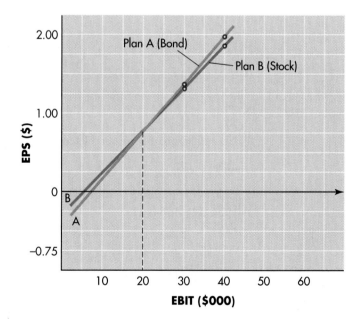

c. The bond plan (Plan A) becomes superior to the stock plan (Plan B) at *around $20,000* of EBIT, as represented by the dashed vertical line in the figure in part **b**. (*Note:* The actual point is $19,200, which was determined algebraically by using the technique described in footnote 22.)

ST12–3 a.

Capital structure debt ratio	Expected EPS (1)	Required return, k_s (2)	Estimated share value [(1) ÷ (2)] (3)
0%	$3.12	.13	$24.00
10	3.90	.15	26.00
20	4.80	.16	30.00
30	5.44	.17	32.00
40	5.51	.19	29.00
50	5.00	.20	25.00
60	4.40	.22	20.00

b. Using the table in part **a**:
   (1) Maximization of EPS: *40% debt ratio*, EPS = $5.51/share (see column 1).
   (2) Maximization of share value: *30% debt ratio*, share value = $32.00 (see column 3).

c. Recommend *30% debt ratio*, because it results in the maximum share value and is therefore consistent with the firm's goal of owner wealth maximization.

Chapter 13

ST13–1 a. Earnings per share (EPS) = $\dfrac{\$2,000,000 \text{ earnings available}}{500,000 \text{ shares of common outstanding}}$

= $4.00/share

Price/earnings (P/E) ratio = $\dfrac{\$60 \text{ market price}}{\$4.00 \text{ EPS}} = 15$

b. Proposed dividends = 500,000 shares × $2 per share = $1,000,000

Shares that can be repurchased = $\dfrac{\$1,000,000}{\$62} = 16,129$ shares

c. *After proposed repurchase:*
Shares outstanding = 500,000 − 16,129 = 483,871

EPS = $\dfrac{\$2,000,000}{483,871} = \$4.13/share$

d. Market price = $4.13/share × 15 = $61.95/share

e. The earnings per share (EPS) are higher after the repurchase, because there are fewer shares of stock outstanding (483,871 shares versus 500,000 shares) to divide up the firm's $2,000,000 of available earnings.

f. In both cases, the stockholders would receive $2 per share—a $2 cash dividend in the dividend case or an approximately $2 increase in share price ($60.00 per share to $61.95 per share) in the repurchase case. [*Note:* The difference of $0.05 per share ($2.00 − $1.95) difference is due to rounding.]

Chapter 14

ST14–1

	Basic data	
Time component	**Current**	**Proposed**
Average payment period (APP)	10 days	30 days
Average collection period (ACP)	30 days	30 days
Average age of inventory (AAI)	40 days	40 days

$$\text{Cash conversion cycle (CCC)} = \text{AAI} + \text{ACP} - \text{APP}$$
$$\text{CCC}_{\text{current}} = 40 \text{ days} + 30 \text{ days} - 10 \text{ days} = 60 \text{ days}$$
$$\text{CCC}_{\text{proposed}} = 40 \text{ days} + 30 \text{ days} - 30 \text{ days} = \underline{40} \text{ days}$$
$$\text{Reduction in CCC} \quad \underline{\underline{20}} \text{ days}$$

Annual operating cycle investment = $18,000,000

Daily expenditure = $18,000,000 ÷ 365 = $49,315

Reduction in resource investment = $49,315 × 20 days = $986,300

Annual profit increase = 0.12 × $986,300 = $\underline{\underline{\$118,356}}$

ST14–2 **a.** *Data:*

$S = 60,000$ gallons

$O = \$200$ per order

$C = \$1$ per gallon per year

Calculation:

$$EOQ = \sqrt{\frac{2 \times S \times O}{C}}$$
$$= \sqrt{\frac{2 \times 60,000 \times \$200}{\$1}}$$
$$= \sqrt{24,000,000}$$
$$= \underline{\underline{4,899}} \text{ gallons}$$

b. *Data:*

Lead time = 20 days

Daily usage = 60,000 gallons/365 days

$\qquad\qquad = 164.38$ gallons/day

Calculation:

Reorder point = lead time in days × daily usage

$\qquad\qquad = 20$ days × 164.38 gallons/day

$\qquad\qquad = \underline{\underline{3,287.6}}$ gallons

ST14–3 Tabular Calculation of the Effects of Relaxing Credit Standards on Regency Rug Repair Company:

Additional profit contribution from sales

[4,000 rugs × ($32 avg. sale price − $28 var. cost)] $16,000

Cost of marginal investment in accounts receivable

Average investment under proposed plan:

$$\frac{(\$28 \times 76{,}000 \text{ rugs})}{365/48} = \frac{\$2{,}128{,}000}{7.6}$$ $280,000

Average investment under present plan:

$$\frac{(\$28 \times 72{,}000 \text{ rugs})}{365/40} = \frac{\$2{,}016{,}000}{9.1}$$ 221,538

    Marginal investment in A/R $ 58,462

    Cost of marginal investment in

    A/R (0.14 × $58,462)   ($ 8,185)

Cost of marginal bad debts

Bad debts under proposed plan

(0.015 × $32 × 76,000 rugs) $ 36,480

Bad debts under present plan

(0.010 × $32 × 72,000 rugs)   23,040

    Cost of marginal bad debts   ($13,440)

Net loss from implementation of proposed plan   ($ 5,625)

Recommendation: Because a net loss of $5,625 is expected to result from relaxing credit standards, *the proposed plan should not be implemented.*

Chapter 15

ST15–1 **a.**

Supplier	Approximate cost of giving up cash discount
X	1% × [365/(55 − 10)] = 1% × 365/45 = 1% × 8 = 8.1%
Y	2% × [365/(30 − 10)] = 2% × 365/20 = 2% × 18 = 36.5%
Z	2% × [365/(60 − 20)] = 2% × 365/40 = 2% × 9 = 18.3%

b.

Supplier	Recommendation
X	8.1% cost of giving up discount < 15% interest cost from bank; therefore, *give up discount.*
Y	36.5% cost of giving up discount > 15% interest cost from bank; therefore, *take discount and borrow from bank.*
Z	18.3% cost of giving up discount > 15% interest cost from bank; therefore, *take discount and borrow from bank.*

c. Stretching accounts payable for supplier Z would change the cost of giving up the cash discount to

$$2\% \times [365/[(60 + 20) − 20]] = 2\% \times 365/60 = 2\% \times 6.1 = 12.2\%$$

In this case, in light of the 15% interest cost from the bank, the recommended strategy in part **b** would be to *give up the discount*, because the 12.2% cost of giving up the discount would be less than the 15% interest cost from the bank.

Chapter 16

ST16–1 a. (1) and (2). In tabular form—after-tax cash outflows in column 3 and present value of the cash outflows in column 5.

End of year (1)	Lease payment (1)	Tax adjustment $[(1-0.40)=0.60]$ (2)	After-tax cash outflows $[(1) \times (2)]$ (3)	Present value factors[a] (4)	Present value of outflows $[(3) \times (4)]$ (5)
1	$5,000	0.60	$3,000	0.917	$ 2,751
2	5,000	0.60	3,000	0.842	2,526
3	5,000	0.60	3,000	0.772	2,316
4	5,000	0.60	3,000	0.708	2,124
5	5,000	0.60	7,000[b]	0.650	4,550
				Present value of cash outflows	$14,267

[a]From Table A–2, *PVIF,* for 9% and the corresponding year.
[b]After-tax lease payment outflow of $3,000 plus the $4,000 cost of exercising the purchase option.

(Calculator solution = $14,269)

b. (1) In tabular form—annual interest expense in column 3.

End of year (1)	Loan payments (1)	Beginning of-year principal (2)	Payments Interest $[0.15 \times (2)]$ (3)	Payments Principal $[(1)-(3)]$ (4)	End-of-year principal $[(2)-(4)]$ (5)
1	$5,967	$20,000	$3,000	$2,967	$17,033
2	5,967	17,033	2,555	3,412	13,621
3	5,967	13,621	2,043	3,924	9,697
4	5,967	9,697	1,455	4,512	5,185
5	5,967	5,185	778	5,189	—[a]

[a]The values in this table have been rounded to the nearest dollar, which results in a slight difference ($4) between the beginning-of-year-5 principal (in column 2) and the year-5 principal payment (in column 4).

(2) In tabular form—after-tax cash outflows in column 9.

End of year (1)	Loan payments (1)	Maintenance costs (2)	Cost of oven (3)	Depreciation percentages[a] (4)	Depreciation $[(3) \times (4)]$ (5)	Interest[b] (6)	Total deductions $[(2)+(5)+(6)]$ (7)	Tax shields $[0.40 \times (7)]$ (8)	After-tax cash outflows $[(1)+(2)-(8)]$ (9)
1	$5,967	$1,000	$20,000	.20	$4,000	$3,000	$8,000	$3,200	$3,767
2	5,967	1,000	20,000	.32	6,400	2,555	9,955	3,982	2,985
3	5,967	1,000	20,000	.19	3,800	2,043	6,843	2,737	4,230
4	5,967	1,000	20,000	.12	2,400	1,455	4,855	1,942	5,025
5	5,967	1,000	20,000	.12	2,400	778	4,178	1,671	5,296

[a]From Table 3.2 on page 106.
[b]From column 3 of table in part **b**(1).

(3) In tabular form—present value of the cash outflows in column 3.

End of year	After-tax cash outflows[a] (1)	Present value factors[b] (2)	Present value of outflows [(1) × (2)] (3)
1	$3,767	0.917	$ 3,454
2	2,985	0.842	2,513
3	4,230	0.772	3,266
4	5,025	0.708	3,558
5	5,296	0.650	3,442
		Present value of cash outflows	$16,233

[a]From column 9 of table in part b(2).
[b]From Table A–2, *PVIF*, for 9% and the corresponding year.

(Calculator solution = $16,237)

c. Because the present value of the lease outflows of $14,267 is well below the present value of the purchase outflows of $16,233, *the lease is preferred*. Leasing rather than purchasing the oven should result in an incremental savings of $1,966 ($16,233 purchase cost − $14,267 lease cost).

ST16–2 a. In tabular form:

Year(s)	Payments (1)	Present value interest factor at 13 percent (2)	Present value [(1) × (2)] (3)
1–25	$ 110[a]	7.330[b]	$806.30
25	1,000	0.047[c]	47.00
		Straight bond value	$853.30

[a]$1,000 at 11% = $110 interest per year.
[b]Present value interest factor for an annuity, *PVIFA*, discounted at 13% for 25 years, from Table A–4.
[c]Present value interest factor for $1, *PVIF*, discounted at 13% for year 25, from Table A–2.

(Calculator solution = $853.40)

b. In tabular form:

Market price of stock (1)	Conversion ratio (2)	Conversion value [(1) × (2)] (3)
$20	40	$ 800
25 (conversion price)	40	1,000 (par value)
28	40	1,120
35	40	1,400
50	40	2,000

c. The bond would be expected to sell at the higher of the conversion value and the straight value. In no case would it be expected to sell for less than the straight value of $853.30. Therefore, at a price of $20, the bond would sell for its straight value of $853.30, and at prices of $25, $28, $35, and $50, the bond would be expected to sell at the associated conversion values (calculated in part **b**) of $1,000, $1,120, $1,400, and $2,000, respectively.

d. The straight bond value of $853.30.

Chapter 17

ST17–1 **a.** Net present value at 11%:

Year(s)	Cash inflow (1)	Present value factor at 11%[a] (2)	Present value [(1) × (2)] (3)
1–3	$20,000	2.444	$ 48,880
4–15	30,000	(7.191 − 2.444)	142,410
		Present value of inflows	$191,290
		Less: Cash purchase price	180,000
		Net present value (NPV)	$ 11,290

[a]Present value interest factors for annuities, *PVIFA*, from Table A–4.

(Calculator solution = 11,289)

Because the NPV of $11,290 is greater than zero, *Luxe Foods should acquire Valley Canning.*

b. In this case, the 14% cost of capital must be used. Net present value at 14%:

Year(s)	Cash inflow (1)	Present value factor at 14%[a] (2)	Present value [(1) × (2)] (3)
1–3	$20,000	2.322	$ 46,440
4–15	30,000	(6.142 − 2.322)	114,600
		Present value of inflows	$161,040
		Less: Cash purchase price	180,000
		Net present value (NPV)	($ 18,960)

[a]Present value interest factors for annuities, *PVIFA*, from Table A–4.

(Calculator solution = $18,951)

At the higher cost of capital, the *acquisition of Valley by Luxe cannot be justified.*

ST17–2   **a.** Lake Industries' EPS without merger:

Year	Earnings available for common		End-of-year value [(1) × (2)] (3)	Number of shares outstanding (4)	EPS [(3) ÷ (4)] (5)
	Initial value (1)	Future value factor at 5%[a] (2)			
2006	$160,000	1.000	$160,000	80,000	$2.00
2007	160,000	1.050	168,000	80,000	2.10
2008	160,000	1.102	176,320	80,000	2.20
2009	160,000	1.158	185,280	80,000	2.32
2010	160,000	1.216	194,560	80,000	2.43
2011	160,000	1.276	204,160	80,000	2.55

[a]Future value interest factors, *FVIF*, from Table A–1.

b. Number of postmerger shares outstanding for Lake Industries:

$$\frac{\text{Number of new}}{\text{shares issued}} = \frac{\text{Initial number of}}{\text{Butler Company shares}} \times \text{Ratio of exchange}$$

$$= \quad 10,000 \times 1.1 \quad = \quad 11,000 \text{ shares}$$

Plus: Lake's premerger shares   80,000

Lake's postmerger shares   91,000 shares

Year	Earnings available for common						
	Butler Company			Lake Industries			
				Without merger	With merger		
	Initial value (1)	Future value factor at 10%[a] (2)	End-of-year value [(1) × (2)] (3)	End-of-year value[b] (4)	End-of-year value [(3) + (4)] (5)	Number of shares outstanding[c] (6)	EPS [(5) ÷ (6)] (7)
2006	$20,000	1.000	$20,000	$160,000	$180,000	91,000	$1.98
2007	20,000	1.100	22,000	168,000	190,000	91,000	2.09
2008	20,000	1.210	24,200	176,320	200,520	91,000	2.20
2009	20,000	1.331	26,620	185,280	211,900	91,000	2.33
2010	20,000	1.464	29,280	194,560	223,840	91,000	2.46
2011	20,000	1.611	32,220	204,160	236,380	91,000	2.60

[a]Future value interest factors, *FVIF*, from Table A–1.
[b]From column 3 of table in part **a.**
[c]Calculated at beginning of this part.

c. Comparing the EPS without the proposed merger calculated in part **a** (see column 5 of table in part **a**) with the EPS with the proposed merger calculated in part **b** (see column 7 of table in part **b**), we can see that after 2008, the EPS *with* the merger rises above the EPS *without* the merger. Clearly, over the long run, the EPS with the merger will exceed those without the merger. This outcome is attributed to the higher rate of growth associated with Butler's earnings (10% versus 5% for Lake).

Chapter 18

ST18–1 MNC's receipt of dividends can be calculated as follows:

Subsidiary income before local taxes	$150,000
Foreign income tax at 32%	− 48,000
Dividend available to be declared	$102,000
Foreign dividend withholding tax at 8%	− 8,160
MNC's receipt of dividends	$ 93,840

a. If tax credits are allowed, then the so-called grossing up procedure will be applicable:

Additional MNC income		$150,000
U.S. tax liability at 34%	$51,000	
Total foreign taxes paid to be used as a credit ($48,000 + $8,160)	− 56,160	− 56,160
U.S. taxes due		− 0
Net funds available to the MNC		$ 93,840

b. If no tax credits are permitted, then:

MNC's receipt of dividends	$93,840
U.S. tax liability at 34%	− 31,906
Net funds available to the parent MNC	$61,934

Appendix C

Answers to Selected
End-of-Chapter Problems

The following list of answers to selected problems and portions of problems is included to provide "check figures" for use in preparing detailed solutions to end-of-chapter problems requiring calculations. For problems that are relatively straightforward, the key answer is given; for more complex problems, answers to a number of parts of the problem are included. Detailed calculations are not shown—only the final and, in some cases, intermediate answers, which should help to confirm whether the correct solution is being developed. Answers to problems involving present and future value were solved by using the appropriate tables; calculator solutions are not given. For problems containing a variety of cases for which similar calculations are required, the answers for only one or two cases have been included. The only verbal answers included are simple yes-or-no or "choice of best alternative" responses; answers to problems requiring detailed explanations or discussions are not given

The problems and portions of problems for which answers have been included were selected randomly; therefore, there is no discernible pattern to the choice of problem answers given. The answers given are based on what are believed to be the most obvious and reasonable assumptions related to the given problem; in some cases, other reasonable assumptions could result in equally correct answers.

1–1 a. Ms. Harper has unlimited liability: $60,000
    c. Ms. Harper has limited liability

1–2 a. $160,000
    b. $150,000

1–5 a. $19,700
    b. $72,800
    c. 21.3%

1–8 e. Total tax liability: $206,400

1–9 a. Earnings after tax: $18,000

1–10 b. Asset X: $100
      Asset Y: $2,000

2–3 a. Net profit after tax: $38,500

2–4 a. Earnings per share: $1.162

2–7   Initial sales price: $9.50

2–8 b. Earnings per share: $2.36
    c. Cash dividend per share: $1.50

2–11 a.

Current ratio	2003: 1.88	2005: 1.79
Quick ratio	2003: 1.22	2005: 1.24

2–13 a. 45.62 days

2–15

	Creek	Industry
Debt ratio	0.73	0.51
Times interest earned	3.00	7.30

2–17 a.

	Pelican	Timberland
(1) Debt ratio	10%	50%
(2) Times interest earned	62.5	12.5

    b.

	Pelican	Timberland
(1) Operating margin	25%	25%
(2) Net profit margin	14.8%	13.8%
(3) ROA	36.9%	34.5%
(4) ROE	41.0%	69.0%

2–20 a.

	Actual 2006
Current ratio:	1.04
Average collection period:	57 days
Debt ratio:	61.3%
Net profit margin:	4.1%
Return on equity:	11.3%

2–22 a. 2006 Johnson ROE = 21.21%
           Industry ROE = 14.46%

2–23 a.

	Actual 2006
Quick ratio:	2.20
Total asset turnover:	2.00
Times interest earned	3.85
Operating profit margin	16.0%
Price earnings ratio	9.8

3–3 a. $16,000
    c. $289,240

3–6 b. $1,620
    c. $13,367

3–8

	April	May
	($000)	
Cash 1 month delay	168	183
Cash 2 months delay	120	134.4
Total disbursements	465.3	413.1

3–14 a. To retained earnings: $146,600
     b. To retained earnings: $157,400

3–16 a. Total assets: $1,383,000
       Total current liabilities: $510,000
       External funds required: $53,000

3–18 a. To retained earnings: $32,500
     c. $11,250

4–3 C: 3 years $< n < 4$ years

4–4 A: $530.60
    D: $78.450

4–6 a. (1) $15,456

4–8 a. $8\% < i < 9\%$

4–11 B: $6,020
     D $80,250

4–18 a. (1) A: $36,217.50
       (2) A: $39,114.90

4–19 a. (1) C: $2,821.70
       (2) C: $3,386.04

4–23 b. $30,950.64

4–25 b. B: $1,000,000
      D: $1,200,000

4–27 a. A: $3,862.50

4–29 b. B: $26,039

4–32 a. $22,215

4–33 b. B: 12.6%
      D: 17.0%

4–34 a.

      (1) Annual: $8,810
           Semiannual: $8,955
           Quarterly: $9,030

4–40 B: $2,439.32

4–43 a. $60,000
     b. $3,764.82

4–45 A: $4,656.58
     B: $10,619.47
     C: $7,955.87

4–49 a. A: $12\% < i < 13\%$
       Calculator solution 12.47%
       C: $2\% < i < 3\%$
       Calculator solution 2.50%

4–51 a. B: $8\% < i < 9\%$
       Calculator solution 8.02%
       D: $10\% < i < 11\%$
       Calculator solution 10.03%

4–56 A: $17 < n < 18$
       Calculator solution 17.79
     D: $18 < n < 19$
       Calculator solution 18.68

5–1 a. X: 12.50%
         Y: 12.36%
5–2 A: 25%
5–4 a. A: 8%
         B: 20%
5–5 a. R: 10%
         S: 20%
     b. R: 25%
         S: 25.5%
5–9 a.
         (4) Project 257 CV: .368
             Project 432 CV: .354
5–10 a. F: 4%
     b. F: 13.38%
     c. F: 3.345
5–12 b. Portfolio return: 15.5%
     c. Standard deviation: 1.511%
5–15 a. 20.73%
     c. 12.89%
5–18 a. 18% increase
     b. 9.6% decrease
     c. No change
5–22 A: 8.9%
     D: 15%
5–24 b. 10%
5–27 b. 12.4%
     c. 10.4%
6–1   3.5%
6–5 a. 20 year bond = 11.5%
         5 year bond = 10.5%
6–8 a. A: 9%
         B: 12%
6–10 b. $175,000
     c. $113,750
6–12 b. $8,789.40
6–13 C: $16,660.00
     D: $9,717.00
6–15 a. $1,156.88
6–19 a. (1) $1,120.23
         (2) $1,000.00
         (3) $896.63
6–22 a. A: approximate: 12.36%
            Calculator solution: 12.71%
         C: approximate: 10.38%
            Calculator solution: 10.22%
         E: approximate: 8.77%
            Calculator solution: 8.95%
6–25 A: $1,152.35
     C: $464.72
     E: $76.11
7–1 b. 800,000 shares
7–3 A: $15.00
     C: $11.00
     D: $25.50

7–6 a. $20
     b. $12
7–8 a. $68.82
     b. $60.95
7–9 A: $24.00
     B: $40.00
     E: $18.75
7–10 a. $37.75
     b. $60.40
7–12 $81.19
7–14 a. $34.12
     b. $20.21
     c. $187.87
7–16 a. (1) $5,021,250
         (2) $5,411,250
         (3) $4,049,331
     b. $2,191,331
     c. $10.96
7–18 a. Book value: $36.00
     b. Liquidation value: $30.20
7–19 a. 9.5%
     b. 14.7%

8–1 a. Operating expenditure
     d. Operating expenditure
     f. Capital expenditure
8–4 Year   Relevant cash flow
      1           $4,000
      2           $6,000
      4           $10,000
8–7 A: $275,500
     B: $26,800
8–8 a. $23,200
     b. @$100,000: $30,720
         @$56,000: $13,120
8–9 a. Total tax: $49,600
     d. Total tax: ($6,400)
8–12 Initial investment $22,680
8–13 a. Initial investment: $18,240
     c. Initial investment: $23,100
8–16 c. Cash inflow, Year 3: $584,000
8–18 b. Incremental cash flow, Year 3: $1,960
8–21 Terminal cash flow: $76,640
8–25 a. Initial investment, Asset B: $51,488
     b. Incremental cash flow, Year 2,
         Hoist A: $8,808
     c. Terminal cash flow,
         Hoist B: $18,600
9–2 a. Machine 1: 4 years, 8 months
         Machine 2: 5 years, 3 months
9–4 a. $3,246 Accept
     b. −$5,131 Reject
9–5 a. $2,675 Accept
     c. −$805 Reject

9–7 **a.** $1,497,650
  b. $385,604
  c. $1,632,400

9–10 **a.** Project A: 3.08 years
  Project C: 2.38 years
  b. Project C: NPV $5,451

9–11 **a.** Project A: 17%
  Project D: 21%

9–14 **a.** NPV = $1,222
  b. IRR = 12%
  c. Accept

9–16 **a.** Project A: payback 3 years 4 months
  b. A: $120,000; B: $105,000
  c. Project B: NPV $51,137
  d. Project A: IRR 19.91%

9–21 **a.** Initial Investment: $1,480,000
  b.

Year	Cash Flow
1	$656,000
2	761,600
3	647,200
4	585,600
5	585,600
6	44,000

  c. 2.1 years
  d. NPV = $959,289
  IRR = 35%

10–2 **a.** $6,183.75

10–4 **a.** Range A: $1,600
  Range B: $200

10–5 **b.** Project A:
  Pessimistic: $73
  Most likely: $1,609
  Optimistic: $3,145

10–7 **a.** Project E: $2,130; Project F: $1,678
  c. Project E: $834; Project F: $1,678

10–10 **a.** Project X: NPV = $14,960
  Project Y: NPV = $2,650

10–12 **a.** Project X: NPV = $2,681
  Project Y: NPV = $1,778
  b. Project X: ANPV = $920.04
  Project Y: ANPV = $1,079.54

10–14 **a.** Value of real options: $2,200
  NPV$_{strategic}$: $500

11–2 **a.** $980
  d. 7.36% after tax

11–4 **a.** A: 4.12% after tax
  D: 3.83% after tax

11–7 **a.** 6%
  b. 12%

11–8 **d.** 16.54%

11–10 **a.** 11.28%
  b. 11.45%

11–13 **a.** 13.55%
  b. 12.985%

11–14 **e.** Breakpoint common stock: $5,880,000
  f. 7.02%
  g. 7.07%

11–18 **a.** WACC 0 to $600,000: 10.52%
  WACC $600,001 to $1,000,000: 10.96%

12–1 1,300

12–4 **a.** 21,000 CDs
  b. $293,580
  d. $10,500

12–6 **a.** 2,000 figurines
  b. −$3,000
  c. $2,000

12–8 **a.** 8,000 units
  b. @ 10,000 units: $95,000

12–11 **b.** 2
  c. 1.25

12–15 **a.** 20,000 latches
  b. $7,200
  e. 225.24

12–20 **a.** Structure A:
  EBIT $30,000: EPS $1.125
  Structure B:
  EBIT $50,000: EPS 2.28

12–23 **a., b., c.**

% Debt	# shs. @@$25	$ Interest expense	EPS
0	1,600,000	0	$3.00
10	1,440,000	300,000	$3.21
40	960,000	1,760,000	$3.90
60	640,000	3,720,000	$4.01

13–4 **a.** $4.75 per share
  b. $0.40 per share

13–7 **a.**

Year	$ Dividend
1997	0.10
2001	0.96
2004	1.28
2006	1.60

  c.

Year	$ Dividend
1997	0.50
2001	0.50
2004	0.66
2007	1.30

13–9 **a.** Common stock: $21,000
  Paid in capital: $294,000
  Retained earnings: $85,000

13–11 **a.** $2.00
  d. $20.00 per share

13–13 **a.** 1,200,000 shares @ $1.50 par
  d. 3,600,000 shares @ $0.50 par

13–16 **a.** 19,047 shares
  b. $2.10

14–1 **a.** OC = 150 days
  b. CCC = 120 days
  c. $9,863,013.70

14–2 **b.** CCC = 70 days
    c. $26,849
14–4 **a.** Average season requirement: $4,000,000
14–6 **a.** 200 units
    b. 121.92 units
    c. 32.88 units
14–9 Loss from implementation: $4,659
14–11 Loss from implementation: $11,972
14–13 **a.** 7 days
    b. $21,450
15–2 **a.** 37.21%
    b. 18.43%
    c. 7.37%
15–6 $1,300,000
15–7 $82,500
15–9 14.29%
15–10 **a.** Effective rate: 12.94%
    b. Effective rate: 11.73%
15–13 **a.** Effective 90-day rate: 2.25%
    b. Effective annual rate: 13.89%
15–17

	Amount remitted
A:	$196,000
C:	$107,800
F:	$176,400
G:	$ 88,200

16–2

Loan	*Year*	*Interest amount*
A	1	$1,400
A	4	$ 402
D	2	$5,822
D	4	$3,290

16–4 **b.** Lease: PV of outflows: $42,934
    Purchase: PV of outflows: $43,896
16–10 A: $1,056.25
16–13 **a.** $832.75
    c. @$9 price: $832.75
    @$13 price: $1,040.00

16–17 **a.** 160 shares; 400 warrants
    b. $1,600 profit; 20% return
    c. $10,000 profit; 125% return
16–19 A: $300
    B: −$50
    C: $500
16–20 **b.** $400 profit
    c. $66 to break even
16–21 **a.** @$46: −$100
    @$40: $120
17–2 **a.** Tax liability: $1,680,000
    b. Total tax savings: $320,000
17–4 **a.** NPV: $19,320
    c. NPV: $15,616
17–6 **a.** EPS Marla's: $1.029
    EPS Victory: $1.852
    d. (a) 10.8
    (b) 12.0
    (c) 13.2
17–8 A: (1) 0.60 (2) 1.20
    B: (1) 1.25 (2) 1.25
    D: (1) 0.25 (2) 1.25
17–10 **a.** 1.125
    c. P/E: 16.89
    d. EPS: $2.529
17–12 **a.** Composition
    b. Extension
    c. Combination
18–1 **a.** $152,425
    b. $100,600
18–3

Effective rates	*U.S.$*	*MP*	*¥*
Euromarket	4.00%	3.20%	3.50%
Domestic	3.75%	2.90%	3.65%

Glossary

ABC inventory system Inventory management technique that divides inventory into three groups—A, B, and C, in descending order of importance and level of monitoring, on the basis of the dollar investment in each. (Chapter 14)

ability to service debts The ability of a firm to make the payments required on a scheduled basis over the life of a debt. (Chapter 2)

accept–reject approach The evaluation of capital expenditure proposals to determine whether they meet the firm's minimum acceptance criterion. (Chapter 8)

accounting exposure The risk resulting from the effects of changes in foreign exchange rates on the translated value of a firm's financial statement accounts denominated in a given foreign currency. (Chapter 18)

accounts payable management Management by the firm of the time that elapses between its purchase of raw materials and its mailing payment to the supplier. (Chapter 15)

accrual basis In preparation of financial statements, recognizes revenue at the time of sale and recognizes expenses when they are incurred. (Chapter 1)

accruals Liabilities for services received for which payment has yet to be made. (Chapter 15)

ACH (automated clearinghouse) transfer Preauthorized electronic withdrawal from the payer's account and deposit into the payee's account via a settlement among banks by the *automated clearinghouse,* or *ACH.* (Chapter 14)

acquiring company The firm in a merger transaction that attempts to acquire another firm. (Chapter 17)

activity ratios Measure the speed with which various accounts are converted into sales or cash—inflows or outflows. (Chapter 2)

after-tax proceeds from sale of old asset The difference between the old asset's sale proceeds and any applicable taxes or tax refunds related to its sale. (Chapter 8)

agency costs The costs borne by stockholders to maintain a *governance structure* that minimizes agency problems and contributes to the maximization of owner wealth. (Chapter 1)

agency problem The likelihood that managers may place personal goals ahead of corporate goals. (Chapter 1)

aggressive funding strategy A funding strategy under which the firm funds its seasonal requirements with short-term debt and its permanent requirements with long-term debt. (Chapter 14)

aging schedule A credit-monitoring technique that breaks down accounts receivable into groups on the basis of their time of origin; it shows the percentages of the total accounts receivable balance that have been outstanding for specified periods of time. (Chapter 14)

all-current-rate method The method by which the *functional-currency-denominated* financial statements of an MNC's subsidiary are translated into the parent company's currency. (Chapter 18)

American depositary receipts (ADRs) Claims issued by U.S. banks representing ownership of shares of a foreign company's stock held on deposit by the U.S. bank in the foreign market and issued in dollars to U.S. investors. (Chapter 7)

angel capitalists (angels) Wealthy individual investors who do not operate as a business but invest in promising early-stage companies in exchange for a portion of the firm's equity. (Chapter 7)

annual cleanup The requirement that for a certain number of days during the year borrowers under a line of credit carry a zero loan balance (that is, owe the bank nothing). (Chapter 15)

annual percentage rate (APR) The *nominal annual rate* of interest, found by multiplying the periodic rate by the number of periods in 1 year, that must be disclosed to consumers on credit cards and loans as a result of "truth-in-lending laws." (Chapter 4)

annual percentage yield (APY) The *effective annual rate* of interest that must be disclosed to consumers by banks on their savings products as a result of "truth-in-savings laws." (Chapter 4)

annualized net present value (ANPV) approach An approach to evaluating unequal-lived projects that converts the net present value of unequal-lived, mutually exclusive projects into an equivalent annual amount (in NPV terms). (Chapter 10)

annuity A stream of equal periodic cash flows, over a specified time period. These cash flows can be *inflows* of returns earned on investments or *outflows* of funds invested to earn future returns. (Chapter 4)

annuity due An annuity for which the cash flow occurs at the *beginning* of each period. (Chapter 4)

articles of partnership The written contract used to formally establish a business partnership. (Chapter 1)

assignment A voluntary liquidation procedure by which a firm's creditors pass the power to liquidate the firm's assets to an adjustment bureau, a trade association, or a third party, which is designated the *assignee*. (Chapter 17)

asymmetric information The situation in which managers of a firm have more information about operations and future prospects than do investors. (Chapter 12)

authorized shares The number of shares of common stock that a firm's corporate charter allows it to issue. (Chapter 7)

average age of inventory Average number of days' sales in inventory. (Chapter 2)

average collection period The average amount of time needed to collect accounts receivable. (Chapter 2)

average payment period The average amount of time needed to pay accounts payable. (Chapter 2)

average tax rate A firm's taxes divided by its taxable income. (Chapter 1)

balance sheet Summary statement of the firm's financial position at a given point in time. (Chapter 2)

bankruptcy Business failure that occurs when the stated value of a firm's liabilities exceeds the fair market value of its assets. (Chapter 17)

Bankruptcy Reform Act of 1978 The governing bankruptcy legislation in the United States today. (Chapter 17)

bar chart The simplest type of probability distribution; shows only a limited number of outcomes and associated probabilities for a given event. (Chapter 5)

basic EPS Earnings per share (EPS) calculated without regard to any contingent securities. (Chapter 16)

behavioral finance A growing body of research that focuses on investor behavior and its impact on investment decisions and stock prices. Advocates are commonly referred to as "behaviorists." (Chapter 7)

benchmarking A type of *cross-sectional analysis* in which the firm's ratio values are compared to those of a key competitor or group of competitors that it wishes to emulate. (Chapter 2)

beta coefficient (*b*) A relative measure of nondiversifiable risk. An *index* of the degree of movement of an asset's return in response to a change in the *market return*. (Chapter 5)

bird-in-the-hand argument The belief, in support of *dividend relevance theory,* that investors see current dividends as less risky than future dividends or capital gains. (Chapter 13)

board of directors Group elected by the firm's stockholders and typically responsible for developing strategic goals and plans, setting general policy, guiding corporate affairs, approving major expenditures, and hiring/firing, compensating, and monitoring key officers and executives. (Chapter 1)

bond Long-term debt instrument used by business and government to raise large sums of money, generally from a diverse group of lenders. (Chapter 1)

bond indenture A legal document that specifies both the rights of the bondholders and the duties of the issuing corporation. (Chapter 6)

book value The strict accounting value of an asset, calculated by subtracting its accumulated depreciation from its installed cost. (Chapter 8)

book value per share The amount per share of common stock that would be received if all of the firm's assets were *sold for their exact book (accounting) value* and the proceeds remaining after paying all liabilities (including preferred stock) were divided among the common stockholders. (Chapter 7)

book value weights Weights that use accounting values to measure the proportion of each type of capital in the firm's financial structure. (Chapter 11)

breakeven analysis Indicates the level of operations necessary to cover all operating costs and the profitability associated with various levels of sales. (Chapter 12)

breakeven cash inflow The minimum level of cash inflow necessary for a project to be acceptable, that is, NPV > \$0. (Chapter 10)

break point The level of *total* new financing at which the cost of one of the financing components rises, thereby causing an upward shift in the *weighted marginal cost of capital (WMCC).* (Chapter 11)

breakup value The value of a firm measured as the sum of the values of its operating units if each were sold separately. (Chapter 17)

business risk The risk to the firm of being unable to cover operating costs. (Chapter 11)

call feature A feature included in nearly all corporate bond issues that gives the issuer the opportunity to repurchase bonds at a stated *call price* prior to maturity. (Chapter 6)

call option An option to *purchase* a specified number of shares of a stock (typically 100) on or before a specified future date at a stated price. (Chapter 16)

call premium The amount by which a bond's *call price* exceeds its par value. (Chapter 6)

call price The stated price at which a bond may be repurchased, by use of a *call feature*, prior to maturity. (Chapter 6)

capital The long-term funds of a firm; all items on the right-hand side of the firm's balance sheet, *excluding current liabilities*. (Chapter 7)

capital asset pricing model (CAPM) The basic theory that links risk and return for all assets; describes the relationship between the required return, k_s, and the nondiversifiable risk of the firm as measured by the beta coefficient, b. (Chapters 5 and 11)

capital budgeting The process of evaluating and selecting long-term investments that are consistent with the firm's goal of maximizing owner wealth. (Chapter 8)

capital budgeting process Five distinct but interrelated steps: *proposal generation, review and analysis, decision making, implementation,* and *follow-up.* (Chapter 8)

capital expenditure An outlay of funds by the firm that is expected to produce benefits over a period of time *greater than* 1 year. (Chapter 8)

capital gain The amount by which the sale price of an asset exceeds the asset's initial purchase price. (Chapter 1)

capital market A market that enables suppliers and demanders of *long-term funds* to make transactions. (Chapter 1)

capital rationing The financial situation in which a firm has only a fixed number of dollars available for capital expenditures, and numerous projects compete for these dollars. (Chapter 8)

capital structure The mix of long-term debt and equity maintained by the firm. (Chapter 12)

capitalized lease A *financial (capital) lease* that has the present value of all its payments included as an asset and corresponding liability on the firm's balance sheet, as required by Financial Accounting Standards Board (FASB) Standard No. 13. (Chapter 16)

carrying costs The variable costs per unit of holding an item in inventory for a specific period of time. (Chapter 14)

cash basis Recognizes revenues and expenses only with respect to actual inflows and outflows of cash. (Chapter 1)

cash bonuses Cash paid to management for achieving certain performance goals. (Chapter 1)

cash budget (cash forecast) A statement of the firm's planned inflows and outflows of cash that is used to estimate its short-term cash requirements. (Chapter 3)

cash concentration The process used by the firm to bring lockbox and other deposits together into one bank, often called the *concentration bank.* (Chapter 14)

cash conversion cycle (CCC) The amount of time a firm's resources are tied up; calculated by subtracting the average payment period from the *operating cycle.* (Chapter 14)

cash disbursements All outlays of cash by the firm during a given financial period. (Chapter 3)

cash discount A percentage deduction from the purchase price; available to the credit customer who pays its account within a specified time. (Chapter 14)

cash discount period The number of days after the beginning of the credit period during which the cash discount is available. (Chapter 14)

cash receipts All of a firm's inflows of cash in a given financial period. (Chapter 3)

Central American Free Trade Agreement (CAFTA) A trade agreement signed in 2003–2004 by the United States and five Central American countries (Costa Rica, El Salvador, Guatemala, Honduras, and Nicaragua). (Chapter 18)

change in net working capital The difference between a change in current assets and a change in current liabilities. (Chapter 8)

Chapter 7 The portion of the *Bankruptcy Reform Act of 1978* that details the procedures to be followed when liquidating a failed firm. (Chapter 17)

Chapter 11 The portion of the *Bankruptcy Reform Act of 1978* that outlines the procedures for reorganizing a failed (or failing) firm, whether its petition is filed voluntarily or involuntarily. (Chapter 17)

clearing float The time between deposit of a payment and when spendable funds become available to the firm. (Chapter 14)

clientele effect The argument that a firm attracts shareholders whose preferences for the payment and stability of dividends correspond to the payment pattern and stability of the firm itself. (Chapter 13)

closely owned (stock) All common stock of a firm owned by a small group of investors (such as a family). (Chapter 7)

coefficient of variation (*CV*) A measure of relative dispersion that is useful in comparing the risks of assets with differing expected returns. (Chapter 5)

collateral trust bonds See Table 6.3 (Chapter 6)

commercial finance companies Lending institutions that make *only* secured loans—both short-term and long-term—to businesses. (Chapter 15)

commercial paper A form of financing consisting of short-term, unsecured promissory notes issued by firms with a high credit standing. (Chapter 15)

commitment fee The fee that is normally charged on a *revolving credit agreement;* it often applies to the average unused balance of the borrower's credit line. (Chapter 15)

common stock The purest and most basic form of corporate ownership. (Chapter 1)

common-size income statement An income statement in which each item is expressed as a percentage of sales. (Chapter 2)

compensating balance A required checking account balance equal to a certain percentage of the amount borrowed from a bank under a line-of-credit or revolving credit agreement. (Chapter 15)

composition A pro rata cash settlement of creditor claims by the debtor firm; a uniform percentage of each dollar owed is paid. (Chapter 17)

compound interest Interest that is earned on a given deposit and has become part of the principal at the end of a specified period. (Chapter 4)

conflicting rankings Conflicts in the ranking given a project by NPV and IRR, resulting from *differences in the magnitude and timing of cash flows.* (Chapter 9)

congeneric merger A merger in which one firm acquires another firm that is *in the same general industry* but neither in the same line of business nor a supplier or customer. (Chapter 17)

conglomerate merger A merger combining firms in *unrelated businesses.* (Chapter 17)

conservative funding strategy A funding strategy under which the firm funds both its seasonal and its permanent requirements with long-term debt. (Chapter 14)

consolidation The combination of two or more firms to form a completely new corporation. (Chapter 17)

constant-growth model A widely cited dividend valuation approach that assumes that dividends will grow at a constant rate, but a rate that is less than the required return. (Chapter 7)

constant-growth valuation (Gordon) model Assumes that the value of a share of stock equals the present value of all future dividends (assumed to grow at a constant rate) that it is expected to provide over an infinite time horizon. (Chapter 11)

constant-payout-ratio dividend policy A dividend policy based on the payment of a certain percentage of earnings to owners in each dividend period. (Chapter 13)

contingent securities Convertibles, warrants, and stock options. Their presence affects the reporting of a firm's earnings per share (EPS). (Chapter 16)

continuous compounding Compounding of interest an infinite number of times per year at intervals of microseconds. (Chapter 4)

continuous probability distribution A probability distribution showing all the possible outcomes and associated probabilities for a given event. (Chapter 5)

controlled disbursing The strategic use of mailing points and bank accounts to lengthen mail float and clearing float, respectively. (Chapter 14)

controller The firm's chief accountant, who is responsible for the firm's accounting activities, such as corporate accounting, tax management, financial accounting, and cost accounting. (Chapter 1)

conventional cash flow pattern An initial outflow followed only by a series of inflows. (Chapter 8)

conversion (or stock) value The value of a convertible security measured in terms of the market price of the common stock into which it can be converted. (Chapter 16)

conversion feature An option that is included as part of a bond or a preferred stock issue and allows its holder to change the security into a stated number of shares of common stock. (Chapters 6 and 16)

conversion price The per-share price that is effectively paid for common stock as the result of conversion of a convertible security. (Chapter 16)

conversion ratio The ratio at which a convertible security can be exchanged for common stock. (Chapter 16)

convertible bond A bond that can be changed into a specified number of shares of common stock. (Chapter 16)

convertible preferred stock Preferred stock that can be changed into a specified number of shares of common stock. (Chapter 16)

corporate bond A long-term debt instrument indicating that a corporation has borrowed a certain amount of money and promises to repay it in the future under clearly defined terms. (Chapter 6)

corporate governance The system used to direct and control a corporation. Defines the rights and responsibilities of key corporate participants, decision-making procedures, and how the firm will set, achieve, and monitor objectives. (Chapter 1)

corporate restructuring The activities involving expansion or contraction of a firm's operations or changes in its asset or financial (ownership) structure. (Chapter 17)

corporation   An artificial being created by law (often called a "legal entity"). (Chapter 1)

correlation   A statistical measure of the relationship between any two series of numbers representing data of any kind. (Chapter 5)

correlation coefficient   A measure of the degree of correlation between two series. (Chapter 5)

cost of capital   The rate of return that a firm must earn on the projects in which it invests to maintain its market value and attract funds. (Chapter 11)

cost of common stock equity, k_s   The rate at which investors discount the expected dividends of the firm to determine its share value. (Chapter 11)

cost of giving up a cash discount   The implied rate of interest paid to delay payment of an account payable for an additional number of days. (Chapter 15)

cost of long-term debt, k_i   The after-tax cost today of raising long-term funds through borrowing. (Chapter 11)

cost of new asset   The net outflow necessary to acquire a new asset. (Chapter 8)

cost of a new issue of common stock, k_n   The cost of common stock, net of underpricing and associated flotation costs. (Chapter 11)

cost of preferred stock, k_p   The ratio of the preferred stock dividend to the firm's net proceeds from the sale of preferred stock; calculated by dividing the annual dividend, D_p, by the net proceeds from the sale of the preferred stock, N_p. (Chapter 11)

cost of retained earnings, k_r   The same as the cost of an *equivalent fully subscribed issue of additional common stock*, which is equal to the cost of common stock equity, k_s. (Chapter 11)

coupon interest rate   The percentage of a bond's par value that will be paid annually, typically in two equal semiannual payments, as interest. (Chapter 6)

coverage ratios   Ratios that measure the firm's ability to pay certain fixed charges. (Chapter 2)

credit monitoring   The ongoing review of a firm's accounts receivable to determine whether customers are paying according to the stated credit terms. (Chapter 14)

credit period   The number of days after the beginning of the credit period until full payment of the account is due. (Chapter 14)

credit scoring   A credit selection method commonly used with high-volume/small-dollar credit requests; relies on a credit score determined by applying statistically derived weights to a credit applicant's scores on key financial and credit characteristics. (Chapter 14)

credit standards   The firm's minimum requirements for extending credit to a customer. (Chapter 14)

credit terms   The terms of sale for customers who have been extended credit by the firm. (Chapter 14)

creditor control   An arrangement in which the creditor committee replaces the firm's operating management and operates the firm until all claims have been settled. (Chapter 17)

cross-sectional analysis   Comparison of different firms' financial ratios at the same point in time; involves comparing the firm's ratios to those of other firms in its industry or to industry averages. (Chapter 2)

cumulative preferred stock   Preferred stock for which all passed (unpaid) dividends in arrears, along with the current dividend, must be paid before dividends can be paid to common stockholders. (Chapter 7)

current assets   Short-term assets, expected to be converted into cash within 1 year or less. (Chapter 2)

current liabilities   Short-term liabilities, expected to be paid within 1 year or less. (Chapter 2)

current rate (translation) method   Technique used by U.S.-based companies to translate their foreign-currency-denominated assets and liabilities into dollars, for consolidation with the parent company's financial statements, using the exchange rate prevailing at the fiscal year ending date (the current rate). (Chapter 2)

current ratio   A measure of liquidity calculated by dividing the firm's current assets by its current liabilities. (Chapter 2)

date of record (dividends)   Set by the firm's directors, the date on which all persons whose names are recorded as stockholders receive a declared dividend at a specified future time. (Chapter 13)

debentures   See Table 6.3 (Chapter 6)

debt capital   All long-term borrowing incurred by a firm, including bonds. (Chapter 7)

debt ratio   Measures the proportion of total assets financed by the firm's creditors. (Chapter 2)

debtor in possession (DIP)   The term for a firm that files a reorganization petition under Chapter 11 and then develops, if feasible, a reorganization plan. (Chapter 17)

degree of financial leverage (DFL)   The numerical measure of the firm's financial leverage. (Chapter 12)

degree of indebtedness   Measures the amount of debt relative to other significant balance sheet amounts. (Chapter 2)

degree of operating leverage (DOL)   The numerical measure of the firm's operating leverage. (Chapter 12)

degree of total leverage (DTL)   The numerical measure of the firm's total leverage. (Chapter 12)

depository transfer check (DTC)   An unsigned check drawn on one of a firm's bank accounts and deposited in another. (Chapter 14)

depreciable life   Time period over which an asset is depreciated. (Chapter 3)

depreciation The systematic charging of a portion of the costs of fixed assets against annual revenues over time. (Chapter 3)

derivative security A security that is neither debt nor equity but derives its value from an underlying asset that is often another security; called "derivatives," for short. (Chapter 16)

diluted EPS Earnings per share (EPS) calculated under the assumption that *all* contingent securities that would have dilutive effects are converted and exercised and are therefore common stock. (Chapter 16)

dilution of ownership Occurs when a new stock issue results in each present shareholder having a claim on a *smaller* part of the firm's earnings than previously. (Chapter 7)

direct lease A lease under which a lessor owns or acquires the assets that are leased to a given lessee. (Chapter 16)

discount The amount by which a bond sells at a value that is less than its par value. (Chapter 6)

discount loans Loans on which interest is paid in advance by being deducted from the amount borrowed. (Chapter 15)

discounting cash flows The process of finding present values; the inverse of compounding interest. (Chapter 4)

diversifiable risk The portion of an asset's risk that is attributable to firm-specific, random causes; can be eliminated through diversification. Also called *unsystematic risk*. (Chapter 5)

divestiture The selling of some of a firm's assets for various strategic reasons. (Chapter 17)

dividend irrelevance theory Miller and Modigliani's theory that in a perfect world, the firm's value is determined solely by the earning power and risk of its assets (investments) and that the manner in which it splits its earnings stream between dividends and internally retained (and reinvested) funds does not affect this value. (Chapter 13)

dividend payout ratio Indicates the percentage of each dollar earned that is distributed to the owners in the form of cash. It is calculated by dividing the firm's cash dividend per share by its earnings per share. (Chapter 13)

dividend per share (DPS) The dollar amount of cash distributed during the period on behalf of each outstanding share of common stock. (Chapter 2)

dividend policy The firm's plan of action to be followed whenever a dividend decision is made. (Chapter 13)

dividend reinvestment plans (DRIPs) Plans that enable stockholders to use dividends received on the firm's stock to acquire additional shares—even fractional shares—at little or no transaction cost. (Chapter 13)

dividend relevance theory The theory, advanced by Gordon and Lintner, that there is a direct relationship between a firm's dividend policy and its market value. (Chapter 13)

dividends Periodic distributions of earnings to the stockholders of a firm. (Chapter 1)

double taxation Occurs when the already once-taxed earnings of a corporation are distributed as cash dividends to stockholders, who must pay taxes of up to a maximum rate of 15 percent on them. (Chapter 1)

DuPont formula Multiplies the firm's *net profit margin* by its *total asset turnover* to calculate the firm's *return on total assets (ROA)*. (Chapter 2)

DuPont system of analysis System used to dissect the firm's financial statements and to assess its financial condition. (Chapter 2)

earnings per share (EPS) The amount earned during the period on behalf of each outstanding share of common stock, calculated by dividing the period's total earnings available for the firm's common stockholders by the number of shares of common stock outstanding. (Chapter 1)

EBIT–EPS approach An approach for selecting the capital structure that maximizes earnings per share (EPS) over the expected range of earnings before interest and taxes (EBIT). (Chapter 12)

economic exposure The risk resulting from the effects of changes in foreign exchange rates on the firm's value. (Chapter 18)

economic order quantity (EOQ) model Inventory management technique for determining an item's optimal order size, which is the size that minimizes the total of its *order costs* and *carrying costs*. (Chapter 14)

economic value added (EVA®) A popular measure used by many firms to determine whether an investment contributes positively to the owners' wealth; calculated as the difference between an investment's *net operating profit after taxes (NOPAT)* and the cost of funds used to finance the investment which is found by multiplying the dollar amount of funds used to finance the investment by the firm's weighted average cost of capital (WACC). (Chapter 11)

effective (true) annual rate (EAR) The annual rate of interest actually paid or earned. (Chapter 4)

effective interest rate In the international context, the rate equal to the nominal rate plus (or minus) any forecast appreciation (or depreciation) of a foreign currency relative to the currency of the MNC parent. (Chapter 18)

efficient market A market that allocates funds to their most productive uses as a result of competition among wealth-maximizing investors that determines and publicizes prices that are believed to be close to their true value; a market with the following characteristics: many small investors, all having the same information and expectations with respect to securities; no restrictions on investment, no taxes, and no transaction costs; and rational investors, who view securities similarly and are risk-averse, preferring higher returns and lower risk. (Chapters 1 and 5)

efficient-market hypothesis   Theory describing the behavior of an assumed "perfect" market in which (1) securities are typically in equilibrium, (2) security prices fully reflect all public information available and react swiftly to new information, and, (3) because stocks are fully and fairly priced, investors need not waste time looking for mispriced securities. (Chapter 7)

efficient portfolio   A portfolio that maximizes return for a given level of risk or minimizes risk for a given level of return. (Chapter 5)

ending cash   The sum of the firm's beginning cash and its net cash flow for the period. (Chapter 3)

enterprise resource planning (ERP)   A computerized system that electronically integrates external information about the firm's suppliers and customers with the firm's departmental data so that information on all available resources—human and material—can be instantly obtained in a fashion that eliminates production delays and controls costs. (Chapter 14)

equipment trust certificates   See Table 6.3 (Chapter 6)

equity capital   The long-term funds provided by the firm's owners, the stockholders. (Chapter 7)

ethics   Standards of conduct or moral judgment. (Chapter 1)

euro   A single currency adopted on January 1, 1999 by 12 of the 15 EU nations, who switched to a single set of euro bills and coins on January 1, 2002. (Chapter 18)

Eurobond   An *international bond* that is sold primarily in countries other than the country of the currency in which the issue is denominated. (Chapters 6 and 18)

Eurobond market   The market in which corporations and governments typically issue bonds denominated in dollars and sell them to investors located outside the United States. (Chapter 1)

Eurocurrency market   International equivalent of the domestic money market. (Chapter 1)

Eurocurrency markets   The portion of the Euromarket that provides short-term, foreign-currency financing to subsidiaries of MNCs. (Chapter 18)

Euromarket   The international financial market that provides for borrowing and lending currencies outside their country of origin. (Chapter 18)

European Open Market   The transformation of the European Union into a *single* market at year-end 1992. (Chapter 18)

European Union (EU)   A significant economic force currently made up of 15 nations that permit free trade within the union. (Chapter 18)

ex dividend   Period, beginning 2 *business days* prior to the date of record, during which a stock is sold without the right to receive the current dividend. (Chapter 13)

excess cash balance   The (excess) amount available for investment by the firm if the period's ending cash is greater than the desired minimum cash balance; assumed to be invested in marketable securities. (Chapter 3)

excess earnings accumulation tax   The tax the IRS levies on retained earnings above $250,000 when it determines that the firm has accumulated an excess of earnings to allow owners to delay paying ordinary income taxes on dividends received. (Chapter 13)

exchange rate risk   The danger that an unexpected change in the exchange rate between the dollar and the currency in which a project's cash flows are denominated will reduce the market value of that project's cash flow; the risk caused by varying exchange rates between two currencies. (Chapters 10 and 18)

exercise (or option) price   The price at which holders of warrants can purchase a specified number of shares of common stock. (Chapter 16)

expectations theory   The theory that the yield curve reflects investor expectations about future interest rates; an increasing inflation expectation results in an upward-sloping yield curve, and a decreasing inflation expectation results in a downward-sloping yield curve. (Chapter 6)

expected return, $\hat{k}$ The return that is expected to be earned on a given asset each period over an infinite time horizon. (Chapter 7)

expected value of a return ($\bar{k}$)   The most likely return on a given asset. (Chapter 5)

extendible notes   See Table 6.4 (Chapter 6)

extension   An arrangement whereby the firm's creditors receive payment in full, although not immediately. (Chapter 17)

external financing required ("plug" figure)   Under the judgmental approach for developing a pro forma balance sheet, the amount of external financing needed to bring the statement into balance. (Chapter 3)

external forecast   A sales forecast based on the relationships observed between the firm's sales and certain key external economic indicators. (Chapter 3)

extra dividend   An additional dividend optionally paid by the firm if earnings are higher than normal in a given period. (Chapter 13)

factor   A financial institution that specializes in purchasing accounts receivable from businesses. (Chapter 15)

factoring accounts receivable   The outright sale of accounts receivable at a discount to a *factor* or other financial institution. (Chapter 15)

FASB No. 52   Statement issued by the FASB requiring U.S. multinationals first to convert the financial statement accounts of foreign subsidiaries into the *functional currency* and then to translate the accounts into the parent firm's currency using the *all-current-rate method*. (Chapter 18)

federal funds   Loan transactions between commercial banks in which the Federal Reserve banks become involved. (Chapter 1)

finance   The art and science of managing money. (Chapter 1)

financial (or capital) lease   A *longer-term* lease than an operating lease that is *noncancelable* and obligates the lessee to make payments for the use of an asset over a predefined period of time; the total payments over the term of the lease are *greater* than the lessor's initial cost of the leased asset. (Chapter 16)

Financial Accounting Standards Board (FASB) Standard No. 52   Mandates that U.S.-based companies translate their foreign-currency-denominated assets and liabilities into dollars, for consolidation with the parent company's financial statements. (Chapter 2)

Financial Accounting Standards Board (FASB)   The accounting profession's rule-setting body, which authorizes *generally accepted accounting principles (GAAP)*. (Chapter 2)

financial breakeven point   The level of EBIT necessary to just cover all *fixed financial costs;* the level of EBIT for which EPS = \$0. (Chapter 12)

financial institution   An intermediary that channels the savings of individuals, businesses, and governments into loans or investments. (Chapter 1)

financial leverage multiplier (FLM)   The ratio of the firm's total assets to its common stock equity. (Chapter 2)

financial leverage   The potential use of *fixed financial costs* to magnify the effects of changes in earnings before interest and taxes on the firm's earnings per share. (Chapters 2 and 12)

financial manager   Actively manages the financial affairs of any type of business, whether financial or nonfinancial, private or public, large or small, profit-seeking or not-for-profit. (Chapter 1)

financial markets   Forums in which suppliers of funds and demanders of funds can transact business directly. (Chapter 1)

financial merger   A merger transaction undertaken with the goal of restructuring the acquired company to improve its cash flow and unlock its hidden value. (Chapter 17)

financial planning process   Planning that begins with long-term, or *strategic,* financial plans that in turn guide the formulation of short-term, or *operating,* plans and budgets. (Chapter 3)

financial risk   The risk to the firm of being unable to cover required financial obligations (interest, lease payments, preferred stock dividends). (Chapter 11)

financial services   The part of finance concerned with the design and delivery of advice and financial products to individuals, business, and government. (Chapter 1)

financing flows   Cash flows that result from debt and equity financing transactions; includes incurrence and repayment of debt, cash inflow from the sale of stock, and cash outflows to pay cash dividends or repurchase stock. (Chapter 3)

five C's of credit   The five key dimensions—character, capacity, capital, collateral, and conditions—used by credit analysts to provide a framework for in-depth credit analysis. (Chapter 14)

fixed (or semifixed) relationship   The constant (or relatively constant) relationship of a currency to one of the major currencies, a combination (basket) of major currencies, or some type of international foreign exchange standard. (Chapter 18)

fixed-payment coverage ratio   Measures the firm's ability to meet all fixed-payment obligations. (Chapter 2)

fixed-rate loan   A loan with a rate of interest that is determined at a set increment above the prime rate and at which it remains fixed until maturity. (Chapter 15)

flat yield curve   A yield curve that reflects relatively similar borrowing costs for both short- and longer-term loans. (Chapter 6)

float   Funds that have been sent by the payer but are not yet usable funds to the payee. (Chapter 14)

floating inventory lien   A secured short-term loan against inventory under which the lender's claim is on the borrower's inventory in general. (Chapter 15)

floating relationship   The fluctuating relationship of the values of two currencies with respect to each other. (Chapter 18)

floating-rate bonds   See Table 6.4 (Chapter 6)

floating-rate loan   A loan with a rate of interest initially set at an increment above the prime rate and allowed to "float," or vary, above prime *as the prime rate varies* until maturity. (Chapter 15)

flotation costs   The total costs of issuing and selling a security. (Chapter 11)

foreign bond   Bond that is issued by a foreign corporation or government and is denominated in the investor's home currency and sold in the investor's home market. (Chapters 1, 6, and 18)

foreign direct investment (FDI)   The transfer by a multinational firm of capital, managerial, and technical assets from its home country to a host country. (Chapters 8 and 18)

foreign exchange manager   The manager responsible for monitoring and managing the firm's exposure to loss from currency fluctuations. (Chapter 1)

foreign exchange rate   The value of two currencies with respect to each other. (Chapter 18)

forward exchange rate   The rate of exchange between two currencies at some specified future date. (Chapter 18)

free cash flow (FCF)   The amount of cash flow available to investors (creditors and owners) after the firm has met all operating needs and paid for investments in net fixed assets and net current assets. (Chapter 3)

free cash flow valuation model   A model that determines the value of an entire company as the present value of its expected free cash flows discounted at the firm's *weighted average cost of capital*, which is its expected average future cost of funds over the long run. (Chapter 7)

friendly merger   A merger transaction endorsed by the target firm's management, approved by its stockholders, and easily consummated. (Chapter 17)

functional currency   The currency of the host country in which a subsidiary primarily generates and expends cash and in which its accounts are maintained. (Chapter 18)

future value   The value at a given future date of a present amount placed on deposit today and earning interest at a specified rate. Found by applying *compound interest* over a specified period of time. (Chapter 4)

future value interest factor   The multiplier used to calculate, at a specified interest rate, the future value of a present amount as of a given time. (Chapter 4)

future value interest factor for an ordinary annuity   The multiplier used to calculate the future value of an *ordinary annuity* at a specified interest rate over a given period of time. (Chapter 4)

General Agreement on Tariffs and Trade (GATT)   A treaty that has governed world trade throughout most of the postwar era; it extends free-trading rules to broad areas of economic activity and is policed by the *World Trade Organization (WTO)*. (Chapter 18)

generally accepted accounting principles (GAAP)   The practice and procedure guidelines used to prepare and maintain financial records and reports; authorized by the *Financial Accounting Standards Board (FASB)*. (Chapter 2)

golden parachutes   Provisions in the employment contracts of key executives that provide them with sizable compensation if the firm is taken over; deters hostile takeovers to the extent that the cash outflows required are large enough to make the takeover unattractive. (Chapter 17)

Gordon model   A common name for the *constant-growth model* that is widely cited in dividend valuation. (Chapter 7)

greenmail   A takeover defense under which a target firm repurchases, through private negotiation, a large block of stock at a premium from one or more shareholders to end a hostile takeover attempt by those shareholders. (Chapter 17)

gross profit margin   Measures the percentage of each sales dollar remaining after the firm has paid for its goods. (Chapter 2)

hedging   Offsetting or protecting against the risk of adverse price movements. (Chapter 16)

hedging strategies   Techniques used to offset or protect against risk; in the international context, these include borrowing or lending in different currencies; undertaking contracts in the forward, futures, and/or options markets; and swapping assets/liabilities with other parties. (Chapter 18)

historical weights   Either book or market value weights based on *actual* capital structure proportions. (Chapter 11)

holding company   A corporation that has voting control of one or more other corporations. (Chapter 17)

horizontal merger   A merger of two firms *in the same line of business*. (Chapter 17)

hostile merger   A merger transaction that the target firm's management does not support, forcing the acquiring company to try to gain control of the firm by buying shares in the marketplace. (Chapter 17)

hybrid security   A form of debt or equity financing that possesses characteristics of *both* debt and equity financing. (Chapter 16)

implied price of a warrant   The price effectively paid for each warrant attached to a bond. (Chapter 16)

incentive plans   Management compensation plans that tend to tie management compensation to share price; most popular incentive plan involves the grant of *stock options*. (Chapter 1)

income bonds   See Table 6.3 (Chapter 6)

income statement Provides a financial summary of the firm's operating results during a specified period. (Chapter 2)

incremental cash flows The *additional* cash flows—outflows or inflows—expected to result from a proposed capital expenditure. (Chapter 8)

independent projects Projects whose cash flows are unrelated or independent of one another; the acceptance of one *does not eliminate* the others from further consideration. (Chapter 8)

individual investors Investors who buy relatively small quantities of shares in order to meet personal investment goals. (Chapter 1)

informational content The information provided by the dividends of a firm with respect to future earnings, which causes owners to bid up or down the price of the firm's stock. (Chapter 13)

initial investment The relevant cash outflow for a proposed project at time zero. (Chapter 8)

initial public offering (IPO) The first public sale of a firm's stock. (Chapter 7)

installation costs Any added costs that are necessary to place an asset into operation. (Chapter 8)

installed cost of new asset The cost of *a new asset* plus its *installation costs;* equals the asset's depreciable value. (Chapter 8)

institutional investors Investment professionals, such as insurance companies, mutual funds, and pension funds, that are paid to manage other people's money and that trade large quantities of securities. (Chapter 1)

intercorporate dividends Dividends received by one corporation on common and preferred stock held in other corporations. (Chapter 1)

interest rate The compensation paid by the borrower of funds to the lender; from the borrower's point of view, the cost of borrowing funds. (Chapter 6)

interest rate risk The chance that interest rates will change and thereby change the required return and bond value. Rising rates, which result in decreasing bond values, are of greatest concern. (Chapter 6)

intermediate cash inflows Cash inflows received prior to the termination of a project. (Chapter 9)

internal forecast A sales forecast based on a buildup, or consensus, of sales forecasts through the firm's own sales channels. (Chapter 3)

internal rate of return (IRR) A sophisticated capital budgeting technique; the discount rate that equates the NPV of an investment opportunity with $0 (because the present value of cash inflows equals the initial investment); it is the compound annual rate of return that the

firm will earn if it invests in the project and receives the given cash inflows. (Chapter 9)

internal rate of return approach An approach to capital rationing that involves graphing project IRRs in descending order against the total dollar investment to determine the group of acceptable projects. (Chapter 10)

international bond A bond that is initially sold outside the country of the borrower and is often distributed in several countries. (Chapter 18)

international equity market A market that allows corporations to sell blocks of shares to investors in a number of different countries simultaneously. (Chapter 1)

international stock market A market with uniform rules and regulations governing major stock exchanges. MNCs would benefit greatly from such a market that is yet to evolve. (Chapter 18)

inventory turnover Measures the activity, or liquidity, of a firm's inventory. (Chapter 2)

inverted yield curve A *downward-sloping* yield curve that indicates generally cheaper long-term borrowing costs than short-term borrowing costs. (Chapter 6)

investment bankers Financial intermediaries who, in addition to their role in selling new security issues, can be hired by acquirers in mergers to find suitable target companies and assist in negotiations. (Chapters 7 and 17)

investment flows Cash flows associated with purchase and sale of both fixed assets and business interests. (Chapter 3)

investment opportunities schedule (IOS) A ranking of investment possibilities from best (highest return) to worst (lowest return); the graph that plots project IRRs in descending order against the total dollar investment. (Chapters 10 and 11)

involuntary reorganization A petition initiated by an outside party, usually a creditor, for the reorganization and payment of creditors of a failed firm. (Chapter 17)

issued shares The number of shares of common stock that have been put into circulation; the sum of outstanding shares and treasury stock. (Chapter 7)

joint venture A partnership under which the participants have contractually agreed to contribute specified amounts of money and expertise in exchange for stated proportions of ownership and profit. (Chapter 18)

judgmental approach A simplified approach for preparing the pro forma balance sheet under which the values of certain balance sheet accounts are estimated, some as a percentage of sales and others by management assumption, and the firm's external financing is used as a balancing, or "plug," figure. (Chapter 3)

junk bonds See Table 6.4 (Chapter 6)

just-in-time (JIT) system Inventory management technique that minimizes inventory investment by having materials arrive at exactly the time they are needed for production. (Chapter 14)

lease-versus-purchase (lease-versus-buy) decision The decision facing firms needing to acquire new fixed assets: whether to lease the assets or to purchase them, using borrowed funds or available liquid resources. (Chapter 16)

leasing The process by which a firm can obtain the use of certain fixed assets for which it must make a series of contractual, periodic, tax-deductible payments. (Chapter 16)

lessee The receiver of the services of the assets under a lease contract. (Chapter 16)

lessor The owner of assets that are being leased. (Chapter 16)

letter of credit A letter written by a company's bank to the company's foreign supplier, stating that the bank guarantees payment of an invoiced amount if all the underlying agreements are met. (Chapter 15)

letter to stockholders Typically, the first element of the annual stockholders' report and the primary communication from management. (Chapter 2)

leverage Results from the use of fixed-cost assets or funds to magnify returns to the firm's owners. (Chapter 12)

leveraged buyout (LBO) An acquisition technique involving the use of a large amount of debt to purchase a firm; an example of a *financial merger*. (Chapter 17)

leveraged lease A lease under which the lessor acts as an equity participant, supplying only about 20 percent of the cost of the asset, while a lender supplies the balance. (Chapter 16)

leveraged recapitalization A takeover defense in which the target firm pays a large debt-financed cash dividend, increasing the firm's financial leverage and thereby deterring the takeover attempt. (Chapter 17)

lien A publicly disclosed legal claim on collateral. (Chapter 15)

limited liability corporation (LLC) See Table 1.2. (Chapter 1)

limited liability partnership (LLP) See Table 1.2. (Chapter 1)

limited partnership (LP) See Table 1.2. (Chapter 1)

line of credit An agreement between a commercial bank and a business specifying the amount of unsecured short-term borrowing the bank will make available to the firm over a given period of time. (Chapter 15)

liquidation value per share The *actual amount* per share of common stock that would be received if all of the firm's assets were *sold for their market value*, liabilities (including preferred stock) were paid, and any remaining money were divided among the common stockholders. (Chapter 7)

liquidity A firm's ability to satisfy its short-term obligations *as they come due*. (Chapter 2)

liquidity preferences General preferences of investors for shorter-term securities. (Chapter 6)

liquidity preference theory Theory suggesting that for any given issuer, long-term interest rates tend to be higher than short-term rates because (1) lower liquidity and higher responsiveness to general interest rate movements of longer-term securities exists and (2) borrower willingness to pay a higher rate for long-term financing causes the yield curve to be upward-sloping. (Chapter 6)

loan amortization The determination of the equal periodic loan payments necessary to provide a lender with a specified interest return and to repay the loan principal over a specified period. (Chapter 4)

loan amortization schedule A schedule of equal payments to repay a loan. It shows the allocation of each loan payment to interest and principal. (Chapter 4)

lockbox system A collection procedure in which customers mail payments to a post office box that is emptied regularly by the firm's bank, who processes the payments and deposits them in the firm's account. This system speeds up collection time by reducing processing time as well as mail and clearing time. (Chapter 14)

London Interbank Offered Rate (LIBOR) The base rate that is used to price all Eurocurrency loans. (Chapter 1)

long-term debt Debts for which payment is not due in the current year. (Chapter 2)

long-term (strategic) financial plans Lay out a company's planned financial actions and the anticipated impact of those actions over periods ranging from 2 to 10 years. (Chapter 3)

low-regular-and-extra dividend policy A dividend policy based on paying a low regular dividend, supplemented by an additional dividend when earnings are higher than normal in a given period. (Chapter 13)

macro political risk The subjection of *all* foreign firms to *political risk* (takeover) by a host country because of political change, revolution, or the adoption of new policies. (Chapter 18)

mail float The time delay between when payment is placed in the mail and when it is received. (Chapter 14)

maintenance clauses Provisions normally included in an operating lease that require the lessor to maintain the assets and to make insurance and tax payments. (Chapter 16) are deducted; the "pure profits" earned on each sales dollar. (Chapter 2)

operating unit   A part of a business, such as a plant, division, product line, or subsidiary, that contributes to the actual operations of the firm. (Chapter 17)

operating-change restrictions   Contractual restrictions that a bank may impose on a firm's financial condition or operations as part of a line-of-credit agreement. (Chapter 15)

opportunity costs   Cash flows that could be realized from the best alternative use of an owned asset. (Chapter 8)

optimal capital structure   The capital structure at which the weighted average cost of capital is minimized, thereby maximizing the firm's value. (Chapter 12)

option   An instrument that provides its holder with an opportunity to purchase or sell a specified asset at a stated price on or before a set *expiration date*. (Chapter 16)

order costs   The fixed clerical costs of placing and receiving an inventory order. (Chapter 14)

ordinary annuity   An annuity for which the cash flow occurs at the *end* of each period. (Chapter 4)

ordinary income   Income earned through the sale of a firm's goods or services. (Chapter 1)

organized securities exchanges   Tangible organizations that act as *secondary markets* where outstanding securities are resold. (Chapter 1)

outstanding shares   The number of shares of common stock held by the public. (Chapter 7)

overhanging issue   A convertible security that cannot be forced into conversion by using the call feature. (Chapter 16)

over-the-counter (OTC) exchange   An intangible market for the purchase and sale of securities not listed by the organized exchanges. (Chapter 1)

paid-in capital in excess of par   The amount of proceeds in excess of the par value received from the original sale of common stock. (Chapter 2)

partnership   A business owned by two or more people and operated for profit. (Chapter 1)

par value (stock)   A relatively useless value for a stock established for legal purposes in the firm's corporate charter. (Chapter 7)

par-value preferred stock   Preferred stock with a stated face value that is used with the specified dividend percentage to determine the annual dollar dividend. (Chapter 7)

payback period   The amount of time required for a firm to recover its initial investment in a project, as calculated from *cash inflows*. (Chapter 9)

payment date   Set by the firm's directors, the actual date on which the firm mails the dividend payment to the holders of record. (Chapter 13)

pecking order   A hierarchy of financing that begins with retained earnings, which is followed by debt financing and finally external equity financing. (Chapter 12)

percentage advance   The percent of the book value of the collateral that constitutes the principal of a secured loan. (Chapter 15)

percent-of-sales method   A simple method for developing the pro forma income statement; it forecasts sales and then expresses the various income statement items as percentages of projected sales. (Chapter 3)

perfectly negatively correlated   Describes two *negatively correlated* series that have a *correlation coefficient* of −1. (Chapter 5)

perfectly positively correlated   Describes two *positively correlated* series that have a *correlation coefficient* of +1. (Chapter 5)

performance plans   Plans that tie management compensation to measures such as EPS, growth in EPS, and other ratios of return. *Performance shares* and/or *cash bonuses* are used as compensation under these plans. (Chapter 1)

performance shares   Shares of stock given to management for meeting stated performance goals. (Chapter 1)

permanent funding requirement   A constant investment in operating assets resulting from constant sales over time. (Chapter 14)

perpetuity   An annuity with an infinite life, providing continual annual cash flow. (Chapter 4)

pledge of accounts receivable   The use of a firm's accounts receivable as security, or collateral, to obtain a short-term loan. (Chapter 15)

poison pill   A takeover defense in which a firm issues securities that give their holders certain rights that become effective when a takeover is attempted; these rights make the target firm less desirable to a hostile acquirer. (Chapter 17)

political risk   Risk that arises from the possibility that a host government will take actions harmful to foreign investors or that political turmoil in a country will endanger investments there. (Chapters 5 and 18)

portfolio   A collection, or group, of assets. (Chapter 5)

positively correlated   Describes two series that move in the same direction. (Chapter 5)

preemptive right   Allows common stockholders to maintain their *proportionate* ownership in the corporation when new shares are issued. (Chapter 7)

preferred stock   A special form of ownership having a fixed periodic dividend that must be paid prior to payment of any common stock dividends. (Chapter 1)

premium The amount by which a bond sells at a value that is greater than its par value. (Chapter 6)

present value The current dollar value of a future amount—the amount of money that would have to be invested today at a given interest rate over a specified period to equal the future amount. (Chapter 4)

present value interest factor The multiplier used to calculate, at a specified discount rate, the present value of an amount to be received in a future period. (Chapter 4)

present value interest factor for an ordinary annuity The multiplier used to calculate the present value of an *ordinary annuity* at a specified discount rate over a given period of time. (Chapters 4 and 11)

president or chief executive officer (CEO) Corporate official responsible for managing the firm's day-to-day operations and carrying out the policies established by the board of directors. (Chapter 1)

price/earnings multiple approach A popular technique used to estimate the firm's share value; calculated by multiplying the firm's expected earnings per share (EPS) by the average price/earnings (P/E) ratio for the industry. (Chapter 7)

price/earnings (P/E) ratio Measures the amount that investors are willing to pay for each dollar of a firm's earnings; the higher the P/E ratio, the greater is investor confidence. (Chapter 2)

primary market Financial market in which securities are initially issued; the only market in which the issuer is directly involved in the transaction. (Chapter 1)

prime rate of interest (prime rate) The lowest rate of interest charged by leading banks on business loans to their most important business borrowers. (Chapter 15)

principal The amount of money on which interest is paid. (Chapter 4)

private placement The sale of a new security issue, typically bonds or preferred stock, directly to an investor or group of investors. (Chapter 1)

privately owned (stock) All common stock of a firm owned by a single individual. (Chapter 7)

pro forma statements Projected, or forecast, income statements and balance sheets. (Chapter 3)

probability The *chance* that a given outcome will occur. (Chapter 5)

probability distribution A model that relates probabilities to the associated outcomes. (Chapter 5)

proceeds from sale of old asset The cash inflows, net of any *removal* or *cleanup costs,* resulting from the sale of an existing asset. (Chapter 8)

processing float The time between receipt of a payment and its deposit into the firm's account. (Chapter 14)

profitability The relationship between revenues and costs generated by using the firm's assets—both current and fixed—in productive activities. (Chapter 14)

prospectus A portion of a security registration statement that describes the key aspects of the issue, the issuer, and its management and financial position. (Chapter 7)

proxy battle The attempt by a nonmanagement group to gain control of the management of a firm by soliciting a sufficient number of proxy votes. (Chapter 7)

proxy statement A statement giving the votes of a stockholder to another party. (Chapter 7)

Public Company Accounting Oversight Board (PCAOB) A not-for-profit corporation established by the *Sarbanes-Oxley Act of 2002* to protect the interests of investors and further the public interest in the preparation of informative, fair, and independent audit reports. (Chapter 2)

public offering The nonexclusive sale of either bonds or stocks to the general public. (Chapter 1)

publicly owned (stock) Common stock of a firm owned by a broad group of unrelated individual or institutional investors. (Chapter 7)

purchase options Provisions frequently included in both operating and financial leases that allow the lessee to purchase the leased asset at maturity, typically for a pre-specified price. (Chapter 16)

put option An option to *sell* a specified number of shares of a stock (typically 100) on or before a specified future date at a stated price. (Chapter 16)

putable bonds See Table 6.4 (Chapter 6)

pyramiding An arrangement among holding companies wherein one holding company controls other holding companies, thereby causing an even greater magnification of earnings and losses. (Chapter 17)

quarterly compounding Compounding of interest over four periods within the year. (Chapter 4)

quick (acid-test) ratio A measure of liquidity calculated by dividing the firm's current assets minus inventory by its current liabilities. (Chapter 2)

quotations Information on bonds, stocks, and other securities, including current price data and statistics on recent price behavior. ((Chapter 6)

range A measure of an asset's risk, which is found by subtracting the pessimistic (worst) outcome from the optimistic (best) outcome. (Chapter 5)

ranking approach The ranking of capital expenditure projects on the basis of some predetermined measure, such as the rate of return. (Chapter 8)

ratio analysis Involves methods of calculating and interpreting financial ratios to analyze and monitor the firm's performance. (Chapter 2)

ratio of exchange The ratio of the amount *paid* per share of the target company to the market price per share of the acquiring firm. (Chapter 17)

ratio of exchange in market price Indicates the market price per share of the acquiring firm *paid* for each dollar of market price per share of the target firm. (Chapter 17)

real options Opportunities that are embedded in capital projects that enable managers to alter their cash flows and risk in a way that affects project acceptability (NPV). Also called *strategic options*. (Chapter 10)

real rate of interest The rate that creates an equilibrium between the supply of savings and the demand for investment funds in a perfect world, without inflation, where funds suppliers and demanders are indifferent to the term of loans or investments and have no liquidity preference, and where all outcomes are certain. (Chapter 6)

recapitalization The reorganization procedure under which a failed firm's debts are generally exchanged for equity or the maturities of existing debts are extended. (Chapter 17)

recaptured depreciation The portion of an asset's sale price that is above its book value and below its initial purchase price. (Chapter 8)

recovery period The appropriate depreciable life of a particular asset as determined by MACRS. (Chapter 3)

red herring A preliminary prospectus made available to prospective investors during the waiting period between the registration statement's filing with the SEC and its approval. (Chapter 7)

regular dividend policy A dividend policy based on the payment of a fixed-dollar dividend in each period. (Chapter 13)

relevant cash flows The *incremental cash outflow (investment) and resulting subsequent inflows* associated with a proposed capital expenditure. (Chapter 8)

renewal options Provisions especially common in operating leases that grant the lessee the right to re-lease assets at the expiration of the lease. (Chapter 16)

reorder point The point at which to reorder inventory, expressed as days of lead time × daily usage. (Chapter 14)

required return The cost of funds obtained by selling an ownership interest; it reflects the funds supplier's level of expected return. (Chapter 6)

required total financing Amount of funds needed by the firm if the ending cash for the period is less than the desired minimum cash balance; typically represented by notes payable. (Chapter 3)

residual theory of dividends A school of thought that suggests that the dividend paid by a firm should be viewed as a *residual*—the amount left over after all

acceptable investment opportunities have been undertaken. (Chapter 13)

restrictive covenants Provisions in a *bond indenture* that place operating and financial constraints on the borrower. (Chapter 6)

retained earnings The cumulative total of all earnings, net of dividends, that have been retained and reinvested in the firm since its inception; earnings not distributed to owners as dividends—a form of *internal* financing. (Chapters 2 and 13)

return The total gain or loss experienced on an investment over a given period of time; calculated by dividing the asset's cash distributions during the period, plus change in value, by its beginning-of-period investment value. (Chapter 5)

return on common equity (ROE) Measures the return earned on the common stockholders' investment in the firm. (Chapter 2)

return on total assets (ROA) Measures the overall effectiveness of management in generating profits with its available assets; also called the *return on investment (ROI)*. (Chapter 2)

reverse stock split A method used to raise the market price of a firm's stock by exchanging a certain number of outstanding shares for one new share. (Chapter 13)

revolving credit agreement A line of credit *guaranteed* to a borrower by a commercial bank regardless of the scarcity of money. (Chapter 15)

rights Financial instruments that permit stockholders to purchase additional shares at a price below the market price, in direct proportion to their number of owned shares. (Chapter 7)

risk The chance of financial loss or, more formally, the *variability of returns associated with a given asset*. (Chapters 1 and 5)

risk (in capital budgeting) The chance that a project will prove unacceptable or, more formally, the degree of variability of cash flows. (Chapter 10)

risk (of technical insolvency) The probability that a firm will be unable to pay its bills as they come due. (Chapter 14)

risk-adjusted discount rate (RADR) The rate of return that must be earned on a given project to compensate the firm's owners adequately—that is, to maintain or improve the firm's share price. (Chapter 10)

risk-averse The attitude toward risk in which an increased return would be required for an increase in risk. (Chapters 1 and 5)

risk-free rate of return, R_F The required return on a *risk-free asset,* typically a 3-month *U.S. Treasury bill.* (Chapter 5)

risk-indifferent The attitude toward risk in which no change in return would be required for an increase in risk. (Chapter 5)

risk-seeking The attitude toward risk in which a decreased return would be accepted for an increase in risk. (Chapter 5)

S corporation (S corp) See Table 1.2 (Chapter 1)

safety stock Extra inventory that is held to prevent stockouts of important items. (Chapter 14)

sale–leaseback arrangement A lease under which the lessee sells an asset for cash to a prospective lessor and then *leases back* the same asset, making fixed periodic payments for its use. (Chapter 16)

sales forecast The prediction of the firm's sales over a given period, based on external and/or internal data; used as the key input to the short-term financial planning process. (Chapter 3)

Sarbanes-Oxley Act of 2002 (SOX) An act aimed at eliminating corporate disclosure and conflict of interest. Contains provisions about corporate financial disclosures and the relationships among corporations, analysts, auditors, attorneys, directors, officers, and shareholders. (Chapter 1)

scenario analysis A behavioral approach that evaluates the impact on the firm's return of simultaneous changes in *a number of variables*. (Chapter 10)

seasonal funding requirement An investment in operating assets that varies over time as a result of cyclic sales. (Chapter 14)

secondary market Financial market in which preowned securities (those that are not new issues) are traded. (Chapter 1)

secured creditors Creditors who have specific assets pledged as collateral and, in liquidation of the failed firm, receive proceeds from the sale of those assets. (Chapter 17)

secured short-term financing Short-term financing (loan) that has specific assets pledged as collateral. (Chapter 15)

Securities and Exchange Commission (SEC) The federal regulatory body that governs the sale and listing of securities. (Chapter 2)

securities exchanges Organizations that provide the marketplace in which firms can raise funds through the sale of new securities and purchasers can resell securities. (Chapter 1)

security agreement The agreement between the borrower and the lender that specifies the collateral held against a secured loan. (Chapter 15)

security market line (SML) The depiction of the *capital asset pricing model* (*CAPM*) as a graph that reflects the required return in the marketplace for each level of nondiversifiable risk (beta). (Chapter 5)

selling group A large number of brokerage firms that join the originating investment banker(s); each accepts responsibility for selling a certain portion of a new security issue on a commission basis. (Chapter 7)

semiannual compounding Compounding of interest over two periods within the year. (Chapter 4)

sensitivity analysis An approach for assessing risk that uses several possible-return estimates to obtain a sense of the variability among outcomes. (Chapter 5)

shark repellents Antitakeover amendments to a corporate charter that constrain the firm's ability to transfer managerial control of the firm as a result of a merger. (Chapter 17)

short-term (operating) financial plans Specify short-term financial actions and the anticipated impact of those actions. (Chapter 3)

short-term financial management Management of current assets and current liabilities. (Chapter 14)

short-term, self-liquidating loan An unsecured short-term loan in which the use to which the borrowed money is put provides the mechanism through which the loan is repaid. (Chapter 15)

signal A financing action by management that is believed to reflect its view of the firm's stock value; generally, debt financing is viewed as a *positive signal* that management believes the stock is "undervalued," and a stock issue is viewed as a *negative signal* that management believes the stock is "overvalued." (Chapter 12)

simulation A statistics-based behavioral approach that applies predetermined probability distributions and random numbers to estimate risky outcomes. (Chapter 10)

single-payment note A short-term, one-time loan made to a borrower who needs funds for a specific purpose for a short period. (Chapter 15)

sinking-fund requirement A restrictive provision often included in a bond indenture, providing for the systematic retirement of bonds prior to their maturity. (Chapter 6)

small (ordinary) stock dividend A stock dividend representing less than 20 to 25 percent of the common stock outstanding when the dividend is declared. (Chapter 13)

sole proprietorship A business owned by one person and operated for his or her own profit. (Chapter 1)

spin-off A form of divestiture in which an operating unit becomes an independent company through the issuance of shares in it, on a pro rata basis, to the parent company's shareholders. (Chapter 17)

spontaneous liabilities   Financing that arises from the normal course of business; the two major short-term sources of such liabilities are accounts payable and accruals. (Chapter 15)

spot exchange rate   The rate of exchange between two currencies on any given day. (Chapter 18)

stakeholders   Groups such as employees, customers, suppliers, creditors, owners, and others who have a direct economic link to the firm. (Chapter 1)

standard debt provisions   Provisions in a *bond indenture* specifying certain record-keeping and general business practices that the bond issuer must follow; normally, they do not place a burden on a financially sound business. (Chapter 6)

standard deviation (σ_k)   The most common statistical indicator of an asset's risk; it measures the dispersion around the *expected value*. (Chapter 5)

statement of cash flows   Provides a summary of the firm's operating, investment, and financing cash flows and reconciles them with changes in its cash and marketable securities during the period. (Chapter 2)

statement of retained earnings   Reconciles the net income earned during a given year, and any cash dividends paid, with the change in retained earnings between the start and the end of that year. An abbreviated form of the *statement of stockholders' equity.* (Chapter 2)

statement of stockholders' equity   Shows all equity account transactions that occur during a given year. (Chapter 2)

stock dividend   The payment, to existing owners, of a dividend in the form of stock. (Chapter 13)

stock options   An incentive allowing managers to purchase stock at the market price set at the time of the grant. (Chapter 1)

stock purchase warrants   Instruments that give their holders the right to purchase a certain number of shares of the issuer's common stock at a specified price over a certain period of time. (Chapters 6 and 16)

stock repurchase   The repurchase by the firm of outstanding common stock in the marketplace; desired effects of stock repurchases are that they either enhance shareholder value or help to discourage an unfriendly takeover. (Chapter 13)

stock split   A method commonly used to lower the market price of a firm's stock by increasing the number of shares belonging to each shareholder. (Chapter 13)

stock swap transaction   An acquisition method in which the acquiring firm exchanges its shares for shares of the target company according to a predetermined ratio. (Chapter 17)

stockholders   The owners of a corporation, whose ownership, or *equity,* is evidenced by either common stock or preferred stock. (Chapter 1)

stockholders' report   Annual report that publicly owned corporations must provide to stockholders; it summarizes and documents the firm's financial activities during the past year. (Chapter 2)

straight bond   A bond that is nonconvertible, having no conversion feature. (Chapter 16)

straight bond value   The price at which a convertible bond would sell in the market without the conversion feature. (Chapter 16)

straight preferred stock   Preferred stock that is nonconvertible, having no conversion feature. (Chapter 16)

strategic merger   A merger transaction undertaken to achieve economies of scale. (Chapter 17)

stretching accounts payable   Paying bills as late as possible without damaging the firm's credit rating. (Chapter 15)

striking price   The price at which the holder of a call option can buy (or the holder of a put option can sell) a specified amount of stock at any time prior to the option's expiration date. (Chapter 16)

subordinated debentures   See Table 6.3 (Chapter 6)

subordination   In a bond indenture, the stipulation that subsequent creditors agree to wait until all claims of the *senior debt* are satisfied. (Chapter 6)

subsidiaries   The companies controlled by a holding company. (Chapter 17)

sunk costs   Cash outlays that have already been made (past outlays) and therefore have no effect on the cash flows relevant to a current decision. (Chapter 8)

supervoting shares   Stock that carries with it multiple votes per share rather than the single vote per share typically given on regular shares of common stock. (Chapter 7)

takeover defenses   Strategies for fighting hostile takeovers. (Chapter 17)

target capital structure   The desired optimal mix of debt and equity financing that most firms attempt to maintain. (Chapter 11)

target company   The firm in a merger transaction that the acquiring company is pursuing. (Chapter 17)

target dividend-payout ratio   A dividend policy under which the firm attempts to pay out a certain *percentage* of earnings as a stated dollar dividend and adjusts that dividend toward a target payout as proven earnings increases occur. (Chapter 13)

target weights Either book or market value weights based on *desired* capital structure proportions. (Chapter 11)

tax loss carryforward In a merger, the tax loss of one of the firms that can be applied against a limited amount of future income of the merged firm over 20 years or until the total tax loss has been fully recovered, whichever comes first. (Chapter 17)

tax on sale of old asset Tax that depends on the relationship among the old asset's sale price, initial purchase price, and *book value,* and on existing government tax rules. (Chapter 8)

technical insolvency Business failure that occurs when a firm is unable to pay its liabilities as they come due. (Chapter 17)

technically insolvent Describes a firm that is unable to pay its bills as they come due. (Chapter 14)

tender offer A formal offer to purchase a given number of shares of a firm's stock at a specified price. (Chapter 13)

term structure of interest rates The relationship between the interest rate or rate of return and the time to maturity. (Chapter 6)

terminal cash flow The after-tax nonoperating cash flow occurring in the final year of a project. It is usually attributable to liquidation of the project. (Chapter 8)

time line A horizontal line on which time zero appears at the leftmost end and future periods are marked from left to right; can be used to depict investment cash flows. (Chapter 4)

times interest earned ratio Measures the firm's ability to make contractual interest payments; sometimes called the *interest coverage ratio.* (Chapter 2)

time-series analysis Evaluation of the firm's financial performance over time using financial ratio analysis. (Chapter 2)

total asset turnover Indicates the efficiency with which the firm uses its assets to generate sales. (Chapter 2)

total cost of inventory The sum of order costs and carrying costs of inventory. (Chapter 14)

total leverage The potential use of *fixed costs, both operating and financial,* to magnify the effect of changes in sales on the firm's earnings per share. (Chapter 12)

total risk The combination of a security's *nondiversifiable* and *diversifiable risk.* (Chapter 5)

transfer prices Prices that subsidiaries charge each other for the goods and services traded between them. (Chapter 10)

treasurer The firm's chief financial manager, who is responsible for the firm's financial activities, such as financial planning and fund raising, making capital expenditure decisions, and managing cash, credit, the pension fund, and foreign exchange. (Chapter 1)

treasury stock The number of shares of outstanding stock that have been repurchased by the firm. (Chapter 7)

trust receipt inventory loan A secured short-term loan against inventory under which the lender advances 80 to 100 percent of the cost of the borrower's relatively expensive inventory items in exchange for the borrower's promise to repay the lender, with accrued interest, immediately after the sale of each item of collateral. (Chapter 15)

trustee A paid individual, corporation, or commercial bank trust department that acts as the third party to a bond indenture and can take specified actions on behalf of the bondholders if the terms of the indenture are violated. (Chapter 6)

two-bin method Unsophisticated inventory-monitoring technique that is typically applied to C group items and involves reordering inventory when one of two bins is empty. (Chapter 14)

two-tier offer A *tender offer* in which the terms offered are more attractive to those who tender shares early. (Chapter 17)

uncorrelated Describes two series that lack any interaction and therefore have a correlation coefficient close to zero. (Chapter 5)

U.S. Treasury bills (T-bills) Short-term IOUs issued by the U.S. Treasury; considered the *risk-free asset.* (Chapter 5)

underpriced Stock sold at a price below its current market price, P_0. (Chapter 11)

underwriting The role of the *investment banker* in bearing the risk of reselling, at a profit, the securities purchased from an issuing corporation at an agreed-on price. (Chapter 7)

underwriting syndicate A group formed by an investment banker to share the financial risk associated with *underwriting* new securities. (Chapter 7)

unitary tax laws Laws in some U.S. states that tax multinationals (both U.S. and foreign) on a percentage of their *total* worldwide income rather than solely on the MNCs' earnings arising within their jurisdiction. (Chapter 18)

unlimited funds The financial situation in which a firm is able to accept all independent projects that provide an acceptable return. (Chapter 8)

unlimited liability The condition of a sole proprietorship (or general partnership) allowing the owner's total wealth to be taken to satisfy creditors. (Chapter 1)

unsecured short-term financing Short-term financing obtained without pledging specific assets as collateral. (Chapter 15)

unsecured, or general, creditors Creditors who have a general claim against all the firm's assets other than those specifically pledged as collateral. (Chapter 17)

valuation The process that links risk and return to determine the worth of an asset. (Chapter 6)

variable-growth model A dividend valuation approach that allows for a change in the dividend growth rate. (Chapter 7)

venture capital Privately raised external equity capital used to fund early-stage firms with attractive growth prospects. (Chapter 7)

venture capitalists (VCs) Providers of venture capital; typically, formal businesses that maintain strong oversight over the firms they invest in and that have clearly defined exit strategies. (Chapter 7)

vertical merger A merger in which a firm acquires *a supplier or a customer*. (Chapter 17)

voluntary reorganization A petition filed by a failed firm on its own behalf for reorganizing its structure and paying its creditors. (Chapter 17)

voluntary settlement An arrangement between a technically insolvent or bankrupt firm and its creditors enabling it to bypass many of the costs involved in legal bankruptcy proceedings. (Chapter 17)

warehouse receipt loan A secured short-term loan against inventory under which the lender receives control of the pledged inventory collateral, which is stored by a designated warehousing company on the lender's behalf. (Chapter 15)

warrant premium The difference between the market value and the theoretical value of a warrant. (Chapter 16)

weighted average cost of capital (WACC), k_a Reflects the expected average future cost of funds over the long run; found by weighting the cost of each specific type of capital by its proportion in the firm's capital structure. (Chapter 11)

weighted marginal cost of capital (WMCC) The firm's weighted average cost of capital (WACC) associated with its *next dollar* of total new financing. (Chapter 11)

weighted marginal cost of capital (WMCC) schedule Graph that relates the firm's weighted average cost of capital to the level of total new financing. (Chapter 11)

white knight A takeover defense in which the target firm finds an acquirer more to its liking than the initial hostile acquirer and prompts the two to compete to take over the firm. (Chapter 17)

wire transfer An electronic communication that, via bookkeeping entries, removes funds from the payer's bank and deposits them in the payee's bank. (Chapter 14)

working capital Current assets, which represent the portion of investment that circulates from one form to another in the ordinary conduct of business. (Chapter 14)

World Trade Organization (WTO) International body that polices world trading practices and mediates disputes between member countries. (Chapter 18)

yield curve A graph of the relationship between the debt's remaining time to maturity (x axis) and its yield to maturity (y axis); it shows the yield to maturity for debts of equal quality and different maturities. Graphically depicts the *term structure of interest rates*. (Chapter 6)

yield to maturity (YTM) The rate of return that investors earn if they buy a bond at a specific price and hold it until maturity. (Assumes that the issuer makes all scheduled interest and principal payments as promised.) (Chapter 6)

zero- (or low-) coupon bonds See Table 6.4 (Chapter 6)

zero-balance account (ZBA) A disbursement account that always has an end-of-day balance of zero because the firm deposits money to cover checks drawn on the account only as they are presented for payment each day. (Chapter 14)

zero-growth model An approach to dividend valuation that assumes a constant, nongrowing dividend stream. (Chapter 7)

Credits

Bold page numbers indicate location of feature.

3:   AP Wideworld Photos

17:   From Robert A. Cooke, "Business Ethics: A Perspective," in *Arthur Andersen Cases on Business Ethics* (Chicago: Arthur Andersen, September 1991), pages 2 and 5. Copyright © 1991 Arthur Andersen. All rights reserved. Reprinted by permission.

45:   Michael Newman/PhotoEdit

51:   Data from *Industry Norms and Key Business Ratios*. Dun & Bradstreet, Inc.

103:   Digital Vision

159:   PhotoDisc

217:   Data from *Stocks, Bonds, Bills, and Inflation, 2004 Yearbook* (Chicago: Ibbotson Associates, Inc., 2004).

223:   Data from *Stocks, Bonds, Bills, and Inflation, 2004 Yearbook* (Chicago: Ibbotson Associates, Inc.), 2004.

225:   Digital Vision

237:   Data from *Value Line Investment Survey* (New York: Value Line Publishing, March 8, 2002).

277:   AP Wideworld Photos; Reprinted from *The Wall Street Journal*, May 19, 2004, p. C12.

320:   Reprinted from *The Wall Street Journal*, May 19, 2004, p. C26.

325:   Corbis RF

375:   Etienne De Malglaive, Lliaison/Getty Images

417:   PhotoDisc

451:   Beth Anderson

497:   © 2004 eBay, Inc.

537:   Corbis/Bettmann

589:   PhotoEdit

627:   Comstock RF

669:   Getty Images/Stone Allstock

707:   Getty Images/Gary C. Caskey/Reuters/Hulton Archive

747:   Beth Anderson

763:   *International Financial Management*, 3/e by Rodriguez/Carter, p. 492. © 1984 Prentice-Hall. Reprinted by permission of Pearson Education, Inc., Upper Saddle River, NJ.

764:   Reprinted from John B. Giannatti, "FAS 52 Gives Treasurers the Scope FAS 8 Denied Them," *Euromoney*, (April 1982), pp. 141–151.

766:   Reprinted from *The Wall Street Journal*, June 29, 2004, p. B8.

772:   *International Financial Management*, 3/e by Rodriguez/Carter, p. 512. © 1984 Prentice-Hall. Reprinted by permission of Pearson Education, Inc., Upper Saddle River, NJ.

791:   Bruce Connolly/Corbis

Index